Kierkegaard's Incarnational Mission

A Study of Søren Kierkegaard as a Missionary
Applied to the Japanese Context

Michio Ogino

© 2025 Michio Ogino

Published 2025 by Langham Academic
An imprint of Langham Publishing
www.langhampublishing.org

Langham Publishing and its imprints are a ministry of Langham Partnership

Langham Partnership
PO Box 296, Carlisle, Cumbria, CA3 9WZ, UK
www.langham.org

ISBNs:
978-1-83973-986-6 Print
978-1-78641-204-1 ePub
978-1-78641-205-8 PDF
DOI: https://doi.org/10.69811/9781839739866

Michio Ogino has asserted his right under the Copyright, Designs and Patents Act, 1988 to be identified as the Author of this work.

All rights reserved. No part of this publication may be reproduced, stored in a retrieval system or transmitted, in any form or by any means, electronic, mechanical, photocopying, recording or otherwise, without the prior written permission of the publisher or the Copyright Licensing Agency.

Requests to reuse content from Langham Publishing are processed through PLSclear. Please visit www.plsclear.com to complete your request.

Unless otherwise specified scripture quotations are from the New Revised Standard Version Bible, copyright © 1989 National Council of the Churches of Christ in the United States of America. Used by permission. All rights reserved.

British Library Cataloguing-in-Publication Data
A catalogue record for this book is available from the British Library

ISBN: 978-1-83973-986-6

Cover & Book Design: projectluz.com

Langham Partnership actively supports theological dialogue and an author's right to publish but does not necessarily endorse the views and opinions set forth here or in works referenced within this publication, nor can we guarantee technical and grammatical correctness. Langham Partnership does not accept any responsibility or liability to persons or property as a consequence of the reading, use or interpretation of its published content.

For Chaa Ogino

LD	*Letters and Documents.* Translated by Henrik Rosenmeier. 1978.
M	*The Moment and Late Writings.* 2009.
P	*Prefaces* and *Writing Sampler.* Edited and translated by Todd W. Nichol. 1998.
PC	*Practice in Christianity.* 1991.
PF	*Philosophical Fragments* and *Johannes Climacus.* 1985.
PV	*The Point of View for My Work as an Author, The Single Individual, On My Work as an Author* and *Armed Neutrality.* 1998.
SLW	*Stages on Life's Way.* 1988.
SUD	*The Sickness unto Death.* 1980.
TA	*Two Ages: The Age of Revolution and the Present Age: A Literary Review.* 1978.
UDVS	*Upbuilding Discourses in Various Spirits.* 1993.
WA	*Without Authority.* 1997.
WL	*Works of Love.* 1962.

Kierkegaard's Journals and Notebooks

JP	*Søren Kierkegaard's Journals and Papers.* Edited and translated by Howard V. Hong and Edna H. Hong, assisted by Gregor Malantschuk. 7 vols. Bloomington: Indiana University Press 1967–1978.
KJN	*Kierkegaard's Journals and Notebooks.* Edited by Niels Jørgen Cappelørn, Alastair Hannay, David Kangas, Bruce H. Kirmmse, George Pattison, Vanessa Rumble, and K. Brian Söderquist. 11 vols. Princeton: Princeton University Press, 2007–2020.
IKC	*International Kierkegaard Commentary.* Edited by Robert L. Perkins. 24 vols. Macon: Mercer University Press, 1984–2010.

Kierkegaard's Secondary Sources

KRSRR	*Kierkegaard Research: Sources, Reception and Resources.* Edited by Jon Stewart. 21 vols (58 titles). Aldershot: Ashgate; London; New York: Routledge, 2007–2017.
KSY	*Kierkegaard Studies Yearbook.* Edited by Heiko Schulz, Jon Stewart, and Karl Verstrynge. Berlin: de Gruyter, 1996–present.

List of Abbreviations

Danish Abbreviations

Pap. *Søren Kierkegaards Papirer*. Edited by Peter Andreas Heiberg, Victor Kuhr, and Einer Torsting. 11 vols. Copenhagen: Gyldendalske Boghandel, Nordisk Forlag, 1909–1948.

SKS *Søren Kierkegaards Skrifter*. Edited by Niels Jørgen Cappelørn, Joakim Garff, Jette Knudsen, Johnny Kondrup, Alastair McKinnon, and Finn Hauberg Mortensen. 28 vols. K1–K28. Copenhagen: Gads Forlag 1997–2013.

English Abbreviations

Kierkegaard's works translated by Howard Vincent Hong and Edna Hatlestad Hong, published by Princeton University Press, or otherwise specified

CA *The Concept of Anxiety*. Translated by Reider Thomte in collaboration with Albert B. Anderson. 1980.

CD *Christian Discourses: The Crisis and a Crisis in the Life of an Actress*. 1997.

CI *The Concept of Irony* together with *Notes on Schelling's Berlin Lectures*. 1989.

CUP I, *Concluding Unscientific Postscript to Philosophical Fragments*.
CUP II 2 vols. 1992.

EO I, *Either/Or*. 2 vols. 1987.
EO II

EUD *Eighteen Upbuilding Discourses*. 1990.

FSE/JFY *For Self-Examination* and *Judge for Yourself!* 1990.

FT/R *Fear and Trembling* and *Repetition*. 1983.

Damon So (2020–2021), who read my early drafts and challenged me to critique Kierkegaard. I am also grateful to Dr. Chris L. Carter and Mrs. Anna Hymes, who proofread my thesis. I am honoured that Prof. John Lippitt and Dr. Joshua Cockayne took on the task of serving as external readers.

This study would not have been possible without the support of many individuals and institutions who helped me –directly and indirectly – in various ways. My heartfelt thanks to the following: my parents, Takeyoshi and Hiroko Ogino; the members of Kumagaya Gospel Christ Church; Mr. and Mrs. Yamada; Dr. Kōichi Kitano; Rev. Yutaka Yoshinaga; Rev. Kazuo Kikuyama; Dr. Hiroshi Horikawa; Rev. Noriyuki Miyake; Dr. Takaya Sutō and the members of the Kierkegaard Study Group in Japan; Mrs. Atsuko Ogino; Dr. Wonsuk Ma; Dr. David Jung and Mrs. Rebecca; Dr. Tim Keene; Dr. Robert Oh; Dr. David Singh; Dr. Jun Guichun; the members of Galilee Marukomachi Christ Church; Rev. Hisao Kashiwazaki; Prof. Jon Stewart; Dr. Roman Kralik; Rev. Derrick Morlan and his wonderful family; Rev. Takashi Arai; my sister Ruth Ngwar and her husband, James Ngwar; Japan Assemblies of God; Central Bible College; Bodleian Library; Ueda Shiritsu Maruko Library; Kwansei Gakuin University Library; Søren Kierkegaard Research Centre; Københavns Indre Mission; Studieskolen; and the Hong Kierkegaard Library. I could not have completed my writing without Starbucks and McDonald's – both in Japan and the UK – where I was able to plug in my laptop.

My heartfelt thanks to Kibō Ogino, who entered the womb when I began my PhD journey and later prayed every night for me to complete my thesis. My deepest thanks to my wife, Chaa Ogino, who has always supported my studies in every way and loves my love for Kierkegaard. I owe her far more than mere words can express.

The Triune God has always been present behind the scenes, working through all the lovely people and institutions mentioned above. My unending thanks and gratitude to him who allowed me to despair and to encounter Kierkegaard. Glory to him who loves me, forsook the infinitely precious life of the Son of God for my sake, gave Kierkegaard talents and inspired him to write as he did, and plans the best for my life's way.

Acknowledgements

I begin by expressing my gratitude to Søren Kierkegaard, who creatively constructed his literary devices. I am also grateful to the successive translators, scholars, editors, and publishers who made it possible for us to read his works in Japanese, English, and Danish. Without their efforts, I would not have been able to access the Kierkegaardian wonderland.

My special thanks to Dr. David Hymes, whom I consulted about my desire to study Kierkegaard. He advised me to work towards a PhD in Kierkegaard and suggested that I study at the Asia Pacific Theological Seminary in the Philippines to improve my English skills and lay the necessary foundation for both Christian faith and rigorous study. He also provided a full scholarship for my studies at the seminary. Furthermore, he planted the "seed" of this work by suggesting that although Kierkegaard actually evangelized intellectuals through his writings, no such study had been carried out yet. How can I fully express my thanks to him?

My gratitude and appreciation to the Oxford Centre for Mission Studies (OCMS), its faculty, staff, and students, who supported me during my PhD studies. I am also grateful to Middlesex University, OCMS's collaborative partner who awarded the degree.

I am deeply grateful to Prof. C. Stephen Evans, my head supervisor. I was greatly encouraged to read his works, in which he refers to Kierkegaard as "a missionary to Christendom." I am thankful that he took on the role of my supervisor. He generously shared his knowledge and was constantly engaged in the process of both my development as a scholar and the present study. My thanks to my three second supervisors: Prof. Pia Søltoft (2013–2016), who taught me how to engage academically; Prof. Niels Jørgen Cappelørn (2017–2019), who passionately discussed Kierkegaard with me; and Dr.

Abstract

This study interprets four published and two unpublished works of Søren Kierkegaard (1813–1855) from the perspective of Kierkegaard as a missionary and applies the Kierkegaardian mission to the Japanese context.

I demonstrate that the interpretation that Kierkegaard was a missionary is a plausible reading of his works. I argue that such an interpretation originates from Kierkegaard's authorial intent and God's Governance. In support of this argument, I establish "an author-oriented method with a critical evaluation" and interpret Kierkegaard's works by closely following this method. I argue that with *Either/Or*, Kierkegaard began his mission strategy with "paganism" to attract many. From a strategic point of view, with *Two Upbuilding Discourses* (1843), Kierkegaard provides a less radical religious view that is palatable and digestible for the readers of *Either/Or*. Further, a sequential reading of *Either/Or* and *Two Upbuilding Discourses* (1843) reveals the nature of Kierkegaard's dual authorship – pseudonymous and signed-religious works, or indirect and direct communication – until 1848. Carefully avoiding any mention of "sin" and "Christ" in both his early pseudonymous and signed works, he finally declares "despair or sin" in *The Sickness unto Death* and "Jesus Christ in His True Form" in *Practice in Christianity*. By doing so, he forces readers into a corner, compelling them to choose between offence or faith in Christ. By studying *The Point of View for My Work as an Author* and *Journals and Notebooks*, I demonstrate that Kierkegaard saw himself as a missionary writer and considered being a missionary an integral part of being a Christian. I also argue that Kierkegaard's strategy can be identified as an incarnational mission that attempts to proclaim Jesus Christ in the same manner that Jesus did on earth. I then define Kierkegaard's mission and apply the Kierkegaardian mission to a Japanese context.

Chapter 10 289
   The Applicability of a Kierkegaardian Mission to Japan
      10.1 David J. Lu's Analysis of Japan......................................291
      10.2 How the Kierkegaardian Mission Can Contribute to
           Evangelization in Japan 298
           10.2.1 How to Overcome the "Self" 300
           10.2.2 How to Overcome "Buddhism Enmeshed in
                   Japanese Culture"...302
           10.2.3 How to Overcome "Myriad Deities of Shintoism"..........306
           10.2.4 How to Overcome "Seeking Perfection without God".......315
           10.2.5 How to Overcome "Invisible Proscription" 321
      10.3 Conclusion 331

Overall Conclusion 335
   A Missionary Is Inevitably an Incarnational Missionary

Appendices

Appendix 1 343
   Chronology

Appendix 2 349
   Categorization of Methods of Kierkegaard Studies

Appendix 3 357
   The Genre of Kierkegaard's Works

Appendix 4 359
   Reading Either/Or

Appendix 5 379
   Reading Two Upbuilding Discourses *(1843)*

Appendix 6 385
   Reading The Sickness unto Death

Appendix 7 399
   Reading Practice in Christianity

Appendix 8 419
   Responses of Individuals to Kierkegaard's Mission

Bibliography...433

Chapter 8 247
  A Selective Study of Journals and Notebooks *with Specific Regard to a View of Kierkegaard as a Missionary*
    8.1 Historical Introduction..248
    8.2 Kierkegaard's References to "(the) Missionary" or "(the) Missionaries"..249
    8.3 Problems Posed in the Previous Section 254
    8.4 Why "Missionary" Instead of Other Terms?.........................258
    8.5 Summary and Conclusion...261

Part 4: Contours of a Kierkegaardian Mission

Chapter 9 267
  Toward a Kierkegaardian Mission
    9.1 Contours of a Kierkegaardian Mission...................................268
      9.1.1 Missionary Assumption 1: The Universality of Despair and the Universal Capabilities to Become a Christian and a Missionary..268
      9.1.2 Missionary Assumption 2: A Human Being Is Becoming..269
      9.1.3 A Missionary Incognito..270
      9.1.4 A Seductive Mission..271
      9.1.5 Not an Instantaneous But a Long-Term Mission 272
      9.1.6 Audience-Oriented Mission (A Servant-Missionary)......273
      9.1.7 A Mission That Prohibits Cheap Grace (The Ideal-Driven Mission) 275
      9.1.8 A Mission That Avoids Objectification or Rationalization of Christianity 276
      9.1.9 The Congruence of the *How* and the *What*.....................277
      9.1.10 An Incarnational Mission 278
      9.1.11 The Congruence of Thought and Practice 278
      9.1.12 Mission as Absolute Devotion to the Triune God 279
      9.1.13 Summary and Conclusion..281
    9.2 A Typology of Mission...282
      9.2.1 A Typology of Missions by Ádám Szabados.....................282
      9.2.2 Modification of Ádám Szabados's Typology of Missions.283

Chapter 6 189
    Practice in Christianity *as Introducing Christianity into Christendom*
        6.1 Historical Introduction 191
        6.2 A Study of *Practice in Christianity* with Specific Regard to
              Kierkegaard the Missionary 192
              6.2.1 An Intended Reader 193
              6.2.2 Faith 195
              6.2.3 A Presentation of Christ in His True Form 203
        6.3 Possible Applications to the Japanese Context 213
        6.4 Conclusion 216
              Section A: Concluding Remarks for a Study of *Practice in
                    Christianity* 216
              Section B: Concluding Remarks on a Combined Study of
                    The Sickness unto Death and *Practice in Christianity* 217

Part 3: A Study of Unpublished Works

Chapter 7 223
    The Point of View for My Work as an Author as a Handbook of
    Mission Strategy
        7.1 Historical Introduction 225
        7.2 Reading *The Point of View for My Work as an Author* 226
        7.3 Those Who Doubt the Trustworthiness of *The Point of
              View for My Work as an Author* 234
        7.4 David R. Law's Middle Position 236
        7.5 The Standpoint of the Present Thesis 237
              7.5.1 Who Kierkegaard Was II 237
              7.5.2 Confession and the Ongoing Journey of Conversion 240
              7.5.3 Is *The Point of View for My Work as an Author*
                    Trustworthy? 241
        7.6 Conclusion 243
              7.6.1 Kierkegaard's Missionary Intention and Authorship 243
              7.6.2 A Unique Characteristic of Kierkegaard the
                    Missionary 244
              7.6.3 Validity of Identifying Kierkegaard's Mission as
                    Incarnational Mission 245

Chapter 4 135
   Two Upbuilding Discourses *(1843) as an Introduction to the Religious Life*
      4.1 Historical Introduction..138
      4.2 A Study of *Two Upbuilding Discourses* (1843) with Specific
          Regard to Kierkegaard the Missionary 139
          4.2.1 Introducing the Religious That the Reader of *Either/
              Or* Can Digest 140
          4.2.2 Who Edifies Whom? 141
          4.2.3 The Polyphonic Voices That Are Capable of
              Addressing Multiple Characters in *Either/Or*...................142
          4.2.4 Dealing with Doubt (*Tvivl*) 147
          4.2.5 Summary of the Religious in *Two Upbuilding
              Discourses* (1843) 149
      4.3 A Possible Application to the Japanese Context..........................150
      4.4 Conclusion 153
          Section A: Concluding Remarks: *Two Upbuilding
              Discourses* (1843) 153
          Section B: Concluding Remarks: *Either/Or* and *Two
              Upbuilding Discourses* (1843) 154
          Section C: Concluding Remarks: the Duplexity of "the
              Whole Authorship"...155

Chapter 5 161
   The Sickness unto Death *as the Rigorous Establishment of Sin*
      5.1 Historical Introduction..162
      5.2 A Study of *The Sickness unto Death* with Specific Regard to
          Kierkegaard the Missionary 163
          5.2.1 The Universality of Sin or Despair 164
          5.2.2 The Consciousness of Sin: The True Gateway and
              Source of Courage to Enter Authentic Christianity..........165
          5.2.3 The Self in Despair: The Need for a Proper Relation
              to God and Self 167
          5.2.4 What Is Not Christianity: Philosophy 168
          5.2.5 What Is Not Christianity: Apologetics 170
          5.2.6 The Dialectic of Faith with Despair, Sin, and Offence......172
          5.2.7 Anti-Climacus as a Preacher...174
          5.2.8 Anyone Who Believes That There Is a Hell Is,
              Eo Ipso, a Missionary 177
      5.3 A Possible Application to the Japanese Context..........................180
      5.4 Conclusion 184

    1.4 The Fetal Period (2004–present) 37
        1.4.1 *The Joy of Kierkegaard* by Hugh Pyper (2004) 37
        1.4.2 "Søren Kierkegaard on Mission in Christendom: Upbuilding Language and Its Rhetoric Understood as the Fundament of Mission" by Pia Søltoft (2007)...........39
        1.4.3 *Truth and Subjectivity, Faith and History: Kierkegaard's Insights for Christian Faith* by Varughese John (2012) 42
        1.4.4 *Kierkegaard: A Christian Missionary to Christians* by Mark A. Tietjen (2016) 50
    1.5 Summary and Conclusion...55

Chapter 2 59
Methodology and Scope
    2.1 Categorization of Methods..60
    2.2 The Need for a Kaleidoscopic Approach 65
    2.3 The Author-Oriented Method 67
        2.3.1 Authorial Intent 67
        2.3.2 Historical and Literary Context..69
        2.3.3 Open-Mindedness towards the Religious Dimension: An Evaluation of Kierkegaard's Thought in Light of Scripture and Christian Traditions and Practices (such as Lutheranism and Pietism) 70
        2.3.4 The Dialectical Structure of Kierkegaard's Corpus 71
    2.4 Critical Evaluation Necessary...77
    2.5 Scope 78

Part 2: A Study of Published Works

Chapter 3 85
Either/Or as an Initial Missionary Task with "Paganism"
    3.1 Historical Introduction..86
    3.2 A Study of *Either/Or* with Specific Regard to Kierkegaard the Missionary 87
        3.2.1 How the Aesthetes Are Able to Will to Allow Themselves to Be Built Up...88
        3.2.2 How to Make Aesthetes Aware of Their Need of the Eternal..106
        3.2.3 Does "The Ordinary Godly Christian" Like B Need to Be Edified? 116
        3.2.4 *Either/Or* as a Whole and Beyond......................................124
    3.3 Conclusion 132

Contents

Abstract xiii

Acknowledgements xv

List of Abbreviations xvii
    Danish Abbreviations xvii
    English Abbreviations xvii
    Kierkegaard's *Journals and Notebooks* xviii
    Kierkegaard's Secondary Sources xviii

Introduction 1
    Who Kierkegaard Was
    Was Kierkegaard a Christian? 5
    Was Kierkegaard a Good Christian? 7
    Was Kierkegaard a Missionary? 10

Part 1: A Preliminary Study

Chapter 1 15
    A History of the Study of Kierkegaard as a Missionary
    1.1 The Embryonic Period (1947–1964) 16
        1.1.1 *Pascal and Kierkegaard: A Study in the Strategy of Evangelism, Vol. II*, by Denzil G. M. Patrick (1947) 17
    1.2 The Chaotic Period (1965–1996) 25
        1.2.1 "Søren Kierkegaard: Missionary to Christendom" by Robert R. Cook (1987) 28
        1.2.2 *Søren Kierkegaard's Christian Psychology: Insight for Counseling and Pastoral Care* by C. Stephen Evans (1990) . 29
    1.3 The Reconsidering Period (1997–2003) 30
        1.3.1 "The Hipness unto Death: Søren Kierkegaard and David Letterman – Ironic Apologists to Generation X" by Mark C. Miller (1997) 30
        1.3.2 "Rejuvenating Apologetics in the Twenty-First Century: Taking Hints from Søren Kierkegaard" by John Depoe (2002) 33
        1.3.3 "Incarnational Mission: Søren Kierkegaard's Challenge to Evangelical Christianity" by Ádám Szabados (2003) 34

It is often overlooked by scholars that Søren Kierkegaard's writing has a missionary focus, seeking to confront each reader with the reality of their existence before God. Kierkegaard's approach is unusual. He attempts to articulate intellectual world views from the inside, adopts pseudonyms and fake interlocuters, and aims to communicate indirectly with his reader. The result can sometimes make Kierkegaard's writings inaccessible or daunting to students and scholars. We can therefore be deeply grateful to Michio Ogino for his important work in helping us to navigate this missional focus of Kierkegaard's writings and for bringing Kierkegaard's work to life in such an accessible way. Dr. Ogino's work has the rare quality of being academically robust while deeply concerned about application, offering fresh insights that can shape missionary practice today. This book is a great gift to both scholarship on Kierkegaard and more broadly, the field of missiology.

Rev. Dr. Joshua Cockayne
Lecturer in Mission and Evangelism,
Cranmer Hall, Durham University, UK

Not many scholars have taken seriously Kierkegaard's claim that he was called to be a kind of missionary. In this penetrating work, Michio Ogino shows how this claim can illuminate an important part of Kierkegaard's authorship. He then goes further by applying these insights to the project of evangelizing his own country, Japan. This is high-quality, important work.

C. Stephen Evans, PhD
Emeritus University Professor of Philosophy and Humanities,
Baylor University Texas, USA

Kierkegaard's Incarnational Mission is an extraordinary book for two reasons. First, as the main title indicates, Kierkegaard is primarily portrayed as a missionary, not just a mission thinker. Second, the book invites Kierkegaard to the Japanese sociocultural context as a unique witness of the Christian message. Ogino is to be commended for this creative work, which may inspire similar explorations in other contexts.

Wonsuk Ma, PhD
Executive Director,
Center for Spirit-Empowered Research,
Distinguished Professor of Global Christianity,
Oral Roberts University, Oklahoma, USA

Introduction

Who Kierkegaard Was

> Kierkegaard is best understood, not primarily as a philosopher, psychologist, theologian, literary critic, or poet, but as a missionary to the pagans in Christendom, those who took it for granted that they were Christians.[1]
>
> – C. Stephen Evans, *Søren Kierkegaard's Christian Psychology*

The quotation above states that although Søren Aabye Kierkegaard (1813–1855) is usually perceived as a philosopher, psychologist, theologian, literary critic, or poet, in reality, he was a missionary. Is that true? In *Kierkegaard Research: Sources, Reception and Resources, Volume 15, Tome I–VI: Kierkegaard's Concepts* – which comprises six volumes and is currently the most exhaustive collection of articles on Kierkegaard's key terms – terms such as "missionary," "mission," "evangelist," and "evangelism" are not found. Although this multi-tome Kierkegaard dictionary includes terms such as "apologetics," "pastor," and "witness," which are indirectly or occasionally related to a missionary or the missionary task, none of these articles view Kierkegaard as someone who attempts to proclaim Christianity.[2] In other words, a view of Kierkegaard as a missionary has not penetrated the consciousness of mainstream Kierkegaard scholarship. Nonetheless, there is a

---

1. Evans, *Kierkegaard's Christian Psychology*, 19.
2. Emmanuel, McDonald, and Stewart, *Kierkegaard's Concepts: Tomes I–VI, KRSRR* 15.

minor trajectory in the Anglophone reception of Kierkegaard that investigates Kierkegaard as a missionary (see chapter 1 of this book). To date, in this minor trajectory, the only academic study of Kierkegaard the missionary is *Pascal and Kierkegaard: A Study in Strategy of Evangelism, Vol II*, written by Denzil G. M. Patrick (1907–1944) and posthumously published in 1947. More recently, in 2016, *Kierkegaard: A Christian Missionary to Christians*, a fine study by Mark A. Tietjen, was published, but Tietjen's intended readers are Christians who are not Kierkegaard experts. In other words, there has been no updated, rigorous study that examines the validity of the claim of Kierkegaard the missionary. The present work is an attempt at an academic investigation of the validity of such a claim.

Additionally, by studying Kierkegaard the missionary, this study attempts to apply its findings to a Japanese context. In fact, there are preceding studies that apply the Kierkegaardian mission to American[3] or Indian[4] contexts. However, one may wonder if Kierkegaard can even be called a missionary and how his strategies – which were carried out in the context of nineteenth-century Christendom in Denmark – can be applied to the Japanese context, where Christianity remains an alien religion to this day. Do Kierkegaard and Japan have something in common? Kierkegaard rarely mentions Japan; if he does, he demonstrates a limited understanding of Japan.[5] Despite this, the Japanese became interested in him quite early on in the history of the international reception of Kierkegaard.[6] キェルケゴールと日本の仏教・哲学 [*Kierkegaard and the Japanese Buddhism and Philosophy*] edited by Masaru Ōtani and Ōya Kenichi (1992), *Kierkegaard Made in Japan* edited by Finn Hauberg Mortensen (1996), and *Kierkegaard and Japanese Thought* edited by James Giles (2008) are collections of treatises that focus on the relationship between Kierkegaard and Japan. The second of these works deals mainly with the reception of Kierkegaard's thought in Japan, while the first and third are comparative studies in which the authors juxtapose Kierkegaard and Japanese philosophy or Buddhism. Despite the rich legacy of Kierkegaard's reception

---

3. Miller, "Hipness unto Death," 38–52. See section 1.3.1 of this book.

4. John, *Truth and Subjectivity*. Kindle, loc. 3279–3434. See section 1.4.3 of this book.

5. *SKS* 2, 286/ *EO I*, 297.

6. See Mortenson, *Kierkegaard Made in Japan*, 27–82; Masugata, 日本に於けるキェルケゴール受容史 [A History of Reception of Kierkegaard in Japan], 265–285; Masugata, "Kierkegaard's Reception in Japan," 31–52.

in Japan, there has been no attempt to apply Kierkegaard's Christian thought to the Japanese context with just one noble exception: *An Elucidation of Soren Kierkegaard's Categories of Communication and Their Application to the Communication of Christian Existence in Japan* by Evyn Merrill Adams (1969).[7] However, there are significant differences between Adams's study and my own. Both Adams and I explore evangelistic applications of Kierkegaard's thought in the Japanese context. However, the primary difference in the scope of our work is that Adams does not address Kierkegaard's missionary self-understanding but, instead, painstakingly studies both Kierkegaard's thought and Japanese religion, culture, history, and ideology. In sum, while Adams deeply engages with both Kierkegaard's and Japanese thought for comparative purposes, I am largely concerned with Kierkegaard the missionary. Furthermore, Adams says, "The conclusion therefore, is the arrival at the beginning, at possibility."[8] In other words, while Adams's study offers deep analysis and insights into Japanese thought and Kierkegaard's thinking, it is far from being immediately applicable to lay Christians and pastors in Japan. In contrast, the present work attempts to provide an analysis of Kierkegaard's mission strategy that can be realistically applied in Japan.[9]

In sum, this study offers a rigorous examination of the validity of labelling Kierkegaard as a missionary and an exploration of appropriate applications of his philosophy to the Japanese context. More specifically, this study will focus on four of Kierkegaard's published works and two of his unpublished works. This work is a study of Kierkegaard the missionary, with specific attention to the following:

1. A set of two published works – *Either/Or* and *Two Upbuilding Discourses* (1843) – in which he attempts to help his contemporary Danes realize the bankruptcy of their lives and introduces religious concepts that are appealing and digestible for them
2. A set of two published works – *The Sickness unto Death* and *Practice in Christianity* – in which he addresses the concepts of

---

7. Adams, *Kierkegaard's Categories of Communication*.
8. Adams, iv.
9. Of course, a Kierkegaardian mission is not applicable only in Japan. Readers can apply this mission in whatever the context of their own lives.

despair and sin and urges his readers to have faith in and imitate Jesus Christ in his true form

3. Kierkegaard's own explanations in his unpublished works *The Point of View for My Work as an Author* and *Journals and Notebooks*

4. The potential applications of the Kierkegaardian mission in the Japanese context

When I gave a presentation on a part of this work to Christian scholars and Kierkegaard experts, it seemed as though we were talking past each other. Upon reflection, I realized that this miscommunication was caused, in part, by the radically different images of Kierkegaard that we held in our minds. For example, an ex-president of a seminary did not regard Kierkegaard as a Christian: "Make sure Kierkegaard is in heaven!"[10] A veteran pastor, who was moved by reading *Practice in Christianity*, said, "Some of his writings are Christianly profound. But I am not sure whether or not he was a faithful Christian until the end of his life."[11] A young pastor said, "We evangelicals hear that he is dangerous." One of my tutors asked me, "How can we reconcile 'Kierkegaard as a missionary' with a standard picture of 'Kierkegaard as the melancholy and gloomy Dane'?" Although I view Kierkegaard as a good Christian who attempted to help his contemporaries become Christians, some Christians are not sure whether or not he was a sincere Christian. Some Kierkegaard experts even view him as a self-torturing man or, at best, a cynical Christian. Because of these wildly divergent views of Kierkegaard, it is important to place our presuppositions about who Kierkegaard was on the table, so to speak, from the outset. Therefore, the remainder of this introduction aims to paint a portrait of Kierkegaard's identity that will help the reader understand the perspective I offer and provide common ground that will aid communication. At the very least, I will make a reasonable attempt to introduce my view, regardless of how the reader views Kierkegaard.

---

10. Perhaps he meant that before studying Kierkegaard, I must ensure he was a Christian and saved.

11. With regard to Kierkegaard's faith on his deathbed (one month before his death), his close friend, pastor Emil Boesen (1821–1881), testifies as follows: [Kierkegaard said,] "'So I pray first for the forgiveness of sins, that everything might be forgiven; then I pray that I might be free of despair at the time of my death' [. . .] [Boesen asked,] 'You believe in Christ and take refuge in Him in God's name?' [Kierkegaard replied,] 'Yes, of course, what else?'" Garff, *Søren Kierkegaard: A Biography*, 787.

Was Kierkegaard a Christian?

According to his self-understanding, Kierkegaard considered himself a Christian.[12] In *Journals and Notebooks*, he explains his pseudonyms and says, "The pseudonym is [Anti-Climacus][13] in contrast to Climacus, who said he was not a Christian. [Anti-Climacus] is the opposite extreme: a Christian on an extraordinary level – but I myself manage to be only a very simple Christian."[14] This quotation immediately raises a couple of issues concerning the interpretation of Kierkegaard. The first issue concerns the genre of his writings.[15] Kierkegaard's reader needs to heed which one of his persona is speaking.[16] As we shall see in detail in chapter 2 of this o, the signed writings and *Journals and Notebooks* represent Kierkegaard's own voice. Therefore, one can take what is said in those writings as Kierkegaard's genuine opinion.

The second issue is Kierkegaard's use of pseudonyms. The context of the quotation in the previous paragraph is that Kierkegaard is inventing his new pseudonym – Anti-Climacus, the author-to-be of *The Sickness unto Death* and *Practice in Christianity*. Kierkegaard created numerous pseudonyms, each with a specific personality and tasks. For instance, Johannes Climacus, who

---

12. Those who are familiar with Kierkegaard's corpus may quote his statements that appear to deny his identity as a Christian: "That, like the Wandering Jew in a beautiful legend, I should lead the pilgrims to the promised land and not enter myself, that I should guide people to the truth of Christianity and that as my punishment for going astray in my younger days I myself would not enter in but would venture only to be an omen of a matchless future" (*JP*, V 5797/ *Pap*. VI B 40:33, *n.d.*, 1845); "I quite literally have no analogy to cite, nothing corresponding in eighteen hundred years of Christianity . . . the only analogy I have before me is Socrates; my task is a Socratic task, to audit the definition of what it is to be a Christian – I do not call myself a Christian, but I can make it manifest that the others are that even less" (*SKS* 13, 404–405 / *M*, 340–341). If the above statements *literally* mean that he did not consider himself a Christian, will a view of Kierkegaard as a missionary be unsustainable? Interestingly, the above statements expound on Kierkegaard's role as a guide to the truth of Christianity or definer of what it is to be a Christian. In other words, these statements *might* be interpreted reflecting a non-Christian self-understanding, but they also seem to point in the direction of a missionary self-understanding.

13. Kierkegaard originally wrote, "The pseudonym is Johannes Anticlimacus in contrast to Climacus, who said he was not a Christian. Anticlimacus is the opposite extreme: a Christian on an extraordinary level." Kierkegaard later removed the word "Johannes" and simply made reference to "Anti-Climacus" by inserting a hyphen between "Anti" and "Climacus." To simplify the explanation, I replace "Johannes Anticlimacus" with "Anti-Climacus."

14. *SKS* 22, 128, NB11:204/ *JP*, VII, 6.174 *n.d.*, 1849. See also *SKS* 16, 116–118/ *PV*, 134–136.

15. As to the "genre" of Kierkegaard's writings, see section 2.3.1 of this book.

16. The pseudonymous authors of Kierkegaard's creation have their own arguments and viewpoints, but their ideas do not necessarily represent Kierkegaard's own views.

is referred to in the above quotation, is the author of the published works *Philosophical Fragments* and *Concluding Unscientific Postscript*, as well as the subject of the unpublished work *Johannes Climacus eller De omnibus dubitandum est* (*Johannes Climacus or Everything Must Be Doubted*). According to Kierkegaard, Climacus is a humorist and a non-Christian.[17] The lower pseudonyms[18] in Kierkegaard's first authorship[19] are generally not Christians. In contrast, Anti-Climacus is distinct from these lower pseudonyms and is a Christian on an extraordinary level.[20]

Finally, Kierkegaard himself claims that he is "a very simple Christian." This statement is not made by one of his pseudonyms. If something is said by one of the pseudonyms, such a statement cannot be considered Kierkegaard's real intention[21] since he says, "Thus in the pseudonymous books there is not a single word by me."[22] Given that Kierkegaard did write the books attributed to his pseudonyms, his statement may seem an exaggeration. However, Carl Henrik Koch points out that we must not wholly disregard what Kierkegaard has said: "Even though these words should be taken with a grain of salt, they still urge carefulness."[23] Therefore, in this book, whenever I quote from pseudonymous works, I refer to the name of the pseudonymous author.[24] Nevertheless, as stated earlier, *Journals and Notebooks* represents Kierkegaard's own voice. Although one may still doubt the trustworthiness of *Journals and*

---

17. On the boundary between "humour" and the religious sphere, see section 2.3.4.1.

18. For lower pseudonyms, see footnote 38 in chapter 2.

19. In general, Kierkegaard's works are classified into first authorship and second authorship according to the date of writing and their character, and it is regarded that Kierkegaard's first authorship is from *Either/Or* to *Concluding Unscientific Postscript*, published from 1843 to 1846. See appendix 1.

20. Kierkegaard regarded himself a Christian but did not consider himself to have reached the ideal height. However, he gave the Anti-Climax, which he created, the role of an embodiment of ideal Christian thought.

21. For instance, it is methodologically inappropriate to view Kierkegaard as a non-Christian solely based on statements made by his pseudonyms, such as when Johannes de Silentio says, "I do not have faith; this courage I lack" (*SKS* 4, 129/ *FT/R*, 34) or Johannes Climacus says, "I am not a religious person but simply and solely a humorist" (*SKS* 7, 454/ *CUP I*, 501).

22. *SKS* 7, 570/ *CUP I*, 625.

23. Koch, *Den Danske Idealisme*, 300.

24. For insightful suggestions on how we should interpret Kierkegaard's pseudonymity, see Evans, *Passionate Reason*, 5–12. For a study of Kierkegaard's pseudonymity in the context of the literary scene in early nineteenth-century Denmark, see Stewart, "Problem of Pseudonymity," 307–338.

Notebooks – and in fact, some do, as discussed later in this book – here we reasonably confirm that *Journals and Notebooks* is reliable and that, therefore, Kierkegaard was very likely a Christian.[25]

Was Kierkegaard a Good Christian?

I view Kierkegaard not just as a Christian but a *good* Christian, a view that is shared by several Kierkegaard experts. David F. Swenson (1876–1940), a member of the first generation to translate Kierkegaard's works into English, along with Walter Lowrie (1868–1959), expresses the following view:

> I refer to [Kierkegaard's] unique power in bringing home a moral challenge to the minds of his readers. The capacity to preach without descending to trivialities, and without ever striking a note of false pathos, is a very rare thing, perhaps the rarest of all accomplishments – especially among the "scientific" theologians. Of the early thinkers in the Christian community perhaps Tertullian and St. Augustine were among those most mighty in moral pathos; in later times Pascal and Luther, the William Law of *A Serious Call to a Devout and Holy Life*, John Bunyan, and several among the mystics. In the English and American literature of the nineteenth century, Ruskin and Emerson and Carlyle were lay preachers of power. Yet in my opinion Kierkegaard easily surpasses all the great names of this list, which has no intention of trying to be exhaustive but only illustrative, in his sensitiveness to the ideal in all spheres of life, in his powers of persuasive delineation, in the firmness of his grip upon essentials, in conceptual clarity and precision, . . . and in reflective sophistication.[26]

Notice that Swenson, in the above quotation, calls Kierkegaard's authorial activity "preaching." Swenson lists the names of great preachers such as Tertullian (160–after 220), Augustine (354–430), Martin Luther (1483–1546),

---

25. See also *SKS* 21, 368, NB10:200/ *JP*, VI 6391 25 April 1849.
26. Swenson, Introduction, vi–vii.

John Bunyan (1628–1688), and William Law (1686–1761), saying that "Kierkegaard easily surpasses all the great names of this list"!

Rev. Walter Lowrie, who was mentioned above, views Kierkegaard like this:

> Having been so indiscreet as to admit that I am a lover of Kierkegaard, I would have it known that *this* is the Kierkegaard I love – not the dissolute and despairing youth, nor the returning prodigal, nor the unhappy lover, not the genius who created the pseudonyms, but the frail man, utterly unfitted to cope with the world, who nevertheless was able to confront the real danger of penury as well as the vain terrors his imagination conjured up, and in fear and trembling, fighting with fabulous monsters, ventured as a lone swimmer far out upon the deep, where no human hand could be stretched out to save him, and there, with 70,000 fathoms of water under him [. . .], and then said distinctly that definite thing he was bidden to say, and died with a hallelujah on his lips. I could not love him as I do unless I could venerate him, and I learned to venerate him only when I saw that he had the courage to die as a witness for the truth.[27]

One can see Lowrie's admiration of Kierkegaard and his view of Kierkegaard as "a witness for the truth."

One of the most prominent Kierkegaard experts in Japan, 大谷愛人 (Ōtani Hidehito, 1924–2018), views Kierkegaard as follows:

> As I have finished reading all of Kierkegaard's works, namely all his religious works, the following question popped up in my mind. In history or Christian history, how many people wrote such great Christian works? Augustine, Luther, John Wesley, and the next should be Kierkegaard. The true "depth" of Kierkegaard's thought will attract the attention of people probably from the next century.[28]

---

27. Lowrie, *Short Life of Kierkegaard*, 208–209.

28. Ōtani, キルケゴール著作活動の研究 後編 – 全著作構造の解明 [A Study on Kierkegaard's Authorship, Part 2 – Investigation in the Structure of the Entirety of his Works], 1593.

As can be seen, Ōtani, like David Swenson, views Kierkegaard as ranking among the spiritual giants of the Christian faith.

After a thorough theological and philosophical investigation of Kierkegaard's thought, Simon D. Podmore makes the following comment:

> I wish to begin by confessing that this project commenced under the belief that the meaning of Kierkegaard's "infinite, radical, qualitative difference" (*uendelig svælgende qualitativ Forskjel*) between humanity and God was essentially *sin*. Mercifully, it concluded with the conviction that the true meaning of the infinite qualitative difference between God and humanity is expressed through *forgiveness*. . . . My initial suspicion that Kierkegaard's God was ultimately a God of despair was itself merely an echo of the discomfort that many readers of his work have felt before. Such a misgiving has found one of its most influential expressions in Karl Barth's warning that those who remain within Kierkegaard's schema have been consumed by it. . . . This Barthian sense of ambivalence toward the melancholy Dane . . ., this oft-repeated legend for Kierkegaard . . ., represents a perception that only sees half the face. . . . But Kierkegaard was able to derive hope by showing in his writings how despair (Dn. *Fortvivelse*) is born from doubt (*tvivl*), and therefore how its spell can be broken by faith in forgiveness and the love of God.[29]

Podmore quite appropriately argues that Kierkegaard, "the melancholy Dane," only represent "half the face" and that Kierkegaard actually proclaimed "faith in forgiveness and the love of God" that breaks the spell of despair.

Of course, individuals are free to hold whatever portrait of Kierkegaard they like in their minds. However, as the above quotations demonstrate, those who have dedicated their lives to studying Kierkegaard often consider him a sincere follower of Christ. I share this view. Of course, the above quotations do not *prove* that Kierkegaard was a good Christian but merely indicate that there were and are some Kierkegaard experts who viewed or view him as a good Christian. This study, which argues that Kierkegaard was a missionary, will indirectly indicate that his Christian faith is authentic and convincing.

---

29. Podmore, *Kierkegaard and the Self*, xi-xii.

Was Kierkegaard a Missionary?

To the surprise of some readers, Kierkegaard refers to himself as "the missionary to Christendom."[30] Through his writings, he sincerely attempted to help his readers to become and continue to be Christians. In *The Point of View for My Work as an Author,* he reflects on his own writings and comments "Once and for all I must earnestly beg the kind reader always to bear in mente [in mind] that the thought behind the whole work is: what it means to become a Christian."[31] According to his retrospective evaluation, the central thought behind all his works is "what it means to become a Christian." Moreover, for Kierkegaard, *being a Christian* entails *being a missionary*. One of his journal entries reads, "According to the New Testament, Christianity is a continuing mission, every Christian a missionary: Go out and proclaim my teaching."[32] The last sentence of this quotation is Kierkegaard's paraphrase of the words spoken by the risen Christ in Matthew 28:20 and Mark 16:15,[33] often known as the Great Commission. Therefore, Pia Søltoft appropriately says, "One could also claim that the whole of his written work is Kierkegaard's attempt to be a missionary."[34] As we shall see in appendix 8 of this book, two anonymous ladies of Kierkegaard's time and three Japanese men today have claimed that they were evangelized or edified by listening to Kierkegaard's sermons or reading his works. Undoubtedly, Kierkegaard was not a traditional missionary who went abroad to proclaim Christianity. He seldom left Copenhagen and remained a writer throughout his life. Therefore, Kierkegaard probably meant that he was *a missionary writer* who proclaimed Christianity within the Christendom of Denmark. This study takes Kierkegaard's self-understanding as "the missionary to Christendom" seriously and, from this starting point, will explore in what sense the label "missionary" fits him. I will argue that Kierkegaard not only proclaimed Jesus Christ but did so in a manner similar to Christ's own proclamation on earth. Just as Jesus Christ incarnated and proclaimed a message that was understandable to the people of his time, Kierkegaard somehow *incarnated* a Christian message that was

---

30. *JP,* III 2649/ *Pap.* IX B 63:13 n.d., 1848.
31. *SKS* 16, 23/ Kierkegaard, *Point of View,* 22.
32. *SKS* 25, 241, NB28:33/ *JP,* III 2730 n.d., 1853. See also "Mission is the task of every member, not just a few." Hale, *On Being a Missionary,* 6.
33. See also Matthew 28:19–20; Mark 16:15–20; Luke 24:47–49; John 20:21; Acts 1:8.
34. Søltoft, "Søren Kierkegaard on Mission," 396.

understandable to his contemporaries. As we shall see in section 1.3.3 of this book, Ádám Szabados describes this as Kierkegaard's method as an incarnational mission.

I imagine that many would object to what I have said above. First, since a missionary should present the gospel "in an understandable fashion within any given culture,"[35] how could anyone possibly imagine that Kierkegaard, a "mysterious Dane who lived in constant inward despair,"[36] could be a missionary? Furthermore, a tradition of interpreting Kierkegaard's central thought of "the single individual" as an asocial individualist who cares for nothing but one's own soul has become the standard interpretation.[37] If this presupposition captures the essence of Kierkegaard's thought and personality, then scepticism about Kierkegaard the missionary is well justified! How indeed could Kierkegaard readers possibly imagine that such a self-interested person was motivated by concern for his neighbours and a passionate desire to evangelize them?[38] The other possible reason that many have not taken Kierkegaard's missionary identity seriously likely arises from the reluctance of evangelicals in Britain and North America to accept his profession of faith at face value.[39] Evangelicals, who ground their identity in their missionary zeal, have long viewed Kierkegaard as an unbeliever – an outsider to the faith – and even as a opponent of that same faith. Consequently, they have been unwilling or unable to recognize the passionate Christian faith and missionary zeal

---

35. Allen, *Playing Both Sides*, 'Communicating Fluently,' para. 3.

36. Vidal and Oubiña, "Spain," 20. This phrase originally seems to have been from Miguel de Unamuno's work, but the location of the reference is unspecified.

37. It is true that "the single individual (*den Enkelte*)" is a key concept of Kierkegaard's thought; see *SKS* 20, 137, NB2:3/ *JP*, IV 4116; *SKS* 16, 77–106/ *PV*, 101–126. The issue is what Kierkegaard means by "the single individual."

38. A study of Kierkegaard as a missionary sheds light on the Kierkegaardian pivotal term "the single individual." See section 1.5 of this book.

39. The term *evangelicalism* should be used carefully. According to Alister McGrath, the German term *evangelisch*, which originally meant *evangelical*, came to be virtually synonymous with *Protestant* and so lost its original meaning. When I refer to "evangelical,"' I do not mean *evangelisch* (mainline Protestant) Christians in Germany. *Evangelicals* in this book signify those who are under the influence of a movement that occurred in Britain and North America from the 1940s onwards. This "evangelical" can be defined as follows: "*Evangelical* is thus the term chosen by evangelicals to refer to themselves, as representing most adequately the central concern of the movement for the safeguarding and articulation of the *evangel* – the good news of God which has been made known and made possible in Jesus Christ." McGrath, *Evangelicalism*, 21–22, emphasis in original.

of self-identity in an archenemy.⁴⁰ Because of these widespread and long-standing assumptions, the idea of Kierkegaard as a missionary has remained largely overlooked. In this book, I will attempt to offer convincing evidence in support of the view of Kierkegaard as a missionary.

---

40. For a discussion of the issue of the common misinterpretation of Kierkegaard among evangelicals in Britain and North America, see Evans, "Misunderstood Reformer," 26–29, and Olson, "Was Kierkegaard an Evangelical?," http://www.patheos.com/blogs/rogereolson/2011/08/was-kierkegaard-an-evangelical-part-1/; http://www.patheos.com/blogs/rogereolson/2011/08/was-kierkegaard-an-evangelical-part-2/; http://www.patheos.com/blogs/rogereolson/2011/09/kierkegaard-as-evangelical-part-3-final/.

Part 1

A Preliminary Study

CHAPTER 1

A History of the Study of Kierkegaard as a Missionary

I am convinced that the missionary theology of a man like Kierkegaard in the nineteenth century, has done more than any dogmatic theologian, perhaps more than all of them put together. Since his time, however, the task which he then recognized as the proper intellectual task of the Church, has become ten times more urgent. . . . Protestant theology, however, still manages to ignore it, and even dismisses the very idea with contempt. This contempt may even prove its own destruction.[1]

– Emil Brunner, *Dogmatik I: Die christliche Lehre von Gott*
[The Christian Doctrine of God: Dogmatics: Vol. 1]

The notion of considering Kierkegaard to have been a missionary has never been mainstream. Nonetheless, a minority trajectory of Anglophone studies adopting this standpoint does exist. In this chapter, I will attempt to trace the historical trajectory of such studies.

---

1. Brunner, *Christian Doctrine of God*, 103.

1.1 The Embryonic Period (1947–1964)

In 1938, Walter Lowrie published *Kierkegaard* – a pioneering monograph in the history of Anglophone Kierkegaard scholarship.[2] Interestingly, several years before Lowrie's *Kierkegaard*, a Presbyterian theologian and missionary named John Alexander Mackay (1889–1983) "interpreted Kierkegaard as a kind of missionary"[3] in a lecture delivered in the years 1931–1932. In this sense, somewhat unexpectedly, the study of Kierkegaard as a missionary has its origins in the early stages of the Anglophone reception of Kierkegaard. In 1946, in his *Dogmatics Volume I: The Christian Doctrine of God*, Emil Brunner (1889–1966) – a renowned Swiss neo-orthodox theologian – highly acclaims Kierkegaard as a missionary theologian, as illustrated in the quotation at the beginning of this chapter. Brunner's view seems to have been known to Anglophone scholars because the English edition of his work was published in 1950, and his view of Kierkegaard as a missionary theologian is respectfully quoted by Howard A. Johnson in the 1966 "Introduction" to Kierkegaard's *Journals and Papers*.[4] However, the first Anglophone monograph that *intensively* studies Kierkegaard as a missionary is perhaps Denzil G. M. Patrick's *Pascal and Kierkegaard: A Study in the Strategy of Evangelism*, published in 1947. This book is not just a pioneering work on Kierkegaard as a missionary but is also almost the lone voice on the subject until the publication of Mark A. Tietjen's *Kierkegaard: A Christian Missionary to Christians* in 2016. Consequently, I consider 1947 – the year Patrick's work was published – the start of the Anglophone study of Kierkegaard as a missionary. I name this first phase of history the "embryonic period" (1947–1964). In 1965, a significant development marked the commencement of a new period – the "Chaotic Period" (1965–1996), which will be discussed in section 1.2.

---

2. Lowrie, *Kierkegaard*.

3. Alessandri, "John Alexander Mackay," 64. Also see 67, 73, 81.

4. "If this elusive Danish theologian is to be captured at all in a phrase, it would be impossible to improve on the one Brunner chose: he is a missionary theologian." Johnson, Introduction to *JP*, xxviii.

1.1.1 *Pascal and Kierkegaard: A Study in the Strategy of Evangelism, Vol. II*, by Denzil G. M. Patrick (1947)

Denzil G. M. Patrick – "a Scotsman who was a returned missionary and takes seriously Kierkegaard's own claim to be a missionary to 'Christendom'"[5] – wrote *Pascal and Kierkegaard: A Study in the Strategy of Evangelism*, which was posthumously published in 1947. This work consists of two volumes. The first volume is about Blaise Pascal (1623–1662), and the second is about Kierkegaard. Hence, the second volume is the object of our interest here. The following is a summary of the second volume.

Patrick begins with a careful study of Kierkegaard's historical, intellectual, and religious environments. He takes account of the political circumstances, spiritual climate (Romanticism, idealism, Hegelianism), and the religious life and thought that characterized Kierkegaard's age.[6] On account of the inseparability of Kierkegaard's thought and life, Patrick devotes a considerable number of pages to his biography[7] through the aid of Kierkegaard secondary literature and Kierkegaard's own posthumously published work (that is, his journals and papers). Before reading Kierkegaard's pseudonymous works, Patrick deliberately examines Kierkegaard's signed commentaries[8] – *The Point of View for My Work as an Author*, *The Single Individual*, and *On My Work as an Author* – where Kierkegaard does not use pseudonymous masks but states the central purpose of all of his writings.[9] After thoroughly studying these signed commentaries, Patrick summarizes Kierkegaard's pseudonymous works primarily. He divides Kierkegaard's works according to Kierkegaard's own categorization found in *The Point of View for My Work as an Author*. In short, Patrick interprets Kierkegaard according to the rubric provided by Kierkegaard himself. His next three chapters summarize Kierkegaard's

---

5. Evans, *Kierkegaard: An Introduction*, 198.

6. Patrick, *Pascal and Kierkegaard*, 1–40.

7. Patrick, 41–158. For instance, Patrick refers to the people most important to Kierkegaard such as his father (pages 41–43) and Regine, "the queen of his heart" (pages 68–85). He also references events that were crucial to him personally such as the "existential manifesto in Gilleleie" (pages 47–49), "the great earthquake" (pages 50–52), his agony of despair (pages 52–62), the Corsair Affair (pages 89–93), the attack on Christendom (pages 139–152), and his death (pages 152–155).

8. For more on the term "signed commentary," see section 2.3.1 of this book.

9. Patrick, 159–176.

aesthetic, philosophical, and Anti-Climacus works.[10] In the last chapter of his survey of Kierkegaard's works, Patrick briefly introduces devotional (religious) and polemic works.[11] He engages critically with Kierkegaard scholars[12] who were active during his time, in light of three essential requirements: reading journals, recognizing the underlying unity of his whole work, and maintaining a positive attitude towards Christianity.[13]

After a general Kierkegaard study, Patrick moves on to argue his main thesis: *Kierkegaard as evangelist or apologist*. Although Kierkegaard himself "had a profound aversion to apologetics,"[14] Patrick dares to define him as an apologist, albeit not a defensive one but a polemical one.

It is worth noting that Patrick evaluates Kierkegaard's missionary task as follows: "Was Kierkegaard's presentation of the Christian faith an essential corrective to contemporary falsifications of the full Christian faith? This certainly is how Kierkegaard himself regarded it."[15] Patrick attaches a high value to the effectiveness of Kierkegaard's evangelism:

> He fought on four different fronts: against the Romantic æsthetic [sic] way of life, against the Idealistic speculative disdain of life, against a trend of civilization towards an order in which personal responsibility would be overwhelmed by the masses, and against a bourgeois, complacent and time-serving Church. There can be no doubt that on each of these fronts he struck a blow of decisive consequence.[16]

Patrick continues to elaborate on the consequences of Kierkegaard's fight on the four fronts mentioned above as follows:

> As against the æsthetic [sic] way of life, he showed the need to enter into true life through the strait gate of a consciousness of

---

10. Patrick, 178–288.
11. Patrick, 289–294.
12. For instance, Patrick argues with Kierkegaard scholars such as Torsten Bolin (1889–1950), Eduard Geismar (1871–1939), Jean Wahl (1888–1974), Walter Lowrie, Emanuel Hirsch (1888–1972), and Hermann Diem (1900–1975). Patrick, 295–301.
13. Patrick, 295.
14. Patrick, 301.
15. Patrick, 306.
16. Patrick, 306–307.

sin and acceptance of grace; as against idealistic speculation, he showed the need for a vital personal relationship to known Christian truth . . . ; as against the dominion of an irresponsible press and an impersonal mob, he steadfastly affirmed the personal responsibility of every man in particular before God; and as against a lukewarm Church, he insisted upon the necessity of taking seriously the absolute demands of the Gospel upon those who profess and call themselves Christians, and especially upon the ministers of the Gospel.[17]

Patrick seems to admire Kierkegaard for the "decisive consequence" of his evangelism: "This was his true vocation; and he fulfilled it to the last breath in his body."[18]

Patrick summarizes Kierkegaard's evangelism as follows:

Kierkegaard . . . "knew how to speak to the melancholy, to Don Juans, to the debauchees, to the faithful husbands; and to each he spoke his own language. Hence the infinite nuances of his writings, sceptical, humorous, full of threats, full of gentleness. And his æsthetic [sic] writings come to grips with a multitude of different men, and yet in a quite individual way with each one." Having arrested their attention, he pointed out to them their truly desperate situation so as to lead them to Christ.[19]

As Patrick studies Pascal in the first volume and Kierkegaard in the second volume respectively, he provides a summary of the strategies of both.

---

17. Patrick, 307.

18. Patrick, 307. While Patrick holds in high estimation the content of Kierkegaard's thought as an essential corrective to the four fronts, the actual impact of Kierkegaard's mission is unknown. However, appendix 8 of this book contains a few testimonies to the actual impact of Kierkegaard's mission both among his contemporaries in Denmark and among the Japanese (outside Denmark) in the twentieth century. For another testimony that shows how Kierkegaard's works have spiritually nourished Danish Christians across generations, see McLuckie, "Pastoral Response," loc. 2591–2602, Kindle. "As an anecdotal claim," C. Stephen Evans says, "Kierkegaard's writings, particularly his attack on the state church, were quickly published in Norway and also translated into Swedish, and had a great impact on the growth of the 'free churches' (non-state churches in Scandinavia)." Evans, personal communication, 16 July 2021.

19. Patrick, *Pascal and Kierkegaard*, 323–324; the quotations within the quotation are originally from Wahl, *Etudes Kierkegaardiennes* [Kierkegaardian Studies], 50, presumably translated by Patrick.

Although "the two thinkers are fundamentally original," Patrick discerns that "real resemblances or parallelisms between them are likely to have more than accidental significance."[20] According to Patrick, "Both Pascal and Kierkegaard were so completely men of their times, and sought so earnestly to meet the specific needs, to combat the specific evils of their age."[21] Patrick further states, "For both of them were conscious Christian missionaries, facing highly cultured and sophisticated people, and deeply conscious of the disunity in the soul of modern man."[22] According to Patrick, both Pascal and Kierkegaard were missionaries who consciously updated their method of evangelism as each of their eras had moved beyond the "good old days."

Patrick summarizes what he learned from Pascal and Kierkegaard:

> The grand strategy of this Christian military science is simple in conception. It is to prepare the way of the Lord, by making contact with the unbeliever in whatever spiritual environment and mood he may be; penetrating his defences by a demonstration of real sympathy with and appreciation of his interests, problems and needs; destroying his camouflage and his line of retreat; bringing him to understand that his real situation is desperate; showing him the one acceptable way of coming to terms with that situation; facing him with a spiritual ultimatum, and finally, helping him to consolidate his new-won position if he had made the right decision.[23]

According to Patrick, two biblical texts sustain a true evangelist or apologist such as Pascal or Kierkegaard: "I determined not to know anything among you, save Jesus Christ, and Him crucified" (1 Cor 2:2 ASV) and "I am made all things to all men, that I might by all means save some" (1 Cor 9:22 KJV).[24] The former verse represents "evangelistic zeal" and the latter "pastoral love," says Patrick.[25] Patrick further elaborates: "On the one hand, [a true evangelist or apologist] declares without fear or favour the whole counsel of God,

---

20. Patrick, *Pascal and Kierkegaard*, 315.
21. Patrick, 315.
22. Patrick, 380.
23. Patrick, 399.
24. Patrick, title page, 401.
25. Patrick, 401.

as revealed in the life, death and resurrection of Jesus Christ. On the other hand, he is filled with a deep interest in, and care for, human beings as such."[26]

Patrick's concluding remark, given below, speaks powerfully to us today.

> The man needed to-day in the service of the Christian Faith is not the heroic adventurer or the brilliant genius – we are going into an unknown future of a kind where neither of these types can bring the help men need – but the missionary, called and sent by God, obedient – nay, inspired with devotion to Him, with the love of Christ and his fellow-men in his heart, anxious only to share with others the infinite gift which God has given and entrusted to him. It is such a man who can hear and learn from the message of Blaise Pascal and Søren Kierkegaard.[27]

Up to now, I have attempted to objectively summarize Denzil G. M. Patrick's *Pascal and Kierkegaard: A Study in the Strategy of Evangelism, Vol. II*.

From here on, I will evaluate this work from my own perspective. One cannot exaggerate the pivotal place this monograph holds in the history of the Anglophone study of Kierkegaard as a missionary. To this day, it remains a pioneering classic on this theme. Patrick's methodology is appropriate since he carefully studies Kierkegaard's historical context, biography, primary sources, and secondary literature. He then applies Kierkegaard's mission strategy to his own context. Patrick prioritizes Kierkegaard's signed commentaries,[28] in which Kierkegaard himself expounds on how his works should be interpreted. Accordingly, throughout his writings, Patrick focuses on Kierkegaard's central and consistent theme – "the problem of becoming a Christian."[29] He leaves no doubt about the importance that he attaches to this theme, saying, "Throughout our study, the problem of becoming a Christian must be borne in mind, not only as the key to the interpretation of Kierkegaard's work, but as the supreme question which Kierkegaard invites us to consider for ourselves, existentially, with him."[30] In this sense, Patrick's work is not just methodologically appropriate but reaches the soul of Kierkegaard.

---

26. Patrick, 401.
27. Patrick, 402.
28. For more on the term "signed commentary," see section 2.3.1 of this book.
29. Patrick, *Pascal and Kierkegaard*, 159–177.
30. Patrick, 160.

Although, to this day, Kierkegaard is commonly labelled the father of existentialism, I believe he would agree with Patrick's evaluation of this label:

> It is no part of my intention to belittle the work of the modern existential philosophy, which has certainly done a great deal to bring thought back into more vital touch with reality. Let that be clearly understood. My sole concern is the sad fate which in the process of its development has befallen Søren Kierkegaard. It cannot be too strongly stated that a system of existence would be no less anathema to him than a system of thought, and that "a secularization and a generalization" of his thought is nothing less than a profanation of it.[31]

A typical example of the above statement is found in "Individual Universal," an address by Jean-Paul Sartre (1905–1980) at a UNESCO Conference in 1963.[32] On the one hand, it is true that Sartre "has certainly done a great deal to bring thought back into more vital touch with reality."[33] On the other hand, the "secularization and generalization" of Kierkegaard's thought cannot be overlooked.[34] Patrick's account (quoted above), which came twenty years before Sartre's address, exposes with penetrating discernment the problems

---

31. Patrick, 377–378. The quotation in double quotation marks is originally from Wahl, *Etudes Kierkegaardiennes* [Kierkegaardian Studies], 433, note. See also Evans, "Kierkegaard: Father of Existentialism," 110–128.

32. Sartre, "L' Universal singulier," 20–63/ 普遍的単独者 [The Singular Universal], 16–50.

33. "For Sartre, Kierkegaard is the 'singular universal' because his inwardness, his singularity, makes him the 'singular universal' who transcends history because his inwardness cannot be reduced to knowledge. Kierkegaard's subjectivity can only be re-received through Sartre's own life and engagement (commitment). In this sense, Kierkegaard is a singular universal as a singular being and a transhistorical 'living being." Minami, 「単独的普遍者」―サルトルのキルケゴール解釈をめぐって― ["'The Singular Universal': on Sartre's Interpretation of Kierkegaard"], 130). For a comprehensible summary of Sartre's address, see Aumann, "Sartre's View of Kierkegaard," 361–372.

34. In the above address, Sartre, as an atheist, plainly states that *we* are not interested in Christ Incarnate. Like Adam sinned and, thereby, we all sinned, Kierkegaard's lived experience becomes ours. For Sartre, Kierkegaard is the "Adam" of human subjectivity and freedom, and so we all inherited that subjectivity and freedom from him. He is the singular universal, says Sartre. My impression is that Sartre is "a non-Christian Judge William" since both absolutize choice – William is convinced that one chooses the good, while Sartre argues that people become themselves –whether good or evil – by choice. As for Judge William, see appendix 4 "Part II: Containing the Papers of B, Letters to A."

in the existentialists' interpretation of Kierkegaard, an interpretation that continues to be generally well known and influential even today.[35]

Regarding his pseudonymous work *Either/Or*, Kierkegaard says, "Each essay in *Either/Or* is only part of a whole, and then the whole of *Either/Or* a part of a whole."[36] Despite this, "The Seducer's Diary," which is a part of *Either/Or*, has been separated from the whole, published, and made into a film.[37] In fidelity to Kierkegaard's intentions, Patrick strongly disapproves of any attempt to isolate "The Seducer's Diary" from its literary and conceptual context, expressing his disapproval with the following words:

> Just as it is a crime to print "The Diary of a Seducer" separately, as a succulent morsel for æsthetic [sic] enjoyment, apart from the setting in which alone its true significance can be not only seen but felt, so it is a failure in intellectual integrity to use portions of Kierkegaard's thought for ends which he could have accepted only with many reservations, while completely ignoring the central purpose of Kierkegaard's literary activity as expressed in the *Point of View*[38]

I agree with Patrick. Therefore, a summary of *Either/Or* as a whole is included in appendix 4 of this book as a safeguard against misinterpreting the central messages that Kierkegaard intended to communicate to readers.[39] Patrick's work is a good example of how to read Kierkegaard's works in the way that Kierkegaard himself wished.

---

35. A Google search on "Kierkegaard" categorizes the following people as "relevant" to this search: Martin Heidegger (1889–1976), Jean-Paul Sartre, Arthur Schopenhauer (1788–1860), Friedrich Nietzsche (1844–1900), Georg Wilhelm Friedrich Hegel (1770–1831), Albert Camus (1913–1960), among others (searched on 31 January 2020). As can be seen, with the exception of Hegel, the list is filled with so-called (atheistic!) existentialists. At any rate, no one would ever associate any of these figures with missionary activity. Even if Patrick is right in identifying Kierkegaard as a missionary, commonly accepted wisdom – as represented by Google – would not lead anyone in this direction.

36. *JP*, V 5905/ *Pap.* VII1 A 118, 1846.

37. See, for instance, Kierkegaard, *Diary of a Seducer*; Kierkegaard and Updike, *Seducer's Diary*; Dubroux, *Le Journal Du Séducteur* [Diary of a Seducer].

38. Patrick, *Pascal and Kierkegaard*, 378.

39. *Either/Or* is *an amusement park* of Kierkegaard's monstrous literary device. In other words, any interpretation can somehow be justifiable. For a variety of interpretations, see David J. Gouwens, 'Kierkegaard's *Either/Or, Part One*: Patterns of Interpretation' in *IKC 3*: Either/Or, Part I. 1995: 5–50. Aiming to do justice to this work, and despite being aware of the dangers of tedium, appendix 4 of this book is devoted to a summary of the entire *Either/Or*.

The proper methods enable Patrick to discern the key features of Kierkegaard's evangelism. According to Patrick, Kierkegaard the missionary determined to know nothing except Jesus Christ (1 Cor 2:2) and made himself a slave to all so that he might win as many as possible to Christ (1 Cor 9:19). As we will see in section 1.3.3, Ádám Szabados calls this aspect of the Kierkegaardian mission "incarnational mission." Although Christ does not appear in Kierkegaard's early and famous pseudonymous works, as I demonstrate in this study, it is possible to argue that the early pseudonymous work *Either/Or* indirectly presents Jesus Christ. These distinctively Kierkegaardian features of his mission strategy were already analyzed by Patrick in the early stages of the Anglophone study of Kierkegaard as a missionary.

Despite the immeasurable value of Patrick's pioneering work, his work also contains some unsatisfactory elements. It is undeniable that Patrick's work is dated as it was published in 1947. Any contemporary student of Kierkegaard must interact with the work of a large number of important scholars after Patrick's time. In this sense, the study of Kierkegaard as a missionary, for which the foundation was laid by Patrick, needs to be updated in light of present scholarship – particularly, current studies of Kierkegaard's relation to Hegel[40] and the debate about the validity of Kierkegaard's interpretation of authorship in his signed works such as *The Point of View for My Work as an Author*.[41] Another problem with Patrick's methods is that he neglects the dialectical structure of the entire work. Appendix 1: Chronology in this book shows the parallels between pseudonymous works and signed-religious works from the first edition of *Either/Or* in 1843 to the second edition in 1849. A chronological reading of Kierkegaard's works would mean reading certain pseudonymous work(s) alongside signed-religious work(s), alternating between the two until the publication of the second edition of *Either/Or*. However, Patrick, like other Kierkegaard scholars, delves mainly into the pseudonymous works (pp. 178–220) and devotes just three pages to signed-religious works (pp. 292–294). This approach is problematic because it violates Kierkegaard's authorial intent, especially his missionary intention.

---

40. See, for instance, Thulstrup, *Kierkegaard's Relation to Hegel*; Stewart, *Kierkegaard's Relations to Hegel Reconsidered*. Although this topic is crucial, this study does not engage with it because our main interest here is Kierkegaard as a missionary, not as a philosopher.

41. See chapter 7.

Kierkegaard seduces the reader with pseudonymous works (indirect communication) and provides digestible Christian messages through his signed-religious works (direct communication). He does not simply continue this dual authorship but also gradually deepens and sharpens the Christian message over time. This dialectical tension between pseudonymous and signed-religious works is a unique aspect of Kierkegaard's missionary authorship. If one studies Kierkegaard's strategy of evangelism, one cannot miss the dialectical structure of the authorship. To compensate for this deficiency, the present book reads Kierkegaard's four published works chronologically, paying special attention to the dialectical structure of his entire body of work.

1.2 The Chaotic Period (1965–1996)

One reason the study of Kierkegaard as a missionary continues to be underdeveloped may be the influence of what I call the "chaotic period" (1965–1996). In 1965, Herbert M. Garelick published *The Anti-Christianity of Kierkegaard: A Study of Concluding Unscientific Postscript*. Garelick believes that Climacus/Kierkegaard "violates the absoluteness of religion" and makes Christianity irrational.[42] In 1972, in *Satan Is Alive and Well on Planet Earth*, Hal Lindsey, an influential American evangelist and writer, says, "Kierkegaard believed that a man comes to a point in his life when he concludes that he cannot find any definite reasons for truth or for life."[43] From this comment, those familiar with Kierkegaard's works may naturally conclude that "Hal Lindsey either never read Kierkegaard or just deliberately misunderstood him."[44] The issue here is that the words of prominent figures significantly influence people and their impact lasts for a long time. One of the most powerful evangelicals who contributed towards a negative image of Kierkegaard is Francis Schaeffer (1912–1984). In his well-read and still influential books – such as *Escape from Reason* (1968), *How Should We Then Live?: The Rise and Decline of Western Thought and Culture* (1976), and *The God Who Is There: Speaking Historic Christianity into the Twentieth Century* (1982) – Schaeffer teaches evangelicals

---

42. Garelick, *Anti-Christianity of Kierkegaard*, 71.

43. Lindsey, *Satan Is Alive*, 88. For recent efforts to recover Kierkegaard's fame in the church community, see Marshall, *Kierkegaard for the Church*, 1–2.

44. Teachman, "'Evangelicals' and Their Gatekeepers," https://medium.com/@newmethos/evangelicals-and-their-gatekeepers-98c4d9477951.

to think philosophically but also warns about the dangers of Kierkegaard's ideas.[45] As Kyle A. Roberts points out, there is not a single direct quotation from Kierkegaard in Schaeffer's writings about Kierkegaard.[46] Schaeffer's recent biography speculates that "it is highly unlikely that Schaeffer ever actually read . . . Kierkegaard."[47] How disconcerting to learn that the views of Lindsey and Schaeffer, who do not seem to have actually read Kierkegaard, became the standard view of Kierkegaard for most evangelicals.

But the situation is not so simple. In 1981, Alasdair MacIntyre published *After Virtue*, which enjoys the status of a classic in moral philosophy. In this work, MacIntyre caricatures Kierkegaard as an irrational fideist who excluded reason and "who first discovered the concept of radical choice."[48] In this sense, "MacIntyre's discussion has, then, acquired a certain status as *the* classic statement of an objection to Kierkegaard which is often also encountered in much less sophisticated forms."[49] In short, one cannot simply claim that it was evangelicals – who probably did not even read Kierkegaard – who paved the way for this view of Kierkegaard as an irrationalist. Garelick's *The Anti-Christianity of Kierkegaard* examines *Concluding Unscientific Postscript*, one of Kierkegaard's pseudonymous works. MacIntyre's *After Virtue* refers not just to Kierkegaard's *Either/Or*, *Fear and Trembling*, and *Philosophical Fragments* but also to Louis Mackey and Gregor Malantschuk, whom he calls "the best Kierkegaard scholars of our own time,"[50] to support his argument.

Are there good grounds for interpreting Kierkegaard as an irrationalist because not just Lindsey and Schaeffer but also Garelick and MacIntyre – who seemed to have read Kierkegaard's works – *also* share this oft-repeated

---

45. In his article, Derek Nutt speculates about who is responsible for "a misunderstanding of Kierkegaard's thought on the relationship of faith and reason" and "a popular view of Kierkegaard as an irrationalist." He says, "This author's anecdotal experience has led him to the conclusion that perhaps the most influential voice in condemning Kierkegaard on this front has been that of Francis Schaeffer. On several occasions, I have engaged with Christian clergy who, in relating this view of Kierkegaard, have cited Schaeffer as their authority on the matter." Nutt, "Kierkegaard's Johannes Climacus," 47–48. I have virtually the same experiences with Nutt here in Japan.

46. See Schaeffer, *Complete Works*, 1:14–17, 43, 51, 54–55, 62, 201, 233, 237–238, 240, 312, 352; 2:79; 4:14, 122, 124; 5:172, 174, 179–180, 188–190, 199, 374.

47. Hankins, *Francis Schaeffer*, 43.

48. MacIntyre, *After Virtue*, 42–43.

49. Davenport and Rudd, *Kierkegaard after MacIntyre*, xx.

50. MacIntyre, *After Virtue*, 39–43, MacIntyre refers to the original Danish titles of Kierkegaard's works: *Enten-Eller*, *Frygt og Baeven*, and *Philosophiske Smuler*.

portrayal? The overall goal of this study is to refute such a view. However, despite this main goal, the study will also introduce Johannes Climacus – a pseudonymous author used by Kierkegaard – who has been accused of promoting subjectivity. In doing so, it will briefly show Climacus defending Kierkegaardian authors. In *Concluding Unscientific Postscript*, Climacus says, "[it is] a poor existence when a thinker, who is indeed also an existing person, has given up imagination and feeling, which is just as lunatic as giving up the understanding."[51] Climacus clearly states that to give up understanding is "lunatic." He warns that "the one-sidedness of thinking produces an appearance of having everything."[52] In other words, he points out that one should not be over-theoretical because both the over-theoretical person and people around may wrongly perceive that such a person has everything. He also critiques a person whom he describes as follows: "A one-sided believer, for example, wants to have nothing to do with thinking."[53] Although MacIntyre accuses Kierkegaard of being an advocate of radical choice, such an idea is refuted by Johannes Climacus, one of the Kierkegaardian pseudonyms! Although Kierkegaardian authors certainly emphasize faith, it is unfair to call Climacus/Kierkegaard an irrationalist. The collection of quotations cited above speaks for itself, showing that Kierkegaard/Climacus urges the reader to balance reason, imagination, and feeling.

In sum, the critiques of Kierkegaard as an irrationalist are not only improper but unwarranted. What is worse, this unwarranted critique has significantly impacted the image of Kierkegaard among evangelical Christians to this day. Thus, Kierkegaard, who is "a grossly misunderstood figure,"[54] might be *the* most profoundly misunderstood among evangelical Christians in this era and thereafter. As C. Stephen Evans lamented in 1984, "Poor Kierkegaard has suffered more than any author I know of from a generation of evangelical ignorance."[55]

---

51. *SKS* 7, 318/ *CUP I*, 348.
52. *SKS* 7, 319/ *CUP I*, 349.
53. *SKS* 7, 319/ *CUP I*, 349.
54. Storm, *Commentary on Kierkegaard*, http://www.sorenkierkegaard.org/kierkegaard-commentary.html.
55. Evans, "Misunderstood Reformer," 28.

1.2.1 "Søren Kierkegaard: Missionary to Christendom" by Robert R. Cook (1987)

After Patrick, the study of Kierkegaard as a missionary seems to have disappeared from Anglophone literature for forty years, until the publication of Robert R. Cook's article "Søren Kierkegaard: Missionary to Christendom" in *The Evangelical Quarterly* in 1987. In this sense, Cook's article was long-awaited. However, I am sceptical about how much this article contributes to the study of Kierkegaard as a missionary. Cook seems to presuppose "Kierkegaard's danger" because he influenced neo-orthodox theologians and religious pluralists (with whom evangelicals are not happy) and because famous evangelical writers such as Francis Schaeffer and Hal Lindsey criticized him.[56] Regrettably, Cook does not seem to critically evaluate whether or not those who claim to have been influenced by Kierkegaard, as well as those who criticize him, are doing him justice. Without engaging in academic discussions, Cook asserts, "[Kierkegaard's] comprehension of Christianity is deficient in many areas.... His deficiencies are obvious enough and, as already observed, his influence has proved dangerous."[57] One may wonder why he published this article: "It is in the way of a testimony; a means of sharing a few of Kierkegaard's penetrating insights which have deeply challenged my life as an evangelical.... In my experience, he still has an important missionary function in challenging us."[58] Cook says that an evangelical Christian can learn about mission from Kierkegaard even if he is somehow dangerous. Cook deals with "three common misconceptions,"[59] claiming that Kierkegaard was not a mystic, Pelagian, or fideist. According to Cook, Kierkegaard's thought is valuable because it teaches evangelicals not to pursue earthly goals but, rather, to pursue God as the supreme good. Kierkegaard also urges readers to stand before God as the single individual by detaching themselves from their loved ones. Furthermore, Cook asserts that Kierkegaard encourages Christians to be subjective so that they can be aware of their need

---

56. Cook, "Søren Kierkegaard," 311–312.
57. Cook, 312.
58. Cook, 312.
59. Cook, 313–317.

for God. Finally, Cook says that Kierkegaard teaches us not to pursue fame but, rather, to will only one thing by purifying the heart.[60]

In summary, the role of Cook's article is ambiguous. In attempting to restore Kierkegaard's damaged reputation, Cook unintentionally demonstrates that he himself is not free from serious prejudices against Kierkegaard that remain common among educated evangelicals in the Anglophone world to this day.

1.2.2 Søren Kierkegaard's Christian Psychology: Insight for Counseling and Pastoral Care by C. Stephen Evans (1990)

C. Stephen Evans is not just a leading American Kierkegaard scholar but also one of the most important figures in the history of the study of Kierkegaard as a missionary.[61] As early as in his concise but pivotal 1984 essay, "A Misunderstood Reformer," Evans says, "Kierkegaard considered himself a missionary whose task was to present the gospel."[62] Here, I will examine *Kierkegaard's Christian Psychology: Insight for Counseling and Pastoral Care*, published in 1990, because this relatively small book exhaustively demonstrates Evans's view of Kierkegaard as a missionary even though its main focus is not his mission but his Christian psychology. Those who are dissatisfied with Kierkegaard studies that tend to de-Christianize or ignore the central purpose of his writings will find this book satisfying. Despite its simplicity, this book demonstrates a deep appreciation and understanding of Kierkegaard's primary and secondary sources. In Evans's view, "Kierkegaard is primarily an evangelist,"[63] and Evans regards Kierkegaard's psychology as "the handmaiden of evangelism" or "an essential tool for evangelism."[64] Assuming that Kierkegaard's central purpose in writing was evangelism, Evans carefully attempts to apply Kierkegaard's Christian psychology to pastoral counselling. Evans's method is not to force Kierkegaard to say what Evans wants to hear but, rather, to allow Kierkegaard to speak for himself.

---

60. Cook, 318–326. See also Luke 10:42.

61. C. Stephen Evans frequently refers to Kierkegaard as a missionary; see Evans, *Pocket Dictionary of Apologetics*, 66; Evans, "Søren Kierkegaard: Philosophical Fragments," 159–160; Evans, *Kierkegaard: An Introduction*, 1–2.

62. Evans, "Misunderstood Reformer," 27.

63. Evans, *Kierkegaard's Christian Psychology*, 25.

64. Evans, 23, 25.

In this way, one can learn the proper procedure to be adopted for drawing insights from Kierkegaard while wisely avoiding distortion of his ideas. However, since the primary focus of Evans's book is Kierkegaard's psychology, and not his mission strategy, the study of Kierkegaard as a missionary is not developed further.

1.3 The Reconsidering Period (1997–2003)

Christian researchers such as Paul L. Holmer (1916–2004),[65] Edward John Carnell (1919–67),[66] Kenneth Hamilton (1917–2009),[67] Vernard Eller (1927–2007),[68] Vernon C. Grounds (1914–2010), and a much younger generation – including the likes of C. Stephen Evans – have introduced a more balanced view of Kierkegaard and helped evangelical Christians take a fresh look at Kierkegaard. They help evangelicals to see Kierkegaard just the way he is, whether or not they finally agree with him on certain philosophical or theological opinions. Thanks to these researchers, evangelicals have been enabled to reconsider Kierkegaard. From 1997 to 2003, a few fine studies in which the authors view Kierkegaard as a missionary were published. I define this period as the "reconsidering period."

1.3.1 "The Hipness unto Death: Søren Kierkegaard and David Letterman – Ironic Apologists to Generation X" by Mark C. Miller (1997)

The article "The Hipness unto Death: Søren Kierkegaard and David Letterman – Ironic Apologists to Generation X," written by Mark C. Miller and published in 1997, is a study of Kierkegaard's apologetics and its possible application to the so-called Generation X in the USA. Miller expounds on Generation X: "Generation X is the name given by novelist Douglas Coupland to Americans born between 1961 and 1981."[69] The Xer is "cynical,

---

65. For example, Holmer, *Kierkegaard and the Truth*.
66. For example, Carnell, *Burden of Søren Kierkegaard*; Silas Morgan, "Edward John Carnell: A Skeptical Neo-Evangelical Reading".
67. For example, Hamilton, *Promise of Kierkegaard*, .
68. For example, Eller, *Kierkegaard and Radical Discipleship*.
69. Miller, "The Hipness unto Death," 27.

wary, ... apathetic, ... suspicious and indifferent, needs nothing."[70] Miller says, "But Xers need the gospel like everyone else. And Søren Kierkegaard is the philosopher-evangelist to give it to them ... I submit that if the church is to communicate meaningfully with Generation X, it must adopt the strategies employed and the convictions passionately held by Kierkegaard."[71] Miller expects that Kierkegaard's tactic can effectively evangelize Generation X. First, Generation X – who found their identity in cynicism (aesthetic), hard work (ethical), or both – is Kierkegaard's audience because he shows the bankruptcy of aesthetic and ethical lives, says Miller.[72] Second, initially jettisoning religious language, Kierkegaard can hook the interest of Xers who regard typical evangelism as "a sales pitch."[73] Third, Kierkegaard's evangelism that employs Socratic irony "to disarm the ironic way of living" will be effective for ironical Xers.[74] Miller says,

> Kierkegaard would then communicate ironically with the reader by detaching himself from his own words. He then was able to speak the language of his reader. "He will be more poetic than any Young German. He will be more Hegelian than any professor of philosophy. He will be more upright than any parson, more exploitive than any Don Juan."[75]

Fourth, Kierkegaard, "the enigmatic Dane," will be more appealing to Xers than "the boomer churches' six steps towards better living."[76] Xers will "agree with Kierkegaard: there are no precise steps to follow. There is only the action of following Christ."[77] Fifth, Kierkegaard restores the relationship between the individual and the neighbour.[78] "Kierkegaard believed that when one stood before God as an individual, he would love his neighbour, and they

---

70. Miller, 27.
71. Miller, 28.
72. Miller, 27–29.
73. Miller, 30.
74. Miller, 31.
75. Miller., 31–32; the quotation within the quotation is originally from Mullen, *Kierkegaard's Philosophy*, 39.
76. Miller, "Hipness unto Death," 34.
77. Miller, 34.
78. Miller, 34–35.

would be bound together . . . 'Restoration of community is the primary need for Generation X.'"[79] Miller also adds,

> His objective was to bring the individual before God, where he would stand naked and alone . . . Here I fear Kierkegaard has been often misunderstood . . . "But to will only one thing, genuinely to will the Good, as an individual, to will to hold fast to God, which things each person without exception is capable of doing, this is what unites" . . . We are united when we seek God wholeheartedly. When we do not submit to one another, when we esteem ourselves, we do not "will the Good" and community suffers. But "[*Love seeks not its own. For the true lover does not love his own individuality. He rather loves each human being according to the other's individuality*]."[80]

Fascinatingly, Miller asserts that by standing before God as individuals, people can be united instead of being individualistic or asocial. In conclusion, Miller expects that the eyes of Xers, who "recognize the bankruptcy of accumulation," will be upon "God and relationships, and they will seek fulfillment outside materialism."[81] This is a summary of Miller's "The Hipness unto Death."

Let me move on to my evaluation of this article. One can see that Miller wisely avoids some common misunderstandings among evangelicals and attractively presents Kierkegaard as "the philosopher-evangelist" who can "communicate meaningfully with Generation X."[82] Miller even contributes to Kierkegaard scholarship in general by demythologizing an image of Kierkegaard as an individualist. Miller bravely applies Kierkegaard's method in the context of the USA in the twentieth century. One may wonder whether or not Kierkegaard's method is applicable in the USA even though both the context of nineteenth-century Denmark and twentieth-century America can be called Christendom. In reality, nineteenth-century Denmark and

---

79. Miller, 35.

80. Miller, 34; the first quotation within the quotation marks is originally from Kierkegaard, *To Will One Thing*, 144; the second quotation within the quotation is originally from *SKS* 9, 268/ *WL*, 251–252, emphasis Kierkegaard's.

81. Miller, "Hipness unto Death," 35.

82. Miller, 28.

twentieth-century America appear dissimilar in many areas, but according to Miller, Kierkegaard's apologetics or evangelism reaches America's cynical Generation X. On the other hand, Miller's article lacks an overt methodology. However, this omission is understandable considering its limited length. In the case of this study, a carefully considered method is required to extract Kierkegaard's thought from his works and apply it to the twenty-first-century Japanese context.

1.3.2 "Rejuvenating Apologetics in the Twenty-First Century: Taking Hints from Søren Kierkegaard" by John Depoe (2002)

In his article "Rejuvenating Apologetics in the Twenty-First Century: Taking Hints from Søren Kierkegaard," published in 2002, John Depoe states that Kierkegaard's thought can rejuvenate weakened apologetics to reach out to modern atheists. Depoe refers to the example of Robert J. Miller, "a voting member of the Jesus Seminar."[83] Robert J. Miller had once engaged in apologetics but later abandoned evangelical faith, disappointed that "apologies almost never reach outsiders."[84] Unlike Robert R. Cook,[85] Depoe does not uncritically agree with Francis Schaeffer: "[Schaeffer] is wrong to suppose that Kierkegaard was an enemy of rationality or applying rigorous thought to Christianity."[86] In Depoe, one can detect a gradually strengthening voice that says "no" to Schaeffer's critique of Kierkegaard among evangelicals.

According to Depoe, the first tactic that the Christian apologist can learn from Kierkegaard is the indirect movement of the audience towards the Christian faith. It is well known that "Kierkegaard saw his fellow Danes existing in three possible stages of life"[87] – that is, the aesthetic, ethical, and religious stages. "Kierkegaard used various pseudonyms to exemplify these life-views and to point his readers to accept the Christian life."[88] The second tactic that can be learned from Kierkegaard is his non-evidentialist approach that did not attempt to prove the *existence* of God but, rather, encouraged the

---

83. Depoe, "Rejuvenating Apologetics." 1.
84. Depoe, 1; originally quoted in Miller, "Stories about Resurrection(s)," 87.
85. See section 1.2.1 of this book.
86. Depoe, "Rejuvenating Apologetics," 2–3.
87. Depoe, 5.
88. Depoe, 5.

reader to *exist* as a true Christian. The third tactic that apologists should learn is "to incorporate humor as part of sharing Christianity."[89] Depoe defends Kierkegaard, arguing that Kierkegaard's notorious term "faith as absurd or paradox" does not mean a strict logical contradiction but, rather, indicates that Christian faith is unthinkable for the human mind.[90] Furthermore, Depoe defends Kierkegaard's discouragement of the historical study of the Gospels, which attempts to ground the Christian faith on a historical foundation. According to Depoe, Kierkegaard meant "that even if there were evidence either completely in favor or none at all for the gospels, it would still require faith to become a Christian."[91] In conclusion, Depoe imagines that if Kierkegaard's tactics were applied, Robert J. Miller would not "[give] up on apologetics and evangelical Christianity."[92]

As can be seen in both Mark C. Miller's "The Hipness unto Death" in section 1.3.1 and Depoe's "Rejuvenating Apologetics in the Twenty-First Century" in section 1.3.2, it seems that evangelicals have gradually learned to critically engage with a common misconception about Kierkegaard. Depoe's approach to interpreting Kierkegaard is a fine example of how to use Kierkegaard's thought for apologetics or evangelism as a foundation for subsequent researchers.

1.3.3 "Incarnational Mission: Søren Kierkegaard's Challenge to Evangelical Christianity" by Ádám Szabados (2003)

In his article "Incarnational Mission: Søren Kierkegaard's Challenge to Evangelical Christianity," published on the internet in 2003, Hungarian pastor Ádám Szabados argues strongly that evangelicals need to learn about incarnational mission from Kierkegaard. Szabados argues that

> Kierkegaard wanted to lead his contemporaries, who lived esthetic and ethical lives, to Christ. Following the example of Jesus, he started the rescue program where the other person was. If he wanted to raise the interest of an esthetic person, he has to give him esthetic writings. He must not criticize directly for by

---

89. Depoe, 7.
90. Depoe, 10.
91. Depoe, 17.
92. Depoe, 18.

that he would lose him. The method should be longer and more indirect. The esthete has to give the criticism himself. As if in a mirror, he must see himself, so that the emptiness might lead to despair. There is solution to the man in despair: "Come unto me, all ye that labour and are heavy laden, and I will give you rest." Kierkegaard writes with a complete existential identification from the point of view of the esthete . . . Kierkegaard does not tell us that the esthete is like this and this. He penetrates the esthete's soul and makes us see him from inside. The esthete introduces himself to us. He himself tells us – in a most natural way – what the world is like for him.[93]

Why does Kierkegaard identify himself with the aesthete and the ethicist in *Either/Or*? He does so to win his readers over to Christ. Szabados says, "Everyone is mistaken who imputed to Kierkegaard the esthetic attitude of Either/Or . . . The whole book is therefore a disguise. Kierkegaard's real I is the missionary."[94]

While Szabados argues that Kierkegaard's aesthetic appearance in *Either/Or* is driven by a missionary purpose, he is also aware of debatable issues concerning Kierkegaard's mission:

As to how much Kierkegaard is responsible for the frequent and general misunderstandings concerning his person and authorship, or if he did not spend too much time with the preparation of the disguise, or if the genius waiting for unfolding in him did not [overdo] the reflexion [sic], or if he was not needlessly obscure sometimes, if he found the healthy balance between directness and indirectness in his writings, or if the perfect

---

93. Szabados, "Incarnational Mission," 37; the quotation within the quotation is originally from Matthew 11:28. How was it possible for Kierkegaard to "[penetrate] the esthete's soul and [make] us see him from inside"? Denzil G. M. Patrick explains this well: "Kierkegaard was a Romantic and an Idealist" and "[the] whole plan of his pseudonymous works is profoundly Romantic." "If he had not known by personal experience the allurements of the æsthetic [sic] way of life, if he had not tasted the delights of Idealistic speculation, he would not have seen able to penetrate to the very bottom of them and disclose the anguish and despair that lurked there." He could penetrate the aesthete's soul from within because he experienced both the pleasure and despair of aesthetic lives (For Kierkegaard, idealistic speculation is also a part of the aesthetic). "It was just because he was so profoundly *en rapport* with the spirit of his times that he knew how to speak effectively to it." Patrick, *Pascal and Kierkegaard*, 311–312.

94. Szabados, "Incarnational Mission," 38.

identification with the esthetic and ethical contemporaries did not become a hindrance for Kierkegaard in the preaching of the gospel: these questions are open to debate.[95]

Szabados admits that there may be deficiencies in Kierkegaard's incarnational mission. But Szabados's point is that evangelicals can learn the *principle* of incarnational mission from him. According to Szabados, *both* sincere compassion for the existential problems of secular people *and* unambiguous proclamation of the gospel are needed in incarnational mission. Szabados compares Christ's method with Kierkegaard's:

> Christ ate with prostitutes and tax collectors because he came to save prostitutes and tax collectors. Kierkegaard wrote *Either/Or* because he knew Christ had come to save esthetes and ethical people for eternal life. They were there so he also needed to go there. Our contemporaries are similarly either in the bondage of morality or in the bondage of the "interesting." More in the latter than the former. Are we ready to become "romantic to the romantic" in a romantic age? Are we ready to hear in our own hearts the cry of the deceived? For Kierkegaard the reflexion [sic] on the esthetic and ethical life was a pastoral task. Incarnational mission is a pastoral task (in the noblest sense of the word): the humility of love, resignation, obedient service, brokenness for others.[96]

Szabados asserts that, like Kierkegaard, we are to weep for the suffering of our contemporaries in order to win them over to Christ. It is clear that Szabados is free from the typical prejudice of many evangelicals against Kierkegaard. He does not merely defend the view of Kierkegaard as a missionary but identifies his strategy as incarnational mission. This identification is quite proper. Since Szabados views incarnational mission as an ideal mission, he does not merely defend Kierkegaard but also urges evangelicals to learn from him. One can see that there is increasing acceptance of Kierkegaard among evangelicals.

---

95. Szabados, 38–39.
96. Szabados, 40.

1.4 The Fetal Period (2004–present)

By the end of the twentieth century, C. Stephen Evans stood almost alone among Kierkegaard experts in his identification of Kierkegaard as a missionary. But from 2004 onwards, Kierkegaard scholars such as Hugh Pyper, Pia Søltoft, Aruthuckal Varughese John, and Mark A. Tietjen refer to Kierkegaard as an evangelist or a missionary. These Kierkegaard scholars have contributed to a study of Kierkegaard as a missionary by publishing articles and monographs in which they intentionally approach Kierkegaard from this missionary angle. I call this period the "fetal period." During this period, the solid ground of modern Kierkegaard scholarship forms the basis for Kierkegaard the missionary to emerge from the shadows.[97]

1.4.1 *The Joy of Kierkegaard* by Hugh Pyper (2004)

In *The Joy of Kierkegaard*, published in 2004, Hugh Pyper, an Old Testament scholar and Kierkegaard expert, describes Kierkegaard in a way that is quite different from the stereotypical portrait of a melancholy and gloomy Dane:

> My strong conviction is that joy is at the heart of what Kierkegaard was about. When I am asked what description best sums up Kierkegaard – philosopher, theologian, religious thinker, a kind of poet, novelist, preacher – these days I have an answer: he is an evangelist, in its root meaning as a bearer of good news.[98]

In view of the similarities between Kierkegaard and Fyodor Dostoevsky (1821–1881), Pyper describes Kierkegaard "a great comic writer."[99] Pyper discerns that "there is in even the darkest passage of Kierkegaard the sheer joy of the writing, the dazzling verbal display, but also so often the teasing tone."[100] Referring to *Either/Or* and *Concluding Unscientific Postscript*, Pyper argues that Kierkegaard's words make his readers laugh and, at the same time,

---

97. I should also refer to Aaron Edwards, who is a prominent figure in the field related to studies of Kierkegaard as a missionary. Although he seems not to refer to Kierkegaard as a "missionary," he imagines Kierkegaard as a pastor in a rural parish or calls him a "Socratic street preacher." However, his focus is more on preaching or homiletics. Edwards, "Kierkegaard's Imaginary Rural Parish," 235–246; Edwards, "Socratic Street Preacher," 280–300.

98. Pyper, *Joy of Kierkegaard*, 1.

99. Pyper, 2.

100. Pyper, 2.

"serve as a warning."[101] Pyper lists the titles of discourses in Kierkegaard's signed-religious work[102] *Christian Discourses*, which emphasizes biblical joy amid sufferings:

> The joy of it, that one suffers only once but is victorious eternally;
> The joy of it, that hardship does not take away but procures hope;
> The joy of it, that the poorer you become the richer you are able to make others;
> The joy of it, that the weaker you become, the stronger God becomes in you;
> The joy of it, that what you lose temporally you gain eternally;
> The joy of it that when I "gain everything" I lose nothing at all;
> The joy of it, that adversity is prosperity.[103]

By referring to the poem[104] of W. H. Auden (1907–1973), who was profoundly influenced by Kierkegaard, Pyper analyzes Kierkegaard's concept of joy as both *absurdity* and *command*. He compares Kierkegaard's joy with the kind of joy described in Habakkuk 3:17–19: "Though the fig tree does not bloom . . . I will rejoice in the Lord."[105] Pyper says that this kind of joy is not a joy of *because* but one of *nevertheless*. He defines Kierkegaard's joy not as his joy but as God's. Pyper describes this biblical and Kierkegaardian joy by saying, "Joy, then, is both duty and gift, both task and reward."[106] Because of the obligation to obey God's command to rejoice, joy is a duty, but joy is also a gift freely given as a reward for obedience to God. In the end, although he thinks it is "an impertinent question," Pyper asks whether or not Kierkegaard really rejoiced during his lifetime.[107] Pyper finds the answer to his query in a touching quotation from Kierkegaard's *Journals and Notebooks*:

> Therefore my voice will shout for joy at the top of my lungs, louder than the voice of a woman who has given birth, louder than the angels' glad shout over a sinner who is converted, more

---

101. Pyper, 3.
102. For an explanation of the term "signed-religious work," see section 2.3.1 of this book.
103. Pyper, *Joy of Kierkegaard*, 4; originally from *SKS* 10, 105/ *CD*, vi.
104. Auden, *Collected Poems*, 319.
105. Pyper, *Joy of Kierkegaard*, 7.
106. Pyper, 11.
107. Pyper, 12.

joyful than the morning song of the birds, for what I have sought I have found, and if men robbed me of everything, if they cast me out of their society, I would still retain this joy. If everything were taken from me, I would still continue to have the best – the blessed wonder over God's infinite love, over the wisdom of his decisions.[108]

Pyper also refers to how Kierkegaard rejoiced in his last days – as testified to by Kierkegaard's nephew Henrik Lund (1825–1889) – and concludes that joy was Kierkegaard's possession. At the same time, Pyper asserts that anybody can be "a prophet of joy."[109]

Pyper's article is quite interesting since no other Kierkegaard scholar has ever emphasized joy in Kierkegaard's thought. This article implies that it is not enough to merely label Kierkegaard as a missionary or evangelist. A study of Kierkegaard's mission must consider the biblical joy that Kierkegaard possessed, a joy that is essential for a missionary spreading the gospel.

1.4.2 "Søren Kierkegaard on Mission in Christendom: Upbuilding Language and Its Rhetoric Understood as the Fundament of Mission" by Pia Søltoft (2007)

In 2007, Pia Søltoft, a Danish Kierkegaard expert and parish priest, published "Søren Kierkegaard on Mission in Christendom: Upbuilding Language and Its Rhetoric Understood as the Fundament of Mission" in *Swedish Missiological Themes*. In this article, Søltoft says, "I have to admit, that mission is not a word Kierkegaard uses very often. But that does not mean that he does not pay any attention to the phenomena."[110] Søltoft says that whenever Kierkegaard refers to a mission, "he does so in a very, very positive way."[111] He adds that Christendom in Denmark was a mission field for Kierkegaard and that he engaged in a specific kind of mission through language and rhetoric. More specifically, Søltoft explains that Kierkegaard's mission had an aspect of intersubjectivity, in which the single individual should influence others. Søltoft affirms that "Kierkegaard is of the firm conviction that mission is an integral

---

108. Pyper, 12; originally from *SKS* 18, 310–311, JJ:510/ *JP*, II 2184 *n.d.*, 1842.
109. Pyper, 13.
110. Søltoft, "Mission in Christendom," 395–396.
111. Søltoft, 396.

part of being a Christian. Maybe that would come as a surprise to those of you who follow the tradition for conceiving of Kierkegaard as the great spokesman for isolated subjectivity."[112] From a philosophical point of view, Søltoft asks how one can influence others through language and rhetoric. For Kierkegaard, a human being is not merely what one is but, rather, something one has to keep on becoming. Becoming oneself is not a once-and-for-all event but a continuing process. Søltoft expounds on this idea: "It is more of a continuous process and in this process the one person can, through communication and speech, be helpful to the other."[113] According to Søltoft's analysis of Kierkegaard, the style of such communication is preaching or upbuilding discourse. Søltoft summarizes her article as follows: "I will first examine Kierkegaard's conception of preaching as a mission in Christendom and then take up his view on rhetoric to see how one person through language can influence the faith of another and thereby be a missionary."[114] According to Søltoft, Kierkegaard's concept of preaching is varied, but his fundamental understanding of it can be found in his pseudonymous work *The Concept of Anxiety*, in which he states,

> But to preach is really the most difficult of all arts and is essentially the art that Socrates praises, the art of being able to converse. It goes without saying that the need is not for someone in the congregation to provide an answer, or that it would be of help continually to introduce a respondent. What Socrates criticized in the Sophists, when he made the distinction that they indeed knew how to make speeches but not how to converse, was that they could talk at length about any subject but lacked the element of appropriation. Appropriation is precisely the secret of conversation.[115]

According to Søltoft, for Kierkegaard, an aspect of appropriation must always be present in any style of mission, and the audience has a responsibility to make a choice. Søltoft refers to Kierkegaard's journal entry:

---

112. Søltoft, 396.
113. Søltoft, 397.
114. Søltoft, 397.
115. Søltoft, 398; originally from *SKS* 4, 323/ *CA*, 16, translation slightly modified by Søltoft.

> To will to allow oneself to be built up [. . .] I am convinced that the person who will allow himself to be built up, even if he heard a perhaps mediocre pastor or read a perhaps mediocre devotional book, will be built up. The danger is that someone may be disturbed in this regard or in remaining, resolute in his choice [. . .] being a good listener [is] just as great as being a good speaker, and perhaps at times the former is even the greater.[116]

According to the above quotation, Kierkegaard believes that the art of listening equals in value the art of preaching, and he even goes one step further in admitting that at times, the greatness of listening may outweigh that of preaching. Søltoft further discusses Kierkegaard's concept of rhetoric or mission as seduction. Rhetoric, which refers to an individual's ability to influence others, lies at the heart of Kierkegaard's concept of mission. From a missionary perspective, rhetoric involves convincing others of Christian truth. In this vein, Søltoft adumbrates a twofold meaning of rhetoric in Kierkegaard's conceptualization of it. On the one hand, for sophists or passionless pastors, rhetoric can mean convincing others of some truth without any personal commitment to that truth. On the other hand, for people like Socrates or the missionaries described in the New Testament, rhetoric involves convincing others of some truth to which one is committed to. Following Plato, Kierkegaard believed that one who believes in and lives by the truth not only *can* but also *ought to* seduce or deceive people into the truth. Søltoft says, "Rhetoric can and should be used by one person, the missionary, to make the other person attentive and perhaps win him/her over to 'the truth.' This is not an assignment for the few, but is in fact an assignment placed on every Christian."[117]

Constructed on the solid foundation of current Kierkegaard studies, Søltoft's short but powerful article is vital. This article explores how Kierkegaard's mission relates to his philosophical discussion on rhetoric and provides important clues that point the way forward for studying Kierkegaard as a missionary. Therefore, discussions of a Kierkegaardian mission should emphasize *listening* and recognize Kierkegaard's *conversational* concept of preaching that facilitates the *appropriation* of the truth by the audience. In

---

116. Søltoft, 400; originally from *Pap.* VI B 133; *TD*, Supplement, 120.
117. Søltoft, 403.

other words, the aim of a Kierkegaardian mission is to seduce the audience into willingly allowing themselves to be built up.

1.4.3 *Truth and Subjectivity, Faith and History: Kierkegaard's Insights for Christian Faith* by Varughese John (2012)

Truth and Subjectivity, Faith and History: Kierkegaard's Insights for Christian Faith by Varughese John, published in 2012, is a philosophical study on Kierkegaard's apologetics and its possible application in the Indian context. Chapter 1, "On the Very Idea of Truth," is the most philosophical and complex part of the book, analyzing the validity of modern and postmodern philosophical frameworks from the Kierkegaardian perspective. John discerns that "the Kierkegaardian method rightly suspects not only the modernistic assumptions but also the arrogant postmodern denials of truth."[118] According to John, Kierkegaard's epistemology is that "depravity or fallenness not only makes humans devoid of truth, but also renders human truth-pursuits, futile."[119] John states that Kierkegaard raised a question about the scheme of modernism, which presupposes so-called objective truth that is indifferent to the pursuer's commitment to the truth. According to John, another problem of modernism is that "much of analytical philosophy sees truth merely in the objective sense, which would also require a God's-eye-view of things to know things as they really are."[120] How about postmodernism? To some degree, "a postmodern hermeneutic of suspicion is a natural successor to Kierkegaard's hermeneutic of finitude,"[121] says John. In this sense, "the postmodern suspicion of truth-claims is understandable."[122] However, John says that the standard-bearers of postmodernism – such as Richard Rorty (1931–2007), Michel Foucault (1926–1984), and Jacques Derrida (1930–2004) – "all seem to touch upon something necessary, and yet each provides a far from satisfactory understanding of truth."[123] But what is a Kierkegaardian perspective? According to John, a Kierkegaardian perspective is to say that "within the givenness of human finitude, truth with no pretension to absoluteness is still

---

118. John, *Truth and Subjectivity*, loc. 464–465, Kindle.
119. John, loc. 767–768, Kindle.
120. John, loc. 397–398, Kindle.
121. John, loc. 505–506, Kindle.
122. John, loc. 457–458, Kindle.
123. John, loc. 400–403, Kindle.

possible. This should lead one neither to a relativism nor to an abandonment of reason."[124] Although both Kierkegaard and postmodernists are suspicious about the human ability to know the truth, a closer look at both epistemologies proves their significant differences: "Whereas, in the Kierkegaardian scheme, the inaccessibility of truth, unlike the relativists, assumes that there is Truth with a capital T, which however, is out of bounds for man because of his finitude and depravity."[125] John argues that "the question then would be, 'how would one know that there is Truth with a capital T, if it is not accessible?'"[126] John continues, "Notably the affirmation of the existence of Truth with a capital T as properly belonging to God could very well function as a basic belief, whose epistemic status is based on faith."[127] Therefore, "Kierkegaard illustrates that truth has to be given from without. The God-man, through the moment of incarnation, makes the transcendent truth, immanent."[128] According to John, it is not through modernistic, objective truth without passion, with its pretension of a God's-eye view, nor by postmodern relativism but, rather, by the God-man Jesus Christ that one comes to the recognition, pursuit, and life of truth within the sphere of human finitude.

In chapter 2, "Truthing through Subjectivity," John examines "Kierkegaard's reconstructive analysis in understanding self." For Kierkegaard, a self is "an unfinished entity that is in a process of becoming." John discerns that Kierkegaard's view of self "provides a biblical alternative to the modern arrogant view of the self."[129] According to John, "Kierkegaard avoids an entirely relativized postmodern view of self and a nihilism that this could entail."[130] As in chapter 1, John emphasizes Kierkegaard's recognition of total depravity, namely, "the complete fallenness of the self – the intellect, will, and passion."[131] Kierkegaardianly speaking, "it is not any choice that defines the self but the choice that pertains to God as its constituter" since "one is always

---

124. John, loc. 469–470, Kindle.
125. John, loc. 489–491, Kindle.
126. John, loc. 495–496, Kindle.
127. John, loc. 501–502, Kindle.
128. John, loc. 769–770, Kindle.
129. John, loc. 931–932, Kindle.
130. John, loc. 933–934, Kindle.
131. John, loc. 975–976, Kindle.

a slave – either to the self (sin) or to God (righteousness)."[132] John argues that Kierkegaard's subjectivity is not relativism but "a network of things, that connect related concepts such as inwardness, self-reflection, passion, will, emotions, etc."[133] So what is subjectivity in Kierkegaard's sense? "One thus becomes subjective to the extent of relating to the God who established the individual in trust and passion."[134] In other words, Kierkegaard's *subjectivity* is the term that defines how one can relate to God in a biblical sense.

As reflected in its title, chapter 3, "Being in the Truth: Re-engaging Climacus's Devout Idolater," deals with an attractive but controversial parable that is told by Johannes Climacus – one of Kierkegaard's pseudonyms. Climacus's parable of the Devout Idolater is as follows:

> If someone who lives in the midst of Christianity enters, with knowledge of the true idea of God, the house of god [sic], the house of the true God, and prays, but prays in untruth, and if someone lives in an idolatrous land but prays with all the passion of infinity, although his eyes are resting upon the image of an idol – where, then, is there more truth? The one prays in truth to God although he is worshipping an idol; the other prays in untruth to the true God and is therefore in truth worshipping an idol.[135]

Interestingly, John says that there is a similarity between Climacus's parable and Jesus's statement in Matthew 8:10–13.[136] John calls attention to the

---

132. John, loc. 960–961, 965, Kindle.

133. John, loc. 1016–1017, Kindle.

134. John, loc. 1376–1377, Kindle.

135. John, loc. 1521–1524, 1529–1533, Kindle; originally from *SKS* 7, 184/ *CUP I*, 201. See also section 10.2.2. Reading the above parable, one of my fellow PhD candidates, himself a Dane, said that he disagreed with Kierkegaard (Climacus) since the *Holy Spirit who dwells in a Christian* allows us to *truly* worship. It is no wonder that *good* Christians struggle to embrace Climacus's parable. On the other hand, this same person, who belongs to one of the free churches in Denmark, said bitterly that the choir members of the Danish State Church prefer to sing on Sunday because they can earn twice as much as singing on weekdays, implying that at least some in the Danish State Church *do not truly worship* but regard church activities merely as an opportunity to earn money. It appears to me that his latter comment unwittingly supports the idea of Kierkegaard (Climacus), who implies the possibility of a Christian who offers untrue worship.

136. John, loc. 1741–1744, Kindle, footnote 1. I would also add Romans 2:12–16. N. T. Wright annotates these verses and says, "God will judge everyone according to where they are, not according to where they are not. Those outside the law (Gentiles, in other words) will be

fact that Kierkegaard wrote a number of books under pseudonyms, in which the pseudonymous authors claim to be non-Christians. Moreover, through these non-Christian pseudonymous works, Kierkegaard attempted to communicate with "Christians, or, at least, to those who claim to be Christians even though they have lost their passion and dedication."[137] In sum, John concludes that "Climacus' purpose in juxtaposing the two worshippers in the parable is not to argue toward a religious pluralism of any kind, but rather it is to argue for the worthlessness or even the depravity of believing in the true God, accompanied by an absence of true devotion."[138] Kierkegaard warns both himself and his fellow Danes that there is no geographical advantage in being born in Christendom. Although Kierkegaard might appear to be a legalist, John argues that Kierkegaard, as he himself says in his journal, believed that every Christian would go to heaven.[139] Kierkegaard did not intend to urge pluralism, determine who would go to heaven or hell, or judge who is superior to whom. In John's view, Kierkegaard's intention was to awaken and edify his fellow Danes within Christendom.

Chapter 4, "Understanding Historical Religious Knowledge of Faith," is "an introductory discussion to the specific issues surrounding history and faith."[140] John refers to the following words of Climacus: "Knowing a historical fact – indeed, knowing all the historical facts with the trustworthiness of an eyewitness – by no means makes the eyewitness a follower, which is understandable, because such knowledge means nothing more to him than the historical."[141] According to Climacus, it is a category mistake to attempt to prove or disprove the divinity of Jesus of Nazareth through a historical

---

judged that way; those inside (Jews) will be judged by the law they possess." Wright, *Paul for Everyone*, page unspecified. What Paul says in Romans 2:12–16 suggests that God is fair and impartial; he judges the devout idolater as outside the law (not according to the law). Thus, Tietjen's and my point is that Johannes Climacus's parable of the Devout Idolater is not that unbiblical.

137. John, *Truth and Subjectivity*, loc. 1684–1685, Kindle.
138. John, loc. 1647–1648, Kindle.
139. John, loc. 1720–1724, Kindle. See below: "Therefore what the old Bishop once said to me is not true – namely, that I spoke as if the others were going to hell. No, if I can be said to speak at all of going to hell then I say something like this: If the others are going to hell, then I am going along with them. But I do not believe that; on the contrary, I believe that we will all be saved, I, too, and this awakens my deepest wonder." *JP*, VI 6947/ *Pap*. XI 3 B57 *n.d.*, 1854. See also *JP*, VI 6934/ *Pap*. XI 2 A244 *n.d.*, 1854.
140. John, *Truth and Subjectivity*, loc. 2270, Kindle.
141. John, loc. 1808–1810, Kindle; originally from *SKS* 4, 261–262/ *PF*, 59.

investigation. John says, "Kierkegaard's corrective seems to address both errors equally and simultaneously."[142] The following quotation serves as a good summary of this chapter:

> From a historical standpoint, one can be reasonably certain about the life of Jesus, who, according to the New Testament writers, claimed to be divine. The truth of that claim, however, is beyond the scope of historical scholarship. The New Testament writer only witnesses to the truth and does not try to prove it.[143]

The divinity of Jesus should not and cannot be proved or disproved by historical scholarship, but it should be and can be *witnessed* to by the apostles. For Climacus, *belief* or *disbelief* in Jesus is based on this witness.

Chapter 5 deals with "Historical Research and Its Sufficiency for Faith."[144] John attempts to define the term *evidence*, stating, "It is one thing to say that 'evidence' refers to coherence between one's beliefs and the historical life of Jesus, and quite another to say that historical evidence demonstrates the truth of one's beliefs. Climacus maintains only the former."[145] John rightly observes that Kierkegaard's position is different from the position of so-called neo-orthodox theologians who draw a sharp distinction between the historical Jesus and the Christ of faith. On behalf of Climacus, John states, "Climacus' position is that historical inquiry does not produce faith, but faith cannot be detached from history."[146] Referring to the argument of Stephen Evans, who examines Climacus's works, John asserts, "Evans argues that the Climacean rejection of historical evidence is to prevent faith from becoming a subject of endless scholarly debate."[147] Quoting from Evans's work, John elucidates Climacus's position as follows:

> Since it is no ordinary occurrence, and as eternal happiness is at stake, no amount of evidence would be sufficient for faith. Further, a Christian "does not have the luxury of waiting for the scholars to reach an agreement, which will never happen in

---

142. John, loc. 1976–1977, Kindle.
143. John, loc. 2087–2089, Kindle.
144. John, loc. 2412, Kindle.
145. John, loc. 2500–2501, Kindle.
146. John, loc. 2506–2507, Kindle.
147. John, loc. 2706, Kindle.

any case," to conclude in the end that there is enough historical evidence for him to now become a believer.[148]

John goes on to say, "[Evans] further suggests that it is the existence of faith that makes the question of evidence meaningful."[149] The historical evidence does not produce faith but faith makes the historical evidence meaningful. In short, "Faith is not established on the basis of historical inquiry, but rather by 'a transforming encounter with Christ, [which] is epistemically antecedent to particular historical beliefs about him.'"[150] "So Kierkegaard writes, 'let miracle be what it is: an object of faith.'"[151] John concludes that the God-man – Christ – is not an object of historical inquiry but of faith.

Chapter 6, "Kierkegaardian Insights for Christian Witness and Apologetics,"[152] is divided into two sections. Section A, titled "Kierkegaard and Apologetics,"[153] attempts to delineate Kierkegaard's apologetics. John argues that "[Kierkegaard] engages in a type of apologetics that provides justification for Christian faith"[154] even though he is not a typical apologist. While Norman Geisler (1932–2019) says that "evangelical Christian theism qualifies as the most systematically coherent theistic view on all three tests; consistency, empirical adequacy, and experiential relevance,"[155] John is sceptical about whether a non-Christian would agree with the arguments and conclusions of Christian apologists. Therefore, John says, "A pivotal question that an apologist should then ask is whether the evidential approach, which views external evidence in conjunction with certain tests for truth as sufficient to determine a given truth-claim, really works."[156] John, learning from Climacus-Kierkegaard, says that "an apologist overestimates the potential of

---

148. John, loc. 2708–2711, Kindle; the quotation within the quotation is originally from Evans, *Faith and the Self*, 160.
149. John, loc. 2716–2717, Kindle.
150. John, loc. 2875–2876, Kindle; the quotation within the quotation is originally from Rae, "Kierkegaard and the Historians," 90.
151. John, *Truth and Subjectivity*, loc. 2883, Kindle; originally from *SKS* 22, 44, NB11:75/ *JP*, III 2720.
152. John, loc. 3023, Kindle.
153. John, loc. 3028, Kindle.
154. John, loc. 3037–3038, Kindle.
155. John, loc. 3099–3100, Kindle.
156. John, loc. 3114–3116, Kindle.

the evidential approach."¹⁵⁷ As far as John is concerned, Kierkegaard emphasizes the radical qualitative difference between a fallen natural intellect and a renewed one. Therefore, Kierkegaard does not encourage Christian apologists to make Christianity logical or probable. Like the apostles, Christians should not attempt to prove but to bear witness to Jesus of Nazareth. John discerns that Kierkegaard's pneumatology plays a vital role in the process that brings one to faith in Jesus. Indeed, in Kierkegaard's eyes, pneumatology replaces rational argumentation; accordingly, he expects the Holy Spirit to work in the hearer to transform their nature and create the conditions necessary for them to recognize the truth.

Section B, titled "Hindu Sense of History and Christian Apologetics," attempts to apply Kierkegaardian apologetics to the Indian context, which I find a valuable resource. Although Kierkegaard was a "missionary in Christendom,"¹⁵⁸ John argues that his apologetics are also relevant in India – a context that is worlds apart from any setting that could be considered "Christian." Indians are generally indifferent to historicity since they view time as cyclical, unlike Westerners who view time as linear. Indians also do not distinguish myth from history. John expounds on the Indian concept of history, stating that "human activities become minuscule and insignificant in comparison. Cyclic time is continuous, without a beginning or an end."¹⁵⁹ John warns the reader not to prejudge the superiority of one world view over another since "each culture has an innate nature, a temper, which must guide all its cultural products from mathematics, to physics, to painting and poetry."¹⁶⁰ John describes several "insights for apologetics in the Hindu context."¹⁶¹ First, he questions the appropriateness of imposing historical rigour in the Indian context. Second, he reminds the reader that the gospel proclaimed by the early church was powerful and effective not because of its historical rigour but because of its salvific value. Third, "the need for a proper appropriation of history within the community of faith is important."¹⁶²

---

157. John, loc. 3122, Kindle.

158. John, loc. 3290, Kindle.

159. John, loc. 3316–3317; originally from Thapar, *Time as a Metaphor*, 5.

160. John, *Truth and Subjectivity*, loc. 3361–3362, Kindle; originally from Nanda, *Postmodernism and Religious Fundamentalism*, 48.

161. John, *Truth and Subjectivity*, loc. 3387, Kindle.

162. John, loc. 3403–3404, Kindle.

John suggests that the practice of Eucharist will help Indians to appropriate history by recalling the past event of the cross and anticipating the future event of Christ's second coming. Finally, "a proper appropriation of history can contribute to the making of history!"[163] By this, John means that the recognition of Christ's death for one's sake will convince a person of their own value. When someone recognizes their significant role in history, they will act according to this renewed world view. John concludes his work by remarking that "a faithful communication of the Christian message will have to take the historical nature of Christian beliefs seriously and yet acknowledge the impossibility of founding faith on historical evidence alone."[164] Accordingly, "a Kierkegaardian response may be summarized in the words of E. Stanley Jones (1884–1973): 'a Christian witness should be just that – a witness of Jesus Christ and not his advocate.'"[165]

There are three points from John's work that are particularly noteworthy for my study. First, John's *Truth and Subjectivity, Faith and History: Kierkegaard's Insights for Christian Faith* ambitiously deals with the issues of modernism and postmodernism, which means that this work attempts to allow Kierkegaard to speak to post-Kierkegaardian philosophers as well. Although some might fault John for leaving his argument open to the charge of anachronism, in my judgment, John appropriately demonstrates that Kierkegaard is still relevant in the postmodern condition. John's work is the most philosophically dense among the literature that explores the topic of Kierkegaard as a missionary or an apologist. However, this does not mean that his work involves speculative philosophizing since such an attempt is not Kierkegaardian. In *The Point of View for My Work as an Author*, Kierkegaard says, "The book describes the second way – *back* from the system, the speculative, etc. to becoming a Christian."[166] It is a Kierkegaardian way (amplification) to *disarm* both modernism and postmodernism philosophically. But how? Based on what? "A believer . . . credits a priori legitimacy to the Scriptures via inspiration."[167] It is not the Kierkegaardian way to critique a certain philoso-

---

163. John, loc. 3412–3413, Kindle.
164. John, loc. 3432–3434, Kindle.
165. John, loc. 3435–3436, Kindle.
166. *SKS* 16, 36/ *PV*, 55, emphasis in original.
167. John, *Truth and Subjectivity*, loc. 1968, Kindle.

phy upon the foundation of another philosophy. The following standpoint of William Stacy Johnson reflects Kierkegaard's own perspective: "The Christian Scriptures set themselves up not so much as truth claims to be defended by philosophical foundations but as witnesses to the transforming power that no truth claim itself can contain."[168] John Kierkegaardianly refutes modernism and postmodernism based on the Scriptures.

Second, to convince others, a person does what they can, which is to bear witness to the truth. According to John, Kierkegaard rejects all attempts at historical proof and, instead, emphasizes witness to Jesus of Nazareth, especially through the missionary's existence. By submitting themselves not to academically persuade but, rather, to bear witness to Jesus of Nazareth based upon the Scriptures, a Kierkegaardian missionary makes way for the Holy Spirit to do his work of renewing the hearer's cognitive ability and convincing them of God's truth.

Third, John bravely applies Kierkegaard's thought to the Indian context. In this sense, his work is one of the most important precedents for this study. John shows how it is possible to apply Kierkegaard's thought to a context that is vastly different from the nineteenth-century Christendom of Denmark. An important lesson to learn from John is that one should learn and apply *the principles* of a Kierkegaardian mission rather than slavishly copying Kierkegaard, especially when targeting a context that is different from Kierkegaard's.

1.4.4 *Kierkegaard: A Christian Missionary to Christians* by Mark A. Tietjen (2016)

Kierkegaard: A Christian Missionary to Christians by Mark A. Tietjen, published in 2016, is the most recent book that studies Kierkegaard as a missionary. Written in plain language, it is aimed at Christians who might be sceptical of the authenticity of Kierkegaard's Christian faith. Tietjen attempts to demonstrate how Kierkegaard's thought is valuable for Christians today. In the first chapter, "Kierkegaard: Friend to Christians?,"[169] Tietjen attempts to restore Kierkegaard's reputation among Christians and help Christian readers rid themselves of some typical misunderstandings about Kierkegaard. He does so

---

168. Johnson, "Reading the Scripture Faithfully," 112.
169. Tietjen, *Kierkegaard: A Christian Missionary*, loc. 291, Kindle.

by addressing the widespread myth, advocated by Francis Schaeffer and other recent evangelicals, that Kierkegaard's ideas were dangerous. Tietjen argues that by criticizing Kierkegaard's concept of faith, Schaeffer unwittingly criticizes the authentic Christian faith described in the New Testament in Hebrews 11. Referring to Kierkegaard's (in)famous concept of a leap of faith, Tietjen says this is not really a central concept in Kierkegaard's thought. If Tietjen is right, there is no basis for labelling Kierkegaard as an "irrationalist"[170] – a label arising from the assumption that Kierkegaard advocates a leap of faith. The following claim made by Tietjen is noteworthy: "Contrary to some of the interpretations of Christians and non-Christians alike, fundamentally Kierkegaard offers nothing new in terms of his theological vision of the biblical view of human life."[171] Tietjen also asserts that Kierkegaard's Christian faith is closely connected to Scripture, the church fathers, and the Reformers, rather than being derived from an eccentric or novel kind of Christianity of his own invention.

The second chapter, "Jesus Christ,"[172] is devoted to describing Kierkegaard's concept of Jesus Christ, which is relatively unheeded in Kierkegaard scholarship. Tietjen identifies three mistaken views of Jesus of Nazareth: the "liberal theology" view, the "Pelagian" view, and the "grace-abuse" view.[173] According to Tietjen, Kierkegaard "critique[d] these problematic theologies"[174] and attempted to restore a sense of the shocking nature of Christian doctrines such as sin and Christ's incarnation. Why did Kierkegaard do this? It is because these doctrines, in particular, seemed unsurprising and unimpressive to Kierkegaard's contemporaries. According to Tietjen, unlike earthly healers who only help those who can *pay*, Jesus – as described in Kierkegaard's *Practice in Christianity* – invites all *unconditionally*. In Tietjen's opinion, Kierkegaard took "seriously Paul's words to Timothy, that God 'desires everyone to be saved' (1 Tim 2:4)."[175] Tietjen concludes his analysis by stating that Kierkegaard's Jesus is both a gentle Saviour and a pattern to be followed.

---

170. Tietjen, loc. 2727, footnote 14, Kindle.
171. Tietjen, loc. 702–703, Kindle.
172. Tietjen, loc. 787, Kindle.
173. Tietjen, loc. 812–814, Kindle.
174. Tietjen, loc. 832, Kindle.
175. Tietjen, loc. 1226–1227, Kindle.

The third chapter, "The Human Self,"[176] is about Kierkegaard's analysis of the human being, a concept that is generally well known among Kierkegaard readers. Tietjen is convinced that "Kierkegaard was of the opinion that Christianity had the most compelling answer to the question 'What does it mean to be human?'"[177] For Kierkegaard, to be human is not a task that can be completed once and for all: "It is a difficult and seemingly endless task, one that speaks to how humans are, in Kierkegaard's language, always in the process of *becoming*."[178] Tietjen applies Kierkegaard's famous theory of three stages to the Christian life. For instance, "Theists can also despair . . . if they love God's creation more than God."[179] Christians can remain trapped in the ethical stage if they have a "strong sense of pride"[180] Therefore, "religion and religious existence cannot be *reduced* to ethics . . . [In] Christianity the truth is not Christ's teaching but rather Christ himself. Religious existence for Kierkegaard is fundamentally about turning to the incarnate God for assistance."[181] Tietjen suggests that, in Kierkegaard's view, to be an authentic human being is to be an authentic Christian.

The fourth chapter, "Christian witness,"[182] is the core of this work. It describes Kierkegaard's mission to his contemporaries and its possible applications for today. In keeping with the previous chapter, where Tietjen argues that truth rests on Jesus himself rather than on his teachings, here he emphasizes that Christian witness requires us to present ourselves rather than limit ourselves to verbal communication. "What one's life proclaims is a hundred thousand times more powerfully effective than what one's mouth proclaims," says Kierkegaard.[183] The following quotation is representative of the central argument of Tietjen's work:

> As a Christian missionary to Christians, Kierkegaard believes that the problem in Christendom is not knowledge of the Christian faith but acting according to that knowledge . . . This,

---

176. Tietjen, loc. 1243, Kindle.
177. Tietjen, loc. 1263, Kindle.
178. Tietjen, loc. 1333–1334, Kindle; emphasis in original.
179. Tietjen, loc. 1519–1520, Kindle.
180. Tietjen, loc. 1690, Kindle.
181. Tietjen, loc. 1650–1652, Kindle; emphasis in original.
182. Tietjen, loc. 1714, Kindle.
183. Tietjen, loc. 1716–1717, Kindle; originally from *SKS* 16, 186/ *FSE /JFY*, 131–132.

> then, explains what Kierkegaard is doing both in the pseudonymous writings but also the signed, religious writings. In the former he aims to awaken a decision and response in the lives of nominal Christians who find themselves attracted to lifestyles and worldviews like the aesthetic or the ethical that are not actually Christian. And in the latter writings he aims to evoke from his reader specifically Christian virtues or actions, such as hopefulness or courage or trust in God.[184]

In the above quotation, Tietjen interprets Kierkegaard's entire authorship from the perspective of Kierkegaard as a Christian missionary to Christians.

The fifth chapter, "The Life of Christian Love,"[185] draws mainly on Kierkegaard's *Works of Love*, through which Tietjen describes Kierkegaard's vision for the Christian life, which is characterized by love, faith, and hope. Ultimately, Tietjen encourages his readers to become more faithful Christians rather than better Kierkegaard scholars: "Looking at what Kierkegaard says about Christian love . . . meets our objective, which is not to become better Kierkegaard scholars but more faithful Christians."[186] According to Tietjen, Kierkegaard believed that love is the mother of all virtues and that it gives birth to faith and hope. Tietjen keenly discerns that in the biblical-Kierkegaardian view, love is not a feeling but a command. Tietjen asserts, "By obeying the command – the emotional side of love will eventually come alongside love's action." Tietjen expounds on this further, saying, "Christians have a word for this process: sanctification. Through obedience to God's commands, one becomes more holy, more like God himself."[187] In other words, love is both a command and a gift from God.

In the "Conclusion," Tietjen asserts that "all Christians are called to mission"[188] since Kierkegaard did not limit the definition of a missionary to someone who is sent to unreached nations by a mission agency. It does not matter whether one's neighbour is an unbeliever or a believer since "mission

---

184. Tietjen, loc. 1748–1753, Kindle.
185. Tietjen, loc. 2094, Kindle.
186. Tietjen, loc. 2134–2136, Kindle.
187. Tietjen, loc. 2189–2192, Kindle.
188. Tietjen, loc. 2523–2525, Kindle; emphasis in original.

work quite simply calls others, *all* others, to God."[189] Furthermore, Tietjen emphasizes Kierkegaard's point about *being* rather than *doing*, saying, "To be a missionary is not simply to convert the lost but to incarnate divine love in obedience to and imitation of Jesus Christ, the God incarnate. This could involve a fresh gospel message, works of love."[190] On behalf of Kierkegaard, Tietjen emphasizes "honesty before God."[191] A Christian has to be coherent both inwardly and outwardly. According to Tietjen, Kierkegaard's *initial* aim was not to convert readers and make them Christians[192] but to help them be honest before God. We must be aware of our own ignorance and learn to know who we are.

As demonstrated by the positive recommendations of several theologians, Tietjen's book is a long-awaited work.[193] Praises for his book are understandable. Tietjen wisely avoids jargon and powerfully demonstrates that Kierkegaard was indeed a missionary and one who remains relevant even today. Tietjen's work certainly represents a milestone in the history of the study of Kierkegaard as a missionary. However, although Tietjen's work is invaluable, my concern is that his intended readership is primarily Christian. In other words, Tietjen's aim in this book does not seem to be to convince non-Christian readers.[194] If it is justifiable to call Kierkegaard a missionary, it should be possible to argue such a point of view irrespective of the religious background of the reader. In this study, I aim to demonstrate the continuing missionary relevance of Kierkegaard to any reader, regardless of their religious background.

What we learn from Tietjen's *Kierkegaard: A Christian Missionary to Christians* is that a Kierkegaardian missionary is not necessarily one who is sent by a mission agency. The Kierkegaardian mission only requires that we

---

189. Tietjen, loc. 2523–2525, Kindle.

190. Tietjen, loc. 2521–2522, Kindle.

191. Tietjen, loc. 2525–2531, Kindle; emphasis in original.

192. Tietjen, loc. 2525, Kindle.

193. See "Praise for Kierkegaard," which is actually praise for Tietjen's work, in Tietjen, loc. 2993–3032, Kindle.

194. His engagement in critical dialogue can be seen in Mark A. Tietjen, *Kierkegaard, Communication, and Virtue: Authorship as Edification*. However, in this work, Tietjen does not attempt to portray Kierkegaard as a missionary but argues that "what Kierkegaard aims to accomplish as a philosopher, theologian, and psychologist – as a writer broadly speaking – is the moral and religious improvement of his reader." Tietjen, *Kierkegaard, Communication, and Virtue*, 2.

call others – all others – to God, whether or not they are already Christians. Why do we invite those who are already Christians to God? Is such a task meaningful? We do so because every individual on earth, including the missionary, is in a process of becoming. Since we are all in the process of becoming, we remain incomplete. Therefore, both Christian missionaries and their neighbours are always encouraged to either become Christians or become more faithful Christians. Kierkegaardianly speaking, truth is Christ himself rather than merely Christ's teachings; therefore, the Kierkegaardian missionary communicates with their neighbours existentially, rather than merely verbally.

1.5 Summary and Conclusion

We have traced the trajectory of previous Anglophone studies of Kierkegaard as a missionary, particularly the work of Denzil G. M. Patrick, Robert R. Cook, C. Stephen Evans, Mark C. Miller, John Depoe, Ádám Szabados, Hugh Pyper, Pia Søltoft, Varughese John, and Mark A. Tietjen. From our survey of this literature, we have learned several important things. First, although studies that view Kierkegaard as a missionary are relatively rare, an increasing number of scholars have adopted this perspective and defended the legitimacy of identifying Kierkegaard as a missionary or an evangelist. "Kierkegaard was an evangelist rather than a theologian" (Patrick). "In my experience, he still has an important missionary function in challenging us" (Cook). "Kierkegaard is best understood . . . as a missionary" (Evans). "Kierkegaard's non-evidentialist message can be an advantageous ally for contemporary apologists and evangelists to heed today" (Miller). "Soren Kierkegaard is the philosopher-evangelist" (Miller). "Kierkegaard's Real I is the missionary" (Szabados). "He is an evangelist" (Pyper), "One could also claim that the whole of his written work is Kierkegaard's attempt to be a missionary" (Søltoft). "Given his acknowledged undertaking was more as a 'missionary in Christendom'" (John). "In a sense Kierkegaard is a Christian missionary to Christians" (Tietjen). These scholars uniformly refer to Kierkegaard as a missionary or an evangelist. If such a claim is justifiable, in what sense and to what extent is it justifiable?

Second, Szabados identifies the nature of Kierkegaard's mission as the *incarnational mission*, which can be compared with Jesus's incarnation.

Although the term "incarnational mission" is not used, Patrick[195] Miller,[196] and Tietjen[197] also recognize this aspect of Kierkegaard's mission. In other words, these four researchers do not merely attempt to prove Kierkegaard's missionary status but, by comparing Kierkegaard's mission with Christ's method, also submit that the Kierkegaardian approach to mission is an ideal model for all Christians to emulate.

Third, Patrick,[198] Miller,[199] and Søltoft[200] assert that Kierkegaard's *single individual* is the one who influences others religiously. Their findings challenge the stereotypical view of Kierkegaard as an asocial individualist. This suggests that a study of Kierkegaard as a missionary is not just personally fulfilling but may also contribute to Kierkegaard studies in general.

Fourth, both Pyper[201] and Tietjen[202] analyze Kierkegaard's views on Christian virtues like joy and love, seeing these as both commands and gifts. According to them, in Kierkegaard's view, when one obeys God's commands to rejoice or love, the fruit of the Holy Spirit – such as joy or love – will be freely given as gifts (Gal 5:22–23). If their interpretation is correct, Kierkegaard seems to reconcile the Lutheran-Pauline view of justification by grace with James's view of justification by action. This is not grace-abuse since obedience to rejoice or to love is demanded. It is not legalism either since joy or love is freely given upon one's absolute obedience. In this way, Kierkegaard resolves the tension between grace and action.

Fifth, well-established methods are necessary to ground a study of Kierkegaard as a missionary on a solid foundation. Studies of Kierkegaard as a missionary remain marginalized and fragmented. With the exception of Patrick, no scholar has discussed in depth what methods are necessary for the study of Kierkegaard as a missionary. Without appropriate methodology, such studies risk being influenced by prejudices – for example, the uncritical view of Kierkegaard as dangerous or the assumption that Kierkegaard was

---

195. Patrick, *Pascal and Kierkegaard*, 323–324.
196. Miller, "Hipness unto Death," 4.
197. Tietjen, *Kierkegaard: A Christian Missionary*, loc. 2521–2522, Kindle.
198. Patrick, *Pascal and Kierkegaard*, 310.
199. Miller, "Hipness unto Death," 6.
200. Søltoft, "Mission in Christendom," 396.
201. Pyper, *Joy of Kierkegaard*, 11.
202. Tietjen, *Kierkegaard: A Christian Missionary*, loc. 2189–2192, Kindle.

an asocial individualist. Such studies can hardly convince either evangelicals or Kierkegaard scholars of the validity of the view of Kierkegaard as a missionary. Therefore, establishing valid methods is vital. Patrick's previous work will serve as Ariadne's thread – a guiding principle – as we attempt to establish these methods. In the next chapter, we will study existing approaches to Kierkegaard, with the aim of establishing the most appropriate methods for this study.

CHAPTER 2

Methodology and Scope

Such works are mirrors: when an ape looks in, no apostle can look out.

Lichtenberg[1] – Søren Kierkegaard, *Stages on Life's Way*

This chapter aims to establish proper methodology and defines the scope of the present work. In the first section, I will categorize the most prominent Kierkegaard studies in the Anglophone world and Japan[2] and then identify the main singular method by drawing on five works that discuss how to read Kierkegaard. However, while identifying the dominant method in these Kierkegaard studies is helpful, there are limitations to these singular approaches to Kierkegaard, who is a man for all disciplines. Therefore, in the second section, I will examine existing Kierkegaard studies that employ plural or multi-layered methods and investigate how and to what extent such an approach does justice to Kierkegaard. In the third section, I will define the author-oriented method, which attempts to allow Kierkegaard to speak for himself by uncovering his multi-layered disciplines and unique aspects of his thought. Section 4 will deal with a critical assessment of this method

---

1. *SKS* 6, 16/ *SLW*, 8; originally written in German, translated by Howard V. Hong and Edna H. Hong, who are translators of Kierkegaard's Writings (Princeton University Press).

2. Japan is one of the most prolific nations when it comes to Kierkegaard research. When it comes to the quality of Japanese Kierkegaard research, Takahiro Hirabayashi states, "In a sense Japanese Kierkegaard research is the world's best. The only problem is that Kierkegaard researchers in other countries do not know what Japanese Kierkegaard research is all about." Hirabayashi, "New Identity," 215.

to address deficiencies in the author-oriented method. Finally, in section 5, I will define the scope of the present study.

2.1 Categorization of Methods

In this section, I will categorize the representative methods of Kierkegaard studies as depicted in the diagram in appendix 2. The material in this section is largely derived from several excellent studies on methodology, including 橋本淳 (Hashimoto Jun's) キェルケゴールにおける「苦悩」の世界 (The World of "Suffering" in Kierkegaard) published in 1976,[3] Hidehito Ōtani's キルケゴール青年時代の研究 (A Study of Kierkegaard's Youth) published in 1966–1968,[4] キルケゴール著作活動の研究 (A Study of Kierkegaard's Authorship) published in 1989–1991,[5] C. Stephen Evans's *Passionate Reason* published in 1992,[6] and David J. Gouwens's *Kierkegaard as Religious Thinker* published in 1996.[7] I will synthesize these studies, include other influential Kierkegaard studies, and arrange the results systematically.

No thought emerges in a vacuum, and this is particularly true of Kierkegaard's thinking. His thought is *existential* and cannot be detached from his life events. In this sense, a Kierkegaard researcher cannot ignore **biographical methods**. These biographical methods can be further divided into three subcategories centred around Kierkegaard's life history, the perceptions of his contemporaries, and his social environment. Those who employ the life-history method usually explore Kierkegaard's personal life and life events chronologically, based on his own perspective, through the evidence contained in his journals. Others take an external, as opposed to an internal, approach, studying Kierkegaard through the eyes of his contemporaries. Such scholars pay careful attention to what was said about Kierkegaard by his contemporaries. Still others choose to approach the biographical aspects of

---

3. Hashimoto, キェルケゴールにおける「苦悩」の世界 [The World of "Suffering" in Kierkegaard], 19–81.

4. Ōtani, キルケゴール青年時代の研究 正 [A Study of Kierkegaard's Youth], 3–43.

5. Ōtani, キルケゴール著作活動の研究 前篇 – 青年時代を中心に行われた文学研究の実態 [A Study on Kierkegaard's Authorship, Part 1 – The Realities of Young Kierkegaard's Own Studies of Literature], 3–83.

6. Evans, *Passionate Reason*, 2–7.

7. Gouwens, *Kierkegaard as Religious Thinker*, 3–25.

Kierkegaard through the lens of his broader exeternal social environment. These students of Kierkegaard take pains to locate him within the wider context of general history, church history, and the history of thought, particularly Scandinavian thought.

Psychological methods can refer to the study of Kierkegaard as either a *patient* or a *psychologist*. Understandably, some researchers attempt to diagnose Kierkegaard as a melancholy man from the perspective of modern psychology. However, Kierkegaard himself seemed to regard the nature of his thought as somehow *psychological*, as evidenced by his frequent use of terms such as "psychology," "psychological," and "psychologically" in the subtitles of chapters, as well as entire works.[8] Therefore, studying Kierkegaard as a psychologist can offer valuable insights into the key elements of his thought.[9]

Kierkegaard is generally referred to as a philosopher, and, therefore, **philosophical methods** are probably the most common approach to studying his work. His fame in philosophical circles – as the father of existentialism – continued to grow globally from the 1920s to the 1960s. Even today, Kierkegaard is often viewed as an existentialist, especially in non-academic settings. However, philosophical studies after the 1960s (that is, after existentialism's dominant period) are not so greatly influenced by existentialism and its aftermath. Instead, modern researchers tend to be interested in studying Kierkegaard more objectively, placing him within the tradition of Western philosophy.

---

8. For instance, the subtitle of *Repetition* is "A Venture in Experimental Psychology"; the subtitle of *The Concept of Anxiety* reads "A Simple Psychologically Orienting Deliberation on the Dogmatic Issue of Hereditary Sin"; and the subtitle of *The Sickness unto Death* is "A Christian Psychological Exposition for Upbuilding and Awakening." Further, the fourth chapter of *Either/Or, Part I* reads "Silhouettes: Psychological Diversion," and in *Stages on Life's Way*, the third chapter – "'Guilty?'/ 'Not Guilty?'" – is made more specific with the subtitle "A Story of Suffering: An Imaginary Psychological Construction by Frater Taciturnus." Inasmuch as the above titles speak for themselves, Kierkegaard regarded his works as somehow psychological. And yet, Takahiro Hirabayashi reminds us that since what "psychology" means for us was established from the late nineteenth century to the early twentieth century, Kierkegaard's "psychology" is different from our concept of "psychology." Hirabayashi relocates Kierkegaard's "psychology" in the context of nineteenth- century Denmark and attempts to deduce what he meant by this term. Hirabayashi, "セーレン・キルケゴールにおける«心理学»の問題―――つの歴史的研究 [On the Problem of Søren Kierkegaard's Psychology: A Historical Study]," 37–56.

9. See, for instance, Popova, "Why Haters Hate," https://internet.psych.wisc.edu/wp-content/uploads/532-Master/532-UnitPages/Unit-06/Popova_Kirkegaard_BrainPickings_2014.pdf.

Theological methods also represent a key approach because Kierkegaard was unquestionably a profound Christian thinker. Along with existentialism, neo-orthodoxy contributed to making Kierkegaard known outside Denmark and creating an image of a neo-orthodox theologian-like Kierkegaard. Once neo-orthodoxy was no longer popular, Kierkegaard's theology was studied in its own right by Kierkegaard experts. David R. Law's *Kierkegaard's Kenotic Christology*, published in 2013, is representative of such sound theological scholarship.

Ecclesiastical interpretation shares similarities with theological studies in that both approaches are Christian interpretations. However, ecclesiastical interpretation is intended more for lay Christians, whereas theological studies are intended for academics.[10] In recent years, the publication of such interpretations has increased, giving Christians greater access to Kierkegaard's thought and more opportunities to apply it to their own Christian lives and spirituality.

In Kierkegaard scholarship, the significance of **literary methods** has often been overshadowed by the popularity of philosophical and theological methods. While philosophical and theological studies are undoubtedly helpful for better understanding Kierkegaard, he did not view himself as an academic professor. Rather, he considered himself a poet, and his pseudonymous works – such as *Either/Or*, *Repetition*, and *Stages on Life's Way* – are not monographs but philosophical *novels*. Philosophical or theological monographs or articles make or clarify statements and propositions using *direct* communication. But Kierkegaard's literature connotes, implies, seduces, provokes, and teases the reader, boldly employing *indirect* communication to do so. Therefore, the nature of Kierkegaard's corpus should be treated as literature rather than as monographs. Literary studies can involve *both* a study of the literary background of Kierkegaard's thought *and* literary criticism. Hidehito Ōtani's *A Study on Kierkegaard's Authorship* uses the former method while Louis Mackey's *Kierkegaard: A Kind of Poet* employs the latter.

---

10. Ronald F. Marshall's *Kierkegaard for the Church* is one of the best books dealing with this kind of approach: "If Kierkegaard's words about Christianity are true, how would they change the way we learn and practice the Christian faith today? My book is an answer to that question. So in these pages I do not enter into a critical discussion over the truth of Kierkegaard's philosophy and theology." Marshall, *Kierkegaard for the Church*, 6–7.

The Frankfurt School's interpretations of Kierkegaard are early, unique, and often harshly critical of Kierkegaard. Interestingly, György Lukács (1885–1971), one of the philosophers associated with the Frankfurt School's critical theory, discusses Kierkegaard before the interwar period of the German Kierkegaard renaissance, which came about due to the popularity of existential philosophies and neo-orthodox theologies. In his *A lélek és a formák* (*Soul and Form*) (orig. 1910/ Eng. 1974), Lukács romantically interprets the tragic love between Kierkegaard and Regine Olsen (1822–1904). In later works, however, his interpretation shifts radically, showing a completely different perspective. *Die Zerstörung der Vernunft* (*Destruction of Reason*) (org. 1954/ Eng. 1980) and *Reason and Revolution* (1941) by Herbert Marcuse (1898–1979) are representative of the Western Marxist interpretation of Kierkegaard. In these works, while Joseph Stalin (1878–1953) is praised, Kierkegaard and the existentialists are accused of inspiring Nazism. In *Kierkegaard: Konstruktion des Ästhetischen* (*Kierkegaard: Construction of the Aesthetic*) (org. 1933/ Eng. 1989), Theodor W. Adorno (1903–1969) astonishingly reverses Kierkegaard's theory of three stages of existence and attributes "to the aesthetic the highest rank both with respect to its truth value and its ethical significance."[11] Although this esoteric work usually has a bad reputation among Kierkegaard scholars,[12] some recognize the value of Adorno's unusual standpoint.[13] The Frankfurt School's interpretation of Kierkegaard seems to be the forerunner of the hermeneutics of suspicion and postmodern interpretations, which attempt to "read Kierkegaard with Kierkegaard against Kierkegaard."[14]

In *Kierkegaard-Myter og Kierkegaard-Kilder* (*Kierkegaard, the Myths and Their Origins*, org. 1976/ partial Eng. 1980), Henning Fenger (1921–1985) attempts to demythologize a *hagiographical*[15] portrayal of Kierkegaard.

---

11. Tonon, "Adorno's Response to Kierkegaard," 185.

12. Merold Westphal famously calls Adorno's *Kierkegaard: Construction of the Aesthetic* "the most irresponsible book ever written on Kierkegaard." Westphal, *Becoming a Self*, 9.

13. See Yoshida, キルケゴールは観念論者か － アドルノのキルケゴール論をめぐって － [Was Kierkegaard an Idealist? In Regard to Adorno's Interpretation of Kierkegaard], 新キェルケゴール研究 第12号 [Kierkegaard Studies, Volume 12], 14–30. For a list of studies that attempt to read Kierkegaard "with the eyes of Adorno," see Yoshida, "Was Kierkegaard an idealist?", 15, footnote 3.

14. Garff, "Eyes of Argus," 73.

15. Alastair Hannay says that "Walter Lowrie's biographies are sometimes described as hagiography." Lowrie, *Short Life of Kierkegaard*, xi.

Borrowing a term from Hans-Georg Gadamer (1900–2002)[16] and Paul Ricœur (1913–2005),[17] I label Fenger's method as **the hermeneutics of suspicion**.[18] Fenger paved the way for the **deconstructive** or **postmodern methods**[19] that became influential from the 1980s onwards. In fact, Kierkegaard's literary techniques: various pseudonyms, which contradict one another; four totally different interpretations of the Abraham-Isaac story in "Exordium" of *Fear and Trembling*;[20] and *Prefaces* – a collection of prefaces to non-existent works[21] – all these literary *plays* – are reminiscent of Jean-François Lyotard's concepts of the delegitimation of grand narratives and the plurality of small narratives.[22] In this sense, Kierkegaard is one of the vital forerunners of postmodernism, and postmodern methods can, therefore, be Kierkegaardian in some respects and thus uniquely able to elucidate his writings.

While it is necessary to discuss methods, the categorization in this section is a rough approximation. In reality, Kierkegaard studies often employ a plurality of methods. For instance, Joakim Garff's *SAK Søren Aabye Kierkegaard: En biografi* (*Søren Kierkegaard: A Biography*, org. 2000/ Eng. 2004) – which is categorized as a biographical method in the diagram in appendix 2 – also fits within the postmodern category. In this way, factual literature frequently utilizes plural methods. Employing plural methods helps us better understand Kierkegaard, who was deeply engaged in various academic disciplines. Thus,

---

16. Gadamer, "Hermeneutics of Suspicion," 313–323.

17. Ricœur, *Freud and Philosophy*, 20–36.

18. See also Tietjen, *Kierkegaard, Communication, and Virtue*, 59–84; Evans, "Kierkegaard among the Biographers," http://www.booksandculture.com/articles/2007/julaug/20.12.html?paging=off.

19. Technically, deconstruction and postmodernism are not synonyms. Deconstruction is an interpretative technique that reads to "seize on some apparently peripheral fragment in the work – a footnote, a recurrent minor term or image, a casual allusion – and work it tenaciously through to the point where it threatens to dismantle the oppositions which govern the text as a whole." However, "Postmodernity means the end of modernity, in the sense of those grand narratives of truth, reason, science, progress and universal emancipation which are taken to characterize modern thought from the Enlightenment onwards." In short, whereas deconstruction is strictly a literary theory, postmodernism is a "cultural and political [reality]." Eagleton, *Literary Theory*, 127, 211, ix. However, both deconstruction and postmodernism are often used interchangeably. Postmodern Kierkegaardian scholars also do not sharply distinguish one from the other. Therefore, both terms will be used in parallel in this work.

20. *SKS* 4, 107–111/ *FT/R*, 9–14.

21. *SKS* 4, 465–527/ *P*.

22. Lyotard, *Postmodern Condition*, 37–41.

the categorization in this section is based on my understanding of the *central* method employed by a particular Kierkegaard scholar.

Indeed, good Kierkegaard secondary literature employs the plural method. For instance, C. Stephen Evans identifies his approach as "literary-philosophical,"[23] while Jun Hashimoto prioritizes "philosophical-theological studies."[24] In the next section, we will proceed with a more realistic investigation by choosing a piece of secondary literature that employs plural or multi-layered methods and examining its validity.

2.2 The Need for a Kaleidoscopic Approach

Kierkegaard readers realize that his ideas include not just plural disciplines but something more – that is, that there is something peculiar in Kierkegaard's thought. One such peculiarity is what is sometimes called the dialectic.[25] Hermann Diem's **study of Kierkegaard's dialectic of existence** is one example in which a plural method (philosophical-theological method) is employed in studying Kierkegaard's dialectic. According to Diem, both existentialist philosophers and neo-orthodox theologians are mistaken in their treatment of Kierkegaard's thought, with the former de-Christianizing his thought and the latter co-opting it in the service of Christian apologetics. Diem views Kierkegaard's dialectic of existence as originating from Socrates. The primitive form of dialectic is a dialogue in the manner of Socrates as vividly portrayed in Plato's dialogues.[26] The function of Kierkegaard's pseudonyms is to allow the reader to have a dialogue with God. Accordingly, a Kierkegaard researcher should not just give a lecture about Kierkegaard but should also make a personal decision about whether to have faith in Jesus Christ or take offence at him. Diem says, "The dialectics which [Kierkegaard] practices stands in an indissoluble dialectical relation to the authoritative

---

23. Evans, *Passionate Reason*, 3.

24. Hashimoto, *World of "Suffering,"* 46–54.

25. For a concise and appropriate explanation of Kierkegaard's dialectic, see Sanchez "'Dialectic," 165–169. For diversity of Kierkegaard's use of *dialectic*, see Diem, *Kierkegaard's Dialectic of Existence*, 8–11.

26. It is a well-known fact that most of Plato's works are written in the form of dialogues, in which Socrates is usually the main participant.

proclamation of the Church."[27] While Diem does not specifically identify Kierkegaard as a missionary, he does recognize an inseparable relationship between Kierkegaard's dialectic of existence and the church's proclamation. As Diem's study on Kierkegaard's dialectic of existence appropriately emphasizes, the reader's accountability in making a decision is indispensable for the study of Kierkegaard as a missionary because a missionary's goal goes beyond intellectual understanding. Indeed, a missionary wants their audience to be transformed by repentance.

This aspect is vital to how we read Kierkegaard. We usually focus on interpretation when discussing Kierkegaard's work. However, the motto of this chapter speaks for itself: Kierkegaard's primary expectation is not that his readers would be curious about the author; rather, he wants readers to reflect on their own lives. Just as a person looks at themselves as reflected in a mirror, Kierkegaard's works reflect the reader's inner self. By only asking how to read Kierkegaard and ignoring the reader's own life, we may misread his works. Of course, this does not mean that we should not critique Kierkegaard. He himself would not have appreciated uncritical admiration. But we must remind ourselves that the true significance of reading Kierkegaard lies in considering the reader's inwardness. As Valdemar Ammundsen (1875–1936), a professor at the University of Copenhagen, says, "Where Kierkegaard was wrong, that is between him and God. Where Kierkegaard was right, that is between God and us."[28]

While appreciating Diem's valuable contribution on how to read Kierkegaard and how we are to be responsible before God, I am aware of the shortcomings of his method; his study does not pay attention to the historical and literary contexts. Diem collects excerpts from Kierkegaard's various works without situating them in their historical and literary contexts. In other words, philosophical-theological methods, particularly with regard to Kierkegaard's dialectics, are still unsatisfactory. A Kierkegaard interpreter must engage with *biographical studies* that pay attention to the historical context. *Literary studies* are also necessary to make us aware of the literary genre of each of Kierkegaard's works. As Mark A. Tietjen says, Kierkegaard is simultaneously a "philosopher, theologian, biblical interpreter, psychologist,

---

27. Diem, *Kierkegaard's Dialectic of Existence*, 100.
28. Johnson, "Kierkegaard and the Church," 79.

prophet, missionary and poet."²⁹ An interpretation of Kierkegaard requires consideration of many disciplines and appreciation of the uniqueness of Kierkegaard's thought.

2.3 The Author-Oriented Method

It is difficult to comprehensively address the unqiue aspects of Kierkegaard's thought. Therefore, an essential principle of interpretation should be "to allow Kierkegaard to speak for himself."³⁰ This approach is common in the writings of Gregor Malantschuk (1902–1978), Hidehito Ōtani, and Jun Hashimoto, and I refer to it as **the author-oriented method**. This section is devoted to defining this method. I synthesize the methods utilized in Gregor Malantschuk's *Dialektik og Eksistens hos Søren Kierkegaard* (*Kierkegaard's Thought*, org. 1968/ Eng. 1971), Jun Hashimoto's *The World of "Suffering" in Kierkegaard* (1976), and Hidehito Ōtani's *A Study of Kierkegaard's Authorship* (1989-1991). The term "author-oriented method" is my own.³¹ This method prioritizes the following four aspects: authorial intent, historical and literary context, open-mindedness to the religious, and the dialectical structure of Kierkegaard's corpus.

2.3.1 Authorial Intent

First and foremost, the author-oriented method respects and prioritizes Kierkegaard's intent. What is Kierkegaard's intent as an author? In *The Point of View for My Work as an Author*, he expounds his authorial intent, saying, "Once and for all I must earnestly beg the kind reader always to bear in mente [in mind] that the thought behind the whole work is: what it means to become a Christian."³² To read Kierkegaard's work in the way he intended

---

29. Tietjen, *Kierkegaard: A Christian Missionary*, loc. 665, Kindle.
30. Hashimoto, *World of "Suffering,"* 70; Ōtani, *Kierkegaard's Authorship, Part 1*, 16, 55.
31. As far as I know, Gregor Malantschuk does not name or label his method. Jun Hashimoto calls his method the "historical method." Hashimoto, *World of "Suffering,"* 67–81. Hidehito Ōtani calls his method the "primary research method." Ōtani, *Kierkegaard's Authorship, Part 1*, 58–65. Although they use different terms, these researchers use a similar method to interpret Kierkegaard. Niels Thulstrup (1924-1988) and Malantschuk are pioneers of this kind of method. Both Hashimoto and Ōtani personally learned from Thulstrup and Malantschuk while studying in Denmark. Four of these researchers emphasize the religious nature of Kierkegaard's works and attempt to read his works in the way that he intended them to be read.
32. *SKS* 16, 23/ Kierkegaard, *Point of View*, 22.

it to be read – without getting lost in the complexity and mystery of his thought – an interpreter must always bear in mind that "the thought behind the whole work is: what it means to become a Christian."

Although readers must always remember Kierkegaard's singular aim of Christian edification, they must also recognize the complexity of his corpus. Therefore, the author-oriented method distinguishes between the genres of Kierkegaard's works: pseudonymous works,[33] signed works,[34] and *Journals and Notebooks*.[35] Since Kierkegaard takes on different personas as his authorial strategy requires, readers must be aware of the genre of each work and read each one with a recognition of which persona is talking. For Kierkegaard's own categorization of his works, see appendix 3 in this book, but note that the diagram there is not an exhaustive list[36] as there are several of Kierkegaard's works that do not fit neatly into these categories.[37]

Kierkegaard scholars debate the nature of his pseudonyms. Some fail to distinguish between the personas, blending quotations from various works into a patchwork of interpretations. At the other extreme, some treat Kierkegaard's pseudonymous works as if each persona were autonomous, ignoring any unity or coherence in his works.[38] Some regard *signed* works as

---

33. While considering himself a simple Christian, Kierkegaard felt the need to present various life-views that were distant from his own. Therefore, the lower pseudonyms represent non-Christians who stand "lower" than Kierkegaard, while the higher pseudonyms represent Christians who stand "higher" than Kierkegaard. The lower pseudonymous works are intended to seduce aesthetes and speculators towards the signed-religious works. The higher-pseudonymous works are intended to present Christianity in a form of the New Testament.

34. While Kierkegaard distanced himself from his pseudonyms, the signed works represent his own voice. The signed-religious works are devotional writings. The signed-polemical works, written during his later years, arose out of his conflict with the Danish National Church. The signed commentaries are Kierkegaard's own explanation of his authorial strategy.

35. One can learn about the young Kierkegaard through his *Journals and Notebooks* since these began to be written in 1833. *Journals and Notebooks* – which consist of his diary, notes, unpublished works, drafts, and memorandums of published works – contain thoughts that do not appear in his published works.

36. For instance, appendix 3 in this book does not include Kierkegaard's early polemical writings, the pseudonymous and signed articles from Danish newspapers such as *Fædrelandet* [The Fatherland] and works such as *From the Papers of One Still Living*, *The Concept of Irony*, *A Literary Review*, and *The Book on Adler*.

37. For now, the fact that some of Kierkegaard's works and articles are not included in appendix 3 is not problematic since these *uncategorized* works and articles lie outside the main subjects of analysis in this study.

38. See Mackey, *Kierkegaard: A Kind of Poet*; Poole, *Kierkegaard: The Indirect Communication*.

parts of *pseudonymous* works – none of his works should be trusted.[39] It is clear that our epistemology shapes our view of Kierkegaard's thought. My own epistemology consist of several steps. First, I establish Kierkegaard's thought based on his signed commentaries and journals, in which he expounds on his authorial strategy. Unless contradicted by factual evidence, I view what is said in his signed commentaries and journals as true. Second, I distinguish Kierkegaard's pseudonymous personas from his own personality, and I also differentiate between pseudonyms. In this study, I distinguish between Victor Eremita, A, Johannes the Seducer, B, Jylland Pastor (the lower-pseudonymous authors of *Either/Or*), Anti-Climacus (the higher-pseudonymous author of *The Sickness unto Death* and *Practice in Christianity*), and Kierkegaard himself (the author of *Two Upbuilding Discourses* [1843], *The Point of View for My Work as an Author*, and *Journals and Notebooks*). Third, I may use the statements of a certain pseudonym to delineate or clarify Kierkegaard's thought provided that the pseudonym's view helps to explain Kierkegaard's own view regarding a specific topic, and vice versa. Fourth, I do not regard Kierkegaard's pseudonymous personas as autonomous but, rather, view each persona as being assigned a specific role by Kierkegaard, who is the real author. For instance, Johannes the Seducer, one of the pseudonymous authors in *Either/Or*, appears destructive and unethical.[40] However, I assume that the real author, Kierkegaard, assigned him a specific role that would help the reader to eventually become a Christian. This aligns with Kierkegaard's overarching purpose as stated in *The Point of View for My Work as an Author*: "Thus my entire work as an author revolves around: becoming a Christian in Christendom."[41]

2.3.2 Historical and Literary Context

Kierkegaard was certainly a creative and unique thinker, but he was also a child of his times, who was influenced by his predecessors and contemporaries.[42]

---

39. See Mackey, *Points of View*.
40. See the paragraph from "The Seducer's Diary" in appendix 4 of this book.
41. *SKS* 16, 69/ *PV*, 90. For an explanation of how the existence of Johannes the Seducer indirectly helps the reader to become a Christian, see sections 3.2.1.3, 3.2.1.5, 3.2.1.6, and 4.2.3 of this book.
42. According to Hidehito Ōtani, Ludvig Holberg (1684–1754) discusses the issue of *den Enkelte* [the single individual] in *Erasmus Montanus* in 1731, a hundred years before Kierkegaard. Ōtani, *Study of Kierkegaard's Youth*, 60. Takahiro Hirabayashi says, "[Kierkegaard's]

By locating Kierkegaard in his historical context, the author-oriented method attempts to prevent unrealistic interpretations. Thus, in chapters 3–8, in my discussion of *Either/Or*, *Two Upbuilding Discourses* (1843), *The Sickness unto Death*, *Practice in Christianity*, *The Point of View for My Work as an Author*, and *Journals and Notebooks*, I carefully consider the historical background of each work. Furthermore, when interpreting specific excerpts from the Kierkegaardian corpus, one must be conscious of the literary context. In other words, one should not take quotations out of their literary context without paying attention to which persona is speaking. To ensure that each persona speaks for himself, I have included summaries of the content of *Either/Or*, *Two Upbuilding Discourses* (1843), *The Sickness unto Death*, and *Practice in Christianity* in appendices 4–7, as well as a summary of *The Point of View for My Work as an Author* in section 7.2. (A summary of the extensive *Journals and Notebooks* is impossible and unnecessary as their use in this study is quite limited.) By doing so, I anchor myself to the historical and literary context of each of Kierkegaard's works to better understand both him and his pseudonyms.

2.3.3 Open-Mindedness towards the Religious Dimension: An Evaluation of Kierkegaard's Thought in Light of Scripture and Christian Traditions and Practices (such as Lutheranism and Pietism)

The author-oriented method requires the researcher to be open-minded towards the religious dimension in Kierkegaard's work. Before elaborating on this idea, I share my personal background because this is relevant to my approach. I am a Christian and a minister of the Japan Assemblies of God, a denomination generally categorized as Pentecostal. Although I have only "met" Kierkegaard through his works, he is like a spiritual father to me because I respect him and have been enormously influenced by him as a Christian. In this sense, it might seem natural for me to presuppose Kierkegaard's faith and God's existence. However, I will attempt to avoid imposing my personal beliefs or appealing to the reader's Christian faith.

---

way of thinking often reminds you of others, most of all Paul Martin Møller (1794–1838)." Hirabayashi, "New Identity," 209.

Instead, I argue that being open-minded towards the religious will help us understand Kierkegaard better.

In *The Point of View for My Work as an Author*, Kierkegaard says, "Thus, time and time again, I have had more joy from my relationship of obedience to God than from the thoughts I produced."[43] Kierkegaard is widely recognized as a profound and prolific writer. But he considered his relationship with and obedience to God far more valuable and joyful than the quality and quantity of his works. A person who reads Kierkegaard's works purely from an academic perspective, without regard for their religious aspects, may not be able to comprehend the true nature of his works in the way that Kierkegaard intended.

Being aware of the religious dimension also plays a significant role in understanding the dialectical structure of Kierkegaard's works. According to Kierkegaard, he did not initially recognize the dialectical structure of his works. Rather, God's "Governance" (*Styrelsen*) guided the whole process of constructing the dialectical structure of his works.[44] In other words, the extent to which a researcher accepts the role of God's Governance in the process of Kierkegaard's literary production influences their view of the organic coherence of his authorship.

Kierkegaard's deep recognition of God's role invites the reader to evaluate Kierkegaard's thought in light of Scripture and Christian traditions. One must examine the Scriptures (Acts 17:11) to see if what Kierkegaard says is biblical. Given Kierkegaard's claim to the religious nature of his works, it is also valid to evaluate his thought from the perspectives of Lutheranism (the official religion of Denmark) and other Christian traditions and practices.

2.3.4 The Dialectical Structure of Kierkegaard's Corpus

The author-oriented method presupposes the dialectical structure of Kierkegaard's corpus.[45] In *Journals and Notebooks*, he says, "I am deeply

---

43. *SKS* 16, 53/ *PV*, 74.
44. *SKS* 16, 56/ *PV*, 76–77.
45. While *dialectic* can mean different things to different people, for many, it naturally brings to mind Hegelian philosophical dialectics with its threefold thesis, antithesis, and synthesis. When Kierkegaard says that his entire authorship has a dialectical structure, he means, first, that each work is in tension with the others. The various works of his corpus thus argue with and confront one another and represent particular life-views in relation to other life-views. Second, his various works do not just contradict one another but also seem to expect

convinced that . . . there is a comprehensiveness in the whole production (especially through the assistance of Governance)."[46] He elaborates on this view in *The Point of View for My Work as an Author*. Building on Kierkegaard's own view, Malantschuk argues that Kierkegaard's entire corpus is governed by the concept of "consistency," with each work having dialectical relationships with the rest.[47] Ōtani develops this view, identifying several dialectical relationships among Kierkegaard's works.[48] Concerning the interpretation of the four published works discussed in this study, the following four dialectical perspectives are pivotal.[49]

2.3.4.1 The Theory of Three Spheres and Two Boundaries

The first dialectical perspective involves the theory of the three spheres or stages of existence – the aesthetic, ethical, and religious – and the theory of the two boundaries of irony and humour. The theory of the three stages is well known, but the theory of the two boundaries is relatively unknown. In *Concluding Unscientific Postscript*, Johannes Climacus says, "There are three existence-spheres: the esthetic, the ethical, the religious. To these three there is a respectively corresponding confinium [border territory]: irony[50] is the

---

Aufhebung (sublation). For Kierkegaard, *Aufhebung* is faith. Third, for Kierkegaard, it is essential that dialectic is not just an abstract concept but something that animates existential movement. One reaches faith as mediated immediacy through existential dialectics such as the suffering of the righteous. In summary, Kierkegaard's view of the dialectical structure of his entire authorship means that his entire work engages in dialogue in order to help the reader to attain faith.

46. *SKS* 21, 276, NB10:38/ *JP*, VI 6346 19 February 1849.
47. Malantschuk, *Kierkegaard's Thought*, 105–122.
48. Ōtani, *Kierkegaard's Authorship, Part 2*, 653–763.
49. Unpublished works – such as *The Point of View for My Work as an Author* and *Journals and Notebooks* – are located outside the dialectical structure of the authorship and serve to annotate each work and the authorship.
50. What does it mean that irony is the boundary between the aesthetic and the ethical? John Lippitt explains this, saying, "The ironist is he who realizes the limitations of living aesthetically. In becoming ironical, the aesthete reveals that he has an *intellectual* understanding of the limitations of his particular object of desire, but he fails to make a further move; one which is not merely intellectual but *existential*; a move beyond irony to truly ethical living. The ethical is the 'way out' of the despair of 'living aesthetically.'" Lippitt, "Existential Laughter," 63–64. The fact that aesthetes can no longer simply enjoy the aesthetic life and become ironical shows their recognition of the limitation of the aesthetic life. However, unless the aesthete changes and starts living ethically, they do not move to the higher sphere. Therefore, irony is the boundary between the aesthetic and the ethical.

confinium between the esthetic and the ethical; humor[51] is the confinium between the ethical and the religious."[52]

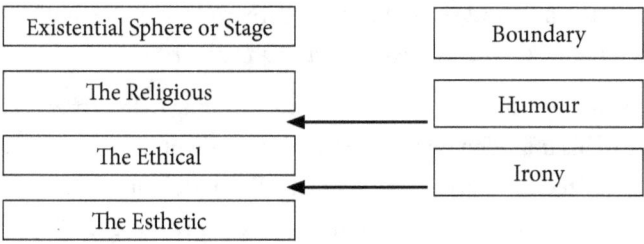

Ideally, Kierkegaard intends for the reader to move on or leap from the aesthetic to the ethical and from the ethical to the religious sphere. This is the basic framework for interpreting Kierkegaard's thought. In other words, Kierkegaard did not simply present various life possibilities and say, "Go ahead and choose whichever you want." Rather, he intended to edify the reader through his works. In the case of the works discussed in this study, the reader is encouraged to move from the aesthetic (*Either/Or, Part I*) to the ethical (*Either/Or, Part II*) and, finally, to the religious (*Two Upbuilding Discourses* [1843]). However, the dialectical relationships within Kierkegaard's corpus are more complicated. Thus, the first dialectical perspective alone is insufficient to reveal the organic relationships in his works.

2.3.4.2 *The Dual Authorship of the Pseudonymous and Signed-Religious Works*

The second dialectical perspective in Kierkegaard's authorship concerns his dual authorship of the pseudonymous and signed-religious works. In *The Point of View for My Work as an Author*, Kierkegaard says,

---

51. What does it mean that humour is the boundary between the ethical and the religious? Drawing on the argument of C. Stephen Evans, John Lippitt says, "The humorist has gained knowledge of the central idea of Christianity, the 'absolute paradox' of the incarnation; but then chooses to smile at this rather than make the 'leap of faith.' What 'limits' him is that he views the incarnation as a *doctrine*; a philosophical idea. [...] However, for the Christian, the incarnation is not merely a doctrine, but rather the source of an existential 'passion.'" Lippitt, "Existential Laughter, 68. While intellectually comprehending the incarnation, which is a central doctrine of Christianity, the humourist shrugs the shoulders instead of placing their faith in Jesus Christ and becoming a Christian. So, the humourist does not yet enter the religious sphere. Accordingly, humour is the boundary between the ethical and the religious.

52. *SKS* 7, 455/ *CUP I*, 501–502. See also *SKS* 6, 439/ *SLW*, 476.

> *Two Upbuilding Discourses* is concurrent with *Either/Or*. The duplexity in the deeper sense, that is, in the sense of the whole authorship, was certainly not what there was talk about at the time: the first and second parts of *Either/Or*. No, the duplexity was: *Either/Or* – and *Two Upbuilding Discourses*.⁵³

The statement above is important when attempting to interpret Kierkegaard according to his intended purpose. Yet, this statement has often been ignored and marginalized by Kierkegaard scholars. Even Malantschuk and Ōtani do not fully conform to this guideline when reading Kierkegaard's works. This study aims to faithfully follow Kierkegaard's instructions in reading his works. Accordingly, it will pay close attention to the dialectical tension between *Either/Or* and *Two Upbuilding Discourses* (1843). Kierkegaard considered signed-religious works qualitatively superior to lower-pseudonymous works, which is supported by the fact that the former are written under his own name while the latter are authored by pseudonymous (deceptive) names. Furthermore, the statement above suggests that the duplexity of *Either/Or* and *Two Upbuilding Discourses* (1843) represents "the whole authorship."⁵⁴ Accordingly, a careful reading of these two works may help to clarify the very nature of dual authorship in Kierkegaard's works as a whole. In other words, Kierkegaard's dual authorship can be expressed in terms of indirect and direct communication. Howard V. Hong (1912–2010) and Edna H. Hong (1913–2007), the English translators of Kierkegaard's works, say,

> The most obvious difference is that whereas the pseudonymous works from *Either/Or* through *Concluding Unscientific Postscript* are indirect communication, the signed discourses from first to last are direct. But the two modes of communication have ultimately the same aim: "to **make aware** of the religious, the essentially Christian."⁵⁵

The quotation above clearly explains the difference between pseudonymous and signed works and also illuminates their shared aim, which is "to

---

53. *SKS* 16, 16/ *PV*, 30.
54. *SKS* 16, 15/ *PV*, 30.
55. Hong and Hong, "Historical Introduction" in *EUD*, xi; the quotation within the quotation is originally from *SKS* 13, 12, asterisk/ *PV*, 6, asterisk, emphasis in original.

make aware of the religious, the essentially Christian." The role of pseudonymous works is to make the reader aware of the truth. Once the reader moves forward towards the truth, the deception should vanish, making way for the signed works that are essentially religious. This function of the pseudonymous works is discussed in the next sub-subsection.

2.3.4.3 *The Concept of Dialectical Self-Stultification*

The third dialectical structure of Kierkegaard's works is the concept of dialectical self-stultification, which applies to his early pseudonymous works from *Either/Or* to *Concluding Unscientific Postscript*. According to Kierkegaard's diagnosis in *The Point of View for My Work as an Author*, his contemporaries in Denmark "have passed into a sophisticated esthetic and intellectual paganism with an admixture of Christianity."[56] Therefore, the treatment of their condition requires Danes to come "away from 'the poet' [the esthetic] or [. . .] away from speculative thought."[57]

According to this perspective,[58] *Either/Or*, *Fear and Trembling*, *Repetition*, and *Stages on Life's Way* make up the aesthetic line that dissolves dialectically. Likewise, *The Concept of Anxiety*, *Philosophical Fragments*, and *Concluding Unscientific Postscript* make up the speculative line, which also dissolves dialectically. All those early pseudonymous works were written to help readers become aware of the vanities of their aesthetic or speculative lives, prompting them to abandon those lives. In other words, these pseudonymous works were intended to prepare readers for their religious life. Kierkegaard did not expect readers to embrace the content of these pseudonymous works; rather these works function as mirrors for readers, reflecting the direction in which they are heading.

---

56. *SKS* 16, 57/ *PV*, 78.
57. *SKS* 16, 57–58/ *PV*, 78.
58. This perspective is initiated by Kierkegaard and expounded by Malantschuk and Ōtani, who claim that their interpretation is an elaboration of Kierkegaard's own explanation. As far as I am concerned, both scholars attempt to follow Kierkegaard's authorial intent closely and conscientiously. This approach seems to be the best way to comprehend Kierkegaard's thought.

The title of pseudonymous work	Perspective
Either/Or	The esthetic line
Repetition	
Fear and Trembling	
Stages on Life's Way	
Dialectical self-stultification	
The Concept of Anxiety	The speculative line
Philosophical Fragments	
Concluding Unscientific Postscript	
Dialectical self-stultification	

2.3.4.4 The Spiritual Deepening throughout the Authorship

The fourth dialectical structure of Kierkegaard's entire thought is the spiritual deepening throughout the authorship. Even though *Two Upbuilding Discourses* (1843) belongs to the religious sphere, it is the lowest religious sphere from the perspective of Kierkegaard's entire work. By repeating this dialectical movement between pseudonymous and signed-religious work, the reader is gradually drawn to the depths of Christian faith as the authorship reflects Kierkegaard's own spiritual development. Kierkegaard neither declares the reader guilty nor proclaims Jesus Christ in *Two Upbuilding Discourses* (1843). Pseudonyms and Kierkegaard gradually produce works that are more decisively Christian through their authorial activities. Finally, on behalf of Kierkegaard, H. H. (higher and higher) and Anti-Climacus – who are closer to Christian ideals than Kierkegaard himself – published deeply Christian works that Kierkegaard himself would aim for. For example, in *The Sickness unto Death*, Anti-Climacus confines all under despair or sin, and in *Practice in Christianity*, he presents Jesus Christ in his true form.

One might ask whether understanding Kierkegaard's thought requires reading his works in chronological order or in a specific order in which he intended them to be read. This is not essential. I myself first read Kierkegaard's *The Sickness unto Death*, followed by either *The Concept of Anxiety* or *Either/Or*. I only read his signed-religious works several years later. Therefore, the Kierkegaard reader is free to choose in which order to read Kierkegaard's works, each of which can be read in its own right. This is evident from the fact that each work was published independently, suggesting that Kierkegaard himself endorsed reading each work on its own. In fact, Kierkegaard initially considered *Either/Or* to be his first and last work as he planned to retire from writing and become a rural pastor. Even during the early to middle period of his authorship, Kierkegaard kept hoping to end his writing career. So from the time he wrote *Either/Or*, his first work as an author, he was ready to retire at any time. This historical fact encourages us to read any work independently as we prefer.

However, as this is a study that purses academic rigour, I assert that the best method to explore what Kierkegaard intended as an author and retrospectively interpreted as a reader (of his own works) is to interpret each work chronologically, paying specific attention to the dialectical structure of the writing.

2.4 Critical Evaluation Necessary

In *Freud and Philosophy*, Paul Ricœur distinguishes between a hermeneutics of faith and a hermeneutics of suspicion.[59] Broadly speaking, the author-oriented method can be classified as a form of hermeneutics of trust. While the author-oriented method is good at faithfully restoring the meaning of the text, it has its limitations. For example, chapter 7 of this book deals with *The Point of View for My Work as an Author*, which, as we will see, was subject to a hermeneutics of suspicion from around 1980 onwards. The author-oriented method or a hermeneutics of trust does not have adequate weapons to fight or defend itself against a hermeneutics of suspicion. While I endorse the author-oriented method, I recognize that it requires certain modifications.

I recognized the weakness of hermeneutics of trust through the following experiences. Commenting on a draft of this thesis, my head supervisor C. Stephen Evans commented that I give "so much credit" to one of the interpreters of the hermeneutics of suspicion. Evans reminded me of a simple historical fact that undermines the foundation of suspicious interpretation.[60] In other words, I place too much trust in the hermeneutics of suspicion!

---

59. Ricœur, *Freud and Philosophy*, 20–36.
60. See section 7.5.3 of this book.

What should I do? To some extent, I must apply a hermeneutics of suspicion against the hermeneutics of suspicion itself.[61]

While the author-oriented method is good at delving into Kierkegaard's thought, one of its deficiencies is its uncritical attitude. Therefore, I have modified and renamed it the **author-oriented method with critical evaluation**. In practice, while usually employing the author-oriented method throughout this work, I also critically assess the hermeneutics of suspicion in section 7.5. By doing so, this work not only delves deep into Kierkegaard's thought but also critically assesses the methodology used.

In conclusion, the kaleidoscopic nature of Kierkegaard's text suggests that the researcher should be author-oriented – being flexible and not hesitating to utilize any method that helps to understand the text – rather than sticking rigidly to one specific discipline or approach. Therefore, I will primarily utilize the author-oriented method, using Diem's study in Kierkegaard's dialectic of existence and literary method as a secondary method since these two methods help to interpret the text faithfully according to its nature. However, a deficiency of the author-oriented method is that it hesitates to critique other scholars, which is why I incorporate critical evaluations. This book aims to study Kierkegaard as a missionary, relying mainly on the author-oriented method with critical evaluation and occasionally using other methods when Kierkegaard's text itself necessitates this for appropriate interpretation.

2.5 Scope

This section defines the scope of the present study. As discussed elsewhere in this book, I will interpret Kierkegaard's *Either/Or*, *Two Upbuilding Discourses* (1843), *The Sickness unto Death*, and *Practice in Christianity* with specific regard to Kierkegaard as a missionary. Why these four works?

Kierkegaard regarded *Either/Or* as the first book in his corpus. Interestingly, he says that a proclamation that begins with orthodoxy would influence only a few. According to Kierkegaard, the proclamation of Christianity in Christendom should begin with "paganism," which is why he started with *Either/Or*.[62]

---

61. "What is needed is . . . a suspicion of that suspicion!" Robinson, "Paul Ricoeur," 12.
62. *SKS* 20, 318, NB4:66/ *JP,* V 6107 *n.d.*, 1848.

As mentioned in section 2.3.4, this study attempts to faithfully follow the logic of the dialectical structure of Kierkegaard's corpus as a whole. Kierkegaard lamented that no one, or almost no one, paid attention to *Two Upbuilding Discourses* (1843) in comparison with the success of *Either/Or*.[63] These two works have generally not been read sequentially. Therefore, this study pays attention to the dialectical tension between the two works. According to Kierkegaard, the title *Either/Or* signifies something beyond *Either/Or* – it includes *Two Upbuilding Discourses* (1843). The duplexity of *Either/Or* and *Two Upbuilding Discourses* (1843) represents the heart of his authorship at least until May 1849 (the publications of the second edition of *Either/Or* and *The Lily in the Field and the Bird of the Air*).[64] In this respect, a continuous reading of *Either/Or* and *Two Upbuilding Discourses* (1843) contributes to revealing the true meaning of the title *Either/Or* and the nature of Kierkegaard's authorship up until that point.

The best way to follow the logic of the dialectical structure of Kierkegaard's works is to read all his books chronologically. However, due to limitations of space, I have chosen the most suitable works for revealing the nature of Kierkegaard's mission strategy within the scope of this study. According to Kierkegaard, his authorship – which aims to win all people for Christianity – started with *Either/Or* and reached its goal with Anti-Climacus's works. In *Journals and Notebooks*, Kierkegaard says,

> What I have understood as the task of the authorship has been done. It is one idea, this continuity from *Either/Or* to Anti-Climacus, the idea of religiousness in reflection. . . . Just one thing more. I hardly need say that by wanting to win men it is not my intention to form a party, to create secular, sensate togetherness; no, my wish is only to win men, if possible all men (each individual), for Christianity.[65]

Therefore, this study takes up Anti-Climacus's two works – *The Sickness unto Death* and *Practice in Christianity* – with the expectation that the choice of these two works will help us to see the *framework* of Kierkegaard's mission

---

63. *SKS* 16, 21/ *PV*, 36.
64. *SKS* 16, 16/ *PV*, 30.
65. *JP*, VI 6770/ *Pap*. X6 B 4:3 1 June 1851, from an unused draft of the preface to *For Self-Examination*.

strategy. Just as *Either/Or* and *Two Upbuilding Discourses* (1843) are concurrent, so are Anti-Climacus's two works. These two works were initially intended to be one work titled *The Radical Cure or the Forgiveness of Sins and the Atonement*[66] but was then divided into two works: *The Sickness unto Death* and *Practice in Christianity*. Therefore, Gregor Malantschuk famously argues that *The Sickness unto Death* and *Practice in Christianity* constitute "a sharpened either/or."[67] Though *The Sickness unto Death* is quite often taken up independently, it is legitimate to read these two works of Anti-Climacus sequentially.

Although the limitations of this study do not permit discussion beyond these four works, I recognize that this exploration is insufficient to follow the whole logic of the grand plan of Kierkegaard's mission strategy. Therefore, in chapters 7 and 8, I will study the unpublished works *The Point of View for My Work as an Author* and *Journals and Notebooks*, with specific focus on the view of Kierkegaard as a missionary. In *The Point of View for My Work as an Author*, Kierkegaard retrospectively interprets his authorship from 1843 to May 1848. *Journals and Notebooks* was written between 1833 (ten years before the publication of *Either/Or*) and 1855 (the year of his death). Therefore, a study of these unpublished works offers important insights into Kierkegaard's overall mission strategy.

This work limits itself to investigating Kierkegaard's thought with specific regard to a view of Kierkegaard as a missionary. In other words, other perspectives may not be unpacked or explored even if they are helpful to the study of *Either/Or*, *Two Upbuilding Discourses* (1843), *The Sickness unto Death*, and *Practice in Christianity*. For instance, one may wish to examine the validity of the claims of scholars who approach *Either/Or* philosophically – for example, the claim that B, one of the pseudonymous authors, represents a Kantian ethicist.[68] Alternatively, others have expended great effort in exploring in depth the relationship between *Either/Or* and Hegel or Danish Hegelianism.[69] Another analytical approach might focus on the role of Kierkegaard's broken engagement to Regine in the creation of "The Seducer's Diary" in *Either/*

---

66. *JP*, VI 6219 N.B./ *Pap.* IX A 176 20 July 1848.
67. Malantschuk, *Kierkegaard's Thought*, 338.
68. Kirkconnell, *Kierkegaard on Ethics*, 3–4, 22–23, 30–33, 37.
69. Stewart, *Kierkegaard's Relations to Hegel*, 182–237.

Or (a biographical method). Although those topics are fascinating, they are unfortunately beyond the scope of this study. Therefore, this book limits itself to what has a direct bearing on the question at hand – that is, the nature of Kierkegaard's mission strategy.

As Ōtani points out, there are intertextual relations not only between the pseudonymous and the signed works but also between one pseudonymous work and another. For instance, the issues that are raised but remain unsolved in *Either/Or* are passed on to the next pseudonymous work, *Fear and Trembling*. While both the ethical and religious spheres are contiguous in *Either/Or, Part II*, both spheres are sharply distinguished in *Fear and Trembling*. To understand and clarify Kierkegaard's concept of the religious sphere, a comparative study of *Either/Or* and *Fear and Trembling* is vital. It is also fascinating to study *Stages on Life's Way* because *Either/Or*'s pseudonymous characters – such as Victor Eremita and Judge William – reappear in this work. In addition, it is fruitful to compare and contrast *The Concept of Anxiety* and *The Sickness unto Death* because the latter can be seen as a continuation and development of the former's theme. However, exploring the intertextual relations among the pseudonymous works is beyond the scope of this study and will not be the focus here.

In summary, I believe that discussing these four works – *Either/Or, Two Upbuilding Discourses* (1843), *The Sickness unto Death*, and *Practice in Christianity* – will reveal some significant features of Kierkegaard's mission. I will supplement this with a study of the unpublished works *The Point of View for My Work as an Author* and *Journals and Notebooks*, which provide a more comprehensive understanding of Kierkegaard's mission strategy.

This concludes "Part 1 (Chapters 1 to 2): A Preliminary Study." Having established the methodology and defined the scope, we will now move to "Part Two (Chapters 3 to 6)," which examines four published works of Kierkegaard according this framework.

Part 2

A Study of Published Works

CHAPTER 3

Either/Or as an Initial Missionary Task with "Paganism"

Then I read *Either/Or* – again, not a particularly good choice if you're looking for [Kierkegaard]'s evangelicalism![1]

– Roger Olson, "Was Kierkegaard an Evangelical? Part 1"

The subject of this chapter is Kierkegaard's "first work in the literature" – *Enten–Eller* (Either/Or).[2] As in the quotation at the head of this chapter, many may wonder, "Why *Either/Or*, if one dares to argue Kierkegaard as a missionary?" Initially, Ádám Szabados also had such an impression: "Years ago I started to read Søren Kierkegaard's [Either/Or].... After reading several pages, I put it down, disappointed.... I did not find any Christian thoughts."[3] Later, however, he had second thoughts about why *Either/Or* does not look like a Christian book: "I know now what the answer is. It is because he loves his neighbors and because he wants to lead them to Christ."[4] What Szabados means here is that the reason for *Either/Or*'s seemingly unchristian nature is

---

1. Olson, "Was Kierkegaard an Evangelical?," http://www.patheos.com/blogs/rogereolson/2011/08/was-kierkegaard-an-evangelical-part-1/.

2. *SKS* 16, 11/ *PV*, 23. Before the publication of *Either/Or*, Kierkegaard had already published *From the Papers of One Still Living* (a book review of H. C. Andersen's *Only a Fiddler*) and *The Concept of Irony* (a master's thesis), but he regarded *Either/Or* as his "first work in the literature."

3. Szabados, "Incarnational Mission," 5.

4. Szabados, 35.

precisely to attract ungodly people and "lead them to Christ." Is that so? Is there evidence for this view? Indeed, Kierkegaard himself endorses this view:

> If one aims to elevate a whole period, one must really know it. That is why the proclaimers of Christianity who begin right off with orthodoxy actually do not have much influence and only on a few. For Christendom is very far behind. One has to begin with paganism. So I begin with *Either/Or*.[5]

According to Kierkegaard, "to begin right off with orthodoxy" is ineffective. Rather, a powerful and effective mission begins with paganism. That is why he began with *Either/Or*. This chapter goes into more detail about this provocative interpretation.

The outline of this chapter is as follows. In the first section, I will provide a historical introduction. (The reader is also reminded that a chapter-by-chapter summary of *Either/Or* is included in appendix 4 to help evaluate whether the interpretations in this chapter are well-founded.) In the second section, I will interpret *Either/Or* from the perspective of Kierkegaard as a missionary and apply some of the findings in *Either/Or* to real-life situations. In the third section, I will conclude this chapter.

3.1 Historical Introduction

On 20 February 1843, *Either/Or* – "a monster of a book" running to 838 pages in the Danish original – was published in Denmark, not under Kierkegaard's name like today but under the pseudonym Victor Eremita.[6] Indeed, Kierkegaard's name did not appear anywhere in the book. By describing the testimony of Kierkegaard's contemporaries – such as H. C. Andersen (1805–1875) – Joakim Garff paints a vivid picture of Kierkegaard's surroundings at the time:

> On February 20, 1843, the very day on which the book was published, Henriette Wulff wrote to Hans Christian Andersen, who

---

5. *SKS* 20, 318, NB4:66/ *JP,* V 6107 *n.d.*, 1848.

6. Garff, *Søren Kierkegaard: A Biography*, 218. The above quotation is originally from J. L. Heiberg's review of *Either/Or* in the article "Litterær Vintersæd" [Literary Winter Seed] in *Intelligensblade*, ed. by J. L. Heiberg, 4 vols. (Copenhagen, 1842–1844; ASKB U 56), vol. 2, no. 24 (March 1, 1843), 288.

was then in Germany: "Recently a book was published here with the title Either/Or! It is supposed to be quite strange, the first part full of Don Juanism, skepticism, et cetera, and the second part toned down and conciliating, ending with a sermon that is said to be quite excellent. The whole book has attracted much attention. It has not yet been discussed publicly by anyone, but it surely will be. It is actually supposed to be by a [Kierkegaard] who has adopted a pseudonym: Do you know him?"[7]

Although Kierkegaard published *Either/Or* pseudonymously, it was not too difficult for his contemporaries to guess the identity of its true author. As Henriette Wulff had predicted, *Either/Or* soon created a sensation. On April 7, Signe Læssøe (1781–1870) wrote to H. C. Andersen saying, "You have no idea what a sensation it has caused. I think that no book has caused such a stir with the reading public since Rousseau placed his *Confessions* on the altar."[8] In *The Point of View for My Work as an Author*, Kierkegaard looks back on the commercial success of *Either/Or* and says,

> In that way I have managed to get the age to go along with me without ever dreaming where it is going or where we now are. But men have become aware of the issues. They cannot get rid of me just because they went along with *Either/Or* so happily.[9]

Where did Kierkegaard intend to take his contemporaries? Of what issues did they become aware? We will tackle these questions in the next section.

3.2 A Study of *Either/Or* with Specific Regard to Kierkegaard the Missionary

In the song "Disciple," to the accompaniment of distorted guitars and thundering drums, the American heavy metal band Slayer yells, "God hates us all; God hates us all."[10] This is a blasphemous challenge to the church's proclamation that "God loves you." What can the church do with people who say such

---

7. Garff, *Søren Kierkegaard: A Biography*, 216–217.
8. Garff, 217.
9. *SKS* 20, 318–319, NB4:66/ *JP*, V 6107 *n.d.*, 1848.
10. "Disciple," *AZLyrics*, http://www.azlyrics.com/lyrics/slayer/disciple.html

things? A good Christian may be offended or may lament over the corruption of the secular world. Perhaps a pastor might even hold up this band as an illustration of a sinful life from the pulpit.[11] What about Kierkegaard? He would attempt to converse with these kinds of people. In *Either/Or*, there is even a passage that would likely resonate with the likes of Slayer:

> But there is yet another demonstration of the existence of God that has hitherto been overlooked. It is introduced by a servant in Aristophanes' The Knights, 32–35 (Demosthenes and Nicias conversing):
>
> [DE. . . . What, do you really think that there are gods?
>
> NIC. I know it.
>
> DE. Know it! How?
>
> NIC. I'm such a wretched god-detested chap.
>
> DE. Well urged indeed].[12]

If they were to read it, this quotation might make Slayer grin at the humorously presented evidence for the existence of gods, demonstrated by divine loathing directed at one unfortunate individual – a thought akin to sentiments expressed in Slayer's lyrics! Should a Christian reader be disappointed with such a blasphemous thought in *Either/Or*? Or should we recognize that Kierkegaard began his rescue programme by meeting readers where they were?[13] According to Kierkegaard, the latter view is what he intended. *Either/Or*'s pagan elements paradoxically demonstrate Kierkegaard's ambitious mission strategy to reach people who were far from Christianity.

3.2.1 How the Aesthetes Are Able to Will to Allow Themselves to Be Built Up

We have two main characters in *Either/Or*. One of these is a formidable antagonist – aesthete A. Can we imagine that A will be built up or edified in any way? Allow me to amend the question with the help of Kierkegaard's

---

11. See also *SKS* 7, 482, asterisk/ *CUP I*, 530–531, asterisk.

12. *SKS* 2, 45–46/ *EO I*, 36–37, the quotation within square brackets was originally written in Greek, translated by the Hongs.

13. *SKS* 16, 27–29/ *PV*, 45–47.

journal: "It is a matter of this choice: to will to allow oneself to be built up."[14] The title *Either/Or* seems to invite the reader to make a choice, implying that the reader can choose edification. But how can aesthetic readers who are somewhat akin to A will to allow themselves to be built up? Moreover, if we can rightly call Kierkegaard a missionary, what kind of mission strategy impels him to create or adopt villains such as A, Don Juan, Faust, and Johannes the Seducer?[15] Since each of these characters has a strong and unbending personality, one may wonder how those aesthetes can will to allow themselves to be built up. Does the creation or adoption of these villains mean that Kierkegaard is, in reality, like them?[16] If he is a kind of missionary, how does he juggle his real existence and literary creativity? What is his motivation? If he is a kind of missionary, why does Kierkegaard not let his villains be converted in the literary world of *Either/Or*? These questions are answered in the following discussion.

3.2.1.1 The Profound Religiousness behind Either/Or

In *The Point of View for My Work as an Author*, written in 1848, Kierkegaard retrospectively describes the approach he adopted when writing *Either/Or*, saying, "I either had to plunge into despair and sensuality or absolutely choose the religious as the one and only – either the world on a scale that would be dreadful or the monastery. That it was the latter I would and must choose was basically decided."[17] The title *Either/Or* urges the reader to make a choice but also represents the author's real situation: "[He] either had to plunge into despair and sensuality or absolutely choose the religious." *Either/Or*'s shallow reader may identify Kierkegaard as a despairing aesthete, but Kierkegaard viewed himself as one who determined a religious identity. According to Kierkegaard's own view, *Either/Or* was, figuratively speaking, written in a monastery: "Strictly speaking, *Either/Or* was written in a monastery."[18] One might object that this is a retrospective interpretation. What is the evidence for such a claim? "I . . . was already in the monastery – an idea concealed in

---

14. *Pap.* VI B 133; *TD*, Supplement, 120.

15. "[Kierkegaard] wrote, especially at the beginning, as a likable scoundrel, generating interest and attracting many readers." Craddock, *Overhearing the Gospel*, 81.

16. See also *JP*, V1 6198/ *Pap.* IX A 155 *n.d.*, 1848.

17. *SKS* 16, 20/ *PV*, 35.

18. *SKS* 16, 20/ *PV*, 35.

the pseudonym *Victor-Eremita* [the Hermit]."[19] According to Kierkegaard, the editor's name – Victor Eremita (Victorious Hermit) – connotes that *Either/Or* was written in the monastery. Amplifying his statement, the real but hidden meaning of *Either/Or* is symbolized by the editor's name – Victorious Hermit – suggesting that both Kierkegaard and the reader can be like a hermit who is victorious alone with God in a monastery. What a paradoxical man Kierkegaard was! Even though *Either/Or* appears to be the most secularized of all Kierkegaard's writings, it was, according to Kierkegaard himself, written in a monastery. Kierkegaard does not mean that he was *physically* in a monastery but, rather, that he wrote *Either/Or* as a man who had abandoned this world and submitted himself to God. In this sense, *Either/Or* is "a poetical emptying" and "a deception."[20]

The fact that Kierkegaard, figuratively speaking, wrote *Either/Or* in a monastery connotes that there is a profound religiousness behind *Either/Or*, even though this is not immediately obvious: "When I began *Either/Or* . . . I was *potentialiter* [in potentiality] as deeply influenced by the religious as I ever became."[21] But how many readers can discern this profound religiousness, which is not immediately apparent, behind the monstrous *Either/Or*? In his *Journals and Notebooks*, Kierkegaard laments the common misunderstanding of *Either/Or* among his contemporaries: "[The age] never dreamed that the author of *Either/Or* had said goodbye to the world long before, that he spent much of the day in fear and trembling reading devotional books, in prayer and supplication."[22] Surprisingly, when Kierkegaard wrote *Either/Or*, he claims that "he was and is conscious of himself as a penitent from the very first line he wrote."[23] In his view, *Either/Or* was, from beginning to end, written with a religious purpose.

3.2.1.2 Was the Publication of Either/Or Successful?

The first printing of *Either/Or* sold well in Denmark. Garff's biography informs us about the literary scene in Denmark seven days after the publication of

---

19. *SKS* 16, 20/ *PV*, 35.
20. *SKS* 16, 20; 39/ *PV*, 35; 58.
21. *SKS* 16, 20/ *PV*, 35.
22. *SKS* 21, 20. NB6:21.b/ *JP*, VI 6206 *n.d.*, 1848.
23. *SKS* 21, 20. NB6:21.b/ *JP*, VI 6206 *n.d.*, 1848.

Either/Or: "Henrik Lund wrote to Peter Wilhelm: 'At my first opportunity I will send you a book that has attracted much attention and is being read "by almost every cultured person." The title of the book is *Either/Or*.'"[24] *Either/Or* is said to have been read by "almost every cultured person"! Although this expression might be an exaggeration, it still demonstrates the commercial success of *Either/Or* at that time.

And yet, Kierkegaard did not seem happy with the sensation caused by *Either/Or*. In *The Point of View for My Work as an Author*, he says, "With my left hand I passed *Either/Or* out into the world, with my right hand *Two Upbuilding Discourses*; but they all or almost all took the left hand with their right."[25] Kierkegaard's statement that *Either/Or* is passed with his left hand means that this work had lesser value in comparison with *Two Upbuilding Discourses* (1843) that is passed with his right hand. However, Kierkegaard thought that all or almost all of his contemporaries took *Either/Or* with their right hand and *Two Upbuilding Discourses* (1843) with their left hand, meaning that his contemporaries misunderstood the true value of each of those two works. Kierkegaard was frustrated by the fact that his contemporaries placed excessive value on *Either/Or*, which he considered to be of lesser value.

On the other hand, despite his frustration with the misconceptions of his contemporaries, Kierkegaard seemed to regard the publication of *Either/Or* and its effect as successful. Notwithstanding the age's numerous misunderstandings, as they so happily went along with Kierkegaard,[26] they were forced to be aware of the issues: "Now they may want to abandon me . . . but it is of no use – they have me for good."[27] It seems that Kierkegaard thought that he could successfully capture their attention and, by so doing, slowly guide them towards Christianity: "If one begins immediately with Christianity, they say: This is nothing for us – and put themselves immediately on guard."[28] The reason Kierkegaard regarded *Either/Or* as successful was because this work could lure those who had no interest whatsoever in Christianity: "But as it says in my last discourses, my whole huge literary work has just one idea,

---

24. Garff, *Søren Kierkegaard: A Biography*, 217.
25. *SKS* 16, 21/ *PV*, 36.
26. *SKS* 20, 318–319, NB4:66/ *JP*, V 6107 *n.d.*, 1848.
27. *SKS* 20, 318–319, NB4:66/ *JP*, V 6107 *n.d.*, 1848.
28. *SKS* 20, 318–319, NB4:66/ *JP*, V 6107 *n.d.*, 1848.

and that is: to wound from behind."²⁹ The secularized surface of *Either/Or* is intended to ambush the reader. Once disarmed – since this work does not appear Christian – the reader is forced to confront the issue and reflect on their existence. *Either/Or*, which falls into the category of paganism, is designed to attack without warning and compel the reader to become aware of the issue, thereby eventually – and unwittingly – encountering Christianity.

3.2.1.3 Seduction

The reason for *Either/Or*'s continued popularity since its first publication³⁰ is partly its seductive power. Why did Kierkegaard create such a seductive literary device? Was it just for his own enjoyment? Or did he have a deeper purpose? Kierkegaard says, "He who *could* not seduce men *cannot* save them either."³¹ According to this explanation, Kierkegaard seduced his contemporaries with *Either/Or* to save them.

3.2.1.3.1 Enigmas as Seductive Elements

The enigmatic elements in *Either/Or* have a seductive appeal for the reader. First, this is a pseudonymous work. Garff comments, "With all its titillating ambivalence, the mystification of the identity of the author succeeded grandly; sales went very briskly and word spread about the unusual book."³² Instead of Kierkegaard's name, the name "Victor Eremita" is printed as the editor of *Either/Or*. This name is Latin, and its meaning was probably not immediately obvious to most readers. Those familiar with Latin may know that this name means "Victorious Hermit." However, understanding the literal meaning and appreciating its significance are two different things. What does "Victorious Hermit" mean? It is less important to solve such enigmas and more important to realize that these enigmas exist to arouse the reader's curiosity.

---

29. *SKS* 20, 318–319, NB4:66/ *JP,* V 6107 *n.d.*, 1848.
30. I am aware that "Kierkegaard was not widely known outside Scandinavia in his lifetime, and was not hugely popular even in Denmark" and that "around the beginning of the twentieth century he exploded upon the European intellectual scene like a long-delayed time bomb." Evans, *Kierkegaard: An Introduction*, 1. For this reason, I am not overestimating Kierkegaard's popularity, but when and where Kierkegaard has been read, *Either/Or* has been popular to this day.
31. *SKS* 21, 148, NB8:8 *n.d.*, 1848, emphasis in original.
32. Garff, *Søren Kierkegaard: A Biography*, 217.

The book begins with Eremita saying that he had accidentally found the papers of *Either/Or*.[33] While Eremita and his story are fictional, this kind of mystery makes *Either/Or* appealing to readers. The first part of *Either/Or* was written largely by Aesthete A, whose name is unspecified anywhere in the papers; the second part was written by Judge William, who is identified as Ethicist B by Eremita. Furthermore, the last chapter of Part I is said to be written by another person, Johannes the Seducer. While A says that the Seducer is the author of the last chapter, Eremita doubts the authenticity of this statement and explains this complication as follows:

> The last of A's papers is a narrative titled "The Seducer's Diary." Here we meet new difficulties, inasmuch as A does not declare himself the author but only the editor. This is an old literary device to which I would not have much to object if it did not further complicate my own position, since one author becomes enclosed within the other like the boxes in a Chinese puzzle.[34]

In reality, there is one more person behind these complex literary layers: the true author, Kierkegaard. If Eremita's position is complicated, Kierkegaard's position is even more so.

In this respect, Kierkegaard's intent is unfathomable. He intended to remain invisible to readers so that they could face the issues of their own existence. In this book I argue that Kierkegaard must have had a specific intention and that this was missionary in nature. My understanding of the authorial layers in *Either/Or* is as follows:

Kierkegaard	Phase 2: A missionary intent	
	Phase 1: His intention is not immediately visible. Through this literary mystery, he helps readers to confront the issues of their existence.	
	↓ a real author	
	Victor Eremita ↓ editor ↓	
	Aesthete A ↓ editor	Ethicist B ↓ editor
	Johannes the Seducer	The Jylland Pastor

---

33. *SKS* 2, 13–14/ *EO I*, 6.
34. *SKS* 2, 16/ *EO I*, 8–9.

Concealing his distinct missionary purpose and using his literary techniques, Kierkegaard enhanced the allure of *Either/Or*.

3.2.1.3.2 Various Seductive Lines in Either/Or

By vividly describing numerous life-views, Kierkegaard intended to seduce various types of people. A depressive person might be allured by the next words of Aesthete A: "But my soul's poisonous doubt consumes everything. My soul is like the Dead Sea, over which no bird is able to fly; when it has come midway, it sinks down, exhausted, to death and destruction."[35] The person who is, has been, or dreams of being in love will enjoy reading A's reflections on the subject: "The most beautiful time is the first period of falling in love, when, from every encounter, every glance, one fetches home something new to rejoice over."[36] A lover of wit or proverbs would appreciate the paragraph below:

> In a theater, it happened that a fire started offstage. The clown came out to tell the audience. They thought it was a joke and applauded. He told them again, and they became still more hilarious. This is the way, I suppose, that the world will be destroyed – amid the universal hilarity of wits and wags who think it is all a joke.[37]

A music lover will enjoy the following *musicalized* words of A:

> Listen to Don Giovanni . . . dancing violin notes, hear the intimation of joy, hear the jubilation of delight, hear the festive bliss of enjoyment. Hear . . . the sighing of erotic love, hear the whisper of temptation, hear the vortex of seduction, hear the stillness of the moment – hear, hear, hear Mozart's Don Giovanni.[38]

The one who enjoys reading novels – or, in modern times, watching movies or playing video or smartphone games – about "saving his beloved by defying the whole world" and longs for such a "knightly love" will be attracted by the following assertion made by B:

---

35. *SKS* 2, 46/ *EO I*, 37.
36. *SKS* 2, 33/ *EO I*, 24.
37. *SKS* 2, 39/ *EO I*, 30.
38. *SKS* 2, 107/*EO I*, 103.

But if the knight has the right to say that the person who does not defy the whole world to save his beloved does not know knightly love, then the married man has the right to say the same. But I must always remind you that every such victory that marital love wins is more esthetically beautiful than the victory the knight wins.[39]

B not only seduces A but also seduces readers to a marital love that is "more esthetically beautiful than the victory the knight wins."[40] The examples above are far from exhaustive. Just as people and their interests vary, the lines in *Either/Or* that one finds seductive may also vary.

3.2.1.3.3 Provoking Seduction

Either/Or did not simply attract readers but also aroused the antipathy of some. This is vividly demonstrated in the following letter, written by Signe Læssøe to H. C. Andersen:

After one has read [Either/Or] one feels disgust for the author, but one profoundly recognizes his intelligence and his talent. We women must be especially angry with him: Like the Mohammedans, he assigns us to the realm of finitude, and he only values us because we give birth to, amuse, and save menfolk. In the first part (this is a work of 838 octavo pages) he is aesthetic, that is, evil. In the second part he is ethical, that is, a little less evil. Everyone praises the second part because it is his alter ego, the better half, which speaks. The second part only makes me the angrier [sic] with him – it is there that he ties women to finitude. In fact, I only understand a small fraction of the book; it is altogether too philosophical.[41]

This letter shows that while Læssøe feels "disgust for the author," she also recognizes "his intelligence and his talent." As a pre-feminist, Læssøe is angry with the author on behalf of women. She calls Aesthete A "evil" and Ethicist B "a little less evil." However, she also says, "The second part only makes me

---

39. *SKS* 3, 119/ *EO II*, 119.
40. *SKS* 3, 119/ *EO II*, 119.
41. Garff, *Søren Kierkegaard: A Biography*, 217, emphasis in original.

the angrier [sic] with him" because "it is *there* that he ties women to finitude." She adds, "In fact, I only understand a small fraction of the book; it is altogether too philosophical."[42] She feels that this work is perplexing and largely beyond her comprehension.

If Læssøe is so upset, why does she not abandon *Either/Or*? In the same letter, she explains, "It is so demonic that one reads and reads [*Either/Or*], puts it aside in dissatisfaction, but always takes it up again, because one can neither let it go nor hold on to it."[43] We see that even disgust for the author or for *Either/Or*'s philosophical perplexity can be seductive for readers. One may recall Kierkegaard's comment "They cannot get rid of me just because they went along with *Either/Or* so happily,"[44] though in Læssøe's case, she goes along with *Either/Or* unhappily. Did Kierkegaard intend this kind of provocative effect? It seems so because Johannes the Seducer says, "Fishing is always best in troubled waters. When a young miss is agitated, one can successfully risk much that otherwise would miscarry."[45]

3.2.1.4 *Sarcasm, Irony, Joke, Wit, Comic, and Humour*

The reader will encounter numerous instances of irony, joke, wit, satire, comic, and humour in *Either/Or*. Kierkegaard consciously used such irony and humour as part of his strategy for proclaiming Christianity and protesting the usual methods of Christian proclamation. As he comments, "By and large it is the most disastrous notion in the world that 'eloquence' has become the medium for the proclamation of Christianity. Sarcasm, irony, humor lie far closer to the existential in Christianity."[46] Kierkegaardianly speaking, the elements of sarcasm, irony, and humour in *Either/Or* serve to existentially proclaim Christianity.

---

42. Garff, 217.
43. Garff, 217.
44. *SKS* 20, 318–319, NB4:66/ *JP,* V 6107 *n.d.*, 1848.
45. *SKS* 2, 312/ *EO I*, 322.
46. *SKS* 22, 133, NB11:215/ *JP*, I 818 *n.d.*, 1849. For more discussion of the difference between irony and humour, see below: "Irony remains aristocratic. (The philosophers.) Humor reconciles with all existence." (*JP*, III B 20 *n.d.*, 1840–1841). Kierkegaard seems to mean that with the terms "[to remain] aristocratic" or "the philosophers," irony is understandable to a few, but with the term "[reconciliation] with all existence," humor is understandable to anyone.

3.2.1.4.1 Irony

Irony plays a vital role in allowing the ideally-exemplified figures in *Either/Or* to freely live. What does irony mean for Kierkegaard? The answer may lie in his MA dissertation, "The Concept of Irony with Continual Reference to Socrates." Completed two years before the publication of *Either/Or*, his study explores how to use "irony as a controlled element."[47] It is characteristic of Kierkegaard to learn an abstract concept through a concrete exemplified figure, and he learned irony through Socrates, the ancient Greek philosopher. Socrates approached his interlocutors with Socratic ignorance or irony, an approach that made them articulate eloquently about subjects in which they claimed to be experts. Similarly, Kierkegaard elegantly uses irony as a tool for indirect communication. Irony allows Kierkegaard to maintain distance from his pseudonyms so that they can freely articulate the views with which he personally disagrees. Irony also allows Kierkegaard to vividly describe his pseudonyms as if they were advocates for the reader.

In the literary universe of *Either/Or*, Victor Eremita plays a Socratic role. Eremita exemplifies "sympathetic irony," standing between the aesthetic and the ethical.[48] Like Socrates, the ironist Eremita lets A and B speak freely on their favourite subjects. In other words, A and B go to extremes to represent the ideal forms of the aesthetic and the ethical through the help of Eremita the ironist: "This is what could be called irony's attempt to mediate the discrete elements – not into a higher unity but into a higher lunacy."[49] Whereas the Hegelian philosophical system mediates the discrete elements into a higher unity, Kierkegaard's irony allows the discrete elements to contradict each other dialectically, resulting in a higher lunacy. In *Either/Or*, A does not prevail over B, or vice versa. The worldviews of both A and B confront each other sharply and never blend but are maintained and advance to a higher lunacy.[50] In other words, as will be explained in section 3.2.1.5, each literary individual in *Either/Or* lives an extremely idealized life. According to Kierkegaard, Victor Eremita (Victorious Hermit) is not the name of a specific

---

47. *SKS* 1, 352–357/ *CI*, 324–329.
48. *SKS* 7, 271/ *CUP I*, 298. See also section 2.3.4.1.
49. *SKS* 1, 295/ *CI*, 257.
50. *SKS* 2, 21/ *EO I*, 14.

person but can refer to anyone who makes their own choice of either/or, thereby becoming a victor:

> He called himself "Victor Eremita," a name that in his opinion would not be a proprium [proper name] for the editor but an apellatinum [descriptive name] for the reader.... If the reader in his self-activity came up with the title Either/Or, there would come a moment when he perhaps would prefer to designate himself as Eremita [eremite, hermit], because more earnest contemplation always creates solitude. Perhaps there would come a next moment when he would call himself Victor.[51]

The sympathetic ironist Eremita does not dare to provide a literary solution, conclusion, or catharsis. If he did so, the reader would not be encouraged to make a choice in their own life. To activate the reader's inwardness, Eremita leaves the obstacle of aporia.[52] By doing so, he engages readers' subjectivity in order to awaken them from their slumber.

3.2.1.4.2 The Comic or Humour

Contrary to the stereotypical image of Kierkegaard as being depressed, he is, in fact, "a great comic writer."[53] In *Either/Or, Part I*, the following extremely funny passage is included along with the more melancholic ones:

> There was a man whose chatter I was obliged to listen to because of the circumstances. On every occasion, he was ready with a little philosophical lecture that was extremely boring. On the verge of despair, I suddenly discovered that the man perspired exceptionally much when he spoke. This perspiration now absorbed my attention. I watched how the pearls of perspiration collected on his forehead, then united in a rivulet, slid down his nose, and ended in a quivering globule that remained suspended at the end of his nose. From that moment on, everything was changed; I could even have the delight of encouraging him to

---

51. *EO II*, Supplement, 421/ *Pap.* IV B 59, 218.

52. Plato's earlier dialogues often end in aporia, and Kierkegaard lauds Plato's use of aporia for its educational or edifying effectiveness. See *SKS* 18, 299–300, JJ:482/ *JP*, IV 4266 n.d., 1846. See also section 3.2.4.2 of this book.

53. Pyper, *Joy of Kierkegaard*, 2.

commence his philosophical instruction just in order to watch the perspiration on his brow and on his nose.[54]

In *Concluding Unscientific Postscript*, Johannes Climacus explains the role of the comic as follows:

> Quite generally, the comic is present everywhere, and every existence can be identified and assigned at once to its specific sphere by knowing how it relates to the comic. Someone who is religious has discovered the comic on the largest scale and yet does not consider the comic the highest, for the religious is the purest pathos. But if he does look on the comic as the highest, then the comic is for him *eo ipso* lower; for what is comic lies always in a contradiction, and when the comic itself is the highest, it lacks the contradiction in which the comic is and in which it shows itself to advantage. That is why it is unexceptionally the case that the more proficiently a person exists, the more he will discover the comic.[55]

According to Climacus, the comic is present everywhere but is not the highest; only the religious is purely the highest. In Kierkegaard's literary framework, the role of the comic or humour is to serve the religious. The one who is on guard can be disarmed by laughter, which may make them more open to the religious. Strictly speaking, as Alejandro Gonzalez says, "Johannes Climacus makes a distinction between two different kinds of humor by naming them 'immature humor' and 'humor in equilibrium between the comic and the tragic.'"[56] The humour exemplified in *Either/Or* is not as advanced as the form of humour personified in Climacus, which "is the condition for properly embracing Christianity."[57] The humour in *Either/Or* is "immature humor [that] is firmly embedded in the aesthetic sphere and is not at the threshold to anything higher."[58] Although it is not an advanced

---

54. *SKS* 2, 288/ *EO I*, 299.
55. *SKS* 7, 420/ Kierkegaard, *Postscript*, 387–388.
56. Gonzalez, "Humor," 176; the quotation within the quotation is originally from *SKS* 7, 266/ *CUP I*, 292.
57. *SKS* 7, 266/ *CUP I*, 292.
58. Gonzalez, "Humor," 176.

form of humour, the comic or humorous elements in *Either/Or* play a vital role in the process of edifying the reader.

3.2.1.5 An Experiment of a Certain Life-View

Kierkegaard's pseudonyms are not just a device to lure his contemporaries. A significant feature of Kierkegaard's pseudonyms is each pseudonym's unwavering faithfulness to a given life-view. The difference between Goethe's and Kierkegaard's treatment of Faust illustrates this well. For some time, Kierkegaard was absorbed in Faust, engaging in intensive study of the various versions of the Faustian legends.[59] For Kierkegaard, Goethe's *Faust* was just one among many Faustian stories in literature. But Kierkegaard was disappointed with the ending of Goethe's *Faust* and says, "In my opinion, Faust is doubt personified. More he should not be, and it certainly is a sin against the idea when Goethe allows Faust to be converted."[60] In Kierkegaard's opinion, Faust was doubt personified, and so he believed that Faust should remain a doubter from the beginning to the end of the story.[61]

Yet, isn't Kierkegaard being cruel? Isn't Goethe's literary rescue, in which Faust converted at the end of the story, more heart-warming? However, as far as Kierkegaard is concerned, the issue is not the salvation of the literary figure but the salvation of the *actual person*. One of his journal entries reflects his belief that it is cruel not to be a missionary if there is no salvation outside the church.[62] Similarly, for Kierkegaard, it would be cruel if a literary figure were saved while an actual person is abandoned. The literary salvation of Faust may ease the reader's mind, but it goes no further since no self-activity would occur in readers because their minds are already at ease. Kierkegaard, however, was concerned with actual people and wanted readers who held problematic life-views to feel unease after reading. Therefore, his characters or personas – each of whom represent certain life-views – had to remain faithful to their respective life-views. The lack of literary rescue, together

---

59. According to Ōtani, 107 Faustian stories are listed in Kierkegaard's personal bibliography. Ōtani, *Kierkegaard's Authorship, Part 2*, 978. See also *SKS* 27, 167, Papir 244/ *JP*, V 5225 *n.d.*, 1837.

60. *SKS* 17, 19, AA:12/ *JP*, V 5092 72 1 June 1835. Kierkegaard probably refers to the fact that Faust is saved at the end of "the Second Part of the Tragedy" in Goethe's *Faust*. See Goethe, *Faust*, 368.

61. For Faust as a Kierkegaardian figure, see Lisi, "Faust," 209–228.

62. *SKS* 25, 223, NB28:13/ *JP*, III 2729 *n.d.*, 1853.

with the unvarnished portrayal of the consequences of their life-views, work together to stir readers to self-reflection and perhaps action. When Faustian figures fail in Kierkegaard's literary world, the reader is invited to experience a life of doubt. On the one hand, this shocks readers; on the other hand, they are urged to reflect on how they should live. In this way, the literary figures in Kierkegaard's writings provoke readers to examine whether or not such a life is worth living.

In order for the aesthetic reader to change their actual life, A needs to be faithful to his life-view until the end of *Either/Or*. Note that in *Either/Or*, the reader does not only encounter A but also numerous other lifestyles. One may encounter exaggerated forms of these lifestyles through various literary figures such as the sympathetic ironist Victor Eremita, the gifted aesthete A, the sensuous lady-killer Don Juan, the skilled seducer Johannes, the unhappiest one, the tragic heroine Antigone, the quiet sad lady Marie Beaumarchais, the emotionally erratic Donna Elvira, the ex-lover-worshipper Margarete, the tragicomical heroine Emmeline, the cruelly abandoned girl Cordelia, and the devoted husband B.[63] These figures make no compromises and remain faithful to their own world views. Readers may identify with certain figures if they find similarities between these figures and themselves. Through such identification, they become involved in a literary experiment that helps them to see clearly where their own lifestyle may lead. As Karsten Harries puts it, "A, the pseudonymous author of the first volume, provided me not only with the portrait of a romantic nihilist, but also with a demonstration of the *necessary failure* of any attempt to find an aesthetic solution to the problem of meaning."[64] Through idealized figures, *Either/Or* provides the reader with an opportunity to existentially reflect upon their own life and demonstrates "the necessary failure" of those figures.[65]

---

63. See appendix 4.

64. Harries, *Between Nihilism and Faith*, XV, emphasis mine.

65. John Milton (1608–1674) famously argues for freedom of speech and says, "Assuredly we bring not innocence into the world, we bring impurity much rather, that which purifies us is trial, and trial is by what is contrary.... Since therefore the knowledge and survey of vice is in this world so necessary to the constituting of human virtue, and the scanning of error to the confirmation of truth, how can we more safely, and with less danger, scout into the regions of sin and falsity than by reading all manner of tractates and hearing all manner of reasons?" Milton, "Areopagitica," 728–729. Whether we like it or not, vice exists in this world. In this sense, Kierkegaardian villains provide the reader with opportunities to "more safely, and with

3.2.1.6 Either/Or *as a Mirror of the Reader's Inner Self*

Kierkegaard expected *Either/Or* to play the role of a mirror in which readers could see their own reflection. For Kierkegaard, *Either/Or* reflects the two dominant lifestyles of his contemporary Danes. Part I reflect the lifestyle of the aesthete, while Part II reflects that of "the ordinary godly Christian."[66] Kierkegaard says that someone who truly wants to help another should listen attentively.[67] *Either/Or* is, in a sense, the result of Kierkegaard's careful listening to his contemporaries.[68] Through careful listening, Kierkegaard constructed *Either/Or* in order to help readers discern themselves more profoundly. Kierkegaard makes a cynical comment on P. L. Møller, saying,

> It is psychologically worthy of note and perhaps also deserves to be perpetuated that a person whose name I will grant a place here in order to carry him along with me, that Herr P. L. Møller quite correctly regarded "The Seducer's Diary" as central to the whole authorship. This reminds me so vividly of the epigraph for *Stages on Life's Way*, the very work that he, with "The Diary of a Seducer" as his point of view, fell upon or fell over – which epigraph I therefore once reminded him of in a little rebuff to him, but which perhaps may fittingly be repeated here again since it appropriately and epigrammatically preserves the memory of Herr. P. L. Møller's esthetic and critical profit from

---

less danger, scout into the regions of sin and falsity" and allowing them to engage with these concepts and potentially transcend vice in their own lives.

66. Watkin, "Judge William," 123.

67. *SKS* 16, 28/ *PV*, 46. In this sense, with *Either/Or*, Kierkegaard somehow plays the role of counsellor. The following explanation by Carl R. Rogers (1902–1987), a prominent psychotherapist who has appropriated Kierkegaard in his own way, helps us to elucidate this dimension of Kierkegaardian therapy: "Real communication occurs, . . . when we listen with understanding. . . . understanding *with* a person, not *about* him – is such an effective approach that it can bring about major changes in personality." Rogers, *On Becoming a Person*, 331–332, emphasis in original. In this book, Rogers often refers to Kierkegaard as one of the major figures who inspired him. The difference between Kierkegaard and Rogers is that whereas the former aims at a religious cure, the latter aims at a religionless cure. For discussion on Kierkegaard's influence on Rogers and the differences between the thoughts of these two figures, see Podmore, "Carl R. Rogers," 238–258; Lippitt, "Philosophical Response," loc. 2064–2418, Kindle.

68. Was Kierkegaard really an asocial individualist? Was he accustomed to associating with his contemporaries? He might have been a lonesome soul, but he also loved to walk and talk with people on the streets. "On these daily walks he meets acquaintances on every street, and many of them will walk along with him, arm in arm, to converse for a while." Carlisle, *Philosopher of the Heart*, loc. 617, Kindle.

my authorship: . . . [Such works are mirrors: when an ape looks in, no apostle can look out.][69]

P. L. Møller was "a writer, poet, and literary critic with academic ambitions."[70] On the one hand, "like Kierkegaard, he spent his youth on varied aesthetic and philosophical studies."[71] However, "Møller had nothing of Kierkegaard's religious and ethical seriousness."[72] This knowledge makes Kierkegaard's ironic comment on Møller clearer. By claiming that "'the Seducer's Diary' [is] central to the whole authorship,"[73] Møller unwittingly reveals his own identity rather than Kierkegaard's. In other words, *Either/Or* revealed to Møller a reflection of himself as a seducer.[74] One can see that Kierkegaard considered *Either/Or* as a book of mirrors that reflected the reader's own image back to them.

3.2.1.7 Summary

How can aesthetes will to allow themselves to be built up? According to Kierkegaard, *Either/Or*, which conceals a profound religiousness behind its complex literary devices (see section 3.2.1.1), greatly amuses the reader (see section 3.2.1.2). *Either/Or* allures the reader with its enigmatic elements, various seductive lines, and provoking seductions (see section 3.2.1.3). Irony makes it possible for Kierkegaard to approach the reader with Socratic ignorance, prompting them to reflect on their own existence (see section 3.2.1.4.1). Humour helps to disarm the reader's defences, encouraging them to open themselves to the ethico-religious (see section 3.2.1.4.2). The reader can experiment with certain life-views through the somewhat extreme and idealized figures who live in the literary world of *Either/Or* (see section 3.2.1.5). *Either/Or* plays the role of a mirror in which readers see their inwardness, prompting them to reflect upon and correct themselves (see section 3.2.1.6).

---

69. *SKS* 16, 71f./ *PV*, 92f; the quotation in square brackets was originally written in German and translated by the Hongs.
70. Hannay, *Kierkegaard: A Biography*, 319.
71. Garff, *Søren Kierkegaard: A Biography*, 386.
72. Hohlenberg, *Søren Kierkegaard*, 179.
73. Garff, *Søren Kierkegaard: A Biography*, 390.
74. This "seducer" does not mean "a seducer into the truth" as Kierkegaard attempts to be. Rather, Kierkegaard means that P. L. Møller's review of Kierkegaard's authorship proves that he is "a seducer in the aesthetic sphere."

What is Kierkegaard's motivation? Why does Kierkegaard deeply engage with the existences of the readers and help them reflect upon and correct themselves? As Johannes Climacus says, "Love ... does not change the beloved but changes itself."[75] Just as Christ changed himself and become flesh out of love, Kierkegaard changes himself and becomes like his contemporaries out of love.

3.2.1.8 Introduction to a Possible Application of the Kierkegaardian Mission

In the previous sub-subsection, I summarized how readers of *Either/Or* will to allow themselves to be built up. Even though Kierkegaard might have managed to skilfully construct literary devices in this way, one may wonder how ordinary people can adopt a Kierkegaardian strategy in their own context. Let me illustrate with a real-life example from the life of Martin Luther and his wife Katharina von Bora (1499–1552). Having lived three centuries before Kierkegaard, Katharina, of course, did not know Kierkegaard at all. But the incident described below demonstrates that this kind of approach was already practised by a Christian in a pre-Kierkegaardian age:

> Martin Luther was a very cheerful man, as a rule; but he had terrible fits of depression.... when he went into the sitting-room, his wise wife Kate, [Katherine] von Bora, was sitting there, dressed in black, and her children round about her, all in black. "Oh, oh!" said Luther, "who is dead?" "Why," said she, "doctor, have not you heard that God is dead? My husband, Martin Luther, would never be in such a state of mind if he had a living God to trust to." Then he burst into a hearty laugh, and said, "Kate, thou art a wise woman. I have been acting as if God were dead, and I will do so no more. Go and take off thy black."[76]

Although Luther is not a so-called aesthete, Kate's strategy resembles Kierkegaard's approach in *Either/Or*. Although there is no funeral, Kate and her children are in black. In short, their appearance is a deception.[77] Kate

---

75. *SKS* 4, 239/ *PF*, 33.

76. Spurgeon, *Complete Works*, loc. 11232–11237, Kindle. See also Markwald and Markwald, *Katharina Von Bora*, 139–140.

77. *SKS* 16, 39/ *PV*, 58.

must have prayerfully intended to edify her husband. Therefore, her profound religiousness lies behind the story (see section 3.2.1.1). Kate dressed herself and her children in clothes appropriate for a funeral because she had calculated that the appearance of his family in mourning garb would provide just the jolt necessary to capture Luther's attention (see section 3.2.1.2). In other words, she seduced her husband (to be built up) (see section 3.2.1.3). As irony conveys a meaning that is the opposite of what is said, her declaration of the death of God reminded Luther that God is alive (see section 3.2.1.4.1). Luther's laughter highlights the comical or humorous aspects of this story (see section 3.2.1.4.2). Kate was faithful to an idealized figure – someone who dressed appropriately to attend the funeral of God – so that Luther might be built up (see section 3.2.1.5). Through Kate's drama, Luther could see his reflection as if in a mirror and realize that he was acting as if God were dead (see section 3.2.1.6).

But might it seem pompous for Kate to dress herself and her children in black despite there being no funeral? I would argue that the more a Kierkegaardian missionary dramatizes, the more powerful edification becomes. Let me share my own experience, which is less bombastic and may seem more relatable. As a driver, I used to complain about bad drivers. One day, I came across a reckless driver. As I was about to grumble, my wife, who was sitting beside me, started impersonating my usual manner of accusing and complaining, doing so in an exaggerated form. The way she acted was funny and endearing, and I began to laugh. And then I began to reflect on my usual behaviour, asking myself, "Is it edifying to complain about other people's driving?" Wisely, my wife did not reproach me directly with reproving words: "You should not speak ill of others as a pastor." If she had done so, I might have defended myself and become hardened. She demonstrated how I looked by becoming like me[78] in an exaggerated and humorous form so that I could reflect upon myself with laughter and *will to allow myself to be built up*. Perhaps all wives have this skill. Could it be that they know how to seduce their husbands to good effect – for their upbuilding?

One might wonder whether these stories about Luther's wife and my wife are emblematic of the Kierkegaardian missionary task? Mark Tietjen says of the Kierkegaardian mission, "The truth is that just as all Christians are

---

78. See 1 Corinthians 9:19–23.

called to mission, so too could *all* Christians use the message and love of the Christian missionary. Mission work quite simply calls others, *all* others, to God."[79] Kierkegaard himself was never sent to a foreign nation by a mission agency. He was a writer. It does not matter whether one is a so-called missionary, a pastor, a layperson, a writer, or a wife. It does not matter whether one is in Christendom or living in a non Christian nation. It does not matter whether the place is a church, a house, or a car. It should not concern a Kierkegaardian missionary whether our neighbour is non-Christian or Christian. The principle of the Kierkegaardian mission is "every Christian a missionary," to whom Christ says, "Go out and proclaim my teaching."[80] Any Christian, regardless of their occupation, can help their neighbours to allow themselves to be built up on all occasions. This is a basic application of the Kierkegaardian missionary task.

3.2.2 How to Make Aesthetes Aware of Their Need of the Eternal

In his letter to A, B penetratively discerns A's problem: "In a certain sense you are right, for nothing that is finite, not even the whole world, can satisfy the soul of a person who feels the need (*Trang*)[81] of the eternal."[82] In saying this, B urges A (and the aesthetic reader) to be aware of their need for the eternal. As far as *Either/Or* is concerned, Kierkegaard seems to identify at least three phases involved in deepening the reader's awareness of this need, with each phase progressively fostering a greater longing for the eternal. First, A's fondness for mythology emphasizes his (unconscious) need for the eternal, but it also signifies the inevitable failure of pursuing the eternal by mythology alone.

---

79. Tietjen, *Kierkegaard: A Christian Missionary*, loc. 2522, Kindle, emphasis in original.

80. *SKS* 25, 241, NB28:33/ *JP*, III 2730 *n.d.*, 1853.

81. *Trang* can mean "1 desire; urge; impulse; 2 need; demand; 3 craving; 4 want, need, poverty" (Pederson, *Danish-English Dictionary*, 1267). A does not consciously seek the eternal; rather, his need remains concealed even from himself. B (Kierkegaard) employs a strategy aimed at leading A (the aesthetic reader) to recognize this need (*Trang*) for the eternal and, ideally, to cultivate "the longing (*Længsel*) for God" (SKS 10, 265–275 / *CD*, 251–261). *Længsel* is defined as "longing, yearning; nostalgia" (Pederson, *Danish-English Dictionary*, 694). In this regard, a central and distinctive aspect of Kierkegaard's missionary approach is his effort to awaken in the reader a longing for the eternal or God by making them conscious of their own desire, need, or hunger for the eternal. For further discussion on the longing for God, see Graham, "Longing for God"; for the sources cited therein, see Graham, 5, fn. 1.

82. *SKS* 3, 195/ *EO II*, 203. Compare Eccl 3:11.

Second, A's appreciation of Romanticism hints at a possible transformation of his (unconscious) need into ethico-religious striving. Third, as A confronts the limitations of aesthetic pursuits, he embodies Ecclesiastes, a text that resonates with his growing realization of the vanity of worldly endeavors and the deeper longing for something beyond them. Although *Either/Or* does not yet introduce a strictly Christian resolution, Ecclesiastes serves as a pivotal moment in A's existential development, pointing him toward a more profound engagement with the eternal.

3.2.2.1 Phase 1: The Roles of the Mythology in Either/Or

In *Either/Or, Part I*, mythology frequently appears in an unforgettable fashion – for example, in the form of figures such as Xerxes, Molbo's eel, Lynceus of Messina, the giants, Apis, Leto, Trophonius, Fenris, Thor, Philoctetes, Hercules, Proteus, Tantalus, Sisyphus, Ancaeus, Hyperboreans, Lethe, Cerberus, Minerva, Jupiter, Venus, Cardea, Aeolus, Ariadne, Nemesis, Aphrodite, Valkyrie, Pyramus, Thisbe, Diana, Alpheus, Amor, Psyche, Alectryon, and Neptune.[83] What are the functions of those mythological figures in *Either/Or*? To explore the roles of mythology in *Either/Or*, I consider a typical example of mythology from *Either/Or, Part I*:

> How dreadful boredom is – how dreadfully boring; I know no stronger expression, no truer one, for like is recognized only by like. Would that there were a loftier, stronger expression, for then there would still be one movement. I lie prostrate, inert; the only thing I see is emptiness, the only thing I live on is emptiness, the only thing I move in is emptiness. I do not even suffer pain. The vulture pecked continually at Prometheus's liver; the poison dripped down continually on Loki; it was at least an interruption, even though monotonous. Pain itself has lost its refreshment for me.[84]

---

83. *SKS* 2; 13; 17; 32 (2); 37; 43 (3); 44; 82; 150; 162; 173; 174 (2); 219 (2); 283; 284; 321 (2); 384; 388 (2)/ *EO I*; 6; 10; 24 (2); 28; 33–34; 34 (2); 35; 77; 151; 164; 175; 177 (2); 226 (2); 294 (2); 332 (2); 396; 400 (2); 404; 425 (4); 436; 440; 443 (2); 445 (2). (Numbers in parentheses indicate multiple mythological figures referenced on the given page).

84. *SKS* 2, 46/ *EO I*, 37. Prometheus and Loki, symbolic-mythical figures of never-ending nightmares, may remind one of *The Myth of Sisyphus* written by Albert Camus, influenced by Kierkegaard, the father of existentialism.

In this powerful expression of perpetual boredom, the mythological figures of Prometheus and Loki play pivotal roles. Prometheus is a Greek mythological figure that has influenced literature worldwide. Prometheus's significance in the quotation above is due to his dreadful situation. According to "Hesiod's hexameter poetry in the *Theogony and Works and Days*," which constitutes "the first literary evidence for the Prometheus myth,"[85] this is the existence that Prometheus was doomed to endure:

> And with painful fetters he [sc. Zeus] bound shifty-planning Prometheus, with distressful bonds, driving them through the middle of a pillar; and he set upon him a long-winged eagle which ate his immortal liver, but this grew again on all sides at night just as much as the long-winged bird would eat during the whole day.[86]

The other mythological figure referred to in the aforementioned quotation from *Either/Or* is the Nordic mythical figure Loki. Matthew Brake summarizes the roles of Loki in Kierkegaard's authorship:

> The gods punished Loki for his mischief by securing him to a rock. They placed a poisonous snake above Loki whose venom dripped down upon him and caused him great pain; however, Loki's wife Sigyn came and stood next to him, holding a bowl over his head. She collected the poison in the bowl, but when she emptied it, the poison dripped down on Loki once more. This story plays a central role in Kierkegaard's appropriation of Loki.[87]

Both Prometheus and Loki represent "almost eternal punishment."[88] While Prometheus's liver is eaten alive perpetually, it grows again on all sides each night. Similarly, in the Nordic myth, earthquakes happen whenever "... the venom drips into [Loki's] face [when his wife Sigyn empties the bowl].

---

85. Pohlmeyer, "Prometheus," 187.

86. Pohlmeyer, 187, originally from Hesiod, 'Theogony, verses 521–5' in Hesiod, *Theogony, Works and Days, Testimonia (Loeb Classical Library) (Reprinted and Corrected Edition)*, ed. and trans. by Glenn W. Most, Cambridge, Massachusetts and London: Harvard University Press 2010, 45.

87. Brake, "Loki," 66.

88. Pohlmeyer, "Prometheus," 192.

Then he writhes against it with such force that all the earth trembles . . ."[89] However, A seems to think that he suffers more than Prometheus and Loki do. For A, Prometheus and Loki still have an interruption of pain. A feels that the agony of boredom is even worse since "pain itself has lost its refreshment for me."[90] This suffering is not the Christian concept of eternity but, rather, some kind of (horrible) perpetuity, in which, nevertheless, the aesthete feels somewhat at home. Why does Kierkegaard use so many mythological figures? Did he simply like them? Or did he have a specific purpose in using them? Did he deploy these figures strategically?

In his classic study of Kierkegaard, Gregor Malantschuk says, "In mythology, as well as in other spheres, Kierkegaard's concern is to find an adequate definition of the concept."[91] According to Malantschuk, Kierkegaard had already come to "the epitomizing definition of the concept 'mythology'"[92] in 1836, seven years before the publication of *Either/Or*. Referring to one of Kierkegaard's journal entries, Malantschuk says, "In this entry we find first of all the encompassing definition of the concept 'mythology': 'Mythology is the compacting (suppressed being) of the idea of eternity (the eternal idea) in the categories of time and space.'"[93] In this definition, Kierkegaard tells us that while mythology contains the idea of eternity, this idea is suppressed because it expresses the eternal within the confines of time and space. Although mythology touches upon the eternal to some degree, this is unsatisfactory because the eternal lies beyond mythology's ability to express it.

If we presuppose Kierkegaard as a missionary, does mythology not confuse the reader in the grand plan of Kierkegaard's mission strategy? Thanks to Pohlmeyer's elucidation of Kierkegaard's uses of Prometheus, we know that confusion was not Kierkegaard's aim in appropriating mythology for his purposes. Although Prometheus is described as the creator in the myth, "Kierkegaard does not take up the idea of Prometheus as the creator of humankind. One reason could be the fact that the establishment of a second

---

89. Snorri Sturluson, *The Prose Edda*. trans. by Arthur Gilchrist Brodeur, New York: The American-Scandinavian Foundation 1916, 77.

90. *SKS* 2, 46/ *EO I*, 37.

91. Malantschuk, *Kierkegaard's Thought*, 21.

92. Malantschuk, *Kierkegaard's Thought*, 22.

93. Malantschuk, 23; the quotation within the quotation is originally from *SKS* 18, 79, FF:24/ *JP*, III 2799.

creator along with the Christian Creator God would have been problematic."[94] The absence of mythological concepts that contradict Christian doctrine testifies to the fact that the missionary Kierkegaard knew what he was doing.

But mythology does present a few problems. First, although mythological motifs effectively capture the attention of the aesthetic reader, the idea of the eternal enshrined in myth cannot satisfy because of its primitive, underdeveloped nature. Second, Kierkegaard's strategy is not to force one to parrot Christian orthodoxy but, rather, to help one "will to allow oneself to be built up."[95]

3.2.2.2 Phase 2: The Roles of Romanticism in Either/Or

Either/Or, Part I is usually referred to as the aesthetic but also can be called the romantic. According to William McDonald, "Most of Kierkegaard's explicit references to Romanticism in his authorship occur early, particularly in *The Concept of Irony* and *Either/Or*."[96] David J. Gouwens summarizes Gerhard vom Hofe's chronological study of Kierkegaard's journal entries concerning the two terms romantic and aesthetic: "Vom Hofe argues that Kierkegaard's early journals on 'the romantic' 'demythologize' the term, and that Kierkegaard increasingly replaces the word 'romantic' with the word 'aesthetic.'"[97] If this is so, the use of the term "aesthetics" in *Either/Or* also signifies Romanticism, along with the direct reference to the term "Romanticism."

What is Kierkegaard's definition of Romanticism? According to Nassim Bravo Jordán,

> Romanticism is impossible to define, because it has no fixed standard and is boundless. It looks for an ideal that cannot be found in given actuality, and as a consequence the romantic

---

94. Pohlmeyer, "Prometheus," 196.
95. *Pap.* VI B 133; *TD*, Supplement, 120.
96. McDonald, "Kierkegaard and Romanticism," 95.
97. David J. Gouwens, "Kierkegaard's *Either/Or, Part One*: Patterns of Interpretation" in *IKC 3*: Either/Or, Part I. 1995, 15, quotations in the single quotation marks are from Gerhard vom Hofe, *Die Romantikkritik Sören Kierkegaards*. Frankfurt am Main: Athenäum 1972, 107 and translated by David J. Gouwens. Kierkegaard "takes [esthetic] to be almost synonymous with Romantic." McDonald, "Kierkegaard and Romanticism," 94. However, my supervisor C. Stephen Evans warns, "Don't equate the romantic with the aesthete conceptually. The correct view is that romantics are a type of modern aesthete, but the aesthetic is a universal category. So romantics are a type of aesthete, but the concepts are not identical." Evans, personal communication, 10 June 2020.

negates reality and becomes restless. In order to quench his frustrated desire, the romantic engages in an endless game of diversity and possibilities.[98]

One can see that the description of Romanticism above almost precisely delineates *Either/Or, Part I*. In short, the first half of *Either/Or* is filled with Romanticism. What about Kierkegaard's evaluation of Romanticism? McDonald states that Kierkegaard's attitude towards Romanticism is ambivalent, including both negative and positive aspects.

> But most importantly, Kierkegaard engages vigorously with Romantic aesthetics, analysing, playing with, and critically transforming some of its central concepts, such as irony, the interesting, reflection, the individual and love, as well as some of the early Romantics' key questions.[99]

This important quotation reinforces the idea that many of the key concepts – for example, irony, the interesting, love – in *Either/Or* derive from Romanticism. The following rich and complex summary by McDonald helps us understand the roles of Romanticism in *Either/Or*:

> [Kierkegaard's vigorous engagement with Romantic aesthetics] include how to distinguish ancient from modern poetry and drama, how to communicate ethical and religious views, how to understand the relative importance of feeling, reason, intuition, sensation and imagination, and how to use the multifarious art of style to represent the unrepresentable, how to rejuvenate religion, and how to become a self in the present age. He shares a love of Socrates and Plato, an admiration for Shakespeare, Cervantes, and Goethe, and a fascination for the mythology of the Middle Ages. He also takes seriously the early German Romantics' view that literature should ultimately serve ethics and religion.[100]

---

98. Jordán, "Romantic." 272.
99. McDonald, "Kierkegaard and Romanticism." 94.
100. McDonald, 94.

As emphasized above, there are many important issues that merit discussion concerning Kierkegaard's relationship to Romanticism. Very briefly, a central aspect of Kierkegaard's mission strategy that seems to draw from Romanticism is the detection of "a perpetual longing for the absolute,"[101] which exists in the heart of the romantic. In *Either/Or*, Kierkegaard seeks to harness this romantic longing and channel it in such a way that it "ultimately serve[s] ethics and religion."[102] In other words, "in Kierkegaard's adaption, romantic longing is transformed into ethical striving."[103] In phase 1, mythology helps the reader to be aware of their unconscious need for the eternal. In phase 2, Romanticism helps the reader not just to perceive their need for the eternal but also to move forward to find what they are looking for. However, as the Irish rock band U2 expresses in *I Still Haven't Found What I'm Looking For*, the Romantic remains in a state of unfulfilled longing.[104] At this stage, one remains trapped in "a perpetual longing for the absolute."[105] In order to move beyond this, one needs the framework of Ecclesiastes, through which *Either/Or* becomes an aesthete-friendly guide to the ethico-religious.

3.2.2.3 Phase 3: The Roles of the Book of Ecclesiastes in Either/Or

In Kierkegaard's strategy to seduce aesthetes into the truth, the book of Ecclesiastes in the Old Testament plays a vital role. One can scarcely help recalling Ecclesiastes while reading *Either/Or, Part I*. For instance, "Vanity of vanities, says the [Qoheleth], vanity of vanities! All is vanity." (Eccl 1:2). A's fist document, "Διαψαλματα" (*Diapsalmata*), opens with the following Ecclesiastes-like epigraph:

> Greatness, knowledge, renown,
> Friendship, pleasure and possessions,
> All is only wind, only smoke:
> To say it better, all is nothing.[106]

---

101. McDonald, 102.
102. McDonald, 94.
103. McDonald, 104.
104. "U2 lyrics." https://www.azlyrics.com/u/u2band.html.
105. McDonald, 102.
106. *SKS* 2, 26/ *EO I*, 18, originally written in French, translated by the Hongs.

One can see that Kierkegaard consciously shaped the atmosphere of *Either/Or, Part I* to resemble that of Ecclesiastes. Not only do both A and Qoheleth share the sense of the vanity of life, they also attempt to enjoy carnal desires to the utmost. Ecclesiastes says, "I said to myself, 'Come now, I will make a test of pleasure; enjoy yourself.' . . . Whatever my eyes desired I did not keep from them; I kept my heart from no pleasure" (Eccl 2:1, 10). Similarly, A is an expert on any form of pleasure, as if he were a faithful disciple of Qoheleth. The epigraph of *Either/Or, Part I* says, "Is reason then alone baptized, are the passions pagans? Young,"[107] which is A's bold declaration that he would pursue the passions (pleasure) as a Christian might pursue God or a rational Christian might pursue speculation. While both Qoheleth and A chase after pleasure or the aesthetic, both know the vanity of pleasure: "But again, [pleasure] also was vanity" (Eccl 2:1); "There are, as is known, insects that die in the moment of fertilization. So it is with all joy: life's highest, most splendid moment of enjoyment is accompanied by death."[108] Therefore, for both Qoheleth and A, to live is to suffer. Depressingly, Qoheleth says, "And I thought the dead, who have already died, more fortunate than the living, who are still alive" (Eccl 4:2) The following excerpt from *Either/Or, Part I* reads like an elaboration of this verse from Ecclesiastes:

> How empty and meaningless life is. – We bury a man; we accompany him to the grave, throw three spadefuls of earth on him; we ride out in a carriage, ride home in a carriage; we find consolation in the thought that we have a long life ahead of us. But how long is seven times ten years? Why not settle it all at once, why not stay out there and go along down into the grave and draw lots to see to whom will befall the misfortune of being the last of the living who throws the last three spadefuls of earth on the last of the dead?[109]

As demonstrated above, there are obvious resemblances between Ecclesiastes and *Either/Or, Part I*. In fact, B says to A, "As for your lecturing

---

107. *SKS* 2, 9/ *EO I*, 1, originally quoted from Edward Young, *The Complaint or Night-Thoughts on Life, Death, and Immortality* (1742–1744), IV, 629 (Howard V. Hong and Edna H. Hong, 'Notes' in *EO I*, 603), slightly modified by Kierkegaard.
108. *SKS* 2, 28/ *EO I*, 20.
109. *SKS* 2, 38/ *EO I*, 29.

and your wisdom, they often remind me of Ecclesiastes . . ., and one would actually think that you occasionally chose your text from it."[110] B even refers directly to Ecclesiastes 1:2, saying to A, "You become erect and more jocular than ever and make yourself and others happy with the gospel *vanitas vanitatum vanitas* [vanity of vanities all is vanity], hurrah!"[111]

In addition, consider the following quotation from Ecclesiastes: "God . . . has also put eternity into the heart of human beings."[112] B diagnoses A according to the theology of Ecclesiastes, saying, "In a certain sense you are right, for nothing that is finite, not even the whole world, can satisfy the soul of a person who feels the need of the eternal."[113] As if speaking on behalf of Qoheleth, B says that since God has put eternity in A's heart, A cannot be satisfied with the finite. Only the eternal God can satisfy A.

In summary, *Either/Or, Part I* is designed to mimic the atmosphere of Ecclesiastes in order to attract those who feel vanity and love pleasure. Further, A is diagnosed to have *a longing for eternity* in his heart according to the theology of Ecclesiastes and therefore, eternity or God is the appropriate spiritual prescription for him.[114]

3.2.2.4 Summary

How can the aesthete become aware of the need for the eternal? According to Kierkegaard's definition, "Mythology is the compacting (suppressed being) of the idea of eternity (the eternal idea) in the categories of time and space."[115] In *Either/Or, Part I*, a multitude of mythological references exposes A's unconscious yearning for eternity and mythology's failure to access it (see section 3.2.2.1). Kierkegaard adapts the concepts of Romanticism in such a way as to transform one's (unconscious) longing for the eternal into ethico-religious striving. The aesthetic reader may thus be able to escape from the state of indifference and embark on a quest for the eternal or attempt to live an

---

110. *SKS* 3, 148/ *EO II*, 150.

111. *SKS* 3, 163/ *EO II*, 166.

112. Ecclesiasts 3:11, taken from *SKS* 8, 126/ *UDVS*, 11.

113. *SKS* 3, 195/ *EO II*, 203.

114. "What the times in the deepest sense *need* can be totally and completely expressed in one single word – the times need: eternity." *SKS* 16, 84/ *PV*, 104, emphasis in original.

115. Malantschuk, *Kierkegaard's Thought*, 23; the quotation within the quotation is originally from *SKS* 18, 79, FF:24/ *JP*, III 2799.

Either/Or as an Initial Missionary Task with "Paganism"   115

ethico-religious life (see section 3.2.2.2). Throughout *Either/Or*, Ecclesiastes plays a pivotal role in both attracting the aesthete – through its references to vanity and pleasure – and introducing the aesthete to the possibility of satisfaction since God can fulfil the desire of the aesthete's heart for the eternal (see section 3.2.2.3).

3.2.2.5 A Possible Application to the Japanese Context

According to our analysis, Kierkegaard uses three phases to make the aesthete aware of their need for the eternal, utilizing mythology, Romanticism, and Ecclesiastes. To fully apply this to the Japanese context and justify such an argument would require more space than is available within the confines of this book. Nonetheless, I will briefly sketch the contours that such an application might follow. In phase 1, one might draw upon Japanese mythology,[116] such as 古事記 (Kojiki)[117] and 日本書紀 (Nihon Shoki),[118] which include the stories of Izanami and Izanagi,[119] Amaterasu and Susanoō,[120] and Ōnamuchi[121] – well-known figures among the Japanese. To capture the heart of the Japanese, a Kierkegaardian missionary could use these Japanese mythologies but adapt them to avoid content that contradicts Christian doctrines. In phase 2, it may be possible to use Japanese Romanticists such as 森鴎外 (Mori Ōgai, 1862–1922), 北村透谷 (Kitamura Tōkoku, 1868–1894), and 島崎藤村 (Shimazaki Tōson, 1872–1943). Since some of these Romanticists were Christians or were influenced by Christianity,[122] utilizing their ideas of perpetual longing may serve as a helpful bridge between Japanese mythology and Christianity. In phase 3, one may be able to use Ecclesiastes for those encountering Christianity for the first time. In my experience, Japanese newcomers to church, who are

---

116. Levin, *Japanese Mythology*.

117. Kurano, 古事記 (Kojiki) [Records of Ancient Matters]; Philippi, *Kojiki*.

118. Kojima, Naoki, Nishimiya, Kuranaka, and Mōri, 日本書紀 1 (Nihonshoki 1) [The Chronicles of Japan 1]; Aston, *Nihongi*.

119. Kurano, 古事記 (Kojiki) [Records of Ancient Matters], 20–34; Philippi, *Kojiki*, 49–73; Kojima, Naoki, Nishimiya, Kuranaka, and Mōri, 日本書紀 1 (Nihonshoki 1) [The Chronicles of Japan 1], 25–35; Aston, *Nihongi*, 1.5–1.12.

120. Kurano, 古事記 (Kojiki) [Records of Ancient Matters], 34–46; Philippi, *Kojiki*, 74–92; Kojima, Naoki, Nishimiya, Kuranaka, and Mōri, 日本書紀 1 (Nihonshoki 1) [The Chronicles of Japan 1], 35–107; Aston, *Nihongi*, 1.13–1.63.

121. Kurano, 古事記 (Kojiki) [Records of Ancient Matters], 47–62; Philippi, *Kojiki*, 93–119.

122. Sasabuchi, 浪漫主義文学 ["Romantic Literature"], 533.

not yet ready to accept strictly Christian doctrines – such as the resurrection of Jesus Christ or the apostle Paul's theology – often feel at home with Ecclesiastes. For instance, the opening paragraph of the eleventh-century Japanese classic *The Tale of Genji*, which most Japanese can probably recite, says this:

> The bells of the Gion monastery in India echo with the warning that all things are impermanent. The blossoms of the sala trees teach us through their hues that what flourishes must fade. The proud do not prevail for long but vanish like a spring night's dream. In time the mighty, too, succumb: all are dust before the wind.[123]

"All things are impermanent" in the above quotation is "諸行無常" (shogyō mujō) in the original Japanese. "無常" (mujō) is a Buddhist term, which can be translated as "transience" or "vanity." Yet, "無常" (mujō) is a key term that expresses the Japanese mentality, regardless of religious background. One might see that Ecclesiastes does not appear foreign but, rather, naturally touches the Japanese heart.[124] Accordingly, using the framework of Ecclesiastes, as B does, may help a Japanese person who admires *mujō*,[125] *wabi-sabi*,[126] or *mono no aware*[127] to become aware of their need for the eternal in the most natural way (See also Eccl 3:1–8, 11).

3.2.3 Does "the Ordinary Godly Christian" Like B Need to Be Edified?

Up to this point, we have focused mainly on the possible edification of aesthetes, represented by A. However, *Either/Or* has one other prominent figure,

---

123. Kajihara and Yamashita, 平家物語 上 [*The Tales of the Heike, Vol. 1*], 5, 9.

124. The following book uses Qoheleth as a Japanese-friendly guide to the world of the Old Testament: Yutaka Ikeda, 旧約聖書の世界 [*The World of the Old Testament*].

125. "Impermanence (*mujō*) is a notion crucial to both Buddhist belief and medieval Japanese values. It is the belief that human (and all) existence is transient, in a constant state of flux between growth and decay." Stalker, *Japan: History and Culture*, 106.

126. "[*Wabi-sabi*] had a philosophical component; it was thought to embody Buddhist concepts like transience and imperfection." Stalker, 129.

127. *Aware* indicates "the appreciation of nature," "[a] person of radiant beauty, a splendid costume, a room subtly redolent of incense." Kondō, "Aware," 240. "*Mono no aware* is not only a living realization of impermanence, but also an aesthetic orientation towards the deep beauty inherent in the transitory nature of existence." Park, "Buddhism and Japanese Aesthetics."

Either/Or as an Initial Missionary Task with "Paganism"   117

Ethicist B, who embodies another dominant lifestyle of Kierkegaard's contemporaries: "the ordinary godly Christian."[128] The question that needs to be asked is this: Does an ordinary godly Christian like B need edification? B seems to be a faithful husband and a good Christian.[129] Did Kierkegaard believe that he needed to proclaim Christianity to the ordinary godly Christian? To answer this question, we need to know more about B. This poses a difficulty. In the literary world of *Either/Or*, we have adequate material to critique A because B – being higher than A – can adequately critique A. However, we lack the resources to construct a critique of B since Kierkegaard does not provide us with a figure who is clearly higher than B[130] and thus able to critique B.[131] Therefore, to adequately critique B, we must go beyond the literary framework of *Either/Or* to find figures who are higher than B.

3.2.3.1 Johannes Climacus's Evaluation of B

In this sub-subsection, we explore the character B through Johannes Climacus, one of Kierkegaard's pseudonyms. Climacus analyzes both the pseudonymous and the signed-religious works published between 1843 and 1845 in an appendix to chapter 1 – "A Glance at a Contemporary Effort in Danish Literature" – of *Concluding Unscientific Postscript*.[132] Climacus, who emphasizes truth as subjectivity, has a specific point of view regarding *Either/Or*. As *Hovedpseudonym* (head pseudonym) and *Dialektiker* (dialectician),[133] Climacus helps us understand B, especially from the perspective of the dialectical structure of Kierkegaard's works. Interestingly, the non-Christian pseudonym, Climacus, probably critiques B more strictly in terms of B's fidelity to Christian doctrine than a professing Christian might have done.

---

128. Watkin, "Judge William," 123.

129. See appendix 4, part II: "Containing the Papers of B, Letters to A."

130. The Jylland Pastor might be higher than B, but the difference between them is not obvious, and since the Pastor does not directly critique B, we apparently lack resources for critiquing B in *Either/Or*.

131. Although B can critique A, it is doubtful that B can critique himself. As Ferreira puts it, "When the Judge raises the question whether the esthete can rightly assess the character and values of the esthetic because he lives in it and only a higher stage can really see a lower one, this indirectly raises the question whether the Judge [B] can rightly assess the ethical [the standpoint of B himself], for the same reason." Ferreira, *Kierkegaard*, 30.

132. *SKS* 7, 228–273/ *CUP* I, 251–300.

133. Ōtani, *Kierkegaard's Authorship, Part 2*, 1051; originally from Malantschuk, *Kierkegaard's Thought*, 3, 209, 211.

First, Climacus has a high opinion of *Either/Or* because this work does not speculatively search for objective truth but, instead, attempts to arouse the reader's interest in inwardness or existence. Climacus sees *Either/Or* as denoting the choice that every human being must make about the nature of their existence. Climacus regards *Either/Or* as the existential possibility of both the aesthete and the ethicist. In his evaluation of *Either/Or*, Climacus pays special attention to the last sentence of the sermon :

> The last word in the whole work . . . reads as follows: Only the truth that builds up is truth for you. This is an essential predicate in relation to truth as inwardness, whereby its decisive qualification as upbuilding for you, that is, for the subject, is its essential difference from all objective knowledge, inasmuch as the subjectivity itself becomes the sign of truth.[134]

Climacus also says, "An individual has come into existence – and only the truth that builds up is truth for you – that is, truth is inwardness, the inwardness of existence, please note, and here in ethical definition."[135] Climacus defines the inwardness of existence as ethical, thereby, approving of Ethicist B's existence to a certain degree. But naturally, one may wonder whether or not the last sentence of the sermon is really B's achievement since this is not said by B but by his friend, the Jylland Pastor.

Second, however, Climacus points out B's problem, which is that a person cannot escape from despair on their own. B instructs A to despair over himself in order to fully develop as an authentic individual.[136] Climacus asserts, "In despairing, I use myself to despair, and therefore I can indeed despair of everything by myself, but if I do this I cannot come back by myself. It is in this moment of decision that the individual needs divine assistance."[137] Climacus believes that no one can overcome despair without divine assistance and seems to critique B for being too autonomous and not truly depending on God.

Third, as far as Climacus is concerned, when a decisive encounter with God occurs, one must hide oneself in a way that differs from A's approach.

---

134. *SKS* 7, 229/ *CUP I*, 252–253.
135. *SKS* 7, 231/ *CUP I*, 254.
136. *SKS* 3, 200/ *EO II*, 208.
137. *SKS* 7, 234/ *CUP I*, 258.

> The terror has to be a new qualification of inwardness, whereby the individual in a higher sphere comes back again to the point where disclosure, which is the life of the ethical, once again becomes impossible, but in such a way that the relation is reversed, so that the ethical, which previously aided disclosure (whereas the esthetic hindered it), is now the hindering element, and it is something else that helps the individual to a higher disclosure over and beyond the ethical.[138]

In order to understand Climacus's point, I will elaborate on the opinions of A, B, and Climacus regarding the concealment of the self. A, in order to aesthetically enjoy his life, hides himself and never reveals himself to anyone. In doing so, A fails to truly become himself. B, as an ethicist, rightly instructs A to reveal himself so that A might see himself as he truly is. For instance, B says that one should be transparent and not hide themselves from their spouse. However, Climacus thinks that B's transparency before others is still a shallow form of religiousity. If a person is deeply committed to the religious life, they cannot fully reveal themselves even to their closest family and friends. Climacus effectively illustrates the need for *Fear and Trembling*, Kierkegaard's next pseudonymous work. In *Fear and Trembling*, Abraham – because he truly fears God – cannot reveal his intention to sacrifice his beloved son to Isaac himself, to Sarah, or to Eliezer. B lacks this deep religious seriousness.[139]

Fourth, Climacus critiques *Either/Or* and both the subsequent pseudonymous works – *Fear and Trembling* and *Repetition* – on the basis that these works lack a clear definition of sin: "Sin was not brought up in any of the pseudonymous books."[140] As the head pseudonym, Climacus explains how the pseudonymous works after *Either/Or* are essential and points out the deficiencies of the three pseudonymous works as a whole.

In conclusion, although Climacus appreciates the final line of the sermon in *Either/Or*, he skillfully identifies the shortcomings in B's religious approach. B suggests that one can overcome despair without divine assistance, which

---

138. *SKS* 7, 235/ *CUP I*, 258–259.

139. Climacus's opinion on religious concealment prompts us to reconsider and rethink certain biblical references that seem unduly strict about one's relationships with God and others (Gen 22:1–19; Ezra 10:1–44; Matt 10:34–37; 19:29; Mark 10:29; Luke 14:26; 18:29).

140. *SKS* 7, 243/ *CUP I*, 268.

Climacus criticizes as overly independent. Additionally, B is too optimistic, believing that one can truly reveal themselves by living religiously, while Climacus contends that true religiousness requires concealment. Above all, B fails to address the concept of sin, which is a crucial aspect of the religious journey.

3.2.3.2 Julia Watkin's Evaluation of B

In this sub-subsection, I will continue my exploration and evaluation of B's character by considering the insights offered in the article "Judge William – A Christian?" by Julia Watkin.[141] This article tells us where B (Judge William) is from and why Kierkegaard was dissatisfied with this ordinary godly Christian.

Watkin compares B's thinking with that of Nikolas Edinger Balle (1744–1816), "a firm adherent of Luther's *Small Catechism*."[142] She introduces Balle's catechism – *Lærebog i den Evangelisk-Christelige Religion Indrettet til Brug i de Danske Skoler* (Textbook in the Evangelical-Christian Religion Arranged for Use in the Danish Schools)[143] – which became a bestseller in Denmark from the late eighteenth to the mid-nineteenth century. According to Watkin, Balle's catechism devotes a "large section of the book ... to 'duties.'"[144] She surveys how Balle's catechism is used throughout Kierkegaard's corpus and concludes that Kierkegaard intended to personify Balle's catechism in the character of B.

B "goes to church regularly,"[145] "appears to know more than the average layman about Church teaching,"[146] and "his ethics are based on Christianity."[147] Watkin summarizes the two intended readers of *Either/Or* as follows: "For when Kierkegaard with *Either/Or* starts from where his readers are (PV, 27), he can be seen as starting from two contemporary lifestyles: that of the aesthete who long ago lost contact with childhood Christianity, and that of the

---

141. Watkin, "Judge William," 113–124.
142. Watkin, 114.
143. Balle, *Lærebog i den Evangelisk-Christelige Religion Indrettet til Brug i de Danske Skoler* [Textbook in the Evangelical-Christian Religion Arranged for Use in the Danish Schools].
144. Balle, 115.
145. Balle, 120.
146. Balle, 120.
147. Balle, 120.

ordinary godly Christian who still finds value in his catechism."[148] Watkin expounds on Kierkegaard's view of B as follows:

> That Kierkegaard treats the Judge as an ethicist rather than as an example of the religious can be seen as due firstly to the basic preoccupation of the book with showing the individual how to move from amoral to moral categories and to the Judge's great emphasis (like Balle) on the ethical element of religion.[149]

Watkin points out B's problems, saying, "The acute altruism and dying to the world belonging to Christian Religiousness A and B (CUP) is not to be found in Judge William's letters any more than it is to be found in the catechism so respected by the Judge."[150] Her analysis suggests that both Balle's catechism and B lack decisive religiousness, such as dying to the self and the world. Watkin elaborates, saying, "Thus it is clear that, in Kierkegaard's view, what is lacking in both the Judge's letters and Balle's catechism is not the basic tenets of Lutheran Christianity, but that vital description of 'what it means in the strictest sense to be a Christian' (PC, 67)."[151] In other words, Kierkegaard's concern is not just orthodoxy but also orthopraxy.

To sum up, Kierkegaard seems to present B as a figure who exemplifies Balle's catechism, which was a well-known work among Kierkegaard's contemporary Danes. Both B and Balle's catechism uphold a doctrinally sound Lutheran faith. However, Kierkegaard considered B's attitude towards the temporal problematic because B would not willingly die to the self and the world and, thereby, lacked the vital elements of "what it means in the strictest sense to be a Christian."[152]

3.2.3.3 Synthesis

Having gathered important insights from both Johannes Climacus's review of *Either/Or* and Julia Watkin's article, we are now ready to answer the following question: Does B need to be edified? First, B, along with the other pseudonyms in *Either/Or*, plays a positive role by helping the reader to be

---

148. Balle, 123.
149. Balle, 123.
150. Balle, 124.
151. Balle, 124.
152. Balle, 124.

subjective. Second, B is not just an ethicist but a Christian ethicist, who represents Kierkegaard's contemporary Danish Christians. Both B and Balle adhere to Luther's *Catechism*, which represents the evangelical Lutheran faith. Third, B's aim is to seduce the aesthete into the ethico-religious. By emphasizing duties, he attempts to help the aesthete to move from the amoral to the moral. Fourth, however, B needs to be edified by learning what it means to become a Christian in the strictest sense. Both Climacus and Watkin point out deficiencies in B's character that must be addressed. These problems may be interconnected. B does not have a concept of sin (according to Climacus), and this deficiency, in turn, causes him to be overly optimistic about the temporal (according to Watkin). Thus, B naively believes that he can reveal his real self to his loved ones (according to Climacus) and does not willingly die to the self and the world (according to Watkin).

In conclusion, B's existence is necessary both as a movement from the amoral to the moral and as a demonstration of the limitations of the ethical.

3.2.3.4 My Personal Application

My response to the above portrait of B includes both provocation and embarrassment. Just as Johannes de Silentio and Johannes Climacus, who claim to be a non-Christians, intensively and passionately pursue faith and the journey of becoming Christians, which must have challenged and stimulated Kierkegaard's contemporaries to reflect on their inner lives, B does the same for me. For instance, I was overwhelmed by these profound words of B: "Every father will also feel that there is more in the child than what it owes to him. Yes, he will feel in humility that it is a trust and that in the most beautiful sense of the word he is only the stepfather."[153] Why is every father

---

153. *SKS* 3, 77/ *EO II*, 73. The interpretation of Karsten Harries, who wrote the commentary on *Either/Or*, is vastly different from mine. Harries suggests that in B's thought, a mother (Mother Mary) plays a more important role than a father (Joseph); a child is a gift, and by living for this gift, the father's pride is cured, and a father is humbled. Harries also says, "It is difficult not to feel a bit sorry for the author of these lines." Whereas I was overwhelmed by these lines, why does Harries "feel a bit sorry"? It is probably because he thinks, "We moderns no longer are sheltered by the theocentric world of the Middle Ages; the modern world-picture has no room for God." Harries, *Between Nihilism and Faith*, 122–123, IX. But if the statement that every father is "the stepfather" signifies the existence of one true Father in heaven, these lines will be rather overwhelming. The justification for my interpretation is as follows: First, in his signed-religious work, Kierkegaard says that because "you" have God who "is called Father in heaven," even "the most loving father" is also "a stepfather." *SKS* 5, 105–106/ *EUD*, 100. Second, regarding his father's death, Kierkegaard's journal entry reads, "My father died – then

only a stepfather? It is because, in the strictest sense, God is the only Father: "And call no one your father on earth, for you have one Father – the one in heaven" (Matt 23:9).[154] I feel that B's words should remain in me so that I will constantly be reminded to make every effort to represent my Father in heaven whenever I approach my son: "Be perfect, therefore, as your heavenly Father is perfect" (Matt 5:48). To be perfect does not mean never making a mistake but, rather, being perfect in representing a loving God who "makes his sun rise on the evil and on the good, and sends rain on the righteous and on the unrighteous" (Matt 5:45).[155]

B's maxim above has become my motto. However, I was astonished when my son said, "I feel like I am always scolded by you." Even though I am a pastor, who loves my son so much and makes every effort to practise B's ethics, it seems that I fail to represent the Father in heaven. Indeed, as the apostle Paul says, "I do not do the good I want, but the evil I do not want is what I do" (Rom 7:19). I know that representing a loving God for my son's sake is a good thing, and it is my dearest desire. However, I am not always able to do this good thing and do what is evil, making my son feel scolded all the time. Christian doctrine has a term for such human unfreedom: "Now if I do

---

I got another father in his place: God in heaven – and then I discovered that my first father actually had been my stepfather and only figuratively my first father." *SKS* 20, 414, NB5:102/ *JP*, VII 6178 *n.d.*, 1848. But is it methodologically appropriate to use the signed-religious work and *Journals and Notebooks* in order to justify my interpretation of B's thought? Remember that B is a personification of Nikolas Edinger Balle, who is "a firm adherent of Luther's *Small Catechism*" (see section 3.2.3.2). Luther's *Small Catechism* expounds on the first line of the Lord's Prayer – "Our Father who art in heaven" – saying, "*What does this mean?* With these words God tenderly invites us to believe that He is our true Father and that we are His true children, so that with all boldness and confidence we may ask Him as dear children ask their dear father." Faith Lutheran Church Thompsons Station, TN, Luther's Small Catechism (Section 1), SC: The Lord's Prayer, https://www.faithlutheran-tn.org/luthers-small-catechism-section-1.html, accessed 23 April 2021. Given that both B and Kierkegaard (author of the signed-religious works and *Journals and Notebooks*) would agree on the doctrine of Lutheran Christianity, I argue that my "overwhelming" interpretation is more fitting than Harries's feeling "a bit sorry."

154. Matthew 23:8–10 originally formed one paragraph and probably means that "the disciples are forbidden the ostentatious use of honorific titles such as 'rabbi,' 'father' (2 Kgs 2:12; 5:13; 6:21; 13:14; Sir 44; Acts 7:2; 22:1), and 'teacher' (or 'tutor;' See also Byrskog 1994; Winter 1991) because no human being is worthy of such honor." Turner, *Matthew*, 549. In other words, "father" in Matthew 23:9 originally does not refer to one's biological father but signifies a kind of teacher (just as a Roman Catholic priest is called "Father"). In the broader sense, one may be able to relate this verse to a biological father who must also be respected.

155. A commentary endorses my interpretation that verse 48 is a summary of verses 43–47: 'This verse [Matt 5:48] appropriately rounds off the final example in vv. 43–47.' France, *Gospel of Matthew*, comment on 5:48.

what I do not want, it is no longer I that do it, but sin that dwells within me" (Rom 7:20). I do not lack knowledge of Christian doctrine, but I am unable to act accordingly. When it comes to practising Christian ethics, one must not make light of sin. Without dealing with the issue of sin, a necessary failure awaits – not only for A's aesthetic life but also for B's ethical life.

3.2.4 *Either/Or* as a Whole and Beyond

While we have dealt with Aesthete A (*Either/Or, Part I*) and Ethicist B (*Either/Or, Part II*) separately, some findings emerge as we consider *Either/Or* as a whole and beyond. In this subsection, by broadening our horizon, we will examine the entirety of *Either/Or* and consider its role in Kierkegaard's works.

3.2.4.1 The Last Words of the Jylland Pastor's Sermon as the Resolution of Entire Either/Or

In his *Journals and Notebooks*, Kierkegaard says, "[The] first διαψαλμα (*diapsalma*) is really the task of the entire work, which is not resolved until the last words of the sermon."[156] According to Kierkegaard, the first paragraph of Διαψαλματα (*Diapsalmata*)[157] represents the entire *Either/Or*, and its problem is resolved by the last words of the sermon given by the Jylland Pastor.[158]

The first question that must be asked is this: What is the task of *Either/Or* as a whole, which the first *diapsalma* represents? For the answer to this question, we must turn to the first *diapsalma*: "What is a poet? An unhappy person who conceals profound anguish in his heart but whose lips are so formed that as sighs and cries pass over them they sound like beautiful music."[159] Kierkegaard further explains this statement: "A total break with actuality is assumed, which does not have its base in futility but in mental depression and its predominance over actuality."[160] This is A's situation. On the surface, *Either/Or, Part I* is like beautiful music with a touch of melancholy. However, A conceals profound anguish within his heart. This represents a complete

---

156. *JP*, V 5629/ *Pap.* IV A216 *n.d.*, 1843/ *EO I*, Supplement, 505. See also *JP*, IV 4847/ *Pap.* IV A 42 *n.d.*, 1843.

157. *SKS* 2, 27/ *EO I*, 19.

158. See also Climacus's explanation of the importance of the last sentence in section 3.2.3.1 of this book.

159. *SKS* 2, 27/ *EO I*, 19.

160. *JP*, V 5629/ *Pap.* IV A 216 *n.d.*, 1843.

disconnection from reality. How will this issue of "a total break with actuality" be resolved by "the last words of the sermon"? The last words of the sermon read, "Only the truth that edifies is truth for you."[161] One might naturally recall the oft-repeated quotation from *Journals and Notebooks*:

> What I really need to be clear about what I am to do, not what I must know except in the way knowledge must precede all action. It is a question of understanding my own destiny, of seeing what the Deity really wants me to do; the thing is to find a truth which is truth for me, to find the idea for which I am willing to live and die.[162]

The destination Kierkegaard seeks for the reader in *Either/Or* is the same place he himself reached when he penned the above journal entry at twenty-two: to discover a truth that is truly *yours*, to find the idea for which *you* are willing to live and die. Kierkegaard himself experienced that "vainly I have sought an anchorage . . . in the bottomless sea of pleasure,"[163] which was unworthy of living and dying for. Understandably, Kierkegaard, under the mask of the Jylland Pastor, urges A (the aesthetic reader) to cross the Rubicon[164] and "begin to act inwardly."[165]

In this sense, the goal of *Either/Or* is to guide to where one rightly starts. As the next sub-subsection shows, *Either/Or* does not provide answers but, rather, helps the reader act inwardly by providing them with the knowledge necessary for action.

3.2.4.2 Is There Salvation in the Aesthete or the Ordinary Godly Christian?

What is remarkable in *Either/Or* is that it poses questions instead of providing answers. These questions can be paraphrased as follows: Is there salvation in the aesthete or the ordinary godly Christian? The epigraph to A's papers reads, "Is reason then alone baptized, are the passions pagans?"[166] *Either/Or, Part I*

---

161. *SKS* 3, 332/ *EO II*, 354, translation modified.
162. *SKS* 17, 24, AA:12/ *KJN* 1, 19, emphasis in original.
163. *SKS* 17, 26, AA:12/ *KJN* 1, 21.
164. *SKS* 17, 30, AA:12/ *KJN* 1, 25.
165. *SKS* 17, 30, AA:12/ *KJN* 1, 24.
166. *SKS* 2, 9/ *EO I*, 1.

is an attempt to baptize the passions, meaning that it seeks salvation in the aesthetic. How about B? Even though B believes that he holds fast to evangelical Lutheran Christianity, he actually attempts to transform a good civil life into a religious life. This seems possible to him because he lacks a proper understanding of sin. Therefore, a question posed by B's existence might be paraphrased as follows: Is there salvation in the ordinary godly Christian? Now, suppose that both A and B pose the following question: "Is there salvation in the aesthete or the ordinary godly Christian?" Does *Either/Or* answer this question? The answer is both *yes* and *no*. The answer is *yes* because the problem of "a total break with actuality" is somehow resolved, as we saw in the previous sub-subsection. The answer is also *no* because the resolution is incomplete, with Climacus articulating some underlying problems with A and B, which are discussed in section 3.2.3.1. The following journal entry sheds light on these unique literary features of *Either/Or*:

> The fact that many of Plato's dialogues end without a result has a far deeper basis than I had thought earlier. They are a reproduction of Socrates' maieutic skill which makes the reader or hearer himself active, and therefore they do not end in a result but in a sting. This is an excellent parody of the modern rote-method which says everything the sooner the better and all at one time, which awakens no self-action but only leads the reader to rattle it off like a parrot.[167]

Kierkegaard would not be satisfied with his readers simply rattling off the tenets of the Christian faith "like a parrot." By structuring *Either/Or* without a definitive solution, Kierkegaard intended to awaken the reader and goad them to self-action. To quote Johannes Climacus, "The merit of [*Either/Or*], if it has any, . . . it must essentially be that it does not provide any conclusion but in inwardness transforms everything."[168]

---

167. *SKS* 18, 299–300, JJ: 482/ *JP*, IV 4266 n.d., 1846.
168. *SKS* 7, 231/ *CUP I*, 254.

3.2.4.3 Exercise of Either/Or

In Kierkegaard's thought, roughly speaking, there seem to be three dimensions of either/or,[169] corresponding to the aesthetic, the ethical, and the religious spheres. More precisely, for Kierkegaard, while there is only one true either/or – a religious either/or – he guides the reader through a gradual process of appropriating this true either/or. An either/or that permeates *Either/Or, Part I* is the aesthetic or A's either/or. In the title "**Either/Or**: An Ecstatic Discourse" of "Διαψαλματα [Diapsalmata]," A says, "Marry, and you will regret it. Do not marry, and you will also regret it. Marry or do not marry, you will regret it either way. Whether you marry or you do not marry, you will regret it either way."[170] For A, the choice itself is problematic because every choice results in regret. Thus, making a choice is the root of all evil. One regrets because one makes a choice. Therefore, A's strategy is to avoid making a choice since avoiding any commitment or responsibility frees one from regret. A regards either/or as the fatal enemy of the aesthetic appreciation of life.

The ethical either/or is B's either/or. B says, "The esthetic is not evil but the indifferent. And that is why I said that the ethical constitutes the choice. Therefore, it is not so much a matter of choosing between willing good and willing evil, as of choosing to will, but that in turn posits good and evil."[171] According to B, the aesthetic way of living cannot be defined as evil because the person does not choose at all. First, one needs to learn to make a choice.[172] B says, "[What] takes precedence in my Either/Or is, then, the ethical."[173] When one learns to make a choice, one moves from the aesthetic sphere to

---

169. Jamie Ferreira explores the multiple possibilities of *Either-Or* (see Ferreira, *Kierkegaard*, 29–30), preferring this translation over *Either/Or* to align with Kierkegaard's original Danish title, *Enten-Eller*. Her discussion is thought-provoking, but I am not convinced that her numerous layers of *Either-Or* align with Kierkegaard's or his pseudonym's original intentions. Here, I present only three layers, each grounded in Kierkegaard's or his pseudonyms' use of the term in the following citations: (1) Aesthete A in "**Either/Or:** An Ecstatic Discourse" (*SKS* 2, 46/ *EO I*, 38, emphasis in original); (2) Ethicist B: "[What] takes precedence in my Either/Or is, then, the ethical" (*SKS* 3, 172/ *EO II*, 176); and (3) Kierkegaard himself: "There are really only two sides to choose between – Either/Or" (*JP* III 2649/ *Pap.* IX B 63:13, n.d., 1848).

170. *SKS* 2, 46/ *EO I*, 38, emphasis in original.

171. *SKS* 3, 165/ *EO II*, 169.

172. B calls this dimension "the baptism of the will." *SKS* 3, 166/ *EO II*, 169. One can find an echo of this thought in A's epigraph: "Is reason then alone baptized, are the passions pagans? Young" *SKS* 2, 9/ *EO I*, 1.

173. *SKS* 3, 172/ *EO II*, 176.

the ethical sphere.[174] By making a choice, B believes that one becomes oneself or chooses oneself absolutely. From the perspective of the aesthetic either/or, this is advancing. However, since B fails to recognize the doctrine of total depravity, he naively believes that once one learns to make a choice, one can choose the good.

The religious either/or, which is Kierkegaard's, does not fully emerge in the literary world of *Either/Or*. In *Journals and Notebooks* he says as follows:

> There are really only two sides to choose between – Either/Or. Well, of course, there are many parties in the practical world [in margin: Not really but only figuratively is there any question of "choosing," since what is chosen makes no difference – one is just as wrong as the other. In the practical world there are many parties] – there are the liberals and the conservatives etc. – and all the strangest combinations, such as the rational liberals and rational conservatives. . . . But in the profoundest sense there really are only two parties to choose between. . . : either in obedience to God, fearing and loving him, to take the side of God against men so that one loves men in God – or to take the side of men against God, so that by distortion one humanizes God and does not "sense what is God's and what is man's" (Matthew 16:23).[175]

Kierkegaard seems to disagree with B's statement that "since the choice is an absolute choice, the Either/Or is absolute."[176] For B, the choice is absolute, but for Kierkegaard, God is absolute. Kierkegaard suggests that both parties may be wrong. Kierkegaard's either/or is the choice between the divine and the human. This either/or is reflected in the title of the last sermon – "The Upbuilding That Lies in the Thought That in Relation to God We Are Always in the Wrong." B says, "In this sermon he has grasped what I have said and what I would like to have said to you; he has expressed it better than I am

---

174. According to C. Stephen Evans, "B thinks that if he can get someone to choose seriously, he/she will choose the good. That is naïve and shows his optimism and failure to understand sin." Evans, personal communication, 10 June 2020.

175. *JP*, III 2649/ *Pap.* IX B 63:13 *n.d.*, 1848. See also *SKS* 11, 26–29/ *WA*, 21–24.

176. *SKS* 3, 173/ *EO II*, 178.

able to."¹⁷⁷ But fortunately or unfortunately, the Pastor goes beyond B's ethical sphere.¹⁷⁸ Whereas B sees the choice as absolute, the Pastor's sermon implies that human choice is always in the wrong unless the choice is to love God. Just as B instructs A to make a choice, Kierkegaard would instruct B to choose to love God alone by dying to oneself and the world. This true either/or is "the embrace that grasps the unconditional."¹⁷⁹

In sum, A's either/or, which is actually a refusal to choose, belongs to the aesthetic sphere. B's either/or, which is to will to choose, belongs to the ethical sphere. Kierkegaard's either/or, which involves a choice between the divine and the human, belongs to the religious sphere. While the title *Either/Or* aptly reflects its content, it also alludes to something that transcends the work itself.

From the perspective of Kierkegaard as a missionary, it can be argued that he gradually guides the reader toward the decisive choice of either having faith in Christ or taking offense at him.¹⁸⁰ The aesthete remains indifferent and must first learn the significance of choosing. The ethicist, by contrast, views the act of choosing as a virtue in itself. However, Kierkegaard ultimately seeks to demonstrate that from a religious standpoint, any choice that does not lead to God is meaningless.¹⁸¹ *Either/Or*, therefore, can be understood

---

177. *SKS* 3, 318/ *EO II*, 338.

178. Ferreira raises an important point: "We need to consider the sermon itself to determine whether it adds anything absolutely new to the picture or in any way forces a choice, or whether William is correct in his judgment that this sermon expresses William's own view." Ferreira, *Kierkegaard*, 31. As can be seen in my discussion above, the sermon is a preliminary glimpse of what is to come after *Either/Or*, which is the religious sphere that is higher than B. That is, "while the Judge presents and recommends it as a summation and explanation of his own views, in fact, the sermon moves beyond the ethical *per se* into the religious sphere." Kirkconnell, *Kierkegaard on Ethics*, 15.

179. *SKS* 13, 132 /*M*, 94.

180. This "ultimatum" is articulated in *Practice in Christianity*: "Jesus Christ is the object of faith; one must either believe in him or be offended." *SKS* 12, 47/ *PC*, 33. Kierkegaard's initial plan was to finish his authorial activity right after *Either/Or* and become a rural pastor. According to him, his appetite for writing and God's Governance made him a religious author. Therefore, it is untrue to say that he *initially* planned to help the reader to learn about making a choice through *Either/Or* and, eventually, to have faith in Jesus Christ in *Practice in Christianity*. As he looked back on his authorship, Kierkegaard retrospectively discovered the dialectical structure of his authorship. He believed that God's Governance made it happen. Furthermore, Kierkegaard himself was being edified by God's Governance, and he notes that this edification is reflected in the process of authorship. Accordingly, a view of *Either/Or* as an initial training to make a choice can be justifiable if one takes into account the role of God's Governance. See *SKS* 16, 56, 65/ *PV*, 76–77, 86.

181. According to C. Stephen Evans, "The Judge thinks that a person who chooses the good has chosen God. The crucial point is that Kierkegaard knows that a person cannot

as a methodical training in decision-making – first, in choosing whether to remain within the aesthetic-ethical framework (*Either/Or*), then in moving toward the religious (*Two Upbuilding Discourses* (1843)), and finally in confronting the decisive choice of faith or offense at Christ: "Indeed, Either/Or is the key to heaven!"[182]

3.2.4.4 Summary

In this subsection, we have considered *Either/Or* in its entirety and even looked beyond it. The last sentence of the Jylland Pastor's sermon deals with the problem of "a total break with actuality," suggesting that resolution is possible if the reader deepens their inwardness (see section 3.2.4.1). Viewed from a different angle, the problem remains unresolved. Instead of providing answers or resolving the issues, *Either/Or* poses the following question: "Is there salvation in the aesthete or in the ordinary godly Christian?" By deliberately leaving the problem unresolved, the text invites the reader to confront and respond to it within their own lived experience (see section 3.2.4.2). *Either/Or* seeks to carefully train its readers to move from the aesthetic sphere (amoral) to the ethical sphere (moral). However, the title *Either/Or* does not mean choosing between A and B but, rather, between *Either/Or* – where the readers currently are – and *Two Upbuilding Discourses* (1843) – the religious. This initial religious either/or will ultimately culminate in the decisive choice: to believe in Jesus Christ or to take offense at him (see section 3.2.4.3).

3.2.4.5 A Possible Application to the Japanese Context

One may be able to adopt Kierkegaard's method of posing choices in terms of either/or to the Japanese. Generally speaking, a pastor at an evangelistic meeting in the church preaches about God, sin, and salvation. A Japanese newcomer who is unfamiliar with the transcendent God is suddenly expected to accept the existence of God, repent of their sin, and believe in Jesus's atonement. Although Kierkegaard was describing the people of nineteenth-century Danish Christendom, the following quotation applies remarkably

---

properly choose God without grace, divine assistance. Again, sin is decisive." Evans, personal communication, 10 June 2020. As we will see in chapters 5 and 6, it makes sense that Kierkegaard needed to address sin in *The Sickness unto Death* before introducing Christ, the God-man, in *Practice in Christianity*.

182. *SKS* 13, 132 /*M*, 94.

well to the Japanese newcomer to the church: "If one begins immediately with Christianity, they say: This is nothing for us – and put themselves immediately on guard."[183] Indeed, one must eventually decide for or against Jesus, but a Kierkegaardian approach may help Japanese missionaries speak in a way that does not immediately alienate non-Christians.

Not making a choice is not a tactic exclusive to A. Similarly, many Japanese people, in varying degrees, are reluctant to commit to religion. Therefore, in imitation of Kierkegaard, a Japanese missionary can take time to cultivate the mind of the Japanese aesthete until they are ready to make a choice. Kierkegaard's first strategy is to make the aesthete feel at home. Instead of preaching and overloading them with a lot of information that may not be digestible, a Kierkegaardian missionary can listen carefully to the Japanese. In an ideal scenario, as the missionary listens attentively, the person will be increasingly willing to talk about their desires. In this way, a Kierkegaardian missionary can be "the astonished listener."[184] This is indirect communication. A Kierkegaardian missionary can indirectly proclaim Jesus without mentioning him explicitly. Just as Christ became flesh and was called "a glutton and a drunkard, a friend of tax-collectors and sinners" (Matt 11:19), a Kierkegaardian missionary does not start with God, sin, and salvation but, instead, begins by establishing rapport with the Japanese.

Once such rapport is established, a Kierkegaardian missionary can seduce the person to move on to the next phase, just as B attempts to allure A to cultivate a decision-making ability. B does not resort to extreme methods. All the aesthete has to do, as a starting point, is to make a choice. The kind of choice depends on the individual. However, whatever decision is made should be appealing and doable, and it should contribute to the edification of the one making the decision.

Eventually, a Kierkegaardian missionary must guide the individual to make a choice between God and human beings. The three phases of either/or serve as a simplified sketch of the Kierkegaardian mission strategy. Through this strategy, a missionary can take their time, slowly nudging a Japanese non-Christian towards a decision. Eventually, however, the missionary must issue a challenge – to make a choice for or against God. The point being emphasized

---

183. *SKS* 20, 318–319, NB4:66/ *JP*, V 6107 *n.d.*, 1848.
184. *SKS* 16, 28/ *PV*, 46.

is the importance of taking time rather than placing a heavy burden on the shoulders of a newcomer right at the outset.

3.3 Conclusion

Published in Denmark in 1843, *Either/Or* was commercially successful. Although Kierkegaard was disappointed that his contemporaries misinterpreted this work, he generally regarded his mission strategy with *Either/Or* as productive. While his contemporaries went along happily with Kierkegaard's ideas, they had no real understanding of where they stood or where they were going. Kierkegaard's strategy was to first amuse his readers and later ambush them. Why did Kierkegaard use villains with strong and unbending personalities, such as Aesthete A, Don Juan, Faust, and Johannes the Seducer? He believed that such a strategy was effective precisely because each character remained faithful to a specific (unchristian) ideal. With its uncompromising description of an idealized aesthetic way of life, *Either/Or* urges the reader to make a choice. In addition, in the literary framework of *Either/Or*, mythology, Romanticism, and Ecclesiastes work together to help the aesthetic reader become aware of their unconscious spiritual thirst and begin striving for the eternal. For Kierkegaard, this strategy encourages readers to will to allow themselves to be built up. Guided by Ethicist B, the aesthetic reader can choose to move from the amoral to the moral. But *Either/Or* is not a book with a neat conclusion. Rather, much like Plato's early dialogues, this book ends with a sting – the ethical sphere of B is not a promised land where the reader should settle down. Both groups of readers – that is those who identify with either A or B, who represent the dominant ways of life in Denmark in Kierkegaard's time – should experience a sense of anxiety. Kierkegaard's contemporaries were confronted, accused, provoked, and guided to awareness by his devastating portrait of the aesthete and the limitations of the ordinary godly Christian life.[185] In this sense, it is wrong to equate any specific character in *Either/Or* with the historical Kierkegaard: "In *Either/Or*, I am just as little, precisely just as little, the editor Victor Eremita as I am the Seducer or the Judge."[186] The creation or adoption of these characters does not mean that

---

185. *SKS* 20, 318, NB4:66/ *JP*, V 6107 *n.d.*, 1848.
186. *SKS* 7, 570/ *CUP I*, 626.

Kierkegaard identifies with them personally; rather, he used these characters for the specific purpose of his mission strategy. In terms of his own existence, *The Point of View for My Work as an Author* testifies that Kierkegaard balanced his real life and literary creativity with fear and trembling – living as one who had abandoned the world and offered himself to God. In terms of literary skills, he masterfully used irony to distance himself from his literary characters, allowing them to live freely in the literary world of *Either/Or*. His underlying motivation was to help the reader become aware of the key issue: the need to become a Christian.

In terms of application, *Either/Or*'s mission strategy makes a unique contribution. We usually assume that evangelism should take place within a church setting and that the content of the evangelistic message must include a declaration about God, sin, and salvation. However, the strategy in *Either/Or* is to begin where the audience is. Like a shepherd who looks for the lost sheep, a Kierkegaardian missionary does not stay in the church but physically or figuratively goes out into the streets, helping people come to awareness.

In conclusion, by designing *Either/Or* as mirrors that reflect the two dominant lifestyles of his contemporary Danes – the aesthetes and the ordinary godly Christians – and reveal the bankruptcy of their lives, Kierkegaard intended to arouse interest in, and perhaps even make them anxious about, their own existence. However, Kierkegaard did not stir up or provoke his contemporaries for no reason. Rather, he had in mind a clear objective: to escort his readers towards a particular destination. That first destination becomes apparent in *Two Upbuilding Discourses* (1843).

CHAPTER 4

Two Upbuilding Discourses (1843) as an Introduction to the Religious Life

> Then followed *Two Upbuilding Discourses* – what is most important often seems so insignificant. The big work, *Either/Or*, which was "much read and even more discussed" – and then *Two Upbuilding Discourses*, dedicated to my late father, published on my birthday (May 5), "a little flower under the cover of the great forest, sought neither for its splendor nor its fragrance nor its food value." There was no one who in the profounder sense paid any attention to or cared about the two discourses.[1]
>
> – Søren Kierkegaard, *The Point of View for My Work as an Author*

The subject of this chapter is *To opbyggelige Taler* [*Two Upbuilding Discourses*], 1843. Although Kierkegaard viewed this work as "most important" – as highlighted in the quotation above – this work has suffered from neglect both during his lifetime and in subsequent Kierkegaard scholarship. Fortunately, in the twenty-first century, Kierkegaard scholars began to pay more attention to the early discourses, including *Two Upbuilding Discourses* (1843).[2] However, discovering the significance of this work is not enough. As emphasized

---

1. *SKS* 16, 21/ *PV*, 36

2. *KSY (2000)*; Pattison, *Kierkegaard's Upbuilding Discourses*; *IKC 5: Eighteen Upbuilding Discourses*. 2003; For a list of literature that studies the early discourses, see Pattison, 2, footnote 1.

elsewhere in this book, "*Two Upbuilding Discourses* is concurrent with *Either/Or*."[3] It is important to read *Either/Or* and *Two Upbuilding Discourses* (1843) sequentially. Thanks to the efforts of the community of Kierkegaard scholars, such studies have advanced in the twenty-first century. For instance, M. W. Sinnett's *Restoring the Conversation* proposes that Kierkegaard embodies Plato's dialogues between sophists – represented by Judge William – and Socrates – represented by *Two Upbuilding Discourses* (1843) or *The Lily in the Field and the Bird of the Air* (an accompanying signed-religious work in the second edition of *Either/Or*). W. Glenn Kirkconnell's *Kierkegaard on Ethics and Religion* reads Kierkegaard's works chronologically from *Either/Or* to *Philosophical Fragments*, attempting to interpret these works with an emphasis on Kierkegaard's historical context by relying mainly on Bruce H. Kirmmse's *Kierkegaard in Golden Age Denmark*.[4] M. Jamie Ferreira's *Kierkegaard* introduces Kierkegaard's main pseudonymous and signed works side by side in chronological order. Unlike my study, which attempts to uncover Kierkegaard the missionary, Ferreira's book aims to help beginners read Kierkegaard's works themselves, engaging with these from a religious, philosophical, psychological, literary, or personal (biographical) perspective.[5] In summary, the works by Sinnett and Kirkconnell are more philosophical readings, while Ferreira's book is more neutral reading. Our task is not just to read *Two Upbuilding Discourses* (1843) together with *Either/Or* but also to read these works faithfully according to Kierkegaard's intent and instruction. In other words, it is vital to read the left-handed work (*Either/Or*) and the right-handed work (*Two Upbuilding Discourses* [1843]) on their own terms, recognizing that for Kierkegaard, the religious was of the highest importance. I will attempt such a reading in this chapter.

As we have seen in section 3.2.4.3, the title *Either/Or* signifies something beyond *Either/Or* itself. Of course, what lies beyond *Either/Or* is none other than the religious, and we received a preliminary glimpse of this in the last sermon of *Either/Or*. With this knowledge, the connection that Kierkegaard makes between *Either/Or* and *Two Upbuilding Discourses* (1843) makes sense. As noted, the title *Either/Or* stands for duplexity. However, this duplexity is

---

3. *SKS* 16, 16/ *PV*, 30.

4. Kirkconnell, *Kierkegaard on Ethics*, 3–37.

5. Ferreira, *Kierkegaard*, 18–40.

not represented by Esthete A and Ethicist B but, rather, by *Either/Or* and *Two Upbuilding Discourses* (1843).[6] Indeed, *Either/Or* is the incognito and the deception. As discussed in section 2.3.4.3, the pseudonymous work *Either/Or* is entirely dissolved. Only in his signed works does Kierkegaard directly[7] declare the truth without pseudonymous masks. Thus, *Two Upbuilding Discourses* (1843) boldly declares the truth that could only be faintly intimated, in a veiled and indirect way, in *Either/Or*. But unfortunately, as D. Anthony Storm puts it, "often his overtly religious writings are overlooked or de-Christianized in favor of the pseudonymous authorship."[8] Nonetheless, this book attempts to sidestep this pitfall by reading the pseudonymous *Either/Or* and signed *Two Upbuilding Discourses* (1843) consecutively. In so doing, it attempts to read Kierkegaard's corpus in the way he intended it to be read.

The outline of this chapter is as follows: The first section provides a historical introduction (see also appendix 5, which is a summary of *Two Upbuilding Discourses* [1843]); the second section interprets *Two Upbuilding Discourses* (1843) from the perspective of Kierkegaard as a missionary; the third section applies some of these findings to the Japanese context; and the fourth section concludes this chapter.

4.1 Historical Introduction

Kierkegaard's initial plan was to become a rural pastor soon after publishing *Either/Or*.[9] However, his passion for writing and providential leading caused

---

6. *SKS* 16, 16/ *PV*, 30.

7. In his remarkable study on early discourses, Pattison says, "I shall claim, the discourses are not quite as direct as Kierkegaard makes them sound, and there is an important sense in which they too are indirect communication." Pattison, *Kierkegaard's Upbuilding Discourses*, 2. See also Strawser, "Indirectness," 73–90; Ferreira, *Kierkegaard*, 2. According to Pattison, Kierkegaardianly speaking, God alone is the teacher, and the best thing that a merely human teacher can do is to employ the Socratic (maieutic) method; consequently, the method that the discourses employ is indirect communication. If we accept Pattison's definition of indirect communication, Kierkegaard's method of discourses can be called indirect communication. However, I still prefer to use the term direct communication for his signed-religious works. This is because what Kierkegaard says in *Two Upbuilding Discourses* (1843) and his other signed works is not dialectically dissolved, but, rather, the content is what he really wants to communicate.

8. Storm, *Commentary on Kierkegaard*, http://www.sorenkierkegaard.org/kierkegaard-commentary.html.

9. See *JP*, V1 6229/ *Pap*. IXA216 *n.d.*, 1848. Kierkegaard graduated from the Royal Pastoral Seminary in 1841, but he was never ordained. Although, at one time, he earnestly desired to

him to remain a writer.¹⁰ As a result, Kierkegaard wrote *Two Upbuilding Discourses* (1843) and published it three months after the publication of *Either/Or*. Unlike *Either/Or*, in which Kierkegaard hides behind the masks of various pseudonyms, *Two Upbuilding Discourses* (1843) is a signed work. In other words, Kierkegaard speaks in his own voice. However, when he speaks in his own voice, he has much less to say – the total number of pages is less than one-tenth that of *Either/Or*.

As quoted at the beginning of this chapter, Kierkegaard regarded *Two Upbuilding Discourses* (1843) as far more important than *Either/Or*. However, with P. L. Møller,¹¹ Kierkegaard's contemporary, at the head of the list, the tradition of paying attention to the more interesting *Either/Or* and other pseudonymous works was handed down from generation to generation. Kierkegaard describes the typical reaction of his contemporaries to *Two Upbuilding Discourses* (1843) with these humorous words:

> There was no one who in the profounder sense paid any attention to or cared about the two discourses; indeed, I even recall that one of my acquaintances came to me and complained that he had in good faith gone and bought them, thinking that since they were by me they must be something rather witty and clever. I also recall that I promised him that he would have his money back if he so desired.¹²

The question remains: Will today's reader pay attention to *Two Upbuilding Discourses* (1843) in the profounder sense, or will they desire to get their money back?

---

be a pastor, this desire was never fulfilled.

10. *SKS* 16, 56; 65/ *PV*, 76–77, 86.
11. For further explanation about P. L. Møller, see section 3.2.1.6.
12. *SKS* 16, 21/ *PV*, 36.

4.2 A Study of *Two Upbuilding Discourses* (1843) with Specific Regard to Kierkegaard the Missionary

Although originally from China, the Japanese consider *Rāmen* noodles to be their national dish. Among the wide variety of *Rāmen*, "Ramen Jiro has achieved something of a cult status in Japan."[13] What is *Rāmen Jirō*?

> Everything about Ramen Jiro is aggressive. Thick-as-udon, tough-as-nails noodles. Pungent mounds of raw chopped garlic. Globs of pork back fat swimming in a soy-sauce based broth. That rich unctuousness that coats your mouth and threatens to bust your gut.[14]

I can vouch for the taste. But would someone feed a baby *Rāmen Jirō*? Such a person, if they existed, would be out of their mind. "[Rāmen Jirō is] ridiculously heavy and fatty,"[15] and may even cause an upset stomach in an adult. The thought of feeding a baby *Rāmen Jirō* is scary.

It is the same with spiritual food. We should not feed a spiritual baby solid food, even though it may be delicious. The apostle Paul says, "And so, brothers and sisters, I could not speak to you as spiritual people, but rather as people of the flesh, as infants in Christ. I fed you with milk, not solid food, for you were not ready for solid food" (1 Cor 3:1–2).[16] The intended readers of *Either/Or* are not ready for solid food. Therefore, Kierkegaard provided *Two Upbuilding Discourses* (1843), which he assumed would be digestible for them.

---

13. K, "Ramen Jiro," http://www.ramentokyo.com/2007/06/ramen-jiro.html.

14. Hoffman, "Cult of Ramen Jiro," https://www.byfood.com/blog/culture/the-cult-of-ramen-jiro.

15. Brzeski, "Ramen Jiro." https://ramenbeast.substack.com/p/ramen-jiro-japans-most-infamous-food.

16. The context of the Corinthians is explained like this in one commentary: "Spiritual persons are those in whom the Spirit has really become a fundamental power of life and who have 'the mind of Christ' (2:16). As σαρκικός (*sarkinos*, fleshly), they are controlled by natural, human impulses rather than the Spirit. Paul does not use the term ψυχικός (*psychikos*) from 2:14, because that describes the natural person completely devoid of the Spirit. As Christians, the Corinthians are not ψυχικός (Refer to Fee, *1 Corinthians*, 123), but their behavior testifies that they are still too much 'of the flesh.' The term σαρκικοί characterizes them as weak and sinful." Garland, *1 Corinthians*, 106. The context of Kierkegaard's intended readers is Christendom. Therefore, the readers are somehow Christians, like σαρκικός in the Corinthian church; their behaviours are weak and sinful (as can be seen in *Either/Or, Part I*). Although the context of the Corinthian church and that of nineteenth-century Denmark are not homogeneous, the terms used in 1 Corinthians 3:1–2 ("people of the flesh," "infants in Christ," "milk," and so on) are metaphorical and effectively illustrate the milder religiousness that Kierkegaard presents in *Two Upbuilding Discourses* (1843).

4.2.1 Introducing the Religious That the Reader of *Either/Or* Can Digest

The discourses begin with prayers, based on specific biblical passages and containing numerous biblical connotations and allusions. In this sense, the discourses are surely religious. However, they also have distinctly poetic or aesthetic flavours that are palatable for the readers of *Either/Or*. In the preface to *Two Upbuilding Discourses* (1843), he says that

> inasmuch as in being published [Two Upbuilding Discourses (1843)] actually remains quiet without moving from the spot, I let my eyes rest on it for a little while. It stood there like a humble little flower under the cover of the great forest, sought neither for its splendor nor its fragrance nor its food value. But I also saw, or thought I saw, how the bird I call my reader suddenly noticed it, flew down to it, picked it, and took it home, and when I had seen this, I saw no more.[17]

The preface likens "*my* reader" to a "bird" and the *Two Upbuilding Discourses* (1843) to "a humble little flower." By employing this poetic form of expression, Kierkegaard hopes that the aesthete will appreciate his writings. Second, there is no severe rebuke or condemnation in *Two Upbuilding Discourses* (1843). In other words, there is no articulation of sin.[18] Rather, it is gently suggested that one's unnamed yearning or desire may be a longing for God. The implication is clear: one can be truly satisfied only by God. Third, Jesus Christ, the true ultimatum, does not appear in these two discourses.[19] For these reasons, the religious elements in the discourses do not radically confront the reader but come across gently. In this way, Kierkegaard makes the religious digestible for the reader of *Either/Or*.

---

17. *SKS* 5, 13/ *EUD*, 5.

18. The concept of sin is introduced briefly in the discourses (see *SKS* 5, 47/ *EUD*, 38) and fully developed in *The Sickness unto Death*.

19. *SKS* 7, 247/ *CUP I*, 272. In *Philosophical Fragments*, published in 1844, Kierkegaard's pseudonym, Johannes Climacus refers to "god" who is the teacher and the saviour; but this "god" is not explicitly identified as Jesus Christ yet. In "Part Three: The Gospel of Suffering: Christian Discourse" in the signed-religious work *Upbuilding Discourses in Various Spirits*, published in 1847, Kierkegaard finally begins to refer explicitly to Christ. One can see how Kierkegaard deliberately and gradually introduces Christ, step by step, throughout his pseudonymous and signed-religious works.

4.2.2 Who Edifies Whom?

Who edifies whom through the discourses? The answer seems to be quite simple. Our common sense tells us that Kierkegaard, as the author, edifies the reader. Surprisingly, however, Kierkegaard did not see it this way. In the discourses, Kierkegaard says, "Yet no person learns this from another but each one individually learns it only from and through God."[20] In his view, it is not he himself who is the teacher but God; and it is God who builds up the reader.[21] The reason Kierkegaard still attempts to hide, even in his signed-religious work, seems to be because he intended to help the reader look to God alone.[22] To be sure, Kierkegaard regarded himself as one lacking authority, partly because he was unordained, a penitent, a poet, and so on.[23] Yet even if he had been ordained, he would still have insisted that God is the one who edifies. Johannes Climacus, one of Kierkegaard's pseudonyms, says that it is ethical and effective when the pastor, who would have been ordained, repents before God from the pulpit.[24] Theologically speaking, if a human being becomes a teacher and judges "an ideal sinner," sin will fall into the quantitative category and will become a matter of comparison. But sin is always sin before God and should fall into the qualitative category. Each individual (the mortal) – including a pastor and a religious author – needs to kneel before God (the immortal). Kierkegaard's authorial activity appears to be a thorough application of the following biblical passage: "But you are not to be called rabbi, for you have one teacher, and you are all students . . . Nor are you to be called instructors, for you have one instructor, the [Christ]" (Matt 23:8; 10).[25] In Kierkegaard's view, he is "a fellow-pupil," and the one who edifies is none other than the Triune God.[26]

---

20. *SKS* 5, 36/ *EUD*, 28.

21. See also 1 Corinthians 3:6–7; *SKS* 9, 219/ *WL*, 216; Pattison, *Kierkegaard's Upbuilding Discourses*, 17.

22. *SKS* 5, 36/ *EUD*, 28.

23. *JP*, IX 6947/ *Pap.* XI. 3B 57; *SKS* 23, 101, NB16:8/ *JP*, VII 6587 n.d., 1850; *SKS* 7, 248/ *CUP I*, 273.

24. *SKS* 7, 482, asterisk / *CUP I*, 530–531, asterisk, translation slightly modified. See also Matthew 7:1–5; Luke 18:9–14.

25. "The reason for the ban is to avoid confusion with the only true 'teacher' they have, Jesus himself." France, *Gospel of Matthew*, comment on 23:8.

26. *SKS* 16, 58/ *PV*, 79.

4.2.3 The Polyphonic Voices That Are Capable of Addressing Multiple Characters in *Either/Or*

George Pattison compares Kierkegaard's discourses with the sermon in general. His comparison yields the following results:

> Most (though not all) preachers are, on the whole, monological. They have something to say, and they say it. Of course they also illustrate it with stories, images, and episodes from history, literature, and life. But the point is to get "the message" across. But for Kierkegaard the point is not to get a "message" across, it is to engage readers in a process of change and, like a therapist, help them become alert to the movements and needs of their own hearts. He is not the one with the answers. He is a fellow learner. And so, beneath the surface of the text, he presents us with a multiple of voices, each representing a different point of view, making objections, posing questions, giving assent. In one discourse, I counted over twenty![27]

Pattison goes on to say,

> Theoretically, this seemed to fit with the Russian literary critic Mikhail Bakhtin's theory of the polyphonic novel (which he saw especially exemplified in Dostoevsky). According to Bakhtin, a polyphonic novel is one that contains a multitude of voices and points of view that crisscross each other in a constant, open, and unfinalizable movement. In such a work there is no final resolution, no grand finale, no concluding chord. Everything remains open; everything is still to be decided. The only possible "resolution," he suggested, was a kind of love big enough to embrace such multiplicity and unselfish enough not to try to impose its own point of view on all the rest. Bakhtin was a reader of Kierkegaard (including his *Works of Love*) and this very possibly shaped his own theory.[28]

Whereas a conventional sermon is generally monological, Kierkegaard's discourses are polyphonic. In his discourses, Kierkegaard attempts to draw

---

27. Jensen and Pattison, *Kierkegaard's Pastoral Dialogues*, xi.
28. Jensen and Pattison, xi. See also Pattison, *Kierkegaard's Upbuilding Discourses*, 8.

the reader nearer to faith, but he also leaves room for various life-attitudes and is willing to wait for their self-action.

Pattison claims to have counted over twenty voices in a single discourse. One may wonder whether, in *Two Upbuilding Discourses* (1843), Kierkegaard addresses the numerous voices corresponding to the various life-views represented in *Either/Or* since he describes these two works as "concurrent."[29] In *Either/Or*, multiple people exemplify various life-views as shown in the table below:

Book	Pseudonymous editor or author	Figure	Sphere or boundary
Preface	Victor Eremita		Irony (boundary)
Either/Or, Part I	A	Don Juan, Faust, the unhappiest one, Antigone, Marie Beaumarchais, Donna Elvira, Margarete, Emmeline	The aesthetic sphere
	Johannes the Seducer	Cordelia	
Either/Or, Part II	B		The ethical sphere
	The Jylland Pastor		The religious sphere

Supposing the diversity of voices in *Two Upbuilding Discourses* (1843) corresponds to the various life-views in *Either/Or*, let us attempt to identify the common or similar voices between these two works. Generally speaking, the multitude of figures in *Either/Or, Part I* are passionate, although they differ greatly in terms of the objects of their passions. The first discourse offers instruction to the passionate who "investigate whether there might not be one wish so certain that he would dare to put his whole soul fervently into it"[30] and informs them that faith alone can satisfy their passions because faith is "the highest good, the most beautiful, the most precious, the most blessed riches of all, not to be compared with anything else, incapable of being

---

29. *SKS* 16, 16/ *PV*, 30.
30. *SKS* 5, 19/ *EUD*, 9.

replaced."³¹ Furthermore, Kierkegaard says that anyone can possess faith: "[Faith] is good in which all are able to share, and the person who rejoices in the possession of it also rejoices in the countless human race, 'because what I possess,' he says, 'every human being has or can possess.'"³² Therefore, the discourse seems to address the general need of the various aesthetes in *Either/Or, Part I* and encourage them to attain faith.

Now let us look more closely and attempt to connect each individual in *Either/Or* with a specific voice in the discourses. In *Either/Or*, A says, "To a knowledge of the truth, I perhaps have come; to salvation, surely not."³³ The term translated as "salvation" in the above quotation is *Salighed* in Danish, which can be also translated as "blessedness," "beatitude," or "bliss."³⁴ A knows the truth, but this knowledge does not lead him to salvation or blessedness. In the discourses, Kierkegaard describes such a person: "What he had come to recognize was the truth, but this truth had not made him happy (*lykkelig*)."³⁵ The discourse seems to expect the existence of a person like A – namely, a person who recognizes the truth but has not yet attained bliss (*Salighed* or *Lykke*³⁶).

What about seducers – such as Don Juan and Johannes the Seducer – in *Either/Or*? In the first discourse, Kierkegaard prays, "We cannot and do not wish to hide from ourselves the thought of the lust of the eye that infatuated."³⁷ The hedonists, such as Don Juan, are included in the intercessory prayer in the discourses. Speaking of seducers, there are also victims of seducers – such as Donna Elvira, who has been abandoned by Don Juan. In *Either/Or*, she says, "No, I will hate [Don Juan]; that is the only way to satisfy my soul, the only

---

31. *SKS* 5, 19–20/ *EUD*, 9–10. Later on, in *Philosophical Fragments*, Kierkegaard's pseudonym Johannes Climacus will call faith "happy passion (*lykkelige Lidenskab*)." *SKS* 4, 261; 263/ *PF*, 59; 61.

32. *SKS* 5, 20/ *EUD*, 10.

33. *SKS* 2, 44/ *EO I*, 35.

34. Bodelsen and Vinterberg, "*Salighed*," *Dansk-Engelsk Ordbog, II N-Ø*, 272.

35. *SKS* 5, 24/ *EUD*, 15.

36. Technically speaking, "Salighed" and "Lykke" are not synonymous. While "Salighed" denotes a deeper, more spiritual sense of blessedness or salvation, "Lykke" represents worldly happiness. Consequently, A is more attuned to his deeper needs than "he" in the discourse. Both are aware that recognizing the truth does not lead to happiness; however, "he" in the discourse feels a lack of "Lykke" (worldly happiness), while A perceives a lack of "Salighed" (spiritual happiness).

37. *SKS* 5, 17/ *EUD*, 7.

way I can find rest and something to occupy me."[38] Again, in the prayer in the discourses, it is said, "We cannot and do not wish to hide from ourselves the thought of . . . the sweetness of revenge that seduced, the anger that made us unrelenting."[39] Kierkegaard seems to expect the presence of a type of Donna Elvira, someone who burns with vengeful thoughts. In *Either/Or*, Margarete still believes Faust, who has made her life tragic: "Faust, O Faust! Come back, satisfy the hungry, clothe the naked, revive the languishing, visit the lonely one!"[40] In the discourses, Kierkegaard is gentle, as though talking to her:

> If there was someone to whom you felt drawn so strongly that you dared to say, 'I have faith in him' . . . Yet you may have been wrong in doing so – not in having faith, not in having faith in this way, but in having faith in a human being in this way.[41]

It is as though Kierkegaard is suggesting that Margarete should keep her passionate faith but with one condition: she must exchange the object of her passion. She must be passionate for God rather than for Faust. In another instance in *Either/Or*, A describes "the unhappiest one," saying, "For there he stands, the envoy from the kingdom of sighs, the chosen favorite of suffering, the apostle of grief, the silent friend of pain, the unhappy lover of recollection."[42] The discourses describe such a despairing person with these words: "And a chill of despair froze your spirit, and its death brooded over your heart. If at times life stirred again in your inner being, savage voices raged there, voices that were not your own but nevertheless came from your inner being."[43] Kierkegaard says that if such despairing persons humble themselves and kneel before God, the heavens will open again, and God will renew their countenance.[44]

What about B, who represents the ethical sphere in *Either/Or, Part II*? At first glance, both B and Kierkegaard share similar thoughts such as "loving

---

38. *SKS* 2, 197–199/ *EO I*, 202–204.
39. *SKS* 5, 17/ *EUD*, 7.
40. *SKS* 2, 207–208/ *EO I*, 213.
41. *SKS* 5, 33/ *EUD*, 24.
42. *SKS* 2, 222/ *EO I*, 229.
43. *SKS* 5, 46/ *EUD*, 38.
44. *SKS* 5, 47/ *EUD*, 38–39.

God in repentance."[45] If this is the case, then does B not need edification? This is not immediately clear, but the discourses seem to aim at edifying B as well. First, while B praises a mother's love,[46] marriage,[47] a woman,[48] and an old woman,[49] the discourses concentrate on God alone. Second, B blends ethical and human categories with religious categories by describing the mother's look as "the benediction of her look."[50] He also says, "salvation comes from woman"[51] and "I am acquiring by purchase an eternal health."[52] Here, B applies religious terms such as "benediction" and "salvation" to a mother or a woman; further, he, who is merely human, purchases eternal health (life). But the discourses do not praise any women or human beings. Furthermore, Kierkegaard would not dare to say that he is the one who purchases eternal life.[53] Therefore, the discourses do intend to edify B by teaching him to focus purely on God and kneel humbly before him.

How about the Jylland Pastor, who preaches in the last chapter of *Either/Or, Part II*? There seem to be affinities between the Pastor and Kierkegaard. To the one who wholeheartedly loves and trusts a human being, both the Jylland Pastor and Kierkegaard suggest that such a person should rather place their wholehearted love and trust in God alone.[54] Furthermore, they both say that

---

45. *SKS* 3, 209/ *EO II*, 217–218; *SKS* 5, 53–54/ *EUD*, 45–46. Compare also *SKS* 3, 195/ *EO II*, 203; Ecclesiastes 3:11; *SKS* 5, 19–20/ *EUD*, 9–10.

46. *SKS* 3, 78–79/ *EO II*, 74.

47. *SKS* 3, 69–71/ *EO II*, 64–66; *SKS* 3, 134/ *EO II*, 135.

48. *SKS* 3, 199/ *EO II*, 207.

49. *SKS* 3, 297/ *EO II*, 314.

50. *SKS* 3, 78–79/ *EO II*, 74.

51. *SKS* 3, 199/ *EO II*, 207.

52. *SKS* 3, 272/ *EO II*, 287. Compare Matthew 26:39; Mark 10:38; Luke 22:42; John 16:21; 18:11; Romans 8:18; Hebrews 12:2.

53. Compare *SKS* 3, 272/ *EO II*, 287 with the following journal entry that, while largely similar, has a few significant differences: "And if the bitter cup of suffering is handed to me, I shall ask that, if possible, it be taken away, and if it is not possible, I shall take it cheerfully, and I shall not fix my gaze upon the cup but upon the one who hands it to me, and I shall not turn my eyes toward the bottom of the cup to see if it is soon empty, but I shall look at him who hands it to me, and while I trustingly raise the goblet I shall not say to any other man: Here's to your health, as I myself am savoring it, but I shall say: Here's to my health, and empty its bitterness, to my health, for I know and am convinced that it is to my health that I empty it, to my health, as I leave not one drop behind." *SKS* 18, 309, JJ:506/ *JP*, V 5562, n.d., 1842. Whereas B dares to say, "I am acquiring by purchase an eternal health," such presumptuous expressions are completely absent in Kierkegaard's journal entry.

54. *SKS* 3, 328/ *EO II*, 349; *SKS* 5, 33/ *EUD*, 24.

if one loves God, they will find that God loves them more than they love him.⁵⁵ In fact, the title of the Jylland Pastor's sermon is "The Upbuilding That Lies in the Thought That in Relation to God We Are Always in the Wrong."⁵⁶ As the title suggests, his sermon intends to edify in the same manner that the discourses do. In addition, one of Kierkegaard's journal entries says that the issue of *Either/Or* is resolved with the last sentence of the sermon.⁵⁷ Though the Jylland Pastor is one of Kierkegaard's pseudonyms, he is also the antidote for what ails the other figures in *Either/Or*. In this sense, the Jylland Pastor can be viewed as representing the religious within *Either/Or* and foreshadowing what is to come in *Two Upbuilding Discourses* (1843).

Clearly, Kierkegaard intentionally created a symmetry that connects *Either/Or* and *Two Upbuilding Discourses* (1843). We have traced some of these lines of symmetry, but we have not yet explored every line exhaustively. Certainly, there are more voices in the discourses, and we have not allowed all of them to speak. Doing so would be difficult, partly because Kierkegaard does not even give every voice in the discourses a proper name, and the voices of *Two Upbuilding Discourses* (1843) do not always perfectly match the personas in *Either/Or*. However, we can say that there are polyphonic voices in the discourses, and Kierkegaard has crafted those voices to address a variety of people such as the various personas in *Either/Or*. Moreover, in certain cases, the voices of *Two Upbuilding Discourses* (1843) very closely match the personas of *Either/Or*.

4.2.4 Dealing with Doubt (*Tvivl*)

Although Kierkegaard's discourses contain multiple voices, this does not mean that the discourses lack a target audience or a central message. First, Kierkegaard's discourses are based on specific biblical passages and, therefore, their central message stems from Scripture and is intended for a specific audience. In this subsection, I will attempt to identify the main target audience; in the next subsection, I will explore the central message.

---

55. *SKS* 3, 331/ *EO II*, 353. Compare I John 4:10.
56. *SKS* 3, 320/ *EO II*, 339.
57. *JP*, V 5629/ *Pap*. IV A216 *n.d.*, 1843/ *EO I*, Supplement, 505.

One of the central issues dealt with in the discourses seems to be doubt (*Tvivl*).[58] In this sense, Faust – who is "doubt personified"[59] – may represent the target audience of the discourses. The first discourse says, "We do not judge you for doubting, because doubt is a crafty passion, and it can certainly be difficult to tear oneself out of its snares."[60] The discourse offers an interesting solution: "What we require of the doubter is that he be silent."[61] Kierkegaard suggests while doubt itself is not judged, doubters should not voice their doubts:

> He surely perceived that doubt did not make him happy – why then confide to others what will make them just as unhappy? And what does he win by this communication? He loses himself and makes others unhappy. [. . .] therefore what he says is not only false in itself but above all on his lips. This is why we pay no attention to him.[62]

The second discourse also tackles doubt directly: "But doubt is sly and guileful, not at all loudmouthed and defiant, as it is sometimes proclaimed to be; it is unassuming and crafty, not brash and presumptuous, and the more unassuming it is, the more dangerous it is."[63] According to Kierkegaard, doubt does not deny the beauty of the biblical text discussed in the discourse: "'Every good and every perfect gift is from above and comes down from the Father of lights, with whom there is no change or shadow of variation.' (James 1:17) [Doubt] merely says that the words are difficult, almost enigmatic."[64] Kierkegaard refutes this statement, saying, "This explanation [of James 1:17] certainly is simple and natural, and yet doubt has craftily concealed itself in it."[65] Kierkegaard never says, "Do not doubt. Just believe." Rather, he allows doubt to deepen until it can sink no lower and vividly describes its craftiness.

---

58. See for instance Law, "The 'Ultimatum' of *Either/Or, Part Two* and *Two Upbuilding Discourses* (1843)" in *IKC 4: Either/Or, Part II*. 1995, 281–283.

59. *SKS* 17, 19, AA:12/ *JP*, V 5092 1 June 1835.

60. *SKS* 5, 31/ *EUD*, 23.

61. *SKS* 5, 31/ *EUD*, 23.

62. *SKS* 5, 31–32/ *EUD*, 23.

63. *SKS* 5, 49/ *EUD*, 41.

64. *SKS* 5, 41/ *EUD* 32

65. *SKS* 5, 49/ *EUD*, 41.

In the second discourse, a solution to doubt is not explicitly given. As Pattison puts it,

> As such, the discourses do not contain Kierkegaard's finished "answer" to his own crises or to the common crisis of modernity or to the question posed by the pseudonyms, but they are engaged with all these in an open-ended way in order to clarify the matter at issue.[66]

As we shall see in the next subsection, Kierkegaard does have a point of view. However, he adopts a gradual approach to dealing with significant problems such as the issue of doubt. As discussed later in this book, Kierkegaard seemed to believe that doubt (*Tvivl*) itself is not the true issue. In his view, the real issue is despair (*Fortvivelse*). Therefore, a definitive answer to doubt is not provided in these two discourses.

4.2.5 Summary of the Religious in *Two Upbuilding Discourses* (1843)

In this subsection, I will define the religious in *Two Upbuilding Discourses* (1843) by summarizing the central message of the two discourses. According to the first discourse, the fervent passion of the aesthete can only be satisfied by faith. However, one cannot give faith to another person. If one gives faith to someone, it is not faith, *eo ipso*. Each person has to strive for faith themselves. By doing so, anyone can attain faith by learning directly from God. And faith overcomes all the struggles and difficulties in one's life.

The second discourse declares that every good and every perfect gift comes from God. Even if prayers are not answered, the words of James 1:17–22 remain true. Instead of granting one's desire, God cultivates a meek heart in the supplicant, enabling them to trust that this biblical word is true:

> [God] did not treat you unfairly when he denied you a wish but in compensation created this faith in your heart, when instead of a wish, which, even if it would bring everything, at most was able to give you the whole world, he gave you a faith by which you won God and overcame the whole world.[67]

---

66. Pattison, *Kierkegaard's Upbuilding Discourses*, 21.
67. *SKS* 5, 45/ *EUD*, 36.

Even if prayer is answered, what one attains is "at most" the whole world. However, when one's wish is denied, faith is created within the person; and this faith enables them to win God and overcome the whole world. Accordingly, both discourses present faith as the supreme good that is not comparable to anything else.

Thus, the overall message of the two discourses is this: As one constantly strives for it, God creates, regenerates, or increases faith within the person, a faith that overcomes every struggle and leads them to God. This is also the definition of the religious that Kierkegaard attempts to introduce in his discourses.

4.3 A Possible Application to the Japanese Context

On one occasion, I preached at an evangelistic meeting. After the meeting, a veteran pastor asked me, "Why did you not mention Jesus's resurrection?" His wife answered for me, "That is why his preaching was effective (for non-believers)." Among Japanese Christians and pastors, opinions vary. Many believe that since Jesus's resurrection is of "first importance" (1 Cor 15:3), it cannot be omitted, *especially* in an evangelistic sermon. However, if one adopts a Kierkegaardian mission strategy, a proclaimer may choose a more circuitous path. In other words, a Kierkegaardian missionary would provide spiritual food that is palatable and digestible for the person before them.

For instance, I once had the opportunity to converse with a person who had lost the will to live. At times, the depth of his depression caused him to despair of life to the extent that he no longer wanted to live. I could not begin by introducing him to the transcendent God. This would have been far more than the average Japanese man with no Christian background could possibly grasp. Therefore, I referred him to the following "stunningly naive but undeniable"[68] biblical verse:

> Therefore I tell you, do not worry about your life, what you will eat or what you will drink, or about your body, what you will wear. Is not life more than food, and the body more than clothing? Look at the birds of the air; they neither sow nor reap nor

---

68. France, *Gospel of Matthew*, 265; cited from Betz, *The Sermon on the Mount*, n.p.

> gather into barns, and yet your heavenly Father feeds them. Are you not of more value than they? And can any of you by worrying add a single hour to your span of life? And why do you worry about clothing? Consider the lilies of the field, how they grow; they neither toil nor spin, yet I tell you, even Solomon in all his glory was not clothed like one of these. But if God so clothes the grass of the field, which is alive today and tomorrow is thrown into the oven, will he not much more clothe you – you of little faith? Therefore do not worry, saying, "What will we eat?" or "What will we drink?" or "What will we wear?" [. . .] So do not worry about tomorrow, for tomorrow will bring worries of its own. Today's trouble is enough for today. (Matt 6:25–31, 34)

First, I hoped that these biblical verses would encourage him to live at least for *today* (day by day). Second, I used this particular passage because Japanese people love the beauty of nature.[69] From experience, I have learned that Jesus's parable of the birds of the air and the lilies of the field touches the Japanese heart. Third, notice that I skipped verses 32–33, which are more overtly religious and demand the hearer's personal commitment. While verses 32–33 are biblically important and crucial for a Christian, they may not be digestible for a non-Christian.

For the person right in front of me – an average Japanese with no Christian background who had lost the will to live – I annotated these biblical verses as follows:

> "[Divide] each of the difficulties under examination into as many parts as possible, and as might be necessary for its adequate solution."[70] To think about life as a whole is too much. If living is too hard for you, just live today. Don't think about tomorrow. Think about tomorrow when it is tomorrow. Do

---

69. *Encyclopedia Britannica*, commenting on *The Tale of Genji*, the eleventh-century classic Japanese literature that represents Japanese mentality, says, 'The work shows supreme sensitivity to human emotions and the beauties of nature." *Encyclopedia Britannica*, "The Tale of Genji," accessed 15 March 2019, https://www.britannica.com/topic/The-Tale-of-Genji. Such an appreciation of nature can also be seen in Japanese cultural activities such as 花見 (*hanami*, cherry blossom viewing in early April) and 俳句 (haiku, Japanese poetry that contains three sentences that constitute 5-7-5 syllables. Haikus must contain 季語 [*kigo*] – that is, seasonal words).

70. Descartes, *Discourse on Method*, loc. 251, Kindle.

what you can today. "Even if I knew that tomorrow the world would go to pieces, I would still plant my apple tree."[71] Does it sound foolish? I don't think so. One can live only today. One cannot change the past; nor can one live in the future. The past is already unchangeable; the future is yet to come. But we can do something today even if it may be a tiny thing. Therefore, day by day, live today.

Although – or perhaps because – the above biblical passage and annotation do not contain what is essentially Christian, he seemed to be encouraged. Later, when he gave a speech in front of ひきこもり (hikikomori),[72] he shared Matthew 6:25–31, 34 along with my annotation.

What is the application of *Two Upbuilding Discourses* (1843) to the Japanese context? Although it appears to be roundabout, a Kierkegaardian missionary does not provide the essentially Christian from the outset but a palatable and digestible religiousness according to the diagnosis of the spiritual condition of the Japanese who is right in front of them. Finally, applying a Kierkegaardian mission strategy in the Japanese mission field should be even more roundabout than Kierkegaard's approach in the Christendom of Denmark. In section 4.2, I referred to 1 Corinthians 3:1–2 and justified Kierkegaard's approach in serving a "milky" religiousness. In Paul's letter to the Corinthians, he categorizes three kinds of people:

1. spiritual people (πνευματικοι), who have the mind of Christ (3:1; 2:16)
2. fleshly people (σαρκινοι), who are infants in Christ (3:1)
3. natural people (ψυχικοι), who do not receive the gifts of God's Spirit (2:14)

We might attempt to evangelize the Japanese by feeding them solid food or *Rāmen Jirō*,[73] which only the spiritual people (πνευματικοι) can digest. On the

---

71. Luther, Martin. goodreads, accessed 6 February 2020, https://www.goodreads.com/quotes/35396-even-if-i-knew-that-tomorrow-the-world-would-go.

72. The definition of *hikikomori* is as follows: "A form of severe social withdrawal, called *hikikomori*, has been frequently described in Japan and is characterized by adolescents and young adults who become recluses in their parents' homes, unable to work or go to school for months or years." Teo and Gaw, "Hikikomori," 444–449.

73. See section 4.2.

other hand, Kierkegaard fed his contemporaries milk since they were fleshly people (σαρχινοι), not yet ready for solid food. In Japan, only 1 percent of the population is Christian; most Japanese are natural people (ψυχικοι). How much more should a missionary in Japan be sensitive to this reality? These people may not even be able to drink milk. In the case of those hearing the gospel for the first time, should a missionary in Japan merely let them *smell* spiritual drink or food? Or should they just show them a *menu* that may stimulate their appetite?

4.4 Conclusion

Section A: Concluding Remarks: *Two Upbuilding Discourses* (1843)

This chapter has attempted to restore Kierkegaard's original intent in writing and publishing *Two Upbuilding Discourses* (1843). Specifically, due attention has been paid to this work, particularly its relationship to, differences from, and superiority over *Either/Or*. Like a skilled cook adding a pinch of spice, Kierkegaard serves poetic and palatable religiousness to the aesthetic reader of *Either/Or* (see section 4.2.1). Kierkegaard assumes the position of a kind of Christian Socrates, a midwife who helps others to give birth to the truth. Thus, Kierkegaard is not a teacher; rather, it is God who edifies the reader (see section 4.2.2). Kierkegaard constructs his discourses polyphonically so that various kinds of people – who we see in *Either/Or* – in different life-stages can engage in their own process of spiritual growth in a natural way (see section 4.2.3). The main target of *Two Upbuilding Discourses* (1843) is Faust – who represents doubt personified – but a definitive solution is yet to emerge since doubt (*Tvivl*) must be intensified until the real enemy – despair (*Fortvivelse*) – makes an appearance (see section 4.2.4). Kierkegaard presents faith in an attractive light. First, one can fervently devote all passions to faith. Second, anyone can have faith because each one learns from God and receives it from God. Third, faith is the supreme good, beyond comparison, because through God's work in creating faith within each individual, they not only gain God but also overcome the whole world (see section 4.2.5).

In terms of application, just as in *Either/Or*, the mission strategy in *Two Upbuilding Discourses* (1843) is to avoid placing a heavy burden on the shoulders of spiritual infants or natural people. When the essentially Christian message is not appetizing or digestible for the audience at a given moment, a Kierkegaardian missionary does not preach rigorous Christianity but, instead, serves a delicious and chewable form of religiousness (see section 4.3).

In conclusion, with *Two Upbuilding Discourses*, Kierkegaard attempted to introduce the religious in a digestible and palatable form for the readers of *Either/Or*, who Kierkegaard diagnosed as the esthete and "the ordinary godly Christians."

Section B: Concluding Remarks: *Either/Or* and *Two Upbuilding Discourses* (1843)

Since I have dealt with *Either/Or* and *Two Upbuilding Discourses* (1843) as a unit, it is appropriate to offer concluding remarks on this unit. Does reading these two works together clarify Kierkegaard's intentions? Indeed, approaching *Either/Or* and *Two Upbuilding Discourses* (1843) as a unit reveals the emergence of an initial and characteristic *religious either/or* within Kierkegaard's authorship. As argued in section 3.2.4.3, the term *religious either/or* suggests that there are broadly three kinds of either/or: aesthetic, ethical, and religious. For Kierkegaard, however, only a *religious either/or* represents the genuine and decisive choice. The term *initial religious either/or* indicates that *Either/Or* marks Kierkegaard's first published attempt to guide the reader toward choosing the religious. Importantly, this initial religious either/or is not a choice between *Either/Or, Part I* and *Either/Or, Part II* but a choice between *Either/Or* and *Two Upbuilding Discourses* (1843). In other words, it is a choice between staying where one is (*Either/Or*) and being willing to venture into the religious sphere (*Two Upbuilding Discourses* [1843]). Since this is an *initial* religious either/or, Kierkegaard is particularly gentle, first guiding the aesthetic reader on how to make a choice before burdening them with a religious either/or – that is, a movement from *Either/Or, Part I* to *Either/Or, Part II*. After learning how to make a choice, the reader is invited to choose the religious over where they currently are – that is, a movement from *Either/Or* to *Two Upbuilding Discourses* [1843]). Since this is an *initial* either/or, this religiousness is not yet strictly Christian but, rather, a *milky* form of religiousness (1 Cor 3:1–2). Even though *Two Upbuilding Discourses* (1843) is a signed-religious work, Kierkegaard does not talk about sin or Christ at this point.

Section C: Concluding Remarks: the Duplexity of "the Whole Authorship"

A single unit of *Either/Or* and *Two Upbuilding Discourses* (1843) is not just an initial either/or but also a *typical* either/or. This initial either/or represents the duplexity of "the whole authorship." Kierkegaard says, "*Two Upbuilding Discourses* is concurrent with *Either/Or*. The duplexity is in the deeper sense, that is, in the sense of the whole authorship."[74] In other words, while this initial religious either/or urges the reader to choose between staying where they are or venturing into the religious sphere, the typical either/or structure is intended be repeated throughout "the whole authorship."

The quotation above is from *The Point of View for My Work as an Author*, which was written in 1848. Therefore, "the whole authorship" here signifies Kierkegaard's works from 1843 to May 1849 – which include the publications of the second edition of *Either/Or* and *The Lily in the Field and the Bird of the Air* – which were in his mind while writing *The Point of View for My Work as an Author*. Here is another important quotation worthy of repetition : "With my left hand I passed *Either/Or* out into the world, with my right hand *Two Upbuilding Discourses*."[75] Amplifying this, Kierkegaard passed subsequent pseudonymous works with his left hand and subsequent signed-religious works with his right hand. As discussed in sections 3.2.1.2 and 4.1, this aspect has often been marginalized and ignored. One reason this aspect has been neglected might be that the repetition of almost the same title for the *Upbuilding Discourses* may create a somewhat insipid impression. To draw proper attention to Kierkegaard's right-handed works, I have inserted the "title" and "main biblical text" under the title of each of the *Upbuilding Discourses* in the following diagram that shows "the whole authorship."[76]

---

74. *SKS* 16, 16/ *PV*, 30.

75. *SKS* 16, 21/ *PV*, 36.

76. The two works by Johannes Climacus – *Philosophical Fragments* and *Concluding Unscientific Postscript* – occupy a unique position, being pseudonymous yet edited by S. Kierkegaard, thereby straddling the boundary between his pseudonymous and signed works.

Year	Age	Authorship	
		Pseudonymous work (written by the left hand)	**Signed work** (written by the right hand)
		First division	
1843	30	*Either/Or* by A and Judge William, edited by Victor Eremita	
			Two Upbuilding Discourses (1. "The Expectancy of Faith" Galatians 3:23–29; 2. "Every Good and Every Perfect Gift Is from Above" James 1:17–21 or 22)
		Fear and Trembling by Johannes de Silentio	*Three Upbuilding Discourses* (1&2. "Love Will Hide a Multitude of Sins" I Peter 4:7–12 (twice); 3. "Strengthening in the Inner Being" Ephesians 3:13–21)
		Repetition by Constantin Constantius	
			Four Upbuilding Discourses (1. "The Lord Gave, and the Lord Took Away; Blessed Be the Name of the Lord" Job 1:20–21; 2&3. "Every Good and Every Perfect Gift Is from Above" James 1:17–21 or 22 (twice); 4. "To Gain One's Soul in Patience" Luke 21:19)
1844	31		*Two Upbuilding Discourses* (1. "To Preserve One's Soul in Patience" Luke 21:19; 2. "Patience in Expectancy" Luke 2:33–40)
			Three Upbuilding Discourses (1. "Think about Your Creator in the Days of Your Youth" Ecclesiastes 12:1; 2. "The Expectancy of an Eternal Salvation" 2 Corinthians 4:17–18; 3. "He Must Increase; I Must Decrease" John 3:30)
		Philosophical Fragments by Johannes Climacus, published by S. Kierkegaard	
		The Concept of Anxiety by Vigilius Haufniensis	
		Prefaces by Nicholaus Notabene	
			Four Upbuilding Discourses (1. "To Need God Is a Human Being's Highest Perfection"; 2. "The Thorn in the Flesh" 2 Corinthians 12:7; 3. "Against Cowardliness" 2 Timothy 1:7; 4. "One Who Prays Aright Struggles in Prayer and Is Victorious – in That God Is Victorious")

Year	Age	Authorship	
		Pseudonymous work (written by the left hand)	Signed work (written by the right hand)
1845	32	*Stages on Life's Way* published by Hilarious Bookbinder	*Three Discourses on Imagined Occasions* ("On the Occasion of a Confession"; "On the Occasion of a Wedding"; "At a Graveside")
		Second division	
1846	33	*Concluding Unscientific Postscript to Philosophical Fragments* by Johannes Climacus, published by S. Kierkegaard	
		Third division	
			A Literary Review: "Two Ages"
1847	34		*Upbuilding Discourses in Various Spirits*
			Works of Love
1848	35	*The Crisis and a Crisis in the Life of an Actress* by Inter et Inter	
			Christian Discourses
1849	36	(The second edition of *Either/Or*)	*The Lily in the Field and the Bird of the Air* "I. "Look at the Birds of the Air; Look at the Lily in the Field'"; "II. "No One Can Serve Two Masters, for He Must Either Hate the One and Love the Other or Be Devoted to the One and Despise the Other"; "III. "Look at the Birds of the Air; They Sow Not and Reap Not and Gather into Barns" - *without Worries about Tomorrow*. "Look at the Grass in the Field, Which Today Is." Matthew 6:24–34

From the outset, Kierkegaard draws our attention to the duplexity of *Either/Or* and *Two Upbuilding Discourses* (1843) and emphasizes "such a sustained duplexity"[77] throughout the authorship. The terms "first division," "second division," and "third division" in the above diagram are Kierkegaard's own, taken from *The Point of View for My Work as an Author*.[78] As shown in

---

77. *SKS* 16, 15/ *PV*, 29.
78. *SKS* 16, 15, asterisk/ *PV*, 29, asterisk.

the diagram, there is more obvious duplexity in the first division. Kierkegaard calls *Concluding Unscientific Postscript* the "turning point."[79] After this, the works in the third division are referred to as "exclusively religious writing[s],"[80] although there are also pseudonymous works such as *The Crisis and a Crisis in the Life of an Actress* and the second edition of *Either/Or*. In the above diagram, shading has been applied to the second division and most of the third divisions, as these sections represent turning points or exclusively religious writings rather than a continuation of the duplexity. Since the focus of this study is the duplexity represented by *Either/Or* and *Two Upbuilding Discourses* (1843), the second division and most of the third divisions are excluded from this discussion.

In the first division, one can observe that Kierkegaard alternated publication of pseudonymous and signed works. My presentation of the titles and main biblical texts of each discourse in the diagram hopefully makes Kierkegaard's original intent with his "right hand" (his signed works) more apparent. While the list of titles and key biblical texts alone may not be sufficient to convince the reader, I draw attention to the words of Paul Martens:

> Kierkegaard's debts to the Bible are so great that Paul Minear and Paul Morimoto, in the first extensive English-language examination of Kierkegaard's use of the Bible, boldly claimed that "we do not hesitate to predict that coming generations will increasingly reckon with him not so much as a philosopher, as a poet, as a theologian, or as a rebel against Christianity, but as an expositor of Scripture."[81]

The title *Either/Or* not only points to *Either/Or* and *Two Upbuilding Discourses* (1843) but also foreshadows subsequent left-handed (pseudonymous) works and subsequent right-handed (signed-religious) works. This provides indirect evidence that Kierkegaard functions as a missionary writer, urging the reader to choose between remaining where they are (subsequent pseudonymous works) and taking a leap into the religious (subsequent religious works).

---

79. *SKS* 16, 17/ *PV*, 31, emphasis in original.

80. *SKS* 16, 17/ *PV*, 31, emphasis in original.

81. Martens, "Kierkegaard and the Bible," 150; Minear and Morimoto, *Kierkegaard and the Bible*, 7–8.

Unfortunately, a detailed investigation of how this basic structure of either/or permeates the whole authorship is beyond the scope of the present work. Thus, we dare to skip Kierkegaard's subsequent twenty works (both pseudonymous and signed works) that were published after *Two Upbuilding Discourses* (1843) and jump into two Anti-Climacus' works that might partly prove if such an either/or-ness is repeated.

Category of either/or		Kierkegaard's work	Published year
Exercise of either/or	Aesthetic either/or (is not to make a choice)	*Either/Or, Part I*	1843
	Ethical either/or (is to take responsibility by making a choice)	*Either/Or, Part I* and *Either/Or, II*	
A true (religious) either/or	(An initial and characteristic) religious either/or	*Either/Or* and *Two Upbuilding Discourses* (1843)	
	(A more advanced) religious either/or	Subsequent pseudonymous (aesthetic) work and signed-religious work mainly in the first authorship	1843–1845; 1849 (The second edition of *Either/Or* and *The Lily in the Field and the Bird of the Air*)
	(A sharpened) religious either/or	*The Sickness unto Death* and *Practice in Christianity*	1849–1850

CHAPTER 5

The Sickness unto Death as the Rigorous Establishment of Sin

> If you would like to write a PhD thesis on Kierkegaard as a missionary, don't take up *The Sickness unto Death*. This work is too depressive.
>
> – Niels Jørgen Cappelørn, in a personal conversation with the present author

The subject of this chapter is *Sygdommen til Døden* (*The Sickness unto Death*). As Niels Jørgen Cappelørn advises, some may not consider it a good idea to take up *The Sickness unto Death*. If one intends to present Kierkegaard as a missionary, it might be a better choice to focus on the more overtly Christian signed-religious works from the second authorship (1846–1851), such as *Christian Discourses* and *The Lily in the Field and the Bird of the Air*. What advantage is there in focusing on *The Sickness unto Death*? Why choose this philosophical and depressive work to argue for Kierkegaard the missionary? Generally speaking, all Kierkegaard's works revolve around what it means to become a Christian. Therefore, each of his works must, in some way, proclaim Christianity. More specifically, in *Practice in Christianity*, Anti-Climacus says, "Admittance is only through the consciousness of sin; to want to enter by any other road is high treason against Christianity."[1] While Kierkegaard's lower pseudonymous works do not specifically address sin, his

---

1. *SKS* 12, 80/ *PC*, 67–68. Compare Mark 2:17 and 1 Timothy 1:15.

mission strategy eventually enters a new phase where sin is a key theme. His missionary task cannot be completed without addressing this dimension. Entering Christianity without consciousness of sin is "high treason against Christianity." Therefore, to argue for Kierkegaard as a missionary, one must engage with *The Sickness unto Death*, which gives a detailed account of the "sickness unto death" – that is, despair or sin.

The outline of this chapter is as follows: In the first section, I will provide a historical introduction. (For a more comprehensive treatment of this work, see appendix 6, which contains a summary of *The Sickness unto Death*.) In the second section, I will interpret this work from the perspective of Kierkegaard as a missionary. In the third section, I will apply some of my findings to the Japanese context. In the fourth section, I will offer some concluding remarks.

5.1 Historical Introduction

Howard V. Hong and Edna H. Hong summarize Kierkegaard's ongoing plan regarding the publication of *The Sickness unto Death* in this way:

> With all the finished writings on hand, Kierkegaard pondered another publication possibility in 1849: to publish everything, "the fruit of the year 1848," in three volumes under his own name and with the common title "The Collected Works of Completion." Volume 1 would be "The Sickness unto Death," with "Armed Neutrality" as an appendix; volume II "Practice In Christianity" in three parts, and volume III "On My Work as an Author," consisting of "Point of View" ("N.B. perhaps not yet"), "Three Notes," "A Note" ("The Accounting"), and "The Whole in One Word."[2]

The Hongs also discuss Kierkegaard's own estimation of the yet-to-be-published work referred to above: "He called [*The Collected Works of Completion*] 'the most valuable I have produced.'"[3] Kierkegaard finally decided to publish *The Sickness unto Death* separately on 30 July 1849 under the pseudonym

---

2. Hong and Hong, "Historical Introduction," in *PV*, xvi; the quotations within double quotation marks are from *Pap*. X5 B 143.

3. Hong and Hong, "Historical Introduction," in *PC*, xviii; the quotation within the quotation is from *SKS* 21, 264, NB10:17/ *JP*, V1 6337.

Anti-Climacus, who embodies the ideal of Christianity and is more Christian than Kierkegaard himself.[4] However, the fact that he had initially considered the possibility of publishing *The Sickness unto Death* under his *own name* and switched to a pseudonym "only at the last minute"[5] indicates that the voice of Anti-Climacus is very close to Kierkegaard's own.[6] Kierkegaard considered *The Sickness unto Death* and *Practice in Christianity* "extremely valuable."[7] Although the term "pseudonym" is used, Anti-Climacus differs significantly from Kierkegaard's early pseudonyms: "The difference from the earlier pseudonyms is simply but essentially this, that I do not retract the whole thing humorously but identify myself as one who is striving."[8] As discussed in section 2.3.4.3, the lower pseudonymous works such as *Either/Or* are dialectically dissolved. However, Anti-Climacus's *The Sickness unto Death* remains an ideal for which Kierkegaard himself was willing to strive.

5.2 A Study of *The Sickness unto Death* with Specific Regard to Kierkegaard the Missionary

During 2020, there were daily news broadcasts about the coronavirus. Everyone was fearful about this virus, which could lead to death. If Kierkegaard had been alive at the time, would he have called the coronavirus "the sickness unto death"? Unlikely. The introduction to *The Sickness unto Death* opens with Jesus's words: "This sickness is not unto death" (John 11:4 NKJV).[9] "This sickness" signifies Lazarus's sickness, which was deadly. "And yet Lazarus did die."[10] Then why did Jesus say that Lazarus's deadly illness was not a sickness unto death? Anti-Climacus says, "Humanly speaking, death

---

4. *SKS* 22, 128, NB11:204/ *JP*, VII, 6433 *n.d.*, 1849.

5. Dunning, *Dialectic of Inwardness*, 214.

6. The following "second-thought" also shows that Anti-Climacus is quite close to Kierkegaard himself: "We know that Kierkegaard expressed regret that he had published under a pseudonym, Anti-Climacus, a text that he later wished he could put under his own name (as he had originally had it in the final draft)." Ferreira, *Kierkegaard*, 9.

7. *SKS* 25, 294, NB10:69/ *JP*, VI 6361, also quoted in *SUD*, xv.

8. *SKS* 22, 151, NB12:9/ *JP*, VI 6446, also quoted in *SUD*, xx.

9. *SKS* 11, 123/ *SUD*, 7. Modern English translations are slightly different. For instance, NRSV translates this, "This illness does not lead to death." However, the Greek original reads, "Αὕτη ἡ ἀσθένεια οὐκ ἔστιν πρὸς θάνατον." This word-for-word translation is as follows: "This sickness is not unto death" (Anti-Climacus's translation, NKJV).

10. *SKS* 11, 123/ *SUD*, 7.

is the last of all, and, humanly speaking, there is hope only as long as there is life."[11] The coronavirus chaos took place because the virus can take away life and, thereby, hope. Anti-Climacus continues, "Christianly understood, however, death is by no means the last of all; in fact, it is only a minor event within that which is all, an eternal life, and, Christianly understood, there is infinitely much more hope in death than there is in life."[12] Therefore, Jesus Christ did not call Lazarus's sickness life-threatening. Anti-Climacus also says, "Christianly understood, then, not even death is 'the sickness unto death.'"[13] The same applies to the coronavirus. In this sense, *The Sickness unto Death* speaks prophetically to us today. The title itself raises a profound question: What is truly frightening? The coronavirus? Or is there another threat? In response to the modern situation of coronavirus chaos, Anti-Climacus would say, "You might say, 'I am scared of the coronavirus.' But you may have been wrong in doing so – not in being scared of something, not in being scared of something in this way, but in being scared of the coronavirus in this way."[14] For, as he reminds us, "the most appalling danger that the Christian has learned to know is 'the sickness unto death.'"[15]

5.2.1 The Universality of Sin or Despair

Who is the intended reader of *The Sickness unto Death*? Is it just those who enjoy gloomy topics? The answer is that it is everyone – non-Christians, Christians, pastors, and even Kierkegaard himself. First, Anti-Climacus argues for the universality of the sickness unto death.[16] Second, for Anti-Climacus, Christians are also in despair if they are not true Christians.[17] Third, Anti-Climacus delivers a harsh critique of a pastor, suggesting that the individual in his illustration – apparently a pastor – must first learn from Socrates the essential lesson of recognizing one's own ignorance.[18] This man believes that he knows the truth, but his actions reveal that he does not truly understand

---

11. *SKS* 11, 124/ *SUD*, 7.
12. *SKS* 11, 124/ *SUD*, 7–8.
13. *SKS* 11, 124/ *SUD*, 8.
14. See *SKS* 5, 33/ *EUD*, 24.
15. *SKS* 11, 125/ *SUD*, 9.
16. *SKS* 11, 138 / *SUD*, 22. Compare Psalm 14:3 and Romans 3:10.
17. *SKS* 11, 138/ *SUD*, 22.
18. *SKS* 11, 204/ *SUD*, 91–92.

what he professes.[19] He must first recognize his own ignorance; only then can he take the next step toward grasping the Christian understanding of sin. In this way, Anti-Climacus argues that the pastor in his illustration is also in despair. Fourth, Kierkegaard "[identifies himself] as one who is striving"[20] – he, too, is one of the intended readers of *The Sickness unto Death*.[21] Therefore, *The Sickness unto Death* declares the universality of despair and sin to everyone, including non-Christians, Christians, pastors, and Kierkegaard himself.

5.2.2 The Consciousness of Sin: The True Gateway and Source of Courage to Enter Authentic Christianity

The Sickness unto Death and *Practice in Christianity* were originally intended to be published together under the title *The Collected Works of Completion*.[22] As a result, these works are now separate and independently published under the pseudonym Anti-Climacus, with Kierkegaard serving as the editor. This production process indicates a coherence and connection between the two texts. It is therefore justifiable to read *The Sickness unto Death* and *Practice in Christianity* as a unified work, with both doctrinal and pedagogical considerations supporting this sequence.

Doctrinally speaking, *The Sickness unto Death* must be read before *Practice in Christianity*. Why did Kierkegaard publish this despairing work?[23] Kierkegaard published *The Sickness unto Death* so that his readers might first pass through the gate of the consciousness of sin, which is the only legitimate gate that leads into Christianity.[24] Thus, by first proclaiming the universality of the sickness unto death– that is, despair or sin[25] – Anti-Climacus lays the

---

19. This formula is often used by heavy metal bands to accuse pastors of hypocrisy and call on them to "practice what you preach." See Lyrics Mode, 'Testament – Practice What You Preach Lyrics." https://www.lyricsmode.com/lyrics/t/testament/practice_what_you_preach.html; "Napalm Death – Practice What You Preach Lyrics," https://www.lyricsmode.com/lyrics/n/napalm_death/practice_what_you_preach.html; "Death – Spiritual Healing Lyrics," https://www.lyricsmode.com/lyrics/d/death/spiritual_healing.html.
20. *JP*, VI 6446/ *Pap*. X1 A 549.
21. See also *SKS* 16, 58/ *PV*, 78–79.
22. *Pap*. X5 B 143; *SKS* 21, 264, NB10:17/ *JP*, V1 6337.
23. *SKS* 12, 49/ *PC*, 36.
24. *SKS* 12, 80/ *PC*, 67–68.
25. See the previous subsection.

groundwork to invite "every single individual" or "all the various kinds [of people]"[26] to Christ through his next work, *Practice in Christianity*.

Pedagogically speaking, too, *The Sickness unto Death* must be read first: "What the natural man catalogs as appalling – after he has recounted everything and has nothing more to mention – this to the Christian is like a jest."[27] The true knowledge of *the* absolute horror makes one courageous: "This is the way a person always gains courage; when he fears a greater danger, he always has the courage to face a lesser one; when he is exceedingly afraid of one danger, it is as if the others did not exist at all."[28] This courage will eventually help one to enter the truly Christian life. *Practice in Christianity* says,

> "But if the essentially Christian is something so terrifying and appalling, how in the world can anyone think of accepting Christianity?" Very simply and, if you wish that also, very Lutheranly: only the consciousness of sin can force one, if I dare to put it that way (from the other side grace is the force), into this horror.[29]

Anti-Climacus presents costly grace[30] in *Practice in Christianity*. As the above quotation states, if the Christianity presented in *Practice in Christianity* is "so terrifying and appalling," it is quite natural to wonder, "[How] in the world can anyone think of accepting Christianity?" The answer lies in comparison. In comparison with sin or despair, which is "the most appalling danger that the Christian has learned,"[31] one "is able to see the gentleness and love and compassion of Christianity."[32]

In summary, Anti-Climacus provides the doctrinal and educative justification for the temporal and logical priority of *The Sickness unto Death*: the

---

26. *SKS* 12, 252/ *PC*, 262.
27. *SKS* 11, 124/ *SUD*, 8.
28. *SKS* 11, 125/ *SUD*, 8–9.
29. *SKS* 12, 79/ *PC*, 67.

30. It is not accidental that the phrase used here reminds us of Dietrich Bonhoeffer (1906–1945). From Kierkegaard, Bonhoeffer inherited the thought-seeds that emphasize the cost of being a disciple of Christ. See Kelly, "Influence of Kierkegaard," 148–154; Law, "Cheap Grace and the Cost of Discipleship in Kierkegaard's *Self-Examination*" 111–142; Law, "Redeeming the Penultimate," 14–26.

31. *SKS* 11, 125/ *SUD*, 9.
32. *SKS* 12, 80/ *PC*, 68.

consciousness of sin is the only legitimate gate to enter Christianity, and it makes one courageous enough to embrace costly grace.

5.2.3 The Self in Despair: The Need for a Proper Relation to God and Self

In the early pages of *The Sickness unto Death*, Anti-Climacus, gives a profound definition of the human being, the spirit, the self, and despair. However, this complex definition is actually a conclusion. One can only understand this definition after reading the entirety of *The Sickness unto Death*. The following formula, stated early on, is repeated at the very end[33] of the book: "The formula that describes the state of the self when despair is completely rooted out is this: in relating itself to itself and in willing to be itself, the self rests transparently[34] in the power that established it."[35] What does this mean? It means that, as a relational, spiritual, and dependent being, the self is in despair unless it wills to become itself by being in proper relationship with both God and itself.

A human being is a synthesis – but what kind of synthesis? "A human being is a synthesis of the infinite and the finite, of the temporal and the eternal, of freedom and necessity, in short, a synthesis. A synthesis is a relation between two."[36] A draft of *The Sickness unto Death* says, "A human being is a psychosomatic synthesis."[37] A human being is not just a psychosomatic synthesis but also a self-relational existence. The self must maintain a balance between the two and is responsible for how it relates to itself. A human being is spirit. Spirit is not merely a synthesis but requires a third active component to carry out the synthesis. When the self fails to maintain the balance between its two components, it is in despair. When the self fails to relate to itself, it is in despair. How can the self properly maintain a balance and relate to itself? By acknowledging its origin and being willing to become who it was originally meant to be, the self can be free from despair.

---

33. *SKS* 11, 242/ *SUD*, 131.

34. Paul R. Sponheim expounds on this, saying, "'Transparently' – it is hard to know what that means, but surely it includes trusting the constituting one in fully conscious faith." Sponheim, *Existing before God*, 62.

35. *SKS* 11, 130/ *SUD*, 14.

36. *SKS* 11, 130/ *SUD*, 14.

37. *SUD*, 142, originally from *Pap*. VIII2 B 170:1 *n.d.*, 1848.

What is the origin of the self? The self is not autonomous but is established by God. Therefore, when the self does not will to become the person that God intended it to be, it is in despair (despair in weakness). When the self wills to become something, but not the thing God intended, it is also in despair (despair in defiance). When the self wills to become someone in a way that God established, then it is no longer in despair. *The Sickness unto Death* is, in a sense, written to destroy the delusion that a human being is completely autonomous. By acknowledging one's dependency and being willing to rely on God, despair is nullified. This despair-free state is called faith. We will come back to this Anti-Climacean dialectic of despair and faith in '5.2.6.'

5.2.4 What Is Not Christianity: Philosophy

Before moving forward to *Practice in Christianity* and its rigorous description of faith in Christ, Anti-Climacus – in *The Sickness unto Death* – explains what Christianity is *not*. According to Anti-Climacus, philosophy (thought) is not Christianity (faith).

An early journal entry testifies that Kierkegaard had already discovered that "philosophy and Christianity can never be united."[38] In keeping with this conviction, Anti-Climacus refines his definition of faith by distinguishing Christianity from philosophy and faith from knowledge. For instance, although Kierkegaard admires and respects Socrates,[39] he ultimately disagrees with this ancient Greek philosopher regarding the definition of sin. For Socrates, sin is ignorance, and knowledge prevents one from sinning. But Christianly speaking, sin does not depend on the presence or absence of knowledge. Rather, sin belongs to the realm of the will. We sin even when possessing knowledge. Therefore, sin is not a problem of thought but of the will.[40]

---

38. *SKS* 17, 30, AA:13/ *JP*, III 3245 17 October 1835. For a detailed discussion on this important journal entry, see Stewart, "Philosophy and Christianity," 291–312. In this article, Stewart says, "Kierkegaard's thesis that 'Philosophy and Christianity can never be united' is best understood as a rejection of the Hegelian claims that philosophy and Christianity are ultimately one in the sense that religion or Christianity constitutes a subordinate part of a single organic philosophical system." Stewart, 309.

39. *SKS* 11, 202/ *SUD*, 89. Socrates – Kierkegaard's favourite pagan philosopher – has a special status in Kierkegaard's thought. Interestingly, 1 Corinthians 8:2 offers the biblical concept of awareness of ignorance: "Anyone who claims to know something does not yet have the necessary knowledge" (1 Cor 8:2). For Kierkegaard's suggestion that Socrates had become a Christian, see *SKS* 16, 36/ *PV*, 54.

40. Compare Romans 7:15–25.

This Socratic confusion regarding the definition of sin infects Christianity through the philosophizing of Christianity.

Anti-Climacus also attacks René Descartes (1596–1650) – the father of modern philosophy – and his famous maxim: "I think therefore I am."[41] Anti-Climacus says,

> And the secret of modern philosophy is essentially the very same, for it is this: *cogito ergo sum* [I think therefore I am], to think is to be (Christianly, however, it reads: according to your faith, be it unto you, or, as you believe, so you are, to believe is to be).[42]

Here, Anti-Climacus Christianly transforms Descartes's phrase "I think therefore I am" into "I believe therefore I am." Anti-Climacus says, "[Christianity] *must* be believed and not comprehended, that *either* it must be believed *or* one must be scandalized and offended by it – is it then so praiseworthy to want to comprehend?"[43] The mere thought cannot save one.

Of course, faith needs content. As Scripture says, "So faith comes from what is heard, and what is heard comes through the word of Christ" (Rom 10:17). Anti-Climacus, or Kierkegaard, does not say that what you believe does not matter but, as can be seen throughout this study, presupposes that the content of faith is a tenet of Christianity and that the object of faith is the Triune God.

Thus, Anti-Climacus does not allow philosophy to destroy the foundation of Christianity. The reader in Socratic confusion may pursue knowledge to be saved from sin. The reader in Cartesian confusion may attempt to understand Christianity instead of believing it. By challenging philosophers[44] such as Socrates and Descartes, Anti-Climacus attempts to eliminate the confusing blend of Christianity and philosophy. He also prepares the way for *Practice*

---

41. *SKS* 11, 206/ *SUD*, 93, originally from Descartes, *Discourse on the Method*, loc. 419; 430, Kindle.

42. *SKS* 11, 206/ *SUD*, 93.

43. *SKS* 11, 210/ *SUD*, 98, emphasis in original.

44. With regard to Kierkegaard's view of philosophy, C. Stephen Evans comments, "I think he rejects philosophy which claims it can be the basis of life and salvation, not philosophical thinking altogether. He uses arguments continually." Evans, personal communication, 12 June 2020. Indeed, Kierkegaard calls himself "a kind of philosopher." *JP*, III 2649/ *Pap.* IX 63:13 *n.d.*, 1848; *JP*, VI 6527 / *Pap.* X 6 B 41 *n.d.*, 1848.

in Christianity, where he introduces the essentially Christian – that is, faith in Christ in its true form.

5.2.5 What Is Not Christianity: Apologetics

The second negative statement that Anti-Climacus makes regarding what Christianity is emphatically not concerns apologetics. Paul Sponheim fittingly says, "Anti-Climacus launches into withering derision over the prospects of apologetics."[45] Indeed, it is abundantly clear that Anti-Climacus rejects not just philosophy but also apologetics.[46] One might understand, to some extent, the Christian rejection of philosophy, but why does Anti-Climacus so thoroughly abhor apologetics?[47] Anti-Climacus says, "Therefore, it is certain and true that the first one to come up with the idea of defending Christianity in Christendom is *de facto* a Judas No. 2: he, too, betrays with a kiss, except that his treason is the treason of stupidity."[48] Here, "a kiss" means that apologetics appears to help Christianity, while "to betray" means that apologetics, contrary to its intention and appearance, destroys the nature of Christianity. Moreover, the "stupidity" of apologetics lies in its misguided belief that it bolsters Christianity when, in reality, it betrays it.[49] For Anti-Climacus, apologetics, despite its sincere intentions, ultimately proves to be a foolish and treacherous enterprise.

So how should one communicate Christianity instead of defending it? According to Anti-Climacus, "If he believes, then the enthusiasm of faith

---

45. Sponheim, *Existing before God*, 96.

46. Despite sharing kindred spirits, the differences between Pascal and Kierkegaard lie in the fact that whereas Kierkegaard abhors apologetics, it seems justifiable to describe Pascal as an apologist. Pascal attempts to *prove* that Christianity is true. See Pascal, *Pascal's Pensées*, loc. 1345–1350.

47. Clarifying the issue, C. Stephen Evans says, "He rejects apologetics as the attempt to make Christianity acceptable to worldly thinking. For him apologetics is falsifying Christianity. But not all apologetics does this." Evans, personal communication, 12 June 2020.

48. *SKS* 11, 200/ *SUD*, 87.

49. For an example of someone who follows Kierkegaard's anti-apologetic stance with a high degree of fidelity, see Penner, *End of Apologetics*. The title *The End of Apologetics* is misleading. Penner aims not to end but to reform apologetics. For instance, in the following quotation, he presents "apologetic witness" that is, in his view, more biblical and effective: "To put another way, when we take prophetic speech as the basis for an apologetic witness, we move from an abstract epistemology of belief to ethics of belief." Penner, 102. Largely relying on Kierkegaard, and through philosophical discussion and engagement with the Christian tradition, Penner proposes a new type of apologetics that is more personal than abstract.

is not a defense – no, it is attack and victory; a believer is a victor."[50] Anti-Climacus seems to be saying that a person will be on the losing side if they attempt to defend Christianity. From his perspective, a true Christian is a believer, and a believer is a victor. And victors do not need to defend themselves, do they?

Anti-Climacus also likens a Christian to a lover:

> Is it not obvious that the person who is really in love would never dream of wanting to prove it by three reasons or to defend it, for he is something that is more than all reasons and any defense: he is in love. Anyone who does it is not in love; he merely pretends to be, and unfortunately – or fortunately – he is so stupid that he merely informs against himself as not being in love.[51]

According to Anti-Climacus, a lover who attempts to prove his love by means of reasons paradoxically "informs against himself as not being in love." Likewise, a Christian does not prove the existence of God but adores God wholeheartedly. One who attempts to defend their love does not truly love the lover.

On the one hand, Anti-Climacus's argument is in line with Scripture. The Bible says that the most important law is to "love the LORD your God with all your heart, and with all your soul, and with all your might" (Deut 6:4–5; See also Matt 22:37; Mark 12:30; Luke 10:27). Thus, the Anti-Climacean ideal of a Christian as a passionate lover of God finds its foundation in Scripture. On the other hand, it is also true that the term "apologetics" has a biblical root: "Always be ready to make your defence to anyone who demands from you an accounting for the hope that is in you" (1 Pet 3:15). The term "defence" in this verse is ἀπολογίαν in the original Greek – a form of ἀπολογία, which means "a speech in defence, defence."[52] As can be seen, the term ἀπολογία is etymologically the origin of *apologetics*. In other words, it is fair to say that Scripture commands us to be engaged in a certain type of apologetics. Kierkegaard

---

50. *SKS* 11, 200/ *SUD*, 87.
51. *SKS* 11, 215/ *SUD*, 104.
52. *An Intermediate Greek-English Lexicon: Founded Upon the Seventh Edition of Liddell and Scott's Greek-English Lexicon. s.v.* "ἀπολογία," Oxford: Oxford at the Clarendon Press 1959, 102.

scholars have reflected at length upon his arguable attitude towards apologetics, and their assessments are diverse.[53]

Anti-Climacus's point is that "those who are unspiritual" (1 Cor 2:14) cannot recognize the truth even if it is right in front of them! On behalf of Anti-Climacus, Johannes Climacus explains this in a more Christianly understandable manner: "If the learner is to obtain the truth, the teacher must bring it to him, but not only that. Along with it, he must provide him with the condition for understanding it."[54] Therefore, "the teacher" not only needs to present the truth but must also provide the condition for understanding it. Everything in the individual – reason, feelings, will, imagination – is corrupted (the universality of sin) unless one is renewed. How can such a renewal occur? By believing in Jesus Christ: "So if anyone is in Christ, there is a new creation: everything old has passed away; see, everything has become new!" (2 Cor 5:17)[55] Anti-Climacus rejects the presupposition that one can recognize the truth without a spiritual transformation.

If one faithfully follows Anti-Climacus's line of thought, apologetics can be seen as an effort to remove offence and make Christianity seem *probable* to a well-educated person. For Anti-Climacus, a Christianity which is merely *probable* or *reasonable* which does not require a personal decision and removes all risk of offense, is no longer Christianity. Therefore, he presents a *scandalous* Christianity – one that requires a personal decision before God.

5.2.6 The Dialectic of Faith with Despair, Sin, and Offence

Anti-Climacus does not simply describe a horrible situation of despair. Although salvation in Christ is fully elaborated on in his next work, *Practice*

---

53. According to Curtis L. Thompson, "Kierkegaard's writings reveal an ambivalence regarding the concept of apologetics." Thompson, "Apologetics," 71. As discussed in chapter 1, many of the preceding studies of Kierkegaard as a missionary regard him as a specific or new kind of apologist – see sections 1.1.1 (Denzil G. M. Patrick), 1.3.1 (Mark C. Miller), 1.3.2 (John Depoe), and 1.4.3 (Varughese John). C. Stephen Evans deals more subtly with this issue, saying, "While I fully agree with Kierkegaard that apologetics alone will never produce a healthy Christian church and that the church needs many things more than it needs apologetics, I do not agree with him that apologetics is not valuable." Evans, *Kierkegaard and Spirituality*, 62, footnote 14; See also Evans, *Kierkegaard on Faith and the Self*, 133–149.

54. *SKS* 4, 223/ *PF*, 14.

55. Some manuscripts read, "So if anyone is in Christ, there is a new creation: everything old has passed away; see, something new came into existence."

in Christianity, he also provides a way out in *The Sickness unto Death*. Anti-Climacus defines the opposite of sin as follows:

> Very often, however, it is overlooked that the opposite of sin is by no means virtue. In part, this is a pagan view, which is satisfied with a merely human criterion and simply does not know what sin is, that all sin is before God. No, the opposite of sin is faith, as it says in Romans 14:23: "whatever does not proceed from faith is sin." And this is one of the most decisive definitions for all Christianity – that the opposite of sin is not virtue but faith.[56]

According to Anti-Climacus, the opposite of sin is not virtue but faith. *The Sickness unto Death* offers a meticulous analysis of a person in despair who does not have faith in Christ. Despair (*Fortvivelse*) is epistemologically an intensified form of doubt (*Tvivl*) in the Danish language. Therefore, the spell of despair (an intensified form of *doubt*) can be broken by faith.

As far as Anti-Climacus is concerned, offence is an intensified form of sin. "Despair of the forgiveness of sins is offense. And offense is the intensification of sin."[57] Therefore, just as despair is the opposite of faith, so also is offence. Anti-Climacus persistently presents Christianity in terms of a required, non-negotiable either/or – faith or offence. He will further develop a discussion of the dialectic of faith and offence in his next work, *Practice in Christianity*. He invites the reader to make a choice rather than philosophizing or defending Christianity.

Anti-Climacus illustrates the dialectic of faith and offence by relating a parable.[58] In this parable, the mightiest emperor and a poor day labourer symbolize God and a human being. The day labourer would certainly be honoured if the emperor wanted to see him. But what if the emperor offered to make the day labourer his son-in-law? Such a situation would require the day labourer to have the courage to believe the offer. Otherwise, the day labourer would be offended. Just as in this parable, one must have the courage to believe the Christian message that one is invited to be a child of God; otherwise, one will be offended. Where faith is required, the possibility of offence

---

56. *SKS* 11, 196/ *SUD*, 82, emphasis in original.
57. *SKS* 11, 235/ *SUD*, 124.
58. *SKS* 11, 197–198/ *SUD*, 84–85.

is unavoidable. Anti-Climacus says, "Therefore, taking full responsibility, I venture to say that these words, 'Blessed is he who takes no offense at me,' belong in the proclamation about Christ."[59] Anti-Climacus, as a proclaimer of Christ, remains faithful to the dialectic of faith and despair/sin or that of faith and offence.

5.2.7 Anti-Climacus as a Preacher

On behalf of many readers, M. Jamie Ferreira describes the impressions that *The Sickness unto Death* typically evokes: "Some find [the title of the book] a somber and disheartening topic, while others feel a pang of recognition because the phrase resonates with something in their own experience."[60] Therefore, we have an impression that *The Sickness unto Death* is dark and depressive. I would argue that we generally overlook the fact that Anti-Climacus functions as a *preacher* in this work. Borrowing a phrase from *Practice in Christianity*, Jakub Marek aptly states, "Anti-Climacus is a 'servant of the Word . . . whose task it is, as far as a human being is capable of it, to draw people to [the Lord Jesus Christ].'"[61] I will now demonstrate this point.

After the "somber and disheartening" title, the book's subtitle – *A Christian Psychological Exposition for Upbuilding and Awakening* – expresses the homiletical aspects of this work. The prayerful motto of the epigraph also endorses the book's attempts to spiritually awaken its readers: "Lord, give us weak eyes for things of little worth, and eyes clear-sighted in all of your truth."[62] In the preface, Anti-Climacus says that though this work appears to be rigorous, all that he says in it is intended to build up the reader, much like "a physician speaks at the sickbed."[63] So this work is meant to edify and offer spiritual healing, rather than to discourage. In the book's introduction, Anti-Climacus does not merely treat the raising of Lazarus as literally true but enthusiastically declares, "The mere fact that [Christ] who is 'the resurrection and the life' (11:25) approaches the grave [signifies] that this sickness is not unto death: the

---

59. *SKS* 11, 239/ *SUD*, 128.

60. Ferreira, *Kierkegaard*, 148.

61. Marek, "Anti-Climacus," 441; the quotation within the quotation is originally from *SKS* 12, 252–253/ *PC*, 262.

62. *SKS* 11, 116/ *SUD*, 3.

63. *SKS* 11, 117/ *SUD*, 5. Compare 1 Corinthians 8:1, 14:26, and Ephesians 4:29.

fact that Christ exists, does it not mean that *this* sickness is not unto death!"⁶⁴ Although the darker passages of *The Sickness unto Death* are well known, this powerful preaching in the introduction seems to be overlooked in academic circles. Anti-Climacus continues his proclamation: "Christianly understood, then, not even death is 'the sickness unto death'; even less so is everything that goes under the name of earthly and temporal suffering: need, illness, misery, hardship, adversities, torments, mental sufferings, cares, grief." How encouraging indeed! To the true Christian, all of these will be "like a jest"⁶⁵ if Christ is with them. "Christianly understood, there is infinitely much more hope in death than there is in life."⁶⁶

Anti-Climacus famously preaches, "What is decisive is that with God everything is possible. This is eternally true and consequently true at every moment."⁶⁷ What a hopeful message! He continues passionately, "But this is the very formula for losing the understanding; to believe is indeed to lose the understanding in order to gain God."⁶⁸

In the following quotation, Anti-Climacus urges his readers as though he were a revivalist,⁶⁹

> And when the hourglass has run out, the hourglass of temporality, when the noise of secular life has grown silent and its restless or ineffectual activism has come to an end, when everything around you is still, as it is in eternity, then – whether you were man or woman, rich or poor, dependent or independent, fortunate or unfortunate, whether you ranked with royalty and wore a glittering crown or in humble obscurity bore the toil and heat of the day, whether your name will be remembered as long as the world stands and consequently as long as it stood or you are nameless and run nameless in the innumerable multitude,

---

64. *SKS* 11, 123/ *SUD*, 7, emphasis in original.
65. *SKS* 11, 124/ *SUD*, 8.
66. *SKS* 11, 124/ *SUD*, 7–8.
67. *SKS* 11, 153/ *SUD*, 38.
68. *SKS* 11, 153–154/ *SUD*, 38.
69. Aaron Edwards offers an appropriate evaluation, saying, "Kierkegaard is occasionally likened to a 'revivalist preacher.' Although he was critical of revivalists per se, at times Kierkegaard also shared their corrective approach to the self-protective malaise of the establishment." Edwards, "Kierkegaard's Imaginary Rural Parish," 241.

whether the magnificence encompassing you surpassed all human description or the most severe and ignominious human judgment befell you – eternity asks you and every individual in these millions and millions about only one thing: whether you have lived in despair or not, whether you have despaired in such a way that you did not realize that you were in despair, or in such a way that you covertly carried this sickness inside of you as your gnawing secret, as a fruit of sinful love under your heart, or in such a way that you, a terror to others, raged in despair. And if so, if you have lived in despair, then, regardless of whatever else you won or lost, everything is lost for you, eternity does not acknowledge you, it never knew you.[70]

As Sponheim aptly says, "Anti-Climacus sets 'earnestness' (*Alvor*) as the tone of his book."[71] As can be seen here, Anti-Climacus earnestly preaches to the reader.

In keeping with his revivalist approach, Anti-Climacus not only confronts the readers with their accountability before God but also offers the hope of forgiveness. Simon D. Podmore aptly captures Kierkegaard's true meaning in a well-known maxim of so-called Kierkegaardian theology: "There is an infinite, radical, and qualitative difference between humanity and God."[72] This difference is initially manifested in sin but eventually, and most importantly, in forgiveness. Anti-Climacus puts it this way: "As sinner, man is separated from God by the most chasmic qualitative abyss. In turn, of course, God is separated from man by the same chasmic qualitative abyss when he forgives sins."[73] One is overwhelmed by the idea that "there is not one single living human being who does not despair a little."[74] However, one is also overwhelmed by the idea that "it is the Deity's joy to forgive sins; just as God is almighty in creating out of nothing, so he is almighty in – uncreating something, for to forget, almightily to forget, is indeed to uncreate

---

70. *SKS* 11, 132–133/ *SUD*, 27–28.
71. Sponheim, *Existing before God*, 50.
72. Podmore, *Kierkegaard and the Self**, xi.
73. *SKS* 11, 233/ *SUD*, 122. In the latter statement, Anti-Climacus means that God's forgiveness, like his holiness, is qualitatively different. God forgives infinitely, in a manner that humans cannot comprehend.
74. *SKS* 11, 138/ *SUD*, 22.

something."⁷⁵ This qualitative difference between God and humanity is thus expressed in forgiveness, as Kierkegaard explains in the above journal entry. Anti-Climacus is ultimately a messenger of forgiveness. In another instance, too, Anti-Climacus speaks on behalf of Christ:

> But in this infinite love of his merciful grace he nevertheless makes one condition: he cannot do otherwise. Precisely this is Christ's grief, that "he cannot do otherwise"; he can debase himself, take a servant's form, suffer, die for men, invite all to come to him, offer up every day of his life, every hour of the day, and offer up his life – but he cannot remove the possibility of offense. What a rare act of love, what unfathomable grief of love.⁷⁶

Sounding almost like an evangelist, Anti-Climacus vividly describes Christ's heart. Accordingly, contrary to unsettling impressions associated with the title *The Sickness unto Death* and widespread images of this work, Anti-Climacus earnestly and passionately preaches to the reader.

5.2.8 Anyone Who Believes That There Is a Hell Is, *Eo Ipso*, a Missionary

According to Anti-Climacus, despair is a perpetual death – a continual dying without ceasing:

> This sickness of the self, perpetually to be dying, to die and yet not die, to die the death. For to die signifies that it is all over, but to die death means to experience dying, and if this is experienced for one single moment, one thereby experiences it forever. If a person were to die of despair as one dies of a sickness, then the eternal in him, the self, must be able to die in the same sense as the body dies of sickness. But this is impossible; the dying of despair continually converts itself into a living. The person in despair cannot die; . . . the self at the root of despair, whose worm does not die and whose fire is not quenched.⁷⁷

---

75. *SKS* 26, 179, NB32:89/ *JP*, II 1224.
76. *SKS* 11, 237/ *SUD*, 126.
77. *SKS* 11, 134/ *SUD*, 18, translation slightly modified.

The description above illustrates the perpetual state of death. Anti-Climacus quotes Jesus's description of hell in the last part of this quotation to signify perpetual death. Compare Anti-Climacus's words with those of Jesus in Mark's Gospel: "And if your eye causes you to stumble, tear it out; it is better for you to enter the kingdom of God with one eye than to have two eyes and to be thrown into hell, where their worm never dies, and the fire is never quenched" (Mark 9:47–48). It seems that the doctrine of hell functions as the inspirational background for Anti-Climacus's notion of despair or the sickness unto death. In this sense, as R. Zachary Manis says in his article,[78] *The Sickness unto Death* contributes to uncomfortable discussion on the doctrine of hell, even though this aspect is rarely referenced by Kierkegaard scholars.

I have three suggestions in this regard. First, *The Sickness unto Death* seems to call for a revival of the recently unpopular doctrine of hell. *National Geographic* reports, "Hell isn't as popular as it used to be" as a new generation of evangelical theologians tend to deny its existence. This article also adds, "A new generation of evangelical scholars are challenging the idea that sinners are doomed to eternal torment – but traditionalists are pushing back."[79] Here, "traditionalists" signifies those who support the view that hell does exist and that it is a place of "everlasting torment." In contrast, "annihilationists" hold that "after death, sinners simply cease to exist, while those who are saved enjoy eternal life under God's grace."[80] Although Anti-Climacus/Kierkegaard belongs among the "traditionalists," his approach and arguments are not traditional. While he occasionally uses the traditional language of sin or hell, he more often uses the modern language of despair or the sickness unto death. Therefore, Anti-Climacus's argument could appeal to "a new generation" and offer a unique contribution to this debate.

Second, *The Sickness unto Death* suggests that the doctrine of hell paradoxically demonstrates the dignity of human existence. Anti-Climacus says that "the eternal in him" does not allow him to die.[81] Anti-Climacus defines

---

78. Manis, "'Eternity Will Nail Him,'" 287–314.

79. Strauss, " Campaign to Eliminate Hell," http://news.nationalgeographic.com/2016/05/160513-theology-hell-history-christianity/.

80. Strauss, http://news.nationalgeographic.com/2016/05/160513-theology-hell-history-christianity/.

81. *SKS* 11, 134/ *SUD*, 18.

a human being as a synthesis of the eternal and the temporal,[82] with the eternal being seen as the essential component of a person's existence. Since human beings are created in God's image,[83] they possess within them the eternal,[84] which God alone can fulfil. Therefore, Anti-Climacus seems to suggest that human beings, who have the eternal within them, are "fearfully and wonderfully made" (Ps 139:14).[85] In other words, eternal torment arises from a person's despairing misuse of the eternal within them.[86]

Third, for Kierkegaard, love – the supreme Christian virtue – is not contradictory to the doctrine of hell; rather, it motivates him to be a missionary. Anti-Climacus believes that God is love,[87] but he seems to have no hesitation about declaring hell. How can he reconcile the God of love with the existence of hell? Although there is not space in this book to debate theodicy, I will pose one question: What if hell does exist?[88] The assumption that hell exists also implies that it would be cruel *not* to talk about hell. A discussion about hell, even though it is unpleasant, is motivated by love. God is love; therefore, he warns against choosing hell. Similarly, Kierkegaard or Anti-Climacus also speaks of hell because of love. In a journal entry, Kierkegaard says, "Anyone who believes that there is a hell, that others go to hell, is *eo ipso* a missionary, that is the least he can do."[89] For Kierkegaard, it is inconceivable that someone who believes in the doctrine of hell would not become a missionary. Accordingly, through "a somber and disheartening topic,"[90] *The Sickness unto Death* paradoxically demonstrates its missionary intention.

---

82. *SKS* 11, 129/ *SUD*, 13.

83. Genesis 1:26–27.

84. "God . . . has also put eternity into the heart of human beings." Ecclesiastes 3:11, taken from *SKS* 8, 126/ *UDVS*, 11.

85. *SKS* 11, 185/ *SUD*, 71.

86. *SKS* 11, 181/ *SUD*, 67.

87. *SKS* 11, 237–240/ *SUD*, 126–129.

88. "'Everlasting torment is intolerable from a moral point of view because it makes God into a bloodthirsty monster who maintains an everlasting Auschwitz for victims whom he does not even allow to die,' wrote the late Clark Pinnock, an influential evangelical theologian." Strauss, "Campaign to Eliminate Hell," ," http://news.nationalgeographic.com/2016/05/160513-theology-hell-history-christianity/.

89. *SKS* 27, 641, Papir 529/ *JP*, VI 6851 *n.d.*, 1854.

90. Ferreira, *Kierkegaard*, 148.

5.3 A Possible Application to the Japanese Context

The concept of despair resonates deeply within Japanese culture, and I have chosen Sensei (which means "Teacher" in Japanese) – a character in the Japanese novel こころ (Kokoro[91]), written by 夏目漱石 (Natsume Sōseki, 1867–1916)[92] – as a cultural touchstone for understanding Japanese despair.[93] In this representative Japanese novel, Sensei's guilt and despair seem to represent a typical Japanese mentality. A summary of Kokoro is given below.

The narrator – who is referred to as "I" – is interested in the character of Sensei, who has no specific occupation. Sensei has a beautiful wife, but he also has a history that includes his former best friend, K. Sensei admires K and considers K superior to him in every aspect. One day, K tells Sensei that he has fallen in love with a girl. Sensei is upset because he loves the same girl. Sensei makes the first move by officially asking the girl's mother for permission to marry her daughter. His wish is granted. Several days after learning about the promise of marriage between Sensei and the girl, K commits suicide. In K's will, he does not blame Sensei at all but thanks him and apologizes for troubling him. After this tragic event, Sensei undergoes a gradually personality change. During this time, the narrator – "I" – meets Sensei. In the end, Sensei decides to commit suicide.[94]

---

91. The Japanese word 心 [Kokoro] literally means *heart*, but "this word signifies also mind, in the emotional sense; spirit; courage; resolve; sentiment; affection; and inner meaning, – just as we say in English, 'the heart of things.'" Hearn, *Kokoro*, 3.

92. Natsume is arguably the most important Japanese novelist ever. "There may not be a more legendary Japanese writer than Natsume Soseki. Beloved by readers from Hokkaido to Okinawa, Soseki has been enjoyed with love and intensity for a hundred years and is arguably held in even higher regard than the Nobel Prize winners, Kawabata [Yasunari] and Oe [Kenzaburo]." McElhinney and Heath, "75 Best Japanese Authors of All Time," https://japanobjects.com/features/japanese-authors.

93. This section will discuss sections from Natsume's novels *Kokoro* and *Wayfarer*, as well as his concept of 則天去私 [Sokuten kyoshi]. which means "Following heaven and departing from the self." Odin, *Social Self*, 52. This follows the order of a discussion by the Japanese prominent theologian Kazō Kitamori in Kitamori, 日本人と聖書 [*Japanese and the Bible*], 176–185. However, while Kitamori emphasizes the aesthetic, my emphasis will be the concept of guilt consciousness.

94. Sensei's suicide is not explicitly described in *Kokoro*. The last chapter of *Kokoro* is Sensei's letter to the narrator, "I." The last part of the letter reads, "By the time this letter reaches you, I shall probably have left this world – I shall in all likelihood be dead." Sōseki Natsume, こころ [*Kokoro*] in 日本の文学13「夏目漱石（二）」[A Treasury of Japanese Literature, vol. 13, Natsume Sōseki, No.2] (『三四郎』[*Sanshirō*], 『それから』[*Sorekara*], 『こころ』[*Kokoro*]), Tokyo: Chūōkōron-sha 1965, 442, See also 526–527; Natsume, *Kokoro*, 96, See also 192.

When Sensei was young, he was betrayed by his uncle. As a result, he viewed his uncle as a bad man. Eventually, however, he began to see himself as even worse for betraying his best friend and causing him to kill himself. Sensei says, "I did not cease to blame myself for K's death. From the beginning, I was afraid of the suffering my own sense of guilt would bring me."[95] He says, "I felt very strongly the sinfulness of man."[96] Recognizing his own guilt, he feels he has no choice but to die. Given that the statistics show that "Japan ranked 14 in suicide rates . . . out of 183 countries,"[97] K and Sensei – who commit suicide in *Kokoro* – seem to reflect a typical Japanese mentality.

In Natsume's other work, *Wayfarer*, a similar kind of struggle is described and the following three options are given: "'To die, to go mad, or to enter religion – these are the only three courses left open for me,' your brother declared at length. At that moment he looked rather like a man riding into the abyss of despair."[98] In Sensei's case, he chooses the option of death. According to this quotation from *Wayfarer*, the other possible choices are to go mad or to enter religion. Although the Japanese are generally viewed as a non-religious people, according to Natsume, they sometimes seem to feel the necessity to enter religion.

Just before his death, Natsume coined the phrase 則天去私 (*Sokuten kyoshi*). Since no literature had included such a phrase before, this phrase is considered Natsume's own creation. Since Natsume died before fully elaborating on the meaning of this phrase, its interpretation varies. At the very least, the literal meaning of 則天去私 seems certain: "Following heaven and departing from the self."[99] Yoshio Nakano (1903–1985), who edited and wrote commentaries on selected works of Sōseki Natsume, speculates that the following quotation from Natsume's letter best elaborates on the meaning of 則天去私:

> There are as many things to dislike, to annoy and to resent as dust bunnies. It is not in human power to cleanse them. If it is

---

95. Natsume, こころ [*Kokoro*], 518–519; Natsume, *Kokoro*, 183.
96. Natsume, こころ [*Kokoro*], 522; Natsume, *Kokoro*, 188.
97. 'Suicide Rates in 2019,' StoryMaps, https://storymaps.arcgis.com/stories/5fea08b4095348cc82f8184735cea228 (accessed 29 Feb 2020).
98. Natsume, 漱石全集 第八巻 [*Soseki Complete Works, Vol. 8*], 412; Natsume, *Wayfarer*, 296.
99. Odin, *Social Self*, 52.

more humanly respectable to forgive them than to fight against them, then I would like us to cultivate that as much as possible.[100]

In *Kokoro*, Sensei's egoism causes an unavoidable conflict with his best friend, destroying their friendship and leading to both K and Sensei taking their own lives. Through the phrase 則天去私, Natsume seems to suggest the possibility of pursuing a religious path as a means of leaving egoism and seeking salvation.[101]

Inspired by Natsume's novels and his existential struggles, I offer three suggestions. First, I suggest deliberately re-evaluating the widespread Christian assumption that the Japanese "rely heavily on shame,"[102] as famously stated by Ruth Benedict (1887–1948). Benedict's *The Chrysanthemum and the Sword* "remains perhaps the most influential English-language book on contemporary Japanese society and culture."[103] Taking Benedict's distinction at face value would lead one to assume that the Japanese rely more heavily on shame than on guilt. This quasi-Benedictine view is considered *common sense* by many Japanese Christians who are concerned about evangelization in

---

100. Nakano, "Commentary," 548.

101. Natsume Soseki's attitude to Christianity is ambivalent. On the surface, he was sceptical and critical of Christianity and had no personal connection with it. However, there lies at the heart of his works a sense of unspoken guilt and a desire for redemption, and a kinship with Christianity. In this sense, his literature mirrors both Japan's superficially stubborn attitude towards Christianity and its deep-seated longing and yearning for God and salvation. See also Park, 夏目漱石とキリスト教 ["Natsume Sōseki and Christianity"], 177–187.

102. Benedict, *Chrysanthemum and the Sword*, 222. Just as the thought of John Calvin and Calvinism are not identical, we should distinguish between Benedict and those who merely take excerpts from her famous quotation out of its literary context, regardless of whether they support or oppose her. In reality, Benedict does not sharply distinguish between shame and guilt cultures. For instance, just before the above quotation, she says, "Japanese sometimes react as strongly as any Puritan to a private accumulation of guilt." Benedict, 222. Although Benedict does not draw a sharp distinction between the two, it is widely assumed that Japanese culture is a shame culture and, therefore, that the Japanese cannot understand guilt. Some emotionally reject Benedict's ideas, assuming that she is prejudiced against the Japanese. While it is true that there are some factual mistakes regarding Japanese culture in Benedict's *The Chrysanthemum and the Sword*, her discreet approach as an anthropologist, the wide range of sources she uses, and her keen intuitive discernment ensure that this work will remain as classic as it has done to this day. Therefore, even though Benedict had never visited Japan when she wrote this book, I believe that both non-Japanese and Japanese readers can learn about the Japanese by reading this work. Therefore, my aim is not to challenge Benedict's original insights but to dispel the misconceptions surrounding the so-called "Benedictine thought" that has taken on a life of its own.

103. Lie, "Ruth Benedict's Legacy of Shame," 249.

Japan.[104] However, Natsume's *Kokoro* seems to present a different view of the Japanese mentality. While Natsume's novel does not prove that the Japanese can understand the Christian concept of guilt or sin, it is significant that one of Japan's most renowned novelists seems deeply concerned with the concept of guilt and that such novels are extremely popular even today. In a comparative study of Kierkegaard and Natsume, 水田信 (Mizuta Makoto) says, "In this way, as Soseki thoroughly experienced resignation, sufferings, and guilt, his last stand is to pose a question of whether or not the existence of *sin itself* can be rooted out. Namely, he could do nothing but to raise a fundamental question about the self itself."[105] The issues of the self, despair, and sin seem to be crucial, not only for Kierkegaard but also for Natsume and the Japanese. In my own experience, I, too, have encountered many non-Christian Japanese who struggle with a guilty conscience. My Burmese wife offers counselling to non-Christian Japanese, and I interpret for her. Some of these counselees cannot forgive themselves for failing to be kind to their families, leading me to question the so-called Benedictine presupposition that the Japanese rely on a shame culture rather than a guilt culture. Instead, I would suggest that the Japanese, as people created in God's image (Gen 1:26–27), are somehow aware of their own sin and guilt. Missiologically speaking, it seems more coherent to base missionary efforts on biblical anthropology rather than on Benedict's secular anthropology.

Second, an unambiguous declaration of sin, based on the revelation of Scripture, is necessary. Anti-Climacus instructs us, saying, "Man has to learn what sin is by a revelation from God."[106] Even if Natsume's novels could mean that the Japanese *can* understand guilt or sin, no one can understand sin in the way that God desires without divine help. "For godly grief produces a repentance that leads to salvation and brings no regret, but worldly grief

---

104. See also Ōhashi, はじめてのキリスト教 [*Christianity for the First Time*], , 死にいたる病「菊と刀」 [The Sickness unto Death 'The Chrysanthemum and the Sword']; Matsuda, 日本の精神風土における福音の「文化内開花（インカルチュレーション）」事例研究—遠藤周作『海と毒薬』の場合— ["Inculturation of the Gospel as seen in the Japanese Spirit and Climate: A Case Study of Shusaku Endo's 'The Sea and Poison'"], 131–132; クリスチャン新聞福音版 [Christian Newspaper Gospel Version] Word of Life Press Ministries 2020. 3, No. 522, 1.

105. Mizuta, 夏目漱石とセーレン・キェルケゴール: 自己への問いと発見 ["Natsume Sōseki and Søren Kierkegaard: Their Quest for 'Self'"], 93; emphasis in original.

106. *SKS* 11, 207/ *SUD*, 95.

produces death" (2 Cor 7:10). The fact that Sensei commits suicide suggests that it could even be dangerous to recognize human guilt without God's revelation.[107] An unambiguous declaration of sin that is based upon revelation (Scripture) is the only safeguard against death or madness since "godly grief produces a repentance that leads to salvation."

Third, even though an unambiguous declaration of sin is necessary, a Kierkegaardian missionary can still engage in some form of indirect communication. In *The Sickness unto Death*, Anti-Climacus describes sin as despair. Since the Japanese may have some awareness of such despair, this work seems to have resonated with them and has been widely read in Japan. According to Hidehito Ōtani, by 1966, *The Sickness unto Death* had been translated into Japanese eight times, been published by over twelve publishers, and sold over seven hundred thousand copies.[108] Recently, in 2017, a new translation of *The Sickness unto Death* was published.[109] All this points to the profound impact of this work on the Japanese. Like Kierkegaard (Anti-Climacus), a Kierkegaardian missionary can present despair or sin in a way that is acceptable to the Japanese, preparing them to embrace the essence of Christianity.

5.4 Conclusion

Hal Lindsey says,

> [Kierkegaard's] writings are a denial of the basic tenets of the Christian faith. . . . He was the first man to launch a system of thought in which despair was the underlying current. . . . *The Sickness unto Death*, the very [title reflects] that mood of despondency.[110]

In this chapter, I have refuted these stereotypical images. The title *The Sickness unto Death* is a creative and updated paraphrase of sin within the sphere of Christian orthodoxy. In this sense, if *The Sickness unto Death* appears depressive, it is because the concept of sin is depressing. While it is true that

---

107. Johannes Climacus critiques B and says that one cannot overcome despair without divine assistance. See the second point in section 3.2.3.1 of this book.
108. Ōtani, *Study of Kierkegaard's Youth*,1: 4.
109. Kierkegaard, 死に至る病 [*The Sickness unto Death*].
110. Lindsey, *Satan Is Alive*, 87–88.

Kierkegaard struggled with melancholy or depression, it is important to note that despair is not technically the same as depression. Gordon Marino suggests a possible application of Kierkegaard's distinction between depression and despair:

> A depressed mother may at times seem to herself to feel nothing for her child. . . . depressed she may be, she can remain free of despair by remembering she is depressed but does not really lack the love she may cease to feel. Once again, she does not surrender her identity to her illness. A depressed one may be able to overcome his or her situation by learning the life of the spirit is something over and above our mental/emotional lives.[111]

As argued in section 5.2.3, the self is relational, and despair occurs because of the self's misrelation. Even if someone is depressed (which may not be their fault because depression can happen with or without a cause), if they, as a self, will to have a proper relationship with God and themselves, they will be free from despair. Once we grasp the distinction between despair and depression, we are able to see the path to hope, enabling us to recover from and overcome despair. Thus, despair signifies "spiritual disorders,"[112] which have been termed "sin" in the Christian tradition. If someone complains about the depressive mood in *The Sickness unto Death*, this suggests that they think that hamartiology[113] should be discussed more cheerfully or that we should avoid talking about sin.

In terms of application, the mission strategy of *The Sickness unto Death* helps us to distinguish between depression and despair. According to Simon D. Podmore, whereas the English term "despair" literally means "without-hope," the Danish *Fortvivlelse* (and the German *Verzweifeln*) literally mean "intensified doubt." However, Podmore calls our attention to the fact that in Kierkegaard's terminology, his despair (*Fortvivlelse*) encompasses both "the Anglo-French sense of despair as 'hopelessness'" and the German-Danish sense of despair as intensified doubt.[114] This etymology of despair corresponds

---

111. Marino, "Making the Darkness Visible," 107.
112. Marino, 107.
113. Hamartiology is a branch of Christian theology, which is the study of sin.
114. Podmore, *Kierkegaard and the Self*, 20–21. See also Gregor Malantschuk, Howard V. Hong, and Edna H. Hong. "Notes, Commentary, and Topical Bibliography." In *Søren*

with the real-life experience of person in despair. Although despair and depression are technically different, when the self experiences misrelation (that is, despair), they may *feel* depressed and be tempted to *surrender* to that depression. Once again, let us consider Anti-Climacus's definition of the despair-free state: "The formula for the state in which there is no despair at all: in relating itself to itself and *in willing* to be itself, the self rests transparently in the power that established it. This formula in turn, as has been frequently pointed out, is the definition of faith."[115] Let us consider the phrase "in willing." Even if someone is depressed, they are still able to *will* to have a proper relation to God and themselves. By doing so despite being depressed, they are not despairing. This distinction helps to clarify the Christian message.

During the COVID-19 pandemic, in Japan, as in other nations, people were panicking – buying masks and toilet paper, and fighting over matters such as coughing etiquette. Why? Because they viewed the coronavirus as a "sickness unto death" and were afraid. However, according to Anti-Climacus, a sickness that may cause a physical death is not the most frightening. Rather, the sickness that can result in a perpetual death – death without end – is the most frightening. Disproportionate fear of physical sickness makes us lose sight of the greatest danger, which is sin, and may cause us not to fear wrongful attitudes and actions such as greed or hurting others. *The Sickness unto Death* reminds us to consider what we should truly fear. According to Anti-Climacus, by understanding what is truly scary, one can be courageous:

> Only the Christian knows what is meant by the sickness unto death. As a Christian, he gained a courage that the natural man does not know, and he gained this courage by learning to fear something even more horrifying. This is the way a person always gains courage; when he fears a greater danger, he always has the courage to face a lesser one; when he is exceedingly afraid of one danger, it is as if the others did not exist at all.[116]

Such courage is most needed in Japan now.

Kierkegaard's Journals and Papers, Volume 2: F–K, edited and translated by Howard V. Hong and Edna H. Hong, assisted by Gregor Malantschuk, Bloomington: Indiana University Press, 1970, 557; Bernier, *Task of Hope*, 64–65.

115. *SKS* 11, 242/ *SUD*, 131, emphasis mine. See also *SKS* 11, 130/ *SUD*, 14.
116. *SKS* 11, 125/ *SUD*, 8–9.

However, Anti-Climacus's Christian proclamation remains incomplete if one considers only *The Sickness unto Death*. It is important to recall that the original title of the work – later divided by Anti-Climacus into two works – was *The Radical Cure or the Forgiveness of Sins and the Atonement*.[117] In light of this original title, *The Sickness unto Death* focuses primarily on the concept of sin. The remaining elements – *The Radical Cure, the Forgiveness,* and *the Atonement* are addressed in *Practice in Christianity*. The next chapter discusses Anti-Climacus's *Practice in Christianity*, which explores these concepts in greater detail.

---

117. *JP*, VI 6219 N.B./ *Pap.* IX A 176 20 July 1848.

CHAPTER 6

Practice in Christianity as Introducing Christianity into Christendom

> *The Sickness unto Death* and *Practice in Christianity* are most fruitfully read as a pair, a poem, a diptych, an either/or: as the works of Anti-Climacus.[1]
>
> – David D. Possen, "The Works of Anti-Climacus"

The subject of this chapter is Kierkegaard's magnum opus – *Indøvelse i Christendom* (*Practice in Christianity*). Whereas most of Kierkegaard's lower pseudonyms represent the perspective of non-Christians, Anti-Climacus – who is the pseudonymous author of both *The Sickness unto Death* and *Practice in Christianity* – is an extraordinary Christian.[2] Therefore, Anti-Climacus's two works represent an ideal of Christianity in the schema of Kierkegaard's authorship. These two works constitute a true ultimatum[3] – an either/or from the perspective of an ideal form of Christianity. This either/or is a choice between the perpetual death caused by despair or sin (*The Sickness unto Death*) and salvation through faith in and imitation of Jesus Christ in his true form (*Practice in Christianity*). I have already argued for the necessity of a sequential reading of *The Sickness unto Death* and *Practice in Christianity*

---

1. Possen, "Works of Anti-Climacus," 209.
2. *SKS* 22, 128, NB11:204/ *JP*, VII, 6431 *n.d.*, 1849.
3. "[*Practice in Christianity*] was an ultimatum." Kirmmse, *Golden Age Denmark*, 379.

elsewhere in this book (see sections 2.4 and 5.2.2). How has the discussion of such a reading been advanced in Kierkegaard scholarship?

Gregor Malantschuk's *Kierkegaard's Thought* covers Kierkegaard's major works almost chronologically and keenly discerns their dialectical structure. Malantschuk was a pioneer, identifying a "sharpened either/or" in these two works of Anti-Climacus.[4]

To my knowledge, Hidehito Ōtani's and Harunori Izumi's キルケゴール 死に至る病 (*Kierkegaard: The Sickness unto Death*) is the only work entirely devoted to analyzing the dialectical structure of Anti-Climacus's two works. Ōtani and Izumi's work can be viewed as an extended and enhanced version of Malantschuk's discussion on Anti-Climacus's two works in *Kierkegaard's Thought*. Ōtani and Izumi see Anti-Climacus's two works as sharply confronting, representing perpetual perdition (*The Sickness unto Death*) and eternal salvation (*Practice in Christianity*).[5]

Building on and modifying Malantschuk's argument, David D. Possen's "The Works of Anti-Climacus" suggests the interpretative possibility that these two works by Anti-Climacus can be read most fruitfully as a single "either/or" unit. According to Possen, Anti-Climacus, on behalf of God, attempts to poetically state a supreme ideal that mere humans are unable to articulate.[6]

According to Stephen N. Dunning's *Kierkegaard's Dialectic of Inwardness*, Anti-Climacus's two works constitute three stages of despair: the first despair is despair about implicit consciousness; the second is the despair of alienation; and the third despair is self-conscious despair before God. According to Dunning, the first and second forms of despair, along with the first half of the third despair, belong to *The Sickness unto Death*, while the latter half of the third despair belongs to *Practice in Christianity*. One might wonder why there is still despair in *Practice in Christianity*. Dunning calls this the *Aufhebung* (sublation) of sin-consciousness. In other words, even once a person saved, their sin-consciousness remains, leading them to rely on grace. Nevertheless, this self is renewed, and such renewal can be viewed as the cure for despair.[7]

---

4. Malantschuk, *Kierkegaard's Thought*, 334–361.

5. Ōtani and Izumi, キルケゴール 死に至る病 [*Kierkegaard: The Sickness unto Death*]; Ōtani, *Kierkegaard's Authorship*, Part 2, 751–754; 1495–1543.

6. Possen, "Works of Anti-Climacus," 187–209.

7. Dunning, *Dialectic of Inwardness*, 214–241.

In summary, by deconstructing the philosophy-theology dichotomy, the studies of Possen and Dunning contribute to uncovering the deep structural connection between *The Sickness unto Death* (usually perceived as a philosophical work) and *Practice in Christianity* (usually perceived as a theological work). Since I do not utilize the philosophical and theological methods, enhancing their studies is outside the scope of this study. Instead, following the methods of Malantschuk and H. Ōtani – who are the pioneers of the author-oriented methods that this work employs – this chapter will explore these two works of Anti-Climacus with special reference to Kierkegaard as a missionary. I contend that Kierkegaard as a missionary is the best perspective for interpreting the uncompromised declaration of sin in *The Sickness unto Death* and a proclamation of grace and discipleship in *Practice in Christianity*. These two works constitute an ultimatum of a "sharpened either/or."

The outline of this chapter is as follows: The first section provides a historical introduction to *Practice in Christianity* (with the literary context being addressed in appendix 7, which is a summary of the work *Practice in Christianity*); the second section interprets *Practice in Christianity* from the perspective of Kierkegaard as a missionary; the third section applies some of the findings to the Japanese context, and; the fourth section offers some concluding remarks.

6.1 Historical Introduction

Chronologically, *Three Discourses at the Communion on Fridays*, which emphasizes Christ's atonement, was published between the two works of Anti-Climacus.[8] This work was a necessary "resting point"[9] in terms of Kierkegaard's existence rather than in relation to the dialectical structure of *The Sickness unto Death*. Therefore, he published *Three Discourses at the Communion on Fridays* not as a pseudonymous work but as a signed one.

---

8. "After publishing *The Sickness unto Death* and before publishing *Practice in Christianity*, [Kierkegaard] established a 'fulcrum,' in which grace is emphasized." "'The position of *Discourses at the Communion on Fridays* is once and for all designated as the fulcrum of the authorship.'" Malantschuk, *Kierkegaard's Thought*, 355; the quotation slightly modified, the quotation within the quotation is originally from *SKS* 22, 322, NB13:79/ *JP*, VI 6519.

9. Malantschuk, *Kierkegaard's Thought*, 356.

The first edition of *Practice in Christianity*, said to have been written by Anti-Climacus and edited by Kierkegaard, was published on 27 September 1850 – over a year after the publication of *The Sickness unto Death*. The fact that Anti-Climacus is the author of both works and Kierkegaard is the editor of both works shows that these two works should be read sequentially, as already pointed out in sections 2.4 and 5.2.2. Since Anti-Climacus is said to be an extraordinary Christian, this work is considered one of Kierkegaard's higher-pseudonymous works, conveying a rigorous Christian message and belonging to the sphere of transcendent religiousness. In *Journals and Notebooks*, Kierkegaard offers this evaluation of *Practice in Christianity*: "Without a doubt it is the most perfect and truest thing I have written."[10] The publication of *Practice in Christianity* was necessary for Kierkegaard to introduce Christianity into Christendom by declaring, "Whoever does not carry the cross and follow [Jesus] cannot be [his] disciple" (Luke 14:27).

6.2 A Study of *Practice in Christianity* with Specific Regard to Kierkegaard the Missionary

David R. Law's *Kierkegaard's Kenotic Christology*, published in 2013, is a long-awaited study. This work focuses on Kierkegaard's "two most overtly Christological works"[11] – *Philosophical Fragment* and *Practice in Christianity*. In his work, Law refers to Donald Dawe's assessment, with which I also agree: "At the core of [Kierkegaard's] message is a bold assertion of the self-emptying of the Christ who meets men as a man. God in the servant form is at the center of Kierkegaard's thought."[12] In this sense, there is some legitimacy in calling Kierkegaard a kenotic theologian. However, the following quotation from Kierkegaard's journal serves as a warning against classifying him as merely an academic theologian:[13]

> Just when the Church really settled down and got it effectually made into dogma that outside the Church there is no

---

10. *SKS* 22, 265, NB12: 196.a/ *JP*, VI 6501 *n.d.*, 1848.

11. Law, *Kierkegaard's Kenotic Christology*, 1.

12. Law, 1.

13. I consent to identifying Kierkegaard as a theologian in the sense conveyed by the following quotation: "There is an old proverb: *oratio, tentatio, meditatiofaciunt theologum* [prayer, trial, meditation make a theologian]." *SKS* 7, 320/ *CUP I*, 350.

salvation – strangely enough, just then there was a settling down. How cruel, then – the more strictly it is taken that there is no salvation outside the Church – not to become a missionary.[14]

According to this journal entry, theological discussion alone is insufficient. Because, for Kierkegaard, "outside the Church there is no salvation," everything culminates in practice; most importantly, true Christian practice will inevitably lead one "to become a missionary." Thus, although it might be justifiable to call Kierkegaard a theologian of kenotic Christology, practice lies closer to his heart than theology – not just any practice, but missionary practice. What term can capture both Kierkegaard's central thought of the self-emptying Christ and his enthusiasm for missionary tasks? I submit that, as Ádám Szabados proposes, "incarnational missionary" is the term that best conveys these two undoubtedly Kierkegaardian features: an incarnated Christ as the content of the message and the method of the mission.

6.2.1 An Intended Reader

In the "Editor's Preface," Kierkegaard writes, "I understand what is said [in *Practice in Christianity*] as spoken to me alone."[15] In other words, Kierkegaard identifies himself not just as an editor but also as an individual reader of *Practice in Christianity*, rather than its author. Therefore, the first intended reader of *Practice in Christianity* is Kierkegaard himself.

Are there other intended readers of this work? The very fact that Kierkegaard published *Practice in Christianity* shows that there are intended readers other than himself. I would argue that the intended readers of *Practice in Christianity* are "every single individual" or "all the various kinds [of people]."[16] In "The Invitation" of "No. I of *Practice in Christianity*," Anti-Climacus movingly elaborates on Matthew 11:28: "Come here, all you who labor and are burdened, and I will give you rest."[17] Like Billy Graham[18] preaching at a revival meeting, Anti-Climacus invites every single individual

---

14. *SKS* 25, 223, NB28:13/ *JP*, III 2729 *n.d.*, 1853.
15. *SKS* 12, 15/ *PC*, 7.
16. *SKS* 12, 252/ *PC*, 262.
17. This is a direct quotation from *Practice in Christianity*, not wording of any Bible translation.
18. "Billy Graham [was] a famous Christian evangelist. As an evangelist, he was committed to spreading the words of Jesus Christ by preaching the Gospel. He emphasized salvation by

to come to Christ. According to Anti-Climacus, Jesus's concern is not that too many people might come to him but that some may not hear his invitation. Since Christ, the God-man, is love, he does not invite only specific people but invites *all*. Like a compassionate preacher, Anti-Climacus calls out to every single individual.[19] Knowing Jesus's heart, Anti-Climacus describes the various types of individuals who are invited: "[You] whom faithlessness deceived, whom human sympathy then made a target for mockery (for human sympathy is rarely long in coming); all you who have been treated unfairly, wronged, insulted, and mistreated."[20] Anti-Climacus is sympathetic to those who suffer and feel that "this is worse than death,"[21] and he calls out, "Come here, here is rest, and here is life!"[22] For those who might still hesitate, Anti-Climacus assures them that Jesus's invitation has no conditions.[23] For Anti-Climacus, the doctrine of the incarnation is not just a creed; it is the action of God's love.[24] Anti-Climacus hopes that every single reader would be convinced that they are invited by the living Christ.

"No. III" of *Practice in Christianity* contains seven discourses or sermons based on John 12:32: "From on high he will draw all to himself."[25] Anti-Climacus concludes *Practice in Christianity* by expressing a wish – the wish that he could pray for every single individual to be drawn wholly to Christ: "So we pray for all. Yet no one is able to name every single individual; indeed, who is able to name all the various kinds!"[26] One can see that Anti-Climacus truly wishes that he could pray for everyone. In summary, the intended reader of *Practice in Christianity* is Kierkegaard himself and "every single individual" or "'all the various kinds [of people].'"[27]

---

faith through personal conversion. Graham's goal was to bring people to Jesus Christ." Donovan, *Billy Graham*, 7

    19. *SKS* 12, 27/ *PC*, 16.
    20. *SKS* 12, 28/ *PC*, 17.
    21. *SKS* 11, 124/ *SUD*, 8.
    22. *SKS* 12, 29/ *PC*, 18.
    23. *SKS* 12, 30/ *PC*, 19.
    24. *SKS* 12, 31/ *PC*, 20.
    25. This is a direct quotation from *Practice in Christianity*, not wording of any Bible translation.
    26. *SKS* 12, 252/ *PC*, 262.
    27. *SKS* 12, 252/ *PC*, 262.

6.2.2 Faith

The "Invocation" in "No. I" beautifully delineates the content of *Practice in Christianity* as follows:

> No, his presence here on earth never becomes a thing of the past . . . if faith is at all to be found upon the earth. . . . [As] long as there is a believer, this person, in order to have become that, must have been and as a believer must be just as contemporary with Christ's presence as his contemporaries were. This contemporaneity is the condition of faith, and, more sharply defined, it is faith.[28]

According to Anti-Climacus, faith is able to transcend time and space and overcome all the challenges of the so-called quest for the historical Jesus. Faith consists in seeing Christ in his true form in all matters. In this sense, *Practice in Christianity* is all about faith. Therefore, this subsection is devoted to scrutinizing Anti-Climacus's concept of faith. To clarify the definition of faith, I will also refer to Kierkegaard's other works and secondary literature as necessary.

6.2.2.1 Faith Is the Epistemological Requirement to Know Christ

For Anti-Climacus, faith is the only *lens* that allows one to see Christ.[29] Anti-Climacus says that Christ is "the object of faith, exists only for faith." He adds, "But all the historical investigation is the communication of *knowledge*; consequently one can come to know nothing about Christ from history."[30] Here, we must be careful. We need to understand Anti-Climacus's definition of "history." Anti-Climacus says, "Here and throughout the book, 'history' is to be understood as profane history, world history, history directly understood in contradistinction to sacred history."[31] When Anti-Climacus rejects *history*, he is rejecting secular historical methods. In contrast, he simply accepts the salvation history in the Bible as true. Although Anti-Climacus rejects

---

28. *SKS* 12, 17/ *PC*, 9.

29. According to Kierkegaard, faith allows one to see the true nature of Christ that even Satan cannot see: "It honors Christ to believe that he succeeded in being neither more nor less than a despised man, an incognito which not ever Satan himself saw through, an incognito which was open only to faith." *SKS* 20, 427, NB5:147/ *JP*, II 1753 *n.d.*, 1848.

30. *SKS* 12, 40/ *PC*, 25, emphasis in original.

31. *SKS* 12, 40, asterisk/ *PC*, 25, asterisk.

secular history or knowledge, his faith is based on the salvation history and knowledge contained in Scripture.

Second, for Anti-Climacus, it is a category mistake to attempt to prove Jesus Christ as God through human-historical investigation. This is because God is qualitatively different from humanity.[32] In other words, if historical investigation – which is merely a human faculty –successfully proved that someone was a god, this would not be the transcendent God but, rather, an immanent god. Since God surpasses all humanly knowable qualities, we could never prove that a human being was God by citing observable qualities. In this sense, the Supreme Being is unknowable. Therefore, when a human being stands before God – who is qualitatively different – the only way to know him is through faith, which can bridge "an infinite chasmic difference between God and man."[33] This is why Anti-Climacus insists that faith is the epistemological requirement to know Christ, the God-man.

6.2.2.2 Faith as the Triune God's Gift, Received through an Act of the Will

From where does faith come? In *Practice in Christianity*, the origin of faith is unclear. Therefore, we turn to *Philosophical Fragment* by Johannes Climacus, another of Kierkegaard's pseudonyms.[34] In *Passionate Reason*, which elucidates the relationship between faith and reason in *Philosophical Fragment*, C. Stephen Evans states, "[Faith] is not an act of will; it is a gift of the god.[35] However, an act of will is necessary if the gift is to be received."[36] Kierkegaard and his pseudonyms view faith as a gift from Christ. However, this does not mean that faith is automatically received. Therefore, "an act of will is necessary

---

32. *SKS* 12, 40–45/ *PC*, 26–31.

33. *SKS* 12, 75/ *PC*, 63.

34. Although Johannes Climacus and Anti-Climacus hold differing views in some areas, both make efforts to define the concept of biblical faith. Therefore, I consider Climacus's explanation of the nature of faith helpful, and I believe that I am justified in using his explanation as the basis on which to understand Anti-Climacus's concept of faith.

35. The reason "god" with a lower-case "g" is used is because *Philosophical Fragment* is written as a thought-project (a hypothetical and philosophical pursuit of how one actively comes to learn the truth) by the non-Christian pseudonym Johannes Climacus. Although Climacus convincingly argues that only "God as teacher and savior" can save a person, he never mentions *Christ* in this work.

36. Evans, *Passionate Reason*, 140.

if the gift is to be received."³⁷ An act of will allows one to receive the gift of faith from Christ. This cycle is repeated throughout one's Christian life. One is always challenged to believe or to be offended. By believing or *willing* to believe, faith is given or increased by Christ. No one can claim that their faith is strong enough. In *Practice in Christianity*, Anti-Climacus says, "It does not follow that you dare to think that he has already drawn you *wholly* to himself. Lord, increase my faith."³⁸ Whether a believer or not, there is always room to grow in faith.

While there are consistent themes in Kierkegaard's exploration of faith, as we have seen, *Concluding Unscientific Postscript* represents "the turning point in the whole authorship."³⁹ In this work, death to oneself and the world is declared to be the condition necessary to become a Christian. This condition is also assumed in Kierkegaard's overtly religious works – including the two works by Anti-Climacus – which were published after *Concluding Unscientific Postscript*. To understand the concept of faith in *Practice in Christianity*, let us consider these words from *For Self-Examination*, which was published two years after *Practice in Christianity*: "And when you died or died to yourself, to the world, then you also died to all immediacy in yourself, also to your understanding . . . then comes the life-giving Spirit and brings faith."⁴⁰

In summary, the nature of faith is twofold. Faith has a divine origin since it is a gift from the Triune God, but it also demands human responsibility since it is given or increased through the act of one's will – especially in the strictly Christian sense through the act of dying to oneself and to the world.

6.2.2.3 Not Faith or Doubt, But Faith or Offence

To Christianly delineate faith, Anti-Climacus scrutinizes the concept of offence in *Practice in Christianity* in greater detail than in any of Kierkegaard's other works.⁴¹ In "The Exposition" of "No. II," Anti-Climacus, as a skilful exegete, elaborates on numerous biblical passages about *offence* – passages that most readers may not have previously paid attention to. By shedding light

---

37. Evans, 140.
38. *SKS* 12, 159/ *PC*, 156.
39. *SKS* 16, 36/ *PV*, 55.
40. *SKS* 13, 103/ *FSE* / *JFY*, 82

41. For more on the concept of offence in Kierkegaard's corpus, see Turchin, "Offense," 7–13.

on the biblical concept of offence, Anti-Climacus attempts to refine the biblical concept of faith: "Just as the concept 'faith' is an altogether distinctively Christian term, so in turn is 'offense' an altogether distinctively Christian term relating to faith."[42]

According to Anti-Climacus, "one turns either to offense or to faith,"[43] and he argues that the opposite of *faith* is not *doubt*, but *offence*.[44] Since faith is given upon one's act of will, Anti-Climacus equips the reader to have faith by avoiding any discussion of faith in the sphere of the intellect – that is, the either/or of faith and doubt. Instead, throughout Anti-Climacus's two works, the battlefield is the realm of the will. While *The Sickness unto Death* deals primarily with the dialectic of faith and despair, *Practice in Christianity* focuses mainly on the dialectic of faith and offence, which is an intensive form of sin or despair.

6.2.2.4 Faith as an Unfinished Task That Rests on Grace

As a Lutheran, Kierkegaard believed in the doctrine of "justification by grace through faith"[45] Since grace is available to all, at the very beginning of *Practice in Christianity*, he invites every single individual. However, Kierkegaard's main concern was the misuse of grace.[46] He believed that one should not merely resort to grace but should *effectively* utilize the freedom that becomes available through salvation by grace. What is an *effective* use of grace? Kierkegaardianly speaking, one can effectively use grace by imitating the abased Christ. Luther himself seems to urge that we do not misuse the freedom that becomes available through Christ's grace. Luther says,

> A Christian is a perfectly free lord of all, subject to none.
> A Christian is a perfectly dutiful servant of all, subject to all.
>
> These two theses seem to contradict each other. If, however, they should be found to fit together they would serve our purpose beautifully. . . . So Christ, although he was Lord of all, was "born of woman, born under the law" [Gal 4:4], and therefore was at

---

42. *SKS* 12, 91/ *PC*, 81.
43. *SKS* 12, 91/ *PC*, 81.
44. *SKS* 12, 91, asterisk/ *PC*, 81, asterisk.
45. Johnson, "The Lutheran Tradition," 668.
46. See also *SKS* 8, 84/ *TA*, 88.

the same time a free man and a servant, "in the form of God" and "of a servant" [Phil 2:6–7].[47]

As can be seen, Kierkegaard's emphasis on imitating Jesus through salvation by grace is faithful to his Lutheran spiritual heritage.

Therefore, faith is not a once-and-for-all task that is completed once one believes in Jesus the Redeemer. Rather, faith is an unfinished task. One should continually strive to imitate Christ. During this striving, one remains continually conscious of how far they are from truly imitating Christ the prototype. Therefore, one must, again and again, resort to grace and more deeply and truly appreciate grace. Merald Westphal explains this well: "Faith is an always unfinished task. But the point is not to reduce faith to striving; it is rather to locate that striving in the place of rest, namely grace."[48] Although one's act of will is required, faith is a gift. The lifelong requirement of faith does not mean that humanity is the origin of faith. Rather, one will learn more and more deeply that faith's origin is divine. The apostle Paul asks the Galatian Christians, "After beginning by means of the Spirit, are you now trying to finish by means of the flesh?" (Gal 3:3 NIV) From beginning to end, faith is a gift from the Triune God. Although faith is not a once-and-for-all completed task but a lifelong striving, it does not forget its origin – namely, God's grace.

6.2.2.5 Faith as Contemporaneity

Anti-Climacus says, "This contemporaneity is the condition of faith, and, more sharply defined, it is faith."[49] In his thought, *contemporaneity* and *faith* are almost synonymous. In this subsection, I will address the overlap between contemporaneity and faith. First, the divinity of Christ makes it possible for one to be contemporary with him and to have faith in him. David J. Gouwens's brilliant summary, which includes a vital journal entry by Kierkegaard, helps us to connect *faith* and *contemporaneity*:

> Christ as God incarnate is present to the believer in faith. This presence or communion follows from the divinity, in contrast to the presence of a "merely historical person." "Believe that

---

47. Luther, "Martin Luther's Treatise on Christian Liberty [The Freedom of a Christian]," 53.

48. Westphal, *Kierkegaard's Concept of Faith*, 254.

49. *SKS* 12, 17/ *PC*, 9.

> Christ is God – then call upon him, pray to him, and the rest comes by itself. When the fact that he is present [*er til*] is more intimately and inwardly certain than all historical information – then you will come out all right with the details of His historical existence ... [Christ is] an eternally present one [*en evig Nærværende*] for he is true God."[50]

For anyone, at any age, encountering Christ is possible because he is the omnipresent God. As the second person of the eternal Triune God, Christ is present and contemporary with every single individual at all times.

Second, through prayer, one can have an intimate and inward relationship with Christ. As Kierkegaard's words – quoted by Gouwens – in the above paragraph show, the divinity of Christ makes it possible to access him through prayer: "Call upon him, pray to him, and the rest comes by itself." Kierkegaard says that for an intimate relationship with Christ, prayer is far more powerful than historical investigation.

Third, the Bible, sensitivity, and imagination play vital roles in faith and contemporaneity. Joakim Garff aptly expresses what *Practice in Christianity* attempts: "In any event, the point is that the text makes its times contemporary with the god's times. And it makes the god contemporary with the text's times. [...] [Anti-Climacus] goes further, situating his idiot God somewhere in Copenhagen in the year 1848."[51] To help his reader to become contemporary with Christ, Anti-Climacus situates us with Jesus of Nazareth in first-century Palestine and situates Jesus in Copenhagen in 1848. Without a knowledge of Scripture, one cannot understand the biblical world or know Christ. Without sensitivity, one cannot feel the atmosphere of either the biblical world or their own times. Without imagination, one cannot freely situate themselves in the biblical world or situate Christ in their daily life. In this sense, contemporaneity and faith become possible through Scripture, sensitivity, and the fully engaged imagination.

Fourth, the communion service plays an indispensable role in helping a believer to become contemporary with Christ. In his article "Contemporaneity and Communion: Kierkegaard on the Personal Presence of Christ," Joshua

---

50. Gouwens, *Kierkegaard as Religious Thinker*, 134; the journal entry shown within quotation marks is from *SKS* 20, 328, NB4:81/ *JP*, I 318 *n.d.*, 1848.

51. Garff, *Søren Kierkegaard: A Biography*, 658.

Cockayne argues that for Kierkegaard/Anti-Climacus, the communion service enables one to have intimate fellowship with, or an inter-subjective relation to, Christ.[52] Indeed, one can predict that communion service will take place after the first exposition of "No. III" in *Practice in Christianity*. In this exposition, Anti-Climacus expects that the Christ who exists amid the communion service will draw all to himself.[53]

In summary, the divinity of Christ, prayer, Scripture, sensitivity, the fully engaged imagination, and the communion service enable one to be contemporary with, and have faith in, Christ. Perhaps one might say that these elements foster intimate fellowship with Christ.

6.2.2.6 Contemporaneity

Although Anti-Climacus somehow equates faith with contemporaneity, the fact that distinct terms are used indicates that each term signifies a specific meaning. While the previous sub-subsection focuses on the close connection between faith and contemporaneity, this sub-subsection is devoted to describing the specific meanings of the term "contemporaneity." First, contemporaneity does *not* mean that one is *born* – in the sense of natural human birth – as Christ's actual contemporary. Contemporaneity is not *a natural-born condition* but, rather, *one's conscious attitude towards Christ*; it is the result of being born again through believing in Jesus Christ.[54]

Second, contemporaneity does *not* mean clinging to an image of a nice-looking Christ:

> "Come here, come here, all, all you who labor and are burdened, come here, see, he is inviting you, he is opening his arms!" When an elegant man dressed in silk says this in such a pleasant, melodious voice that it gives a lovely echo in the beautiful vaulted ceiling, a silken man who spreads honor and esteem upon listening to him; when a king in purple and velvet says this against

---

52. Cockayne, "Contemporaneity and Communion," 41–62.
53. *SKS* 12, 160/ *PC*, 156.
54. Anti-Climacus strongly disapproves of the notion that if a person had been born in the same generation as Jesus Christ, they would certainly have recognized him: "The majority of people living in Christendom today no doubt live in the illusion that if they had been contemporary with Christ they would have recognized him immediately despite his unrecognizability." *SKS* 12, 132–133/ *PC*, 128.

the background of a Christmas tree hung with the glorious gifts he is about to distribute.[55]

For Anti-Climacus, having an image of Christ like the one described above is not being contemporary with Christ. Such a "fancy" Christ is neither the abased Christ who was born in a stable nor the glorified Christ who will return riding on a white horse at his second coming. The one who clings to this image of a fancy Christ has never truly known Christ.

Third, contemporaneity means becoming like Christ in his lowliness. To become a Christian is to "become so contemporary with him in his abasement."[56] Anti-Climacus imagines that one thousand eight hundred years ago, the resemblances to their master, Jesus, made it easy for people to recognize his disciples as Χριστιανός (Christian, a follower of Christ).[57] Contemporaneity is to suffer with Christ. It moves one to *want* to suffer with him. The opportunity to suffer like Christ may be given to any disciple, at any time. However, even if such an opportunity is not given, the heart of the matter is the *willingness* to suffer like Christ.[58] Therefore, contemporaneity means imitating the abased Christ through voluntary suffering that resembles his own.

Fourth, contemporaneity is a risky business. To be contemporary with Christ is to be scorned by the *wise* of this world and risk losing everything for the sake of Christ.[59]

Fifth, contemporaneity is the only condition for truly knowing Christ and being a Christian. "In relation to the absolute, there is only one time, the present; for the person who is not contemporary with the absolute, it does not exist at all."[60] The God-man is absolute, and one can encounter him only in the present – namely, through contemporaneity. By urging readers to personally encounter Christ *now*, Anti-Climacus attempts to help them become contemporary with Christ.[61]

---

55. *SKS* 12, 51/ *PC*, 38.
56. *SKS* 12, 50/ *PC*, 37.
57. *SKS* 12, 115/ *PC*, 107.
58. *SKS* 12, 175/ *PC*, 172.
59. *SKS* 12, 64/ *PC*, 52.
60. *SKS* 12, 75/ *PC*, 63.
61. *SKS* 12, 76–77/ *PC*, 64–65.

In summary, no one is born to contemporaneity. Instead, one becomes a contemporary of Christ through the act of will, by believing in him. Contemporaneity does not allow one to cling to a fancy Christ but requires imitating Christ's lowliness and may also invite persecution or mockery. Contemporaneity is the only way to truly know Christ and, therefore, the only way to be a Christian.[62]

6.2.3 A Presentation of Christ in His True Form

In the previous subsection, I stated that in *Practice in Christianity*, Anti-Climacus passionately urges the reader to have faith. But just any faith will not do. Throughout *Practice in Christianity*, he also labours to demonstrate the authentic Christ, who represents the only proper object of that faith. While reading *Practice in Christianity*, the reader may naturally recall Christological passages such as Matthew 11:28–30, Philippians 1:29 and 2:6–11, 1 Peter 2:19–25, and Hebrews 12:1b–2. While *Practice in Christianity* is all about faith (as demonstrated in section 6.2.2), this work is all about Christ. Therefore, I devote this subsection to describing the Jesus Christ who is presented in *Practice in Christianity*. To more faithfully sketch a portrait of Anti-Climacus's Christ, I will also refer to other works from Kierkegaard's corpus and secondary literature where necessary.

---

62. Joshua Cockayne makes a significant contribution to the concept of Kierkegaard's contemporaneity: "Søren Kierkegaard's claim that religious faith requires being contemporary with Christ is one of the most important, yet difficult to interpret claims in his entire authorship." Cockayne, "Contemporaneity and Communion," 1. In his article "Contemporaneity and Communion," Cockayne refutes Stephen Evans's model of "a kind of mystical experience" (Cockayne, 7) and Patrick Stokes's model of "a kind of imaginative mode of cognition," (Cockayne, 2) and he presents his own model – "Christ's true presence at the Eucharist" (Cockayne, 10). What is the standpoint of this study? As discussed in section 6.2.2.6, we affirm all three models. Kierkegaard's presupposition of the omnipotence of the God-man naturally affirms a mystical experience. See also *SKS* 20, 328, NB4:81/ *JP*, I 318 n.d., 1848; *SKS* 11, 153/ *SUD*, 38. A fully-engaged imagination always plays a pivotal role in Kierkegaard's experience of Christ. See also section 6.2.2.6 of this book; Gouwens, *Dialectic of the Imagination*. Anti-Climacus preaches that Christ, in the midst of the communion, draws all to himself (the first discourse of 'III' in *Practice in Christianity*). Therefore, we do not need to choose between these three models because "he uses the most varied things as a way of drawing to himself." *SKS* 12, 159/ *PC*, 155), a point that Cockayne also affirms. Cockayne, "Contemporaneity and Communion," 14.

6.2.3.1 Faith or Contemporaneity Precedes Historical Rigour

At first glance, Anti-Climacus appears quite negative regarding the historicity of Jesus.[63] However, a closer look reveals that Anti-Climacus does not deny the historicity of Jesus but, rather, presupposes that the four Gospels and other descriptions of Jesus in the Bible are historical. Given this fact, in what sense does Anti-Climacus say that "one can come to know nothing about Christ from history"?[64] Anti-Climacus insists that one can know Christ only by faith. When he refers to faith as the only means to know Jesus, this does *not* mean that whatever someone believes about Christ is necessarily true. Rather, Anti-Climacus's concept of faith presupposes the historicity of Scripture. Therefore, it is a terrible mistake to group Kierkegaard with Rudolf Bultmann (1884–1976), who is known for his radical scepticism about the historicity of the Gospels and the Bible.[65] David Crump aptly summarizes the issue as follows:

> Kierkegaard would not have any sympathy for either Bultmann's historical-critical methods or his anti-supernaturalism.... Unlike Bultmann, Kierkegaard insists that belief in the gospel miracles, especially the supernatural events of Jesus' incarnation, bodily resurrection, and ascension, is essential for any faith claiming to be Christian.[66]

In *Practice in Christianity*, the faith of Kierkegaard/Anti-Climacus is orthodox, aligning with to Scripture, the early church fathers, and the Apostles' Creed.[67]

---

63. *SKS* 12, 40/ *PC*, 25.

64. *SKS* 12, 40/ *PC*, 25.

65. The following are representative views of educated evangelicals and Catholics who group Kierkegaard and Bultmann with radical scholars who deny the historicity of Jesus: "Christology from above is basically fideistic. Particularly in the form expounded by Brunner and other existentialist theologians [presumably such as Bultmann], it draws heavily upon the thought of Søren Kierkegaard." Erickson, *Christian Theology*, 690; "At the other extreme from the maximalists are such writers as Gotthold Ephraim Lessing (1729–1781), Søren Kierkegaard (1813–1855), and Rudolf Bultmann (1884–1976), who have given minimalist answers to the historical questions about Jesus." Collins, *Christology*, loc. 229.

66. Crump, *Encountering Jesus*, 11.

67. *SKS* 12, 170/ *PC*, 167.

How does Kierkegaard view the relationship between the historical Jesus and the Christ of faith?[68]

> Such contemporaneity makes the believing individual obediently available to Christ. Knowledge and research alone can never accomplish this. I may investigate the minutiae of peasant life in first-century Palestine, learn Aramaic, and memorize ancient texts, but none of this will make me Jesus' contemporary. But if I make myself obediently available to the presence of Christ in my life, that will make me his contemporary.[69]

As Crump says in the quotation above, Anti-Climacus/Kierkegaard acknowledges the necessity of being trained in various disciplines. However, Anti-Climacus's point is that faith in, or contemporaneity with, Jesus Christ is more important than the rigour of historical investigation. Crump paraphrases what Anti-Climacus means: "*If my Christian faith had led me to a true relationship with Jesus Christ, then the Christ I now know by faith is the true Jesus of history.*"[70] Crump believes – and I agree – that Kierkegaard held a similar conviction. The quest for the historical Jesus might argue that the more one investigates historically, the closer one gets to understanding the historical Jesus. But Kierkegaard would argue that the historical investigation is always approximate. Even if someone knows all the historical details, that does not mean that they will know Jesus in his true form since even his contemporaries misunderstood him. Kierkegaard reverses the logic. To understand his thinking, consider the following parable: To truly know your spouse, you should spend time with them rather than hiring a private detective or interviewing their family or friends. Similarly, if someone has faith in Jesus Christ or becomes contemporaneous with him – that is, personally spends time with him – they will get to know the historical Jesus more fully.

---

68. In relation to the terms "historical Jesus" and the "Christ of faith," consider the following: "[Albert Schweitzer's *The Quest of the Historical Jesus*] has provided a label for the post-Enlightenment attempts to reconstruct the life and teaching of Jesus of Nazareth by critical historical methods. The phrase implies a contrast in Christological definitions ('the dogmatic Christ') and other Christian accounts of Jesus ('the Christ of faith')." Cross and Livingstone, *Oxford Dictionary*, 779. See also Schweitzer, *Quest of the Historical Jesus*; Kähler, *So-Called Historical Jesus*; Meyer and Hughes, *Jesus Then and Now*; O'Collins, *Christology*.

69. Crump, *Encountering Jesus*, 71.

70. Crump, 2, emphasis in original.

6.2.3.2 *The Holy Spirit Who Is the Guarantor of the Truth*

The argument in the previous sub-subsection will hardly convince twenty-first-century readers. How can one be sure that the Christ we know through faith is indeed the historical Jesus? In other words, what guarantees the trustworthiness of the Christ of faith? I would argue that for Kierkegaard, the Holy Spirit is the guarantor of the truth.

Kierkegaard never attempts to give a rational explanation for Christianity. Instead, he witnesses to the Christian faith through his signed works. Why does Kierkegaard make no attempt to offer a rational argument for the truth of Christianity? In discussing Kierkegaard's pneumatology,[71] John says, "The Spirit endows the believer with a capacity for the faith that is not accessible within the former self or natural human reasoning."[72] According to John's explanation of Kierkegaardian pneumatology, knowing the truth does not depend on (fallen) human reason but, rather, on the Spirit who renews a person's cognitive ability and convinces them of the truth. While agreeing with John, I will elaborate further. For instance, in concluding *Philosophical Fragment*, which is a unique "thought project" concerning the doctrine of Christ's incarnation, Johannes Climacus says,

> No philosophy (for it is only for thought), no mythology (for it is only for the imagination), no historical knowledge (which is for memory) has ever had this idea – of which in this connection one can say with all multiple meanings *that it did not arise in any human heart (Dn. at det ikke opkom i noget Menneskes Hjerte)*.[73]

According to Climacus, no one and no academic discipline could ever have come up with the idea of Christ's incarnation and Christian truth. Compare the emphasized part of the above quotation with the emphasized part of the

---

71. In comparison to his abundant references to the Father God and Jesus Christ, Kierkegaard rarely refers to the Holy Spirit except in Part III of *For Self-Examination*. SKS 13, 95–108/ FSE /JFY, 73–87. See also Stan, "Holy Spirit," 157–161. However, one cannot underestimate the role of the Holy Spirit in Kierkegaard's theology. In Part III of *For Self-Examination*, Kierkegaard urges one to die to oneself and the world so that the Spirit brings faith, hope, and love. This schema implies that in Kierkegaard's authorship, whenever he urges one to die to oneself and the world, he anticipates the work of the Holy Spirit. Furthermore, since the Spirit brings faith, hope, and love, whenever Kierkegaard elaborates on these three theological virtues, he assumes that the Holy Spirit is at work behind the scenes.

72. John, *Truth and Subjectivity*, loc. 3273. Kindle.

73. *SKS* 4, 305/ *PF*, 109, emphasis mine.

following 1 Corinthians 2:9: "But as is written: what no eye has seen, no ear has heard, *and has not arisen in any human heart (Dn. og ikke er opkommet i noget Menneskes Hjerte)*, what God has prepared for those whom he loves."[74] There is a clear parallel between Climacus's words and Paul's words in 1 Corinthians 2:9. In short, Climacus implies that God reveals the doctrine of Christ's incarnation (and salvation) to the human heart. The 1 Corinthians passage goes on to explain *how* God reveals this truth:

> But God revealed it to us through his Spirit; for the Spirit searches all things, even the depths of God. Which human knows what is in the human except for the human's spirit within? So no one knows what is in God except for the Spirit of God. And we have received not the spirit of the world but the Spirit from God, on that we could know what is given to us by God; which we also speak, not with a word that human wisdom teaches, but with a word that the Holy Spirit teaches, as we interpret spiritual thing with spiritual word. (1 Cor 2:10–13)[75]

The way God reveals "the depths of God" to human beings is "through his Spirit." A comparison between Climacus's earlier words and 1 Corinthians 2:9–13 suggests that, for Climacus, God reveals the truth through the Spirit. According to Kierkegaard's schema, it is not (fallen) human reason but the Spirit who convinces us of the truth. The Spirit works within the hearer, laying the necessary foundation for them to accept the truth. To make room for the Spirit, Kierkegaard abandoned rational persuasion. His bewildering abhorrence of apologetics is, in a sense, the expression of his deep respect for the Spirit. Naturally, one might object, asking why Kierkegaard, if he believed that the Spirit is the guarantor of the truth, mentions the Spirit so few times in his works? But Kierkegaard himself explains, "I have so much respect for the Spirit that I have not dared speak of him."[76] Paradoxically, the fact that Kierkegaard does not mention the Spirit frequently demonstrates his respect for the Spirit. Therefore, it is logical to conclude that, for Kierkegaard, the

---

74. New Testament 1819 revision during the reign of King Frederik VI, originally in Danish, emphasis mine.

75. New Testament 1819 revision during the reign of King Frederik VI, originally in Danish.

76. *SKS* 24, 469, NB25:48/ *JP*, VI 6792; see also *SKS* 25, 312–313, NB29:23/ *JP*, VI 6862.

Spirit is the guarantor of truth, as one of his journal entries states: "There is only one proof for the truth of [Christianity] – the inner proof, *argumentum spiritus sancti* [the argument of the Holy Spirit]."[77]

In conclusion, what guarantees that the Christ we know in faith is the historical Jesus? Our guarantor is neither human reason nor Kierkegaard but the Holy Spirit. Therefore, Kierkegaard presents himself not as a teacher but as a fellow pupil, giving the Holy Spirit space to work within the heart of the reader. As the psalmist says, "The unfolding of your words gives light; it imparts understanding to the simple" (Ps 119:130). The Holy Spirit illuminates Scripture for us. As we learn about the historicity of Jesus through Scripture, preaching, and testimonies, the Holy Spirit enables us to recognize the truth.

6.2.3.3 *The Existential Significance of Jesus Christ, the God-Man*

In *Practice in Christianity*, Anti-Climacus frequently refers to Christ as the "God-man."[78] For Anti-Climacus, Christ is the incarnated God – fully divine and fully human. Anti-Climacus conforms to orthodox Christology. However, he does not engage in speculation or apologetics to defend the truth of the doctrine of the God-man. When someone stands before the God-man, they will respond personally – they will either believe in or be offended by Christ. Therefore, Anti-Climacus talks about Christ, the God-man, in the context of the possibility of offence:[79] "But whether faith is abolished or whether the possibility of offense is abolished, something else is also abolished: the God-man. And if the God-man is abolished, Christianity is abolished."[80] *Faith that is paired with the possibility of offence*, *Christ the God-man*, and *Christianity* form a close-knit triad.

---

77. *SKS* 22, 108, NB11:179/ *KJN*, 6, 105. According to C. Stephen Evans, Kierkegaard holds a very similar view to Alvin Plantinga, who argues more apologetically in a way that modern evangelicals can accept. In his *Warranted Christian Belief*, Plantinga argues that "[by] virtue of the inward instigation of the Holy Spirit, we see that the teachings of Scripture are true." Evans, "Externalist Epistemology, Subjectivity, and Christian Knowledge: Plantinga and Kierkegaard" in Evans, *Kierkegaard on Faith and the Self*: 183–205; Plantinga, *Warranted Christian Belief*, 150, 404.

78. *SKS* 12, 90, 91–96, 101–103, 113–115, 120, 123, 127–147, 185, 195–196, 199, 207, 217–218/ *PC*, 78, 81–87, 93–94, 105–106, 113, 116, 120–144, 186, 196–197, 202, 210, 223.

79. *SKS* 12, 92; 146–147/ *PC*, 81; 143–144.

80. *SKS* 12, 147/ *PC*, 144.

Anti-Climacus emphasizes the fact that Christ's dual nature requires faith. This is an unusual approach. On the one hand, Christ's dual nature is focused on in the classroom of a Bible College or seminary, and we tend to speculate or argue rather than emphasizing faith. On the other hand, faith in Christ is emphasized in the church, where we are seldom deeply engaged in the dual nature of Christ. Anti-Climacus's *Practice in Christianity* demonstrates that Christology is not just a theological issue but it is a vital question for the true Christian life. The dual nature of Christ requires one to have faith in him.

6.2.3.4 *The Existential Significance of Christ the Redeemer and the Prototype*

At first glance, as Anti-Climacus repeatedly urges the reader to imitate the abased Christ, *Practice in Christianity* may seem to overemphasize Christ as the prototype. However, a closer look reveals that Anti-Climacus's Christ is both the redeemer and the prototype. In the "Editor's Preface," Kierkegaard acknowledges that he needs to learn not only to resort to grace but also not to misuse grace.[81] In other words, while acknowledging that all of us need to resort to grace, he warns against taking grace for granted. As far as Anti-Climacus is concerned, the ideal of imitating Christ should be declared without compromise. By striving precisely for what Scripture requires, one effectively uses grace or respectfully resorts to grace. The following journal entry makes this point clearer:

> By becoming contemporaneous with Christ (the prototype), you simply discover that you are not like it at all, not even in what you call your best moment; for in such a moment you are not in the corresponding tension of actuality but are spectating. The result is that you effectively learn to flee to faith in grace. The prototype is that which requires itself from you; alas, and you feel the unlikeness horribly; then you flee to the prototype that he may have compassion upon you. In this way the prototype is simultaneously the one who infinitely judges you most rigorously – and also the one who has compassion upon you.[82]

---

81. *SKS* 12, 15; 85, 153/ *PC*, 7, 73; 149.
82. Possen, "Voice of Rigor," 169; originally from *SKS* 21, 12–13, NB6:3/ *JP*, I 692; See also *JP*, II 1909/ *Pap*. X4 A491, *n.d.*, 1852.

This journal entry demonstrates that Kierkegaard's Christianity is not legalistic; rather, it offers salvation by grace and is concerned with the effective use of grace. To put it differently, Christ the redeemer relates to the past, while Christ the prototype points to the future: "Christ the Atoner. This is continually in relation to the past. But at the same moment he is the Atoner for the past he is 'the prototype' [Forbilledet] for the future."[83] In other words, Christ is a gift (the redeemer) and a task (the prototype).[84] As *Practice in Christianity* presents Christ as both the redeemer and the prototype, this work serves the twofold function of both evangelism and discipleship.

6.2.3.5 A Necessary Emphasis on Christ the Prototype in the Context of the Nineteenth-Century Christendom of Denmark

In the previous sub-subsection, we considered Kierkegaard's journals and discovered that he has a well-balanced view of Christ as both redeemer and prototype. However, his contemporaries did not have access to his journals. Even though Kierkegaard, in his journals, presents Christ as both the redeemer and the prototype, in *Practice in Christianity*, Anti-Climacus emphasizes Christ as a prototype much more than as a redeemer.[85] Why is this? Was Kierkegaard unaware that Anti-Climacus, in *Practice in Christianity*, presents an unbalanced Christology? The following journal entry testifies that Kierkegaard intentionally proclaimed an unbalanced Christology that emphasized the prototype:

> This is the mission in our time. It is not necessary to proclaim Christianity, it has been proclaimed enough, I am sure, but it is the "You shall" that is what the missionary in Christendom has to proclaim. But the bishops and preachers have not understood this, and, even if they had understood it, they would not have dared to do it. Of course, to go out into the world in the consciousness or at least with the hope and prospect that the "You

---

83. *SKS* 25, 158, NB27:44/ *JP*, II 1919/ *Pap*. X5 A44, *n.d.*, 1852; See also *SKS* 25, 157–158, NB27:44/*JP*, II 1918 *n.d.*, 1852.

84. Gouwens, *Dialectic of the Imagination*, 248; *SKS* 23, 26–27, NB15:32/*JP*, II 1862 *n.d.*, 1849.

85. Roughly speaking, "The Invitation" of "No. I" refers exclusively to Christ the redeemer. *SKS* 12, 19–33/*PC*, 11–22. The rest of *Practice in Christianity* is devoted to elucidating Christ the prototype. *SKS* 12, 15–18, 35–253/*PC*, 7–10, 23–262.

shall" which one proclaims will make one influential, powerful: well, now, that is appealing to a man. But to go out in the world in the consciousness that for proclaiming this "You shall" they may put you to death, and even if they do not do that you will never get to rule over others, since the "You shall" applies to you yourself – this teaching has no appeal to men.[86]

Kierkegaard understood that the missionary task in Christendom is not to proclaim an indulgent Christianity but, rather, a "You shall" Christianity. *Practice in Christianity* demonstrates the supreme ideal of the "You shall" and emphasizes Kierkegaard's identity as a missionary rather than a systematic theologian. In *Practice in Christianity*, Kierkegaard has Anti-Climacus focus on the abased Christ in an unbalanced manner because the historical context required him to adopt this approach.[87]

In summary, Anti-Climacus does not deliver a comprehensive lecture on Christology but, rather, proclaims what his audience needs to hear. A Kierkegaardian mission is deeply concerned with the spiritual condition of its audience.[88]

6.2.3.6 Homiletics

Somewhat harshly, Anti-Climacus says, "I still have never heard any discourse or sermon about which I, if the question were put to me before God, unconditionally would dare to say that it was Christian."[89] Why is he so disappointed with contemporary sermons? Anti-Climacus wants to bring existential commitment back into the sermon. The admirer may observe

---

86. *SKS* 20, 260–261, NB3:32/ *JP*, 3477 N.B. *n.d.*, 1847.

87. See also Patrick, *Pascal and Kierkegaard*, 306.

88. In *Overhearing the Gospel*, Fred Craddock asserts that "[the] ego of the teacher or preacher very often prevents the necessary concentration on the listener" and adds that the teacher and the preacher in the Christendom of the United States should learn from Kierkegaard to respect their audience and pay attention to their situation. Craddock, *Overhearing the Gospel*, 68. Certainly, Kierkegaard was acutely conscious of the method of communication and took special care to understand the needs of the recipients. Kierkegaard's journal shows that he intensively studied Aristotle's *Rhetoric*, which analyzes the basis of rhetoric by considering three functions: ethos, logos, and pathos. Aristotle, *Rhetoric*, 7–8. According to Kierkegaard, "ethos" corresponds to the communicator, "logos" to the content of the communication, and "pathos" to the emotion of the recipient. Interestingly, Kierkegaard was frustrated with Aristotle for not paying sufficient attention to the recipient, which Kierkegaard believed was the most important function. *SKS* 27, 340, Papir 326:3/ *JP*, V 5782 *n.d.*, 1845.

89. *SKS* 12, 222/ *PC*, 228.

and praise the beauty of Christ's life as one might appreciate art. While this may sound Christian, it is not so for Anti-Climacus. The imitator, however, engages personally with the life of Christ.[90] Christ is not just a sermon subject but the model that the preacher must imitate in every aspect: "God in human form, that this divine teaching, that these signs and wonders, which would have made even Sodom and Gomorrah repent if they had happened there, actually produce the very opposite effect, that the teacher is shunned, hated, held in contempt."[91] According to this statement, even Christ – the best proclaimer of the gospel – was not able to produce repentance through his preaching. To imitate Christ as a preacher means recognizing that the success or failure of a mission does *not* depend on how many people are converted. What are the criteria for determining success when it comes to the proclamation of the gospel? As an imitator of Christ, all that truly matters is one listener – the omnipotent God. Anti-Climacus claims that the preacher is required to have fear and trembling before God:[92] "The proclaimer of the Christian truth ... steps forward into a place where, even if the eyes of all are not focused on him, the eye of an omniscient one is."[93] Again, one's personal involvement in preaching is required: "His task is: to be himself, and in a setting, God's house, which, all eyes and ears, requires only one thing of him – that he should be himself, be true."[94] The preacher is required not only to preach sound doctrine but also to be true to oneself before God.

But the preacher is an imitator, not Christ himself. What if the preacher, who is always imperfect, falls short of the ideal that should be preached? Anti-Climacus would not dare to ask the preacher to dilute the requirements of Christianity. "[The] requirement should indeed be stated, presented, and heard."[95] Instead of compromising the content or pretending to be a perfect Christian, a preacher should admit, confess, and repent in the pulpit, recognizing that they preach a Christianity that is far higher than themselves.[96] Anti-Climacus insists on the preacher's sincerity, that they either embody

---

90. *SKS* 12, 228/ *PC*, 234.
91. *SKS* 12, 65/ *PC*, 53.
92. *SKS* 12, 228–229/ *PC*, 234–235.
93. *SKS* 12, 229/ *PC*, 235.
94. *SKS* 12, 229/ *PC*, 235.
95. *SKS* 12/ *PC*, 7.
96. *SKS* 12, 229/ *PC*, 235.

what they preach or demonstrate a genuine striving toward that ideal. "That he should be true, that is, that he himself should be what he proclaims, or at least strive to be that."[97] While admitting that one falls far short, one must also strive to be like the prototype. This is the spirituality of preachers that Anti-Climacus proposes. Thus, for Anti-Climacus, Christ is not just a sermon subject but the model for the preacher in every aspect.

6.3 Possible Applications to the Japanese Context

What are the possible applications of *Practice in Christianity* to the Japanese context? First, Jesus Christ as a gentle Saviour needs to be proclaimed. The consciousness of sin should be immediately followed by faith in Jesus Christ in his true form. No sooner the hearer is "cut to the heart" (Acts 2:37) through preaching on sin, the essential Christian message needs to be presented. Only when someone learns of the extreme danger (that is, despair or sin) will they have the courage to face the lesser danger (that is, what is essentially Christian). The essentially Christian is not easy, but when one understands the despair that has made them misuse eternity and nailed them to perpetual death, they will understand that the essentially Christian is grace and leniency. Many Japanese have only read *The Sickness unto Death*.[98] A Kierkegaardian missionary should not leave the hearer with just the consciousness of sin. We should prevent a tragedy like the death of Sensei in Natsume's *Kokoro* from taking place.[99] We should bring the help that the gospel offers to address other social problems, such as the increasing number of people suffering from depression,[100] the high suicide rate,[101] and the *hikikomori*.[102] Perhaps just hearing Anti-Climacus's invitation, "Oh, a sigh is enough; that you sigh

---

97. *SKS* 12, 229/ *PC*, 235.
98. See section 5.3.
99. For a discussion of Sensei in Natsume's *Kokoro*, see section 5.3.
100. Honkawa, 社会実情データ図録: うつ病・躁うつ病の総患者数 ["Honkawa Data Tribune: Total Numbers of Depressive and Manic-Depressive Patients"], http://www2.ttcn.ne.jp/honkawa/2150.html.
101. "Japan ranked 14 in suicide rates . . . out of 183 countries. . . ." "Suicide Rates in 2019," StoryMaps, accessed 29 Feb 2020, no longer available (URL: [https://storymaps.arcgis.com/stories/5fea08b4095348cc82f8184735cea228]).
102. For an explanation of the term *hikikomori*, see footnote 72 in section 4.3.

for him is also to come here,"¹⁰³ would be sufficient to help depressed and helpless people who feel they are at the end of their rope to move towards faith and come to Jesus. This kind of invitation, which we see in *Practice in Christianity*, must be extended to the people in Japan.¹⁰⁴

Second, a Kierkegaardian missionary should present Jesus Christ in his *true* form. How many proclaimers of Christianity speak in the manner that Anti-Climacus describes below?

> They defended Christianity and said, "Do not reject Christianity; it is a gentle teaching, containing all the gentle consolations that everyone can easily come to need in life. Good Lord, life is not always smiling, we all need a friend, and such a friend is Christ. Do not reject him; he is kindly disposed toward you."¹⁰⁵

It is worthwhile for the proclaimer of Christianity to evaluate the content of their proclamation in light of Anti-Climacus's outspoken criticism. I am afraid that we also, to some extent, tend to present Christ in a way that avoids *offending* our hearers. Must we offend people? It is not necessary. What is important is to present Jesus Christ as the God-man, which involves the possibility of biblical offence. According to Anti-Climacus, the confusion prevalent in the modern age is far more dangerous. If Christians fall asleep in their faith and forget the God-man, Anti-Climacus shockingly reminds us that the very fact that both the Ebionites and the Gnostics were offended by the God-man is evidence that a true proclamation was being made at that time.¹⁰⁶ Where there is the possibility of offence at the God-man, true proclamation exists. We may need to scrutinize the Scriptures, not to find keys to building a megachurch but to undesrstand what it means to present Jesus Christ in his true form.

Third, a Kierkegaardian missionary should proclaim faith in Jesus Christ. One should not attempt to rationalize or philosophize Christology. Instead, faith should be proclaimed. As far as Anti-Climacus is concerned, faith is the only lens through which one can see Jesus Christ in his true form. When we

---

103. *SKS* 12, 33/ *PC*, 22.

104. See the third point in appendix 8, section II D. *Practice in Christianity* has contributed to evangelizing some Japanese.

105. *SKS* 12, 225/ *PC*, 231.

106. *SKS* 12, 128/ *PC*, 123.

rely on reasoning and present an academically justified Jesus, in the process, we end up emptying Christianity of its true meaning.

Fourth, if Ant-Climacus is right, a proclaimed Christ precedes the quest for the historical Jesus. While this quest may be necessary and important for teachers and professors at a Bible college or seminary, when proclaiming Christ, we must proclaim not merely a historical figure but the omnipotent God-man who personally meets each individual today. This God-man is the historical Jesus. According to Anti-Climacus, the secular historical method brings confusion and cannot enable one to meet the true historical Jesus.

Fifth, the proclamation of Christianity must be combined with discipleship. Some evangelicals do emphasize this aspect.[107] Evangelicals generally focus on evangelism, but the inseparability of evangelism and discipleship has increasingly been recognized and given prominence. "Each believer is a disciple (learner) and must be nurtured and helped to grow and develop in the Christian faith."[108] Some say this because they view the crisis of the church from a practical viewpoint. Others, considering the matter from a biblical viewpoint, say this because they see no dichotomy between evangelism and discipleship in the Bible.[109] The fact that Japan's Christian population has not been increasing shows that while some come to church through evangelism, just as many are leaving the church. Like Anti-Climacus's approach in *Practice in Christianity*, a combination of evangelism and discipleship may encourage those who come to church not to leave and to faithfully continue being Christ's disciples.

Sixth, one ought to imitate Christ. This is the core of *Practice in Christianity*. We should be ashamed of the fact that we Protestants do not have obvious figures like Francis of Assisi (1182–1226) or Mother Teresa (1910–1997) who even outsiders of the church somehow know that Jesus Christ must have been similar to them. Not just a Catholic but also a Protestant should imitate Jesus Christ. We should not just verbally proclaim Christ but also imitate him existentially.

---

107. Edgemon, "Evangelism and Discipleship," 539–547; Root, "Evangelism and Discipleship," http://www.lausanneworldpulse.com/themedarticles-php/717/05-2007; Burns, "Evangelism vs Discipleship," https://scottburns.wordpress.com/2013/02/19/evangelism-vs-discipleship/.

108. Edgemon, "Evangelism and Discipleship," 539.

109. See Matthew 28:18–20.

6.4 Conclusion

Section A: Concluding Remarks for a Study of *Practice in Christianity*

We have argued that it makes good sense to view *Practice in Christianity* from the perspective of Kierkegaard the missionary. A brief look at the content of *Practice in Christianity* speaks for itself. In "The Invitation" in "No. I," Anti-Climacus personally invites each individual to come to Christ. In "No. II," he urges the reader to have faith in Jesus Christ and not be offended at him. In "No. III," he delivers seven discourses that preach Christ who draws all to himself from on high. Therefore, we conclude that one of the most striking features of *Practice in Christianity* is that Kierkegaard, under the mask of Anti-Climacus, acts as an evangelist. Another important aspect of *Practice in Christianity* is the concept of *imitatio Christi*.[110] With this concept in mind, consider the following journal entry: "If Christianity is to be reintroduced into Christendom, it must again be proclaimed unconditionally as imitation, as law . . . if this is to be realized . . . , there could be a person who . . . becomes the missionary, the missionary to Christendom."[111] This journal entry eloquently demonstrates that through *Practice in Christianity*, Kierkegaard – under the higher-pseudonymous mask of Anti-Climacus – attempts to be a missionary by uncompromisingly proclaiming the imitation of Christ as law.

In terms of application, the mission strategy in *Practice in Christianity* is to avoid compromise and proclaim the uncompromising ideal of the New Testament. In this postmodern age, a missionary might be afraid to urge an audience towards a religious commitment. However, *Practice in Christianity* does not water down the radicality of the Christian message. This work, like the New Testament, challenges us by showing that such a bold message is more attractive than a diluted or compromised message.

In conclusion, with *Practice in Christianity*, Anti-Climacus attempts to introduce Christianity into Christendom of Denmark[112] by forcing up 'the

---

110. Kierkegaard acquires "a Danish translation of Thomas's *The Imitation of Christ* in 1848." But "none of Kierkegaard's direct references to Thomas in the journals refer explicitly to imitation and Kierkegaard never acknowledges the influence of Thomas's thought on his own writings." Cockayne, "Imitation and Contemporaneity," 5, 15, footnote 16.

111. *SKS* 25, 156, NB27:42/ *JP*, 401, *n.d.*, 1852.

112. *SKS* 12, 49/ *PC*, 36.

requirement for being a Christian' 'to a supreme ideality'[113] or presenting faith in and imitation of Jesus Christ in the true form.

Section B: Concluding Remarks on a Combined Study of *The Sickness unto Death* and *Practice in Christianity*

In *The Sickness unto Death*, Anti-Climacus says, "[Christianity establishes] sin so securely as a position that now it seems to be utterly impossible to eliminate it again – and then it is this very Christianity that by means of the Atonement wants to eliminate sin as completely as if it were drowned in the sea."[114] This quotation can be viewed as a summary of Anti-Climacus's two works. The subject of establishing of sin is dealt with in *The Sickness unto Death*, while the question of eliminating sin is addressed in *Practice in Christianity*. Therefore, with *The Sickness unto Death*, the reader is made fully aware of sin and spiritually equipped, while *Practice in Christianity* helps them to believe in the forgiveness of sin and teaches them how to become and continue to be a Christian. *The Sickness unto Death* and *Practice in Christianity* function as a single unit that exemplifies the Christian message of *sin* and *salvation*.

This connection between *The Sickness unto Death* and *Practice in Christianity* is also apparent when Anti-Climacus calls Christ "[the one] who is able to rescue from the . . . life-threatening sickness."[115] In *Practice in Christianity*, the "life-threatening sickness" for Anti-Climacus is not a physical or mental sickness but despair and sin.[116] *The Sickness unto Death* is entirely devoted to describing this "life-threatening sickness." In *Practice in Christianity*, Anti-Climacus describes faith in and imitation of Jesus Christ as the only means of rescue from the sickness unto death.[117]

In some ways, the relationship between *The Sickness unto Death and Practice in Christianity* resembles that of *Either/Or* and *Two Upbuilding Discourses* (1843). *Either/Or* offers initial training that prepares one to make the real choice in *Two Upbuilding Discourses* (1843), but that choice only becomes clear through a sequential reading. Similarly, a sequential reading

---

113. *SKS* 12, 15/ *PC*, 7.
114. *SKS* 11, 212/ *SUD*, 100.
115. *SKS* 12, 22/ *PC*, 12, translation modified.
116. See *SKS* 11, 123–125/ *SUD*, 7–9.
117. See also *SKS* 11, 123/ *SUD*, 7.

of Anti-Climacus's two works reveals a "sharpened either/or,"[118] to borrow Malantschuk's phrase. In other words, with *The Sickness unto Death*, Anti-Climacus confines everyone under the sentence of the life-threatening sickness, despair, or sin, while with *Practice in Christianity*, he urges them to have faith in and imitate Jesus Christ, who saves everyone from sickness, despair, or sin.

With the initial religious either/or presented in *Either/Or* and *Two Upbuilding Discourses* (1843), Kierkegaard, as a missionary, gently guides the reader to choose between remaining in the aesthetic or embracing the ordinary godly life (*Either/Or*), and to venture toward the first religious leap (*Two Upbuilding Discourses* [1843]). With the "sharpened either/or"[119] of *The Sickness unto Death* and *Practice in Christianity*, Kierkegaard delivers the true ultimatum, challenging readers to choose between the perpetual death caused by despair or sin (*The Sickness unto Death*) and salvation by faith in and imitation of Jesus Christ in his true form (*Practice in Christianity*).

Since he does not refer to Jesus Christ in the early pseudonymous and signed-religious works, why does he emphasize presenting Christ in his true form in *Practice in Christianity*? Is it because "the religious is something one turns to when one has become older"?[120] Kierkegaard refuted this kind of view and insisted that he is a religious author from the outset. The result of the present study up to now also endorses his view. Therefore, a single unit of *Either/Or* and *Two Upbuilding Discourses* (1843) and that of *The Sickness unto Death* and *Practice in Christianity* can be seen as the practise of Kierkegaard's incarnational mission. Namely, a single unit of *Either/Or* and *Two Upbuilding Discourses* (1843) represents the how of the incarnational mission. Just like Jesus Christ established rapport with townspeople, Kierkegaard did so with 19th century Danes. A single unit of *The Sickness unto Death* and *Practice in Christianity* represents the what of the incarnational mission. Anti-Climacus wholeheartedly presented Jesus Christ in the true form. Thus, these four works demonstrate the congruence of the how and the what of the incarnational mission.

---

118. Malantschuk, *Kierkegaard's Thought*, 338.
119. Malantschuk, 338.
120. *SKS* 13–14, asterisk/*PV*, 8, asterisk.

Practice in Christianity as Introducing Christianity into Christendom   219

This concludes Part 2. Although many other works by Kierkegaard could contribute original insights to the field of missiology, the scope of this study is limited and does not extend to further analysis of his other published writings. Instead, in the next section, we turn to Kierkegaard's unpublished work, with the aim of uncovering new aspects of Kierkegaard as a missionary – dimensions not evident in his published works.

Part 3

A Study of Unpublished Works

CHAPTER 7

The Point of View for My Work as an Author as a Handbook of Mission Strategy

> For though I am free with respect to all, I have made myself a slave to all, so that I might win more of them. To the Jews I became as a Jew, in order to win Jews. To those under the law I became as one under the law (though I myself am not under the law) so that I might win those under the law. To those outside the law I became as one outside the law (though I am not free from God's law but am under Christ's law) so that I might win those outside the law. To the weak I became weak, so that I might win the weak. I have become all things to all people, so that I might by any means save some. I do it all for the sake of the gospel, so that I may share in its blessings.
>
> – The apostle Paul, 1 Corinthians 9:19–23, NRSV[1]

---

1. The counterpoint to this verse is found in Galatians 2:11–14. Thomas R. Schreiner summarizes the issues as follows: "[Some argue] that Paul wrongly condemned Peter, for Peter followed the principle of accommodation set out by Paul himself in 1 Cor 9:19–23.... But [their] argument is seriously flawed." I agree with Schreiner. While 1 Corinthians 9:19–23 expresses Paul's mission strategy, Galatians 2:11–14 addresses "the independence and authority of his gospel." Schreiner, *Galatians*, 139, footnote 7. Paul's mission strategy is *incarnational* – that is, to proclaim Christ in the same way Christ himself did on earth (1 Cor 9:19–23). In Galatians 2:11–14, however, Peter behaves as if faith alone is not enough and circumcision is necessary for complete salvation and purification. This behaviour might suggest a *syncretic mission*, even

The helper must first humble himself under the person he wants to help and thereby understand that to help is not to dominate but to serve, that to help is not to be the most dominating but the most patient. . . . Or, if you are able to do so, portray the esthetic with all its bewitching charm, if possible captivate the other person, portray it with the kind of passionateness whereby it appeals particularly to him, hilariously to the hilarious, melancholically to the melancholy, wittily to the witty, etc. – but above all do not forget one thing, the number carried that you have, that it is the religious that is to come forward. Just do it; do not fear to do it; for truly it can be done only in much fear and trembling.[2]

– Søren Kierkegaard, *The Point of View for My Work as an Author*

The two quotations above reveal a striking parallel between the mission strategies of the apostle Paul and Kierkegaard. A proclaimer of Christianity should be, in the words of Paul, "a slave to all" or, in Kierkegaard's phrasing, a helper should humble oneself. Thus, the first common point is the emphasis on being a servant missionary. Paul commands this attitude so that one "might win more of them." Kierkegaard endorses the same attitude so that one might take "captive the other person." The second common point is the effectiveness of servant mission. Paul's strategy for accomplishing this involves becoming as a Jew to the Jews, as one under the law to those under the law, as one outside the law to those outside the law, and weak to the weak. Similarly, Kierkegaard's strategy is to "portray the esthetic with all its bewitching charm . . . hilariously to the hilarious, melancholically to the melancholy, wittily to the witty." This, then, is the third common point: "To sense the audience's private world as if it were the missionary's own, but without ever losing the 'as if' quality."[3] What is the purpose of this chameleon-like appearance? Paul does this "all for

---

if Peter did not intend to. For a discussion of the terms "incarnational" or "syncretic" mission, see section 10.1.2.

2. *SKS* 16, 28/ *PV*, 46, translation slightly modified.

3. This is a paraphrase of the following quotation: "To sense the client's private world as if it were your own, but without ever losing the 'as if' quality." Rogers, *On Becoming a Person*, 284.

the sake of the gospel," and Kierkegaard does it for a religious purpose. The fourth common point focuses on the missionary purpose. As the comparison above shows, one can read Kierkegaard's *The Point of View for My Work as an Author* as his own explanation of his mission strategy, which is built on Paul's example. Furthermore, as we will see in this chapter, Kierkegaard himself compares his mission strategy with Christ's, thereby revealing *The Point of View for My Work as an Author* for what it truly is – a handbook on Kierkegaard's mission strategy.

The subject of this chapter is *Synspunktet for min Forfatter-Virksomhed* (*The Point of View for My Work as an Author*). The outline of this chapter is as follows: In the first section, I will provide a historical introduction. In the second section, I will summarize *The Point of View for My Work as an Author*. The reader will see that this summary speaks for itself and demonstrates that this work is a handbook on Kierkegaard's mission strategy. But is its true character as self-evident as it appears? Unfortunately, not everyone involved in Kierkegaard scholarship uses the hermeneutics of trust. Therefore, in the third section, we will briefly consider those who doubt the trustworthiness of *The Point of View for My Work as an Author*. In the fourth section, we will examine one possible solution, proposed by David Law, to resolve the contradiction between the hermeneutics of trust and doubt. In the fifth section, I will establish the standpoint of this study through a thorough discussion. Finally, in the sixth section, I will offer some concluding remarks on this chapter.

7.1 Historical Introduction

The genre of *The Point of View for My Work as an Author* is signed commentary.[4] This work was written in 1848, and Kierkegaard pondered the possibility of publishing *The Collected Works of Completion*, which would include this work. His journal entries show that his will or feelings about this wavered and fluctuated. He worried that "[this work says] too much about him so that he would appear as an extraordinary."[5] In other words, people's perceptions of Kierkegaard as a playboy or, at best, a literary genius – but not a serious

---

4. For the term "signed commentary," see section 2.3.1.
5. Hong and Hong, "Historical Introductio'" in *PV*, xiv, see *SKS* 21, 244–246, NB9:74/ *JP*, VI 6325; *SKS* 21, 340–341, NB10:169/ *JP*, VI 6383; *SKS* 22, 298–299, NB13:37/ *JP*, VI 6511.

man – were a good disguise for him. This implies that Kierkegaard preferred not to be admired personally, but rather to increase the chances that readers would be unexpectedly confronted and edified through an encounter with his works. As a result, in 1851, Kierkegaard published a shortened version of *The Point of View for My Work as an Author*, which he titled *On My Work as an Author*. *The Point of View for My Work as an Author* remained unpublished during Kierkegaard's lifetime and was posthumously published in 1859, four years after his death, by his brother, Peter Kierkegaard. The subtitle of this work – *A Direct Communication: Report to History* – implies that Kierkegaard does not communicate indirectly with the reader using the mask of a pseudonym but, instead, directly explains his works as the author.

7.2 Reading *The Point of View for My Work as an Author*

"There is a time to be silent and a time to speak,"[6] says Kierkegaard. Now the time to speak has come; it is a time to unlock the secret of Kierkegaard's authorship. In his introduction, Kierkegaard says, "The content, then, of this little book is: what I in truth am as an author, that I am and was a religious author, that my whole authorship pertains to Christianity, to the issue: becoming a Christian."[7] Kierkegaard guarantees the truth of his statement and says that he was and is a religious author, with the subject of becoming a Christian being the underlying theme of his works. As stated elsewhere in this work, this work was written in 1848. In other words, he had seven more years to go as an author before his death in 1855.[8] Accordingly, whenever Kierkegaard explains his "whole authorship" in *The Point of View for My Work as an Author*, this term refers to the works that were published between 1843 and May 1849 – until the publication of the second edition of *Either/Or* and *The Lily in the Field and the Bird of the Air*.

Kierkegaard makes an interesting request: "I request everyone who truly has the cause of Christianity at heart, and I request more urgently him who has it at heart more earnestly, to become acquainted with this little book,

---

6. *SKS* 16, 11/ *PV*, 23. Compare Ecclesiastes 3:7.
7. *SKS* 16, 11/ *PV*, 23.
8. See appendix 1.

not inquisitively, but thoughtfully, as one reads a religious book."[9] One can see that Kierkegaard regarded this book not just as a commentary but also as a work that is religious or pious in nature. As we will see later, this book has sparked great debate about whether or not we should trust its words. However, we should keep in mind Kierkegaard's reminder as we read the book. Kierkegaard reveals who he is, saying,

> I am a religious author, it, of course, is, on the whole, a matter of indifference to me whether a so-called esthetic public has found or would be able to find some enjoyment through reading the esthetic works, or through reading the esthetic in the works, which is the incognito and the deception in the service of Christianity.[10]

According to Kierkegaard, as a religious author, he produced literary works in the guise of an aesthetic author. Therefore, his aesthetic works are "the incognito and the deception." He also confesses the inner motivation behind his authorship:

> But I also know with God that precisely my work as an author was the prompting of an irresistible inner need, the only possibility for a depressed person, an honest indemnifying attempt by one deeply humbled, a penitent, to make up, if possible, for something by means of every sacrifice and effort in the service of the truth.[11]

According to Kierkegaard's confession, his "irresistible inner need" prompted him to write; as a penitent, he willingly sacrificed everything to serve the truth.

In "Part one," Kierkegaard compares his incognito approach with Jesus Christ's incarnation: "To use the supreme example: Christ's whole life here on earth would indeed have become a game if he had been so incognito that he had gone through life totally unnoticed – and yet he truly was incognito."[12] Christ is the transcendent God. But he humbled himself, and

---

9. *SKS* 16, 11/ *PV*, 23.
10. *SKS* 16, 39/ *PV*, 23–24.
11. *SKS* 16, 12/ *PV*, 24.
12. *SKS* 16, 19/ *PV*, 34.

his true status was hidden. The lowly Christ achieved rapport with so-called sinners, tax collectors, prostitutes, the demon-possessed, Samaritans, and so on. Therefore, the Pharisees and the scribes called him "a glutton and a drunkard, a friend of tax-collectors and sinners" (Matt 11:19). Kierkegaard created various pseudonyms to achieve rapport with his contemporaries. Ádám Szabados defines Kierkegaard's mission as an incarnational mission, and Denzil G. M. Patrick, Mark C. Miller, and Mark A. Tietjen concur with this assessment.[13] In fact, Kierkegaard himself initiated the impulse to think of his work in terms of an incarnational mission by comparing his lower pseudonymous works with Christ's incarnation. One can see that Kierkegaard consciously imitated Christ's incarnational method to establish rapport with his contemporary Danes.

Kierkegaard calls our attention to the duplexity of *Either/Or* and *Two Upbuilding Discourses* (1843), which helps us to understand the duplexity of "the whole authorship."[14] He raises the question whether it is more plausible to regard him as an aesthetic writer or as a religious writer. According to Kierkegaard, the publication of *Two Upbuilding Discourses* (1843) right after *Either/Or* (the "first work in the literature"[15]) and "such a sustained duplexity"[16] throughout the authorship well explain that he is a religious author.[17] Assuming that the reader agrees with Kierkegaard's view of himself as a religious author, he then moves on to "Part Two: The Authorship Viewed as a Whole, and from the Point of View that the Author is a Religious Author." In chapter 1 of the book, Kierkegaard divides his works into three categories: the aesthetic writings, *Concluding Postscript*, and the religious writings; he also annotates each category.

Kierkegaard begins by repeating the aim of his authorship: "Once and for all I must urgently request this kindly disposed reader continually to bear *in mente* [in mind] that the total thought in the entire work as an author is this: becoming a Christian."[18] Why did he start with *Either/Or*, which is so aesthetic? It is because Kierkegaard observed that people live in the

---

13. See sections 1.1.1, 1.3.1, and 1.4.4.
14. *SKS* 16, 16/ *PV*, 30.
15. *SKS* 16, 11/ *PV*, 23.
16. *SKS* 16, 15/ *PV*, 29.
17. *SKS* 16, 19–20/ *PV*, 34.
18. *SKS* 16, 23, asterisk/ *PV*, 41, asterisk.

aesthetic sphere. "'Christendom' is an enormous illusion"[19] in Kierkegaard's view. Lutheran Christianity is officially the state religion of Denmark. Yet Kierkegaard discerned that, in reality, the Danes lived according to aesthetic – or at the most ethical – values, rather than according to strictly Christian values.

Kierkegaard explains his strategy: "If one is truly to succeed in leading a person to a specific place, one must first and foremost take care to find him where he is and begin there."[20] He wished to successfully lead his fellow citizen to religious life, a life of Christianity as found in the New Testament. Therefore, he needed to write various kinds of aesthetic and ethical writings to begin where his contemporaries were. Kierkegaard describes his imaginary dialogue partner talking to him as follows:

> My dear friend, you are still rather young – and then to want to begin such a project, a project that, if it is to have any success at all, would require at least a dozen well-trained missionaries, a project that amounts to neither more nor less than wanting to introduce Christianity again – into Christendom.[21]

Although the above quotation does not indicate whether this is truly Kierkegaard's own view, it indirectly supports our interpretation of him as a missionary. The imaginary dialogue partner regards Kierkegaard's authorial activity as fulfilling the work of (at least) a dozen well-trained missionaries – that is, the task of introducing Christianity into Christendom.

Kierkegaard goes on to explain the secret of the art of helping:

> This is the secret in the entire art of helping. Anyone who cannot do this is himself under a delusion if he thinks he is able to help someone else. In order truly to help someone else, I must understand more than he – but certainly first and foremost understand what he understands. If I do not do that, then my greater understanding does not help him at all. If I nevertheless want to assert my greater understanding, then it is because I am vain or proud, then basically instead of benefiting him I really want to

---

19. *SKS* 16, 23, the title of § 1/ *PV*, 41, the title of § 1.
20. *SKS* 16, 27, the title of § 2/ *PV*, 45, the title of § 2, emphasis Kierkegaard's.
21. *SKS* 16, 24/ *PV*, 42.

> be admired by him. But all true helping begins with a humbling. The helper must first humble himself under the person he wants to help and thereby understand that to help is not to dominate but to serve, that to help is not to be the most dominating but the most patient, that to help is a willingness for the time being to put up with being in the wrong and not understanding what the other understands.[22]

According to Kierkegaard, "in order truly to help someone else," the helper must "understand more than" that person and "first and foremost understand what [they understand]." The helper should not assert their own "greater understanding." If they do, this springs from pride. If one wants to help or lead someone, one must start with humility.

Kierkegaard provides vivid illustrations: "Consider a person who is impassioned about something, granted that he actually is in the wrong." Kierkegaard suggests that instead of preaching, one should be "a willing and attentive listener" and adds, "If you cannot do that, you cannot help him either. He shuts himself off from you, shuts himself up in his innermost being – and then you merely preach to him."[23] Does preaching without listening really help someone?

> Perhaps by personal power you will be able to force him to confess to you that he is in the wrong. Ah, my dear fellow, the very next moment he sneaks around by another path, a secret path, to a rendezvous with the secret passion, for which he now longs all the more; yes, he has almost become afraid that it would have lost some of its seductive fervor – for now by your behavior you have helped him to fall in love once again, namely, which his unhappy passion – and then you only preach![24]

For someone trapped in the delusion of a sinful life, preaching may have the opposite effect. By preaching without listening, the seductive fervour of the sinful life may grow more powerful than before! "So it is also with

---

22. *SKS* 16, 27/ *PV*, 45.
23. *SKS* 16, 28/ *PV*, 45.
24. *SKS* 16, 28/ *PV*, 46.

becoming a Christian."²⁵ Therefore, Kierkegaard advises, "Be the astonished listener who sits and listens to what delights that other person, whom it delights even more that you listen in that way."²⁶ However, the helper should not forget the purpose of being the astonished listener – it is to lead the person to the religious. The term "missionary" is far more frequently used in *Journals and Notebooks*. Kierkegaard states that those who recognize themselves as true Christians inevitably become missionaries: "If it is true that there actually are so few true Christians in Christendom then these are *eo ipso* [precisely thereby] obligated to be missionaries."²⁷

Kierkegaard knew that he could not force anyone to enter into eternal bliss. However, he says, "Even though a person refuses to go along to the place to which one is endeavoring to lead him, there is still one thing that can be done for him: compel him to become aware."²⁸ The decision is up to each individual, but Kierkegaard can at least compel the reader to become aware of the issue.

After explaining the aesthetic writings (the first division), Kierkegaard moves on to the commentary on the *Concluding Unscientific Postscript*

> [*Concluding Postscript*] forms, to repeat again, the turning point in the whole authorship. It poses the issue: becoming a Christian. After first having appropriated all the pseudonymous esthetic writing as a description of one way along which one may go to becoming a Christian – back from the esthetic to becoming a Christian, the book describes the second way – back from the system, the speculative, etc. to becoming a Christian.²⁹

After *Concluding Unscientific Postscript*, Kierkegaard moves on to the explanation of the "exclusively religious books" (the third division):

> As early as *Concluding Postscript*, I could be very brief when the point of view for all the work as an author is that the author is a religious author; what needed explanation there was how the

---

25. *SKS* 16, 28/ *PV*, 46.
26. *SKS* 16, 28/ *PV*, 46.
27. *SKS* 16, 29/ *PV*, 47.
28. *SKS* 16, 32, the title of § 4/ *PV*, 50, the title of § 4.
29. *SKS* 16, 36/ *PV*, 55.

esthetic writing is to be interpreted on this assumption. And what needs no explanation at all on this assumption is of course the latter part, the purely religious writing, which specifically provides the point of view.[30]

Kierkegaard says that clarification of his religious writings is unnecessary because they speak for themselves and demonstrate that they have a religious author. He chronologically divides the authorship into three groups: aesthetic writings, *Concluding Unscientific Postscript*, and exclusively religious writings. He claims that he wrote each work in these three groups as a religious author.

In Chapter 2, Kierkegaard explains his authorship from the perspective of his existence: "Here was a religious author, but one who began as an aesthetic author, and this first part was the incognito, was the deception."[31] If his real *I* is taken into consideration, the entire aesthetic works are a deception because he was, in reality, a religious author. Kierkegaard says, "This book [*Concluding Postscript*] constitutes the turning point in my entire work as an author, inasmuch as it poses the *issue*: becoming a Christian. Thereafter the transition to the second part is made, the series of exclusively religious books."[32] After *Concluding Unscientific Postscript*, the second phase of his authorship began, and most of his works during this period are overtly religious. Accordingly, from the standpoint of his actual existence, the aesthetic writings served as a deliberate form of deception, while *Concluding Unscientific Postscript* marks the turning point that presents the issue of becoming a Christian. His existence corresponds to the writings that follow *Concluding Unscientific Postscript* because these works are overtly religious.

In chapter 3 he explains the role of God's Governance in his authorship. As if he is released from some kind of bondage, Kierkegaard starts joyfully praising God and speaking of his personal relation to him.[33] Further, he steps into the explanation of the specific role of God's Governance in his authorship:

> But in this accounting I must in an even more precise sense bring out Governance's part in the authorship. If, for example, I were to go ahead and say that I had had an overview of the whole

---

30. *SKS* 16, 37/ *PV*, 55.
31. *SKS* 16, 39/ *PV*, 58.
32. *SKS* 16, 44/ *PV*, 63; emphasis in original.
33. *SKS* 16, 50/ *PV*, 71.

> dialectical structure from the very beginning of the whole work as an author ... it would be a denial and an unfairness to God.[34]

Kierkegaard's works are dialectically related to one another and work together beautifully towards a single purpose: to make the readers aware of and, hopefully, seduce them into the Christian faith. However, Kierkegaard says that he did not see that far at the beginning of his authorship. According to him, it was God's Governance that looked ahead from the beginning and allowed his works to be dialectically related in this way. He says, "It is Governance that has brought me up, and the upbringing is reflected in the writing process."[35] Kierkegaard's works not only edify his readers but also shape and form him. Since God planned his entire authorship, and the writing process played a formative role in his own spiritual development, how does Kierkegaard identify himself?

> And now I, the author, in my judgment what relation then do I have to the age? Am I perhaps "the apostle"? Abominable! I have never given occasion for such an idea; I am a poor, lowly human being. Am I then the teacher, the one who does the upbringing? No, not that either. I am the one who himself has been brought up, or the one whose authorship describes what it means to be brought up to become a Christian; just as bringing and accordingly as the upbringing puts pressure on me, I in turn put pressure on the age, but teacher I am not – only a fellow-pupil.[36]

As God was in charge of Kierkegaard's authorship, Kierkegaard was neither an apostle nor a teacher. He regarded himself as "a fellow-pupil" who was brought up by God.

In summary, *The Point of View for My Work as an Author* presents Kierkegaard's belief that the single aim of his various writings is to help the reader become a Christian. He was, in fact, a religious writer; his aesthetic writings were "the deception" and "incognito,"[37] which can be compared

---

34. *SKS* 16, 56/ *PV*, 76–77.
35. *SKS* 16, 56/ *PV*, 77.
36. *SKS* 16, 58/ *PV*, 78–79.
37. *SKS* 16, 39/ *PV*, 58.

with Christ's incarnation and were meant to seduce his fellow citizens to the religious. In order to help, one must begin with humility and become like the aesthetic to the aesthetic. Although no one can force others to enter eternal bliss, Kierkegaard intended to compel awareness in them. He felt profoundly that God was in control of his authorship and did not consider himself a teacher but, rather, a fellow pupil.

7.3 Those Who Doubt the Trustworthiness of *The Point of View for My Work as an Author*

According to *The Point of View for My Work as an Author*, there is a unified voice behind all of Kierkegaard's seemingly perplexing works, and that voice invites the reader to become a Christian. Summarizing the views of scholars on *The Point of View for My Work as an Author*, C. Stephen Evans says, "Most writers about Kierkegaard in English have accepted this point of view, at least until [the mid-1980s] or so."[38] After the mid-1980s, however, Kierkegaard's self-portrait contained in *The Point of View for My Work as an Author* came under heavy fire. A pioneering work that attempts to demythologize Kierkegaard's self-portrait is Henning Fenger's *Kierkegaard, the Myths and Their Origins*. The original edition of this work was published in 1976, and its English edition was published in 1980. Fenger presents a detailed and carefully constructed case for questioning the veracity of what Kierkegaard says in *Journals and Letters*, as well as what scholars say about him based on these documents. Similarly, Louis Mackey's *Points of View* published in 1986, Roger Poole's *Kierkegaard: The Indirect Communication* published in 1993, and Joakim Garff's *SAK Søren Aabye Kierkegaard: En biografi* (*Søren Kierkegaard: A Biography*) published in 2000 (with its English edition published in 2005) are suspicious, deconstructive, or postmodern studies that are influential in Kierkegaard scholarship.

In *Points of View*, Louis Mackey says, "When a man fabricates as many masks to hide behind as Kierkegaard does, one cannot trust his (purportedly) direct asseverations. And when he signs his own name, it no longer has the effect of the signature."[39] Drawing on a statement by Peter, Søren

---

38. Evans, *Kierkegaard: An Introduction*, 12.
39. Mackey, *Points of View*, 188.

Kierkegaard's brother, Mackey says, "Søren Kierkegaard was one of his pseudonyms."[40] If the name "Søren Kierkegaard" is also one of his pseudonyms, then who was the historical Kierkegaard? Mackey makes an astonishing statement: "Søren was never the same person. At most a free variable (an x), he is at last an absolute absence. A constant [evanescence]."[41] According to Mackey's analysis, the historical Kierkegaard vanishes from view, and it is uncertain who he truly was.

At the outset of his *Søren Kierkegaard: A Biography*, Joakim Garff prepares the way for his subject matter by referencing a comment given by Kierkegaard's secretary:

> Israel Levin, who had served as Kierkegaard's secretary for years, surveyed the problem from the opposite side – absolutely from within, so to speak – . . . "Anyone who wants to deal with Søren Kierkegaard's life must take care not to burn his fingers; This is a life so full of contradictions that it will be difficult to get to the bottom of his character. He often refers to double reflections; all his own words were more than sevenfold reflection. He fought to achieve clarity for himself, but he was pursued by all manner of moods and was such a temperamental person that he often alleged things that were untrue, deceiving himself into believing that they were the truth."[42]

According to Israel Levin, who knew Kierkegaard "absolutely from within," Kierkegaard deceived himself into believing that untrue things were the truth. Garff goes on to say,

> Levin's reminder is important because it emphasizes the capricious nature of the source materials and indirectly reveals the infinite care with which Kierkegaard planned his posthumous rebirth. So if one wishes to write a biography of Kierkegaard, one must come to terms with the fact that over much of the expansive terrain one is crisscrossing an already existing autobiography. Consequently the danger of being an unintentional

---

40. Mackey, 188.
41. Mackey, 187.
42. Garff, *Søren Kierkegaard: A Biography*, xx–xxi.

collaborator in writing the myth of Kierkegaard lurks everywhere in the materials, as they provide optimal conditions for uncritical praise of his genius.[43]

According to Garff, Kierkegaard carefully fabricated his self-portrait in a way that would ensure that later generations would evaluate him as he wanted them to. If this is true, one cannot take it for granted that what is said in Kierkegaard's corpus is true. In Garff's view, one must demythologize both Kierkegaard's corpus and existing biographies of Kierkegaard to reveal the historical Kierkegaard.

In summary, Fenger, Mackey, Garff, and some other postmodern readers challenge the traditional reading of Kierkegaard. For them, Kierkegaard's self-portrait is not *the* point of view but *a* point of view. According to Garff, Kierkegaard scholars tend to admire his genius and, therefore, tend to approach him uncritically. By doing so, his admirers unwittingly collaborate with Kierkegaard in fabricating a myth. To avoid this, Kierkegaard's allegedly falsified documents must be doubted and deconstructed. By doing this, we can reveal who Kierkegaard truly was – or was not.

7.4 David R. Law's Middle Position

In his article "A Cacophony of Voices: The Multiple Authors and Readers of Kierkegaard's *The Point of View for My Work as an Author*,"[44] David R. Law evaluates both conservative and radical views and concludes that "our reading of *The Point of View* occupies a middle position"[45] between a radical view (Roger Poole) and a conservative view (Walter Lowrie, Julia Watkin, Michael Theunissen, and Wilfried Greve).[46] According to Law, "[Emanuel Hirsch] and [Joakim Garff] come closest to an accurate characterization of *The Point of View* in their description of the work as strange and chameleon-like."[47]

According to Law, *The Point of View for My Work as an Author* contains both external and internal aporia. An example of external aporia is the

---

43. Garff, xx–xxi.
44. Law, "Cacophony of Voices," 22:44.
45. Law, 22:44.
46. Law, 22:44–45.
47. Law, 22:46.

reference to the fact that by revealing the secret of his pseudonymous work that is supposed to deceive the reader into the truth, the intended deception does not work anymore: "Kierkegaard seems like a magician who is revealing his tricks."[48] The internal aporia springs from the existence of a multitude of authorial voices and multiple intended readers. According to Law, *The Point of View for My Work as an Author* has co-authors – Kierkegaard and God – and seven types of intended readers: the ideal reader, the single individual, God, Kierkegaard's contemporaries, the general public, Kierkegaard's "lover," and Kierkegaard himself.

Law's point is that *The Point of View for My Work as an Author* is not an authoritative interpretation but "a snapshot of this struggle for self-understanding at a particular point in Kierkegaard's life."[49] He further states that ". . . this retrospective understanding has arguably not yet been fully established in *The Point of View*."[50] In reality, Kierkegaard did not publish *The Point of View for My Work as an Author*, instead, he published *On My Work as an Author*. And Law believes that in *On My Work as an Author*, Kierkegaard has resolved the tensions that confound readers of *The Point of View for My Work as an Author*.[51]

7.5 The Standpoint of the Present Study

We have two seemingly contradictory and mutually exclusive views: first, Kierkegaard's own view that he served Christianity through his writings (see section 7.2) and, second, the view that Kierkegaard was a falsifier who craftily prepared his documents in anticipation of a kind of posthumous rebirth (see section 7.3). David Law suggests a middle position (see section 7.4). What is the view adopted in this study?

7.5.1 Who Kierkegaard Was II

I will now repeat a question posed in the introduction to this book: Who was Kierkegaard? We have already examined this question in relation to the

---

48. Law, 22:21.
49. Law, 43.
50. Law, 45.
51. Law, 46.

possibility of calling Kierkegaard a missionary. However, we have not yet formed a clear picture of him at that point in time. We have briefly considered the validity of calling him a missionary, but now we turn to the issue of understanding Kierkegaard the man.

I believe that both conservative and radical portraits of Kierkegaard help us learn who Kierkegaard was. It is not unusual for there to be both positive and negative impressions about any person, especially someone like Kierkegaard, with his mysterious and eccentric personality. For instance, Mackey cites the opinion of Søren's brother,[52] and Garff refers to the opinion of his secretary;[53] but these portrayals of Kierkegaard seem to contradict his own portrayal in his autobiography, *The Point of View for My Work as an Author*. However, there is another type of contemporary impression of Kierkegaard that seems to align well with *The Point of View for My Work as an Author*. For instance, when Kierkegaard was hospitalized in his last days, his niece Henriette Lund (1829–1909) visited her uncle in hospital. In his well-read biography, Walter Lowrie says that Lund "was overwhelmed by the gleam of light which seemed to radiate from [Kierkegaard's] face: 'Never in such a way have I seen the spirit break through the earthly husk and impart to it a glory as of the transfigured body on the resurrection morning.'"[54] Lowrie also refers to the reports of Lund's half-brother, Trols Lund (1840–1921), and Kierkegaard's best friend, Pastor Emil Boesen.[55] The words of Lund and Boesen substantiate the portrait of Kierkegaard found in *The Point of View for My Work as an Author*. We need to value both the supportive and critical perspectives on the portrait of Kierkegaard presented in *The Point of View for My Work as an Author*. By valuing the witness of both positive and negative sources, one can form a clearer picture of the historical Kierkegaard. Reading Garff's biography, Roger Olson synthesizes two seemingly contradictory views and visualizes Kierkegaard as follows:

---

52. "One might almost be tempted to think that even what was signed 'S.K.' might not for certain be his final words, but only a point of view. – Peter Christian Kierkegaard." Mackey, *Points of View*, 160.

53. See Garff's citation of the words of Kierkegaard's secretary, Israel Levin, in section 7.3 of this book.

54. Lowrie, *Short Life of Kierkegaard*, 253–4.

55. Lowrie, 254–255.

> [Kierkegaard] was extremely intense, isolated, somewhat bitter, resentful, elusive, prone to angry outbursts, obsessive-compulsive, etc.... Nevertheless, in spite of these personal flaws and failures, what always shines through is [Kierkegaard]'s insightfulness into the human condition and his commitment to finding true Christianity and living it out to the greatest extent possible.[56]

In her recent biography, Clare Carlisle offers a similar portrait of Kierkegaard:

> His books give his readers high expectations; his lyrical religious discourses describe exquisite ideals, like how a pure human heart reflects God's goodness as truly as a calm, still sea reflects the heavens. Yet in his journals he rehearsed his petty fixations, his jealousy of his rivals' success, his bitter fury at those who slighted him, his debilitating pride. He often felt sorry for himself, justified himself, blamed others for his disappointments.
>
> Does this make him a hypocrite who preached something he did not practise or experience? On the contrary: Kierkegaard's remarkable ability to invoke the goodness, purity and peace for which he longed was inseparable from the storms that raged and twisted in his soul – connected by precisely this longing for what he knew he lacked.... And like every human being, his life was a mixture of elements both petty and profound, which could exert equally powerful claims upon him; he struggled to synthesize them, though they frequently collided in flashes of comic or tragic absurdity.[57]

The portraits of Kierkegaard presented by Olson and Carlisle seem fair and adequate since they allow us to evaluate contemporary testimonies as widely and fairly as possible. In other words, we should not choose between Kierkegaard's self-portrayal in *The Point of View for My Work as an Author*

---

56. Olson, "Was Kierkegaard an Evangelical?," http://www.patheos.com/blogs/rogereolson/2011/08/was-kierkegaard-an-evangelical-part-1/.

57. Carlisle, *Philosopher of the Heart*, xvii.

and more sceptical or postmodern interpretations, but instead consider both in order to gain a fuller picture of who Kierkegaard was.[58]

7.5.2 Confession and the Ongoing Journey of Conversion

Although we concluded in the previous subsection that referring to both conservative and radical views is helpful for realistically visualizing who Kierkegaard was, some aspects cannot easily be synthesized. For instance, one cannot take a middle position between the two views of whether Kierkegaard was a Christian or a falsifier because both views seem mutually exclusive. Is there a reasonable explanation, or at least a hypothesis, that could resolve this tension?

Although the quotation below is Jean-François Lyotard's analysis of Augustine's *Confessions*, does it sound accurate if "Augustine" is replaced with "Kierkegaard"?

> The strike of conversion is not one single blow delivered once and for all; it is not shower of repeated blows either. No, confessive writing bears the fissure along with it. Augustine confesses his God and confesses himself not because he is converted: he becomes converted or tries to become converted while making confession. Conversion is the fissure in the grain of confession, it is not the substitution of an amended, luminous version for a blind, poor version of profane life. No longer will there be night and day for the confessant; henceforth it is fissured day and fissured night. And it is the minuscule chink of this fissure that the stilus is styled, in the precarious, reciprocal balance of enigma and demonstration.[59]

Just as "Augustine confesses his God and confesses himself" in *Confessions*, in *The Point of View for My Work as an Author*, Kierkegaard confesses, "I must also confess that my whole life has been an indescribable joy or satisfaction, which is also why in praying to God I always thank him for the indescribable good he has done to me, far more than I had expected."[60] Remember that

---

58. See also Torrance, *Freedom to Become*, 10, footnote 24.
59. Lyotard, *Confession of Augustine*, 49–50.
60. *PV*, 212, originally from *SKS* 22, 296, NB13:35/*Pap.* X2 A104 *n.d.*, 1849.

one of the seven groups of intended readers of this work, according to Law, is "God." Whereas both conservative and radical views appear contradictory and irreconcilable, Lyotard's description of Augustine's *Confessions* sheds light on the real situation in relation to Kierkegaard without patronizing or ignoring either side. As shown in section 7.3, there *might* be some aspects that appear unchristian, dishonest, or mystifying in Kierkegaard's life and writings (although I do not agree with some of the claims of those holding radical views). However, this does not mean that the Christian aspects of his writings should be rejected. In *The Point of View for My Work as an Author*, to paraphrase Lyotard's words, "Kierkegaard confesses his God and confesses himself not because he is converted: he becomes converted or tries to become converted while making confession." Moreover, Lyotard's description of Augustine's faith resonates with Kierkegaard's concept of faith. Lyotard says, "The strike of conversion is not one single blow delivered once and for all." This sounds like an elaboration of Kierkegaard's concept of conversion. A vital aspect of Kierkegaard's concept of Christian faith is that conversion is not a once-and-for-all experience. Instead, one is always *becoming* a Christian. One has flaws and deficiencies, but one is always striving, willing to be and become a Christian. I believe this is true not just of Augustine and Kierkegaard but of all Christians! While the radical view certainly sheds light on some aspects of the historical Kierkegaard, it is also true that *The Point of View for My Work as an Author* is his sincere attempt to be and become a Christian.

7.5.3 Is *The Point of View for My Work as an Author* Trustworthy?

While I learned a great deal from Law's article and agree with his conclusion that "*The Point of View* is a work in progress and gives us a snapshot of an important transitional phase in Kierkegaard's authorship,"[61] I disagree with his underestimation of the credibility of Kierkegaard's account of his authorship in *The Point of View for My Work as an Author*. In my view, some of the cacophonies of voices that Law detects in this work are not problematic. Both *The Point of View for My Work as an Author* and *Journals and Notebooks* are valuable precisely because they are raw and unfinished. In fact, these works may even be more valuable than Kierkegaard's finalized published works.

---

61. Law, "Cacophony of Voices," 22:43.

Law also recognizes the value of *Journals and Notebooks* and refers to this work in his argument.[62] Since both *The Point of View for My Work as an Author* and *Journals and Notebooks* are unfinished, it is not surprising that they are sometimes contradictory or fragmented. Certainly, "a cacophony" is detectable in these works. However, amid these unpolished, fragmented, and sometimes contradictory elements, we see a Kierkegaard who is less obscured by the refinement of his published works. Indeed, is there any human existence that is not riddled with contradictions? *Journals and Notebooks* contains multiple snapshots of a living Kierkegaard – a figure immersed in plans, self-realization, self-discovery, and the reinterpretation of his authorship. *The Point of View for My Work as an Author* is one of those snapshots. All those snapshots do not "reimpose the straitjacket of authorial intention"[63]; rather, they humbly and humorously help us understand Kierkegaard better.

With due respect to Law, *On My Work as an Author* is not so helpful for this study because it lacks the detailed description of the strategy and background of Kierkegaard's authorship that is found in part 1 and in chapter 1 of part 2 of *The Point of View for My Work as an Author*. For practical reasons, we need *The Point of View for My Work as an Author* to delineate Kierkegaard's mission strategy. In conclusion, the snapshot of Kierkegaard's struggles to understand his authorship in *The Point of View for My Work as an Author* is helpful and illuminating for understanding the nature of Kierkegaard's mission.

A more concrete reason for appreciating *The Point of View for My Work as an Author* is based on the mere fact that *Two Upbuilding Discourses* (1843) was published three months after *Either/Or*. Law partly adopts Fenger's demythologization: "Fenger may be right in claiming that Kierkegaard did not have a religious purpose in mind from the outset."[64] I detect an inconsistency in Law's argument. As for Fenger, he denies Kierkegaard's religious purpose from the outset by the fact that *Two Upbuilding Discourses* (1843) was published three months after *Either/Or*. On the other hand, Law does not buy Fenger's idea because Law thinks a three months hiatus is needed simply

---

62. Law, 22:16, 29, 30, 34, 36, 41, 43–44.
63. Law, 22:20.
64. Law, 45.

for Kierkegaard to write the discourses.[65] Here Law himself (unwittingly) confirms Kierkegaard's religious purpose from the outset (at the time of the publication of *Either/Or* that is "first work in the literature"[66]). In *The Point of View for My Work as an Author*, Kierkegaard plainly says,

> Let us make the attempt; let us try to explain this whole authorship on the assumption that it is the work of an esthetic author. It will readily be seen that from the beginning this explanation is not in accord with the phenomenon but promptly runs aground on *Two Upbuilding Discourses*. If, however, we attempt to explain the authorship by assuming that it is the work of a religious author, we will see that step by step it tallies at every point.[67]

The fact that Kierkegaard's first signed-religious work, *Two Upbuilding Discourses* (1843), was published three months after *Either/Or* eloquently testifies to his religious purpose from the outset.[68] Although the hermeneutics of suspicion is influential in Kierkegaard scholarship today, it seems unnatural to deny Kierkegaard's religious purpose from the outset. The undeniable historical fact is that he published his religious writings – including *Two Upbuilding Discourses* (1843) – from the outset, which dispels any doubts about his original intention as a religious writer.

Therefore, I confidently align myself more closely with the conservative view adopted by Lowrie, Watkin, Theunissen, and Greve and conclude that Kierkegaard was a religious author from the outset.

7.6 Conclusion

What can we learn about Kierkegaard the missionary from *The Point of View for My Work as an Author*?

---

65. Law, 27.
66. *SKS* 16, 11/ *PV*, 23.
67. *SKS* 16, 19–20/ *PV*, 34.
68. Thanks to C. Stephen Evans's supervision, I was reminded of this simple but powerful fact.

7.6.1 Kierkegaard's Missionary Intention and Authorship

Did Kierkegaard have a missionary purpose from the outset? In section 7.5.3, we noted that the fact that *Two Upbuilding Discourses* (1843) was published three months after his first work (*Either/Or*) can be seen as evidence of his religious purpose from the outset. But what about Kierkegaard's missionary intention? Does the fact that he was a religious author from the outset mean that he was a missionary as well? On the one hand, Kierkegaard himself admits, and even emphasizes, that he did not see that far from the beginning. Therefore, it would be an overestimation to claim that he had a clear vision and a fully developed mission strategy from the outset. On the other hand, it is also fair to say that his authorship can be interpreted from the perspective of Kierkegaard as a missionary. Law, while denying a religious purpose from the outset, states, "The fact is that a religious interpretation *can* be placed upon the authorship."[69] Applying Law's logic, we can argue that a missionary interpretation *can* be placed upon the authorship, and this is supported by Kierkegaard's retrospective interpretation.[70] According to Kierkegaard, he wrote *Either/Or* to effectively proclaim Christianity within Christendom. He retrospectively estimates that *Either/Or*'s strategy is far more effective than starting directly with orthodoxy. Thus, agreeing with Kierkegaard's own view, we can place a missionary interpretation on his authorship.

7.6.2 A Unique Characteristic of Kierkegaard the Missionary

Thanks to Law's detection of a cacophony of voices in *The Point of View for My Work as an Author*, a unique aspect of Kierkegaard as a missionary becomes more visible. Kierkegaard was a missionary who hid his identity as a missionary, at least in his early published works. Law says, "If we take indirect communication and the notion of hidden inwardness seriously, then it is not up to Kierkegaard to 'explain' his authorship, for it is quite simply none of his business how I react to his authorship and use it in my own spiritual journey."[71] This makes it clear why Kierkegaard did not reveal his missionary intention in his published works – it was so that he could be consistent with

---

69. Law, "Cacophony of Voices," 45, emphasis in original.
70. *SKS* 20, 318, NB4:66/ *JP*, V 6107 *n.d.*, 1848.
71. Law, "Cacophony of Voices," 22:19.

his indirect communication, which attempts to nurture hidden inwardness in the reader. As Mark C. Miller aptly says,

> Kierkegaard wants to arouse a sense of self in the good, in God. But Xers, in their sensuality, forget who God is. What's more, if they suspect you're going to tell them about God or their need for him, they hear a sales pitch coming. They have been a target market for too long. They will not listen. If they are to hear the gospel, they must be told subversively, and not know what they are hearing until it is too late.[72]

If there is such a thing as a Kierkegaardian mission strategy, a pivotal aspect of such a strategy is not introducing oneself as a missionary. If Kierkegaard had introduced himself as a missionary, he would no longer be Kierkegaard. Therefore, he could only discuss the importance of the missionary task in his unpublished works, to which his contemporaries had no access.

7.6.3 Validity of Identifying Kierkegaard's Mission as Incarnational Mission

In "Incarnational Mission: Søren Kierkegaard's Challenge to Evangelical Christianity," Ádám Szabados describes a Kierkegaardian mission as "incarnational mission."[73] Is such an identification valid? Is there solid evidence that Kierkegaard consciously imitated Christ's ministry on earth? First, as discussed in section 7.2, Kierkegaard compares *his hidden identity as a religious author* to *Christ's hidden identity on earth.*[74] Here, one sees Kierkegaard's self-claimed analogy between his authorial strategy and Christ's incarnation.

Second, there seems to be indirect evidence that Kierkegaard was an incarnational missionary in the parallel between the apostle Paul's mission strategy (1 Cor 9:19–23) and Kierkegaard's description of mission tactic (*SKS* 16, 28/ *PV*, 46), as already mentioned at the beginning of this chapter. But do New Testament scholars view Paul's strategy in 1 Corinthians 9:19–23 as an imitation of Christ's incarnational method of making friends with sinners? Some New Testament scholars are sceptical about how much Paul knew about the

---

72. Miller, "Hipness unto Death," 3.
73. Szabados, "Incarnational Mission," 40. See also section 1.3.3.
74. *SKS* 16, 19/ *PV*, 34.

historical Jesus. However, recent commentaries on 1 Corinthians interpret this passage as Paul's *imitatio Christi*.[75] Therefore, although not all scholars agree, a significant number do view Paul's mission strategy in 1 Corinthians 9:19–23 as an imitation of Christ's method.

In making an overall evaluation, there is direct evidence (Kierkegaard's own comparison of his method with Christ's incarnation) and indirect evidence (the similarity between Kierkegaard's description of mission strategy and Paul's incarnational mission strategy in 1 Corinthians 9:19–23) to support the view that Kierkegaard imitated the methods of the incarnated Christ. Thus, viewing Kierkegaard as an incarnational missionary is a plausible interpretation.

Although this study contends that Kierkegaard was a missionary, the reader may notice that there is not even a single quotation where Kierkegaard directly uses the term "missionary" in *Either/Or*, *Two Upbuilding Discourses* (1843), *The Sickness unto Death*, or *Practice in Christianity*. In *The Point of View for My Work as an Author*, there are at least a few such references,[76] but this work functions largely as a commentary on Kierkegaard's mission strategy and does not rely on explicitly missionary terminology. At the same time, this study has cited several instances where Kierkegaard directly uses the term "missionary," revealing his conviction that the missionary task is both an integral part of Christianity and his self-identification as a missionary. Indeed, these direct references to "missionary" are found exclusively in *Journals and Notebooks*. Although this vast literary work – which occupies roughly one-third of Kierkegaard's oeuvre – is clearly beyond the scope of this study, the next chapter will provide a detailed and comprehensive account of Kierkegaard's direct references to "missionary" in *Journals and Notebooks*.

---

75. "Jesus himself is the paradigm for such servanthood. Free, in order to become slave to all – this is surely the ultimate expression of truly Christian, because it is truly Christlike, behavior." Fee, *Corinthians*, 426. "This self-lowering is homologous with the law/pattern of Christ, who also became a slave (cf. Phil. 2:6–8) in obedience to God." Hays, *First Corinthians*, 155. "What are the implications of viewing 1 Cor 10:32–11:1 as a recapitulation of 1 Cor 9:19–23? The correlation suggests that Paul's accommodation described in 1 Cor 9:19–23 was modelled after Christ's example." Rudolph, *Jew to the Jews*, 176.

76. *SKS* 16, 24/ *PV*, 42; *SKS* 16, 29/ *PV*, 47.

CHAPTER 8

A Selective Study of *Journals and Notebooks* with Specific Regard to a View of Kierkegaard as a Missionary

For Kierkegaard there was no doubt that true Christianity must always have a universal and missionary character. "According to the New Testament, Christianity is a continuing mission, every Christian a missionary: Go out and proclaim my teaching." If one forgets this task and settles down in repose, Christianity loses its significance for him and the falling away begins. Kierkegaard thinks that the individual needs to be reminded again of this task. "Christianity in repose is *eo ipso* not Christianity. As soon as anything of that sort appears, it means: 'Become a missionary.'"[1]

– Howard V. Hong, Edna H. Hong, and Gregor Malantschuk

The subject of this chapter is Kierkegaard's *Journaler og Papirer* (*Journals and Papers* [The Hongs's and Malantschuk's edition, 1978] or *Journals and Notebooks* [the latest edition, 2020]). As stated above, the Hongs and Malantschuk thematically edited Kierkegaard's *Journals and Papers* and

---

1. Howard V. and Edna H. Hong, Gregor Malantschuk, *s.v.* "*mission*" in *Søren Kierkegaard's Journals and Papers, Volume 3, L-R.* ed. and trans. by Howard V. and Edna H. Hong, assisted by Gregor Malantschuk, Bloomington: Indiana University Press 1975, 820; the two quotations within double quotation marks are originally from *SKS* 25, 241, NB28:33/ *JP*, III 2730 *n.d.*, 1853; *SKS* 26, 16, NB31:17/ *JP*, III 2731 *n.d.*, 1854.

provide a concise summary of the theme of "mission" in this literature. The task of this chapter is to examine whether this summary is accurate.

The outline of this chapter is as follows: In the first section, I will provide a historical introduction. In the second section, I will examine and annotate important journal entries that refer to the term "missionary." In the third section, I will attempt to resolve several issues raised in the previous section. In the fourth section, I will explore alternative terms synonymous with "missionary," considering whether Kierkegaard might have chosen a more fitting label for himself than the somewhat peculiar self-identification as "missionary." In section five, I will offer some concluding remarks.

8.1 Historical Introduction

"Before Kierkegaard's death, Emil Boesen [Kierkegaard's close friend] asked him about his various manuscripts and papers [*Journals and Notebooks*]. His reply was: 'No, let come what may; it depends upon chance.'"[2] It was God's providence that ensured *Journals and Notebooks* survived and was published posthumously. *Af Søren Kierkegaards Efterladte Papirer* (*From Søren Kierkegaard's Posthumous Papers*) – the first edition of Kierkegaard's *Journals and Notebooks* – were published between 1869 and 1881. These papers – written between 1833 (ten years before the publication of *Either/Or*) and 1855 (the year of Kierkegaard's death) – are sources that offer unparalleled insights into Kierkegaard's life, ranging from his youth to his later years. *Journals and Notebooks* contains various kinds of writings, such as his personal translation of the New Testament from Greek to Latin, prayers, diary entries, notes, descriptions of his relationship with Regine, unpublished works, drafts, notes on published works, plans for lectures, daily remarks, and other reflections – particularly on the topic of a missionary, as we shall explore in this chapter – that are not found in his published works. In *Journals and Notebooks*, one can see the living Kierkegaard in his description of the darkest moments and the supreme experience of Christian faith, in literary fragments and scribbles, and even in things that have been erased or torn off. Some entries are dated, others are not. Furthermore, Kierkegaard often reread and revised his *Journals and Notebooks*. The editors of the latest edition of *Journals and Notebooks*

---

2. Hong and Hong, "Translator's Preface" in *JP*, I xv.

offer this explanation: "Further reflections could be – and very often were – added later, sometimes much later, often on several subsequent occasions, e.g., when Kierkegaard read or thought of something that reminded him of something he had written earlier."[3] As a result, *Journals and Notebooks* contains a vast amount of material – over seven thousand pages – and a forest of profound thoughts. It is beyond the scope of this study to comprehensively examine this document. Therefore, we will narrow our focus and concentrate on Kierkegaard's direct references to "(the) missionary" or "(the) missionaries," where he either discusses the missionary task as an integral part of Christianity or identifies himself as a missionary.

8.2 Kierkegaard's References to "(the) Missionary" or "(the) Missionaries"

In this section, we will examine Kierkegaard's reference to "(the) missionary" or "(the) missionaries" in *Journals and Notebooks*, as well as his concept of a missionary in this work.[4] First and foremost, we must remember that Kierkegaard's entire authorship focuses on the issue of becoming a Christian. As he begins *The Point of View for My Work as an Author*, he explains, "The content, then, of [*The Point of View for My Work as an Author*] is: what I in truth am as an author, that I am and was a religious author, that my whole authorship pertains to Christianity, to the issue: becoming a Christian."[5] Not

---

3. Kirmmse, "Introduction to the English Language Edition" in *KJN* 1, xiv.

4. To be precise, there are some other references to "missionary (*Missionair*)," "the missionary (*Missionairen*)," "missionaries (*Missionairer*)" or "the missionaries (*Missionairerne*)" that are not discussed or quoted in this book. Since the following unmentioned references are either not directly related to the themes of the present study or are ambiguous, I believe that not mentioning these references does not misrepresent Kierkegaard's view of the term "missionary": *SKS* 6, 318/ *SLW*, 342; *SKS* 7, 549/ *CUP I*, 605; *SKS* 7, 551/ *CUP I*, 606; *SKS* 10, 222/ *CD*, 214; *SKS* 12, 104/ *PC*, 95–96; *SKS* 16, 24/ *PV*, 42; *SKS* 17, 262, DD:143/ *JP*, III 2738 Sep 17, 1838; *SKS* 18, 26, EE:60/ *JP*, V 5382, May 11, 1839; *SKS* 24, 207, NB23:4/ *JP*, III 2758, *n.d.*, 1851; *SKS* 28, 162, Letter 84/ *JP*, V 5548 Letters, no. 62 January 16 [1842]; *SKS* 20, 237, NB2:258/ *JP*, V 6070, *n.d.*, 1847. Even if the content is vital for the theme of the present study, due to the limited space, some entries are not mentioned in this book: *SKS* 16, 29/ *PV*, 47; *SKS* 20, 309, NB4:47/ *JP*, I 473 *n.d.*, 1848; *SKS* 23, 209, NB17:63/ *JP*, III 3569, *n.d.*, 1850; *SKS* 24, 363, NB24:68/ *JP*, III 3521 *n.d.*, 1851. Consequently, there are plenty of journal entries where Kierkegaard discusses a missionary task as an integral part of Christianity or views himself as a missionary.

5. *SKS* 16, 12/ *PV*, 23.

just one work or a few works but all of Kierkegaard's works dialectically serve to clarify what it means to become a Christian.

Second, in the following journal entry, Kierkegaard says that anyone who is willing to be deeply involved in Christianity will inevitably become a missionary: "If, however, you feel a deeper need to become involved with Christianity, well, then, get out in the character of the essentially Christian, in character in the strictest sense of the word – witness to the teaching like a missionary among the heathen or in 'Christendom.'"[6] This quotation also suggests that a Christian's location or context – whether among unbelievers or in Christendom – should not impact their role as a missionary. While Kierkegaard's proclamation was made in Christendom – and it seems likely that his strategy would have been different had he laboured among unbelievers – Kierkegaard strongly believed that Christians must proclaim Christianity regardless of their context. In this sense, if the central issue underlying Kierkegaard's oeuvre is becoming a Christian, this necessarily means that the central issue underlying his work is also about becoming a missionary. In the following journal entry, Kierkegaard proposes that if someone is uncertain about their love for God, they should become a missionary: "Finally, if you doubt that you will be kept from loving God . . . then become a missionary, which every Christian really is, after all."[7] As far as Kierkegaard is concerned, the missionary task must be carried out not because Christians are few or because someone is good at it but simply because one is a Christian.

Third, *a missionary* is an example of the "single individual" in Kierkegaard's thought.

> A single individual, gripped by Christianity, becomes a missionary, and that is why Christianity has spread so remarkably, something scarcely to be found in any other religion, no more than it occurs to the single individual in any other religion to want, *mir nichts und Dir nichts*,[8] to spread his religion.[9]

---

6. *SKS* 27, 593, Papir 464/ *JP*, III 3581 *n.d.*, 1853–1854.

7. *SKS* 27, 658, Papir 554/ *JP*, IV 4730 *n.d.*, 1855.

8. The German idiom is *mir nichts, Dir nichts* and its literal translation is "nothing for me, nothing for you"; the commentary to *SKS* translates this "without further ado, for no reason." *Kommentarer til SKS* 24, 135m, 7.

9. *SKS* 24, 135, NB22:61.a/ *JP*, III 2727 *n.d.*, 1850.

Kierkegaard, who is the originator of the term "single individual," says that the single individual *religiously influences others*.[10] Furthermore, he says that "Christianity has spread so remarkably" *because* a Christian is the single individual. It seems clear that Kierkegaard's "single individual" is not an asocial individualist but, rather, a prominent proponent of the Christian gospel. It would not be an overstatement to say that one cannot properly understand what Kierkegaard meant by "a single individual" without understanding his concept of a "missionary." However, as far as I am aware, no published study has connected these two concepts. This represents a lacuna in Kierkegaard scholarship that I hope to address in this work. According to the journal entry below, until Kierkegaard, Socrates was the only person to utilize the concept of "the single individual." However, Kierkegaard does not slavishly imitate Socrates; rather, he transforms this concept into the missionary within Christendom:

> The single individual – this category has been used only once before (the first time) in a decisively dialectical way, by Socrates in disintegrating paganism. In Christendom it will be used a second time in the very opposite way, to make men (the Christians) Christians.[11] It is not the missionary's category with respect to the pagans to whom he proclaims Christianity, but it is the missionary's category within Christendom itself, for the inward deepening of being and becoming a Christian. When he, the missionary, comes, he will use this category. If the age is waiting for a hero, it waits in vain; instead there will more likely come one who in divine weakness will teach men obedience – by means of their slaying him in impious rebellion, him, the one obedient to God.[12]

---

10. See also *SKS* 22, 396–397, NB14:89/ *JP*, II 2019 n.d., 1849.

11. It sounds redundant to *make the Christians Christians*. What Kierkegaard means is that his contemporary Danes are cultural or untrue Christians. Therefore, Kierkegaard attempts to help them become and be true Christians. As Johannes Climacus, one of Kierkegaard's pseudonyms, says, although in the Christendom of Denmark "[it] is assumed that we are all Christian," "to become a Christian is actually the most difficult of all tasks." *SKS* 7, 55; 343/ *CUP I*, 50; 377.

12. *SKS* 20, 281–282, NB3:77/ *JP*, II 2004 n.d., 1847.

The above quotation suggests that a missionary within Christendom will teach people obedience to God by being slain in divine weakness. Therefore, the fourth unique concept of the Kierkegaardian missionary found in *Journals and Notebooks* is that a missionary is willing to be a *martyr*.

Like Hans Lassen Martensen (1808–1884), a contemporary of Kierkegaard, some may ask the question, "Cannot a witness to the truth be stoned in a manner other than by the throwing of actual stones?"[13] Kierkegaard is not suggesting that a martyr must always be stoned to death. Jack Mulder Jr. concisely summarizes Kierkegaard's concept of "Martyrdom/Persecution": "Anti-Climacus and Kierkegaard will concede that in the logical sense not everyone can be a martyr, but that at minimum one must experience a 'martyrdom in possibility.'"[14] Therefore, the point is not whether one is actually stoned to death but whether they are *willing* to sacrifice their life for Christian truth. In Kierkegaard's view, a martyr is one who is willing to live and die for Christian truth.[15] The following journal entry also affirms that "the single individual," "the missionary," and "the martyr" are interconnected:

> "The martyr," this "martyr of the future" ("the missionary"), who uses the category "the single individual" educationally, will by all means have within himself what is appropriate to the age ("the age of reflection") – a superior reflection and, in addition to the faith and the courage to risk, will need the work or the preliminary work of infinite reflection in becoming or in order to become a martyr.[16]

Fifth, as the above quotation shows, a Christian who is "the missionary," "the single individual," and "the martyr" will "by all means have within himself what is appropriate" to "the age of reflection." The quotation below from *Journals and Notebooks* confirms once again that, in Kierkegaard's thought,

---

13. Garff, *Søren Kierkegaard: A Biography*, 736.

14. Mulder, "Martyrdom/Persecution," 128; the quotation within the quotation is originally from *SKS* 12, 220–221/ *PC*, 226. Mulder also suggests referring to *SKS* 22, 100, NB11:170 / *JP*, I 504.

15. See the following reflection upon his role as a martyr: "I seemed to understand that the world, or Denmark, needed a martyr. I had everything ready in writing and really thought about whether it was possible to back up my writing in the most decisive manner, by laying down my life." *SKS* 21, 367, NB10:200/ *KJN* 5, 378 25 April 1849.

16. *JP*, III 2649/ *Pap*. IX B 63:13 *n.d.*, 1848.

the martyr and the missionary are conceptually connected, and that such a person undoubtedly has within themselves what is appropriate to the age of reflection:

> "The martyr" ("the missionary") will by all means have within himself what is appropriate to the age, "the age of reflection" – an infinite reflection as a servant in respect to *becoming* a martyr, so that, knowing the times from the bottom up, he succeeds in falling at the right spot and assures that his death wounds in the right spot.[17]

What is "the age of reflection"? In Kierkegaard's usage, this signifies "the present age."[18] For Kierkegaard, reflection is a key feature of the present age. He problematized reflection, which just wonders, hesitates, and does not produce a decision, and diagnosed this phenomenon as a sickness in the present age: "Action and decision are just as scarce these days."[19] However, reflection is not always negative in Kierkegaard's view. As David Lappano rightly points out, "It is not reflection itself that Kierkegaard opposes but 'stagnation in reflection.'"[20] For Kierkegaard, reflection that results in a leap into the religious is a good thing and can guide one towards eternal salvation: "Reflection is a snare in which one is trapped, but in and through the inspired leap of religiousness the situation changes and it is the snare that catapults one into the embrace of the eternal."[21] Therefore, in Kierkegaard's thought, a missionary is suitable to the present age (the age of reflection) because their existence may prompt people to reflect on their lives and, hopefully, embrace the eternal.

Finally, while the references in this section point to Kierkegaard's self-recognition as a missionary, there are also a few instances where he seems to *deny* his missionary identity: "But I was bound to the idea of trying to introduce Christianity into Christendom, albeit poetically and without authority

---

17. *JP*, III 2648/ *Pap.* IX B 63:12 *n.d.*, 1848, emphasis in original.

18. See "The Present Age" of "III Conclusions from a Consideration of the Two Ages" in *SKS* 8, 66–106/ *TA*, 68–112.

19. *SKS* 8, 69/ *TA*, 71.

20. Lappano, "Press/Journalism," 127; the quotation within the quotation is originally from *SKS* 8, 92 / *TA*, 96.

21. *SKS* 8, 85/ *TA*, 89.

(namely, not making myself a missionary)."²² In this quotation, Kierkegaard seems to shrink back from the idea of himself as a missionary. However, his reason for "not making myself a missionary" is that he sought to emphasize his lack of formal authority. His recognition that was "bound to the idea of trying to introduce Christianity to Christendom" certainly aligns with what one might call the missionary task. Although Kierkegaard graduated from seminary, he remained unordained throughout his life, and his method was to proclaim Christianity indirectly, rather than directly. Therefore, the journal entry cited earlier does not really contradict Kierkegaard's identity as a missionary, even though it may appear to do so. Instead, Kierkegaard is expressing that, without authority, he seeks to introduce Christianity into Christendom in an indirect manner.

In conclusion, the quotations in this section speak for themselves, showing that Kierkegaard took his role as a missionary in the Christendom of Denmark very seriously. His understanding of the term "missionary" has a broader meaning. While Kierkegaard was not a missionary sent to a foreign country by a missionary organization, he probably viewed himself as a missionary writer within Christendom. In this way, Kierkegaard asserts that every Christian can and should be a missionary in their own context. Using whatever means or methods available, each person is tasked with proclaiming Christianity to their neighbors.²³

8.3 Problems Posed in the Previous Section

Our investigation in the previous section raises several problems. The first concerns the location of Kierkegaard's frank discussions about his missionary identity – namely, all these are found in his unpublished works, particularly *Journals and Notebooks*, which were not published during Kierkegaard's lifetime. The second problem concerns the period during which these missionary references were written. The dates of the journal entries – which are indicated in the footnotes in the previous section – show that Kierkegaard's

---

22. *SKS* 21, 289, NB10:60/ *JP*, VI 6536 *n.d.*, 1849. See also *SKS* 23, 272, NB18:33/ *JP*, VI 6616 *n.d.*, 1850.

23. See below: "All of us are called to be first-class witnesses all of our lives wherever we are." Hale, *On Being a Missionary*, 8.

references to "missionary" relate only to the last several years of his journal writing (1847–1855) and not to the entire period (1833–1855). Third, although we have confirmed Kierkegaard's belief that the single individual rapidly spreads the gospel, common sense demands an explanation for how this single individual relates to other people. Fourth, although Kierkegaard suggests that a missionary who is the single individual and martyr can effectively proclaim Christianity in the age of reflection, how this works in practice remains unclear. Fifth, although Kierkegaard's references to "missionary" have been systematically listed in the previous section, he sometimes discusses the concept of the missionary without explicitly using the term "missionary" – for example, references to "proclaiming Christianity" (*at forkynde Christendommen*) or "spreading Christianity" (*at udbrede Christendommen*). In that case, limiting the investigation to direct references to 'missionary' may result in a partial understanding. This section will address these five problems.

First, although Kierkegaard occasionally refers to "(the) missionary" or "(the) missionaries" in his published works, he never calls his authorship a missionary task; and in his published works, he never explicitly states that the missionary task is an integral part of Christianity. As discussed in the introduction to this book, a view of Kierkegaard as a missionary has been marginalized, which is not surprising since, in his published works, he never explicitly describes his authorship a missionary task or asserts that the missionary task is central to Christianity. The surprisingly rich references to his conviction that every Christian (including himself) is called to be a missionary – which were highlighted in the previous section – can *only* be found in his unpublished works, particularly *Journals and Notebooks*. But what does this mean? One might speculate that Kierkegaard did not want his contemporaries to know about his missionary intentions. The fact that he reveals his zeal for Christian mission only in the unpublished works – and never in the published works – suggests that his intention was, in his own words, "to wound from behind."[24] Behind the masks of multiple pseudonyms, he pretended to be an aesthetic writer but had a hidden missionary agenda. The contrast between Kierkegaard's eloquence as he discusses his missionary intention in *Journals and Notebooks* and his silence on this topic in his published works suggests a deliberate missionary tactic to ambush the reader

---

24. *SKS* 20, 318–319, NB4:66/ *JP*, V 6107 *n.d.*, 1848.

by never officially introducing himself as a missionary, which aligns with our observations on *The Point of View for My Work as an Author* in section 7.6.2.

The second problem relates to the period of his journal references to "(the) missionary" or "(the) missionaries." Although many journal entries support Kierkegaard's missionary self-understanding, all the references that explicitly mention this occur from 1847 to 1855 – namely, during his second authorship.[25] In other words, 1847 is the earliest date of any of the journal entries that testify to Kierkegaard's missionary self-understanding. Considering that his journal entries begin in 1833 and that his early entries reveal certain patterns of thought that are idiosyncratic to him and pervasive in his writings, it is strange that no references to "(the) missionary" or "(the) missionaries" appear before 1847. Was Kierkegaard aware of the importance of missionary tasks in 1847? Should we conclude that he did not have a missionary intention during his first authorship (1843–1846) and only gradually began to realize the importance of the missionary task, eventually seeing himself as a missionary writer only during his second authorship (1846–1851)? His silence on the topic of missionary intention before 1847 and his testimony of retrospective realization about his entire authorship suggest that he did not have a clear vision of his mission strategy from the outset. This finding also aligns with our observations on *The Point of Work for My Work as an Author* in section 7.6.1. However, one *could* interpret his *whole* authorship from the perspective of Kierkegaard as a missionary. Since Kierkegaard saw himself as a co-author with God, the reader can only do justice to Kierkegaard's text by paying attention to the pivotal role of God's Governance. Accordingly, our examination of *Journals and Notebooks* reveals that, whether consciously or unconsciously, Kierkegaard's missionary agenda began before he explicitly acknowledged it.

The third and fourth problems will be addressed together. How does it make sense that the single individual can (sociably?) spread the gospel and also function as a martyr who appropriately proclaims Christianity in the age of reflection? Although space does not allow me to delve into how the terms "Christian," "missionary," "the single individual," and "martyr" are interconnected in Kierkegaard's thought or how the figure who embodies these identities is well-suited to the age of reflection, I offer a possible hypothesis,

---

25. See the dates of the journal entries in the footnotes of section 8.2.

backed by a legitimate biblical argument that draws on Johannine theology. John 21:15–23 records a conversation between the risen Christ and the apostle Peter. Three times, the risen Christ asks Peter, "Do you love me?" Peter answers, "You know that I love you" (21:15–17). Since a Christian is one who loves Jesus, this conversation reaffirms that Peter is a *Christian*.[26] Next, Christ commands Peter to feed or tend his sheep (vv. 15–17), which means that Christ assigns Peter to be a pastor or missionary who feeds Jesus' sheep with spiritual food. Then, although Peter worries about another disciple, Christ reminds Peter not to be concerned with others but to concentrate on individually following Jesus (vv. 20–22). In other words, Christ is the originator of *the single individual* before Kierkegaard. Further, Christ foretells Peter's martyrdom (vv. 18–19). So Peter is a martyr. Finally, during his ministry on earth, Jesus says as follows: 'Very truly, I tell you, unless a grain of wheat falls into the earth and dies, it remains just a single grain; but if it dies, it bears much fruit.' (John 12:24) According to Jesus, a martyr's death bears much fruit. Kierkegaard viewed that such a martyr is needed in the age of reflection:

> What the age needs is not a genius – it surely has had geniuses enough – but a martyr, one who in order to teach men to obey would himself become obedient unto death, one whom men put to death; but, see, just because of that they would lose, for simply by killing him, by being victorious in this way, they would become afraid for themselves. This is the awakening which the age needs.[27]

According to the above quotation, a person like the apostle Peter – a Christian (one who loves Jesus), a missionary (one who feeds others with spiritual food), the single individual (one who personally follows Jesus), and a martyr – can spiritually awaken people in the age of reflection. In other words, whether everyone agrees or not, this is how Kierkegaard's logic works. In sum, the concept of "Christian," "missionary," "the single individual," and "martyr" are seamlessly connected in both Christ's and Kierkegaard's thoughts. Furthermore, in and through the way such a figure lives and dies, reflecting upon such a missionary can bear much spiritual fruit (to

---

26. For example, John 14:15; 15:10.
27. *SKS* 20, 254, NB3:19/ *JP*, III 2636 *n.d.*, 1847.

use Johannine language) or awaken and edify one's contemporaries (to use Kierkegaard's language).

Fifth, although I have systematically collected Kierkegaard's references to "missionary," this survey does not include the journal entries that discuss the concept of the missionary without using the term "missionary." For example, consider the following quotation: "But something else preoccupies me: . . . do I dare profit temporally by proclaiming – Christianity, which is renunciation of things temporal."[28] Although this quotation does not use the term "missionary," it deals with a missionary task. Furthermore, it introduces a new aspect of Kierkegaard's concept of the missionary – the question of a missionary's wage. I must admit that the present chapter does not deal comprehensively with Kierkegaard's concept of the missionary in *Journals and Notebooks*. Ideally, we should include all journal entries that are related to the concept of the missionary, but such an exhaustive study is beyond the scope of this work. Further studies are needed to clarify Kierkegaard's concept of the missionary in *Journals and Notebooks*.

8.4 Why "Missionary" Instead of Other Terms?

Some readers may continue to wonder: is "missionary" the best term, even if Kierkegaard might have attempted to proclaim Christianity through his writings? What about other terms related to a missionary, such as "evangelist," "preacher," "apologist" or "witness to the truth"? Did Kierkegaard use a more suitable term to identify his task and position? We turn now to these questions.

The term "missionary" is *Missionair* in the Danish of Kierkegaard's time and *missionær* in modern Danish. In the third edition of *Dansk-Engelsk Ordbog* (*English-Danish Dictionary*), *missionær* is simply "missionary."[29] In the nineteenth edition of *Politikens Nudansk Ordbog* (*Politiken's New Danish Dictionary*), *missionær* is "a person who is sent out from a church or a religious sect in order to proclaim the church's or the sect's faith."[30] Thus, there is no significant difference between the concept of the English "missionary" and the Danish *Missionair* or *missionær*. Kierkegaard probably understood

---

28. *JP*, VI 6843/ *Pap.* X5 A 146, 13 Octover 1853.
29. "*missionær*," Pedersen, *Dansk-Engelsk Ordbog*, 746.
30. "*missionær*," *Politikens Nudansk Ordbog*, 750.

"missionary" in the same way we understand it today. In other words, he probably recognized the awkwardness of using this term to describe his position or task. But why does he use this term rather than other synonyms or seemingly more appropriate terms?

The term "evangelist" is *Evangelist* in the Danish at Kierkegaard's time and *evangelist* in modern Danish. In the nineteenth edition of *Politikens Ordbog*, *evangelist* is defined first as "each of the four authors of gospels in the New Testament, Matthew, Mark, Luke, and John" and second as "a preacher of the gospel in certain free religious community."[31] In English, "evangelist" shares these same two meanings – either *an author of one of the four Gospels in the New Testament* or *one who proclaims Christianity*. But our focus here is on the latter meaning, which relates to Kierkegaard's calling or occupation, even though Kierkegaard does use *Evangelist* in its first sense twice. However, Kierkegaard does not use *Evangelist* to signify his vocation. A related word – "Evangelism" or *Evangelium* in Danish – occurs 159 times in Kierkegaard's published works and 88 times in his *Journals and Notebooks*. But most of these occurrences refer to the gospel in the New Testament or to the title of his book *Lidelsernes Evangelium* (*The Gospel of Suffering*), which is found in the third part of his *Upbuilding Discourses in Various Spirits*, which was published in 1847. These statistics show that Kierkegaard does not use *Evangelist* or *Evangelium* to speak of his self-understanding of his position or task.

What about the term "preacher" (*forkynder* or *prædikant*) that the Danish dictionary lists under synonyms of *Evangelist*? In the nineteenth edition of *Politikens Ordbog*, preacher (*forkynder*) means "a person who seeks to spread out religious teaching or an idea, for example through sermons (*prædikener*),"[32] which seems fitting to describe Kierkegaard's mission through authorship. "*Forkynder*" can be both a present-tense verb and a noun, but only the noun concerns us because it is the noun form that would be used in language that is explicitly about self-identity or vocation. Since nouns were capitalized in Kierkegaard's age, we are specifically interested in occurrences of *Forkynder* in Kierkegaard's corpus. There are only a few such occurrences in Kierkegaard's writings – for instance, he uses *Forkynder* to critique contemporary pastors or to discuss the authenticity of such persons, but he does

---

31. "*evangelist*," 290.
32. "*forkynder*," 348.

not use this term to describe his own position. In the nineteenth edition of *Politikens Ordbog*, preacher (*prædikant*) means "a person who seeks to propagate religion and gain new followers."[33] *Prædikant* occurs twenty times in Kierkegaard's corpus. Its usage is similar to *Forkynder*, and it is not used to signify Kierkegaard's position.

Kierkegaard's thought seems more apologetic than missionary as it is highly intellectual. However, the term *Apologet* (apologist) never occurs, and he does not use the related term *Apologetik* (apologetics) very much either. Surprisingly – or unsurprisingly for the reader of this book – whenever Kierkegaard does use *Apologetik*, he always does so negatively, with just one exception.[34] Kierkegaard also abhors the related term "*at forsvare Christendommen* (to defend Christianity)."[35] He would certainly not have allowed anyone to call him either an apologist or a defender of Christianity. These terms would not have aligned with his self-understanding of his task.

Another possible term to describe Kierkegaard's self-understanding of his task is *Sandhedsvidne (truth's witness)* This term occurs more than 50 times in his corpus and is arguably a pivotal concept for Kierkegaard. Although he had used this term already in 1844, his use of it became (in)famous through his attack upon Christendom launched by the publication of an article titled "Was Bishop Mynster a 'Truth-Witness,' One of 'the Authentic Truth-Witnesses' – Is This the Truth?" Of course, an expected answer to the question of this article's title is – no. Kierkegaard himself speaks about the application of this title to himself saying, ". . . in the strictest sense I am not a witness to the truth."[36] Kierkegaard indeed attempts to serve Christian truth with all his might, but it is not his preference to call himself a witness to the truth.

Having considered various terms and labels that might be applied to Kierkegaard, we return to the question posed at the beginning of this section: Why should we call Kierkegaard a missionary rather than an evangelist, preacher, apologist, or witness to the truth? The answer is simply that Kierkegaard himself seemed to have felt most at home with the term "missionary," rather than any of these other related terms. Some may prefer to use

---

33. "*prædikant*," 904.
34. *SKS* 24, 338, NB24:35/ *JP*, IV, 3842.
35. *SKS* 11, 200/ *SUD*, 87.
36. *SKS* 21, 368, NB10:200/ *JP*, VI 6391 25 April 1849.

a different term to describe Kierkegaard's work and life, not caring whether he would have approved of their nomenclature. After all, he might have misunderstood his task, and later generations might find a more suitable term for his work; or perhaps his usage of the term "missionary" seems too peculiar, dated, or not in keeping with our modern culture. Nevertheless, it is worth attempting identify his role with a name that he would have approved of.

8.5 Summary and Conclusion

This chapter has explored *Journals and Notebooks* to establish the logical foundation upon which our understanding of Kierkegaard as a missionary rests. After the historical introduction in the first section, we examined Kierkegaard's journal entries that refer to "(the) missionary" or "(the) missionaries" in the second section. Our investigation showed that Kierkegaard was a strong advocate of the missionary task. For Kierkegaard, the single individual carries out the missionary task even if it leads to martyrdom. Thus, from Kierkegaard's perspective, to become a Christian is to become a missionary. Although he was not a missionary in the traditional sense of being sent to a foreign country by a mission agency, Kierkegaard considered himself a missionary to the Christendom of Denmark.

In the third section, we discussed several problems that militate against a simple affirmation of Kierkegaard's missionary identity. One problem is that he clearly states his missionary self-understanding only in *Journals and Notebooks* (an unpublished work). This supports our observations on *The Point of View for My Work as an Author* (see section 7.6.2) – Kierkegaard is the kind of a missionary who does not officially claim such a title (in his published works) but attempts to skilfully ambush his readers to win them over to Christ. Another problem is that the dates of the journal entries in which his missionary self-understanding appear were written between 1847 and 1855. Perhaps his intention and zeal to become a missionary were not present during his first authorship and only arose during his second authorship. This aligns with our observations on *The Point of View for My Work as an Author* (see section 7.6.1); in this posthumous work, he confesses that although he was a religious writer from the outset, he did not plan the organic coherence of his entire work from the beginning. Rather, he claims that God's Governance guided his upbringing, which is evident in his authorship. The fact that Kierkegaard's references to the term "missionary" began in 1847 suggests that he might have been unconsciously involved in missionary tasks as a writer before 1847 and began to more consciously engage in missionary tasks as a writer only after 1847. The dates of his journal entries testify that his conviction of his vocation as a missionary lasted until the final year of his life (1855). Another issue is the legitimacy of Kierkegaard's claim that a missionary who is both the single individual and a martyr possesses the qualities necessary for the age of reflection. Since Christ commanded the apostle Peter – who affirmed his Christian faith – to individually follow him and become a missionary and a martyr, we have a plausible argument for the biblical authenticity of Kierkegaard's claim. Further, such a missionary-martyr is needed in the age of reflection to awaken people from their spiritual slumber. Finally, this chapter examined *Journals and Notebooks* with specific focus on Kierkegaard's direct references to the term "missionary" and not consider all his discussions about the concept. Therefore, further studies are necessary to explore this subject more fully.

In the fourth section, we examined the dictionary definitions of the terms "missionary" (*Missionair*), evangelist (*Evangelist*), preacher (*Forkynder* or *Prædikant*), apologist (*Apologet*), and truth's witness (*Sandhedsvidne*). We then investigated the frequency with which Kierkegaard employs these words in his corpus. We found that Kierkegaard mostly feels at home with the term "missionary" (from 1847 to 1855) rather than the synonymous terms available to him. Although some may hesitate to call him a missionary since he certainly does not fit the traditional definition of a missionary, we are content to call him a special species of missionary.

Finally, let us reflect on why Kierkegaard used the term *Missionair* (missionary). For Kierkegaard, this term reflects the dignity of wholeheartedly following Jesus. Although Jesus was the transcendent God, he humbled himself and became a human being. Furthermore, he was not born in a palace but became the slave of all. He crossed the boundary between God and humans. Similarly, a Christian (an imitator of Christ) must step outside their comfort zone and cross the boundary between the self ("I") and the other. This is Kierkegaard's concept of mission, which can only be expressed by the term "missionary." A so-called missionary goes abroad and learns the language, culture, and customs of the people there. A Kierkegaardian missionary goes beyond self ("me") and learns the language, culture, and customs of their neighbours. In other words, Kierkegaard's term "missionary" expresses his recognition of the foreignness of others. Just like Jesus Christ, Christians – who are imitators of Christ – should humble themselves, put themselves in the shoes of the other, and proclaim a *translated* gospel in the world of the other, where *language* and *culture* are essentially different.

In conclusion, although Kierkegaard does not explicitly call himself a missionary in his published works, in *Journals and Notebooks*, he reveals his conviction that being a missionary is an integral part of the Christian faith and affirms that he himself is a missionary.

This concludes part 3. Having learned about Kierkegaard as a missionary by studying Kierkegaard's published works (part 2) and unpublished works (part 3), our study now moves to the final section (part 4), where we will summarize Kierkegaardian insights and apply them to the Japanese context.

Part 4

Contours of a Kierkegaardian Mission

CHAPTER 9

Toward a Kierkegaardian Mission

In the N.T. Christianity is always a mission, every Christian a missionary: Go forth and proclaim my teaching – and nowadays we are all Christians in such a way that it does not in the least way occur to any of us to become missionaries – apart from some unfortunate wretches who grasp at it as a last way out – frightful satire![1]

– Kierkegaard, *Journals and Notebooks*

In the above quotation, Kierkegaard laments that Christians in Christendom seldom accept the burden to proclaim Christianity. He asserts that, as far as the New Testament is concerned, "every Christian [is] a missionary."

Although such a claim is not common in traditional studies of Kierkegaard, this study argues that it is legitimate to identify Kierkegaard as a missionary. This chapter will summarize the findings of this study and define the Kierkegaardian mission. The first section will outline the contours of this mission; the second will broaden our perspective by classifying this mission using critically examined typology.

---

1. *SKS* 25, 241, NB28:33/ *KJN* 9, 243 *n.d.*, 1853, translation slightly modified.

9.1 Contours of a Kierkegaardian Mission

9.1.1 Missionary Assumption 1: The Universality of Despair and the Universal Capabilities to Become a Christian and a Missionary

Kierkegaard's missionary assumptions are grounded in one universal phenomenon and two universal capacities of human beings. A human being is universally in despair. The theme of despair is always present in Kierkegaard's works, from *Either/Or* to *The Sickness unto Death*. Despair is described as the unavoidable companion of the aesthete in *Either/Or* and ultimately analyzed as a universal phenomenon among the human species in *The Sickness unto Death*. Despair is a form of perpetual death. Mercifully, everyone is invited to Christ, who eradicates despair. "The Invitation" – the opening section of *Practice in Christianity* – is Christ's universal and yet personal invitation to each individual. While "there is not one single living human being who does not despair a little,"[2] "every single individual" or "all the various kinds [of people]"[3] are invited to Christ. Since Christ himself is the truth, he is the cure. To remain in him is the cure for despair. Therefore, each individual is invited to become a Christian. Furthermore, a universal invitation is extended to every human being to become a missionary. For Kierkegaard, being a Christian inevitably means becoming a missionary. Anti-Climacus presupposes that not only pastors but also lay Christians are obligated to draw others to Christ.[4] It is "cruel . . . not to become a missionary" if one knows that there is no salvation outside the church.[5] "Christianity in repose is *eo ipso* not Christianity."[6] Therefore, "to become involved with Christianity" is to "witness to the teaching like a missionary among the unbelievers or in 'Christendom.'"[7]

In other words, for Kierkegaard, what makes a missionary a missionary is not their surroundings but on their identity. We may presuppose that missionary zeal arises because many people around us are not Christians.

---

2. *SKS* 11, 138/ *SUD*, 22.
3. *SKS* 12, 252/ *PC*, 262.
4. *SKS* 12, 252–253/ *PC*, 262.
5. *SKS* 25, 223, NB28:13/ *JP*, III 2729 *n.d.*, 1853.
6. *SKS* 26, 16, NB31:17/ *JP*, III 2731 *n.d.*, 1854. See also *SKS* 20, 220, NB2:203/ *JP*, I 468, *n.d.*, 1847.
7. *SKS* 27, 593, Papir 464/ *JP*, III 3581 *n.d.*, 1853–1854.

Kierkegaard does not share this view. In his view, we should become missionaries even if everyone around us were true Christians. Of course, if one is surrounded by unbelievers, this should motivate them to become missionaries. But the quantity or quality of Christians around must not be the factor that stirs missionary zeal. As the recruiter of missionaries, Kierkegaard seems to say, "Remember who you are. Then, become a missionary." In other words, anyone who is a Christian is, *eo ipso*, a missionary. "To be a Christian means essentially to be a missionary."[8]

The Kierkegaardian implications here presuppose the universality of despair and the universal human capabilities to become both a Christian *and* a missionary. Everyone needs the cure of despair by believing in Jesus Christ. Besides, every Christian is potentially a missionary whose missionary zeal burns because of who they are, not for external reasons.

9.1.2 Missionary Assumption 2: A Human Being Is Becoming

Another Kierkegaardian missionary assumption is that a human being is not a static being but one who is always in a process of becoming. This presupposition means, first, that becoming a Christian is not a instantenous, once-and-for-all event. In Kierkegaard's thought, no one is *already a Christian*; rather, they are in the process of *becoming a Christian*. This explains why Kierkegaard, in *The Point of View for My Work as an Author*, says, "Thus my entire work as an author revolves around: becoming a Christian in Christendom."[9] For him, one is always becoming, and so he could address the issue of becoming a Christian throughout the entire body of his work. Therefore, one must always strive towards becoming and being a Christian because the task of becoming a Christian is never completed during one's lifetime (see also Phil 2:12; 3:12–14).

Second, this presupposition relativizes the believer-unbeliever dichotomy. We usually perceive Christians as already being edified and non-Christians as needing edification. A missionary may see oneself as already saved and in charge of proclamation, while viewing their audience as not saved and needing to be edified. However, Kierkegaard does not make a sharp distinction

---

8. *SKS* 26, 16, NB31:17/ *JP*, III 2731 *n.d.*, 1854.
9. *SKS* 16, 69/ *PV*, 90.

between these two groups. For him, both the audience and the missionary are "becoming" and, therefore, in need of edification. This is why the Triune God alone, and not the missionary, is the one who edifies (see also Matt 23:8–10; 1 Cor 3:6–7). A missionary is a fellow pupil and should repent before God rather than rebuking another.

Third, the presupposition that a human being is not static means that just as a sinner may be transformed into a Christlike Christian, a Christian may become a nominal Christian or even backslide. This is why Kierkegaard became a missionary to Christendom – because anyone in Christendom, including himself, could never be settled.[10] A person is a Christian as long as they are striving. In this way, the presupposition that one is always becoming underpins Kierkegaard's mission.

The Kierkegaardian implication here is that we need to be reminded of both the warning and the hope that anyone may fail and anyone may be saved because a human being is always in the process of becoming.

9.1.3 A Missionary Incognito

Kierkegaard was a missionary incognito. In his published works, the words "missionary" and "missionaries" occur only a few times. Furthermore, in such instances, Kierkegaard does not even express what one might call "missionary zeal." However, turning to his unpublished works, one sees a whole new face of Kierkegaard. As C. Stephen Evans and Robert C. Roberts say, "In his *Point of View for My Work as an Author*, [. . .] Kierkegaard makes it clear that he thinks of himself as a kind of missionary to 'Christendom' and regards his writings as the chief vehicle of his missionary work."[11] In this work, Kierkegaard compares his missionary method to Christ's incarnation; in addition, his explanation of mission strategy resembles the apostle Paul's incarnational mission described in 1 Corinthians 9:19–23. Kierkegaard's unique application of Christ's and Paul's methods explains how he became a missionary who pretended not to be a missionary. Like Christ, who "truly was incognito,"[12] Kierkegaard was incognito in his pseudonymous works. Like Paul, who "[became] all things to

---

10. "Christianity in repose is *eo ipso* not Christianity." *SKS* 26, 16, NB31:17/ *JP*, III 2731 n.d., 1854.

11. Evans and Roberts, "Ethics," 223. See also, 228.

12. *SKS* 16, 19/ *PV*, 34.

all people" (1 Cor 9:22), Kierkegaard became like the aesthetes and "the ordinary godly Christians." Although pseudonymous authorship was common in the Danish Golden Age, Kierkegaard used it as a vehicle for his Christian missionary task. *Journals and Notebooks*, written from 1847 onwards, confirms that Kierkegaard regarded himself as a missionary and that his missionary task was an integral part of his Christian faith. Therefore, the overall picture of Kierkegaard in both his published and unpublished works is that of a missionary incognito. Since he does not appear to be a missionary, the non-religious audience is more interested in his person and authorship. Like an animal or insect that simulates something completely different from what it is, Kierkegaard obscured his identity and ambushed the reader.

The Kierkegaardian implication here is that one does not to be officially assigned as a missionary but may have a hidden agenda to proclaim Christianity wherever one is in everyday life, using whatever methods or tools are available.

9.1.4 A Seductive Mission

Instead of using traditional Christian terms, Kierkegaard preferred to use terms like "deception to the truth" or "seduction to the truth." In other words, the sphere of Kierkegaard's target audience includes those who are unpromising. (In section 3.2, I suggested that Kierkegaard might even seduce Slayer, a radical heavy metal band that seems furthest away from Christianity.) To achieve this task, Kierkegaard presented Christianity in a way that was far from boring. He systematically studied "the interesting" and applied the result of this study to proclaim Christianity. His peculiar identity as "a missionary incognito" (see section 9.1.3) is also a part of the strategy to attract those who are far from Christianity. To seduce the reader into the truth, Kierkegaard presented Christianity in a sensational manner, using the complexity and mystique of his personality and authorship. For instance, his pseudonymity is one of his most seductive elements. The vivid descriptions of the aesthetic, ethical, and religious spheres and individuals are undoubtedly appealing. In his works, likeable villains magnetically attract and entice the reader. Even the confrontational elements in his works – such as provocation and threat – are appealing. His irony, jokes, and humour are intoxicating. Well-known melancholic or depressive passages antipathetically or sympathetically bewitch the reader with charm. His skilful rhetoric makes his books extremely readable. On the other hand, his signed-religious works beautifully demonstrate simplicity of thought and purity of heart. In these signed-religious works, Kierkegaard speaks personally, in a way that appeals directly to each individual. A Christian cannot resist reading his godly descriptions of humility, courage, faith, hope, and love in these works. In both his pseudonymous and signed-religious works, Kierkegaard musicalizes words and writes as if he were singing.[13] The enthusiasm and passion in Kierkegaard's works profoundly impress the reader. His readers also enjoy the beauty of the ideal portrayed in Kierkegaard's works, which earnestly urge readers to be themselves. His works are intellectual, philosophical, stimulate the imagination, and urge the reader to earnestly make a decision before God. Even the weirdness and eccentricity of his existence stimulate the reader's curiosity. All these features contribute to the effectiveness of Kierkegaard's missionary tasks.

The Kierkegaardian implication here might be that we should "present [our] bodies as a living sacrifice" (Rom 12:1) so that God's Governance can use our whole being, along with whatever we do, for the sake of his kingdom.

9.1.5 Not an Instantaneous But a Long-Term Mission

Kierkegaard's mission is not an instantaneous but a long-term mission. He does not proclaim God, sin, and salvation from the outset. Instead, his mission starts from the standpoint of paganism.[14] The readers of *Either/Or* had no idea where Kierkegaard intended to lead them.[15] But Kierkegaard retrospectively interprets that God's Governance was slowly guiding both himself and his readers towards the depths of profound Christianity. As one of his journal entries says, "God creates out of nothing – marvelous, you say. Yes, of course, but he does something more marvelous – he creates saints . . . out of sinners."[16] Imagine the time it takes for sinners to be transformed into saints. This patient missionary never places a heavy burden on his readers' shoulders

---

13. For instance, *The Concept of Irony* is, as a thesis or dissertation, one of the most academic writing styles among Kierkegaard's corpus but he still "sings" at this work: "And if something should be found, particularly in the first part of the dissertation, that one is generally not accustomed to come across in scholarly writings, the reader must forgive my jocundity, just as I, in order to lighten the burden, sometimes sing at my work." *CI*, Supplement, 441/ *Pap*. III B 3. If he "sings" at his dissertation, what can possibly stop him "singing" at any kinds of works?

14. *SKS* 20, 318, NB4:66/ *JP*, V 6107 *n.d.*, 1848.

15. *SKS* 20, 318–319, NB4:66/ *JP*, V 6107 *n.d.*, 1848.

16. *SKS* 18, 104. FF: 154.a/ *JP*, II 88 *n.d.*, 1838.

but, rather, offers them options – such as not making a choice (*Either/Or, Part I*), just being willing to choose (*Either/Or, Part II*), or making a more palatable, digestible religious choice (*Two Upbuilding Discourses* [1843]). After the publication of twenty books, Kierkegaard – through Anti-Climacus's two works – finally issues an ultimatum: perdition (*The Sickness unto Death*) or salvation (*Practice in Christianity*). While he allows his audience to start slowly, he ambitiously takes these same people to the highest spiritual peaks in *Practice in Christianity*. In this way, Kierkegaard's mission is indirect and long-term.

The Kierkegaardian implication here might be that we should not force a spiritual baby to eat solid food from the outset. Just as loving parents provide their child with the appropriate food at the proper time, a Kierkegaardian missionary should first feed people milk, gradually offer baby food, and, over time, eventually feed them solid food.

9.1.6 Audience-Oriented Mission (A Servant-Missionary)

Kierkegaard's mission is more audience-oriented than any other mission I know. First, he deeply respects the subjectivity of his audience. Kierkegaard was not someone who decided to edify his readers. Instead, he wanted readers to *will to allow* themselves to be built up.[17] He was a missionary who made "excessive concessions,"[18] as John Lippitt puts it. The motivation behind the task is well captured by David Gouwens's expression "maieutic form of love."[19] Like Socrates, Kierkegaard did not provide answers directly but played the role of a midwife, helping the reader to give birth to the truth. He was willing to patiently wait for such a birth, and this Kierkegaardian patience was motivated by a sincere love for his readers. In this way, he constructed a literary device that allowed each of his readers to find the path of their own spiritual journey.

Second, Kierkegaard emphasizes the importance of listening to his audience (readers). Since his mission strategy is highly audience-oriented, he needed to know his audience. A Kierkegaardian missionary should listen before preaching. A missionary is encouraged to "be the astonished listener."[20]

---

17. *Pap.* VI B 133; *TD*, Supplement, 120.
18. Lippitt, "Philosophical Response," loc. 2242, Kindle.
19. Gouwens, *Kierkegaard as Religious Thinker*, 206–208.
20. *SKS* 16, 28/ *PV*, 46.

Just as a shepherd must first find where the lost sheep is by being "a willing and attentive listener,"[21] Kierkegaard (spiritually speaking) attempted to find where the audience was and began his rescue programme there.

Third, a Kierkegaardian mission is conversational. Usually, a Christian proclamation is monological. A missionary has a message that they feel obligated to deliver without fail. However, because Kierkegaard highly respected his audience, he did not directly deliver a message. Kierkegaard's text is like a faithful companion. Wherever the reader may wonder, halt, be still, be happy, be anxious, reflect, or make a decision, Kierkegaard's text patiently waits. Reading Kierkegaard's works is like conversing with a Christian Socrates, where the reader engages in a dialogue.

Fourth, a Kierkegaardian mission affirms and ignites passion in an audience. Kierkegaard does not force an audience but allows their passion to be the guide that move them to the religious sphere. With *Either/Or*, he seduces divergent aesthetes without directly or overtly judging them. Kierkegaard presupposes the possibility that anyone's desire might be able to lead them to God. One can be satisfied only by God because of the way human beings are created – as the title of one of his upbuilding discourses expresses it, "to need God is a human being's highest perfection."[22]

Fifth, Kierkegaard's mission emphasizes the audience's decision-making power. As the title *Either/Or* suggests, Kierkegaard urges his readers to make a choice to act, and to live the truth. Appropriation is always Kierkegaard's concern.

In conclusion, the fact that Kierkegaard highly respected the reader means that he humbled himself. He was a servant-missionary. He listened willingly to his readers, engaged in dialogue with the audience, ignited their passion that would guide them to God – who alone could satisfy them – and was concerned with the audience's appropriation of the truth.

The Kierkegaardian implication here is well explained in his own words: "But all true helping begins with a humbling. The helper must first humble himself under the person he wants to help and thereby understand that to help is not to dominate but to serve."[23]

---

21. *SKS* 16, 27/ *PV*, 45.
22. See *SKS* 5, 291/ *EUD*, 297.
23. *SKS* 16, 27/ *PV*, 45.

9.1.7 A Mission That Prohibits Cheap Grace (The Ideal-Driven Mission)

In Kierkegaard's mission, cheap grace is prohibited. While he did not pressure a spiritual infant, this does not mean that he cheapened grace. While he was slow to present the whole message of the gospel, this does not mean that he distorted the Christian proclamation or held back from declaring the harsher messages of Scripture. Kierkegaard urged both himself and the reader not to misuse grace. If someone takes for granted that their sins are forgiven simply because Christ forgives, they risk misusing grace and freedom. Grace is costly because salvation by grace was purchased through the infinitely precious life of the Son of God. To casually sin is to behave blasphemously and is like crucifying Jesus on the cross again. Therefore, one must strive for the ideal that is described in the New Testament – to imitate Christ, who humbled himself infinitely. By earnestly striving for this ideal, one will certainly realize how far they fall short of this ideal even in their best moments. In such moments, grace and unconditional forgiveness are offered. In this way, Kierkegaard's proclamation strictly prohibits cheapening grace . His audience are taught not to blaspheme grace but, instead, to learn to effectively use and rely on grace.

In other words, Kierkegaard's mission is an ideal-driven mission. A typical mission strategy might aim to skilfully win as many souls as possible to Christ. However, while Kierkegaard's mission does include creative strategies to reach as many as possible – such as beginning with paganism or using seduction and polyphony – its main focus is not the number of converts. This is because what mattered to Kierkegaard was not the number of converts but, rather, serving the truth. For instance, Anti-Climacus says that a preacher should not care about the number of listeners but focus on just one listener: the omniscient God who knows their private life and listens to their sermons. Anti-Climacus or Kierkegaard served the ideal of Christianity and would not flatter or compromise to gain more converts. In the "Editor's Preface" to *Practice in Christianity*, Kierkegaard declares that "a supreme ideality" of "the requirement for being a Christian" must "be stated, presented, and heard."[24] In this way, he profoundly discerned the spiritual condition of his contemporaries, constructed literary devices to effectively proclaim Christianity, and desired as many as possible to become Christian. At the same time, his mission was

---

24. *SKS* 12, 15; 85; 153/ *PC*, 7; 73; 149, emphasis in original.

driven by ideality. Climacus's statement expresses this well: "My intention is to make it difficult to become a Christian, yet not more difficult than it is."[25]

The Kierkegaardian implication here might be that what concerns a missionary should not be the number of converts but the ideal-driven message. Instead of presenting grace cheaply, a missionary should offer costly grace and serve the ideal.

9.1.8 A Mission That Avoids Objectification or Rationalization of Christianity

Reading Kierkegaard is an intellectually challenging experience. However, Kierkegaard did not attempt to objectify or rationalize Christianity to convince his readers. Rather, he deconstructed philosophical or apologetic forms of Christianity and attacked and rejected objectification or rationalization of Christianity that does not require a decision of faith or offence. He presupposed that the Christian battlefield is not the sphere of the intellect but that of the will. According to Kierkegaard's theological anthropology, a person is incapable of accepting Christianity not because of a lack of knowledge but because of the sickness of the will. Therefore, by fighting on the battlefield of the intellect, both the missionary and the audience make a category mistake. If a missionary attempts to rationally prove the truth of Christianity, what the audience accepts would be an inauthentic Christianity. To avoid these numerous confusions, Kierkegaard had his pseudonyms present the gospel as "absurd" or "unthinkable" from the perspective of the natural human mind. He did not attempt to rationally defend Christianity but became a witness to Christ in his signed-religious works and higher-pseudonymous works. For Kierkegaard, argumentation is not the missionary's job.

The Kierkegaardian implication here might be that a missionary should not attempt to rationally argue for Christianity but, rather, present it "through the foolishness of our proclamation" (1 Cor 1:21), allowing God to reveal the truth of Christianity "through the Spirit" (1 Cor 2:10).

9.1.9 The Congruence of the *How* and the *What*

Kierkegaard was a careful communicator who believed that the communication might fail if the method was contradictory to the content of the message.

---

25. *SKS* 7, 506/ *CUP I*, 557.

Therefore, for him, the congruence of the *how* and the *what* was an absolute must. For example, in the second chapter of *Either/Or*, he describes Don Juan through the medium of musicalized language. For Kierkegaard, Don Juan was absolutely musical. Therefore, it is practically impossible to portray him with language that is not musical (sensual) but logical (intellectual). Ambitiously, using the mask of the pseudonym A, Kierkegaard attempts to allow readers to "hear" Don Juan by unreflective, sensuous language that does not cross the boundary between the sensuous and the intellect but, rather, provokes music to spring from language itself. To present Don Juan, who is absolutely musical (the *what*), Kierkegaard uses musicalized, unreflective, sensuous language (the *how*). Above all, to establish rapport with non-Christians, Kierkegaard created various non-Christian pseudonyms. He did not claim to be the best Christian to proclaim Christianity. To present something interesting to non-Christians (the *what*), Kierkegaard uses the medium of non-Christian pseudonyms (the *how*). The congruence of the *how* and the *what* allows Kierkegaard to powerfully and effectively win the heart of the reader.

A Kierkegaardian application here might be that a missionary should reflect upon whether their message is presented with congruence of the *how* and the *what*. For example, if the good news is presented with a gloomy face, even though the content (the *what*) is joyful, the medium (the *how*) contradicts the message, and such a presentation would be ineffective. When the gospel is presented, both the message (the *what*) and the missionary (the *how*) should be joyful. To be a successful communicator, the congruence of the *how* and the *what* should penetrate every aspect of the communication.

As the next subsection shows, in terms of Kierkegaard as a missionary, the most important congruence of the *how* and the *what* in his communication is the presentation of Jesus Christ.

9.1.10 An Incarnational Mission

This is the core of Kierkegaard's mission: it is incarnational. All his literary devices are aimed at presenting an incarnated Christ in his true form. While all missionaries know that they need to present Jesus Christ, they are usually focused on the verbal content (the *what*). Kierkegaardianly speaking, Christ must be presented through the congruence of the *how* and the *what*. This is the way to present the incarnated Christ in his true form. To give an extreme example, if a perfect Christology is presented arrogantly, although the content of the message (the *what*) may be correct, there is a fatal mistake in the method (the *how*). Paradoxically, Kierkegaard deliberately refrains from mentioning Christ in *Either/Or* and *Two Upbuilding Discourses* (1843) because he was embodying the method of the incarnated Christ. Just as Christ emptied himself, became flesh, and established a rapport with sinners, tax collectors, prostitutes, the demon-possessed, and Samaritans, Kierkegaard became like his contemporaries, both the aesthetes and "the ordinary godly Christians." By not mentioning Christ at all in these works, Kierkegaard imitates the method of the incarnated Christ. However, Kierkegaard's incarnational mission did not stop with the *how*. In fact, with *Practice in Christianity*, he presents the *what* of Christ. The reader is urged to have faith in Christ and imitate Christ's humility. There is no compromise. The ideality of the New Testament is presented as it is. In this way, the core of Kierkegaard's mission is to present the incarnated Christ (the *what*) through the manner of Christ's ministry on earth (the *how*).

The Kierkegaardian implication here might be that a missionary is encouraged to proclaim Jesus Christ with congruence of the *how* and the *what*. In other words, they should proclaim Christ in the same manner that Christ presented himself on earth.

9.1.11 The Congruence of Thought and Practice

Kierkegaard's mission is characterized by an inseparability of thought and action. In Kierkegaard's thought, Christology and mission are intertwined. David J. Bosch (1929–1992) famously says, "Theology ceases to be theology if it loses its missionary character."[26] For Kierkegaard, there is no such dichotomy of thought and practice. Neither *theory without practice* nor *action without thought* are Kierkegaardian. *Discussing theology without being a missionary* and *being a missionary without thinking* were both problematic for him. He did not make a distinction between systematic theology (Christology) and practical theology (mission). His reflections on Christ inevitably pushed him to become a passionate missionary, proclaiming Christ in an elegant unity of the *how* and the *what*.

---

26. Bosch, *Transforming Mission*, 494. Compare *SKS* 25, 223, NB28:13/ *JP*, III 2729 n.d., 1853.

A Kierkegaardian implication here might be that, on the one hand, a professor of systematic theology should strive to be a passionate missionary and inspire their students to do the same. On the other hand, a missionary should delve deep into various disciplines to guard against separating practice from thought and to make use of multiple disciplines to seduce the audience into the truth.

9.1.12 Mission as Absolute Devotion to the Triune God

Kierkegaard's mission is marked by absolute devotion to the Triune God. First, while making greatest efforts to carry on missionary work, he also recognized God's omnipotence and his own nothingness. *Concluding Unscientific Postscript* clarifies that it is vital to recognize one's nothingness before God.[27] If a human being can do nothing, should we do nothing? "The religious person does not preach indulgence but proclaims that the greatest effort is nothing – but also requires it."[28] This dialectic – recognizing one's own nothingness and making the greatest efforts – lies in the heart of a Kierkegaardian missionary. Only a few people may come to the difficult realization that they can do nothing without God. Yet, an even greater difficulty follows: being "capable of it with God."[29] It is only through this recognition that one who is capable of nothing can, paradoxically, do everything with God. This is the profound secret at the heart of the Kierkegaardian missionary task.

Second, while he did everything he could to draw others to Jesus Christ, Kierkegaard recognized that it is Jesus alone who draws people to himself and is able to use everything and everyone to draw them to himself.[30] It is widely known that Kierkegaard respected Socrates. But in *Christian Discourses*, he says that it is blasphemous to compare Jesus and Socrates. "As soon as I think about the matter of my eternal salvation, then he, the simple wise man [Socrates], is a very unimportant person, a sheer nonentity, a nobody."[31] Kierkegaard goes on to say,

---

27. *SKS* 7, 391/ *CUP I*, 430.
28. *SKS* 7, 421/ *CUP I*, 463–464.
29. *SKS* 7, 441/ *CUP I*, 486.
30. *SKS* 12, 253/ *PC*, 262.
31. *SKS* 10, 248/ *CD*, 241.

> I truly can answer the question, to whom do I owe most – should I not know to whom I owe most, most of all, most beyond all comparison? To him, namely, in whom I have believed, to him who has given his life also for me, give his life, not as one person may do for another in order to *preserve* the other one's life – no, in order to *give* me life. Without him it is a matter of indifference whether I live or die; it is an empty phrase to say that someone has saved my life when this life he saved for me still amounts to being dead. But he is life; in the eternal sense I owe him life, him in whom I believe.[32]

Devotion to and worship of Jesus Christ lies behind Kierkegaard's authorial mission activities.

Third, because he infinitely respected the Holy Spirit,[33] Kierkegaard discarded all rational arguments and simply became a witness to Jesus Christ: "There is only one proof for the truth of [Christianity] – the inner proof, *argumentum spiritus sancti* [the argument of the Holy Spirit]."[34] Furthermore, the Holy Spirit is the dispenser of grace, and no one can truly imitate Christ without his help. "Grace is the everlasting fountain – and the Holy Spirit the dispensator, the Comforter. The Holy Spirit is the Comforter also in the sense that Christ as the prototype is a requirement which no human being meets."[35] An impossible task becomes possible because of the Holy Spirit. Accordingly, Kierkegaard believed that it was the Triune God who infinitely helped him in his task as a missionary writer and that he could do everything through the grace of this Triune God.

The Kierkegaardian implication here might be that a missionary should not seek self-actualization or be discouraged by "failure" but, instead, offer all their missionary efforts to God as a pleasing sacrifice.

9.1.13 Summary and Conclusion

This section summarizes the findings of this study and defines a Kierkegaardian mission. Kierkegaard's mission presupposes three universalities of human

---

32. *SKS* 10, 248/ *CD*, 242, emphasis in original.
33. *SKS* 24, 469, NB25:48/ *JP*, VI 6792; see also *SKS* 25, 312–313, NB29:23/ *JP*, VI 6862.
34. *SKS* 22, 108, NB11:179/ *KJN*, 6, 105.
35. *SKS* 23, 80–81, NB15:114/ *JP*, II 1654 *n.d.*, 1850.

beings. All human beings are universally in despair, and every single person is universally and graciously invited by Christ, who is the cure for despair. Furthermore, each person is universally invited to be a missionary because, for Kierkegaard, being a missionary is an integral part of being a Christian (see section 9.1.1). In his anthropology, a human being is always in the process, of becoming. No one is absolutely safe, and no one should be given up on (see section 9.1.2). Kierkegaard was a missionary incognito – a missionary who did not officially introduce himself as a missionary but pursued a hidden agenda to guide his contemporaries towards the truth (see section 9.1.3). His mission is seductive. Within the vortex of excitement and enjoyment, the audience is unwittingly guided towards the truth (see section 9.1.4). His mission is not an instantaneous one but a long-term mission. An audience should first be fed with spiritual milk, then baby food, and, eventually, solid food (see section 9.1.5). His mission is highly audience-oriented. A Kierkegaardian missionary is a servant-missionary (see section 9.1.6). In his mission, cheap grace is sternly prohibited, and a missionary must serve the ideal (see section 9.1.7). Contrary to popular belief, objectification or rationalization of Christian belief is sternly prohibited in his mission. In the devices found within Kierkegaard's literary world, the Holy Spirit is the only arguer (see section 9.1.8). Whenever Kierkegaard communicated in his works, he did so with the congruence of the *how* and the *what* (see section 9.1.9). His mission is best expressed by the term "incarnational mission," which is a mission that attempts to present Christ in the manner that Christ presented himself on earth (see section 9.1.10). For Kierkegaard, thought and practice are inseparable. Thought inevitably produces practice, and practice is the result of profound reflection (see section 9.1.11). Kierkegaard's missionary activity as an author is absolute devotion to the Triune God, and engaging in missionary tasks is a pleasing sacrifice to the Triune God. For Kierkegaard, engaging in a missionary task is precious in itself and is already rewarded regardless of success or failure from a human perspective (see section 9.1.12)

Although Kierkegaard was a genius, and it may seem almost impossible for ordinary people to imitate him, his mission is a realistic possibility and could contribute to contemporary missionary efforts.

9.2 A Typology of Mission

In the previous section, we defined Kierkegaard's mission. In this section, we expand our horizons by comparing and contrasting Kierkegaard's mission with other types of missions. From this wider perspective, what are the features of Kierkegaard's mission? In the first subsection, we will examine Ádám Szabados's typology of missions.[36] In the second subsection, we will critically examine his typology.

9.2.1 A Typology of Missions by Ádám Szabados

In his article "Incarnational Mission: Søren Kierkegaard's Challenge to Evangelical Christianity," Ádám Szabados proposes a typology for categorizing a Kierkegaardian mission. According to Szabados, there are three types of evangelism: docetic mission, kenotic mission, and incarnational mission. The *docetic mission*, which is often adopted by evangelicals, is holiness without compassion. Docetic missionaries substitute methods for the pain of identification. They attempt to efficiently win souls to Christ through various methods but lack sympathy for the existential problems of non-Christians. According to Szabados, the secular world is frustrated with a docetic mission that does not follow the way of Christ. Another extreme is *kenotic mission*, which is "identification with loss of identity."[37] Kenotic missionaries identify with secular people but sacrifice holiness, which is central to the identity of a Christian.[38] The *incarnational mission*, which is "identification without

---

36. For a more exhaustive typology of mission, see "tentative, suggesting rather than defining the contours of a new model" in Bosch, *Transforming Mission*, 368–510. For another good typology of mission, which highlights substantial differences and advantages of incarnational mission, see Langmead, *Word Made Flesh*, 266–268. I take up Ádám Szabados's typology, which is much simpler than the other two, because a full-length discussion of a typology of mission is beyond the scope of this work. We need a typology of mission that is manageable in length and content, and which serves the needs and scope of this study.

37. Szabados, "Incarnational Mission," 8.

38. A New Testament scholar, who is also my friend, read the draft of my thesis and said, "One may question whether holiness represents the essence of Christian identity. For Paul, the indwelling of the Holy Spirit is Christian identity. For him, holiness is a symptom of Christian identity, not its root." Soteriologically speaking, if holiness were a *condition* of salvation, my friend is right, and such Christianity would no longer be Protestant Christianity. However, Szabados probably means that "holiness matters because, without holiness, you will have lost your savor and the power to convert sinners who are grasping for the gospel." Becker, *Like Christ by Grace*, xvi. Both the Old Testament (for example, Leviticus 11:45) and the New Testament (for example, Romans 12:1–2) emphasize separation from the world and devotion to God,

loss of identity"³⁹ is the ideal form of evangelism. Just as Christ did not lose his holiness, neither do incarnational missionaries. By writing *Either/Or*, Kierkegaard identifies with both the aesthete and the ethicist without losing holiness. In this way, Szabados argues that an incarnational mission is the ideal mission and categorizes Kierkegaard's mission as such an ideal mission.

9.2.2 Modification of Ádám Szabados's Typology of Missions

As seen in the previous subsection, Szabados categorizes three types of missions – docetic, kenotic, and incarnational mission – and identifies Kierkegaard's mission with the last type. Szabados's typology helps us to identify the features of Kierkegaard's mission in a broader context that also includes other types of missions. Moreover, his contention that Kierkegaard's mission strategy imitates Christ's method accords with the argument that has been developed throughout this study. However, the validity of Szabados's chosen terms is questionable.

First, the term "docetic" is a theological term that signifies heresy, but the doctrine underlying the docetic mission is not heretical. Therefore, I propose the term *"imperialistic mission"* as a substitute for docetic mission (mission without compassion). Historically, the term *imperialistic mission* seems appropriate in the context of caricatures of missionaries who came from *civilized* Christendom to *uncivilized* "heathen" nations to impart the gift of Western culture – as for example the first Catholic missionaries to Japan in the sixteenth century and the first Protestant and Eastern Orthodox missionaries in the nineteenth century.⁴⁰ However, it is an oversimplification to view those missionaries solely as agents of imperialism or colonization and ignore their missionary fervour and religious zeal. In reality, those historical missionary activities often stemmed from a mix of motivations. A closer look at historical records reveals that motivations varied even among people from the same religious group during the same period. Therefore,

---

which is the biblical essence of holiness. In this light, Szabados's characterization of holiness as the identity of a Christian is well justified.

39. Szabados, "Incarnational Mission," 9.

40. For a study of the encounter between Japan and Christianity and a neutral perspective on this struggle, see Baskind, キリスト教から見た日本の宗教 ["A Look at Japanese Religion Through a Christian Lens: In Contrast with the Japanese Perspective on Christianity"], 90–120.

we must be cautious not to hagiographically describe missionaries as saints or to deny their religious missionary zeal altogether. Having said that, with the term *imperialistic mission*, I intend to signify not simply a mission that is linked to imperialism or colonization but any type of mission that remains arrogant or foreign, regardless of whether such missionary efforts are carried out by foreigners or the Japanese. Kierkegaardianly speaking, if missionaries do not humble themselves, their "greater understanding does not help [the recipients] at all."[41] In the case of Japan, this could result in "a gospel that 'smells like butter' [foreign], causing alienation because it is fundamentally discontinuous with Japanese cultural history."[42] This long-term failure to appropriately contextualize Christianity on Japanese soil is expressed in the following stereotypical image that many Japanese may share: "We do not need Christianity that is from the West because we have Japanese religions (such as Shintoism and/or Buddhism)." I call this kind of mission, which fails to be humble and, thereby, fails to contextualize Christianity on Japanese soil, an imperialistic mission. Sadly, as Szabados says, many Christian churches and many missionary efforts fall into this category, and the situation may be even worse in Japan.

Second, the term "kenotic" in "kenotic mission" is a theological term that refers to Christ's incarnation. Therefore, this term is inappropriate to express a "mission that loses holiness" because it could be confused with an incarnational mission.[43] Therefore, I propose the terms "secularized mission" (holiness-free mission) and "syncretic mission" (identity-free mission) as substitutes and subcategories of the kenotic mission.

My choice of the term *secularized mission* is inspired by the renowned British preacher D. Martyn Lloyd-Jones (1899–1981). Lloyd-Jones states,

---

41. *SKS* 16, 27/ *PV*, 45.

42. Lee, "Paradigm Shifts," 48.

43. Philippians 2:7 reads, "ἑαυτὸν ἐκένωσεν" [he emptied himself]. The last word in Greek is κενόω (kenō), which means, "to empty, evacuate," and when used together with ἑαυτὸν (himself), means "to divest one's self of one's prerogatives, abase one's self." Mounce, "κενόω," in "Mounce's Complete Expository Dictionary of Old and New Testament Words* https://www.billmounce.com/greek-dictionary/kenoo. In short, κενόω (kenō) signifies the orthodox interpretation of the act of Christ's incarnation. Therefore, its adjective form "kenotic" and noun "kenosis" should be retained to preserve the authentic theological understanding of Christ's incarnation.

> The fact is that the world expects us to be different; and this idea that you can win the world by showing that after all you are very similar to it, with scarcely any difference at all, or but a very slight one, is basically wrong not only theologically but even psychologically.[44]

According to my interpretation, if a missionary is sinning or exceedingly impolite, such a mission is theologically and psychologically inappropriate. Theologically speaking, if a missionary is motivated just to win the secular people over to Christ and therefore, they compromise with sin (to become equal to them), it is a betrayal of a Christian's own nature. Psychologically speaking, such a missionary is not appreciated in the secular world either because secular people somehow expect Christians to be holy.

Syncretic mission signifies a movement that attempts to merge with the indigenous religion and culture but ends up becoming syncretic or heretical. Mark Mullins writes about a study on indigenous Christian movements in Japan. Contrary to the imperialistic mission, the Christian movements that are introduced in his monograph – *Christianity Made in Japan: A Study of Indigenous Movements* – attempt to allow Christianity to take root in Japanese soil (culture, history, mentality, religion, etc.). Sadly, almost all movements introduced in Mullins's work are examples of syncretism or heresy, with the exception of the Mukyōkai movement founded by Kanzō Uchimura. What does this mean? It means that almost no movements of Christian orthodoxy in Japan are regarded as significant attempts to make Christianity indigenous.

Third, some theologians and missiologists feel uncomfortable with the term *incarnational mission* because the incarnation is, strictly speaking, doable only by the God-man.[45] Indeed, the Son of God alone can become

---

44. Lloyd-Jones, *Preaching and Preachers*, 139.

45. For a positive evaluation of the term *incarnational mission*, see Sherwood G. Lingenfelter and Marvin K. Mayers, *Ministering Cross-Culturally: An Incarnational Model for Personal Relationships (Second Edition)*. Grand Rapids: Baker Academic 1986, 2003; John R. W. Stott, *The Contemporary Christian: Applying God's Word to Today's World*. Downers Grove: IVP 1992, 358; Langmead, *The Word Made Flesh*; Mick Pope, '10. Grappling for Christ: Incarnational Mission at the Margins of the Church' in *We Are Pilgrims: From, in and with the Margins of Our Diverse World*. ed. by Darren Cronshaw and Rosemary Dewerse, Dandenong, Victoria: Urban Neighbours of Hope 2015: 151–63; Samuel Wells, *Incarnational Mission: Being with the World*. Norwich: Canterbury Press 2018. For a negative evaluation of the term *incarnational mission*, see Tim Chester, 'Why I don't believe in incarnational mission.' http://timchester.wordpress.com/2008/07/19/why-i-dont-believe-in-incarnational-mission/ (accessed 20 June

incarnate, which means that God becomes flesh. However, ultimately, I consider that the term *incarnational* is not that problematic because whereas "incarnation" as a noun strictly signifies the unrepeatable incarnation of Christ, "incarnational" as an adjective loosely implies something related to the incarnation of Christ. For instance, we might use the term *Christ-like* Christian to describe a Christian who resembles Christ. But we do not view the term *Christ-like* as blasphemy. Rather, this adjective powerfully grasps some unique concepts that cannot be expressed otherwise. With the term Christ-like, *we do not call anyone Christ* but just simply *describe a character or personality* of a certain Christian. One may object that there is an infinite gap between an adjective of *Christ-like* (that compares to a *character* or *personality* of Christ) and that of *incarnational* (that compares to *making the impossible possible*, which is that transcend God made flesh). Having said that, by not using the term *incarnational*, how can we express the following command by the Apostle Paul?

> Let the same mind be in you that was in Christ Jesus,
>   who, though he was in the form of God,
> did not regard equality with God
>   as something to be exploited,
> but emptied himself,
>   taking the form of a slave,
>   being born in human likeness.
> And being found in human form,[46]
> he humbled himself
>   and became obedient to the point of death –
> even death on a cross (Phil 2:5–8).

2013); Eckhard J. Schnabel, *Early Christian Mission: Jesus and the Twelve*. Downers Grove: InterVarsity Press 2005, 1574–5. For a more neutral assessment, see Craig Ott, Stephen J. Strauss with Timothy C. Tennent, *Encountering Theology of Mission: Biblical Foundations, Historical Developments, and Contemporary Issues (Encountering Mission)*. Grand Rapids: Baker Academic 2010, 97–104.

46. Moisés Silva translates verse 7 as follows: "Instead, he made himself nothing by assuming the form of a servant, that is, by becoming ⌜incarnate.⌝" Silva, *Philippians*, 94. *Note: Corner brackets indicate words supplied by the translator to clarify the meaning.*

Paul, whom all theologians rely on, simply urges us to imitate Christ by describing his incarnation.[47] The above quotation illuminates how we should obey this command without being blasphemous. Verse 5 urges us to have the same mind that was in Christ Jesus.[48] Verses 6–8 describe a mission that is impossible for us, a mission that only the Son of God could accomplish: Christ, who was "in the form of God," was born in human form. However, these verses also describe certain attitudes that Christians are urged to imitate: to take the form of a slave, to humble oneself, and to become obedient to the point of death. Logically speaking, Paul must be saying something that we *should* and *can* follow since he urges us to have the mind of Christ in verse 5. While the aspects of the incarnation that only the Son of God can do might be termed *qualitative humility*, the aspects of the incarnation that Christians ought to follow could be described as *quantitative humility*. The term "incarnational mission" signifies an aspect of *quantitative humility* that Paul urges to imitate. Indeed, I have considered whether suitable yet less problematic terms such as *Christlike, Christ-centred,* or *Christocentric* mission might be used as a substitute for "incarnational mission" (identification without loss of identity). However, I could not find an adjective that comprehensively and elegantly captures the features of a Kierkegaardian mission better than the term *incarnational mission*. Therefore, unless we find a better term that captures the Kierkegaardian functions and causes less offence to other Christians, we will choose to use the term *incarnational mission*.

In this subsection, we have modified Ádám Szabados's typology – renaming "docetic mission" as "imperialistic mission" and "kenotic mission" as "secularized mission" and "syncretic mission" – and confirmed the appropriateness of the term "incarnational mission" through critical investigation. We now consider the following questions: Is the Kierkegaardian incarnational

---

47. Moisés Silva, arguing that these verses are not just an appeal to be united with Christ but an appeal to imitate Christ's attitude, says, "We should note in this regard Paul's desire to share in the sufferings of Christ (Phil 3:10). Even though these words clearly speak of union with Christ, they hardly preclude the idea that believers suffer as Jesus suffered (1 Thess 2:14–15). Those who are united with Christ live as he did (See 1 John 2:6), and so the notion of Jesus as an ethical example is implicit in Phil. 2:5 by the very nature of the subject matter." Silva, 97.

48. F. F. Bruce annotates this verse, saying, "The words that follow, celebrating the self-emptying and self-humbling of Christ in becoming man and consenting to endure death by crucifixion, suggest strongly that his example in this regard is being recommended to his followers." Bruce, *Philippians*, 66.

mission suited to contemporary Japan? How can we evaluate this? We will tackle these questions in the next chapter.

CHAPTER 10

The Applicability of a Kierkegaardian Mission to Japan

> But how does Jesus communicate in Japan? This is our central question.
>
> No one is more qualified to lead us at this point than Kierkegaard.[1]
>
> – Evyn Merrill Adams, "An Elucidation of Soren Kierkegaard's Categories of Communication and Their Application to the Communication of Christian Existence in Japan"

In the above quotation, Evyn Merrill Adams boldly declares that if Jesus is to be communicated in Japan, "no one is more qualified to lead us at this point than Kierkegaard." I agree with Adams that Kierkegaard can help us effectively seduce the Japanese into Christianity.

Kurt Cobain (1967–1994) once said, "There are some pop songs I hate but I can't get them out of my head. Our songs also have the standard pop format: Verse, chorus, verse, chorus, solo, bad solo."[2] Just as Cobain had planned, his band, Nirvana – which sold seventy-five million records worldwide – was extremely successful. He knew how to craft a tune that would stick in

---

1. Adams, *Kierkegaard's Categories of Communication*, 7.
2. "NIRVANA Bio (DGC)," LiveNIRVANA.com, accessed March 23, 2022, https://livenirvana.com/documents/bioDGC.html.

people's minds, whether they liked it or not. Similarly, Kierkegaard devised a strategy that made Christianity stick in the minds of his contemporaries, whether they liked it or not.

A Kierkegaardian style of mission in Japan can accomplish similar results by packaging the gospel in a form that is easily memorable for the Japanese. For instance, at a Christmas party at our church in Japan, we played Led Zeppelin's "Good Times Bad Times" and 美空ひばり (Misora Hibari)'s 川の流れのように ("Like the Flow of the River"). The former is my favourite style of hard rock music, but the latter is a popular traditional Japanese style known as 演歌 (*enka*). Although I do not usually enjoy this traditional style of music, we played it to attract older people to the church. One week after the Christmas party, I found that the tune that stuck in my head during that entire week was not "Good Times Bad Times" but "Like the Flow of the River"! Does this mean that even though I usually listen to and enjoy hard rock, the "Japaneseness" within me makes me feel at home with *enka*? Perhaps traditional forms such as the *enka* can help Kierkegaardian missionaries to Japan to strategically formulate and deliver a Christian message that the Japanese cannot get out of their minds.

Johannes Climacus says, "*It is easier to become a Christian if I am not a Christian than to become a Christian if I am one, and this decision is reserved for the person who has been baptized as an infant.*"[3] Fortunately, the majority of Japanese are not baptized as infants and are not natural-born Christians. Therefore, it is easier for them to become Christians. Climacus's statement can encourage and inspire us in our task of bringing Christianity to Japan.

"Just one more comment, no doubt unnecessary, but nevertheless I will make it."[4] When I gave a presentation on part of the present study, some people assumed that my goal was to have the Japanese read Kierkegaard's works. But to apply the Kierkegaardian mission in Japan, do the Japanese have to read his works? This is not necessary. I merely attempt to apply the principles of a Kierkegaardian mission to Japan. It is not even necessary to mention Kierkegaard's name and give him the spotlight since he himself "constantly [desired] to be considered someone who is absent."[5] Our concern

---

3. *SKS* 7, 333/ *CUP* 366, emphasis in original.
4. *SKS* 11, 118, *SUD*, 6.
5. *SKS* 28, 480/ *LD*, 383.

is not that the Japanese come to know Kierkegaard but, rather, Jesus Christ, who is their true Saviour.

In the first section, we will examine David J. Lu's *Overcoming Barriers to Evangelization in Japan*, in which he claims that there are five barriers preventing Japan from being evangelized. In the second section, we will explore how Kierkegaardian principles might be applied to help overcome these barriers. In the third section, we will summarize this chapter and briefly discuss the issues of 日本的キリスト教 (Japanese Christianity) from a Kierkegaardian perspective.

10.1 David J. Lu's Analysis of Japan

This chapter will explore how the Kierkegaardian mission can be applied in contemporary Japan. To carry out this task, we need a concise but comprehensive analysis of the spiritual milieu of Japan, for which we turn to *Overcoming Barriers to Evangelization in Japan*, written by David J. Lu, a Taiwanese Christian scholar. Why this book? First, Lu is a renowned scholar of Japan studies – who served as the director of the Center for Japanese Studies from 1965 to 1994 – and his book *Japan: A Documentary History* (2 volumes) is used as a standard textbook in secular universities.

Second, Lu's analysis of Japan in *Overcoming Barriers to Evangelization in Japan* is concise, comprehensive, and far more persuasive than any other book I have read on this topic. Lu's unique background, which makes his arguments convincing and reliable, is introduced in his own words as follows:

> I have had the advantage of being able to observe Japanese society from within (uchi). . . .
>
> Born in Taiwan in 1928 when it was under Japanese rule, I was a Japanese citizen through my high school years, receiving their best education. In my academic career as a Japan specialist, I developed close contact with all strata of Japanese society. It was by luck that I got to know seventeen prime ministers personally. The Nobel Laureate Sato Eisaku became a close personal

friend. I visited 120 businesses and factories, but did not neglect to observe the homeless.[6]

Third, Lu is a conservative Christian with a deep passion for evangelization in Japan. His mission strategy is not imperialistic, secularized, or syncretic, but incarnational – even though he does not use the term "incarnational mission" – and his approach and Kierkegaard's are compatible. Therefore, summarizing Lu's book is the most effective way for me to describe the Japanese spiritual milieu within this limited space and to naturally connect the Kierkegaardian mission to Japan.

According to Lu, there are five barriers to evangelization in Japan: "self," "Buddhism enmeshed in Japanese culture," "myriad deities of Shintoism," "seeking perfection without God," and "invisible proscription."[7] The first barrier, "self," is not external but internal, existing within the missionary. Lu asks, "When we try to tell others about Christ, don't we sometimes have a notion that we are better than they, because we know Christ? That is a dangerous attitude, because when we have that arrogance, our listeners will know it instantly."[8] He warns, "Hubris is a dangerous enemy."[9] Therefore, missionaries must first be aware of their own arrogance and reconsider their (unconscious) self-centred approach. Missionaries are, of course, enthusiastic about the proclamation of a Christian message that gives eternal life. But Lu suggests going slowly: "The needs of others must come first before your own."[10] Instead of proclaiming the gospel first, he advises, "You must be a good listener. For a minister or a missionary to succeed, the first lesson to learn is to listen."[11] This is also the way of Christ: "Their life experiences are very important to them and should be to you as well, who serve them. Follow the example set by our servant Messiah. Be ready to wash their feet. That will go a long way toward your own success."[12] He warns, "If we go to Japan only to condemn its culture's darkness, our mission will invariably

---

6. Lu, *Overcoming Barriers*, x.
7. Lu, 1–84.
8. Lu, 1–2.
9. Lu, 2.
10. Lu, 3.
11. Lu, 3.
12. Lu, 3.

fail."¹³ According to Lu, "The greatest hindrance to our success comes from our own inadequacies and dispositions."¹⁴

The second barrier is "Buddhism enmeshed in Japanese culture." To some extent, Lu admires the efforts of Japanese Buddhists because they were successful in contextualizing Buddhism on Japanese soil. Lu refers to the apostle Paul's mission strategy and elaborates as follows:

> Paul the apostle, who was a great missionary, will support this step you take. "For though I am free from all men, I have made myself a servant to all, that I might win the more; and to the Jews I became a Jew, that I might win Jews; to those who are under the law, as under the law, that I might win those who are under the law." (1 Cor 9:19–20) To lead your Buddhist friends to Christ, you must immerse yourself into their midst to understand them. Once that step is taken a serious conversation can begin.¹⁵

Since Lu's mission strategy is to listen first, he suggests that missionaries listen to Buddhists and "[immerse themselves] into their midst to understand them." Lu argues that this is an authentic mission strategy that can be seen in 1 Corinthians 9:19–20. For instance, Lu finds a bridge between Buddhism and Christianity in 歎異抄 (*Tannishō*), written by a Japanese Buddhist monk 親鸞 (*Shinran*, 1173–1263): "If he repents of his desire to depend on his own power and becomes solely reliant on Amida, he can then attain salvation in the True Land of Recompense."¹⁶ Lu comments, "This is a beautiful confession of faith which always reminds me of the thief on the cross with Christ."¹⁷ Lu finds both similarities and differences between Christianity and Buddhism. He notes that "no matter how great he was, Amida remained one of the many Buddhas. Therefore he was not absolute. In Christianity, there was only one son of God, and he is absolute. *Solus Christus!*"¹⁸ Lu challenges the

---

13. Lu, 7.
14. Lu, 1.
15. Lu, 19.
16. Lu, 20, originally from Shinran, *Tannishō, Shūjishō*, 20. In *Japan: A Documentary History*, David J. Lu explains, "True Land of Recompense is used almost synonymously with the term 'Pure Land,' or 'Pure Land of Perfect Bliss.' It is in recompense to the Original Vow of Amida and not to any particular individual's act of faith." Lu, *Japan*, 135, footnote 14.
17. Lu, *Overcoming Barriers*, 20.
18. Lu, 21.

assumption that Christianity is a Western religion and invites us to imagine a possible historical alternative:

> If early Christianity had not developed in the Roman world under Hellenism, but rather took roots to the East traveling through the Silk Road and beyond, it certainly would have taken a different shape and expression. It is time for us to help our Christian brothers to find ways to express our Christian thoughts and values in the Japanese language more consistent with their daily lives.[19]

The third barrier is the "myriad deities of Shintoism." Lu offers an interesting suggestion regarding an event that recurs every year in relation to Shintoism:

> Yasukuni has spring (April 21–23) and autumn (October 17–20) festivals. In war-time Japan, these were the dates that the emperor came in person to worship at the shrine. In recent years, visits, or "worship," by a sitting prime minister have become quite a hot political issue. I hope you will pay close attention whenever this issue is raised. It provides an excellent opportunity to discuss who our God is.[20]

Lu seems to recommend seizing every opportunity to arouse Japanese interest in Christianity. Shintoism is not only a vehicle to transmit the gospel to the Japanese heart; Lu also learns from their strategy – although he clearly distinguishes between the doctrines of Christianity and Shintoism.

> The Shinto precinct is easily accessible and is a friendly place to visit. Everyone can enter its gate. Without having any regular worship services, Shintoism still has been able to maintain close ties (*musubi*) with its *ujiko* (parishioners) due to this openness. It claims that all residents of the local community are *ujiko*, and everyone is welcomed to its festivals. Do our churches have this sense of close ties with the local communities? Why do our Japanese friends continue to have a perception that churches are

---

19. Lu, 36.
20. Lu, 40.

only for their believers and that their doors are closed to others? "Come to me, all you who labor and are heavy laden, and I will give you rest" (Matt 11:28). This sweet and powerful invitation of our Lord is for all who seek him. Missional churches must find ways to open their gates.[21]

Shintoism is naturally close to the heart of the Japanese. When the church humbly learns from the positive aspects of Shintoism, we may be better able to reach unreached Japanese.

The fourth barrier is "seeking perfection without God." Lu identifies Confucian thought behind the Japanese mentality of seeking perfection without God. On the one hand, the Japanese today are usually recognized as being polite and kind.

> On March 11, 2011, Northeast Japan was devastated by a magnitude 9 earthquake, which was followed by a tsunami and a nuclear disaster, resulting in the death and injury of 24,590 persons. It was the worst natural disaster in Japan's post-war history. The world witnessed a sight seldom seen elsewhere. In spite of their own suffering, losing loved ones and properties, victims of the disaster yielded to one another. On the television screen, all could be seen was the rectitude, self-sacrifice, and a willingness to help others.[22]

Lu observes, "These characteristics of Japanese people I have just described make them the most desirable candidates to receive the word of God."[23] On the other hand, this "national hubris" can be a barrier to accepting Christianity: "This national hubris is what we have to counter. It could reject Christianity in this fashion: 'We have such and such wonderful virtues in our hands. So, we really don't need your God.'"[24] Therefore, Lu regards this barrier as more problematic than the barriers of Buddhism and Shintoism:

> Earlier in this book I dealt with the barriers presented by Buddhism and Shintoism, but the greatest barrier may be

---

21. Lu, 51–52.
22. Lu, 57.
23. Lu, 57.
24. Lu, 58.

found in the attitude of self-reliance nurtured by Confucianism because it has given the Japanese people a sense of general satisfaction with their own tradition.[25]

How should we approach this Confucian atheistic perfectionism? In the Japanese edition of his book, Lu suggests, "Many pearls of wisdom for everyday life are included in Japanese traditional culture. Why don't you try holding a meeting at which you read Japanese proverbs together with Proverbs and Ecclesiastes?"[26] He adds, "There are so many stories in Japanese history, literature, and even in children's literature which are imbued with the Confucian sense of right and wrong. They can be incorporated into a sermon to interpret Christian values."[27] He also gives the example of a person who once abandoned playing the 琴 (*koto*, Japanese traditional instrument) as she believed this was improper for a Christian. However, she was later given the opportunity to play the *koto* at church, where her musical talent was used for evangelization. Lu says, "Just like *koto* is not heresy, a traditional culture itself is not heresy."[28] In the Japanese edition of his book, Lu encourages the reader:

> Like Nitobe elaborates, voices to cry out to God are hidden in traditional culture in Japan. Try looking for that opportunity. In the process of evangelism, you can experience the same joy that Paul experienced when he shared the gospel to Athenians who were worshipping "the unknown god" (Acts 17:22–24).[29]

The fifth barrier is "invisible proscription." Lu expands on this idea with reference to a historical event:

> In 1612, these words were prominently displayed on the public board (*takafuda*) in Nagasaki: "No one is allowed to become a follower of the padre. Offenders shall be severely punished." A year later all priests were expelled from the country and in 1614, proscription against Christianity became the law for all of Japan. Today Japan does not proscribe Christianity and its

---

25. Lu, 58.
26. Lu, 日本宣教を阻む5つの障壁 [*Overcoming Barriers to Evangelization in Japan*], 68.
27. Lu, *Overcoming Barriers*, 66.
28. Lu, 日本宣教を阻む5つの障壁 [*Overcoming Barriers to Evangelization in Japan*], 72.
29. Lu, 74.

constitution guarantees freedom of religion. However, there are invisible proscriptions, just as the United States has experienced proscriptions through the guise of political correctness.[30]

Although Christianity is not officially prohibited in Japan, Lu discerns the existence of an "invisible proscription." According to Lu, "invisible proscription" is assumed to be politically correct even though freedom of religion is constitutionally guaranteed. Lu explains that although "invisible proscription" is not yet fully realized, peer pressure could emerge in due course. Against this fifth barrier, Lu adopts a confrontational approach. He offers three suggestions: "The first and clearest answer is to pray for the people who created these proscriptions."[31] He goes on, "The second step you must take is to take a serious look at your Bible, and read it as if you are one of those who are persecuted."[32] Even though there is currently no religious persecution in Japan, we do not know when persecution might occur again. According to Lu, we must be prepare for this eventuality by learning from the Bible what we should do in such a situation. Lu says, "The third step will involve your community."[33] He urges us to fight against social evil, guided by Scripture, and also help victims of social evil: "My suggestion for your church is to create a counseling center for your community."[34]

By referring to 俳句 haiku[35] Japanese literature, and pivotal historical events in Japan, Lu concisely but convincingly argues that there are five barriers to evangelization in Japan. In the next section, we will explore how the Kierkegaardian mission could contribute to overcoming those barriers and evangelizing contemporary Japanese.

---

30. Lu, *Overcoming Barriers*, 73.
31. Lu, 78.
32. Lu, 79.
33. Lu, 79.
34. Lu, 80.
35. For haiku, see footnote 69 in section 4.3.

10.2 How the Kierkegaardian Mission Can Contribute to Evangelization in Japan

In the previous section, we discussed David J. Lu's *Overcoming Barriers to Evangelization in Japan*. According to Lu, there are five barriers to evangelization in Japan. In this section, we will consider how the Kierkegaardian mission might be applied to overcome those barriers. Below are three general observations.

First, the Kierkegaardian mission suggests that a Christian missionary must venture outside the church. One of Kierkegaard's journal entries reads, "Luther was absolutely right in saying that preaching really should not be done in churches but on the street. The whole modern concept of a pastor who preaches in a church is pure hallucination."[36] Both Kierkegaard and Lu recommend listening before proclamation. To listen to non-Christians, a missionary needs to go outside the church. In *Practice in Christianity*, Anti-Climacus describes Christ's incarnation, saying, "He walks – but no, he has walked, but infinitely farther than any shepherd and any woman – indeed, he walked the infinitely long way from being God to becoming man; he walked that way to seek sinners!"[37] Anti-Climacus compares Christ's incarnation with the shepherd and the woman in Christ's parables. In Luke 15:4–32, Christ tells the Pharisees and the scribes three parables: the lost sheep, the lost coin, and the prodigal son. Anti-Climacus refers to the shepherd and the woman in the first two parables. What does the Kierkegaardian mission suggest? A Japanese Christian might previously have waited for the Japanese to come to the church. But this method does not imitate Christ's incarnation. Christ's method was to "go after the one that is lost until he finds it" (Luke 15:4) and "search carefully until she finds it" (15:8). We need to change our mindset. A missionary must not wait at the church but go out into the streets. In the subsequent subsections, we will suggest ways of doing this in the Japanese context.

Second, the Kierkegaardian mission suggests that Japanese religions and cultures are not enemies to combat but, rather, vehicles that carry the Christian message to the hearts of the Japanese people. Kierkegaard used mythology and Romanticism to attract his Danish contemporaries and convert their passion

---

36. *JP*, I 287/ *Pap*. VIII 2 B 85.
37. *SKS* 12, 31/ *PC*, 20.

into ethico-religious striving. We can use Japanese religions and culture in a similar way when dealing with contemporary Japanese, who are typically aesthetes who avoid religious commitment.[38] A Kierkegaardian mission possesses the ability to draw them toward Christianity by appealing to their aesthetic sensibilities. However, we must be careful not to mix Christian doctrine with the doctrines of other religions. While Kierkegaard boldly used pagan ideas, he carefully avoided doctrines that were inconsistent with Christianity.

Third, the Kierkegaardian mission emphasizes that the congruence of the *how* and the *what* is the most effective way to communicate the message of Jesus Christ in a way that touches the heart of the Japanese. The proclamation of Christ in his true form is the core of Kierkegaard's mission, and this approach is well-suited to contemporary Japan. The *what* of Christ (Christian proclamation) alone may not be appreciated in Japan, but the *how* of Christ (listening, humbling oneself, and becoming like the Japanese) will be appreciated by the Japanese. When they encounter the gospel embodied in a humble person, their resistance may weaken, and they may be more willing to accept the gospel. The strength of this method is that when the *what* of Christ (Christian proclamation) is presented in a timely way, it is likely to speak powerfully to the hearts of the Japanese people since they already *know* Christ through the humility of a Christlike missionary. This demonstrates the congruence of the *how* and the *what*.

As pointed out in the previous section, Lu analyzes five barriers to evangelization in Japan: "self," "Buddhism enmeshed in Japanese culture," "myriad deities of Shintoism," "seeking perfection without God," and "invisible proscription." Can a Kierkegaardian mission contribute to overcoming those barriers? What suggestions does the Kierkegaardian mission offer for evangelization in contemporary Japan? Since Kierkegaard knew almost nothing about Japan and passed away 170 years ago, the following applications to twenty-first-century Japan are an amplification based on my interpretation of Kierkegaard's thoughts.

One might naturally wonder: Can we bridge the huge gap between the historical context of nineteenth-century Denmark and twenty-first-century Japan? Can we adopt and apply Kierkegaard's strategy in a completely different

---

38. Kazō Kitamori (1916–1998) categorizes the predominant way of life among the Japanese as that of the aesthete. See Kitamori, 日本人と聖書 [*Japanese and the Bible*], 186–211.

context? The answer to both questions is yes. Kierkegaard's strategy was to establish rapport with his contemporaries, just as Christ became flesh, and just as the apostle Paul identified with both Jews and Greeks. It is important not to simply copy Kierkegaard but, rather, to learn and apply the principles of the Kierkegaardian mission. For example, if we attempt to become like nineteenth-century Danes to evangelize twenty-first-century Japanese, such an *imitation of Kierkegaard* would not be effective. But if we become like our contemporaries, just as Kierkegaard became like his contemporaries, this is an application of a Kierkegaardian principle of mission. Therefore, I would argue that the vast gap between the contexts of nineteenth-century Denmark and twenty-first-century Japan is not problematic because the fundamental principles of the Kierkegaardian mission are applicable in almost any context. Now let us see one by one how the Kierkegaardian mission may be able to contribute to overcoming the five barriers to evangelization in Japan.

10.2.1 How to Overcome the "Self"

> However strong he is otherwise, there is one enemy that is stronger – himself; there is one enemy he cannot conquer by himself, and that is himself.[39]
>
> – Søren Kierkegaard, *Two Upbuilding Discourses* (1843)

According to David Lu's *Overcoming Barriers to Evangelization to Japan*, the first barrier to mission in Japan is the "self" within the missionary. How can a Kierkegaardian mission contribute to overcoming this formidable enemy of the "self" within a missionary?

10.2.1.1 Christian Self-Denial

First, Kierkegaard would urge us to imitate the incarnated Christ and, thereby, to deny self. Indeed, the central strategy of the Kierkegaardian mission is to imitate the self-denial of the incarnated Christ. In *The Point of View for My Work as an Author*, Kierkegaard says,

> Only the one who personally understands what true self-denial is, only he can solve my riddle and see that it is self-denial. [. . .]

---

39. *SKS* 5, 27/ *EUD*, 18.

> There is unconditionally one thing that can be understood neither by a noisy assembly nor by an esteemed public, not in a half-hour, and that is: what Christian self-denial is. In order to understand this, much fear and trembling, quiet solitude, are required, and for a long time.[40]

This quotation shows that self-denial plays a central role in Kierkegaard's authorship. Furthermore, he invites the reader to practise self-denial, even though this is not an easy task.

10.2.1.2 Careful Listening

Second, Kierkegaard would suggest listening attentively. According to him, a missionary must be "a willing and attentive listener"[41] and "the astonished listener who sits and listens to what delights that other person, whom it delights even more that you listen in that way."[42] A Christian denies self, closes their mouth, listens attentively, and learns about their neighbour.

> To be a teacher is not to say: This is the way it is, nor is it to assign lessons and the like. No, to be a teacher is truly to be the learner. Instruction begins with this, that you, the teacher, learn from the learner, place yourself in what he has understood and how he has understood it.[43]

It is a beautiful idea to deny self and learn from the other, but how can one practise this in reality?

10.2.1.3 Self-Recognition as a Penitent

Third, a Kierkegaardian missionary should recognize themselves as a penitent. This self-recognition as a sinner is a decisive difference between the incarnated Christ and an incarnational missionary. Jesus Christ "knew no sin" (2 Cor 5:21) and did not need to repent. Although the apostle Paul was proud to be an imitator of Christ (1 Cor 11:1), he recognized himself as the "foremost" among sinners (1 Tim 1:15). Kierkegaard says, "My life was most

---

40. *SKS* 16, 13/ *PV*, 25.
41. *SKS* 16, 28/ *PV*, 45.
42. *SKS* 16, 28/*PV*, 46.
43. *SKS* 16, 28/*PV*, 46.

properly used in doing penance."[44] His devotion to repentance was not a fleeting aspect of his spirituality but rather a lifelong commitment. In this way, he remained faithful to the spiritual heritage of Lutheranism, his national religion. On 31 October 1517, Luther nailed the 95 Theses to the door of the Castle Church in Wittenberg, marking the beginning of Protestantism. The first thesis says, "When our Lord and Master Jesus Christ said, 'Repent' (Mt 4:17), he willed the entire life of believers to be one of repentance."[45] According to Lutheran tradition, a person should repent throughout their entire life. Therefore, this self-recognition as a penitent is not just Kierkegaard's inclination but something that every true Christian should have.[46]

In summary, how can one overcome the first barrier, "self"? According to Kierkegaard, one should imitate Christ and deny oneself. Practically speaking, this requires attentive listening to and learning from the other. Finally, one's self-recognition as a sinner and a penitent may be able to weaken the stubborn self, making it conquerable.

10.2.2 How to Overcome "Buddhism Enmeshed in Japanese Culture"

> If someone who lives in the midst of Christianity enters, with knowledge of the true idea of God, the house of God, the house of the true God, and prays, but prays in untruth, and if someone lives in an idolatrous land but prays with all the passion of infinity, although his eyes are resting upon the image of an idol – where, then, is there more truth? The one prays in truth to God

---

44. *SKS* 16, 61/*PV*, 82.

45. "95 Theses," https://www.luther.de/en/95thesen.html.

46. Of course, since a Christian belongs to Christ, they are forgiven and released from sin. But Kierkegaardianly speaking, "there is not one single living human being who does not despair a little." *SKS* 11, 138/ *SUD*, 22. In other words, when Christians are honest before God, they recognize that they cannot achieve perfection while they remain on earth. It is spiritually healthy to discover sins and transgressions in one's daily life. Thanks to possessing a new secure status (justification) in relation to God, Christians can be honest, sensitive, and penitent before God. At the same time, they are *becoming* people who must behave in a manner that is appropriate to their newly won position (sanctification). Eventually, the day will come, in heaven, when they are completely free of guilt (glorification).

although he is worshipping an idol; the other prays in untruth to the true God and is therefore in truth worshipping an idol.[47]

– Johannes Climacus, *Concluding Unscientific Postscript*

The above quotation[48] has acquired a bad reputation among some Christians. Some think that this quotation demonstrates Kierkegaard's relativism because it suggests that a devout idolater may possess more truth than a lazy Christian.

First, it is important to note that this statement is uttered by Johannes Climacus, not Kierkegaard himself. Climacus claims that he is not a Christian. In addition, Kierkegaard says, "Thus in the pseudonymous books there is not a single word by me."[49] Why did Kierkegaard engage in such mental gymnastics? He did this to "deceive" the reader into the truth. "What, then, does it mean 'to deceive'? It means that one does not begin *directly* with what one wishes to communicate but begins by taking the other's delusion at face value."[50] The Kierkegaardian concept of pseudonymous works can be likened to the term *upāya* (方便) in Buddhism. According to Daigan and Alicia Matsunaga, *upāya* "has a dual connotation, being both:

1. A method for the enlightened one's communication of his experience, and
2. A method of spiritual awakening for the 'ignorant' sentient being."[51]

Applied to Japan, a Kierkegaardian missionary ought to affirm *whatever truths they find in Buddhism* rather than flatly denying *all things* simply because it is not Christian. In other words, one can become like a Buddhist to the Buddhist (1 Cor 9:20–21). Although Paul, in Athens, "was deeply distressed to see that the city was full of idols" (Acts 17:16), he approached them saying, "Athenians, I see how extremely religious you are in every way" (17:22). Our goal is to win Buddhists over to Christ. Therefore, we can concede on all other arguments and disputes and just aim for *that* goal.

---

47. *SKS* 7, 184/ *CUP I*, 201.

48. See the summary of chapter 3 of Varughese John's *Truth and Subjectivity* in section 1.4.3.

49. *SKS* 7, 570/ *CUP I*, 625.

50. *SKS* 16, 36/ *PV*, 54, emphasis in original.

51. Matsunaga and Matsunaga, "Concept of Upāya," 72.

Second, the quotation at the beginning of this section is a statement made in the context of the Christendom of Denmark. Climacus does not encourage idol worship but warns the Danes against any notion of geographical superiority or advantage, thereby endeavouring to provoke them to worship the true God in truth.

According to David Lu's *Overcoming Barriers to Evangelization to Japan*, the second barrier that hinders evangelization in Japan is "Buddhism enmeshed in Japanese culture." How can we apply the Kierkegaardian mission to evangelize Japanese Buddhists?

10.2.2.1 Respect for Buddhists

First, we respect Buddhists who are not yet born again and acknowledge the truths present in their tradition. When we despise them as idol worshippers or judge them in our hearts, they will sense such attitudes even if we do not actually voice them aloud. Such attitudes may indirectly present Christianity in an unappealing manner. We can respect Buddhists who truly live in immanent truth, and we can learn from them. Climacus's "Devout Idolater" reminds me of 佐々井秀嶺 (Sasai Shūrei), a Japanese-born monk[52] who suffered greatly during his youth but, today, has contributed significantly to the "untouchable" liberation movement and the revival of Buddhism in India. The knowledge of a Buddhist like Sasai Shūrei should inspire Christians, humble them, and encourage them to be appropriately respectful of Buddhists.

10.2.2.2 Affirming Buddhists' Faith Temporarily and Guiding Them to Shift Their Faith to Christ

Second, a Kierkegaardian missionary temporarily affirms the Buddhist's faith and then helps them to switch the object of their faith[53] to Christ. For instance, Kierkegaard says to the one who has been betrayed by someone they truly trusted,

---

52. As for 佐々井秀嶺 (Sasai Shūrei), see Sasai, 必生 闘う仏教 [*Live without Fail, Fighting Buddhism*]; Yamagiwa, 破天 – インド仏教徒の頂点に立つ日本人 [*Unprecedented: A Japanese Who Stands on the Top of Indian Buddhists*].

53. The object of a Buddhist's faith may vary. In original Buddhism and Theravada Buddhism, Shakamuni-butsu (BCE 563–483 or 480–400) is the sole Buddha in the world and the only object of faith. But the 浄土宗 [*Jōdō* sect], which is the most popular Buddhist sect in Japan, may say that 法然 (Hōnen, 1133–1212) or 阿弥陀仏 (*Amidabutsu*) is the object of faith. Namikawa, ブッダたちの仏教 [*Buddhism of Buddhas*], 126–130.

> If there was someone to whom you felt drawn so strongly that you dared to say, "I have faith in him" . . . Yet you may have been wrong in doing so – not in having faith, not in having faith in this way, but in having faith in a human being in this way.[54]

Here, Kierkegaard affirms the person's faith but then gently guides them to switch the object of their faith from a human being to God. Paul was once a persecutor of the church. He passionately persecuted Christ but, later, passionately worshipped Christ. He was passionate both as a Jew and as a Christian. Similarly, there is a biblical and Kierkegaardian way to affirm, rather than criticize, the passion of Buddhists while also seducing them into directing their passion to Christ. But how can this be done?

10.2.2.3 Prayer in Truth to the True God

Third, the seduction of Buddhists to Christ may be achieved by praying in truth to the true God. A Christian who worships the true God in truth can influence their Buddhist neighbours: "What one's life proclaims is a hundred thousand times more powerfully effective than what one's mouth proclaims."[55] When Christians become aware of their own untrue worship and are inspired to worship the true God in truth, this can have a profound effect on those who observe the change in their lives. In other words, when Christians repent and are renewed, the effects of this renewal are not limited to themselves. The renewal of authentic worship indirectly but effectively influences Buddhists.

Above all, prayers allow the hand of the Almighty to move. Kierkegaard believed that while human beings (Christians) can provide opportunities for others (Buddhists), God alone can do the work of regeneration and lead people to recognize the truth. Therefore, we humans must recognize the limitations of the role God has assigned to us. We must pray in truth and sincerity, while allowing God to do the work that only he can do. Anti-Climacus concludes *Practice in Christianity* with the following prayer to Jesus:

> And we pray for the lay Christians, that they . . . may not think poorly of themselves, as if it were not allotted to them also to draw others to you as far as a human being is capable of it. As

---

54. *SKS* 5, 33/ *EUD*, 24.
55. *SKS* 16, 186/ *FSE* /*JFY*, 131–132.

> far as a human being is capable of it – for indeed you are the only one who is capable of drawing to yourself, even if you are able to use everything and everyone to draw all to yourself.[56]

Indeed, only the Triune God can draw Buddhists to himself by using everything and everyone.

In summary, how can one overcome the second barrier, "Buddhism enmeshed in Japanese culture"? A Kierkegaardian missionary first affirms the faith of Buddhists, respects those who practise Buddhism, and learns from them. Second, a Kierkegaardian missionary can affirm the passion or devotion of Buddhists while simultaneously guiding them to switch the object of their faith to Christ. Third, a Kierkegaardian missionary prays to the true God in truth so that their life powerfully proclaims Christianity, while recognizing that, ultimately, it is the hand of the Triune God that will draw Buddhists to himself.

10.2.3 How to Overcome "Myriad Deities of Shintoism"

> That pantheism constitutes a surmounted factor in religion, is the foundation for it, seems now to be acknowledged, and hereby also the error in Schleiermacher's definition of religion as remaining in pantheism, in that he makes the extra-temporal fusion factor of the universal and the finite – into religion.[57]
>
> – Søren Kierkegaard, *Journals and Notebooks*

Some define Shintoism as pantheism;[58] others do not.[59] However, both parties will admit that Shintoism can be loosely described as *pantheistic* because the world view of Shintoism suggests that "gods are a mountain, a sea, wind, a tree, a rock, a fall, thunder, etc., all elements that constitute great nature."[60]

---

56. *SKS* 12, 253/ *PC*, 262.

57. *SKS* 17, 219, DD:9/ *JP* IV, 3849 *n.d.*, 1837.

58. Koami Jinja. "神道の汎神論上価値観こそ、和と調和を生み現在の日本の繁栄に導いた" ["It Is Precisely the Values of Shinto's Pantheism That Gave Birth to Harmony and Balance, Leading to Japan's Present Prosperity"]. *Koami Jinja Blog*. Last modified March 19, 2022. https://blog.goo.ne.jp/koamijinja/e/2347d5bcaefcd2cce2965775b60be56f.

59. Shinto Kokusai Gakkai. "神道とは" ["What Is Shintoism?"]. *Shinto Kokusai Gakkai*. Accessed March 19, 2022. http://www.shinto.org/wordjp/?page_id=2.

60. Toya, 神道入門 [*Introduction to Shintoism*], 15.

Therefore, I will proceed on the assumption that the above quotation, in which Kierkegaard discusses pantheism, can be loosely related to Shintoism. Missionaries and philosophers often view the pantheistic world view of Shintoism and the monotheistic world view of Christianity as mutually exclusive and wholly incompatible. However, the quotation at the beginning of this subsection suggests that Kierkegaard, while regarding pantheism as something that should be transcended, also acknowledges it as the foundational stage in the development of religious consciousness. In short, Kierkegaard sees not just differences but also some degree of continuity between pantheism and Christianity. In fact, when Paul gave his speech before the Areopagus in Athens, he did not adopt a confrontational approach but a conciliatory attitude to pantheism: "Indeed [God] is not far from each one of us. For 'In him we live and move and have our being'[61]; as even some of your own poets have said,/ 'For we too are his offspring'"[62] (Acts 17:27–28). Here, Paul quotes two non-biblical religious sources that express a pantheistic world view. However, Paul does not criticize these views but uses these pantheistic quotations to support his message. In contrast, the Christian approach to Shintoism has been often been confrontational or even offensive, as seen in Fabian Fucan's 妙貞問答 (*Myōtei* Dialogues)[63] in 1605 and Tsunehiko Sano and Nicolas's 教法問答 (*Doctrinal Dialogues*)[64] in 1890. In accordance with Scripture, we can proclaim, "Indeed God is not far from each one of us. For Shintoists have said, 'For we too are his offspring'" (See Acts 17:27–28).[65] The Kierkegaardian conciliatory approach to Shintoism is innovative and biblical.[66] According to

---

61. "The language here is quoted from an address to Zeus by his son Minos: 'In thee we live and move and have our being.'" Bruce, *Acts of the Apostles*, 338. If that is the case, Paul was referring positively to a pagan poem devoted to Zeus, a pantheistic god.

62. This is a quotation from the Stoic poem Aratos' Φαινόμενα (Phainomena). According to 田川建三 (Tagawa Kenzō), Hellenistic Jewish missionary literature preferred to quote from Stoic pantheism such as Aratos' Φαινόμενα (Phainomena) – namely, Aristobulus of Alexandria (fl. c. 181–124 BC). Tagawa, 新約聖書 訳と注2下 使徒行伝 [*The New Testament, Translation and Commentary, volume 2(2): Acts*], 491–492.

63. Fucan, 妙貞問答 ["*Myōtei* Dialogues"], 128–143.

64. Sano and Nicolas, 教法問答 [*Doctrinal Dialogues*]. cf. 世のため、人のため - 経彦さま伝 [For People in the Society: Biography of Tsunehiko] in 新理教応援HP [Home Page to Support Teaching of Divine Principle] http://sinri.sub.jp/tsune/H16-2.html.

65. "Shintoism sees the omnipresence of gods in all things in nature and also views humans as gods." Toya, 神道入門 [*Introduction to Shintoism*], 17.

66. When I claim that the method of Paul's ministry in Athens is "biblical," some may not agree, citing several reasons. First, since Paul did not initially intend to proclaim the gospel

David Lu's *Overcoming Barriers to Evangelization to Japan*, the third barrier that hinders evangelization in Japan is the "myriad deities of Shintoism." How can we apply the Kierkegaardian mission to evangelize Japanese Shintoists?

10.2.3.1 Shintoists' Adoration of Nature as Points of Contact

A Kierkegaardian mission to Shintoists must, first, use Shintoistic sensitivity, which involves adoring nature and viewing gods or God as being present in nature as "points of contact." One missiologist defines "points of contact" as "bridges for communicating the gospel across the various cultures of the world yet unreached with the gospel."⁶⁷ The grove of the village shrine demonstrates the Japanese view of nature and gods, a view that has been passed down from ancient Shintoism: "The grove of the village that 神社 [shrine] is present, is not just the natural forest but the holy forest that gods abide. A long time ago when they were not aware of ecology, the Japanese who felt gods in nature enshrined shrine in the forest nearby."⁶⁸ In his discourses on "The Lily of the Field and the Bird of the Air" (Matt 6:25–34), Kierkegaard describes the sense of the reality of the divine in nature as follows:

> The sun shines for you and for your sake, that when it becomes weary the moon begins to shine and the stars are lit; that winter comes, that all nature disguises itself, plays the game of stranger,

---

in Athens, his sermon was not well-prepared. Second, he gained only a few converts, which implies that his mission in Athens was a failure. Third, reflecting on this apparent failure, Paul critiques (Greek) philosophy and, in the first four chapters of 1 Corinthians, declares his decision to proclaim a simple gospel. Although these views may be popular in some Christian circles, most biblical scholars do not accept these ideas. "The idea, popular with many preachers, that his determination, when he arrived in Corinth, to 'know nothing' there 'except Jesus Christ and him crucified' (1 Cor 2:2), was the result of disillusionment with the line of approach he had attempted in Athens, has little to commend it." Bruce, *Book of the Acts*, 344. "Luke's summary of Paul's time in Athens ends with this note of some positive response. While certainly not an overwhelming success, nothing about what Paul does or says is viewed negatively or as a failure (Weiser 1985: 477; Polhill 1992: 379)." Bock, *Acts*, page unspecified. "Contrary to what some scholars have inferred, there is no reason to view Paul's mission in Athens as a failure. Indeed, far from intending to present this occasion as a failure, Luke provides it as a model for apologetic." Keener, *Acts*, page unspecified.

67. Sanders, "Point of Contact Theory," 1.

68. Takashi Sakurai, 神道の立場から [From the Perspective of Shintoism] in 2014 年 国際神道セミナー キリスト教と神道との対話 二つの宗教が探る協調への道筋 – 過去・現在から未来へむけて – [International Shintoism Seminar in 2014, Dialogues between Christianity and Shintoism, The Collaborating Path that Two Religions Seeks for: from Past, Present to Future]. ed. by International Shintoism Studies Association, Tokyo: Shinano Publishing House, 2015, 27.

and in order to delight you; that spring comes, that the birds return in great flocks, and in order to give you joy; that the leaves bud, the forest adorns itself and stands like a bride, and in order to give you joy; that autumn comes, that the birds fly away... that the forest hides its adornment for the sake of next time, that is so that it can give you joy next time.... If this does not give you joy, then there is nothing to rejoice over.[69]

A love of nature is always present in the works of traditional Japanese artists – 歌人 (poets) such as 西行法師 (Saigyō Hōshi, 1118–1190) and 芭蕉 (Bashō, 1644–1694), and 水墨画家 (wash-drawing painters) such as 雪舟 (Sesshū, 1420–1502). To connect with the divine through nature is second nature to the Japanese. Accordingly, a Kierkegaardian mission to the Japanese must appreciate nature's vastness, solemnity, silence, and absolute obedience to God.[70] This kind of spirituality is a natural way to introduce the Christian God to Shintoists.

However, Kierkegaard's words cited at the beginning of this subsection suggest that pantheism should be surmounted. Similarly, the apostle Paul not only builds bridges between Greek pantheism and Christianity but also surmounts pantheism by proclaiming that whereas the Greeks worship an unknown god, God is creator, spirit, and giver of life, (Acts 17:23–25). Similarly, a Kierkegaardian missionary can surmount pantheistic elements of Shintoism through Christian proclamation.

10.2.3.2 Christian Proclamation to Shintoists

Second, a Kierkegaardian mission to Shintoists should follow the apostle Paul's lead and proclaim what they worship as unknown. For example, when he visited 伊勢神宮 (Ise Grand Shrine), *Saigyō Hōshi*, a famous Japanese monk and poet, said, "何事の おわしますかは 知らねども かたじけなさに 涙こぼるる" (What it is I know not /But with the gratitude/ My tears fall).[71] This poem well represents what the Japanese experience when they visit shrines. Shintoism does not have a founder, sacred texts, or doctrines.

---

69. *SKS* 11, 43–44/ *WA*, 39–40.
70. Posch, "Nature/Natural Science," 229.
71. Salinger, *Raise High the Roof Beam*, https://mixi.jp/view_diary.pl?id=1959831813&owner_id=1737245.

Therefore, 山折哲雄 (Yamaori Tetsuo), a scholar of religious studies, comparing and contrasting Western religion with Japanese religion, notes that the West has a religion of faith while Japan has a religion of intuition. The average Japanese is not too concerned about whom they worship.[72] They turn to gods only in times of trouble or when they want to experience something extraordinary. Christians are responsible to proclaim "what it is" so that Shintoists can know whom they are worshipping.

The Kierkegaardian mission takes time. If we start with an orthodox proclamation of God, sin, and salvation, it is hard for a non-Christian Japanese to accept this message. A Kierkegaardian mission does not demand a person's decision and commitment in the early stages of a mission but, instead, slowly offers a spirituality that is palatable and digestible for the Japanese. Kierkegaard is tolerant towards and accepting of aesthetes who avoid commitment and patient about slowly cultivating the ability of *either/or* in them. We can learn from him how to plant the seeds of *either/or* in the Japanese.[73] In this way, we must take the time to patiently present Christian doctrines in the way that Scripture does. Among these Christian doctrines, the most challenging and important message is the third point, which we will discuss in the next subsection.

10.2.3.3 Cultivating a Culture of Repentance for War Crimes

Third, a Kierkegaardian missionary could guide Shintoists to repent of war crimes committed by Japan in the name of State Shinto from 1868 to 1945.[74] "We [Christians and Shintoists] should have opportunities to talk about State Shinto and wars at some future date. We cannot avoid political issues."[75] Let

---

72. Of course, each shrine is dedicated to a specific god(s) – for instance, Ise Grand Shrine to 天照大御神 (Amaterasu-Ōmikami), 靖国神社 (Yasukuni Shrine) to the war dead, 明治神宮 (Meiji Jingū) to 明治天皇 (Meiji Emperor). However, the majority of worshippers seem not to know to whom the shrine is dedicated. Watanabe, 日本の宗教人口: 2億と2–3割の怪の解 ["Religious Demographics in Japan: The Mystery of Two Hundred Million and the Enigma of 20–30%"], 27–28, 33.

73. See section 3.2.4.3.

74. "State Shintō, Japanese Kokka Shintō, nationalistic official religion of Japan from the Meiji Restoration in 1868 through World War II. [. . .] State Shintō was abolished in 1945 by a decree of the Allied occupation forces that forbade government subsidy and support to Shintō shrines and repudiated the emperor's divinity." *Encyclopedia Britannica*, s.v. "State Shintō," accessed 23 March 2022, https://www.britannica.com/topic/State-Shinto.

75. John Breen, "問題提起『これまでの歴史を振り返って』" [Posing the Question: 'Reflecting on History So Far'], in *Dialogues between Christianity and Shintoism: International*

me begin by sharing a personal experience that demonstrates how the typical Japanese is ignorant of wars that have been fought in the name of State Shinto. While I was studying at a seminary in the Philippines, I had an opportunity to preach at a local church. The pastor introduced me to the congregation, saying, "Previously, Japan was an enemy and the Imperial Japanese Army tortured Filipinos by Bataan Death March (in 1942).[76] Today we have the same Japanese but as a friend. He is going to share the word of God with us." I was embarrassed that I did not know what atrocities my nation had committed against Filipinos and was now suddenly faced with the knowledge of these monstrous crimes of the Japanese. I was disturbed that descendants of the victims of these crimes welcomed me with a smile. I could not just start preaching as if nothing had happened. Before preaching, I apologized for what Japan has done against the Filipinos in the past. Although I could not hold back my tears, I felt fortunate that I had this opportunity to learn what my nation had done and apologize to the Filipinos. The brutality of the Japanese in the Philippines – even though it happened thirty years before I was born – still shocked me.

Two years before his death, the Shōwa Emperor (1901–1989) confessed his anguish over his responsibility for the war to his chamberlain, 小林忍 (Kobayashi Shinobu, 1923–2006).[77] It is impossible to imagine his heartache. He could not have experienced peace of mind since he must have known about the atrocities committed by the Imperial Japanese Army. There is much debate about how to judge the war responsibility of the Shōwa Emperor, who functioned both as the head of the political state and as 現人神 (a living god)

Shintoism Seminar in 2014, ed. International Shintoism Studies Association (Tokyo: International Shintoism Studies Association, 2014), 21.

76. "The surrendered Filipinos and Americans soon were rounded up by the Japanese and forced to march some 65 miles from Mariveles, on the southern end of the Bataan Peninsula, to San Fernando. The men were divided into groups of approximately 100, and the march typically took each group around five days to complete. The exact figures are unknown, but it is believed that thousands of troops died because of the brutality of their captors, who starved and beat the marchers, and bayoneted those too weak to walk. Survivors were taken by rail from San Fernando to prisoner-of-war camps, where thousands more died from disease, mistreatment and starvation." "Bataan Death March," *History*, accessed March 25, 2025, https://www.history.com/topics/world-war-ii/bataan-death-march.

77. Kobayashi and Kyōdō News Crew, 昭和天皇 最後の侍従日記 [*Shōwa Emperor's Last Chamberlain's Diary*], 192.

over the Shinto State. Although General Headquarters (GHQ)[78] decided not to prosecute the Shōwa Emperor, the war was fought in the name of the emperor. In Dostoevsky's *Crime and Punishment*, Raskolnikov commits murder. Prior to confessing his sin, he suffers from a fever of unknown origin. But after surrendering himself to the police and being sent to Siberia, he experiences a kind of resurrection akin to the resurrection of Lazarus in chapter 11 of the Gospel of John, which Sonya has previously read for him. Not having an opportunity to confess one's sin and choose to repent is a form of torture.

The atomic bombings of Hiroshima and Nagasaki made Japan the only country to have experienced atomic bombs. Since then, many Japanese have held on to a sense of victimization instead of taking responsibility for the actions of Imperial Japan and the crimes that ordinary Japanese were forced to commit.[79] The Holocaust, in which Nazi Germany killed six million Jews, is widely condemned. But what about Imperial Japan's actions, which led to the death of twenty million people across the Asia Pacific region at the hands of Japanese soldiers?

---

78. "Japan accepted the terms of the Potsdam Declaration on 15 August 1945 (Showa 20), that ended Pacific War. Japan then was placed under the occupation of the Allied Powers, led by the United States. Thereafter, the General Headquarters, Supreme Commander for the Allied Powers (GHQ/SCAP) issued directives to the Japanese Government, implementing various reforms based on the major policies of demilitarization and democratization." "Modern Japan in Archive: Political History from the Opening of the Country to Post-War" "Chapter 5: Reconstruction of Japan" "(a) End of the Ward and Allied Occupation" ed. by National Diet Library. Japan. https://www.ndl.go.jp/modern/e/cha5/index.html (accessed 23 March 2022).

79. 香月泰男(Kazuki Yasuo, 1911–1974), a Japanese painter known for his "Siberia Series," offers important insights. He experienced being sent to Manchuria as a soldier and later to Siberia as a prisoner of war. Although Japan surrendered on August 15, 1945, World War II was not yet over for soldiers in Manchuria, which was occupied by the Soviet Union. Japanese POWs were transported to Siberia. On the train journey from Manchuria to Siberia, Kazuki witnessed a horrific sight – a "red corpse" that resembled an anatomical model of human muscles. He speculated that a local Chinese person had taken personal revenge by skinning the Japanese victim either alive or after death. Kazuki believed that ordinary Japanese were coerced into participating in war, forced to kill, and ultimately became unwilling perpetrators. As a consequence, they took on what he saw as an inevitable role of atonement by becoming the "red corpse." He contrasted this with the "black corpse" – the charred remains of victims from the atomic bombings of Hiroshima and Nagasaki. Upon his return from Siberia, Kazuki was disturbed that the Japanese focused solely on saying "No more Hiroshima," as if other tragedies of war did not exist. To him, the "red corpse" more profoundly embodied the overall misery of war than the "black corpse." If it had been possible, he wished he could have carried the "red corpse" across Japan to ensure that no one would ever desire war again. Instead, as an artist, he expressed this anguish through his paintings in the *Siberia Series*.

Japanese Christians must take the initiative and repent.[80] And this repentance should begin by confessing and repenting of the national sins committed during the war. This is necessary because, thus far, Japan has failed to show appropriate contrition and sorrow over its role in the war. As Richard Lloyd Parry, a British foreign correspondent, notes, "The Japanese have failed in the task so successfully managed by the Germans, of persuading their former enemies that they are sorry."[81] Japan needs a good example of a true apology, and not just for the sake of formalities. Japanese Christians have an obligation to offer a sincere apology on behalf of themselves, Shintoists, and the nation of Japan. Furthermore, we should repent because we failed to say "no" to war during World War II. "Following the 1930s, the Japanese Christian Church stated that pledging allegiance to the Emperor and the nation did not contradict Christian faith, and subsequently, it gradually and actively cooperated with the war effort."[82] Both as *Japanese* and as *Christians*, even those born in a generation after WWII have a political and religious responsibility to address wrongdoing that took place during this period.

Kierkegaard allows his pseudonym Johannes Climacus to speak on how one can influence others to plead guilty:

> In the religious discourse there sometimes are instances of the opposite tactic. The religious speaker, thundering guilt upon the individual's head, wants to force the individual comparatively into the totality of the guilt-consciousness. That just cannot be done; the more he thunders, the more he makes the individual feel more loathsome *than* others, and the less it is accomplished, and when he gesticulates most vehemently, he is furthest from

---

80. "It is one of Japan's greatest failures in 75 years of postwar success that it remains unreconciled with the countries in the world with which it has the closest physical, linguistic and cultural proximity. The tragedy is that it is now too late: everyone who carried individual responsibility for the war is dead, or soon will be." Parry, "Akihito," https://www.lrb.co.uk/the-paper/v42/n06/richard-lloyd-parry/akihito-and-the-sorrows-of-japan. Undoubtedly, reconciliation efforts may be "too late," but to the extent to which we recognize our responsibility and guilt, we are accountable. Granted, we may not be able to reconcile with our neighbouring lands; however, Kierkegaardianly speaking, we still have a responsibility before God.

81. Parry, "Akihito." The contexts of Japan and Germany are vastly different; therefore, Japan cannot simply mimic the German path but needs to find its own path as it seeks to earn the trust of ex-enemy nations. See also Nakamasa, 日本とドイツ - 二つの戦後思想 [*Japan and Germany: Two Post-war Thinkings*].

82. Takahashi, 靖国問題 [*Yasukuni Issue*], 133–134.

it. . . . Another way is better, when the religious speaker, "humble before God, submissive to the royal majesty of the ethical," himself in fear and trembling for his own person, joins the guilt together with the conception of an eternal happiness. Then the listener is not incited but is influenced indirectly, since it seems to him as if the pastor were speaking only about himself. . . . in the pulpit it is better to beat one's own chest, especially when the discourse is about the totality of guilt, because if the pastor beats his own chest, he hinders any comparison; if he points to himself, then we have the comparative again.[83]

In the midst of daily life, a Kierkegaardian missionary should be like the preacher who beats his own chest in the above quotation. Climacus says, "The task appears in everyday life and in the living room." He adds, "It is in the living room that the battle must be fought, because the victory must be that the home becomes a shrine."[84] There are over eighty thousand 神社 (Shinto Shrines) in Japan, and the Japanese naturally come across Shinto Shrines everywhere in Japan. If each Japanese Christian's home "becomes a shrine," the number of "Christian shrines" in Japan would be well over one million and, theoretically, a Japanese person would be able to come across a "Christian shrine" more often than a Shinto Shrine. Nevertheless, relying solely on numbers is not the Kierkegaardian way. Rather, we should be encouraged to repent as "the single individual" before God, alone with God, because God "uses the single individual to prod the established order out of self-complacency."[85] When a Kierkegaardian missionary sincerely acknowledges their responsibility and guilt before God, especially on days such as 15 August – when the nation of Japan commemorates the end of the war in the Pacific – and in their daily life, Shintoists and the descendants of those who committed war crimes under the name of State Shinto may be guided to reflect on their own responsibility and guilt. This, in turn, may encourage Japan to take responsibility for and repent of its crimes against humanity, which will lead to international recognition that Japan has reconciled with its

---

83. *SKS* 7, 482, asterisk / *CUP I*, 530–531, asterisk, emphasis in original, translation slightly modified. Compare Matthew 7:1–5 and Luke 18:9–14.

84. *SKS* 7, 422/ *CUP I*, 465

85. *SKS* 12, 98/ *PC*, 90.

past. Above all, such repentance will prepare Shintoists to enter Christianity, which is our primary goal. "Admittance is only through the consciousness of sin; to want to enter by any other road is high treason against Christianity."[86] Recognition of their own guilt will help Shintoists to enter Christianity. As Paul writes, "Where sin increased, grace abounded all the more" (Rom 5:20).

In summary, how one can overcome the third barrier, the "myriad deities of Shintoism"? First, the Kierkegaardian mission is not to be confrontational but, rather, must seek to connect the Shintoistic pantheistic appreciation of nature to the Christian appreciation of God's beautiful creation. Second, since Shintoists are largely unaware of what kind of divinity they worship, Christians can slowly introduce them to the "unknown god" in a way that is digestible and appropriate. Third, the Kierkegaardian mission is to help Shintoists to repent of their wrongful actions between 1868 to 1945 in the name of State Shinto. How can a Kierkegaardian missionary help? They can help by encouraging Japanese Christians to take the initiative in repenting for Japan's war crimes against humanity from 1868 to 1945, as well as for Christian cooperation with State Shinto when they should have opposed it. Sincere repentance before God may indirectly but effectively influence others to be sincerely sorry for the past. This process may also help Japan to gain the trust of neighbouring nations. Above all, this may prepare Shintoists to enter Christianity.

10.2.4 How to Overcome "Seeking Perfection without God"

> The more we think we are able to or harden our hearts to be able to dispense with the eternal, all the more do we stand basically in need of just that.[87]
>
> – Søren Kierkegaard, *"The Single Individual"*:
> *Two "Notes" concerning My Work as an Author*

According to David Lu's *Overcoming Barriers to Evangelization to Japan*, the fourth barrier that hinders evangelization in Japan is "seeking perfection without God." Despite the influence of Buddhism and Shintoism – two

---

86. *SKS* 12, 80/ *PC*, 67–68. Compare Mark 2:17 and 1 Timothy 1:15.
87. *SKS* 16, 84/ *PV*, 104.

great religions in Japan – many modern Japanese people claim to have "no religion."[88]

In this context, it is relevant to discuss Confucianism. According to Confucian scholars, Confucianism is not just a system of ethics but also contains religious elements.[89] But the very fact that scholars have to defend and argue for the religious nature of Confucianism elucidates the manner in which Japan has received Confusion thought. Namely, Japan has imported Confucianism mainly as moral education. Lu seems to associate this mode of reception with the phenomenon of non-religiousness in Japan – intimating its Confucian origins.[90]

In addition, there is a slight difference between Western atheists and the non-religious Japanese. While an atheist in the West positively denies the existence of a God or gods, in Japan, the line between a believer and a non-believer is often unclear. It is quite normal for Japanese who faithfully visits a shrine or temple on New Year's Day to consider themselves "non-religious." Therefore, it may be more accurate to call such a person a "self-proclaimed non-religious person." Some Japanese attempt to harden themselves against the eternal by claiming to be non-religious, thereby illustrating Kierkegaard's statement at the beginning of this subsection. However, the longing for the eternal within them prompts them to seek divine help on occasions such as New Year's Day or when they encounter crises in life.

---

88. Although the current population of Japan is 127 million, religious affiliation in Japan exceeds 200 million. The reason for this contradiction is that a large section of the Japanese population is counted both as Shintoist *and* Buddhist. So does this mean that the Japanese are extremely religious because they believe in both Shintoism and Buddhism? Strangely enough, surveys show that only 20 to 30 percent of the population claim to be adherents of a specific religion, with the rest (70 to 80 percent of the population) claiming to be non-religious. This shows that many Japanese are culturally Shintoists *and* Buddhists. See Watanabe, 日本の宗教人口: 2億と2–3割の怪の解 ["Religious Demographics in Japan: The Mystery of Two Hundred Million and the Enigma of 20–30%"].

89. Kaji, 沈黙の宗教 – 儒教 [*Religion of Silence: Confucianism*], 4.

90. Confucianism certainly has atheistic or agnostic elements: "季路問事鬼神。子曰、未能事人、焉能事鬼。曰、敢問死。曰、未知生、焉知死。[Ji Lu asked about serving the spirits of the dead. The Master [Confucius] said, 'While you are not able to serve men, how can you serve their spirits?' Ji Lu added, 'I venture to ask about death?' He was answered, 'While you do not know life, how can you know about death?']' ("諸子百家 (*Chinese Text Project*)" "《先進 - Xian Jin》" https://ctext.org/analects?searchu=未知生. 荀子 [Xunzi, BCE 310–238], one of the great Confucius philosophers, says, "雩而雨, 何也? 曰: 無佗也, 猶不雩而雨也。[If a rainmaking sacrifice is held, and then it rains, what of it? I say, there is no reason. It would still rain even if we do not hold the sacrifice]." Tavor, "12 Religious Thought," 277; originally from Xianquian Wang, 荀子集解 [Xunzi Jijie]. Beijing: Zhonghua Shuju 1988, 316.

10.2.4.1 *Engaging the Non-Religious Through Captivating Topics*

A Kierkegaardian mission to the self-proclaimed non-religious Japanese must begin by engaging such people through captivating and culturally relevant topics. Kierkegaard says, "If one begins immediately with Christianity, they say: This is nothing for us – and put themselves immediately on guard."[91] We can begin immediately with Christianity if the person in front of us is already open to faith. But just as one cannot force someone who is not hungry to eat, starting with Christian orthodoxy for someone who is not interested in faith would be counterproductive. Kierkegaard wrote the pseudonymous work *Either/Or* to attract secular people. On the surface, this work – especially *Part I* – appears to have nothing to do with the devout Christian life. However, this entire work, which is filled with non-religious appeal, was prayerfully constructed to proclaim Christianity. Similarly, Japanese Christian churches can prayerfully prepare interesting events, without religious elements, to attract self-proclaimed non-religious Japanese – for example, English classes, children's cafeterias, counselling centres, lectures on current topics, festivals, and game events. For instance, one Kierkegaardian mission strategy could be to invite Japanese people to study Christ as a path to nurturing and fulfilling their virtue. In *Chrysanthemum and Sword: Patterns of Japanese Culture*, her classic work in Japanology, Ruth Benedict describes the Japanese as "unprecedentedly polite [. . .] [but] also insolent and overbearing."[92] In short, although the Japanese are "unprecedentedly polite," they have a dual nature. Despite their courteous appearance, many Japanese have not really humbled themselves. This may reflect the status quo, with the Japanese unable to practise what 孔子 (Confucius) (BCE 551–479) says in 論語 (The Analects): "子曰、人而不仁、如禮何、[The Master [Confucius] said, 'If a man be without the virtues proper to humanity, what has he to do with the rites of propriety?']."[93] But if the Japanese learn the ways of Jesus Christ, the virtue of humility may be able to permeate both the outward and the inward. Then 本音 (one's true feelings) and 建前 (one's official stance) would be in accord. In short, Christianity need not necessarily be perceived as a Western religion; it

---

91. *SKS* 20, 318–319, NB4:66/ *JP*, V 6107 *n.d.*, 1848.
92. Benedict, *Chrysanthemum and the Sword*, 1.
93. "諸子百家 (*Chinese Text Project*)" " 《八佾 - Ba Yi》 " https://ctext.org/analects/ba-yi/ens.

also calls for an ethical life that contributes to nurturing and accomplishing Japanese virtues. 中沢新一 (Nakazawa Shinichi), a Japanese philosopher, says, "I felt Christianity was less authentic. I like Jesus though."[94] We should not limit the study of Jesus to the sphere of what is commonly considered "Christian." A Kierkegaardian missionary might facilitate a Bible study group that considers Jesus's ethics and is open to self-proclaimed non-religious people. Such people may be interested in studying Jesus Christ from an ethical perspective. It is importance not to focus on a religious commitment at the outset. Over time, they may realize their spiritual hunger.

10.2.4.2 Religious Music

As a second step, a Kierkegaardian mission to self-proclaimed non-religious Japanese could approach them through religious music. This approach is already practised in many churches. Aesthete A, one of Kierkegaard's literary creations, describes the power of music as follows:[95] "Where the rays of the sun do not reach, the tones still manage to come."[96] Religious music can sneak into the heart of a self-proclaimed non-religious person and help them realize their need of the eternal. For instance, J. S. Bach (1685–1750) – who is sometimes called the "fifth evangelist" (after Matthew, Mark, Luke, and John) – communicates the gospel through his music. In his letter, Friedrich Nietzsche, the father of atheist existentialism, writes, "This week I heard [Bach's] *St Matthew Passion* three times and each time I had the same feeling of immeasurable admiration. One who has completely forgotten Christianity truly hears it here as Gospel."[97] Some may say that since both Bach and Nietzsche were Germans, it is not surprising that Nietzsche was moved by Bach's music. However, I would argue that music can overcome both atheism and language barriers. When 立花隆 (Tachibana Takashi, 1940–2021), a critic and journalist who claimed to be agnostic, visited Spain and happened to

---

94. Watanabe, 宗教と現代がわかる本 [*The Book You Can Understand Religion and Modern Age*], 17.

95. Although Esthete A and Kierkegaard differ in some respects, I believe that they share the same views when it comes to music: "We ought to be careful about attributing [A's] views [of music] to Kierkegaard, but in fact nothing Kierkegaard or his other pseudonyms says elsewhere contradicts the views of A." McDonald, "Music," 214.

96. *SKS* 2, 50/ *EO I*, 41.

97. Friedrich Nietzsche's letter to Erwin Rhode, quoted in Gardiner, *Bach*, page unspecified.

drop in to a cathedral on a weekday, when it was almost empty, he heard an organist practising Bach's *Grosse Fuge*. He describes his experience as follows:

> I did not know why but I burst into tears. Once I shed a tear, tears flew endlessly. Even if I am asked why I shed tears at that time, I cannot explain. [. . .] Until now this incident remains in my heart as one of the mysterious experiences in my life. [. . .] Nothing can express what Bach exactly does, how small a human being is when he/she is present before God. Did Bach's musical effect like that knock on my heart at that time?[98]

This statement does not sound anything like Tachibana, who claimed to dislike religion. We can explain why he shed tears. It is because "the more he thinks he is able to or harden his heart to be able to dispense with the eternal, all the more does he stand basically in need of just that."[99] In this way, music has the potential to touch a person's heart beyond their beliefs. Kierkegaard speaks through the mouth of Aesthete A: "It cannot be denied that in every detail the music often can be seductive enough. But so it ought to be, and this is precisely its greatness."[100] Kierkegaard views *missionary tasks* as *seduction to the truth*. Christian music may be able to seduce a self-proclaimed non-religious Japanese to Christianity. If a church has a concert featuring godly music by composers such as Bach, Handel, or Beethoven, self-proclaimed non-religious Japanese may be happy to attend. For instance, when our church had a concert with violin and piano duets featuring Bach, the church was filled with people who would not usually come to the church. However, it is not enough to merely attract self-proclaimed non-religious people. We must at least make them aware of the deeper issues and, hopefully, move them towards the religious. How can we do this?

10.2.4.3 Switch from Indirect Communication to Direct Communication at the Right Moment

As a third step, a Kierkegaardian mission to the self-proclaimed non-religious Japanese must switch from indirect to direct communication once the

---

98. Tachibana, 思索紀行 [*Thought Journey*], 56–57
99. A paraphrase of *SKS* 16, 84/ *PV*, 104.
100. *SKS* 2, 118/ *EO I*, 115.

non-religious person becomes aware of their spiritual hunger and despair. As Nietzsche says, "One who has completely forgotten Christianity truly hears it here as Gospel," and a Kierkegaardian missionary can offer spiritual food. If someone, without understanding why, bursts into endless tears, a Kierkegaardian missionary can provide palatable and digestible food for spiritual upbuilding. As soon as a Kierkegaardian missionary discerns the signs of these spiritual conditions in the non-religious person, they can switch from indirect to direct communication. In other words, they can directly share the gospel in the way the person needs.

According to Kierkegaard, all humanity is in despair. Even if someone seems happy and free from despair, happiness is despair's preferred dwelling place. The wide popularity of *The Sickness unto Death* in Japan suggests that the Japanese somehow recognize the truth of the Anti-Climacean claim regarding the universality of despair. The Japanese might sense that they are in despair. However, whereas *The Sickness unto Death* sells well in Japan, *Practice in Christianity* does not.[101] This suggests that while the Japanese people easily recognize their despair, they are less inclined to hear and respond to the invitation of Jesus Christ. Nevertheless, the Kierkegaardian missionary can boldly present Jesus Christ, who is the only healer of despair, when the Holy Spirit prompts them to do so.

In summary, how can one overcome the fourth barrier, "seeking perfection without God"? One possible application of the Kierkegaardian mission is to attract people with non-religious elements that interest them. Second, a Kierkegaardian missionary can seduce self-proclaimed non-religious people with religious music. Godly music, like that of Bach, can sneak into their hearts and may make them aware of their need for the eternal. Third, a Kierkegaardian missionary can switch from indirect to direct communication

---

101. As of 2022, while three secular publishers in Japan offer a pocket edition (*bunko*) of *The Sickness unto Death*, only one Christian publisher offers a paperback edition of *Practice in Christianity*. Therefore, a Japanese reader has more opportunities to encounter the former work and is unlikly to see a dialectical relationship between the two works. See Søren Kierkegaard, 死に至る病 [*The Sickness unto Death*], translated by Shinji Saitō, Tokyo: Iwanami-bunko 1939, 1957; Søren Kierkegaard, 死に至る病 [*The Sickness unto Death*], translated by Keisaburō Masuda, Tokyo: Chikuma-bunko 1996; Søren Kierkegaard, 死に至る病 [*The Sickness unto Death*], translated by Yūsuke Suzuki; Søren Kierkegaard, キリスト教の修練 [*Practice in Christianity*], translated by Yoshio Inoue, Tokyo: Shinkyō-shuppan-sha, 2004.

when they discern that the non-religious Japanese person has become aware of their spiritual hunger and despair.

10.2.5 How to Overcome "Invisible Proscription"

> If the age is waiting for a hero, it waits in vain; instead there will more likely come one who in divine weakness will teach men obedience – by means of their slaying him in impious rebellion, him, the one obedient to God.[102]
>
> – Søren Kierkegaard, *Journals and Notebooks*

Edwin Reischauer (1910–1990), an expert on the history and culture of Japan and East Asia, describes the impact and result of Japan's first contact with Christianity as follows:

> First introduced by the famous Jesuit missionary, Saint Francis Xavier, in 1549, [Christianity] spread more rapidly in Japan during the next several decades than in any other Asian country, and Christians came to number close to half a million, a much larger percentage of the population of that time than they are today. But Hideyoshi and the early Tokugawa shoguns came to view Christianity as a threat to political unity and suppressed it ruthlessly, creating in the process a large number of Japanese martyrs but virtually stamping the religion out by 1638.[103]

In 1873, the ban on Christianity was lifted. Today 日本国憲法 (the Constitution of Japan) guarantees freedom of religion.[104] However, Lu says that peer pressure keeps Christianity at distance. He calls this phenomenon "invisible proscription." Japanese Christians might experience "invisible

---

102. *SKS* 20, 281–282, NB3:77/ *JP*, II 2004 *n.d.*, 1847.
103. Reischauer and Jansen, *Japanese Today*, 212.
104. "Article 20. Freedom of religion is guaranteed to all. No religious organization shall receive any privileges from the State, nor exercise any political authority.
    No person shall be compelled to take part in any religious act, celebration, rite or practice. The State and its organs shall refrain from religious education or any other religious activity." Constitution of Japan, Article 20, Accessed April 7, 2025. https://japan.kantei.go.jp/constitution_and_government_of_japan/constitution_e.html.

proscription" through the Danka system,¹⁰⁵ Buddhist funerals, Shinto festivals, and family disapproval of their faith. Although the gospel is the source of hope and joy, Japanese Christians might also experience hatred because of Jesus's name (Luke 21:17).

To examine this issue further, I will take up 遠藤周作 (Endō Shūsaku)'s 沈黙 (*Silence*). As stated earlier, Christianity was first brought to Japan in 1549 by the Jesuit missionary Francis Xavier. The historical setting of Endō's *Silence* is the seventeenth century, a time when persecution of Christianity was at its most severe, following the Shimabara Rebellion.¹⁰⁶

According to David Lu's *Overcoming Barriers to Evangelization to Japan*, the fifth barrier that hinders a mission to Japan is "invisible proscription." How can we apply the Kierkegaardian mission to overcome "invisible proscription"?

---

105. "The danka system (檀家制度, *danka seido*) . . . is a system of voluntary and long-term affiliation between Buddhist temples and households in use in Japan since the Heian period. In it, households (the danka) financially support a Buddhist temple which, in exchange, provides for their spiritual needs. Although its existence long predates the Edo period (1603–1868), the system is best known for its repressive use made at that time by the Tokugawa, who made the affiliation with a Buddhist temple compulsory to all citizens. During the Tokugawa shogunate, the system was turned into a citizen registration network; supposedly intended to stop the diffusion of Christianity and help detect hidden Christians, it soon became a government-mandated and Buddhist temple-run system to monitor and control the population as a whole. For this reason, it survived intact long after Christianity in Japan had been eradicated. The system as it existed in Tokugawa times is sometimes called terauke system (寺請制度, *terauke seido*) because of the certification (or terauke, because the tera, or temple would issue an uke, or certificate) issued by a Buddhist temple that a citizen was not a Christian. The mandatory danka system was officially abolished during the Meiji period, but continues nonetheless to [exist] as a voluntary association between the two sides, constitutes a major part of the income of most temples and defines as before the relationship between households and temples." "Danka System." *DBpedia*. https://dbpedia.org/page/Danka_system.

106. "Shimabara Rebellion, (1637–38), uprising of Japanese Roman Catholics, the failure of which virtually ended the Christian movement in 17th-century Japan and furthered government determination to isolate Japan from foreign influences.
The revolt began as a result of dissatisfaction with the heavy taxation and abuses of local officials on the Shimabara Peninsula and the Amakusa-rettō Islands. Most of the peasants in the Shimabara vicinity had been converted to Catholicism by Portuguese and Spanish missionaries, and the rebellion soon took on Christian overtones. With the support of large numbers of rōnin, samurai whose lords had been dispossessed, the rebels fought so zealously that an army of 100,000 troops was unable to quell them, and the Japanese government had to call in a Dutch gunboat to blast the rebel stronghold. Following this incident the government vigorously enforced its proscription of all Christian beliefs and activities." Amy Tikkanen, "Shimabara Rebellion," *Britannica*, last modified [or revised] date not given, accessed March 24, 2022, https://www.britannica.com/event/Shimabara-Rebellion.

10.2.5.1 A Distinction between Absolute and Relative Crises

A Kierkegaardian approach to "invisible proscription" begins by distinguishing between absolute and relative crises. Kierkegaard, in nineteenth-century Denmark, offered insight into how people sometimes fail to recognize a crisis or appreciate how critical a situation is. In my opinion, in contemporary Japan, too, the real crisis is often not recognized as a crisis as many focus on relative crises. As a result, Christian churches in Japan may focus on treating symptoms rather than identifying and addressing the root causes.

Specifically, is it a really a crisis that the Christian population in Japan is still less than 1 percent? Japanese Christians may envy Christian countries where Christians are a majority because they think that it would be comforting to be part of a large Christian community. Kierkegaard cried out about a crisis in Denmark, a country where most of the population was already Christian. Therefore, according to Kierkegaard, the size of the Christian population is not the critical issue. If Kierkegaard is right, then by mistaking *missionary stagnation* for an absolute crisis, we may be blinded to a crisis that is, in fact, far worse.

If stagnation in mission is not the real crisis, what *is* the real crisis? What crisis might we overlook by misidentifying stagnation in mission as the main crisis? What crisis might unwittingly creep into the church? There are two types of crises we must consider: 1) crises that pastors may cause, and 2) crises that ordinary Christians may cause.

10.2.5.1.1 Crises That Pastors May Cause

The first crisis that pastors may cause is compromising the very concept of Christian mission. To quote Anti-Climacus, "As I go up into that holy place – whether the church is packed or as good as empty"[107] is not the most important question. Whether we live in a country with a Christian majority or in a country with a minority of Christians, where missionary progress is slow, is not the most important issue. What, then, is most important?

> I have one listener more than can be seen, an invisible listener, God in heaven, whom I certainly cannot see but who truly can see me. This listener, he pays close attention to whether what I am saying is true, whether it is true in me, that is, he looks

---

107. *SKS* 12, 228/ *PC*, 234.

to see ... whether my life expresses what I am saying. And although I do not have authority to commit anyone else, I have committed myself to every word I have said from the pulpit in the sermon – and God has heard it. Truly it is a risk to preach![108]

Annual reports of the ever-increasing number of church members is not so important. Pastors lose sight of what is truly risky when the annual report of the number of church members becomes their primary concern, whether this is driven by the pure motive of soul-winning or the impure motive of vanity. We, pastors, more than anyone else, must first and foremost humble ourselves before the truth of the gospel and try to live by it; and when we fail to do so, we must honestly admit it from the pulpit.

Kierkegaard, too, intended and hoped for the salvation of as many people as possible through his writings. However, for him, his most important mission was, with God's help, to present the content of the Christian mission correctly.[109] He recognized that distorting the message or failing to live according to it would lead to a real crisis.

10.2.5.1.2 Crises That Ordinary Christians May Cause

The next crisis Christians may cause is to become "a Church triumphant" instead of "a militant Church."[110] One of the reasons that Endō's *Silence* is highly acclaimed is that the reality of "a militant Church" is demonstrated through the description of cruel persecutions and Christian's sufferings. Although this novel is fictitious, the reader can learn some truth about "a militant Church" in the history of the reception of Christianity in Japan. In *Practice in Christianity*, Anti-Climacus states that "only the Church militant is truth – the Church triumphant ... [is] an illusion."[111] He describes "a Church triumphant" as follows:

> The fact that he was the truest Christian would be recognizable by his having the most work to do, having the most assistants,

---

108. *SKS* 12, 228–229/ *PC*, 234–235.
109. *SKS* 13, 23–24/ *PV*, 16.
110. *SKS* 12, 205/ *PC*, 209.
111. *SKS* 12, 214/ *PC*, 219.

and perhaps the king and queen and the whole royal house, or at least clergy, had their shoes made by him.[112]

What are the problems in the situation described above?

> Christ has never wanted to be *victorious in this world*. He came into the world in order to suffer; *that* he called being victorious. But when human impatience and brazen impertinence in imputing to Christianity its own thoughts and conceptions instead of letting its thoughts and conceptions be transformed by Christianity, when this has gained the upper hand, then in the old human way to be victorious comes to mean to be victorious in this world, and then Christianity is abolished.[113]

In the guise of the higher pseudonym Anti-Climacus, Kierkegaard insists on this radical form of Christianity amid the semblance of peace in the nineteenth-century Christendom of Denmark. At present, Japan also appears peaceful. It seems like just a dream that Christianity was once banned and inhuman persecutions were commonplace. However, in the complacency of peace and security, Anti-Climacus warns that allowing the world's victory to infiltrate the church will ultimately destroy Christianity.

According to Anti-Climacus, each Christian needs to overcome the trials of life on their own. One cannot be like an "ass in a lion's skin,"[114] taking pride in victories won by the earthly Jesus or the apostles. They overcame *their* trials. However, we cannot claim *their* victories as though they were *our* war trophies. Each person needs to start from scratch and learn to overcome the trials in their own life. No pain no gain. Anti-Climacus describes "a militant Church" as follows:

> I thought that the very beginning of the test to become and to be a Christian is to become a turned inward that it seems as if all the others do not exist at all for a person, so turned inward that one is quite literally alone in the whole world, alone before

---

112. *SKS* 12, 210–211/ *PC*, 215.
113. *SKS* 12, 219/ *PC*, 224, emphasis in original.
114. Aesop, "The Ass in the Lion's Skin," in *Aesop's Fables*.

God, alone with Holy Scripture as a guide, alone with the prototype before one's eyes.[115]

This quotation invites Japanese Christians to seriously consider the implications of following Christ: "If any want to become my followers, let them deny themselves and take up their cross and follow me" (Mark 8:34).

10.2.5.2 Christianity Should Transform Japan Rather Than Japan Transforming Christianity

Second, a Kierkegaardian mission regarding "invisible proscription" does not mean that Japan is a "swamp" that "sucks up all sorts of ideologies, transforming them into itself and distorting them in the process."[116] Instead, Christianity must transform Japan and bring it to completion. In *Silence*, Ferreira, a senior Portuguese priest who is an apostate, says to Rodrigo, his pupil:

> This country is a swamp. In time you will come to see that for yourself. This country is a more terrible swamp than you can imagine. Whenever you plant a sapling in this swamp the roots begin to rot; the leaves grow yellow and wither. And we have planted the sapling of Christianity in this swamp.[117]

While Endō's *Silence* aligns well with Kierkegaard's concept of a militant church, the above quotation goes in the opposite direction. The mistake of the victorious church was "human impatience and brazen impertinence in imputing to Christianity its own thoughts and conceptions instead of letting its thoughts and conceptions be transformed by Christianity."[118] Here, Ferreira refers to the same kind of problem. Christianity should transform Japan and not the other way around.

Interestingly, 鈴木大拙 (Suzuki Daisetsu, 1870–1966) says Shintoism does not reflect true Japanese spirituality; however, Zen Buddhism does afford one an opportunity to get a glimpse of Japanese spirituality in a pure form.[119] We can learn from him that the spirituality that existed in ancient Japan is

---

115. *SKS* 12, 219–220/ *PV*, 225.
116. Endo, *Silence*, xix.
117. Endō, 沈黙 [*Silence*], 189; Endo, *Silence*, 225.
118. *SKS* 12, 219/ *PC*, 224.
119. Suzuki, 日本的霊性 [*Japanese Spirituality*], 21–22; Suzuki, *Japanese Spirituality*, 18–19.

not necessarily pure Japanese spirituality. Besides, we claim that the best is still to come in the following sense. According to Christian theology, God created everything – including Japan. If so, *only* God knows what Japan and the Japanese are. The best destiny for Japan is that Japan becomes what God has designed and planned. We claim that Japan has not yet become what it truly is. Japan needs Christianity to become what God originally meant it to be. In other words, our perspective should be renewed by God's eschatological horizon. "To historically understand the essence of Japanese culture is to see its completion in the eschatological possibility in the future and to understand Japan as still being in the process of formation now."[120] A Kierkegaardian missionary expands the horizon and sees God's plan of redemption in the future, recognizing that we live in the midst of history, which progresses to completion. One should not be near-sighted nor should they be discouraged by the fact that ministry does not seem to bear fruit. Japan today is in process. Authentic Japan is not completed yet. Christianity should not be transformed by anything but should transform everything – including Japan. In this way, Christianity will bring Japan to completion according to God's original plan of creation.

10.2.5.3 Missionary Martyrs

Third, a Kierkegaardian mission regarding "invisible proscription" calls missionaries to embrace martyrdom. However, this recommendation does not encourage Christians to be suicidal. In 学問のすゝめ (An Encouragement of Learning), 福沢諭吉 (Fukuzawa Yukichi, 1835–1901) says,

> In ancient Japan, many died in battle and committed hara-kiri. In either case, each man is highly acclaimed as a loyal retainer but the reason why he laid down his life is usually for the sake of his lord struggling to gain political power or dying glorious death to take revenge of his lord. This may appear to be splendid but in fact, they do not make a difference in the world.[121]

In 武士道 (*Bushidō*), 新渡戸稲造 (Nitobe Inazō, 1862–1933) says,

---

120. Kondō, キリスト教弁証学 [*Christian Apologetics*], 315.
121. Fukuzawa, 学問のすゝめ [*An Encouragement of Learning*], 113.

Death for a cause unworthy of dying for, was called a "dog's death." "To rush into the thick of battle and to be slain in it," says a Prince of Mito, "is easy enough, and the merest churl is equal to the task; but," he continues, "it is true courage to live when it is right to live, and to die."[122]

What is worth dying for? As the quotation at the beginning of this subsection shows, a missionary in Christendom teaches people obedience to God by sacrificing one's life in humble submission to God. In other words, glorifying God is worth dying for.

Anti-Climacus verbalizes a question that many of us may want to ask: "'But,' I hear someone say, 'you who are speaking here, do you have the strength to become a martyr this way?'"[123] One of the fundamental issues raised in Endō's *Silence* is that not all Christians are strong enough to become martyrs. Endō suggests that ordinary or weak Christians need a maternal form of religion that accepts even apostates.[124] If Anti-Climacus forces all Christians to become martyrs, he would just be repeating the paternal religion that Endō profoundly rejects in his *Silence*.

Anti-Climacus explains what he really wants to communicate to the reader: "I have never enjoyed 'alarming'; I am aware that I am able to speak gently and reassuringly to the suffering, the sick, the sorrowful; I know that I have had my joy in so doing."[125] He makes it clear that he does not intend to fuel anxiety. Instead, he is happy to talk gently to the weak and provide godly comfort to them. He says, "I have never asserted that every Christian is

---

122. Nitobe, *Bushido, the Soul of Japan*, 29–30. https://www.sacred-texts.com/shi/bsd/bsd09.htm.

123. *SKS* 12, 221/ *PC*, 226

124. 山本博文 (Yamamoto Hirofumi), an expert on early modern history in Japan, critically investigates historical documents surrounding the period of the historical backdrop of Endō's *Silence*. According to his investigation, over four thousand Christians died as martyrs in Japan within a period of half a century. Martyrs in Japan are incomparably large in number in the history of Christianity. Yamamoto speculates that this large number of martyrs was due to the Bushido ethos and the attractiveness of Christian doctrine. He also notes that historical records provide no evidence of a missionary resembling Endō's Rodrigo, who mourned the martyrdom of Japanese Christians. Instead, foreign missionaries were proud of the martyrdom of Japanese Christians. Yamamoto, 殉教 – 日本人は何を信仰したか [*Martyrdom: What Did Japanese Believe?*], 250–251.

125. *SKS* 12, 221/ *PC*, 226.

a martyr, or that no one was a true Christian who did not become a martyr."[126] Then why does he use the term "martyr"? Anti-Climacus seems to suggest two things: humble admission and experience of "a martyrdom in possibility."[127] One reason he uses the term "martyr" is that this compels us to admit and confess humbly before God that we fall far short of the ideal Christianity that requires dying for Christ. Anti-Climacus says, "I think that every true Christian should – and here I include myself – in order to be a true Christian, make a humble admission that he has been let off far more easily than true Christians in the strictest sense, and he should make this admission."[128] This quotation is interesting. According to Anti-Climacus, every true Christian is not a true Christian without one condition. This condition is to admit that they fall short of the ideal of the true Christian. Anti-Climacus seems to reject Endō's dualism of strong and weak Christians. Whether it is Anti-Climacus, Kierkegaard, Augustine, St. Francis of Assisi, Luther, Mother Teresa, or any other spiritual giant whom we might recall, no one is strong enough to become a martyr. To the lone voice in Endō's *Silence* that cries out "I am not strong enough to become a martyr," Anti-Climacus would say, "You are right. Making that humble admission is the very condition one must meet in order to be a true Christian."

Another reason Anti-Climacus uses the term "martyr" is because while it is true that every true Christian should make confession and admission, it is also true that every true Christian experiences "a martyrdom in possibility."[129] What does this mean? It means that no one knows how they are going to die, but a true Christian knows that they have something more important than their own life. 星野富弘 (Hoshino Tomihiro, 1946–2024), a renowned Christian painter and poet, says, "いのちが一番大切だと思っていたころ 生きるのが苦しかった/いのちより大切なものがあると知った日 生きているのが嬉しかった" [When I thought life was the most important thing, living felt painful. The day I realized there was something more important than life, I felt joy in living.] I interpret "a martyrdom in possibility" as follows: a Kierkegaardian missionary knows that "we have this treasure in clay

---

126. *SKS* 12, 221/ *PC*, 226–227.
127. *SKS* 12, 220–221/ *PC*, 226.
128. *SKS* 12, 221/ *PC*, 227.
129. *SKS* 12, 220–221/ *PC*, 226.

jars" (2 Cor 4:7) and, therefore, *wills* to embrace an attitude of martyrdom, and *this* attitude brings joy that the world cannot take away.

In speaking of Abel, Scripture says, "He died, but through his faith he still speaks" (Heb 11:4). Kierkegaard says, "The tyrant dies and his rule is over, the martyr dies and his rule begins."[130] Some may die for the truth."[131] Some may die of other causes like Kierkegaard himself. But the cause of death does not define a true Christian. While Kierkegaard was alive, he became the object of ridicule and called himself "the martyr of laughter."[132] A Kierkegaardian missionary does not know how they are going to die, but they live as a martyr in possibility. As the title of one of Kierkegaard's discourses in his signed-religious works says, "The joy of it, that one suffers only once but is victorious eternally."[133] Or in the apostle Paul's words, "For to me, living is Christ and dying is gain" (Phil 1:21).

In summary, how can one overcome the fifth barrier, "invisible proscription"? First, a Kierkegaardian mission reminds Japanese Christians that the church on earth is not the church triumphant but a militant church. Second, Japan is not a swamp in which the plant of Christianity withers and rots. Instead, Christianity transforms Japan and brings it to completion. Third, a Kierkegaardian mission is a call to become a martyr. The severity of this call allows a person to humbly admit their inadequacy, which is itself a mark of a true Christian. Furthermore, when one realizes that they have something more precious than their own life, they experience "martyrdom in possibility," which results in a life of joy that the world cannot take away.

---

130. Kierkegaard, *Journals of Kierkegaard*, 151.

131. "On the evening of February 28, 1909, a steam locomotive began its accent of Shiokari Pass as it headed for Asahikawa from Nayoro. As the train began to climb the steep slope, the coupling connecting the end carriage to the locomotive worked loose and the carriage became disconnected and rolled backward down the hill. If the carriage gained speed there would have been a danger of it derailing on one of the bends on the mountain. As screams echoed around the carriage, railway employee Nagano Masao got up from his seat and ran to the deck and tried to operate the hand brake manually. His attempts were unsuccessful, so just before the bend, Nagano threw himself in front of the wheel in a bid to stop it. The carriage did indeed stop, but Nagano was killed in the process." "Shiokari Pass," http://kai-hokkaido.com/en/feature_vol35_sidestory4/. In this way, Nagano Masao (1880–1909) truly sacrificed his life to save the life of passengers on the train. 三浦綾子 (Miura Ayako), a famous Christian author, wrote the novel *Shiokari Pass* based on this historical event. Miura, 塩狩峠 [*Shiokari Pass*].

132. *SKS* 21, 279, NB10:42/ *JP*, IV 6348.

133. *SKS* 10, 105/ *CD*, vi.

10.3 Conclusion

In this chapter, we have explored various ways in which one might engage in a Kierkegaardian mission in twenty-first-century Japan. We have learned from David Lu's *Overcoming Barriers to Evangelization in Japan* and examined Kierkegaard's insights in relation to five barriers that hinder evangelization in Japan. According to our speculative application, the Kierkegaardian mission contributes uniquely to overcoming these five barriers. The hubris of the "self" (the first barrier) will be removed when a missionary imitates Christ and humbles oneself. Buddhism, Shintoism, and Confucianism (the second, third, and fourth barriers) will be transformed from obstacles into mediums that can help to convey Christian messages naturally to the hearts of the Japanese. Kierkegaard's concept of a militant church and a martyr in possibility will help the Japanese to fight against "invisible proscription" (the fifth barrier) and move Japan towards completion.

In conclusion, let me discuss the issue of 日本的キリスト教 (Japanese Christianity).[134] Since this book argues that missionaries must become like the Japanese to the Japanese, it stands to reason, prima facie, that Japanese Christianity must be thoroughly and authentically Japanese. However, we must admit that, thus far, Japanese Christianity has been a great failure in

---

134. There are all sorts of 日本的キリスト教 [Japanese Christianity]. On the assumption that Japanese Christianity has something to do with State Shinto, 山口陽一 (Yamaguchi Yōichi) groups Japanese Christianity into five types: syncretism, compatibility, mutual inspiration, confrontational compatibility, and confrontation. In 日本基督教の精神的伝統 [*Spiritual Tradition of Japan Christianity*], 魚木忠一 (Uoki Tadakazu, 1892–1954) nobly attempts to establish Japanese Christianity. While his methodology appears to be appropriate, the outcome appears inevitably syncretic. A more appropriate approach might be the one taken by Kanzō Uchimura and 矢内原忠雄 (Yanaihara Tadao, 1893–1961). However, one might hesitate to agree fully with their "Japanese Christianity" and conclude that there are fundamental issues with their attempt to establish a "Japanese Christianity." In my view, Kierkegaard can be positioned between Uchimura and Katsuhiko Kondō. Although Kondō does not accept Uchimura's idea, Kierkegaard would probably have been sympathetic towards Uchimura's affirmation of the faith of Japanese Buddhists such as Hōnen, Shinran, and 源信 (942–1017, Genshin) and been happy to learn from their faith just by redirecting it to Christ. But Kierkegaard would not have endorsed Uchimura's idea of the necessity of establishing Japanese Christianity. See Yamaguchi, 「日本的キリスト教」の考察 ["Consideration of 'Japanese Christianity'"], 11–37; Uoki, 日本基督教の精神的伝統 [*Spiritual Tradition of Japan Christianity*]; Lee, 魚木忠一の「日本基督教」を再考する：挫折した土着化神学への試み ["Reconsidering 'Christianity in Japan' of Tadakazu Uwoki: An Attempt of Indigenous Theology Dwindled"], 91–115; Ohara, 内村鑑三の生涯 – 日本的キリスト教の創造 [*Biography of Kanzō Uchimura: Creation of Japanese Christianity*]; Kikukawa, 矢内原忠雄の「日本的基督教」：土着化論再考 ["'Japanese Christianity' of Tadao Yanaihara: Reconsidering Indigenization"], 91–104; Kondō, キリスト教弁証学 [*Christian Apologetics*], 309–449.

this regard. According to 土肥昭夫 (Dohi Akio, 1928–2008), a historian of Christianity in Japan, Japanese Christianity "discusses returning to Japan, reevaluates Japanese classics such as Shinto and other traditions. Some forms of Japanese Christianity find their spiritual roots in those Japanese historical heritages."[135] If Kierkegaard were to carry out a mission in Japan, he might creatively use Japanese classics such as 古事記 (Kojiki) and 歎異抄 (Tannnishō). He might create pseudonymous authors or bloggers who present parodies of Norinaga Motoori (expert on the *Kojiki*) or Shinran (author of *Tannnisho*). He might publish these signed works or post them on Facebook. While these signed works would initially present a simple Christian faith, free of any pagan elements, over time, he would gradually reveal the fullness of Christianity. After a few years of authorial or blogging activity, he might boldly proclaim, "Thus in the pseudonymous books [or blogs] there is not a single word by me."[136] In short, these pseudonymous works or blogs would attract readers, encourage them to develop inward reflection, prompt them to examine their lives, and reveal the inevitable futility of spiritual pursuits rooted in Japanese classics. If he were to present the gospel in these signed works and higher-pseudonymous works (or blogs), his goal would not only be to present a simple Christianity but also to refine Christianity by purifying Christianity if it has become entangled with pagan elements.

In 1 Corinthians 9:20–22, Paul begins by saying, "To the Jews I became as a Jew." The use of "as" (ὡς) is important. Paul did *not become* a Jew *but* became *like* (ὡς) a Jew. When he talks about winning Jews, one under the law, he always uses "as" (ὡς). But he omits "as" (ὡς) when he says, "To the weak I became weak." This shows that Paul identified with the weak but distinguished himself from both Jews – who were bound by the law – and Gentiles – who were not bound by the law. If Paul had really become a Jew who was under the law – and not just "as" (ὡς) such a person – he would not have rebuked Peter for avoiding the uncircumcised according to Jewish custom (Gal 2:11–14).

Accordingly, a Kierkegaardian answer to the issue of Japanese Christianity is this: A Kierkegaardian mission involves becoming *like* a Japanese to the

---

135. Yamaguchi, 「日本的キリスト教」の 考察 ["Consideration of 'Japanese Christianity'"], 13, originally from Akio Dohi, *s.v.* "日本的キリスト教 [Japanese Christianity]" in 日本キリスト教歴史大辞典 [Japan Christian History Encyclopedia]. Tokyo: Kyōbunkan, 1998, page unspecified.

136. *SKS* 7, 570/ *CUP I*, 625.

Japanese, but it does not mean that he would attempt to establish Japanese Christianity. In a mission in Japan, a Kierkegaardian missionary would dialectically resolve[137] the elements of Japaneseness that attract the Japanese and gradually introduce Christianity in its true form. If confronted with a Japanese Christianity that was a mix of Christian and non-Christian elements, the Kierkegaardian missionary would attempt to refine it by removing impurities from it.

In a nutshell, a Kierkegaardian mission should thoroughly imitate the incarnated Christ. On the one hand, just as Jesus Christ became flesh and was called "a glutton and a drunkard, a friend of tax-collectors and sinners" (Matt 11:19), a Kierkegaardian missionary will become like the Japanese and establish rapport with them. On the other hand, just as Jesus Christ did not change his divine nature and knew no sin, a Kierkegaardian missionary will dialectically resolve idolatrous (sinful) elements, refining the existing form of Christianity and, ultimately, presenting Christianity (and Jesus Christ) in its true form.

This concludes part 4, where we have examined Kierkegaardian insights and applied them to the Japanese context. Since the particular tasks of this study are now complete, we will move on to the overall conclusion of the entire work.

---

137. For the term "to dialectically resolve," see section 2.3.4.3.

Overall Conclusion

A Missionary Is Inevitably an Incarnational Missionary

> For a long time the strategy employed was to utilize everything to get as many as possible, everyone if possible, to accept Christianity – but then not to be so very scrupulous about whether what one got them to accept actually was Christianity. My strategy was: with the help of God to utilize everything to make clear what in truth Christianity's requirement is – even if not one single person would accept it.[1]
>
> – Søren Kierkegaard, *On My Work as an Author*

As observed in the introduction to this book, the study of Kierkegaard as a missionary has been a neglected subject. While there is a minor trajectory of studies on the subject, there has been no rigorous academic study on this topic except what is found in chapter 1 of Denzil G. M. Patrick's *Pascal and Kierkegaard: A Study in the Strategy of Evangelism* (1947). Therefore, the aim of this study was to critically investigate the subject of Kierkegaard the missionary in light of recent Kierkegaard scholarship. Kierkegaard can be viewed in a great variety of ways: philosopher, theologian, literary critic, social critic, psychologist, poet, religious pluralist, fideist, irrationalist, subjectivist, ironist,

---

1. *SKS* 13, 23–24/ *PV*, 16.

falsifier, or proto-postmodernist. Therefore, in this postmodern or metamodern age, it is not surprising to propose yet another label: "missionary." But the issue is how one can rigorously justify a view of Kierkegaard as a missionary. Although I was aware from my personal reading that Kierkegaard is a missionary (and, in fact, I came to faith in Jesus Christ by reading his works; see appendix 8, II, C), I had to *unlearn* this presupposition in order to analyze Kierkegaard objectively and establish a rigorous methodology. I adopted an author-oriented method with critical evaluation, which binds the researcher to the authorial intent and critically evaluates the methodology (see chapter 2). This approach revealed that Kierkegaard's four published works – *Either/Or* and *Two Upbuilding Discourses* (1843) as a single unit and *The Sickness unto Death* and *Practice in Christianity* as a single unit – are missionary works that proclaim Christ after the manner of Christ (that is, the congruence of the *how* and the *what*). In other words, Kierkegaard was not just a missionary but an ambitious, far-reaching, and profound missionary (see chapters 3 to 6). The study of Kierkegaard's unpublished works also revealed that he introduces himself as a missionary, states that the missionary task is an integral part of being a Christian, and imitates Christ's incarnational method. Furthermore, this study uncovered similarities between Kierkegaard's missionary strategy and the apostle Paul's incarnational mission, particularly as seen in 1 Corinthians 9:19–23 (see chapters 7 and 8). Thereafter, the findings of this study were summarized and Kierkegaard's mission defined and categorized according to critically examined typology (see chapter 9). Finally, this study confirmed that a Kierkegaardian mission could contribute to the evangelization of contemporary Japan (see chapter 10). Therefore, I conclude that the Kierkegaardian mission is not a relic of the past to be displayed in a museum but, rather, a concept that sheds light on and is applicable to contemporary situations.

Was Kierkegaard a missionary? If so, in what sense does the appellation "missionary" fit him? Varughese John describes Kierkegaard's epistemology as follows: "Kierkegaard illustrates that truth has to be given from without. The God-man, through the moment of incarnation, makes the transcendent truth, immanent."[2] Jesus Christ *is* the truth, and no human can transmit this transcendent truth to another. Therefore, the only possible way for someone

---

2. John, *Truth and Subjectivity*, Kindle, loc. 769–770.

to access this truth is to personally know Christ. The only possible way to transmit *this* truth (Christ) to others is to imitate the path of the incarnated Christ. Mark A. Tietjen describes Kierkegaard's practices of incarnational mission, saying, "To be a missionary is not simply to convert the lost but to incarnate divine love in obedience to and imitation of Jesus Christ, the God incarnate. This could involve a fresh gospel message, works of love."[3] Here, "to incarnate" does not signify Christ's incarnation but a missionary's incarnational approach to their neighbours. The incarnational mission is to imitate the incarnated Christ, which involves both verbally and existentially proclaiming Christ to our neighbours. Kierkegaard's mission principle connotes that the truth of Christ can be properly communicated only incarnationally. Therefore, this study concludes that Kierkegaard not only qualifies to be called a missionary but also that he redefined the very concept of missionary. Without an incarnational approach, a missionary cannot appropriately transmit the truth of Christ to their neighbours.

In this study, I make several contributions to Kierkegaard scholarship. First, I reconsider the methodology for studying Kierkegaard's work. To restore Kierkegaard's original intention, I adopt a sequential reading of the single units of both *Either/Or* and *Two Upbuilding Discourses* (1843) and *The Sickness unto Death* and *Practice in Christianity*. By adopting this approach, the either/or-ness *throughout* his writings is revealed, which provides justification for interpreting Kierkegaard as a missionary. In other words, Kierkegaard urges readers to make a choice: to remain where they are or to take a leap into the religious. Second, this study demonstrates that the study of Kierkegaard as a missionary is a lacuna in Kierkegaard scholarship that is worth exploring in greater depth. Failure to do so may lead to fundamental misinterpretations of his works and ideas. For example, the term "the single individual" has sometimes been taken to mean an asocial individualist, whereas Kierkegaard views "the single individual" as playing the role of a missionary who spreads the gospel. Another example is the contribution I make to the understanding of significances of Kierkegaard's pseudonymous works. From a perspective of Kierkegaard as a missionary, Kierkegaard used his (lower) pseudonymous works to establish rapport with non-Christian readers and to lead them to signed-religious works. Third, I demonstrate that while Kierkegaard might

---

3. Tietjen, *Kierkegaard: A Christian Missionary*, loc. 2521–2522, Kindle.

appear to be an unparalleled genius who seems almost impossible to imitate, his mission strategy offers significant and practical insights that are relevant to contemporary evangelization efforts.

One of Kierkegaard's most significant suggestions is that to become a missionary means becoming who we truly are, as God designed us to be. This calling to become a missionary does not always mean being an official missionary or pastor. For instance, Kierkegaard was a writer, who, for the most part, remained in his own country, Denmark. While we cannot turn back history, *if* Kierkegaard had become a rural pastor, would he have become who he was? Nobody knows, but I suspect that he might have failed to become who he was and who he was supposed to be. Kierkegaard believed that God's Governance did not allow him to become a rural pastor – even though he himself desired this – and that God guided him to remain as an author. Kierkegaard's mission was effective because, presumably, he became who God intended him to be. Similarly, while some of us may be called to be official missionaries or pastors, others are called to different occupations. But occupation or status does not hinder a person from being a missionary. If we become who God has designed us to be, our potential is maximized, and our mission will be effective, regardless of the tools or methods we use.

Second, by calling every Christian a missionary, Kierkegaard both challenges Christians and offers hope to the contemporary missionary landscape. An American friend of mine, having conversed with Japanese pastors, told me that he sensed their feelings of defeat over the failure of missionary efforts in Japan. For many years, Japanese Christians have struggled to achieve missionary breakthroughs in Japan, where only 1 percent of the population is Christian. According to Kierkegaard, every Christian – no matter who they are – is called to be a missionary. In Japan, there are at least one million Christians, which means that there are one million missionary candidates. The existence of one million missionary candidates in Japan could be the very breakthrough we have been seeking. As of 2023, statistics indicates that there are 2.5 billion Christians in the world, or about 31.2% of the world's population.[4] So, in the world, there are 2.5 billion missionary candidates. Perhaps we should consider the possibility that the following prayer has been

---

4. 世界の宗教人口 ["The World's Religious Population"]. *Aikido World*, accessed April 4, 2025, https://aikido.mixh.jp/world-religious-statics-2/

both prayed and answered: "The harvest is plentiful, but the labourers are few; therefore ask the Lord of the harvest to send out labourers into his harvest" (Matt 9:37b–38). God may be saying, "I have already sent out plenty of labourers into my harvest." Now it is a matter of the labourers *awakening* from their slumber: "Besides this, you know what time it is, how it is already the moment for you to wake from sleep. For salvation is nearer to us now than when we became believers" (Rom 13:11).

Third, this study found an alternative reward for a missionary. Having said that Kierkegaard's mission can contribute to the contemporary situation, it is difficult to estimate how far Kierkegaard's mission was successful.[5] But one thing is for sure: he did not care much about the results as can be seen at the top of this concluding chapter. He aimed to serve the ideal; to imitate Christ in every area. As a result, his mission strategy *also* resembled Christ's. Therefore, by imitating Christ, whether such a mission is, humanly speaking, successful or not, one can be complete in themselves by personally and wholeheartedly following Jesus no matter what the situation is. The reward is not necessarily to produce many converts but to follow Christ:

> Yet whatever gains I had, these I have come to regard as loss because of Christ. More than that, I regard everything as loss because of the surpassing value of knowing Christ Jesus my Lord. For his sake I have suffered the loss of all things, and I regard them as rubbish, in order that I may gain Christ and be found in him, not having a righteousness of my own that comes from the law, but one that comes through faith in Christ, the righteousness from God based on faith. I want to know Christ and the power of his resurrection and the sharing of his sufferings by becoming like him in his death, if somehow I may attain the resurrection from the dead. (Phil 3:7–11)

Let me be clear. As Kierkegaard says, a missionary's desire is that everyone should become a Christian. But the desired result should not dictate the missionary's method. A mission that imitates Christ without compromise is more likely to produce the best results on the mission field under God's Governance.

---

5. See also Appendix 8.

Appendices

APPENDIX 1

Chronology

Year	Age	Personal Life	Authorship		
			Pseudonymous works	Signed works	Journals and Notebooks, unpublished work
1813	0	Birth			
1828	15	Confirmed by J. P. Mynster in the Church of Denmark			
1830	17	Entering the University of Copenhagen as a theology student			
1833	20	First journal entry			Journals
1835	22	Great earthquake			
1838	25		From the Papers of One Still Living		
1840	26	Engagement to Regine Olsen, breaking the engagement the next year			
1841	27	Successfully defending his master's thesis, *The Concept of Irony*			
			First authorship		
1843	30		*Either/Or* by A and Judge William, edited by Victor Eremita		
				Two Upbuilding Discourses	
			Fear and Trembling by Johannes de Silentio	*Three Upbuilding Discourses*	
			Repetition by Constantin Constantius		
				Four Upbuilding Discourses	

Chronology

Year	Age	Personal Life	Authorship		Journals and Notebooks, unpublished work
			Pseudonymous works	**Signed works**	*Journals* →
1844	31			Two Upbuilding Discourses	
				Three Upbuilding Discourses	
			Philosophical Fragments by Johannes Climacus, published by S. Kierkegaard		
			The Concept of Anxiety by Vigilius Haufniensis		
			Prefaces by Nicholaus Notabene		
				Four Upbuilding Discourses	
1845	32			Three Discourses on Imagined Occasions	
			Stages on Life's Way published by Hilarious Bookbinder		
1846	33	The Corsair affair	Concluding Unscientific Postscript to Philosophical Fragments by Johannes Climacus, published by S. Kierkegaard		
			Second authorship		
				A Literary Review: "Two Ages"	
1847	34			Upbuilding Discourses in Various Spirits	
				Works of Love	

Year	Age	Personal Life	Pseudonymous works	Signed works	Journals and Notebooks, unpublished work
1848	35	Spiritual awakening	The Crisis and a Crisis in the Life of an Actress by Inter et Inter	Christian Discourses	The Book on Adler The Point of View for My Work as an Author
1849	36		(The second edition of Either/Or by A and Judge William, edited by Victor Eremita) Two Ethico-Religious Treatises by H. H. The Sickness unto Death by Anti-Climacus, published by S. Kierkegaard	The Lily in the Field and the Bird of the Air Three Discourses at the Communion on Fridays	Armed Neutrality
1850	37		Practice in Christianity by Anti-Climacus, published by S. Kierkegaard	An Upbuilding Discourse	
1851	38			On My Work as an Author Two Discourses at the Communion on Fridays For Self-Examination	Judge for Yourselves!
1852	39	The silent period			
1853	40				

Chronology

Year	Age	Personal Life	Authorship		
			Pseudonymous works	Signed works	*Journals and Notebooks,* unpublished work
1854	41			*Was Bishop Mynster "a Witness to the Truth," One of 'the True Witnesses to the Truth' – Is This the Truth?*	Journals →
		The Attack upon Christendom		*This Must Be Said, So Let It Be Said*	
1855	42			*The Moment*	
				Christ's Judgement on Official Christianity	
				God's Unchangeability: A Discourse	
		Death			

APPENDIX 2

Categorization of Methods of Kierkegaard Studies

How to approach Kierkegaard	Author	Title of works and "articles"	Published year	
			Original	English
		(1) Biographical methods		
A study of Kierkegaard's life history	Johannes Hohlenberg	*Søren Kierkegaard*	1940	1954
	Walter Lowrie	*Kierkegaard*	1938	
		A Short Life of Kierkegaard	1965	
	Josiah Thompson	*Kierkegaard*	1973	
	Jun Hashimoto	憂愁と愛 [Melancholy and the Unhappy Love]	1985	-
	Joakim Garff	*SAK Søren Aabye Kierkegaard: En biografi* [Søren Kierkegaard: A Biography]	2000	2005
	Alastair Hannay	*Kierkegaard: A Biography*	2001	
	Clare Carlisle	*Philosopher of the Heart: The Restless Life of Søren Kierkegaard*	2019	
	Stephen Backhouse	*Kierkegaard: A Single Life*	2016	
A study of how Kierkegaard is seen by his contemporaries	T. H. Croxall	*Glimpse and Impressions of Kierkegaard*	1959	
	Bruce H. Kirmmse and Virginia R. Laursen	*Encounters with Kierkegaard: A Life as Seen by His Contemporaries*	1996	

How to approach Kierkegaard	Author	Title of works and "articles"	Published year	
			Original	English
A study of Kierkegaard's external social environments	Hidehito Ōtani	キルケゴール青年時代の研究 [A Study of Kierkegaard's Youth]	1966–1968	–
	Bruce H. Kirmmse	Kierkegaard in Golden Age Denmark	1990	
	Satoshi Nakazato	キルケゴールとその思想風土 －北欧のロマンティークと敬虔主義 [Kierkegaard and the Climate of the Traditional Thoughts – Romanticism and Pietism in Northern Europe]	1994	–
	Jon Stewart	Kierkegaard and His Contemporaries: The Culture of Golden Age Denmark	2003	
(2) Psychological methods				
A study of Kierkegaard's psyche	Ib Ostenfeld	Søren Kierkegaards Psykologi [Søren Kierkegaard's Psychology]	1972	1979
	Kresten Nordentoft	Kierkegaards psykologi [Kierkegaard's Psychology]	1972	1978
A study of Kierkegaard as a psychologist	Sven Hroar Klempe	Kierkegaard and the Rise of Modern Psychology	2014	
	Vincent A. McCarthy	Kierkegaard as a Psychologist	2015	

How to approach Kierkegaard	Author	Title of works and "articles"	Published year	
			Original	English
				Published year of the original language edition
		(3) Philosophical methods		
A study of Kierkegaard as father of existentialism	Karl Jaspers	*Psychologie der Weltanschauungen* [Psychology of Worldview] (1919), *Die geistige Situation der Zeit* [Man in the Modern Age] (1931), *Vernunft und Existenz* [Reason and Existence] (1935), *Der philosophische Glaube angesichts der Offenbarung* [Philosophical Faith and Revelation] (1962), *Kierkegaard: A Discourse at Pen Club in Basel* (1951), "Kierkegaard" in *Kierkegaard and Evil* (1955), "Kierkegaard" in *Kierkegaard vivant* [Kierkegaard Alive] (1964)		
	Martin Heidegger	*Sein und Zeit* [Being and Time] (1927), *Nietzsche* (1936–1946), "Nietzsches Wort, Gott ist tot [A Word of Nietzsche: God is Dead]" (1943), *Schellings Abhandlung Über das Wesen der Menschlichen Freiheit* [Schelling's Treatise on the Essence of Human Freedom] (1971)		
	Jean-Paul Sartre	*L'Être et le Néant* [Being and Nothingness] (1943), *L'existentialisme est un humanisme* [Existentialism is Humanism] (1945), *Questions de méthode* [Question of Method] (1960), "L'Universal singulier [The Singular Universal]" in *Kierkegaard vivant* [Kierkegaard Alive] (1966)		

Categorization of Methods of Kierkegaard Studies 353

How to approach Kierkegaard	Author	Title of works and "articles"	Published year Original	English
A philosophical study of Kierkegaard after existentialism	Mark C. Taylor	Journeys to Selfhood: Hegel & Kierkegaard	1980	
	Michael Theunissen	Der Begriff Verzweiflung: Korrekturen an Kierkegaard [Kierkegaard's Concept of Despair]	1993	2005
	Michael Weston	Kierkegaard and Modern Continental Philosophy: An Introduction	1994	
	Alastair Hannay	Kierkegaard and Philosophy: Selected Essays	2003	
	Jon Stewart	Kierkegaard's Relation to Hegel Reconsidered	2003	
	C. Stephen Evans	Kierkegaard's Ethic of Love: Divine Commands and Moral Obligations	2004	
	George Pattison	The Philosophy of Kierkegaard	2005	
	Jacob Howland	Kierkegaard and Socrates	2006	
	Patrick Stokes	Kierkegaard's Mirrors: Interest, Self and Moral Vision	2009	
	John Lippitt	Kierkegaard and the Problem of Self-Love	2013	
(4) Theological methods			Published year of the original language edition	
A study of Kierkegaard as inspirer of neo-orthodox theology	Karl Barth	Der Römerbrief. 2. Aufl [The Epistle to the Romans, second edition] (1922), "Dank und Reverenz [A Thank You and a Bow – Kierkegaard's Reveille]" (1963), "Kierkegaard und die Theologen [Kierkegaard and the Theologians]" (1963), Kirchliche Dogmatik [Church Dogmatics] (1932–1967)		
	Rudolf Bultmann	Theologie des Neuen Testaments [Theology of the New Testament] (1948–1953), Das Evangelium des Johannes [The Gospel of John] (1941)		
	Paul Tillich	The Courage to Be (1952), Systematic Theology (1951–1963), A History of Christian Thought (1968–1972)		

How to approach Kierkegaard	Author	Title of works and "articles"	Published year	
			Original	English
A theological study of Kierkegaard after neo-orthodox theology	Louis Dupré	*Kierkegaard as Theologian: The Dialectic of Christian Existence*	1963	
	Arnold B. Come	*Kierkegaard as Theologian: Recovering My Self*	1997	
	Silvia Walsh	*Kierkegaard: Thinking Christianly in an Existential Mode*	2009	
	Murray Rae	*Kierkegaard and Theology*	2010	
	Christopher Ben Simpson	*The Truth is the Way: Kierkegaard's Theologia Viatorum (Veritas)*	2011	
	Simon D. Podmore	*Kierkegaard and the Self before God: Anatomy of the Abyss*	2011	
	David R. Law	*Kierkegaard's Kenotic Christology*	2013	
	Merold Westphal	*Kierkegaard's Concept of Faith*	2014	
	ed. by Aaron Edwards and D. J. Gouwens	*T&T Clark Companion to the Theology of Kierkegaard*	2019	
(5) Ecclesiastical interpretation				
	William T. Rivere	*A Pastor Looks at Kierkegaard: The Man and His Philosophy*	1955	
	David J. Gouwens	*Kierkegaard as Religious Thinker*	1996	
	George Pattison, Helle Møller Jensen	*Kierkegaard's Pastoral Dialogues*	2012	
	Ronald F. Marshall	*Kierkegaard for the Church: Essays and Sermons*	2013	
	Christopher B. Barnett	*From Despair to Faith: The Spirituality of Søren Kierkegaard*	2014	
	C. Stephen Evans	*Kierkegaard and Spirituality: Accountability as the Meaning of Human Existence*	2019	

How to approach Kierkegaard	Author	Title of *works* and "articles"	Published year	
			Original	English
		(6) Literary method		
A study of literary background of Kierkegaard's thought	Hidehito Ōtani	キルケゴール著作活動の研究 [A Study on Kierkegaard's Authorship]	1989–1991	–
	Eric Ziolkowski	*The Literary Kierkegaard*	2011	
Literary criticism	Louis Mackey	*Kierkegaard: A Kind of Poet*	1971	
	György Lukács	*A lélek és a formák* [Soul and Form]	1910	1974
		(7) Frankfurt School's interpretation		
	Herbert Marcuse	*Die Zerstörung der Vernunft* [Destruction of Reason]	1954	1980
	Herbert Marcuse	*Reason and Revolution: Hegel and the Rise of Social Theory*	1941	
	Theodor W. Adorno	*Kierkegaard: Konstruktion des Ästhetischen* [Kierkegaard: Construction of the Aesthetic]	1933	1989
		(8) The hermeneutics of suspicion		
	Henning Fenger	*Kierkegaard-Myter og Kierkegaard-Kilder* [Kierkegaard, the Myths and Their Origins]	1976	1980
	Joakim Garff	"The Eyes of Argus: The Point of View and Points of View with Respect to Kierkegaard's 'Activity as an Author'"	1991	
		(9) Deconstructive or postmodern interpretation		
	Louis Mackey	*Points of View: Reading of Kierkegaard*	1986	
	Jacques Derrida	*Donner la mort* [The Gift of Death]	1992	1995

How to approach Kierkegaard	Author	Title of works and "articles"	Published year	
			Original	English
	Roger Poole	*The Indirect Communication*	1993	
	Sylviane Agacinski	*Aparté: Conceptions and Death of Søren Kierkegaard*	1998	
	ed. by Elsebet Jegstrup	*The New Kierkegaard*	2004	
	Steven Shakespere	"Kierkegaard and Postmodernism"	2013	
(10) A study of Kierkegaard's dialectic of existence				
	Hermann Diem	*Die Existenzdialektik von Sören Kierkegaard* [Kierkegaard's Dialectic of Existence]	1950	1978
(11) Author-oriented method				
	Gregor Malantschuk	*Dialektik of Eksistens hos Søren Kierkegaard* [Kierkegaard's Thought]	1968	1971
	Jun Hashimoto	キェルケゴールにおける「苦悩」の世界 [The World of "Suffering" in Kierkegaard]	1976	-
	Hidehito Ōtani	キルケゴール著作活動の研究 [A Study on Kierkegaard's Authorship]	1989–1991	-

APPENDIX 3

The Genre of Kierkegaard's Works

Category	Subcategory		Title of Work	Authorial Features	Relation to Kierkegaard	Published Year
Pseudonymous Works	Lower-Pseudonymous Works	Aesthetic Works	Either/Or, Fear and Trembling, Repetition, Prefaces, Stages on Life's Way, The Crisis and a Crisis in the Life of an Actress	Aesthetes ironists, an ethicist, and humorists	Lower than Kierkegaard	1843–1848
		Speculative Works	The Concept of Anxiety, Philosophical Fragments, Concluding Unscientific Postscript	A humorist	Lower than but close to Kierkegaard	1844, 1846
	Higher-Pseudonymous Works	Works of H. H. (Højre og Højre [Higher and Higher])	Two Minor Ethical-Religious Essays	A Christian on a higher level	Higher than but close to Kierkegaard	1849
		Anti-Climacus's Works	The Sickness unto Death, Practice in Christianity	A Christian on an extraordinary level	Higher than but close to Kierkegaard	1849–1850

Signed Works	Signed-Religious Works	*Two Upbuilding Discourses* (1843), *Three Upbuilding Discourses* (1843), *Four Upbuilding Discourses* (1843), *Two Upbuilding Discourses* (1844), *Three Upbuilding Discourses* (1844), *Four Upbuilding Discourses* (1844), *Three Discourses on Imagined Occasions*, *Upbuilding Discourses in Various Spirits*, *Works of Love*, *The Lily in the Field and the Bird of the Air*, *Three Discourses at the Communion on Fridays*, *An Upbuilding Discourses*, *Two Discourses at the Communion on Fridays*, *God's Unchangeability: A Discourse*, *For Self-Examination: Recommended to the Contemporary Age*, *Judge for Yourselves! Recommended to the Present Time for Self-Examination. Second series*	Kierkegaard himself (his authentic voice)	1843–1855
	Signed-Polemical Works	*Was Bishop Mynster 'a Witness to the Truth,' One of 'the True Witnesses to the Truth' – Is This the Truth?, This Must Be Said, So Let It Be Said, The Moment, Christ's Judgement on Official Christianity*		1851, 1854, 1855
	Signed Commentaries	"A First and Last Declaration" in *Concluding Unscientific Postscript*, *The Single Individual*, *The Point of View for My Work as an Author*, *Armed Neutrality*, *On My Work as an Author*		1851, 1859
		Journals and Notebooks		Written between 1833 and 1855 and posthumously published

APPENDIX 4

Reading *Either/Or*

Preface by Victor Eremita

The preface to *Either/Or* opens with the following philosophical riddle: "It may at times have occurred to you, dear reader, to doubt somewhat the accuracy of that familiar philosophical thesis that the outer is the inner and the inner is the outer."[1] *Either/Or* is said to be edited and published by Victor Eremita. According to Eremita, the manuscripts of *Either/Or* were found by chance in a secret chamber of a writing desk that he had purchased in a second-hand shop. In order to obtain permission to publish, Eremita attempted to find the unknown authors, but his efforts were in vain. Finally, he decided to publish the papers. Eremita invested "the honorarium on behalf of the unknown authors in order, if they should ever come forward, to be able to give them the whole amount together with interest and interest on the interest."[2]

Either/Or, which is the title given by Eremita, is divided into two parts. The first part is a collection of various aesthetic writings, with no mention of the author's name. The second part contains ethical writings, and the author is identified as Judge William. Yet Eremita prefers to refer to the author of the aesthetic writings as "A" and the author of the ethical writings as "B." In *Either/Or*, the world views of both Aesthete A and Ethicist B sharply confront each other, ending with no resolusion. Eremita comments on this peculiar literary style of *Either/Or*: "When the book is read, A and B are forgotten;

---

1. *SKS* 2, 11/ *EO I*, 3.
2. *SKS* 2, 20/ *EO I*, 12.

only the points of view confront each other and expect no final decision in the particular personalities."[3]

"Part I: Containing A's Papers"

The epigraph of "Part I: Containing A's Papers" says, "Is reason then alone baptized, are the passions pagans? Young."[4] What does this mean? First, is it possible for reason alone to be baptized? Does A imply that the Christianity of the intended reader is too rational and should be more passionate? A poses a question but does not answer it; there is no definite resolution. In any case, it seems that A demands the idealization of the aesthetic. Thus, Part I of *Either/Or* shows A's ambitious attempt to replace the worship of God with the worship of the aesthetic, through the aestheticization of Christianity.

The first chapter, "Διαψαλματα [Diapsalmata]," opens with the following epigraph:

> Greatness, knowledge, renown,
> Friendship, pleasure and possessions,
> All is only wind, only smoke:
> To say it better, all is nothing.[5]

This chapter is a collection of aphorisms. Some of these aphorisms are witty: "What philosophers say about actuality [*Virkelighed*] is often just as disappointing as it is when one reads on a sign in a secondhand shop: Pressing Done Here. If a person were to bring his clothes to be pressed, he would be duped, for the sign is merely for sale."[6] Some are sarcastic or cynical: "The best demonstration of the wretchedness of life [*Tilværelse*] is that which is obtained through a consideration of its glory."[7] Others are melancholic: "Life for me has become a bitter drink, and yet it must be taken in drops, slowly, counting."[8] Still others are depressing: "My life is like an eternal night; when

---

3. *SKS* 2, 21/ *EO I*, 14.

4. *SKS* 2, 9/ *EO I*, 1, originally quoted from Edward Young, *The Complaint or Night-Thoughts on Life, Death, and Immortality* (1742–1744), IV, 629 ('Notes' by Howard V. Hong and Edna H. Hong in *EO I*, 603), slightly modified by Kierkegaard.

5. *SKS* 2, 26/ *EO I*, 18, originally written in French, translated by the Hongs.

6. *SKS* 2, 41/ *EO I*, 32.

7. *SKS* 2, 37/ *EO I*, 28.

8. *SKS* 2, 34/ *EO I*, 26.

I die, I shall be able to say with Achilles: You are fulfilled, nightwatch of my life."[9] Some aphorisms are comical: "Old age fulfills the dreams of youth. One sees this in Swift: in his youth he built an insane asylum; in his old age he himself entered it."[10] The opinions expressed in each paragraph often contradict what has been said in adjacent paragraphs, and the resulting conflicting logic exemplifies the inconsistency of A's – and anyone's – feelings and moods. As Eremita says, "It seemed to me that ['Διαψαλματα'] could best be regarded as preliminary glimpses into what the longer pieces develop more coherently."[11] "Διαψαλματα" is an introduction to what will come later in *Either/Or, Part I*.

The second chapter, "The Immediate Erotic Stages, or the Musical-Erotic," is a *rhapsodic* yet brilliant review of Mozart's opera *Don Giovanni or Don Juan*.[12] By elegantly using biblical motifs with an aesthetic twist, A praises Mozart's *Don Giovanni*: "Mozart with his *Don Giovanni* stands highest among those immortals, of those visibly transfigured ones, whom no cloud takes away. From the eyes of men; with Don Giovanni he stands supreme among them. This last assertion, as I said above, I shall attempt to demonstrate."[13] "The Immediate Erotic Stages" is A's ambitious attempt to play music with language rather than instruments. Yet, how can such an attempt be possible? A is fully aware that language cannot convey music since language belongs to the intellect and music to the senses. Therefore, he does not allow himself to cross the boundary between the intellect and the senses, but he flirts with the boundary by allowing his admiration of music to permeate his language. By doing so, he expects, so to speak, to delineate the kingdom of music:

> What I want to do, however, is in part to illuminate the idea from as many sides as possible and its relation to language and thereby continually to encompass more and more the territory where music is at home, to provoke it, so to speak, to declare itself, without my being able to say, when it can be heard, any more than: Listen.[14]

---

9. *SKS* 2, 45/ *EO I*, 35–36; the last sentence was originally written in German, translated by the Hongs.

10. *SKS* 2, 26/ *EO I*, 21.

11. *SKS* 2, 15/*EO I*, 8.

12. Furtwängler, *Mozart – Don Giovanni*.

13. *SKS* 2, 59/*EO I*, 51, cf. Matthew 17:1–6 and Acts 1:9.

14. *SKS* 2, 91/ *EO I*, 85.

Aesthete A ambitiously attempts to musicalize language, allowing the reader to "hear" Don Juan, who is "absolutely musical."¹⁵

In this chapter, A begins to develop the concept of the seducer through exemplified figures such as Don Juan and Faust. The primitive concept of seduction is exemplified by the figure of Don Juan. According to A, Don Juan is strictly a deceiver rather than a seducer because he captures a woman sensuously rather than intellectually: "Don Juan, then, is the expression for the demonic qualified as the sensuous; Faust is the expression for the demonic qualified as the spiritual that the Christian spirit excludes."¹⁶ A sees the ideal form of the reflective seducer in the medieval mythical figure of Faus, who intellectually seduces a woman,

> in the fact that Faust, who reproduces Don Juan, seduces only one girl, whereas Don Giovanni seduces by the hundreds; but in intensity this one girl is seduced and destroyed in an entirely different way than all those Don Giovanni deceived – precisely because Faust as a reproduction has an intellectual-spiritual quality.¹⁷

This chapter, exemplified by Don Juan, is "absolutely musical"; it is the best demonstration of the immediate seducer or the sensuous deceiver. The reflective seducer will be fully demonstrated in "The Seducer's Diary," which is the eighth chapter of *Either/Or, Part I*.

The next three chapters are said to be "delivered before the Συμπαρανεκρωμενοι [Fellowship of the Dead]."¹⁸ Συμπαρανεκρωμενοι is a group that meets together at night in order to praise night, death, and despair. The title of the third chapter of *Either/Or* is "The Tragic in Ancient Drama Reflected in the Tragic in Modern Drama"; its subject is Antigone who is a daughter of Oedipus in Greek tragedy. Who is Antigone? A biography of Antigone is as follows.¹⁹ As Laius was warned by the Delphic oracle that

---

15. *SKS* 2, 105/ *EO I*, 102.
16. *SKS* 2, 95/*EO I*, 90.
17. *SKS* 2, 103/*EO I*, 99.
18. *SKS* 2, 137/ *EO I*, 137.
19. Sophocles, *Sophocles I, Antigone, Oedipus the King, Oedipus at Colonus (The Complete Greek Tragedies)*. Trans. by Mark Griffith and David Grene, Chicago: University of Chicago Press 2013.

his son would eventually kill him and would marry his wife, he ordered the infant child to be taken away to a mountain where exposed to the elements, he expected the child to die. But this baby survived. After growing up, he who was named Oedipus, not knowing his origin, killed his father Laius and married his mother Jocasta. Antigone is Oedipus's daughter born of the incestuous relationship between Jocasta and Oedipus. And in the destiny of Antigone, the speaker of Συμπαρανεκρωμενοι discerns an ideal tragedy and idolizes her using esthetically modified Christian terms:

> There are analogies to this. We speak, for example, of a bride of God; in faith and spirit she has the content in which she rests. In a perhaps still more beautiful sense, I would call our Antigone a bride – indeed, she is almost more, she is a mother. Purely esthetically, she is *virgo mater* [virgin mother]; . . . She is proud of her grief, she is jealous of it, for her grief is her love. But yet her grief is not a dead, static possession; it is continually in motion; it gives birth to pain and is born in pain.[20]

As for the term "a bride of God" in the above quotation, its origin lies in Scripture, which refers to Christians as the bride of Christ or the bride of God (Matt 9:15; 25:1-13; Mark 2:19; Luke 5:34; John 3:29; Rev 3:12; 19:7; 21:2, 9-10; 22:17). As to *virgo mater* (virgin mother), this term refers to Mary, who conceived Jesus Christ while a virgin (Matt 1:18-25; Luke 1:31-35). As can be seen, the speaker uses Latin, the official language of the Catholic Church. In Catholic tradition, *virgo mater* (virgin mother) has a distinctive status. By calling Antigone "a bride of God" and "*virgo mater*," the speaker aesthetically adores her.

"Silhouettes" is the title of the second address before the Συμπαρανεκρωμενοι. The speaker clarifies the meaning of the title: "I call them silhouettes [*Skyggerids*], partly to suggest at once by the name that I draw them from the dark side of life and partly because, like silhouettes, they are not immediately visible."[21] The subjects of this chapter are three sorrowful ladies: Marie Beaumarchais from Goethe's *Clavigo*,[22] Donna Elvira from Mozart's *Don*

---

20. *SKS* 2, 156/ *EO I*, 157-158.
21. *SKS* 2, 170/ *EO I*, 173.
22. von Goethe, *Clavigo*.

Juan,²³ and Margarete from Goethe's *Faust*.²⁴ These three ladies, abandoned by their lovers, reflect unceasingly on their sorrows. Marie Beaumarchais's quiet and hidden sadness is illustrated using the analogy of a nun in a monastery:

> [Marie Beaumarchais] takes the veil. She does not enter the convent, but she takes the veil of sorrow, which hides her from every alien glance. Outwardly she is quiet. The whole affair is forgotten; her words give no hint. She herself takes the vow of sorrow, and now she begins her lonely, hidden life.²⁵

Through the hand of the speaker, Beaumarchais's anguish is turned into a tragic-religious art.

The speaker lets the reader hear Donna Elvira's inner voice: "Forget [Don Juan], that is what I want; rip his picture out of my soul"; "No, I will hate him; that is the only way to satisfy my soul, the only way I can find rest and something to occupy me"; "He was no deceiver; he had no idea of what a woman can suffer. If he had had that, he never would have forsaken me."²⁶ Elvira is tormented by her own contradictory feelings.

Margarete idolizes Faust, who has forsaken her:

> Faust, O Faust! Come back, satisfy the hungry, clothe the naked, revive the languishing, visit the lonely one! I certainly know that my love had no meaning for you, but, after all, neither did I demand that. My love lay down humbly at your feet; my sigh was a prayer, my kiss a thank offering, my embrace adoring worship. Will you forsake me for this? Did you not know it beforehand? Or is it not, then, a reason to love me that I need you, that my soul languishes when you are not with me?²⁷

Margarete *worships* Faust in an aesthetic-tragic mode.

"The Unhappiest One" is the third and final address before the Συμπαρανεκρωμενοι. Despair reaches "a higher lunacy" in this chapter.²⁸ "The

---

23. Furtwängler, *Morzart – Don Giovanni*.
24. von Goethe, *Faust*.
25. *SKS* 2, 180/ *EO I*, 183.
26. *SKS* 2, 197–199/ *EO I*, 202–204.
27. *SKS* 2, 207–208/ *EO I*, 213.
28. *SKS* 1, 295/ *CI*, 257. For the term "higher lunacy," see section 3.2.1.4.1.

unhappiest one" is introduced as follows: "As is well known, there is said to be a grave somewhere in England that is distinguished ... by a short inscription – 'The Unhappiest One.' It is said that the grave was opened, but no trace of a corpse was found."[29] The speaker wonders whether the unhappiest one, not finding peace even in the grave, still wanders through the earth. Or, perhaps this person is unable to die and is, therefore, called the unhappiest one since "we know a worse calamity, and first and last, above all – it is to live"[30] If to live is a worse calamity, the one who cannot die must be the unhappiest one. The speaker lists tragically modified figures such as Niobe,[31] Antigone, Job, the father of the prodigal son, the blended identities of the apostles Peter and Judas Iscariot, and the blended identities of Marie Beaumarchais, Donna Elvira, and Margarete. Yet none of them can be awarded the grave of the unhappiest one but only "the place closest to it."[32] Who, then, is the unhappiest one? The speaker does not specify. But the unhappiest one brings to mind the medieval mythical figure Ahasverus, who cannot die and exemplifies despair.[33] The speaker lifts up the unhappiest one as if he were Jesus

---

29. *SKS* 2, 213/ *EO I*, 219.

30. *SKS* 2, 214/ *EO I*, 220.

31. Niobe is "in Greek mythology, a queen of Thebes, daughter of Tantalus, and wife of Amphion. Having boasted that she had twelve children and Leto (L. Latona) only two, she was slain by Leto's children, Artemis and Apollo. Niobe was turned into a stone image (on Mt. Sipylos, named after one of her children) that wept continually." Howard V. Hong and Edna H. Hong, 'Notes' in *EO I*, 635, see Paul Friedrich A. Nitsch, *Neues Mythologisches Wörterbuch II* [New Mythological Dictionary II], rev. by Friedrich Gotthilf Klopfer, Leipzig: Soran, 1821, 326–30).

32. *SKS* 2, 222/ *EO I*, 229.

33. Ahasverus is also called the "Wandering Jew." The legend says that he is not allowed to die but must live under the spell of a curse until the day of Jesus's second coming. This is because he scolded Jesus when Jesus, who was on the way to Golgotha, tried to rest at the post of Ahasverus's house. Ahasverus is the unhappiest one because he cannot die and cannot find peace in the grave. One of Kierkegaard's journal entries says, "Representing life in its three tendencies, as it were, outside of religion, there are three great ideas (Don Juan, Faust, and the Wandering Jew)." *SKS* 27, 134, Papir 140/ *JP*, I 795 March 1836. As can be seen above, Don Juan, Faust, and Ahasverus are brought together by Kierkegaard. For Kierkegaard, Don Juan is sensuousness personified; Faust is doubt personified, and Ahasverus is despair personified. In *Either/Or*, the first two figures appear to be more prominent. Yet, Ahasverus is probably the most important figure of "three great ideas" for Kierkegaard since his masterpiece *The Sickness unto Death* deals exclusively with despair, which is exemplified by Ahasverus. "While nowhere does [*The Sickness unto Death*] mention the Wandering Jew, it is difficult not to think of him in the context of the description of the despair of the one who hopes for death, who despairs over himself to the point that he wishes to rid himself of himself, but cannot die." Ballan, "Wandering Jew," 243. See also Walsh, "Patterns for Living Poetically," 288; Podmore, *Kierkegaard and the Self*, 92.

Christ. Or, is the unhappiest one a blended identity of Ahasverus and Christ? As for the grave of the unhappiest one, the speaker says, "See, the stone is rolled away."[34] Clearly, the speaker equates the empty tomb of the unhappiest one with that of Jesus of Nazareth. The speaker's attempt to Christianize the aesthetic despair reaches its apex in these words:

> For there he stands, the envoy from the kingdom of sighs, the chosen favorite of suffering, the apostle of grief, the silent friend of pain, the unhappy lover of recollection, confused in his recollection by the light of hope, frustrated in his hope by the ghosts of recollection. His brow is troubled, his knees are slack, and yet he leans on himself alone. He is exhausted, and yet how full of energy; his eyes do not seem to have shed, but to have drunk, many tears, and yet they flame with a fire that could consume the whole world, but not a splinter of sorrow in his own breast; he is bowed down, and yet his youth portends a long life; his lips smile at the world, which does not understand him. Arise, dear Συμπαρανεκρωμενοι; bow down, you witnesses of sorrow, in this solemn hour. I hail you, great unknown, whose name I do not know; I hail you with your title of honor: the unhappiest one.[35]

The sixth chapter, "The First Love," is a review of *The First Love: A Comedy in One Act*, written by the French writer Eugene Scribe (1791–1861). To better understand this chapter, here is a summary of Scribe's *The First Love*. In this story, Emmeline's father wants her to get married to Rinville, but she remains captivated by Charles, the first love of her childhood. As time goes by, both Rinville and Charles take advantage of the fact that they have been away from home for a long time and cannot be recognized by anyone. To win Emmeline's love, Rinville pretends to be Charles (Emmeline's first love). Charles, on the other hand, who is not trusted by Emmeline's father, pretends to be Rinville. In the story, Emmeline remains committed to her first love, Charles – who is, in fact, Rinville – and detests Rinville – who is, in fact, her first love, Charles. When she is informed that Charles has been married to another woman, she decides to marry Rinville (who is, in fact, Charles).

---

34. *SKS* 2, 222/ *EO I*, 230.
35. *SKS* 2, 222/ *EO I*, 229.

Finally, both identities are revealed, and Emmaline agrees to marry the real Rinville, saying, "I suppose I mistook the past for the future."[36] According to A, Emmeline lives in a state of illusion or confusion, unable to recognize Charles, whom she claims to truly love, and, furthermore, is easily misled into believing that Rinville is Charles:

> [Emmeline] has all possible qualities for becoming a heroine, not substantially, however, but negatively. She is, then, comic, and because of her the play is a comedy. She is in the habit of controlling, as befits a heroine, but that which she controls is a fool of a father, the staff of servants, etc. She has pathos, but since its content is nonsense, her pathos is essentially chatter; she has passion, but since its content is a phantom, her passion is essentially madness; she has enthusiasm, but since its content is nothing, her enthusiasm is essentially frivolity; she wants to sacrifice everything for her passion – that is, she wants to sacrifice everything for nothing. As a comic heroine, she is unparalleled. With her, everything revolves around a fantasy, and everything outside her revolves in turn around her and thereby around her fantasy. It is easy to see how thoroughly comic the whole action must become; watching it is tantamount to gazing into an abyss of the ridiculous.[37]

Like a skilled literary critic, A analyzes Scribe's puzzling comedy with dazzling words, making readers gaze "into an abyss of the ridiculous."

In the seventh chapter, "Rotation of Crops," A says, "Boredom is the root of all evil."[38] For A, boredom is *sin* and arbitrariness is *salvation*. A advises his readers to "guard against contracting a life relationship" such as friendship or marriage because one will eventually get bored; he also warns against seeking any "official post" or "title."[39] Instead, he says, "Attach great importance to all the pursuits that are compatible with aimlessness; all kinds of

---

36. Scribe, *First Love*, 16.
37. *SKS* 2, 246/ *EO* I, 253.
38. *SKS* 2, 275/ *EO* I, 286; this is a parody of the biblical verse "the love of money is a root of all kinds of evil'" (1 Tim 6:10).
39. *SKS* 2, 286–287/ *EO* I, 297–298.

unprofitable pursuits may be carried on."⁴⁰ The title "Rotation of Crops" signifies A's method of avoiding boredom. Just as a farmer does not continually grow the same crops or vegetables in the same field, one should constantly change one's viewpoint in order to move from a boring routine to one that is interesting. "When sentimental people, who as such are very boring, become peevish, they are often amusing. Teasing in particular is an excellent means of exploration."⁴¹ What a mean man A is!

The eighth chapter, "The Seducer's Diary" is a narrative that is said to be written by Johannes the Seducer. But Eremita suspects that this chapter is also written by A.⁴² If we take it at face value, a diary, the main part of the chapter is written by Johannes the Seducer and a short introduction to the diary by A. In the diary, Cordelia, the object of Johannes' seduction, is perceptively described: 'How lovely she was in her plain, blue-striped calico housedress, with a freshly picked rose on her bosom. A freshly picked rose – no, the girl herself was like a freshly picked blossom, so fresh was she, so recently arrived!'⁴³ Johannes's strategy of seduction is this: he pretends as if he is not interested in her at all. It is because "fishing is always best in troubled waters. When a young miss is agitated, one can successfully risk much that otherwise would miscarry."⁴⁴ The strategy of Johannes's seduction is not to force her but to orchestrate things so that she freely gives herself to him. Johannes is not only a gifted poet, but he poetises everything he had experienced in order to esthetically enjoy it again. He poetises Cordelia, his love, and himself. Therefore, although a diary is supposed to be a description of reality (indicative mood), his diary looks as if it is a dream or an imaginative story (subjunctive mood). Johannes is successfully engaged to Cordelia, and after that, he manipulates her in order to induce her to call off the engagement. In his letter to her, Johannes says, "Only when no alien suspects our love, only then does it have meaning . . ."⁴⁵ Johannes says that the engagement is a declaration of love but love wants to be hidden. Johannes influences her to think that the engagement means nothing (Remember A's life-theory is to "guard

---

40. *SKS* 2, 287/ *EO I*, 298.
41. *SKS* 2, 287/ *EO I*, 299.
42. *SKS* 2, 16–7/ *EO I*, 8–9.
43. *SKS* 2, 362/ *EO I*, 373.
44. *SKS* 2, 312/ *EO I*, 322.
45. *SKS* 2, 413/ *EO I*, 425.

against contracting a life relationship."[46] The engagement certainly constitutes such a relational contract. One needs to avoid it; otherwise, they run the risk of boredom. No wonder Eremita suspects that the diary is written by A. Whoever the real author is, the avoidance of boredom motivates the breaking of the engagement). Johannes artfully contrives to reap the maximum possible enjoyment from Cordelia and her love by first manipulating and then abandoning her. A describes Johannes and says, 'For him, individuals were merely for stimulation; he discarded them as trees shake off their leaves – he was rejuvenated, the foliage withered.'[47]

"Part II: Containing the Papers of B, Letters to A"

"Part II: Containing the Papers of B, Letters to A" is said to be written by B, an older friend of A who is sincerely concerned about him. The longest parts of the documents in this section are B's letters to A. The epigraph of "Part II" says, "The great passions are hermits, and to transport them to the desert is to hand over to them their proper domain. Chateaubriand."[48] This is a quotation from *Atala*, written by François-René de Chateaubriand (1768–1848), a French Romanticist. In Chateaubriand's story, Atala runs away with her lover and roams the desert. Sadly, she dies in the desert.[49] By quoting this passage, is B warning that A's excessive passions will lead A to the "desert" – which is a metaphor for a miserable life – that will eventually ruin him?[50]

In the first extended letter, "The Esthetic Validity of Marriage," B speaks warmly to A, who is his friend.[51] B is well aware that A is skilled at mocking consequential questions to evade responsibilities.[52] A seems to visit B frequently, and B, in his letter, sometimes refers to their common memories. B summarizes his letter as follows: "There are two things that I must regard as my particular task: to show the esthetic meaning of marriage and to show how

---

46. *SKS* 2, 286–7/ *EO I*, 297–8.
47. *SKS* 2, 297/ *EO I*, 308.
48. *SKS* 3, 9/ *EO II*, 1, originally written in French, translated by the Hongs.
49. Chateaubriand, *Atala/René*.
50. I learned this interpretation from Ōtani, *Kierkegaard's Authorship, Part 2*, 843–845.
51. *SKS* 3, 15–16/ *EO II*, 5–6.
52. *SKS* 3, 15/ *EO II*, 5.

the esthetic in it may be retained despite life's numerous hindrances."[53] For B, the aesthetic does not disappear in marriage but is retained and transformed into what the aesthetic is supposed to become. B believes that what he writes in the letter could not be written without his wife's existence. He feels that he owes his entire existence to her. To him, his relationship with her includes the aesthetic, the ethical, and the religious.

B points out A's problems, sayings, "What you lack, altogether lack, is faith. Instead of saving your soul by entrusting everything to God, instead of taking this shortcut, you prefer the endless roundabout way, which will never take you to your destination."[54] According to B's analysis, A abhors divine intervention in the relationship between him and his lover because he worries that the religious will ruin its aesthetic beauty. Therefore, A plays the role of fate or the Lord God, creating arbitrary situations from which he can repeatedly reap aesthetic enjoyment. As far as B is concerned, A's worries are groundless. For B, aesthetic love is unattainable without God.[55] According to B, a man should not view himself as a conqueror but as one who receives his lover as a gift from God's hand.[56]

God mediates between lovers and between parents and children, perfecting their relationships.[57] B describes the aesthetic beauty of the relationship between a mother and her child in a way designed to touch even an individual such as A.

> I have seen a poor woman – she had a little business, not in a shop or in a stall, but she stood in the open square; she stood there in rain and wind with a little one in her arms; she herself was neat and clean and her baby was carefully wrapped up. I have seen her many times. A fine lady came along who practically scolded her because she did not leave the child at home, and all the more so because it was just a hindrance to her. A clergyman came along the same street and approached her; he wanted to find a place for the child in an orphanage. She thanked

---

53. *SKS* 3, 18/ *EO II*, 8.
54. *SKS* 3, 23/ *EO II*, 14.
55. *SKS* 3, 66–68/ *EO II*, 57–58.
56. *SKS* 3, 66/ *EO II*, 57.
57. *SKS* 3, 77/ *EO II*, 73.

him graciously, but you should have seen the way she looked down and gazed at the child. Had it been frozen, her look would have thawed it; had it been dead and cold, her look would have thawed it; had it been exhausted from hunger and thirst, the benediction of her look would have refreshed it. But the child slept, and not even its smile could reward the mother . . . She really does not need either gold or fine ladies, or orphanages and clergymen. . . . She needs nothing at all, except that the child will at some time love her with the same tenderness, and she does not need this either, but it is the reward she has deserved, a blessing that heaven will not fail to give her.[58]

In the above quotation, B illustrates a mother's love not only aesthetically but also religiously by using the term "benediction" to describe "her look."

As far as B is concerned, marriage has no finite goal or "telos." For example, one should not view marriage as a "school for character" even if marriage may produce maturity.[59] Furthermore, one should not marry because of the desire for a home, children, a remedy for loneliness, or any other finite benefit that is external to the marriage itself. Indeed, even if one were to marry in order "to bear a savior for the world, this marriage would be just as unesthetic and immoral and irreligious."[60] The *only* admissible reason for marriage is a couple's love for each other.

In his diatribe style, B anticipates A's objections and counterarguments. A will no doubt come up with dramatic examples of difficulties and failures in marriage. However, to refute A's arguments, B describes the aesthetic beauty of a marriage in which a husband loves his wife all the more amid troubles.[61] B's point of view is summarized in these words: "And although this cannot be portrayed artistically, then let your consolation be, as it is mine, that we are not to read about or listen to or look at what is the highest and the most beautiful in life, but are, if you please, to live it."[62] According to B, the truly aesthetic life – which is married life – cannot be expressed as art because the

---

58. *SKS* 3, 78–79/ *EO II*, 74.
59. *SKS* 3, 69–71/ *EO II*, 64–66.
60. *SKS* 3, 70/ *EO II*, 65.
61. *SKS* 3, 124/ *EO II*, 124.
62. *SKS* 3, 137/ *EO II*, 139.

daily patience and cross-bearing it requires cannot be portrayed through poetry or art.[63] In other words, B argues that an actual and responsible life far surpasses all other forms of arts, no matter how splendid.

Both A and B aim to rescue the aesthetic. A regards duty as the fatal enemy of the aesthetic and attempts to avoid it. In contrast, B argues that duty is the best friend of the aesthetic and claims that it helps one to actualize the aesthetic in real life.[64] B concludes his letter with his warm greetings to A.[65]

In the next letter, which is even longer, "The Balance between the Esthetic and the Ethical in the Development of the Personality," B addresses the relationship between the aesthetic and the ethical. In the course of his discourse, B warns A, who is always hiding the real *self*, that "midnight" will come, at which point he will no longer be able to hide. According to B, those who always hide themselves can no longer know who they truly are. B says, "But the person who can scarcely open himself cannot love, and the person who cannot love is the unhappiest of all."[66] B discerns A's dire situation.[67] B warns that A will be in trouble because he does not make a decision. B likens A to philosophers who live as outsiders to real life. As far as B is concerned, philosophy belongs to the same category as logic, history, necessity, and mediation, while human freedom resides in its own category – that of either/or.[68] Echoing Matthew 16:26, B says, "[A philosopher] wins the whole world and he loses himself."[69] From B's perspective, his way of life has a value that can be transmitted from one generation to the next. Thus, B expects, in his final hours, to leave the inheritance of either/or to his son. According to B, one must choose the absolute, which means refusing the aesthetic; but in doing so, the aesthetic reappears in its relative form. By this, B probably means that while one should not aim for the aesthetic for its own sake (as A does), the one who chooses the absolute (as B does) can eventually gain the aesthetic as a by-product. B continues by affirming that the time will come when we

---

63. *SKS* 3, 134/ *EO II*, 135.
64. *SKS* 3, 150/ *EO II*, 153.
65. *SKS* 3, 151/ *EO II*, 154.
66. *SKS* 3, 158/ *EO II*, 160.
67. *SKS* 3, 158/ *EO II*, 160.
68. *SKS* 3, 170/ *EO II*, 175.
69. *SKS* 3, 171/ *EO II*, 176. Compare Matthew 16:26, Mark 8:36, and Luke 9:25.

will all stand before the eternal and, irrespective of our wealth or poverty, face the same question – whether we chose the self or not.

B analyzes the life of the Roman emperor Nero, saying, "Nero's nature was *depression* [*Tungsind*] . . . because only in the moment of pleasure does he find rest."[70] B warns A that if he does not change his life, his life, like Nero's, will be ruined! "What, then, is depression? It is hysteria of the spirit."[71] Why is one depressed? One can neither explain nor understand why. B claims that depression might be either sin or sickness, or both. According to B, depression is a sickness that tends to affect those who are gifted – for example, it spreads among young German and French Romanticists. B says, "Consequently, it is manifest that every esthetic view of life is despair, and that everyone who lives esthetically is in despair, whether he knows it or not."[72] According to B, when one humbles oneself before the eternal power, depression will be eliminated.

Nevertheless, for B, not all despair is created equal. He distinguishes between different types of despair, saying, "But there is a difference between despair and despair."[73] In short, there are different kinds of despair. The painter who loses his sight will despair. But this despair is different from A's: "[A's despair] is not despair involving something actual but a despair in thought."[74] Paradoxically, the fact that A cannot be satisfied with anything implies that he "feels the need of the eternal."[75] B insightfully observes that A's boredom is the very evidence that he needs the eternal: "In a certain sense you are right, for nothing that is finite, not even the whole world, can satisfy the soul of a person who feels the need of the eternal."[76] A's self is too valuable to be dealt with casually: "But the spirit does not allow itself to be mocked, and the gloom of depression thickens around you, and the lightning flash of a demented witticism only shows you yourself that it is even more dense,

---

70. *SKS* 3, 180/ *EO II*, 185–186.
71. *SKS* 3, 183/ *EO II*, 188.
72. *SKS* 3, 186/ *EO II*, 192.
73. *SKS* 3, 188/ *EO II*, 194.
74. *SKS* 3, 188/ *EO II*, 194.
75. *SKS* 3, 195/ *EO II*, 203. Compare Ecclesiastes 3:11.
76. *SKS* 3, 195/ *EO II*, 203.

even more terrible."⁷⁷ B analyzes A's actions, saying, "This joy you have now chosen, the laughter of despair."⁷⁸

B religiously idealizes the role of women, which is different from A's poetic idealization: "Believe me, as surely as corruption comes from man, salvation comes from woman."⁷⁹

B advises A to gain himself. But how? B says, "I have only one answer: Despair, then!"⁸⁰ How can A gain himself by despairing? "And in despairing a person chooses again, and what then does he choose? He chooses himself...."⁸¹ B encourages A to learn to exercise his will, take responsibility, and choose himself instead of avoiding those tasks and fleeing to the interesting.

According to B, repentance will guide one to find oneself in God, and *that* self is the authentic self: "He repents himself back into himself, back into the family, back into the race, until he finds himself in God. Only on this condition can he choose himself. And this is the only condition he wants, for only in this way can he chose himself absolutely."⁸² B categorizes a wide range of loves, each with a specific definition. According to B, while each kind of love has certain features, love for God has a distinct quality. B says that to love God means to repent: "The greater the freedom, the greater the guilt."⁸³

B asserts that everybody has a unique calling and duty that belongs to them alone: "I never say of a man: He is doing duty or duties; but I say: He is doing *his* duty; I say: I am doing *my* duty, do *your* duty."⁸⁴ Duty is universal and yet personal in a truer sense: "...I can discharge the duty and yet not do *my* duty, and I can do *my* duty and yet not discharge the duty."⁸⁵ The world view of B's ethical life is beautifully described as follows:

---

77. *SKS* 3, 197/ *EO II*, 205.
78. *SKS* 3, 197/ *EO II*, 205.
79. *SKS* 3, 199/ *EO II*, 207.
80. *SKS* 3, 200/ *EO II*, 208.
81. *SKS* 3, 203/ *EO II*, 211. C. Stephen Evans expounds on this as follows: "B's idea is that since A is in despair, he must choose himself, take responsibility for his despair. Then his despair will be different, not just a condition that afflicts him but part of his identity that he can then remake as he embarks on the task of becoming a self. That must begin by choosing to take responsibility for who he is." Evans, personal communication, 10 June 2020.
82. *SKS* 3, 207/ *EO II*, 216.
83. *SKS* 3, 209/ *EO II*, 218.
84. *SKS* 3, 251/ *EO II*, 263, emphasis in original.
85. *SKS* 3, 251/ *EO II*, 264, emphasis in original.

> And when the cup of suffering is handed to me, I shall not fix my gaze upon the cup but upon the one who hands it to me, and I shall not stare at the bottom of the cup to see whether I have quickly emptied it but steadfastly at the one who hands it to me. I shall gladly take the cup in my hand; I shall not empty it to somebody else's health as on a festive occasion when I myself delight in the delicious drink. No, I shall taste its bitterness, and while I am tasting it I shall cry out to myself "To my health," because I know and am convinced that with this drink I am acquiring by purchase an eternal health.[86]

According to the above quotation, God will hand B the cup of suffering. B does not pay attention to how long that suffering continues, how horrible it is, or whether or not he can really bear it. Instead, B will fix his eyes on God alone and embrace the suffering with the confidence that, through this suffering, he will eventually gain eternal life.

In the quotation below, B praises a faithful old woman and pays obeisance to her:

> What contributed to enhancing my joy and made the impression of the divine worship in this church complete for me was ... an elderly woman who likewise appeared every Sunday. She was accustomed to coming a little before the service began, and I likewise ... As she walked by, I always arose and bowed to her, or, as it says in the Old Testament, I did obeisance [*neiede*] to her. For me this bow implied so very much; it was as if I wanted to entreat her to include me in her intercessions. She entered her pew; she nodded graciously to the sexton; she remained standing a moment, she bowed her head, briefly held a handkerchief to her eyes for a prayer – it would take a powerful preacher to make as strong and beneficent an impression as the solemnity of that venerable woman did.[87]

---

86. *SKS* 3, 272/ *EO II*, 287, emphasis in original. Compare *SKS* 18, 309, JJ:506/ *JP*, V 5562, n.d., 1842. For the biblical images and allusions in this quotation, see Matthew 26:39, Mark 10:38, Luke 22:42, John 16:21 and 18:11, Romans 8:18, and Hebrews 12:2.

87. *SKS* 3, 297/ *EO II*, 314.

For B, no matter what one's duty is, those who fervently devote their whole being to their duty are as edifying as a powerful preacher. But perhaps B is also claiming that women are, by nature, more religiously devoted than men: "Woman believes that for God all things are possible; man believes that for God something is impossible."[88]

B summarizes his letter by saying, "What I wanted to do was to show how the ethical in the mixed territories is so far from depriving life of its beauty that it expressly gives it beauty."[89] B provides an interpretative clue and says, "consider it as notes to Balle's catechism."[90] According to B, what he has written is akin to the catechism (*Lærebog*) written by Nicolai Edinger Balle (1744–1816).[91] Like the previous letter, B concludes his letter with warm greetings: "I hope to see you at my house just as often as before."[92]

"Ultimatum" is B's final short letter, in which he introduces an unpublished sermon written by B's friend, a Jylland Pastor. B believes that this pastor conveys what B wants to say better than B can. The title of the sermon is "The Upbuilding That Lies in the Thought That in Relation to God We Are Always in the Wrong." The sermon begins with a prayers "Father in heaven! Teach us to pray rightly so that our hearts may open up to you in prayer … by always joyfully thanking you as we gladly confess that in relation to you we are always in the wrong. Amen."[93] This sermon is based on Luke 19:41–48, where Jesus weeps over the destruction of Jerusalem. The pastor includes Luke 13:1–4 in his discussion and says that one should not think of the destruction of Jerusalem as a punishment. He also refers to Job 40:2, saying, "You are not to argue with God," and adds that one should not insist that they are right in relation to God.[94]

---

88. *SKS* 3, 298/ *EO II*, 315.

89. *SKS* 3, 305/ *EO II*, 323.

90. *SKS* 3, 305/ *EO II*, 323.

91. See *SKS* 3, 253–257/ *EO II*, 266–270. For a discussion of Balle's catechism and its relationship to Kierkegaard's thought and authorship, see Watkin, "Judge William"; Watkin, *Historical Dictionary*, 21–23; Barnett, "Nicolai Edinger Balle," 23–39. See also section 3.2.3.2.

92. *SKS* 3, 314/ *EO II*, 333.

93. *SKS* 3, 321/ *EO II*, 341.

94. *SKS* 3, 324/ *EO II*, 344.

What does the title of this sermon mean? The pastor gives the example of a woman who truly loves her lover.[95] She cannot be happy with the thought that her lover is in the wrong. Out of love, she would rather wish to be in the wrong herself. The more she loves her lover, the less she thinks that he is in the wrong. How much would this be true if one truly loves God?[96] The more one loves God, the more one can freely, out of love, recognize that they are in the wrong. The thought that God is always in the right will *forcefully (rationally)* make one think that they are in the wrong. Yet if one loves God, one can *freely (personally)* acknowledge that they themselves are in the wrong. The pastor seems to believe that it is not apologetics (defending the doctrine of God's justice) but only love for God that enables a person to properly acknowledge their own wrong. In other words, the reader is encouraged to meet God with the heart, not with the head.

When someone loves God, they will immediately realize that they can never love God in the way that God loves them. By *that* realization, one will understand that God loves them in such a profound way that it lies beyond anything that they could ever fathom. That understanding will help one to overcome self-pity, the trials of life, and further to rejoice in, praise God.[97] The thought that we are always in the wrong in relation to God will edify in a twofold way. First, it helps one to overcome doubt, and second it animates action.[98] This thought edifies a person and "only the truth that edifies is truth for you."[99] This is the very last sentence of *Either/Or*.

---

95. *SKS* 3, 327/ *EO II*, 347–348. One may suspect that Kierkegaard speaks to his former fiancée, Regine Olsen, under the mask of the Jylland Pastor.

96. *SKS* 3, 328/ *EO II*, 349.

97. *SKS* 3, 329–330/ *EO II*, 351.

98. *SKS* 3, 330/ *EO II*, 351.

99. *SKS* 3, 332/ *EO II*, 354, translation modified.

APPENDIX 5

Reading *Two Upbuilding Discourses* (1843)

Preface

The fact that this work is dedicated to his father, Michael Pederson Kierkegaard (1756-1838),[1] and was published on Søren Kierkegaard's birthday[2] indicates its personal significance to Kierkegaard. As the title indicates, this work includes two discourses. Both discourses are expositions of specific Bible passages. However, Kierkegaard himself refuses to call these discourses "sermons."[3] In the preface, he says,

> Although this little book (which is called "discourses," not sermons, because its author does not have authority to preach, "upbuilding discourses," not discourses for upbuilding, because the speaker by no means claims to be a teacher) wishes to be only what it is, a superfluity, and desires only to remain in hiding, just as it came into existence in concealment.[4]

---

1. *SKS* 5, 11/ *EUD*, 3.

2. *SKS* 5, 13/ *EUD*, 5; the printed date of publication is 5 May, which is Søren's birthday. But the actual date of publication was 16 May.

3. For a discussion about whether the discourses should be called sermons or not, see Pattison, *Kierkegaard's Upbuilding Discourses*, 21–26; Law, "The 'Ultimatum' of Kierkegaard's *Either/Or, Part Two*, and the *Two Upbuilding Discourses* of 16 May 1843" in *IKC 4: Either/Or, Part II*. 1995, 262–3.

4. *SKS* 5, 13/ *EUD*, 5.

The discourses are written in a conversational style, with Kierkegaard gently and personally addressing the reader in the second person. His famous term "single individual" first appears in this work: "[This work] finally met that single individual [*hiin Enkelte*] whom I with joy and gratitude call *my* reader."[5] Here, Kierkegaard personifies his work, suggesting that it has found its intended audience who he calls "single individual."

"The Expectancy of Faith: New Year's Day"

The title of the first discourse is "The Expectancy of Faith: New Year's Day." As we have seen in the preface, this work was published in May, but Kierkegaard chose to subtitle the first discourse "New Year's Day." By doing so, Kierkegaard seems to cue the reader to expect something new or some kind of renewal. The first discourse opens with the following prayer:

> Once again a year has passed, heavenly Father! We thank you that it was added to the time of grace ... because we trust in your mercy. The new year faces us with its requirements, and even though we enter it downcast and troubled because we cannot and do not wish to hide from ourselves the thought of the lust of the eye that infatuated, the sweetness of revenge that seduced, the anger that made us unrelenting, the cold heart that fled far from you, we nevertheless do not go into the new year entirely empty-handed, since, we shall indeed also take along with us recollections of the fearful doubts that were set at rest, of the lurking concerns that were soothed, of the downcast disposition that was raised up, of the cheerful hope that was not humiliated.[6]

This discourse is based on Galatians 3:23–29.[7] Kierkegaard describes person who is earnestly looking for something worthy of the investment of all their passions and energy: "He perhaps would go there to reflect again and

---

5. *SKS* 5, 13/ *EUD*, 5; emphasis in original.
6. *SKS* 5, 17/ *EUD*, 7.
7. In our conversation, Niels Jørgen Cappelørn said this: "Interestingly, Kierkegaard refers to the biblical verse; 'The law was our disciplinarian until Christ come' (Gal 3:24) in his first discourses. He understood what he was doing. What he was doing with discourses was 'a disciplinarian until Christ came,' a sort of help for the reader to get closer to Christianity."

to investigate whether there might not be one wish so certain that he would dare to put his whole soul fervently into it without holding back any part of it for another wish."[8] According to Kierkegaard, such a passionate person can be satisfied only by faith that is the supreme good: "About *faith* there is a different kind of talk. It is said to be the highest good, the most beautiful, the most precious, the most blessed riches of all, not to be compared with anything else, incapable of being replaced."[9] However, is not faith something that only the pious can have? "Faith is qualitatively different. It is not only the highest good, but it is good in which all are able to share, and the person who rejoices in the possession of it also rejoices in the countless human race, 'because what I possess,' he says, 'every human being has or can possess.'"[10]

Everybody and anyone can have faith, says Kierkegaard. At the same time, "One person can do much for another, but he cannot give him faith."[11]

> Then he discovered that life was beautiful, that it was a new gloriousness of faith that no human being can give it to another, but that every human being has what is highest, noblest, and most sacred in humankind. It is original in him, and every human being has it if he wants to have it – it is precisely the gloriousness of faith that it can be had only on this condition. Therefore, it is the only unfailing good, because it can be had only by constantly being appropriated and can be appropriated only by constantly being generated.[12]

Then how can one possess faith? According to Kierkegaard, faith is a gift that is available to everyone, but no one can give their faith to another. Mysteriously, anyone can appropriate faith by being constantly renewed.

If someone acquires faith, what will happen to them? "The expectancy of faith, then, is victory!"[13] Faith can overcome everything: "Faith expects victory in everything, in all battles and spiritual trials – or, more correctly, it expects

---

8. *SKS* 5, 19/ *EUD*, 9.
9. *SKS* 5, 19–20/ *EUD*, 9–10, emphasis in original.
10. *SKS* 5, 20/ *EUD*, 10.
11. *SKS* 5, 22/ *EUD*, 12.
12. *SKS* 5, 24/ *EUD*, 14, translation slightly modified.
13. *SKS* 5, 29/ *EUD*, 19.

to be victorious without a struggle."[14] The one who constantly strives for and attains faith from God is victorious. Such a person can say,

> There is an expectancy that the whole world cannot take from me; it is the expectancy of faith, and this is victory. I am not deceived, since I did not believe that the world would keep the promise it seemed to be making to me; my expectancy was not in the world but in God.[15]

"Every Good and Every Perfect Gift Is from Above"

The title of the second discourse is "Every Good and Every Perfect Gift Is from Above." This discourse opens with the following beautiful prayer:

> From your hand, O God, we are willing to receive everything. You reach it out, your mighty hand, and catch the wise in their foolishness. You open it, your gentle hand, and satisfy with blessing everything that lives. And even if it seems that your arm is shortened, increase our faith and our trust so that we might still hold fast to you. And if at times it seems that you draw your hand away from us, oh, then we know it is only because you close it, that you close it only to save the abundant blessing in it, that you close it only to open it again and satisfy with blessing everything that lives. Amen.[16]

According to Kierkegaard, this discourse is based on James 1:17–22:

> Every good gift and every perfect gift is from above and comes down from the Father of lights, with whom there is no change or shadow of variation. According to his own counsel, he brought us forth by the word of truth, that we should be a first fruit of his creation. Therefore, my beloved brethren, let every man be quick to hear, slow to speak, slow to anger, because a man's anger does not work what is righteous before God. Therefore put away

---

14. *SKS* 5, 29/ *EUD*, 20.
15. *SKS* 5, 32/ *EUD*, 24.
16. *SKS* 5, 41/ *EUD*, 31.

all filthiness and all remnants of wickedness and receive with
meekness the word that is implanted in you and that is powerful
for making your souls blessed.[17]

Kierkegaard says that people often work and succeed in their business without recognizing to whom they owe their success. According to Kierkegaard, understanding James's message is not difficult, but those who hear this message might say, "Now we have understood them; now bring on new thougths that we have not understood."[18] However, speaking in such a way reveals that they do not understand this passage. Kierkegaard says that those who truly comprehend the meaning of this passage will come to the following realization: "The more they were capable of sinking their souls into [this biblical passage], the more they felt themselves strengthened and filled with confidence."[19] As far as Kierkegaard is concerned, this passage in James can continually strengthen a person, and no one should ever think that they have "graduated" from it. However, some may experience disappointment. Someone may have prayed sincerely to God all day long and yet have received no answer or sign at all. To such a person, Kierkegaard says,

> Then you acknowledged with humble joy that God was still the almighty Creator of heaven and earth, who not only created the world from nothing but did something even more marvelous – from your impatient and inconstant heart he created the imperishable substance of a quiet spirit.[20]

What a thought! God not only created the world from nothing but did something even more marvellous – from our "impatient and inconstant" hearts, he created "the imperishable substance of a quiet spirit." Kierkegaard declares that something more marvellous than creation *ex nihilo* will take place when a person sinks their soul deep into this biblical passage.

"The apostle Paul says, 'Everything created by God is good if it is received with thankfulness.'"[21] Kierkegaard expands these passages and says, "It is

---

17. *SKS* 5, 41–42/ *EUD*, 32.
18. *SKS* 5, 43/ *EUD*, 34.
19. *SKS* 5, 43/ *EUD*, 34.
20. *SKS* 5, 45/ *EUD*, 36. See also *SKS* 18, 104. FF:154.a/ *JP*, II A 758 *n.d.*, 1838.
21. *SKS* 5, 50/ *EUD*, 42, originally from I Tim 4:4.

beautiful that a person prays . . . without ceasing, but it is more blessed always to give thanks. Then you have worthily interpreted those apostolic words more gloriously than if all the angels spoke in flaming tongues."[22] Kierkegaard urges his readers to treasure the apostolic words in their hearts: "Did you treasure them in a pure and beautiful heart and refuse to be ransomed, for any price or any wily bribe on the part of prudence, from the deep pain of having to confess again and again that you never loved as you were loved?"[23] Kierkegaard urges the reader to be courageous to stand firm on these biblical passages against any of the difficulties of life: "The courage to understand that every good and every perfect gift is from above, the courage to explain it in love, the faith to receive this courage, since it, too, is a good and a perfect gift."[24]

Kierkegaard invites the reader to wade deep into spirituality:

> [A] person can truly love God only when he loves him according to his own imperfection. Which love is this? It is the love that is born of repentance, which is more beautiful than any other love, for in it you love God . . . In repentance, you receive everything from God, even the thanksgiving that you bring to him . . . Was it not so, my listener? You wanted to give thanks to God at all times, but even this was very imperfect. Then you understood that God is the one who does everything in you and who then grants you the childlike joy of regarding your thanksgiving as a gift from you . . . [A] person becomes as happy as a child in God.[25]

Human beings are imperfect; and for imperfect people, true love can only be experienced by loving God in repentance. One may wish to give thanks to God constantly. One may imagine that the Father is happy to receive such thanksgiving. But *everything* – even our thanksgiving – is given from above as a gift from our heavenly Father. Recognizing this truth, we can find joy as a child of the Father.

---

22. *SKS* 5, 51/ *EUD*, 43.
23. *SKS* 5, 52/ *EUD*, 44.
24. Ibid.
25. *SKS* 5, 53–54/ *EUD*, 45–46.

APPENDIX 6

Reading *The Sickness unto Death*

Motto

The Sickness unto Death opens with an unforgettable, prayerful epigraph: "Lord, give us weak eyes for things of little worth, and eyes clear-sighted in all of your truth."[1] This epigraph seems to presuppose that we are usually concerned about unworthy things, despite their being unnecessary, and blind to godly truth, despite its great value. Anti-Climacus prays – and invites the reader to pray as well – that God may give us "weak eyes" for the former and make us "clear-sighted" for the latter.

Preface

Anti-Climacus says, "From the Christian point of view, everything, indeed everything, ought to serve for upbuilding."[2] *The Sickness unto Death* might appear to be rigorous, but it serves to upbuild because, for Anti-Climacus, whatever a Christian does should serve the purpose of upbuilding. He offers a vivid example: "Everything essentially Christian must have in its presentation a resemblance to the way a physician speaks at the sickbed; even if only medical experts understand it, it must never be forgotten that the situation

---

1. *SKS* 11, 116/ *SUD*, 3; this quotation was originally by Nicolaus Ludwig von Zinzendorf (1700–1760), but Kierkegaard only knows the verse from a sermon by Johan Baptist von Albertini (1769–1831). See *Kommentarer til SKS* 11, 116, 1. This is originally quoted by Kierkegaard in German, and the above translation is by the Hongs. Compare John 9:39–41.
2. *SKS* 11, 117/ *SUD*, 5. Compare 1 Corinthians 14:26 and Ephesians 4:29.

is the bedside of a sick person."³ Although a physician might sometimes say something that sounds severe or technical, whatever is said at the sickbed is intended to be beneficial, to *cure* the sickness of the patient. Similarly, while the content of *The Sickness unto Death* might be severe or technical, this book serves as a cure for spiritual sickness and is aimed at upbuilding the reader. Anti-Climacus adds, "Thus, also in Christian terminology, death is the expression of the greatest spiritual misery, and healing is just to die, to die."⁴ Death is dialectical: "Death is the expression of the greatest spiritual misery," but it is also the fount from which healing springs. While the first part of this sentence is understandable, the latter part may seem unclear. What does it mean? Presumably, it means that healing can occur by dying to sin.⁵ In Christian terminology, dying to sin signifies to will to sin no more after being freed from sin's dominion through Christ's atonement. If, figuratively speaking, a person dies with Christ and dies to sin, they are no longer slaves of sin. Anti-Climacus presumably had in mind the following biblical passage:

> Should we continue in sin in order that grace may abound? By no means! How can we who died to sin go on living in it? . . . We know that our old self was crucified with him so that the body of sin might be destroyed, and we might no longer be enslaved to sin (Rom 6:1b–2, 6).

As this Scripture shows, this freedom comes through Christ's atonement and one's death to sin. To use Anti-Climacus's terminology, healing from despair and sickness comes through dying to sin.

---

3. *SKS* 11, 117/ *SUD*, 5.

4. *SKS* 11, 118/ *SUD*, 5, translation modified.

5. I am indebted to Niels Jørgen Cappelørn for bringing the following points to my attention: The Hongs' translation says, "To die, to die to the world." But there is no "to the world" in the Danish original. It simply says, "at døe, at afdøe [to die, to die]," and the Hongs have interpretatively added "to the world." According to Cappelørn, the reason for this addition is 1 Peter 2:24, which includes the phrase "døde fra synden [died from sin]." If Kierkegaard had this verse in mind, then such a translation makes more sense since *The Sickness unto Death* urges the reader to be cured of *despair* or *sin*. Therefore, Anti-Climacus probably means here that healing is *not* to die to the world *but* to die from sin (see also Romans 6:2, which includes the phrase "døde fra synden [died from sin]"). The next question is this: What does dying to sin mean? As far as I know, Andrew B. Torrance provides the best explanation: "In faith, he is *cured* from the despair of sin by *dying to* his untrue self (the self that embraces sin) and becoming a true self who is made alive in relationship with God." Torrance, *Freedom to Become*, 29–30.

"Introduction"

To explain the meaning of the title *The Sickness unto Death*, Anti-Climacus refers to the New Testament story of the raising of Lazarus in the Gospel of John:

> "This sickness is not unto death" (John 11:4). And yet Lazarus did die; when the disciples misunderstood what Christ added later, "Our friend Lazarus has fallen asleep, but I go to awaken him out of sleep" (11:11), he told them flatly "Lazarus is dead" (11:14). So Lazarus is dead, and yet this sickness was not unto death; he was dead, and yet this sickness is not unto death.[6]

Lazarus was once physically dead. But Anti-Climacus repeats Jesus's words: "This sickness is not unto death." By doing so, Anti-Climacus excludes physical death from his definition of "the sickness unto death." In the Bible story, Jesus raised Lazarus from the dead by approaching the grave and crying out "with a loud voice, 'Lazarus, come out!'" (John 11:43).[7] However, Anti-Climacus lets his imagination take him beyond what is written in the Bible. According to Anti-Climacus, Lazarus's sickness is not a sickness unto death (even though Lazarus dies physically) not because Christ raised Lazarus from the dead but because Christ, who is "the resurrection and the life" (John 11:25), approached the grave.[8] As a passionate preacher, Anti-Climacus proclaims, "No, it may be said that *this* sickness is not unto death, not because Lazarus was raised from the dead, but because He exists; therefore this sickness is not unto death."[9] According to Anti-Climacus, wherever Christ is present, there is no death. Anti-Climacus also defines the sickness unto death negatively by listing what it is *not*. According to him, neither suffering nor even death itself fits within the category of the sickness unto death.[10] To explain this, he uses the analogy of a child and an adult to compare the natural person with a Christian.[11] Although a child may fear many things, this fear

---

6. *SKS* 11, 123/ *SUD*, 7.
7. *SKS* 11, 123/ *SUD*, 7.
8. *SKS* 11, 123/ *SUD*, 7.
9. *SKS* 11, 124/ *SUD*, 7, emphasis in original.
10. *SKS* 11, 124/ *SUD*, 8.
11. *SKS* 11, 124–125/ *SUD*, 8–9. In his supervision, Cappelørn commented that 1 Corinthians 2:6–16 underpins Anti-Climacus's argument. In 1 Corinthians 2, the apostle Paul states, "But, as it is written, 'What no eye has seen, nor ear heard,/ nor the human heart

is often indiscriminate and unreasonable. A child does not yet know which things ought to call forth horror. An adult is no longer fearful of things that scare a child but knows full well what is *truly* to be feared. Similarly, the natural person does not even know the proper objects of fear. Things that hold no terror for a Christian often terrify the natural person. Suffering and death cannot frighten a Christian in the same way that they frighten the natural person. Anti-Climacus whispers omniously, "But the most appalling danger that the Christian has learned to know is 'the sickness unto death.'"[12]

"Part One: The Sickness unto Death Is Despair"

At the beginning of "**A. Despair Is the Sickness unto Death**," Anti-Climacus gives a complex definition of the human being:

> A human being is spirit. But what is spirit? Spirit is the self. But what is the self? The self is a relation that relates itself to itself or is the relation's relating itself to itself in the relation; the self is not the relation but is the relation's relating itself to itself.[13]

Anti-Climacus defines a human being as spirit and spirit as the self. The self is relational, but it is not static. The self is not a finished state; rather, it *is* in a continual process of *becoming*. As Anti-Climacus explains, the true self is found in the relation between the two paradoxical elements of the self. By maintaining the dialectical balance or tension between these elements, the self continually relates to itself in order to become its authentic self.

After defining the human being as relational, Anti-Climacus expands this definition by adding synthesis to it: "A human being is a synthesis of the infinite and the finite, of the temporal and the eternal, of freedom and

---

conceived,/ what God has prepared for those who love him' – these things God has revealed to us through the Spirit; for the Spirit searches everything, even the depths of God. [. . .] Those who are natural do not receive the gifts of God's Spirit, for they are foolishness to them, and they are unable to understand them because they are discerned spiritually" (1 Cor 2:9–10, 14). Cappelørn's comment helps me to summarize Anti-Climacus's logic as follows: As God reveals his revelation through the Spirit, *The Sickness unto Death* aids spiritual discernment so that its readers can recognize what is truly terrifying. In this way, this work, under the guidance of the Holy Spirit, helps the natural person to become a Christian. See also section 6.2.3.2.

12. *SKS* 11, 125/ *SUD*, 9.
13. *SKS* 11, 129/ *SUD*, 13.

necessity, in short, a synthesis. A synthesis is a relation between two."[14] In this way, Anti-Climacus presents the self as a third party that relates to both extremes – that is, the infinite and the finite. The self not only maintains a balance between these extremes but also relates to *itself*.

Anti-Climacus raises the question of *who* establishes the self that relates to itself: "Such a relation that relates itself to itself, a self, must either have established itself or have been established by another."[15] He responds by saying that the self is established by another.[16] For Anti-Climacus, a human being is not immediately who they are supposed to be. They must *become* the self they are intended to be according to the standard of selfhood that has been established by another – that is God, or at least something beyond the human faculty of reason. Based on this understanding, Anti-Climacus describes how despair can be rooted out: "The formula that describes the state of the self when despair is completely rooted out is this: in relating itself to itself and in willing to be itself, the self rests transparently in the power that established it."[17] When the human being – who is positioned between the two extremes and who relates to the self – wills to depend completely on God, who has established them, despair can be rooted out.

Next, Anti-Climacus defines despair as a sickness of the self. For Anti-Climacus, when the self does not relate well to God and, therefore, to itself, it is sick, and this sickness is called despair. Anti-Climacus says, "The possibility of this sickness is man's superiority over the animal"[18] because only a spirit can have this sickness. While the *possibility* of despair sets humans in a superior position, above animals, the *actuality* of despair is "not only the worst misfortune and misery – no, it is perdition."[19]

Third, Anti-Climacus defines despair as "the sickness unto death." For Anti-Climacus, this sickness does not end with physical death but persists as an ongoing death. Since a human being is a synthesis of the temporal and the eternal, one cannot get rid of the eternal. Therefore, this sickness, which

---

14. *SKS* 11, 129/ *SUD*, 13.
15. *SKS* 11, 129/ *SUD*, 13.
16. *SKS* 11, 130; 132/ *SUD*, 13; 16. "The self does not create itself." Dunning, "Dialectical Structure," 50.
17. *SKS* 11, 130/ *SUD*, 14.
18. *SKS* 11, 131/ *SUD*, 15.
19. *SKS* 11, 131/ *SUD*, 15, translation modified.

springs from the synthesis of the temporal and the eternal, will continue perpetually unless it is cured: "This is the state in despair. No matter how much the despairing person avoids it . . . – eternity nevertheless will make it manifest that his condition was despair."[20] Anti-Climacus describes the awfulness of this perpetual dying.[21]

In "B. The Universality of This Sickness (Despair)" Anti-Climacus argues the universality of the sickness unto death: "Just as a physician might say that there very likely is not one single living human being who is completely healthy, so anyone who really knows mankind might say that there is not one single living human being who does not despair a little."[22] Previously, Anti-Climacus says, "to be aware of this sickness is the Christian's superiority over the natural man; to be cured of this sickness is the Christian's blessedness."[23] But here he says, "In any case, no human being ever lived and no one lives outside of Christendom who has not despaired, and no one in Christendom if he is not a true Christian, and insofar as he is not wholly that, he still is to some extent in despair."[24] Anyone, who lives whether in a heathen nation or in Christendom, is in despair except for a true Christian, says Anti-Climacus: "That one is in despair is not a rarity; no, it is rare, very rare, that one is in truth not in despair."[25] One may object to Anti-Climacus' assertion as there are many happy people who look as though they do not despair. However, Anti-Climacus says,

> happiness is not a qualification of spirit, and deep, deep within the most secret hiding place of happiness there dwells also anxiety, which is despair; it very much wishes to be allowed to remain there, because for despair the most cherished and desirable place to live is in the heart of happiness.[26]

Happiness does not prove that one is not in despair. To be cured of despair, a person must first realize that they are in despair. Anti-Climacus says that

---

20. *SKS* 11, 136/ *SUD*, 21.
21. *SKS* 11, 134/ *SUD*, 18.
22. *SKS* 11, 138/ *SUD*, 22.
23. *SKS* 11, 131/ *SUD*, 15.
24. *SKS* 11, 138/ *SUD*, 22.
25. *SKS* 11, 139/ *SUD*, 23.
26. *SKS* 11, 141/ *SUD*, 25.

joy or sorrow in life may blind a person to what is ultimately essential.[27] He emphasizes that being aware that one is before God – an awareness that is gained only through despair – is of the greatest importance.

In "C. The Forms of This Sickness (Despair)," Anti-Climacus categorizes despair into two types. The first category is an observation of despair in terms of the self as a synthesis – the synthesis of infinitude and finitude, the synthesis of temporal and eternal, or the synthesis of possibility and necessity. The second is an observation of despair in terms of one's consciousness. In the first category, despair can be defined as the spirit's failure to maintain balance between two elements. When one views human beings as a synthesis of infinitude and finitude, it becomes clear that despair arises because of an imbalance – that is, one lacks either infinitude or finitude. To be more specific, infinitude requires that one be aware of the self before God, while finitude requires that one be conscious of one's situation of despair. To avoid despair, both dimensions must be present. From another angle, if we think of humans in terms of a synthesis of possibility and necessity, a person who is in despair lacks either possibility or necessity. Anti-Climacus explains the lack of possibility, saying, "Fatalism and determinism lack possibility for the relaxing and mitigating, for the tempering of necessity, and thus lack possibility as mitigation."[28] To more fully and clearly explain this relationship, Anti-Climacus uses the following simile: "Possibility is like a child's invitation to a party; the child is willing at once, but the question now is whether the parents will give permission – and as it is with the parents, so it is with necessity."[29] Necessity signifies "our concrete embeddedness in a context, most of which we cannot change (e.g., where and to whom we are born, the particularities of our physical and intellectual constitution)"[30] – to use Jamie Ferreira's phrase – while possibility stands for God's omnipotence and negotiability:

> What is decisive is that with God everything is possible. This is eternally true and consequently true at every moment. This is indeed a generally recognized truth, which is commonly expressed in this way, but the critical decision does not come

---

27. *SKS* 11, 142–143/ *SUD*, 26–27.
28. *SKS* 11, 156/ *SUD*, 41.
29. *SKS* 11, 152/ *SUD*, 37.
30. Ferreira, *Kierkegaard*, 155.

until a person is brought to his extremity, when, humanly speaking, there is no possibility. Then the question is whether he will believe that for God everything is possible, that is, whether he will believe. But this is the very formula for losing the understanding; to believe is indeed to lose the understanding in order to gain God.[31]

In Anti-Climacus's view, believing is the exercise of one's freedom and the actualization of possibility. Anti-Climacus views human beings as a synthesis of two extremes and regards the functions of both extremes as indispensable for their existence.

Anti-Climacus moves on to an observation of the forms of despair from the perspective of one's consciousness. From this perspective, one is either unaware or aware of despair. As Anti-Climacus has already stated in the previous section, happiness does not signify that one is free from despair:

> An individual is furthest from being conscious of himself as spirit when he is ignorant of being in despair. But precisely this – not to be conscious of oneself as spirit – is despair, which is spiritlessness, whether the state is a thoroughgoing moribundity, a merely vegetative life, or an intense, energetic life, the secret of which is still despair. In the latter case, the individual in despair is like the consumptive: when the illness is most critical, he feels well, considers himself to be in excellent health, and perhaps seems to others to radiate health.[32]

This unconscious despair is spiritless despair. Since the person is unaware of their despair, it is not really despair in the true sense. Rather, it is despair that is unaware of its despair. What about one who *is* aware of their despair? In such an instance, there are two forms of despair. The first is the despair where the self does not will to be itself. The second is the despair where the self wills to be itself. Anti-Climacus refers to the former as despair in weakness.[33] This is despair over the earthly or over something earthly.[34] For Anti-Climacus,

---

31. *SKS* 11, 153–154/ *SUD*, 38, emphasis in original.
32. *SKS* 11, 159–160/ *SUD*, 44–45.
33. *SKS* 11, 165/ *SUD*, 49.
34. *SKS* 11, 165/ *SUD*, 50. The difference between the two is explained as follows: "to despair over the earthly (the category of totality) and to despair over something earthly (the

this is not a true form of despair since "there is no infinite consciousness of the self."³⁵ He explains further: "Its dialectic is: the pleasant and the unpleasant; its concepts are: good luck, bad luck, fate."³⁶ The second stage of weak despair is the despair over the eternal or over oneself.³⁷ In a sense, despair deepens, but in another sense, one gets closer to salvation:

> Ultimately, this is still a step forward, although in another sense, simply because this despair is more intensive, it is in a certain sense closer to salvation. It is difficult to forget such despair – it is too deep; but every minute that despair is kept open, there is the possibility of salvation as well.³⁸

Since one is conscious of the eternity within or the self, this despair is qualitatively deep; at the same time, the possibility of salvation is kept open.

Instead of moving on to salvation, Anti-Climacus then addresses a more intense form of despair, where one wills to be oneself by despairing. Anti-Climacus calls this despair defiance.³⁹ What does this despair look like? "No, in hatred toward existence, [the self] wills to be itself, wills to be itself in accordance with its misery."⁴⁰ Anti-Climacus vividly describes this defiantly-despairing person as follows:

> Figuratively speaking, it is as if an error slipped into an author's writing and the error became conscious of itself as an error – perhaps it actually was not a mistake but in a much higher sense an essential part of the whole production – and now this error wants to mutiny against the author, out of hatred toward him, forbidding him to correct it and in maniacal defiance saying to him: No, I refuse to be erased; I will stand as a witness against you, a witness that you are a second-rate author.⁴¹

---

particular).*" SKS* 11, 174–5/ *SUD*, 60
35. *SKS* 11, 165/ *SUD*, 50.
36. *SKS* 11, 166/ *SUD*, 51.
37. *SKS* 11, 175/ *SUD*, 60.
38. *SKS* 11, 177/ *SUD*, 62.
39. *SKS* 11, 181/ *SUD*, 67.
40. *SKS* 11, 187/ *SUD*, 73.
41. *SKS* 11, 187/ *SUD*, 74.

The "author" in the above quotation signifies God and the "error" that becames "conscious of itself as an error" signifies a defiantly-despairing person. Despair as defiance is a person's absolute rejection of both divine assistance and self-transformation.[42]

"Part Two: Despair Is Sin"

In "Part Two," Anti-Climacus defines despair as sin: "Sin is: *before God, or with the conception of God, in despair not to will to be oneself, or in despair to will to be oneself.*"[43] According to Anti-Climacus, sin is always sin *before God*:

> The point that must be observed is that the self has a conception of God and yet does not will as he wills, and thus is disobedient. Nor does one only occasionally sin before God, for every sin is before God, or, more correctly, what really makes human guilt into sin is that the guilty one has the consciousness of existing before God.[44]

Anti-Climacus develops an interesting argument about the opposite of sin. According to Anti-Climacus, the opposite of sin is not virtue but faith.[45]

Sin is always sin before God. Sin can be forgiven only by God's grace through faith. Accordingly, faith is the only means through which one can attain forgiveness. However, where faith is required, the possibility of offence is unavoidable. Anti-Climacus passionately describes Christ's incarnation:

> For this very person's sake, God comes to the world, allows himself to be born, to suffer, to die, and this suffering God – he almost implores and beseeches this person to accept the help that is offered to him! Truly, if there is anything to lose one's mind over, this is it![46]

---

42. Regarding despair as defiance, one may recall some fascinating Dostoevskian figures such as Nikolai Vsevolodovich Stavrogin from *Demons* and Ivan Karamazov from *The Brothers Karamazov*.
43. *SKS* 11, 191/ *SUD*, 77, emphasis in original.
44. *SKS* 11, 194/ *SUD*, 80.
45. *SKS* 11, 196/ *SUD*, 82.
46. *SKS* 11, 198–199/ *SUD*, 85.

Anti-Climacus offers the reader a fresh look at the incarnation of Christ, which had been taken for granted by nominal Christians in Kierkegaard's time.

To craft a Christian definition of sin, Anti-Climacus begins with the Socratic definition of sin: "Sin is ignorance. This, as is well known, is the Socratic definition."[47] However, Anti-Climacus promptly refutes the Socratic definition: "Socrates does not actually arrive at the category of sin."[48] In what sense is the Socratic definition of sin unsatisfactory? "Socrates actually gives no explanation at all of the distinction: not *being able* to understand and not *willing* to understand."[49] If sin were *ignorance*, as Socrates defines it, *knowledge* would save one. However, the issue is that one who possesses knowledge may not *will* to act according to this knowledge. Anti-Climacus says, "That is why Christianity begins in another way: man has to learn what sin is by a revelation from God; sin is not a matter of a person's not having understood what is right but of his being unwilling to understand it, of his not willing what is right."[50] In contrast to the Socratic definition, Anti-Climacus defines sin in a rigorously Christian fashion: "Sin has its roots in willing, not in knowing, and this corruption of willing affects the individual's consciousness."[51] A definition of sin as a sickness of the *will* inevitably means that "sin is not a negation but a position."[52] Sin is not "merely negative – weakness, sensuousness, finitude, ignorance, etc."[53] Whenever one sins, one *wills* to sin.

In "B: The Continuance of Sin," Anti-Climacus asserts, "Every state of sin is a new sin, or, to express it more precisely, as will be done in this next section, the state of sin is the new sin, is the sin."[54] In the usual sense, to despair over one's sin seems ethical since this should lead to the avoidance of sin – that is, ethical behaviour. However, Anti-Climacus insists that despair over one's sin *is* sin: "Sin is despair; the intensification is the new sin of despairing over one's sin."[55] Anti-Climacus explains the difference between sin and despair

---

47. *SKS* 11, 201/ *SUD*, 87.
48. *SKS* 11, 202/ *SUD*, 89.
49. *SKS* 11, 207/ *SUD*, 95, emphasis in original.
50. *SKS* 11, 207/ *SUD*, 95. Compare Romans 7:15–20.
51. *SKS* 11, 208/ *SUD*, 95.
52. *SKS* 11, 209/ *SUD*, 96.
53. *SKS* 11, 209/ *SUD*, 96.
54. *SKS* 11, 217/ *SUD*, 105.
55. *SKS* 11, 221/ *SUD*, 109.

over sin: "Sin itself is severance from the good, but despair over sin is the second severance."[56] While it is sin to turn away from what is good, despair over one's sin causes one to lose the opportunity to turn to what is good. Therefore, despair over sin is further away from what is good. Anti-Climacus adds, "To describe the intensification in the relation between sin and despair over sin, the first may be termed the break with the good and the second with repentance."[57] If one truly understands that despair over sin is a more intensified form of sin, "he may not say: I can never forgive myself (as if he had previously forgiven himself sins – a blasphemy)."[58] As far as Anti-Climacus is concerned, when God forgives sin, it is blasphemous not to humbly accept God's offer of forgiveness.[59]

Next, Anti-Climacus discusses "the sin of despairing of the forgiveness of sins."[60] This is a sin that is more intensified than despair over sin because this sin is "that after God has taken this step it should be taken in vain."[61] To forgive one's sin, God became a human being, suffered, and died on the cross.[62] Despair over one's forgiveness is to treat all God's deeds out of love as *nothing*. Therefore, Anti-Climacus names this despair "the most dreadful of all blasphemies."[63] Anti-Climacus finally comes to "the sin of dismissing Christianity *modo ponendo* (positively), of declaring it to be untruth."[64] According to Anti-Climacus, this is the most intensified sin: "This is sin against the Holy Spirit. Here the self is at the highest intensity of despair; it not only discards Christianity totally but also makes it out to be a lie and untruth."[65] Needless to say, Anti-Climacus talks about "sin against the Holy Spirit" not to condemn the reader but to eventually guide them to Christianity. Therefore,

---

56. *SKS* 11, 221/ *SUD*, 109.
57. *SKS* 11, 221/ *SUD*, 109.
58. *SKS* 11, 224/ *SUD*, 112.
59. Compare the following: 1 Corinthians 4:3; "It is the error of believing that the self can itself decide what sin is and decide the extent of the *possible* reach of forgiveness." Podmore, *Kierkegaard and the Self*, 167.
60. *SKS* 11, 225/ *SUD*, 113.
61. *SKS* 11, 229/ *SUD*, 117.
62. See Philippians 2:6–8.
63. *SKS* 11, 229/ *SUD*, 117.
64. *SKS* 11, 236/ *SUD*, 125.
65. *SKS* 11, 236/ *SUD*, 125. See also Matthew 12:32.

Anti-Climacus praises God's love and refers to the possibility of offense, which causes God to grieve.[66]

Although the offence is "greater ever than sin," Anti-Climacus does not engage in speculative theology or apologetics that attempt to remove the possibility of offence by rationally expounding on Christianity. Instead, he leaves the decision up to the reader by offering the biblical either/or of faith and offence.

Anti-Climacus concludes *The Sickness unto Death* with a contemplation of the despair-free state referred to elsewhere in this work: "The formula for the state in which there is no despair at all: in relating itself to itself and in willing to be itself, the self rests transparently in the power that established it. This formula in turn, as has been frequently pointed out, is the definition of faith."[67] In Anti-Climacus's schema, despair and faith are absolute opposites. Therefore, where faith is present, there is no despair.

---

66. *SKS* 11, 237/ *SUD*, 126.
67. *SKS* 11, 242/ *SUD*, 131. Compare *SKS* 11, 130/ *SUD*, 14.

APPENDIX 7

Reading *Practice in Christianity*

Motto

The motto on the title page of *Practice in Christianity* says, "Away, away, O unhallowed ones,"[1] as if warning the reader and hinting at the offensive nature of this work.[2]

"Editor's Preface"

Practice in Christianity comprises three parts, each containing a distinct type of literature: "No. I," "No. II," and "No. III."[3] An "Editor's Preface," written by Kierkegaard, which appears at the beginning of each part, says,

> In this book, originating in the year 1848, the requirement for being a Christian is forced up by the pseudonymous author to a supreme ideality.

---

1. *SKS* 12, 13/ *PC*, 5, originally written in Latin, translated by the Hongs. This phrase appears again in "The Halt" in *SKS* 12, 37/ *PC*, 23.

2. According to Kierkegaard, J. P. Mynster (1775–1854), the renowned bishop with whom the Kierkegaard family was personally associated, read *Practice in Christianity* and said, "The book has made me very indignant; it is playing a profane game with holy things." *JP*, VI 6691/ *Pap*. X3 A 563 *n.d.*, 1850; *PC*, supplement, 356–358. For an account of the relationship between Kierkegaard and Mynster with regard to the publication of *Practice in Christianity*, see Christian Fink Tolstrup, "'Playing a Profane Game with Holy Things': Understanding Kierkegaard's Critical Encounter with Bishop Mynster" in *IKC 20*: Practice in Christianity. 2004: 245–274.

3. "*Practice in Christianity* consists of three parts which Kierkegaard had worked on separately and in the beginning regarded as three different works, as is clearly indicated in the . . . journal." Malantschuk, *Kierkegaard's Thought*, 347.

> Yet the requirement should indeed be stated, presented, and heard. From the Christian point of view, there ought to be no scaling down of the requirement, nor suppression of it instead of a personal admission and confession.
>
> The requirement should be heard – and I understand what is said as spoken to me alone – so that I might learn not only to resort to grace but to resort to it in relation to the use of grace.
>
> S. K.[4]

According to Kierkegaard in his role as editor, Anti-Climacus – the pseudonymous author of *Practice in Christianity* – holds up as the supreme ideal the requirement to be a Christian. Such a requirement must be declared without any compromise. Kierkegaard, who claims to be the editor, expresses his willingness to be the sole recipient of this demand. Considering this requirement enables a reader to recognize how far they fall short of it, prompting personal admission and confession. Kierkegaard believed that this was the way to humbly resort to grace instead of abusing it.

"No. I: 'Come Here, All You Who Labor and Are Burdened, and I Will Give You Rest' – For Awakening and Inward Deepening"

"No. I," the first book of *Practice in Christianity*, consists of "Invocation," "The Invitation," "The Halt," and "The Moral." "Invocation" is a concise summary that outlines the entire theme of *Practice in Christianity*. For Anti-Climacus, being a true Christian means believing in Christ or becoming contemporary with Christ.[5] The latter half of "Invocation" is a prayer that says, "Lord Jesus Christ, would that we, too, might become contemporary with you in this way, might see you in your true form and in the surroundings of actuality as you walked here on earth."[6] Although this is a prayer, Anti-Climacus uses it to sharply and humorously criticize Christendom, accusing it of twisting and

---

4. *SKS* 12, 15; 85; 153/ *PC*, 7; 73; 149, emphasis in original.
5. *SKS* 12, 30/ *PC*, 19.
6. *SKS* 12, 17/ *PC*, 9.

distorting the image of Christ.[7] He concludes this prayer by saying, "Again and again in concern you had to repeat, 'Blessed is the one who is not offended at me.' Would that we might see you in this way and that we then might not be offended at you!"[8] While *Practice in Christianity* carefully describes Christ in his true form, it also delves deeply into the concept of offence, which is indispensable if one is to have a truly biblical understanding of Christ.

"The Invitation" takes the form of a heartfelt sermon that elaborates on Matthew 11:28: "Come here, all you who labor and are burdened, and I will give you rest."[9] Like a variation in a musical composition, Anti-Climacus develops this theme through repeating Christ's invitation but with a slight alteration in the form of the invitation with each repetition. According to Anti-Climacus, Jesus's invitation is unique. He beckons as if he is the one who desperately needs help. Moreover, he does not discriminate against anybody and freely offers help. Therefore, Anti-Climacus movingly says, "These words, which seem to have been designed for him from the beginning of the world, he does in fact say: Come here, all you."[10] Ultimately, Anti-Climacus points to the identity and nature of Christ in the invitation that he offers: "Come here to me, all you who labor and are burdened. This he says, and those who lived with him saw and see that there truly is not the slightest thing in his way of life that contradicts it."[11] Anti-Climacus further analyzes Christ's invitation and concludes, "'I will give you rest.' – Amazing! Then those words 'Come here to me' presumably must be understood in this way: Remain with me, I am that rest, or to remain with me is that rest."[12] Anti-Climacus marvels at this because although a helper is not usually identical with the help itself, in the case of Jesus, the helper *is* the help.[13] For Anti-Climacus, this message holds special significance for the socially marginalized.

---

7. For instance, Anti-Climacus humorously criticizes a so-called quest for the historical Jesus that is in the initial stage (at his time) and says that "a historical-talkative remembrance has distorted [Christ]." SKS 12, 17/ PC, 9. For a fine study of Kierkegaard's discernment of the quest of historical Jesus, see Murray A. Rae, "The Forgetfulness of Historical-Talkative Remembrance in Kierkegaard's *Practice in Christianity*" in *IKC 20*: Practice in Christianity. 2004: 69–94.

8. *SKS* 12, 18/ *PC*, 10.
9. *SKS* 12, 21/ *PC*, 11.
10. *SKS* 12, 23/ *PC*, 13.
11. *SKS* 12, 24/ *PC*, 14.
12. *SKS* 12, 25/ *PC*, 15.
13. *SKS* 12, 25/ *PC*, 15.

> Come here also you, "you whose residence has been assigned among the graves," you who in the eyes of society are regarded as dead but are not missed, are not lamented – not buried, yet dead – that is, belonging neither to life nor to death; you to whom human society cruelly locked its doors and for whom no grave has yet mercifully opened; you, too, come here, here is rest, and here is life![14]

Anti-Climacus is concerned that there may be someone who does not have the strength to stand and walk towards Christ. To such a person, Anti-Climacus says that "a sigh is enough" because "that you sigh for him is also to come here."[15]

"The Invitation" reads like an evangelistic call; but the atmosphere suddenly changes with "The Halt." While "The Invitation" portrays Christ as a gentle Saviour, "The Halt" shows that there are people who come to Christ but later abandon him.[16] Why do they abandon Christ? It is because they realize the cost of discipleship, which requires imitating the abased Christ. In "The Halt," Anti-Climacus focuses on *the inviter*. According to Anti-Climacus, people assume that they know who Christ is; but in reality, they do not. Christendom may take it for granted that the God-man must be glorified even on earth. But Anti-Climacus emphasizes that Christ lived in lowliness on earth. In other words, Christ's divine nature was incognito, as a result of which many of his contemporaries were offended. For Anti-Climacus, Christ was and is the sign of offence. He helps the reader to imagine how offensive it would have been for Christ's contemporaries to hear the words of Matthew 11:28 coming from the mouth of the abased Christ: "It is the abased Jesus Christ who is speaking. It is historically true that *he* said these words."[17] Anti-Climacus seems to suggest that Christendom mistakenly puts Matthew 11:28 in the mouth of a fanciful or fictional Christ, rather than the poor and beaten Christ of history. Therefore, Anti-Climacus attempts to put Matthew 11:28 back into the mouth of the historical Jesus Christ.

---

14. *SKS* 12, 29/ *PC*, 18.
15. *SKS* 12, 33/ *PC*, 22.
16. *SKS* 12, 37/ *PC*, 23.
17. *SKS* 12, 51/ *PC*, 37.

Anti-Climacus's message about the lowliness of Christ and the requirements for being his disciple leads his readers to the conclusion that they must become like Christ; in a sense, becoming his contemporaries – humble, poor, and abused. Anti-Climacus says, "In relation to the absolute, there is only one time, the present; for the person who is not contemporary with the absolute, it does not exist at all."[18] By being contemporary with Christ, one can personally encounter him: "The qualification that is lacking – which is the qualification of truth (as inwardness) and of all religiousness is – **For you.**"[19] Anti-Climacus helps the reader to be essentially Christian by urging them to personally encounter Christ.[20] From Anti-Climacus's perspective, Christ had lived on earth one thousand eight hundred years before. In a sense, lifestyles had become more convenient during that time period. However,

> what God understands by human misery, which in both cases is altogether different from what people understand thereby and is something everyone in every generation to the end of time must learn for himself from the beginning, beginning at exactly the same point as every contemporary with Christ and practicing it in the situation of contemporaneity.[21]

If Anti-Climacus is right, the practice in Christianity would undergo the same process regardless of the era in which one lives. There is neither an advantage nor a disadvantage to living in a particular era, and regardless of the time period, a person must start from scratch to be contemporary with Christ. As far as Anti-Climacus is concerned, the practice in Christianity, as he understood it, which was effective one thousand eight hundred years ago, is equally effective in his own era and will continue to be effective until the end of time.

In "The Moral," which is short and placed at the end of "No. I," Anti-Climacus explains how the presentation of this requirement works:

> "And what does all this mean?" It means that each individual in quiet inwardness before God is to humble himself under what

---

18. *SKS* 12, 75/ *PC*, 63.
19. *SKS* 12, 76/ *PC*, 64, emphasis in original.
20. *SKS* 12, 77/ *PC*, 65.
21. *SKS* 12, 77/ *PC*, 65–66.

it means in the strictest sense to be a Christian, is to confess honestly before God where he is so that he still might worthily accept the grace that is offered to every imperfect person – that is, to everyone.[22]

Following the steps of the abased Christ, who is the supreme ideal, is a requirement for being a Christian. Through this uncompromising requirement, Anti-Climacus expects his readers to recognize and confess their own imperfections. The requirement needs to be heard so that one might *humbly* resort to the grace that is freely given to every imperfect person through their faith in Christ. Upon this humble admission, one can earnestly strive for ideality by imitating Christ. In this way, presenting the highest requirement effectively helps one to believe in and suffer for Christ, thereby helping a person to be a true Christian.

"No. II: 'Blessed Is He Who Is Not Offended at Me' – A Biblical Exposition and Christian Definition"

"No. II," the second book of *Practice in Christianity*, consists primarily of "The Exposition" and "The Categories of Offence, That Is, of Essential Offense."[23] As the title indicates, this book attempts to define the concept of taking offence at Christ from a biblical perspective. In "The Exposition," Anti-Climacus deals with three kinds of offence. The first type of offence is not essential; it existed only while Christ was on earth one thousand eight hundred years ago (from Anti-Climacus's perspective). Christ as the single individual was destined to collide with the established order. Anti-Climacus refers to Matthew 15:1–12, where "the Pharisees *were offended*"[24] because Christ criticized their facade of piety and urged true and inward piety. Anti-Climacus, comparing Hegel and the Pharisees, says that "[Hegel] deified the established order"[25] and

---

22. *SKS* 12, 79/ *PC*, 67.

23. "No. II" also contains an "Editor's Preface," "Exordium," and "A Brief Summary of the Contents of This Exposition," which are relatively shorter than the other main sections. For more on the "Editor's Preface," see "Editor's Preface" in appendix 7. The "Exordium" and "A Brief Summary of the Contents of This Exposition" are not addressed in this study due to limited space.

24. *SKS* 12, 95/ *PC*, 86, originally from Matthew 15:12, emphasis is Anti-Climacus's.

25. *SKS* 12, 96/ *PC*, 87. According to Robert L. Perkins, Hegel's *The Philosophy of History* that Kierkegaard had in hand contains the following sentence: "In the Protestant world there is

that the Pharisees did the same. Anti-Climacus rejects the idea that God's will is revealed in the established order. Instead, he says that God "uses the single individual to prod the established order out of self-complacency."[26] Anti-Climacus asserts that "[the] deification of the established order is the secularization of everything."[27] In such a situation, what is the role of the single individual? The single individual "in unconditional obedience and with unconditional obedience, by being persecuted, by suffering, by dying, keeps the established order in suspense."[28] While this description of the single individual certainly aligns with the portrait of the earthly Christ, it is not his *unique* role as *the God-man*. Christ is more than just a martyr – he is the Redeemer. Accordingly, Anti-Climacus concludes that this first type of offence does not yet touch the essential nature of Christ.

The second offence, which is essential, is being offended by Christ's divine actions. One must face the possibility of this offence in order to have authentic faith in Jesus Christ. Anti-Climacus refers to Matthew 11:3–6, where John the Baptist asks, "Are you the one who is to come?" and Christ answers, "The blind see and the lame walk, the lepers are cleansed and the deaf hear, the dead are raised up, and the good news is preached to the poor, ... and blessed is he who is not *offended* at me."[29] Why does Christ answer in this indirect manner? Why does warn his hearers not to be offended? According to Anti-Climacus, the assumption that Christ's divinity was immediately obvious is *a delusion of Christendom*.[30] When Christendom takes it for granted that Christ was viewed as God in everyone's eyes, the possibility of offence is removed: "[In] order to become a believer he must have passed by the possibility of offense."[31] Anti-Climacus single-mindedly attempts to help the reader become a contemporary with Christ:

---

no sacred, no religious conscience in a state of separation from, or perhaps even in hostility to, Secular Right." Originally from Hegel, *Philosophy of History*, 456, quoted by Robert L. Perkins, 'Kierkegaard's Anti-Climacus in His Social and Political Environment' in *IKC 20: Practice in Christianity*. 2004, 281.

26. *SKS* 12, 98/ *PC*, 90.
27. *SKS* 12, 99/ *PC*, 91.
28. *SKS* 12, 99/ *PC*, 91.
29. *SKS* 12, 103/ *PC*, 94, originally from Matthew 11:5–6, emphasis is Anti-Climacus's.
30. *SKS* 12, 103/ *PC*, 95.
31. *SKS* 12, 107/ *PC*, 99.

But, again to repeat, if one has only a fantastic figure of Christ, one perhaps finds it quite in order for him to forgive sins without one's being aware of the possibility of offense. But in actuality, in truth, that is, in the situation of contemporaneity, that an individual human being like everybody else, that he wants to forgive sins! There is only one way to avoid offense, by having faith.[32]

One can see Anti-Climacus's emphasis on the God-man. If one had lived at the same time as Christ, one would have encountered a situation where someone who seemed to be merely a man was acting as God.[33] The only way to overcome this offence is to believe in him. The second offence is essential because it relates to Christ's dual nature as both God and man. One faces the possibility of offence because the carpenter's son acts as God and, even though indirectly, declares himself as God.

The third offence, which is also essential, involves being offended because Christ, who claims to be God, lives in lowliness and dies in weakness. As with the second offence, one has to pass through the possibility of this offence to truly believe. Anti-Climacus refers to Matthew 13:55–57 (or Mark 6:2–3): "'Is this not the carpenter's son? Is his mother not called Mary? And his brothers James and Joseph and Simon and Judas? And are all his sisters not with us? Whence, then, did that man get all this?' And they *were offended* at him."[34] One can understand the confusion of his contemporaries, who only see Christ the man. According to Anti-Climacus, Christ agonized when people were offended: "'This night you will all *be offended* at me.' . . . Ah, what infinite pain, a pain that no human being can comprehend. . . . alas, his suffering, alas, his most oppressive suffering, which is precisely this, that all are going to be offended at him."[35] Christ came to this world to save all those who believe in him (John 3:16). Therefore, the fact that one of his beloved ones is offended is his most oppressive agony: "Ah, abysmal suffering, unfathomable to human

---

32. *SKS* 12, 109/ *PC*, 101.

33. For example, see Mark 2:1–12.

34. *SKS* 12, 111/ *PC*, 103, originally from Matthew 13:55 (or Mark 6:3), emphasis is Anti-Climacus's.

35. *SKS* 12, 112–113/ *PC*, 104, emphasis is Anti-Climacus's; Christ's words within single quotation marks is originally from Matthew 26:31 or Mark 14:27 in the Danish translation. English translations vary: "shall be offended" (KJV, ASV), "will be made to stumble" (NKJV), "will all fall away" (NASB, NIV, RSV), or "will all become deserters" (NRSV).

understanding – to have to be the sign of offense in order to be the object of faith!"[36] The third offence is essential because it relates to the *lowliness* of Christ, who is the God-man. The possibility of offence arises because this God-man comes in weakness: "But the possibility of offense is precisely the repulsion in which faith can come into existence if one does not choose to be offended."[37] As far as Anti-Climacus is concerned, the possibility of offence dialectically helps one to have genuine faith.

"The Categories of Offense, That Is, of Essential Offense" is the most perplexing section in *Practice in Christianity*. At the beginning of this section, Anti-Climacus sheds light on the possibility of offence from the perspective of church history. For Anti-Climacus, the problem in (his) modern age is that the possibility of offence has been removed: "In the entire modern age, which so unmistakably bears the mark that it does not even know what the issue is, the confusion is something different and far more dangerous."[38] Anti-Climacus reflects on the history of the early church *in terms of offence at the God-man*. Surprisingly, he diagnoses that his contemporaries – namely, the Christendom of Denmark – face a crisis that is far more dangerous than that caused by notorious heretics such as the Ebionites[39] or the Gnostics.[40] On the one hand, the Ebionites and the Gnostics – despite being heretics – were somehow *appropriately offended* by Christ the God-man. What about the Christendom of Denmark? "[We] take Christ's teaching – and abolish Christ. This is to abolish Christianity."[41] According to Anti-Climacus, the early church heresies *somehow contributed to the truth* because they were offended by the God-man or, to put it differently, were offended by the essential nature of Christ. The modern church, however, focuses on Christ's teaching but forgets that Christ is the God-man. In Anti-Climacus's view, to forget Christ's dual nature as both God and man is to abolish Christianity.

---

36. *SKS* 12, 113/ *PC*, 105.
37. *SKS* 12, 127/ *PC*, 121.
38. *SKS* 12, 128/ *PC*, 123.

39. Anti-Climacus defines Ebionitism as a doctrine where, "with respect to the God-man . . . , the term 'God' was taken away" (*SKS* 12, 128/ *PC*, 123). Essentially, Ebionitism denies the divinity of Christ.

40. Similarly, Anti-Climacus defines Gnosticism as a doctrine where, "with respect to the God-man . . . , the term 'man' was taken away" (*SKS* 12, 128/ *PC*, 123). In essence, Gnosticism denies the humanity of Christ.

41. *SKS* 12, 128/ *PC*, 123–124.

Anti-Climacus takes further steps to scrutinize the categories of offence. According to his analysis, there are seven such categories. First, "the God-man is a *sign*."[42] According to Anti-Climacus, Christ draws attention to himself; and once attention is directed to him, he reveals his nature, which contains a contradiction[43] – namely, the infinite qualitative distinction between God and humanity that is evident when Christ presents himself as the *God-man*, thereby revealing *a contradiction*. But it is easy for people to lose sight of this contradiction. Because of Christ's miracles and his claims to be God, Anti-Climacus's contemporaries easily forget that Christ is the God-man and a sign of contradiction.[44]

Second, "the form of a servant is unrecognizability (the incognito)."[45] Anti-Climacus gives a simple definition of "unrecognizability" : "Unrecognizability is not to be in the character of what one essentially is – for example, when a policeman is in plain clothes."[46] The God-man, who has two qualitatively different natures within him, is profoundly incognito. Christ is hidden from human eyes so that only the eyes of faith can recognize him. If he had simply revealed himself as God, there would have been no self-denial. According to Anti-Climacus, Christ is perfectly incognito because he completely denies himself. Anti-Climacus also claims that Christ is *almightily in incognito*, meaning that his divinity is not just perfectly hidden but also "[he] is not, therefore, at any moment beyond suffering but is actually in suffering."[47] For Anti-Climacus, Christ is not a superman who never feels pain. Rather, Christ experiences pain like everyone else does because he almightily humbles himself and perfectly becomes a human being.

The third category of offence is the "impossibility of direct communication."[48] Since the God-man appears to be a man, he cannot directly communicate to disclose his divinity. Anti-Climacus terms this method of Kierkegaardian pseudonymous authorship "indirect communication." According to

---

42. *SKS* 12, 129/ *PC*, 124, emphasis in original.
43. *SKS* 12, 130/ *PC*, 125.
44. *SKS* 12, 130–131/ *PC*, 126.
45. *SKS* 12, 131/ *PC*, 127.
46. *SKS* 12, 131/ *PC*, 127.
47. *SKS* 12, 136/ *PC*, 132.
48. *SKS* 12, 137/ *PC*, 133.

Anti-Climacus, the pseudonym is "a zero, a nonperson,"[49] which means that both the believer and the atheist can find "the most zealous supporter"[50] in the pseudonymous writings. By making their own choice, both the believer and the atheist disclose who they are. This is the function of indirect communication. Anti-Climacus further explains indirect communication through the concept of "reduplication," where the communicator exists through what is communicated. This means that the communicator's essence and actions are intrinsically tied to the message being conveyed. But this does not yet fully meet the requirements of indirect communication.[51] According to Anti-Climacus, the credibility of indirect communication is that the communicator is "a sign, the sign of contradiction" and that "he is unrecognizable."[52] The God-man has this quality. "If someone says directly: I am God; the Father and I are one, this is direct communication."[53] The *content* of the above communication is direct communication. However, *when this statement is made by an ordinary person*, it becomes indirect communication because the communicator is both a sign of contradiction and unrecognizable. Since direct communication is impossible, one either believes in or is offended by Christ.[54] Anti-Climacus's Christ is a kind of mirror that reveals the heart of the hearer: "[The] thoughts of your heart are disclosed as you choose whether you will believe or not."[55]

Fourth, "in Christ the secret of sufferings is the impossibility of direct communication."[56] Christ's sufferings, how he was mocked, scourged, and crucified, have been much and often discussed, especially in earlier times. But in all this, an entirely different kind of suffering seems to be forgotten, the suffering of inwardness, suffering of soul, or what might be called the secret of the sufferings that were inseparable from his life in unrecognizability from the time he appeared until the very last.[57]

---

49. *SKS* 12, 137/ *PC*, 133.
50. *SKS* 12, 137/ *PC*, 133.
51. *SKS* 12, 138/ *PC*, 134.
52. *SKS* 12, 138/ *PC*, 134.
53. *SKS* 12, 138/ *PC*, 134.
54. *SKS* 12, 138/ *PC*, 134.
55. *SKS* 12, 140/ *PC*, 136.
56. *SKS* 12, 140/ *PC*, 136.
57. *SKS* 12, 140/ *PC*, 136–137.

Anti-Climacus argues that Christ suffered not just in the garden of Gethsemane and on the cross but that his whole life was a suffering of the soul. The fact that Christ is an object of faith means that one might be offended unless they believe in him. This is unbearable agony for Christ because he suffers more over the sad destiny of his beloved ones (that is, each individual) than from his own sufferings. Although Anti-Climacus profoundly describes Christ's suffering in this way, he realizes that his description is inadequate and, in some sense, futile since "[no] human being can comprehend this suffering; to want to comprehend it is presumption."[58] Christ's inward suffering is ultimately unrecognizable and belongs to the realm of the divine mystery.

Fifth, "the possibility of offence is to deny direct communication."[59] The possibility of offence is everywhere since there is an infinite qualitative distance between God and humanity.[60] Direct communication requires that both parties be of the same kind. However, because of the qualitative difference between God and human beings, a leap of faith – which is paired with the possibility of offence – is the only way for a human being to reach the God-man.

Sixth, "to deny direct communication is to require *faith*."[61] In the case of direct communication, one does not need to *believe* because one can simply *know*. However, in the case of indirect communication, one is required to have faith in order to reach the God-man, who is qualitatively different: "But only the God-man cannot do otherwise and, as qualitatively different from man, must insist upon being the object of faith."[62] The impossibility of direct communication means that faith is the only way to know Christ.

Seventh, "the object of faith is the God-man precisely because the God-man is the possibility of offense."[63] Anti-Climacus hammers out the dialectic of faith and offence. The fact that Christ is the object of faith inevitably involves the possibility of offence.[64]

In "No. II," Anti-Climacus emphasizes the pivotal importance of the possibility of offence. True faith is coupled with the possibility of offence; one can

---

58. *SKS* 12, 142/ *PC*, 138.
59. *SKS* 12, 142/ *PC*, 139.
60. *SKS* 12, 142–143/ *PC*, 139.
61. *SKS* 12, 143/ *PC*, 140, emphasis in original.
62. *SKS* 12, 146/ *PC*, 143.
63. *SKS* 12, 146/ *PC*, 143.
64. *SKS* 12, 146/ *PC*, 143.

have faith only by confronting and passing through the possibility of taking offence at the God-man.

"No. III: From on High He Will Draw All to Himself – Christian Expositions"

"No. III," the third book of *Practice in Christianity*, consists of seven discourses or sermons. The first discourse was, in fact, delivered by Kierkegaard at Von Frue Kirke [Our Lady Church] in 1848.[65] Each discourse begins with a prayer and the citation based on John 12:32: "From on high he will draw all to himself." Like variations on a common musical theme, Anti-Climacus repeats this verse and develops this theme throughout the book.

In "I," Anti-Climacus speaks as a preacher. He presupposes the existence of an audience who cannot forget their worries and suggests to them that they fix their eyes on Jesus. According to Anti-Climacus, by fixing their eyes on Jesus, his readers will be able to forget their worries because Christ draws them powerfully towards himself, completely overcoming the tug which the vanities of daily life exert on them. It seems that a communion service will take place after this discourse, and Anti-Climacus expects that Christ, who is present in this service, will draw the audience to himself.

It is significant that it is not the exalted Christ who promises to draw all to himself from on high but, instead, the abased Christ who makes this promise. Here, once again, we encounter the possibility of offence. If one loves only the exalted Christ, this means that one does not truly love him. Such a person loves the truth only when it is victorious. On the other hand, if one loves only the debased Christ, one does not truly love him either. Such a person loves the truth with "heavy-mindedness [*Tungsind*]."[66] Christ is the same whether he is in lowliness or lifted up. The hearer ought to both love the abased Christ and hope for his coming in glory.

In the one thousand eight hundred years since Christ's first coming, many things had changed. During this time, Christ was not resting on high, but "he is working, is occupied and concerned with drawing all to himself."[67]

---

65. *SKS* 12, 155, asterisk/ *PC*, 151, asterisk.
66. *SKS* 12, 158/ *PC*, 154.
67. *SKS* 12, 159/ *PC*, 155.

Though God's work is invisible, it is real. Without God's work, everything and everyone would fall apart. Likewise, Christ's work cannot be seen, but it is there. Without Christ's continuing work, no one would be able to come to him. In celebration of this ongoing work of Christ, Anti-Climacus offers a prayer-wish for his readers: may "God grant that at the sacred moment you might feel wholly drawn to him, be aware of his presence, the presence of him who is present there."[68] Through these words, Anti-Climacus encourages his hearers not to forget Christ; but he also reassures them that even if they do forget, Christ will not forget about them and will never stop drawing them to himself.

In "II," Anti-Climacus calls the reader's attention to the biblical context of Christ's words in John 12:32:

> But who is the speaker? Is it the uplifted one who is the speaker? By no means, then the words would have to read differently; then they would have to read: "I, who am lifted up, I will draw all to myself." On the contrary, they read: "But I – when I am lifted up." Consequently, the I speaking is not the uplifted one. I, that is, I, the abased one, when I am lifted up, I will draw all to myself. The uplifted one will do it, but the abased one is the one who said that he will do it.[69]

Further, Anti-Climacus emphasizes that from on high, Christ tells us nothing; rather, everything we hear from him was said when he was in lowliness. Anti-Climacus illustrates this using the seemingly modified story of Kierkegaard's father, Michael. A boy is neglected because of his poverty, but he believes that he will become rich and that people will recognize him when this happens. According to Anti-Climacus, it is important that the boy makes this statement while he is still poor. Similarly, one must recognize that Christ makes his statement while he is in lowliness. Anti-Climacus also calls our attention to the difference between the former poor boy and Christ. While the poor boy – presumably Kierkegaard's father as a boy – hopes that his desire expressed in words may prompt God to grant his wish, Christ speaks with the absolute certainty that God would lift him up. Anti-Climacus also

---

68. *SKS* 12, 160/ *PC*, 156.
69. *SKS* 12, 165/ *PC*, 161.

notes that the poor boy might speak in bitterness when he says that people will recognize him when he becomes rich. Christ, however, has no bitterness when he speaks the words of John 12:32 but does so in lowliness because he is love. While the former poor boy may forget his past, Christ, who is eternal, recognizes every moment – right now, as well as every moment of the past one thousand eight hundred years. Accordingly, Christ, who says that from on high he draws all to himself, *is* the abased one. One cannot bypass either the abased Christ or the Christ of glory.

In "III," Anti-Climacus urges the reader not to merely be an observer but to imitate the lowliness of Christ. He warns the reader to refrain even from shedding tears for Christ. Instead, one should *act* in the way that Christ lived on earth. Anti-Climacus gives the illustration of a woman who loves a man who has suffered before meeting her. When she comes to know him, he is already victorious. While he was suffering, she did not yet know him. But if she truly loves him, she will feel guilty about her unawareness of his past agony.

> But as far as Jesus Christ is concerned, certainly no one can say that he first became acquainted with him when he had come on high; for everyone who has learned to know him learns to know him in his lowliness, and if he truly learns to know him, he learns to know him first in his lowliness.[70]

Anti-Climacus attempts to convince the reader that to truly love Christ, one must love the whole Christ, which includes his lowliness.

Anti-Climacus clearly articulates what kind of suffering a disciple of Christ should bear:

> Whether you, namely, or some person has adversities in life, whether things perhaps go downhill for him, or whether he perhaps loses the beloved: this is not called suffering like that of Jesus Christ. Such sufferings are universally human, in which the pagans are tried as much as Christians.[71]

Universal suffering cannot be equated with Christ's suffering. So, what is Christian suffering? "To suffer in a way akin to Christ's suffering is not to put

---

70. *SKS* 12, 175/ *PC*, 172.
71. *SKS* 12, 175/ *PC*, 173.

up patiently with the inescapable, but it is to suffer evil at the hands of people because as a Christian or in being a Christian one wills and endeavors to do the good."[72] When one voluntarily and persistently keeps doing good even if one is persecuted, this suffering is akin to Christ's suffering.[73]

In "IV," Anti-Climacus summarizes the life of Christ as follows:

> Let us look at him and his life; let us speak altogether humanly about it; he was, after all, truly human. He began his life in lowliness, led his life in lowliness and abasement to the very end, then ascended on high – what does this mean? It means that temporality in its entirety was suffering and abasement; not until eternity is there victory, loftiness.[74]

Christ remained in lowliness until the final moment of his life. He ascended on high only *after* completing his abased life on earth. The life of Christ provides a pattern to which the lives of his followers ought to conform. Indeed, conforming to this pattern is the standard by which we ought to evaluate our lives as Christians. Kierkegaard expresses this thought with these words : "[The] greatest examination a human being has to take, to which his whole life is assigned, is to become and to be a Christian."[75] According to Anti-Climacus, becoming and being a Christian is the most difficult task assigned to human beings. One must strive to be a Christian until the final moment of one's life on earth.

It seems that a modified version of Kierkegaard's biography is used as an illustration: "Let us now assume that that youth of whom we have been speaking, who, although not many years have passed, has already become like an old man."[76] Under the pseudonymous mask of Anti-Climacus, Kierkegaard reflects on his own life by comparing it with the life of Christ. His comparison focuses particularly on the moment when Christ felt forsaken on the cross: "[Let] us assume that he, trusting that even if it should happen that God forsook him it would nevertheless be only for a moment."[77] Through this

---

72. *SKS* 12, 175/ *PC*, 173.
73. For example, see 1 Peter 2:19–21.
74. *SKS* 12, 182/ *PC*, 182.
75. *SKS* 12, 183/ *PC*, 183.
76. *SKS* 12, 194/ *PC*, 195.
77. *SKS* 12, 194/ *PC*, 195.

comparison, Anti-Climacus deals with the common Christian experience of God's silence or what might seem like abandonment. In these circumstances, a disciple of Christ should say two things: "in a little while" and "at last."[78] God's abandonment is "for a little while," and eternity will, "at last," be one's reward:

> But to return to our assumption, this young or old man, however long he lived, persevered to the end. When the little while was over, he at last entered (after having passed the test to become and continue to be a Christian) into eternal happiness, ultimately came to him who from on high drew him to himself.[79]

Anti-Climacus seems to invite the reader to envision the conclusion of their own life – a life that, ideally, fulfills the requirement of becoming and remaining a true Christian.

In "V," Anti-Climacus claims that the church should not be triumphant but should struggle in this world. He reminds the reader that Christ is "the way" and "the truth." According to Anti-Climacus, Christ's contemporaries mistakenly view the truth as *the result*, but *the process* should be prioritized since Christ is the way and the truth: "If one wants to maintain this, which is indeed Christ's own statement, that the truth is the way, one will more and more clearly perceive that a Church triumphant in this world is an illusion, that in this world we can truthfully speak only of a militant Church."[80] For Anti-Climacus, a triumphant church attempts to seize in advance what is only given in eternity,[81] and to do so is "to abolish Christianity."[82]

A Christian should be transformed into Christlikeness and obedient to the point of death. Anti-Climacus reinforces this point by saying, "I have never asserted that every Christian is a martyr, or that no one was a true Christian who did not become a martyr."[83] In that case, what is Anti-Climacus's intention? Why does he emphasize being a martyr? He says, "I think that every true Christian should – and here I include myself – in order to be a true Christian, make a humble admission that he has been let off far more easily

---

78. *SKS* 12, 194/ *PC*, 195.
79. *SKS* 12, 194/ *PC*, 196.
80. *SKS* 12, 205/ *PC*, 209.
81. *SKS* 12, 207–208/ *PC*, 211.
82. *SKS* 12, 207/ *PC*, 211.
83. *SKS* 12, 221/ *PC*, 226–227.

than true Christians in the strictest sense."[84] Christians may or may not be slain physically. Martyrdom is not the criterion to judge whether or not one is a true Christian. But all true Christians will strive to meet "Christianity's requirement to die to the world, to surrender the earthly,"[85] and to die to the self. As a result, every true Christian will humbly confess and admit that they fall short of this requirement.

In "VI," Anti-Climacus distinguishes between the admirer of Christ and the imitator of Christ. Christendom is filled with admirers of Christ, but the admirer of Christ abolishes Christianity. According to Anti-Climacus, the true Christian, in the strictest sense, is an imitator of Christ. Anti-Climacus attempts to show how admiration is inappropriate: "Here admiration is totally inappropriate and ordinarily is deceit, a cunning that seeks evasion and excuse. If I know a man whom I must esteem because of his unselfishness, self-sacrifice, magnanimity, etc., then I am not to admire but am supposed to be like him."[86] For Anti-Climacus, to imitate Christ is not a matter of one's gift or ability; it is equally difficult for anyone to overcome themselves. Anti-Climacus shocks the reader by saying, "Who, if he has any knowledge at all of human nature, can doubt that Judas was an admirer of Christ!"[87] Anti-Climacus believes that the admirer is far more dangerous than readers might think. About the admirer in Christendom, Anti-Climacus says, "The admirer really assumes a pagan relation to Christianity, and this is also how admiration, in the middle of Christendom, gave birth to a new paganism – Christian art."[88] The admirer views Christ as if he were an object of art but does not attempt to demonstrate the abased Christ through their way of living. Anti-Climacus concludes section "VI" by saying, "In the strictest sense the admirer is indeed not the true Christian; only the imitator is that."[89]

In "VII," which concludes "No. III," Anti-Climacus says, "How the sacred words just read are to be understood we have shown from various sides, not as if their meaning has thereby become different, no, but we have tried to

---

84. *SKS* 12, 221/ *PC*, 227.
85. *SKS* 12, 244/ *PC*, 252.
86. *SKS* 12, 235/ *PC*, 242.
87. *SKS* 12, 238–239/ *PC*, 246.
88. *SKS* 12, 246/ *PC*, 254.
89. *SKS* 12, 249/ *PC*, 257.

come from various sides to the one and the same meaning of the words."[90] Anti-Climacus's variations on the common musical theme of John 12:32 are now moving toward an epilogue. Anti-Climacus prays for the sake of various people – for instance, the infant, those "who have renewed their covenant with [God],"[91] the lovers, the husband, the wife, the elderly, the happy one, the sufferer, and the one who needs conversion. Finally, Anti-Climacus prays for "servants of the Word" and "lay Christians" to be drawn to Christ *and* to draw others to Christ "as far as a human being is capable of it."[92] Why does he add "as far as a human being is capable of it"? Anti-Climacus explains that this is because Christ is the only one who is capable of drawing all to himself. In his prayer, Anti-Climacus speaks to Christ: "As far as a human being is capable of it – for indeed you are the only one who is capable of drawing to yourself, even if you are able to use everything and everyone to draw all to yourself."[93]

---

90. *SKS* 12, 250/ *PC*, 259.
91. *SKS* 12, 251/ *PC*, 260.
92. *SKS* 12, 252–253/ *PC*, 262.
93. *SKS* 12, 253/ *PC*, 262.

APPENDIX 8

Responses of Individuals to Kierkegaard's Mission

And while his roundabout style was not entirely elusive to his readers, it may well have been better grasped by another generation in another place.[1]

> – Mark C. Miller, "The Hipness unto Death:
> Søren Kierkegaard and David Letterman –
> Ironic Apologists to Generation X"

Kierkegaard was and is an enigma. As Mark C. Miller suggests above, "his roundabout style" must have been elusive to his contemporaries. However, it was "not entirely elusive." If, as this book claims, Kierkegaard was a missionary, there had to be an audience who was able to receive his Christian proclamation. We will examine the testimonies of such contemporaries in the first section. While it is true that Kierkegaard wrote primarily for his contemporary Danes, he also expected that his works would be read outside Denmark after his death.[2] The international reception of Kierkegaard's work proves that he was right about this expectation. In Miller's phrase, Kierkegaard's mission "may well have been better grasped by another generation in another place."

---

1. Miller, "Hipness unto Death," 27.

2. That is, in his *Journals and Notebooks*, Kierkegaard talks about one of his pseudonymous works, *Fear and Trembling*, as follows: "Once I am dead, *Fear and Trembling* alone will be enough for an imperishable name as an author. Then it will be read, translated into foreign languages as well." *SKS* 22, 235, NB12:147/ *JP*, VI 6491 *n.d.*, 1849.

The second section of this appendix considers another generation – the twentieth century – in another place – Japan.

I. Responses of Kierkegaard's Contemporaries

Kierkegaard – who graduated from the Royal Pastoral Seminary in 1841 but remained unordained – preached from the pulpit only six times in his life.[3] The last of these sermons was delivered at Citadel Church on 18 May 1851. Three days later, Kierkegaard received two anonymous letters thanking him for both his works and his sermon. These letters are precious testimonies that shed light on how Kierkegaard's mission was received. This section will examine these letters.

A. A Letter from 'e – e' (an Anonymous Woman), Written on 21 May 1851 to S. Kierkegaard

> Copenhagen
>
> May 21, 1851
>
> e – e
>
> Dear Magister,
>
> ... In the frivolous, or perhaps, as you remark somewhere, the melancholy spirit of the times, I long ignored God and my relation to him, but this was an unhappy state of affairs, as I soon realized. I sought comfort in prayer, but I felt that God would not hear me; I went to church, but my scattered thoughts would not follow those of the preacher; I tried, in the philosophy books that I could understand, to find rest for my lost soul, and I found

---

3. Pia Søltoft describes Kierkegaard's lifetime of preaching experiences as follows: "His first sermon was given as a part of the instruction at the Pastoral Seminary on January 12, 1841 in Holmens Church. His *Demis-prædiken* [the graduation test in the art of preaching] from the Pastoral Seminary was given on February 24, 1844 in Trinitatis Church. On Friday, June 18, 1847 he preached at the communion in Our Lady's Church and did so again on Friday, August 27 of the same year, in the same church. Once again, on September 1, 1848, Kierkegaard preached at the communion on Friday in Our Lady's Church, while his activity as public preacher was completed with a sermon on May 18, 1851 in the Citadel's Church. Moreover, he published this sermon during his final, most violent attack on the Danish Church, under the title *The Changelessness of God*, on September 3, 1855." Søltoft, "Power of Eloquence," 247, footnote 3.

some. I had read *Either/Or* with profound admiration, and I tried to obtain some of your works by borrowing since I could not afford to buy them. I received the *Christian Discourses* of 1848, which were not what I had wanted, but I read them – and how can I ever thank you enough? In them I found the source of life that has not failed me since. When I was troubled, I sought refuge there and found comfort; when need or chance brought me to church and I walked away downcast, conscious of one more sin for having been in the House of the Lord without reverence and humility, then I would read your discourses and find comfort. In everything that happened to me, in sorrow or in joy, this small portion of the riches you have bequeathed to the world became the constant source from which I drew comfort and sustenance.

Last Sunday you were listed as the preacher in the Citadel. What could I do but walk out there, and I was not disappointed. This was not one of those sermons I have heard so often and forgotten before it was concluded. No, from the rich, warm heart the speech poured forth, terrifying, yet upbuilding and soothing at the same time; it penetrated the heart so as never to be forgotten but to bear the eternal fruits of blessing in rich measure. . . . I have heard that you often preach in various churches. . . . If I were a man I would apply to you directly . . . But I am a woman and dare only approach you under an assumed name. . . .[4]

A lady who called herself "e – e" had a problem similar to Kierkegaard's. She felt melancholy and distant from God. She sought God through prayer and by listening to sermons, but her efforts seemed in vain. However, she found some hope in Kierkegaard's pseudonymous work *Either/Or*. Thereafter, she obtained Kierkegaard's signed-religious work *Christian Discourses*. Here, she "found the source of life that has not failed [her] since." When she heard that Kierkegaard would be preaching at Citadel Church, she attended the service expectantly. For her, that sermon bore "the eternal fruits of blessing in rich measure."

---

4. *SKS* 28, 475–476/ *LD*, 379–380.

First, for "e – e," the pseudonymous work *Either/Or* seemed to work as a seduction to the truth rather than merely aesthetic enjoyment. Second, the signed-religious work *Christian Discourses* helped her to continually establish a close relationship with God. Third, Kierkegaard's sermon – which would be published as a signed-religious work under the title *God's Unchangeability: A Discourse* four years later – also edified her. In summary, Kierkegaard effectively proclaimed Christianity to one of his contemporaries through his works and this sermon.

B. A Letter from S.F. (an Anonymous Woman), 21 May 1851 to S. Kierkegaard

On the same day that he received a letter from "e – e" (an anonymous woman), Kierkegaard also received a letter from S.F. (another anonymous woman). Below is an excerpt from this letter:

> May 21, 1851
>
> [. . .] I know very well . . . that what you proclaim is not really a new discovery you have made but something that has endured as have eternal truths since – since eternity, of course. But in spite of this, inasmuch as nobody has proclaimed those truths to *me* before you did so in such a way that I could hear them, with the ears of my soul to that they dwelt with me and became my eternal possessions, then surely I am entitled to feel grateful to you who inspire and enrich my thought! [. . .]
>
> From the very outset when you began to publish your pseudonymous works, I mean, from the time when you began that work of love of sharing your divine inspiration with mankind, *I* have pricked up my ears and listened lest I should miss any sound, of these magnificent harmonies, for everything resounded in my heart. [. . .] And then this enchanting irony that renders you so indescribably superior and has an almost intoxicating effect on me – oh, please do not become angry at my speaking my mind, but it is really remarkable how talented you are – that is *the* marvel! For I doubt that there is a single string in the human heart that you do not know how to pluck,

any recess that you have not penetrated. I thought I knew what it means to laugh, before 1843 as well, but no, it was not until I read *Either/Or* that I had any idea what it meant to laugh from the depths of my heart; and it is with my heart that I have come to an overall understanding of everything you have said. Many a time I have been almost embarrassed to hear clever people say that they did not understand S. Kierkegaard, for I always thought I understood him; I had to make myself appear stupider than I was so as not so appear conceited. I am never lonely, even when I am by myself for long periods of time, provided only that I have the company of these books, for they are, of all books, those the most closely resemble the company of a living person. But please do not think that these books have only taught me to laugh; oh no, please believe that again and again I have been roused by them to see myself more clearly and to understand my duty, to feel myself ever more closely tied to "the truth, the way, and the life"; I have become infinitely liberated just by musing on them. . . .

Please believe as well that I have been struck with terror by those supreme demands of the ideal which you know how to throw into such sharp relief – and my distance from them!, . . . but I swear to you that I never sleep off awareness of my sins, thanks to that "gadfly of the times" who has understood so thoroughly how to awaken it. But it is no easy task to remake one's whole congenital nature – as I hope you will concede – indeed, it would be impossible without grace and if God did not grant growth where we but sow and plant.

. . . You! you who constantly desire to be considered someone who is absent – but one can still write occasionally to someone who is absent. . . . it is merely to the author of your works and to the man who delivered your sermon last Sunday in the Citadel, for when all is said and done, it is he who made the cup run over for me. If you would preach more often, but please, always with your name posted, for you cannot know how many souls you may save from perdition by so doing. It is your clear duty. For me that day was a festival day of upbuilding, and I think many came to feel as I did. . . .

One of your most devoted female readers,

– S.F.[5]

S.F. was well aware of Kierkegaard's genius and recognized that what he proclaimed was not a new discovery but eternal truths. However, she felt that nobody had proclaimed these truths to *her* until she read Kierkegaard's works. She had been attentive to Kierkegaard from his first publication and viewed his authorship as a "work of love of sharing [his] divine inspiration with mankind." Unlike "clever people" who said that they did not understand Kierkegaard, she had always felt that she understood him. She was not only entertained by *Either/Or* but felt "ever more closely tied to 'the truth, the way, and the life.'"[6] In addition, she was not just comforted but also "struck with terror by those supreme demands of the ideal." She confessed, "Indeed, it would be impossible without grace and if God did not grant growth where we but sow and plant." When she heard Kierkegaard's sermon at Citadel Church, she urgently requested that he preach more often and told him, "For you cannot know how many souls you may save from perdition by so doing."

First, S.F. regarded Kierkegaard's thought not as a proclamation of a new discovery but as a declaration of eternal truths. She also felt that Kierkegaard's works personally proclaimed those eternal truths to her. Second, like "e – e," S.F. also regarded Kierkegaard's works – including the pseudonymous work *Either/Or* – as being not merely for entertainment but also for upbuilding. Third, she believed that Kierkegaard's sermon – which later became a signed-religious work – could edify many. In summary, both "e – e" and S.F. testify that Kierkegaard successfully proclaimed Christianity to some of his contemporaries in an extraordinary way.

C. Implications of These Two Anonymous Letters

W. Glenn Kirkconnell asks, "But his original readers had no access to his journals; and they knew nothing of the books which were to come later, whether from his pen or others. How would Kierkegaard's thought have appeared

---

5. *SKS* 28, 477–480/ *LD*, 381–384, emphasis in original.
6. See John 14:6.

to them?"⁷ Here are two examples that show how Kierkegaard's thought appeared to his original readers and audience. As Kirkconnell states above, when these two women wrote their letters in 1851, they had no access to either *The Point of View for My Work as an Author* or *Journals and Notebooks*, which were both published posthumously. There were no biographies or secondary sources available either. These women might have heard some discussions, rumours, or gossip about Kierkegaard's person and authorship. Yet, being thoughtful, receptive, and above all, deep longing for God, they found Kierkegaard's works and sermons fulfilled their spiritual needs.

Although Joakim Garff suggests that "Kierkegaard planned his posthumous rebirth"⁸ by craftily preparing his unpublished work, the letters from these two anonymous women suggest that this was unlikely. These two letters serve as solid evidence that some of Kierkegaard's contemporaries already viewed him as a proclaimer of Christianity. The fact that such a view already existed while Kierkegaard was alive suggests that his unpublished works were not prepared for a posthumous rebirth but, rather, as a *confirmation* of the view of Kierkegaard as a proclaimer of Christianity. In light of the existence of these two letters, the following paraphrase of the apostle Paul's statement may speak on behalf of Kierkegaard: "Have you been thinking all along that [I] have been defending [myself] before you? [I am] speaking in Christ before God. Everything [I] do, beloved, is for the sake of building you up" (2 Cor 12:19).

We must remember that reading Kierkegaard is, in a sense, not that difficult. The letters from these two women correspond with the ideas conveyed by *The Point of View for My Work as an Author* and *Journals and Notebooks*. Since these two women did not know the content of Kierkegaard's unpublished works or secondary literature about Kierkegaard, their letters are indeed valuable. We could say that Kierkegaard's works were not primarily intended to provoke scholarly discussion but, rather, to edify ordinary people who need eternity.⁹

In the next section, I will examine the testimonies of three Japanese who came to or confirmed their Christian faith by reading Kierkegaard. Their

---

7. Kirkconnell, *Kierkegaard on Ethics*, 1.
8. Garff, *Søren Kierkegaard: A Biography*, xxi.
9. *SKS* 16, 84/ *PV*, 104.

testimonies demonstrate that Kierkegaard's writings could potentially impact Japan, although, as I have already argued, a Kierkegaardian mission to Japan does not require this.[10]

II. Responses of Japanese Kierkegaard Readers

In the previous section, we considered the responses of some of Kierkegaard's contemporary Danes. Posthumously, Kierkegaard's work gradually became known outside the Denmark/Nordic Protestant context. *KRSRR Volume 8: Kierkegaard's International Reception* names a total of thirty-four nations with a history of Kierkegaard's reception. Surprisingly, "Japan has a long, comprehensive tradition of reading [Kierkegaard] among both experts and laymen."[11] In this entirely different context of Japan, has anyone been led to faith through reading Kierkegaard's works?

A. Jun Hashimoto

Jun Hashimoto is a prominent Kierkegaard scholar in Japan,[12] who "reads Kierkegaard in Danish and does not interpret him on the basis of German idealism."[13] He is one of the key figures who shaped the Japanese view Kierkegaard in his native Danish context rather than through the lens of German idealism.

Hashimoto says that, as far as he can remember, he was in despair since his teens.[14] He converted to Christianity in upper secondary school.[15] He was

---

10. See my "unnecessary comment" at the beginning of chapter 10.

11. Mortensen, *Kierkegaard Made in Japan*, 12.

12. Jun Hashimoto's major literary works include: キェルケゴールの「苦悩」の世界 (The World of "Suffering" in Kierkegaard, 1976); セーレン・キェルケゴール年表 (A Chronological Table of Søren Kierkegaard, 1976); 逍遥する哲学者 – キェルケゴール紀行 (The Wandering Philosopher – Kierkegaard's Life and Authorship, 1979); キェルケゴール―憂愁と愛 (Kierkegaard – Melancholy and Love, 1985); and デンマークの歴史 (ed., A History of Denmark, 1999). Notable articles include: 殉教のキリスト教 –「認容」の問題を巡って (Christianity of Martyrdom in Regard to the Issue of Admission, 1979). Translations include: Kierkegaard's 背後から傷つける思想 (Thoughts That Wound from Behind – for Upbuilding, 1976); Kierkegaard's セーレン・キェルケゴールの日誌 第 1 巻 (Journals, Vol. 1, 1985); and Patrick Gardiner's キェルケゴール (Kierkegaard, 1996).

13. Hashimoto, "Prophet," 177.

14. Hashimoto, 遥かなデンマーク – キェルケゴールの国 ["A Far Denmark: Kierkegaard's Country"], 304.

15. Hashimoto, "Prophet," 178.

passionate about his Christian faith and entered Kwansei Gakuin University to study theology. While studying theology, however, he lost his "pure" Christian faith. Fortunately, Kierkegaard's works helped him to regain his Christian conviction.[16] In retrospect, he says that Kierkegaard's works – especially *Practice in Christianity* – taught him how to be a witness to the truth and transformed his denial of life into salvation. Hashimoto earned a PhD from Kwansei Gakuin University, and his dissertation title was キェルケゴールにおける「苦悩」の世界 (The World of "Suffering" in Kierkegaard). Kierkegaard studies become his life's work. An overview of his writings concerning despair and salvation shows that he has not been completely released from despair by his Christian faith or by reading Kierkegaard, and he seems to experience a continual spiritual tug-of-war between despair and his Christian faith. However, for Hashimoto, studying Kierkegaard has brought some measure of healing. His engagement with the Christian faith and existential study of Kierkegaard have brought him releaf from despair.

First, Kierkegaard's works helped Hashimoto to return to the Christian faith when he experienced a crisis of faith while studying theology. Second, while his faith before reading Kierkegaard was a naive faith, after reading Kierkegaard, his faith became more reflective as he struggled with despair and suffering in life. Third, his study of Kierkegaard did not only strengthen his Christian convictions but also became his life's work. Both Kierkegaard's proclamation of Christianity and his study of Kierkegaard have helped Hashimoto to obtain a measure of healing for despair and remain grounded in Christian salvation.

B. Takashi Arai

Takashi Arai is a retired pastor who has published several Christian books and articles about issues of physical sickness and disability.[17] Arai has suffered

---

16. Hashimoto, 逍遙する哲学者 – キェルケゴール紀行 [*The Wandering Philosopher – Kierkegaard's Life and Authorship*], 9.

17. Takashi Arai's major works and articles include:「病気」(Sickness) in 新聖書辞典 (New Bible Dictionary, 1985);「〔懸賞論文〕福音と文化 – 文化のフェティシズムと福音宣教 – 」("Essay Contest" Gospel and Culture: Culture of Fetishism and Gospel Proclamation) in 福音主義神学 19号 (Evangelical Theology, vol. 19, 1988); 病気の時にどう祈るか (How to Pray When You Are Sick, 1990); 障害者と教会 – 聖書に学ぶ「人間の弱さ」と障害者問題 (Disabled People and Church: "The Fragility of Human Beings" Learning from Scripture and Disability Issues, 1991);「病気」(Sickness) in 新キリスト教辞典 (New Christian Dictionary,

from tuberculosis since his elementary school years. After graduating from high school under the old system of education, he was hired by a sewing company. Two years later, his mother passed away. The day after his mother's funeral, Arai fell ill with a fever, which turned out to be pleurisy, and had to take leave from work for six months. After recovering from pleurisy, he went back to the work. In his late twenties, he had renal tuberculosis, and one of his kidneys had to be removed.

As part of his spiritual journey, Arai read Immanuel Kant's *Critique of Pure Reason* but could not understand it. He then read Wilhelm Windelband's *History of Philosophy*, where he encountered philosophical thought for the first time. In his early thirties, he began reading Kierkegaard's works. Although he read *Either/Or* and *The Sickness unto Death*, he was not inspired by these works. *Fear and Trembling* was the first of Kierkegaard's works that appealed to him, and this work also attracted him to Abraham and the Bible. An article about the book of Isaiah in 福音と世界 (Gospel and World), a Christian magazine, also aroused his interest. This prompted him to start reading parts of the Bible, such as the book of Isaiah (especially from chapter 40 onwards), the Gospels, and Genesis (the stories about Abraham). His experience with the Bible transcended mere reading; he felt that God was speaking to him, saying, "If you follow me, your life is going to be OK." One day, he found a selective translation (only sections I and II) of *Practice in Christianity* at a second-hand bookship and purchased it. The Japanese edition, titled イエスの招き (Jesus's Invitation), made a strong impression on him. This work begins with an impressive elaboration of Matthew 11:28 (NRSV): "Come to me, all you that are weary and are carrying heavy burdens, and I will give you rest." Arai was strongly convinced that Jesus was inviting him, and since he felt invited by Jesus, he thought about going to church. While thinking about this on the way to work, he was handed a leaflet about an evangelism campaign at a Christian church. He felt as though God knew everything and had planned this encounter for him. That Friday night, Arai attended the evangelism meeting at the church. Although he did not understand everything of the sermon, he decided to return to that church. The next day, 10 October

---

1991); あなたの小さなやさしさを‐障害者への心くばり (Your Small Kindness Is Needed: Considerations for Disabled People, co-authored, 1999); and 「聖書的に考えられる「決断」とその機能」 ("Decision" Biblically Conceivable and Its Function) in 心病む人に教会ができること (What Church Can Do for Mentally Ill People, 2006).

1964, was the opening ceremony of the Tokyo Olympics. As he looked up at the sky, which had unexpectedly cleared, Arai felt as if all the problems in his life had been solved. Formerly, he had felt shut off, as if there was always an invisible wall before him and he was unable to find a way out. But now, he could see a future and felt a sense of peace beyond comprehension. He knew he could walk this new path.[18]

First, Kierkegaard's works were one of the vital sources that prompted Arai to turn to Scripture. Second, reading Kierkegaard's *Practice in Christianity* made him feel invited by Jesus Christ and led him to church. Third, while wondering about which church to attend, he received a Christian evangelic leaflet, which prompted him to attend an evangelic campaign; and the next day, as he looked up at the sky that had "incredibly" cleared up, he became convinced of his salvation.

C. Michio Ogino (author of this book)

Although I was born into a Christian home and attended church every Sunday, I was a depressed teenager. The more I heard new converts testify about the joy of salvation, the more depressed I became because I did not experience such joy. My problem was that no one, including devout Christians, could not understand my agony. While my mind acknowledged that Christianity was the solution, this recognition did not aid my anguished soul. In an attempt to *heal* my melancholy, I turned to heavy metal music and reading, which I enjoyed. But at times, both music and books no longer held any meaning for me, becoming nothing to my senses. During this time, while in my early twenties, I read Kierkegaard's *The Sickness unto Death* for the first time. I immediately connected with Kierkegaard and began reading his works one after another. Through this process, I found that my depression was gradually and tangibly fading away. One day, I encountered the following words in *Practice in Christianity*:

> Come here, all you who labor and are burdened, and I will give you rest . . . "*Come here!*" However tired and weary you are of the labor, or of the long, long and yet up until now futile going for help and rescue, even if you could not succeed in taking one

---

18. Michio Ogino, in a personal conversation with Takashi Arai, Ueda, January 2021.

more step, could not keep on one moment longer without collapsing – oh, just one step more and here is rest! – "*Come here!*" Alas, but if there is someone so wretched that he cannot come, oh, a sigh is enough; that you sigh for him is also to come here.[19]

Before encountering these words, I had felt that although Jesus Christ was the Saviour for all people, he was not for *me*. Although I knew this was contradictory, I could not help *feeling* this way. In the above quotation, Anti-Climacus says that "a sigh is enough." At least I could sigh. If to "sigh for him is also to come to [Christ]," then I could come to Christ. In this way, Kierkegaard – especially through this passage – helped me to *personally* accept Jesus Christ as my Saviour and *feel* the truth of salvation.

First, as a depressed teenager, I was attracted by *The Sickness unto Death* because I felt that this title really captured what I was feeling. Second, as I read Kierkegaard's works, I felt that I was gradually being released from melancholy. Third, Anti-Climacus's invitation at the beginning of *Practice in Christianity* played a decisive role in my personally accepting Jesus Christ as my Saviour.

D. Implications of These Japanese Kierkegaard Readers' Experiences

First, Kierkegaard's works can provide an opportunity for even the Japanese to embrace the Christian faith. In other words, although Kierkegaard primarily wrote for his contemporary Danes, his translated works may appeal to people who live in non-Danish cultures and in different eras. Second, all three readers cited above had previously experienced the kind of despair that *The Sickness unto Death* addresses. As Anti-Climacus asserts, despair is a universal phenomenon, and the symptoms of despair were evident in these readers. Third, all three readers were convinced of the Christian faith by reading *Practice in Christianity*.

---

19. *SKS* 12, 33/ *PC*, 22, emphasis in original.

III. Conclusion

We have examined a total of five testimonies from people who claim to have been evangelized or edified by Kierkegaard – two of his contemporaries and three Japanese readers from the twentieth century. Admittedly, this appendix cannot fully explain the effectiveness of Kierkegaard's mission since the number of testimonies is limited. Nevertheless, the existence of these five testimonies suggests that there may be many more who were evangelized and edified by Kierkegaard's mission.

In conclusion, just as Kierkegaard's mission proved effective for some of his contemporaries, it can also be effective in different cultured contexts such as Japan. This statement could be elaborated on in more detail as follows. First, these testimonies contribute to modern Kierkegaard scholarship by highlighting that Kierkegaard wrote for the upbuilding of his readers and demonstrating that both his contemporaries and readers from different cultural contexts can be edified in line with his intentions. His thoughtful and profound works will remain a subject of interest for research in the future. However, the following question is important: Is the term "Kierkegaard studies" justified if we consciously or unconsciously lose sight of Kierkegaard's central focus of serving Christian truth? Second, the aim of this study was not to spark a Kierkegaard Renaissance but to encourage a modern application of the Kierkegaardian mission. These testimonies of actual and successful missions to Kierkegaard readers demonstrate the potential of applying the Kierkegaardian mission in modern contexts. Third, another aim of this study was to consider how the Kierkegaardian mission could be applied in Japan. Since Japanese readers also read Kierkegaard in order to have or deepen their Christian faith, it is hoped that Kierkegaardian mission can be effectively applied in Japan.

Bibliography

"The 95 Theses." Accessed 14 March 2022. https://www.luther.de/en/95thesen.html.

Adams, Evyn Merrill. "An Elucidation of Soren Kierkegaard's Categories of Communication and Their Application to the Communication of Christian Existence in Japan." PhD thesis, Drew University, 1969.

Adorno, Theodor. キルケゴール – 美的なものの構築 [*Kierkegaard: Construction of the Aesthetic*]. Translated by Yasuo Yamamoto. Tokyo: Misuzu-shobō, 1988.

Akihara, Kazukuni. 明暗と則天去私 ["*Meian* and the Idea of *Sokuten Kyoshi*"]. In 漱石文学 – その文学と思想 [*Sōseki's Literature – His Literature and Thought*], 262–277. Tokyo: Hanawa-shobō, 1980.

Akker, Robin van den, Alison Gibbons, and Timotheus Vermeulen, eds. *Metamodernism: Historicity, Affect, and Depth after Postmodernism*. Radical Cultural Studies. London: Rowman & Littlefield, 2017.

Alessandri, Mariana. "John Alexander Mackay: The *Road* Approach to Truth." In *Kierkegaard's Influence on Theology: Tome II: Anglophone and Scandinavian Protestant Theology*, Vol. 10 of *Kierkegaard Research: Sources, Reception and Resources*. edited by Jon Stewart, 63–84. London; New York: Routledge, 2012.

Allen, Diogenes. *Three Outsiders: Pascal, Kierkegaard, Simone Weil*. Eugene: Wipf & Stock, 1983.

Allen, Richie. *Playing Both Sides of the Fence: A Missionary's Journey in Search of the Supra-Cultural Gospel*. Bloomington: WestBow, 2015.

Ama, Toshimaro. *Why Are the Japanese Non-Religious?: Japanese Spirituality: Being Non-Religious in a Religious Culture*. Translated by Michihiro Ama. Lanham: University Press of America, 2005.

———. 日本人はなぜ無宗教なのか [*Why Are the Japanese Non-Religious?*]. Tokyo: Chikuma-shinsho, 1996.

Arai, Takashi. 〔懸賞論文〕福音と文化 – 文化のフェティシズムと福音宣教 ["'Essay Contest' Gospel and Culture: Culture of Fetishism and Gospel

Proclamation"]. 福音主義神学 19号 [*Evangelical Theology, vol. 19*], November 1988, 143–164.

———. 障害者と教会 – 聖書に学ぶ「人間の弱さ」と障害者問題 [*Disabled People and Church: "The Fragility of Human Beings" Learning from Scripture and Disability Issues*]. Tokyo: Inochino Kotoba-sha, 1991.

———. 聖書的に考えられる「決断」とその機能 ["'Decision' Biblically Conceivable and Its Function"]. In 心病む人に教会ができること [*What Church Can Do for Mentally Ill People*], 104–112. Tokyo: Inochino Kotoba-sha, 2006.

———. 病気 ["Sickness"]. In 新キリスト教辞典 [*New Christian Dictionary*], edited by S. Uda, A. Suzuki, T. Tsutada, G. Nabetani, R. Hashimoto, and N. Yamaguchi, 1069–1071. Tokyo: Inochino Kotoba-sha, 1991.

———. 病気 ["Sickness"]. In 新聖書辞典 [*New Bible Dictionary*], edited by A. Izuta, S. Uda, Y. Hattori, S. Funaki, and N. Yamaguchi, 1045–1049. Tokyo: Inochino Kotoba-sha, 1985.

———. 病気の時にどう祈るか [*How to Pray When You Are Sick*]. Tokyo: Inochino Kotoba-sha, 1990.

Arai, Takashi, Norifumi Kageyama, Minoru Sakurai, and Kiyoshige Miura. あなたの小さなやさしさを – 障害者への心くばり [*Your Small Kindness Is Needed: Considerations for Disabled People*]. Tokyo: Inochino Kotoba-sha, 1999.

Aristotle. *Rhetoric*. Edited by W. D. Ross. Translated by Rhys Roberts. New York: Cosimo, 2010.

Asano, Hitoshi, Masanori Makino, and Takahiro Hirabayashi, eds. デンマークの歴史・文化・社会 [*Danish History, Culture, and Society*]. Tokyo: Sōgen-sha, 2006.

Auden, W. H. *Collected Poems*. Edited by Edward Mendelson. London: Faber & Faber, 1994.

Augustine. *The Confessions of St. Augustine*. Translated and edited by Albert Cook Outler. Mineola: Dover, 1955; 2002.

Aumann, Antony. *Art and Selfhood: A Kierkegaardian Account*. Lanham: Lexington Books, 2019.

———. "Sartre's View of Kierkegaard as Transhistorical Man." *Journal of Philosophical Research* 31 (2006): 361–372.

Bakhtin, Mikhail. *Problems of Dostoevsky's Poetics (Theory and History of Literature, Volume 8)*. Edited and translated by Caryl Emerson. Minneapolis: University of Minnesota Press, 1984.

Ballan, Joseph. "The Wandering Jew: Kierkegaard and the Figuration of Death in Life." In *Kierkegaard's Literary Figures and Motifs: Tome II: Gulliver to Zerlina*. Vol. 16 of *Kierkegaard Research: Sources, Reception and Resources*, edited by Katalin Nun and Jon Stewart, 235–248. London; New York: Routledge, 2015.

Balle, Nikolai Edinger. *Lærebog i den Evangelisk-Christelige Religion Indrettet til Brug i de Danske Skoler* [*Textbook in the Evangelical-Christian Religion Arranged for Use in the Danish Schools*]. Copenhagen: Johan Frederik Schultz 1791; 1793; 1795; 1801; 1802; 1805; 1814; 1860; Copenhagen: Gyldendal 1854.

Barnett, Christopher B. *From Despair to Faith: The Spirituality of Søren Kierkegaard*. Philadelphia: Fortress, 2014.

———. *Kierkegaard, Pietism and Holiness*. Farnham: Ashgate 2011.

———. "Nicolai Edinger Balle: The Reception of His *Lærebog* in Denmark and in Kierkegaard's Authorship." In *Kierkegaard and His Danish Contemporaries: Tome II: Theology*. Vol. 7 of *Kierkegaard Research: Sources, Reception and Resources*, edited by Jon Stewart, 23–39. London; New York: Routledge, 2009.

Barrett, Lee C., and Jon Stewart, eds. *Kierkegaard and the Bible: Tome II: The New Testament*. Vol. 1 of *Kierkegaard Research: Sources, Reception and Resources*. Farnham: Ashgate, 2010.

Barth, Karl. 教会教義学 – 和解論 I/4 [*Church Dogmatic: The Dogmatic of Reconciliation I/4*]. Translated by Yoshio Inoue. Tokyo: Shinkyō-shuppan-sha, 1959.

———. 教会教義学 – 和解論 II/4 [*Church Dogmatic: The Dogmatic of Reconciliation II/4*]. Translated by Yoshio Inoue. Tokyo: Shinkyō-shuppan-sha, 1972.

———. *The Epistle to the Romans*. Translated by Edwyn C. Hoskyns. Oxford: Oxford University Press, 1932.

———. *The Epistle to the Romans*. Translated by Ian W. Robertson. London: SCM, 1960.

———. ロマ書 [*The Epistle to the Romans*]. Translated by Keiji Ogawa and Tetsuo Iwanami. Tokyo: Kawade-shobō, 1968.

———. "A Thank You and a Bow – Kierkegaard's Reveille (Translated by H. Martin Rumscheidt)". *Canadian Journal of Theology* 11 (1965): 3–7.

———. キルケゴールと私 ["A Thank You and a Bow – Kierkegaard's Reveille"] and キルケゴールと神学者 [*Kierkegaard and the Theologians*]. Translated by Keiji Ogawa. In キルケゴール研究 – キルケゴール著作集別巻 [*The Studies of Kierkegaard: Kierkegaard's Works Supplement*], edited by Shinsaburō Matsunami and Munetaka Iijima. Tokyo: Hakusui-sha, 1968.

Baskind, James. キリスト教から見た日本の宗教 ["A Look at Japanese Religion through a Christian Lens: In Contrast with the Japanese Perspective on Christianity"]. In 日本宗教史 2 – 世界のなかの日本宗教 [*History of Japanese Religions 2: Japanese Religions in Global Context*], edited by Susumu Uejima and Kazuhiko Yoshida, 90–120. Tokyo: Yoshikawa Kōbunkan, 2021.

"Bataan Death March." *History*. 9 November 2009. https://www.history.com/topics/world-war-ii/bataan-death-march.

Bauckham, Richard. *God Crucified: Monotheism and Christology in the New Testament*. Grand Rapids: Eerdmans, 1999.

Becker, Carl. *Like Christ by Grace: Pursuing the Prize of Christlikeness by God's Grace*. Bloomington: WestBow, 2012.

Benedict, Ruth. *The Chrysanthemum and the Sword: Patterns of Japanese Culture*. Boston: Houghton Mifflin, 1974.

Bernier, Mark. *The Task of Hope in Kierkegaard*. Oxford: Oxford University Press, 2015.

Betz, H. D. *The Sermon on the Mount: A Commentary on the Sermon on the Mount, including the Sermon on the Plain (Matthew 5:3–7:27 and Luke 6:20–49) (Hermeneia Commentary)*. Minneapolis: Augsburg/Fortress, 1995.

Bevans, Stephen. "Seeing Mission through Images." *Missiology* 19, no. 1 (1991): 45–57.

「日本的キリスト教」を超えて [*Beyond "Japanese Christianity"*]. Edited by Shinshū Summer Mission. Tokyo: Inochi no kotoba-sha, 2016.

Bock, Darrell L. *Acts*. Baker Exegetical Commentary on the New Testament. Ada: Baker Academic, 2007.

Bodelsen, Carl Adolf, and Hermann Vinterberg, eds. *Dansk-Engelsk Ordbog, II N-Ø [Danish-English Dictionary II N-Ø]*. København: Gyldendalske Boghandel, 1956.

Borg, Marcus J., and N. T. Wright. *The Meaning of Jesus: Two Visions (Plus): The Leading Liberal and Conservative Jesus Scholars Present the Heart of the Historical Jesus Debate*. New York: HarperCollins, 1999.

Bosch, David J. *Transforming Mission: Paradigm Shifts in Theology of Mission*. Maryknoll: Orbis Books, 1991.

Brake, Matthew. "Loki: Romanticism and Kierkegaard's Critique of the Aesthetic." In *Kierkegaard's Literary Figures and Motifs: Tome II: Gulliver to Zerlina*. Vol. 16 of *Kierkegaard Research: Sources, Reception and Resources*, edited by Katalin Nun and Jon Stewart, 65–74. London; New York: Routledge, 2015.

———. "Soren Kierkegaard and Pentecostalism: A Dialogue." Master's thesis, Regent University, 2009.

Bruce, F. F. *The Acts of the Apostles: Greek Text with Introduction and Commentary*. Grand Rapids: Eerdmans, 1951; 1990.

———. *The Book of the Acts*. New International Commentary on the New Testament. Grand Rapids: Eerdmans, 1988.

———. *Philippians*. Understanding the Bible Commentary Series. Grand Rapids: Baker Books, 1989.

Brunner, Emil. *The Christian Doctrine of God: Dogmatics: Vol. 1*. Translated by Olive Wyon. Philadelphia: Westminster, 1950.

Brzeski, Patrick, ed. "Ramen Jiro: Japan's Most Infamous Food Cult." *Ramen Beast* (blog). 12 February 2021. https://ramenbeast.substack.com/p/ramen-jiro-japans-most-infamous-food.

Buber, Martin. "The Question to the Single One." In *Between Man and Man*, 40–82. Translated by Ronald Gregor Smith. New York: Macmillan, 1965.

Bultmann, Rudolf. ヨハネの福音書 [*The Gospel of John*]. Translated by Tasuku Sugihara. Tokyo: Nihon Kirisuto Kyōdan-shuppan-kyoku, 2005.

———. イエス [*Jesus*]. Translated by Seiichi Yagi and Junshirō Kawabata. Tokyo: Shinkyō-shuppan-sha, 1963.

———. 新約聖書神学〈2〉(ブルトマン著作集 第4巻) [*The Theology of the New Testament vol. 2 (Bultmann Works Vol. 4)*]. Translated by Junshirō Kawabata. Tokyo: Shinkyō-shuppan-sha, 1966.

Burns, Scott. "Evangelism vs Discipleship." *Work in Progress* (blog). 19 February 2013. https://scottburns.wordpress.com/2013/02/19/evangelism-vs-discipleship/.

Cailliet, Emile. "Review of *Pascal and Kierkegaard: A Study in the Strategy of Evangelism*, by Denzil G. M. Patrick, 2 vols." *Theology Today* 6, no. 1 (April 1949): 127–129.

Camus, Albert. *The Myth of Sisyphus*. Translated by Justin O'Brien. 2nd Vintage International ed. New York: Vintage Books, 1955; 1983; 2018.

Cappelørn, Niels Jørgen, Joakim Garff, Johnny Kondrup, Tonny Aagaard Olesen and Steen Tullberg. eds. *Søren Kierkegaards Skrifter*. 55 vols. Copenhagen: Gad, 2007–2013. Accessed 11 February 2017. http://sks.dk/forside/indhold.asp.

Caputo, John D. *How to Read Kierkegaard*. New York: Norton, 2007.

Carlisle, Clare. *Philosopher of the Heart: The Restless Life of Søren Kierkegaard*. London: Penguin Books, 2019. Kindle.

Carnell, Edward John. *The Burden of Søren Kierkegaard*. Edward Carnell Library. Eugene: Wipf & Stock, 2007.

Charlesworth, James H. *The Historical Jesus. Essential Guides*. Nashville: Abingdon, 2008.

Chateaubriand, François-René de. *Atala/René*. Translated by Irving Putter. Berkeley: University of California Press, 1952.

"諸子百家 (*Chinese Text Project*)." Accessed 23 April 2022. https://ctext.org/analects.

Chester, Tim. "Why I Don't Believe in Incarnational Mission." Accessed 20 June 2013. http://timchester.wordpress.com/2008/07/19/why-i-dont-believe-in-incarnational-mission.

クリスチャン新聞福音版 [*Christian Newspaper Gospel Version*]. Word of Life Press Ministries (March 2020) no. 522.

"Christianity." *Japan-Guide.Com*. Accessed 28 February 2020. https://www.japan-guide.com/e/e2298.html.

Cockayne, Joshua. "Contemporaneity and Communion: Kierkegaard on the Personal Presence of Christ." *British Journal for the History of Philosophy* 25, no. 1 (2017): 41–62.

———. "Imitation and Contemporaneity: Kierkegaard and the Imitation of Christ." *Heythrop Journal* 63 (2022): 553–566.

Coe, David Lawrence. *Kierkegaard and Luther*. Lanham: Lexington Books/Fortress Academic, 2020.

Coogan, Michael D., Marc Z. Brettler, and Carol Newsom, eds. *The New Oxford Annotated Bible: New Revised Standard Version with Apocrypha*. 4th ed. Oxford: Oxford University Press, 2010.

Cook, Robert R. "Søren Kierkegaard: Missionary to Christendom." *The Evangelical Quarterly* 59, no. 4 (October–December 1987): 311–327.

Conway, Daniel W., and K. E. Gover, eds. *Søren Kierkegaard: Authorship and Authenticity: Kierkegaard and His Pseudonyms*. Vol. 1 of *Critical Assessments of Leading Philosophers*. London; New York: Routledge, 2002.

———. *Søren Kierkegaard: Epistemology and Psychology: Kierkegaard and the Recoil from Freedom*. Vol. 2 of *Critical Assessments of Leading Philosophers*. London; New York: Taylor & Francis, 2002

Craddock, Fred. *Overhearing the Gospel*. Rev. and exp. ed. St. Louis: Chalice 1978; 2002. Kindle.

Cross, Frank Leslie, and Elizabeth A. Livingstone, eds. *The Oxford Dictionary of the Christian Church*. Oxford: Oxford University Press, 2005.

Crump, David. *Encountering Jesus, Encountering Scripture: Reading the Bible Critically in Faith*. Grand Rapids; Cambridge: Eerdmans, 2013.

"Danka System." *DBpedia*. https://dbpedia.org/page/Danka_system (accessed 23 March 2022).

Davenport, John, and Anthony Rudd, eds. *Kierkegaard after MacIntyre: Essays on Freedom, Narrative, and Virtue*. Chicago; LaSalle: Open Court, 2001.

Davis, Bret W. 日本哲学とは何か − その定義と範囲を再考する試み − ["What Is Japanese Philosophy? Rethinking Its Definition and Scope"].日本哲学史研究 第16号 [*Studies in Japanese Philosophy, vol. 16*]: 1–20.

Davis, Ellen F., and Richard B. Hays, eds. *The Art of Reading Scripture*. Grand Rapids: Eerdmans, 2003.

Dazai, Osamu. *No Longer Human*. Translated by Donald Keene. New York: New Directions, 1958.

———. 人間失格 [*No Longer Human*]. Tokyo: Gutenberg 21, 2007.

Depoe, John. "Rejuvenating Apologetics in the Twenty-First Century: Taking Hints from Søren Kierkegaard." Waco: Baylor University, 2002.

Derrida, Jacques. *Of Grammatology*. Translated by Gayatri Chakravorty Spivak. Repr. ed. Baltimore: Johns Hopkins University Press, 1998.

———. *Writing and Difference*. Translated by Alan Bass. Chicago: University of Chicago Press, 1980.

Descartes, René. *Discourse on the Method of Rightly Conducting One's Reason and of Seeking Truth in the Sciences*. Translated by John Vietch. Project Gutenberg, 2008. Kindle.

Dewey, Bradley R. *The New Obedience: Kierkegaard on Imitating Christ*. Washington, D.C.: Corpus, 1968.

Diem, Hermann. *Kierkegaard's Dialectic of Existence*. Translated by Harold Knight. Edinburgh: Oliver & Boyd, 1959.

Dillenberger, John, ed. *Martin Luther: Selections from His Writings*. New York: Anchor Books, 1961.

"Disciple." *AZLyrics*. Accessed 24 February 2016. http://www.azlyrics.com/lyrics/slayer/disciple.html.

Dohi, Akio. s.v. "日本的キリスト教 [Japanese Christianity]" in 日本キリスト教歴史大事典 [Japan Christian History Encyclopedia]. Tokyo: Kyōbunkan, 1998.

Donovan, Sandra. *Billy Graham*. Minneapolis: Twenty-First Century Books, 2007.

Dostoevsky, Fyodor. *The Brothers Karamazov* (Norton Critical Editions). Edited and with a revised translation by Susan McReynolds. 2nd ed. New York: Norton, 2011.

———. *Demons*. Translated by Richard Pevear and Larissa Volokhonsky. New York: Vintage Books, 1995.

———. *The Idiot*. Translated by David McDuff. London: Penguin Books, 2004.

Dubroux, Danièle. *Le Journal Du Séducteur* [*Diary of a Seducer*]. Fox Lorber. Movie 1996.

Dunning, Stephen Northrup. "The Dialectical Structure of Consciousness. The Anti-Climacus Writings." In *Epistemology and Psychology: Kierkegaard and the Recoil from Freedom*. Vol. 2 of *Søren Kierkegaard: Critical Assessments of Leading Philosophers*, edited by Daniel Conway and K. E. Gover, 49–71. London; New York: Taylor & Francis, 2002.

———. *Kierkegaard's Dialectic of Inwardness: A Structural Analysis of the Theory of Stages*. Princeton: Princeton University Press, 1985.

Duriez, Colin. *Francis Schaeffer: An Authentic Life*. Downers Grove: InterVarsity Press, 2008.

Eagleton, Terry. *Literary Theory: An Introduction*. Hoboken: Wiley & Sons, 2011.

Ebisawa, Arimichi, and Saburō Ōuchi. 日本キリスト教史 [*The History of Christianity in Japan*]. Tokyo: Nihon Kirisuto Kyōdan-shuppan-kyoku, 1970.

Edgemon, Roy T. "Evangelism and Discipleship." *Review & Expositor* 77, no. 4 (December 1980): 539–547.

Edwards, Aaron. "Kierkegaard as Socratic Street Preacher?: Reimagining the Dialectic of Direct and Indirect Communication for Christian Proclamation." *Harvard Theological Review* 110, no. 2 (April 2017): 280–300.

———. "Life in Kierkegaard's Imaginary Rural Parish: Preaching, Correctivity, and the Gospel." *Toronto Journal of Theology* 30, no. 2 (Fall 2014): 235–246.

Eller, Vernard. *Kierkegaard and Radical Discipleship*. Princeton Legacy Library. Princeton: Princeton University Press, 1967; 2015.

Emmanuel, Steven M., William McDonald, and Jon Stewart, eds. *Kierkegaard's Concepts: Tome I: Absolute to Church*. Vol. 15 of *Kierkegaard Research: Sources, Reception and Resources*. London; New York: Routledge, 2016.

———. *Kierkegaard's Concepts: Tome II: Classicism to Enthusiasm*. Vol. 15 of *Kierkegaard Research: Sources, Reception and Resources*. London; New York: Routledge, 2016.

———. *Kierkegaard's Concepts: Tome III: Envy to Incognito*. Vol. 15 of *Kierkegaard Research: Sources, Reception and Resources*. London; New York: Routledge, 2016.

———. *Kierkegaard's Concepts: Tome IV: Individual to Novel*. Vol. 15 of *Kierkegaard Research: Sources, Reception and Resources*. London; New York: Routledge, 2014.

———. *Kierkegaard's Concepts: Tome V: Objectivity to Sacrifice*. Vol. 15 of *Kierkegaard Research: Sources, Reception and Resources*. London; New York: Routledge, 2015.

———. *Kierkegaard's Concepts: Tome VI: Salvation to Writing*. Vol. 15 of *Kierkegaard Research: Sources, Reception and Resources*. London; New York: Routledge, 2016.

Encyclopedia Britannica. Accessed 17 December 2019. https://www.britannica.com.

Endō, Shūsaku. *Silence*. Translated by William Johnston. New York: Taplinger, 1980.

———. 沈黙 [*Silence*]. Tokyo: Shinchō-bunko, 1981.

Erickson, Millard J. *Christian Theology*. 2nd ed. Grand Rapids: Baker Books, 1998.

Eriksen, Niels Nymann. *Kierkegaard's Category of Repetition: A Reconstruction*. Berlin; New York: de Gruyter, 2000.

Etō, Jun. 漱石神話と則天去私 ["The Sōseki Myth and *Sokuten Kyoshi*"]. In 決定版 夏目漱石 [*A Definitive Edition, Natsume Sōseki*], 11–19. Tokyo: Shinchō-bunko, 1979.

Evans, C. Stephen. "Kierkegaard among the Biographers: The Hermeneutics of Suspicion." *Christianity Today/Books & Culture*, 2007. http://www.booksandculture.com/articles/2007/julaug/20.12.html?paging=off.

———. *Kierkegaard: An Introduction*. Cambridge: Cambridge University Press, 2009.

———. *Kierkegaard and Spirituality: Accountability as the Meaning of Human Existence* (Kierkegaard as a Christian Thinker). Grand Rapids: Eerdmans, 2019.

———. "Kierkegaard: Father of Existentialism or Critic of Existentialism?" In *Søren Kierkegaard: Theologian of the Gospel*, edited by Todd Speidell, Greg Marcar, and Andrew Torrance, 110–128. Eugene, Oregon: Wipf & Stock, 2021.

———. *Kierkegaard on Faith and the Self: Collected Essays*. Waco: Baylor University Press, 2006.

———. "A Misunderstood Reformer." *Christianity Today*, 21 September 1984, 26–29.

———. *Passionate Reason: Making Sense of Kierkegaard's Philosophical Fragments*. Bloomington: Indiana University Press, 1992.

———. *Pocket Dictionary of Apologetics and Philosophy of Religion*. Downers Grove: InterVarsity Press, 2002.

———. "Søren Kierkegaard: Philosophical Fragments." In *Central Works of Philosophy: The Nineteenth Century*, edited by John Shand, 159–181. Montreal; Kingston; London; Ithaca: McGill-Queen's University Press, 2005.

———. *Søren Kierkegaard's Christian Psychology: Insight for Counseling and Pastoral Care*. Grand Rapids: Ministry Resources Library, 1990.

Evans, C. Stephen, and Robert C. Roberts. "Ethics." In *The Oxford Handbook of Kierkegaard*. edited by John Lippitt and George Pattison, 211–229. Oxford: Oxford University Press, 2013.

Fee, Gordon D. *The First Epistle to the Corinthians*. Grand Rapids: Eerdmans, 1987.

Fenger, Henning. *Kierkegaard, the Myths and Their Origins: Studies in the Kierkegaardian Papers and Letters*. Translated by George C. Schoolfield. New Haven; London: Yale University Press, 1980.

Ferreira, M. Jamie. *Kierkegaard*. Oxford: Blackwell, 2009.

世のため、人のため – 経彦さま伝 [For People in the Society: Biography of Tsunehiko] in 新理教応援HP [Home Page to Support Teaching of Divine Principle] http://sinri.sub.jp/tsune/H16-2.html (accessed 22 March 2022).

Forte, Bruno. *The Portal of Beauty: Towards a Theology of Aesthetics*. Translated by David Glenday and Paul McPartlan. Grand Rapids: Eerdmans, 2008.

France, R. T. *The Gospel of Matthew*. The New International Commentary on the New Testament. Grand Rapids; Cambridge: Eerdmans, 2007.

Frankl, Viktor E. *Man's Search for Meaning: An Introduction to Logothrapy*. Translated by Ilse Lasch. 4th ed. Boston: Beacon, 1959. Reprint 1962, 1984, 1992.

Fucan, Fabian. 妙貞問答 ["Myōtei Dialogues"]. In 日本思想体系25 キリシタン書 排耶書 [*Japanese System of Thought 25: Kirishitan Book, Christian Book*], edited by Arimichi Ebisawa, Hubert Cieslik, Tadao Doi, and Mitsunobu Ōtsuka, 128–143. Tokyo: Iwanami, 1970.

Fujino, Hiroshi. キルケゴール ‒ 美と倫理のはざまに立つ哲学 [*Kierkegaard: The Philosophy of Standing in between the Aesthetic and the Ethical*]. Tokyo: Iwanami-shoten, 2014.

Fukuzawa, Yukichi. 学問のすゝめ [*An Encouragement of Learning*]. Edited by Masao Suzuki. Tokyo: Kōdan-sha Gakujutsu-bunko, 2006.

Furnal, Joshua. *Catholic Theology after Kierkegaard*. Oxford: Oxford University Press, 2016.

Furtwängler, Wilhelm. *Mozart ‒ Don Giovanni*. Directed by Alfred Travers. New York: Unitel, 2001.

Gadamer, Hans-Georg. "The Hermeneutics of Suspicion." *Man and World* 17 (1984): 313‒323.

Gardiner, John Eliot. *Bach: Music in the Castle of Heaven*. New York: Vintage Books, 2014.

Gardiner, Patrick. キェルケゴール [*Kierkegaard*]. Translated by Jun Hashimoto and Takahiro Hirabayashi. Tokyo: Kyōbunkan, 1996.

Garelick, Herbert M. *The Anti-Christianity of Kierkegaard: A Study of Concluding Unscientific Postscript*. New York: Springer, 1965.

Garff, Joakim. "The Eyes of Argus: The Point of View and Points of View with Respect to Kierkegaard's 'Activity as an Author.'" Translated by Bruce H. Kirmmse. In Kierkegaardiana 15. 29–54. Copenhagen: C. A. Reitzels forlag, 1991.

———. *Søren Kierkegaard: A Biography*. Princeton: Princeton University Press, 2005.

Garland, David E. *I Corinthians*. Baker Exegetical Commentary on the New Testament. Grand Rapids: Baker Academic, 2003.

Garrard, David J. "Questionable Assumptions in the Theory and Practice of Mission." *Journal of the European Pentecostal Theological Association* 26, no. 2 (2006): 102–112.

Georges, Jayson, and Mark D. Baker. *Ministering in Honor-Shame Cultures: Biblical Foundations and Practical Essentials*. Downers Grove: IVP Academic, 2016.

Giles, James, ed. *Kierkegaard and Japanese Thought*. Basingstoke; New York: Palgrave Macmillan, 2008.

Givens, John. "A Narrow Escape into Faith? Dostoevsky's *Idiot* and the Christology of Comedy." *The Russian Review* 70, no. 1 (January 2011): 95‒117.

Gladwin, Michael. "Mission and Colonialism." In *The Oxford Handbook of Nineteenth-Century Christian Thought*, edited by Joel D. S. Rasmussen, Judith Wolfe, and Johannes Zachhuber, 282–304. Oxford: Oxford University Press, 2017.

Goethe, Johann Wolfgang von. *Clavigo*. Dinslaken: Atenemedia Verlag, 2014.

———. *Faust: A Tragedy in Two Parts with Urfaust*. Translated by John R. Williams. Ware: Wordsworth Editions, 1999; 2007.

———. ファウスト（一）[*Faust, First Part*]. Translated by Yoshitaka Takahashi. Tokyo: Sinchō-bunko, 1967.

———. ファウスト（二）[*Faust, Second Part*]. Translated by Yoshitaka Takahashi. Tokyo: Sinchō-bunko, 1968.

Goldin, Paul R., ed. *Routledge Handbook of Early Chinese History*. London; New York: Routledge, 2018.

Gonzalez, Alejandro. "Humor." In *Kierkegaard's Concepts: Tome III: Envy to Incognito*. Vol. 15 of *Kierkegaard Research: Sources, Reception and Resources*, edited by Steven M. Emmanuel, William McDonald, and Jon Stewart, 175–182. London; New York: Routledge, 2016.

Gouwens, David J. *Kierkegaard as Religious Thinker*. Cambridge; New York: Cambridge University Press, 1996.

———. *Kierkegaard's Dialectic of the Imagination*. New York: Lang, 1988.

Graham, Billy. *Peace with God: The Secret Happiness*. Rev. ed. Edinburgh: Nelson 1953; 1984; 2000.

Graham, Glen. "Kierkegaard and the Longing for God." PhD thesis, McMaster University, 2011.

Grøn, Arne. *The Concept of Anxiety in Søren Kierkegaard*. Macon: Mercer University Press, 2008.

Hale, Thomas. *On Being a Missionary*. Pasadena: William Carey Library, 1995.

Hamilton, Kenneth. *The Promise of Kierkegaard*. Philadelphia; New York: Lippincott, 1969.

Hankins, Barry. *Francis Schaeffer and the Shaping of Evangelical America*. Grand Rapids: Eerdmans, 2008.

Hannay, Alastair. *Kierkegaard: A Biography*. Cambridge: Cambridge University Press, 2001.

Hannay, Alastair, and Gordon D. Marino, eds. *The Cambridge Companion to Kierkegaard*. Cambridge: Cambridge University Press, 1998.

Harries, Karsten. *Between Nihilism and Faith: A Commentary on* Either/Or. Kierkegaard Studies Monograph Series 21. Berlin; New York: de Gruyter, 2010.

Hashimoto, Jun. キェルケゴールにおける「苦悩」の世界 [*The World of "Suffering" in Kierkegaard*]. Tokyo: Mirai-sha, 1976.

———. キェルケゴール－憂愁と愛 [*Kierkegaard – Melancholy and Love*]. Tokyo: Jimbun Shoin, 1985.

———. 殉教のキリスト教－「認容」の問題を巡って ["Christianity of Martyrdom in Regard to the Issue of Admission"]. 理想 [*Riso*] 555 (August 1979): 50–61.

———. 逍遙する哲学者－キェルケゴール紀行 [*The Wandering Philosopher – Kierkegaard's Life and Authorship*]. Tokyo: Shinkyō-shuppan-sha, 1979.

———. セーレン・キェルケゴール年表 [*A Chronological Table of Søren Kierkegaard*]. Tokyo: Mirai-sha, 1976.

———, ed. デンマークの歴史 [*A History of Denmark*]. Tokyo: Sōgen-sha, 1999.

———. 遥かなデンマーク－キェルケゴールの国 ["A Far Denmark: Kierkegaard's Country"]. In キェルケゴールとキリスト教神学の展望 [*New Perspective of Studies on Kierkegaard and the Scope of Contemporary Christian Theology*], edited by Shinichi Matsuki, 293–321. Hyogo: Kwansei Gakuin University Press, 2006.

———. "Prophet in a Mass Society." In *Kierkegaard Made in Japan*, edited by Finn Hauberg Mortensen, 176–184. Odense: Odense University Press, 1996.

Hays, Richard B. *First Corinthians*. Interpretation: A Bible Commentary for Teaching and Preaching. Louisville: Westminster John Knox, 1997.

Hearn, Lafcadio (Koizumi Yakumo). *Kokoro: Hints and Echoes of Japanese Inner Life*. Lincoln: Zea Books, 1896; 2022.

Hegel, Georg Wilhelm Friedrich. *The Phenomenology of Spirit*. Edited and translated by Terry Pinkard. Cambridge: Cambridge University Press, 2018.

———. *The Philosophy of History*. Translated by J. Sibree. New York: Dover, 1956.

Heidegger, Martin. *Being and Time*. Translated by John Macquarrie and Edward Robinson. Oxford: Blackwell, 1962.

———. シェリング [*Schelling's Treatise on the Essence of Human Freedom*]. Translated by Gen Kida and Kenichi Sakoda. Tokyo: Shinshokan, 1999.

———. 存在と時間 [*Being and Time*]. Translated by Yū Hara. Tokyo: Chūō Kōron-sha, 1980.

———. ニーチェII [*Nietzsche II*]. Translated by Haruyuki Enzou. Tokyo: Sōbun-sha, 2004.

———. ニーチェの言葉『神は死せり』ヘーゲルの『経験』概念 [*Nietzsche's Word "God is Dead," Hegel's Concept of Experience*]. Translated by Sadao Hosoya. Tokyo: Risō-sha, 1954.

Hesiod, *Theogony, Works and Days, Testimonia (Loeb Classical Library) (Reprinted and Corrected Edition)*, ed. and trans. by Glenn W. Most. Cambridge: Harvard University Press, 2010.

Hill, Harriet. "Incarnational Ministry: A Critical Examination." *Evangelical Missions Quarterly* 26, no. 2 (1990): 196–201.

Hinkson, Craig. "Luther and Kierkegaard: Theologians of the Cross." *International Journal of Systematic Theology* 3, no. 1 (March 2001): 27–45.

Hirabayashi, Takahiro. セーレン・キルケゴールにおける«心理学»の問題－一つの歴史的研究 ["On the Problem of Søren Kierkegaard's Psychology: A Historical Study"]. 理想 [*Riso*] 676 (March 2006): 37–56.

———. "New Identity." In *Kierkegaard Made in Japan*, edited by Finn Hauberg Mortensen, 203–216. Odense: Odense University Press, 1996.

Hirsch, Emanuel. *Kierkegaard-Studien, I.* Gütersloh: 1933; repr., Vaduz: Topos Verlag, 1978.

Hoffman, Rika. "The Cult of Ramen Jiro: Legend, Lore, and Lingo." Culture (blog). 19 June 2019 Updated: August 27, 2020, https://www.byfood.com/blog/culture/the-cult-of-ramen-jiro (accessed 31 May 2021).

Hogg, Chris. "Japan Quake: Disaster Tests Country's Famed 'Stoicism.'" *BBC News*, 20 March 2011. https://www.bbc.co.uk/news/world-asia-pacific-12798799.

Hohlenberg, Johannes. *Sören Kierkegaard*. Translated by T. H. Croxall. New York: Pantheon Books, 1954.

———. *Søren Kierkegaard*. København: Minerva-Bøgerne, 1963.

Holmer, Paul L. *Communicating the Faith Indirectly: Selected Sermons, Addresses, and Prayers*. Vol. 3 of *The Paul L. Holmer Papers*. Edited by David J. Gouwens and Lee C. Barrett. Eugene: Wipf & Stock, 2012.

———. *On Kierkegaard and the Truth*. Vol. 1 of *The Paul L. Holmer Papers*. Edited by David J. Gouwens and Lee C. Barrett. Eugene: Wipf & Stock, 2012.

———. *Thinking the Faith with Passion: Selected Essays*. Vol. 2 of *The Paul L. Holmer Papers*. Edited by David J. Gouwens and Lee C. Barrett. Eugene: Wipf & Stock, 2012.

Honkawa, Yutaka. 社会実情データ図録: うつ病・躁うつ病の総患者数 ["Honkawa Data Tribune: Total Numbers of Depressive and Manic-Depressive Patients"]. Accessed 23 October 2012. http://www2.ttcn.ne.jp/honkawa/2150.html.

Houe, Poul, and Gordon D. Marino, eds. *Søren Kierkegaard and the Word(s): Essays on Hermeneutic and Communication*. Copenhagen: Reitzel, 2003.

Ichizawa, Masanori. キルケゴールにおける殉教の意義 ["The Meaning of Martyrdom in the Thought of Kierkegaard"] in 清泉女学院短期大学研究紀要 第20号 [Bulletin of Seisen Jogakuin Junior College, vol. 20] (June 2001): 49–69.

Ikeda, Yutaka. 旧約聖書の世界 [*The World of the Old Testament*]. Tokyo: Iwanami Gendai-bunko, 2001.

Illmer, Andreas. "World Cup: Japan Fans Impress By Cleaning Up Stadium." *BBC News*, 20 June 2018. https://www.bbc.co.uk/news/world-asia-44492611.

"Important Documents: Nirvana Bio (DGC)" https://livenirvana.com/documents/bioDGC.html#:~:text=%22There%20are%20some%20pop%20songs,Black%20Flag%20and%20Black%20Sabbath.%22 (accessed 23 March 2022).

International Shintoism Studies Association, ed. 2014. 年 国際神道セミナー キリスト教と神道との対話 二つの宗教が探る協調への道筋 – 過去・現在から未来へむけて [*International Shintoism Seminar in 2014: Dialogues between Christianity and Shintoism, The Path of Cooperation Sought by Two*

Religions—From Past and Present to the Future]. Tokyo: Shinano Publishing House, 2015.

Ishikawa, Yuki. スマホ廃人 [*Smartphone Zombies*]. Tokyo: Bunshun-bunko, 2017.

Itō, Kiyoshi. キルケゴールの教育倫理学 [*Kierkegaard's Educational Ethics*]. Tokyo: Daigaku Kyōiku-shuppan, 2015.

Jackson, Timothy P. "Judge William and Professor Browning: A Kierkegaardian Critique of Equal-Regard Marriage and the Democratic Family." In *The Equal-Regard Family and Its Friendly Critics: Don Browning and the Practical Theological Ethics of the Family*, edited by John Witte Jr., M. Christian Green, and Amy Wheeler, 123–150. Grand Rapids: Eerdmans, 2007.

Jaspers, Karl. キルケゴール ["Kierkegaard"]. In 生けるキルケゴール [*Kierkegaaard Alive*], 63–72. Translated by Genji Yasui. Kyōto: Jimbun Shoin, 1967.

———. キルケゴール ["Kierkegaard"]. In キルケゴールと悪 [*Kierkegaard and Evil*], 3–19. Translated by Hiroyuki Kitano. Ōsaka: Tōhō-shuppan, 1982.

———. キルケゴール ‐ バーゼルのペンクラブでの講演 ["Kierkegaard – A Discourse at Pen Club in Basel"]. In キルケゴール研究 ‐ キルケゴール著作集別巻 [*The Studies of Kierkegaard: Kierkegaard's Works Supplement*], 483–508. Translated by Eiichi Kitō. Tokyo: Hakusui-sha, 1951.

———. 現代の人間 [*Man in the Modern Age*]. Translated by Munetaka Iijima. Tokyo: Risō-sha, 1971.

———. 世界観の心理学 (上) [*Psychology of Worldviews vol. 1*]. Translated by Tadao Kamimura and Toshio Maeda. Tokyo: Risō-sha. 1971.

———. 世界観の心理学 (下) [*Psychology of Worldviews vol. 2*]. Translated by Tadao Kamimura and Toshio Maeda Tokyo: Risō-sha, 1971.

———. 理性と実存 [*Reason and Existence*]. Translated by Masao Kusanagi. Tokyo: Risō-sha, 1972.

Jensen, Helle Møller, and George Pattison. *Kierkegaard's Pastoral Dialogues*. Eugene: Wipf & Stock, 2012.

Jespersen, Knud J. V. *A History of Denmark*. Translated by Ivan Hill. London: Palgrave Macmillan, 2004.

John, Varughese. *Truth and Subjectivity, Faith and History: Kierkegaard's Insights for Christian Faith*. Eugene: Pickwick, 2012.

Johnson, Howard A. "Kierkegaard and the Church." *Kierkegaardiana* 8, edited by Niels Thulstrup, 64–79. København: Munksgaard, 1971.

Johnson, William Stacy. "Reading the Scripture Faithfully in a Postmodern Age." In *The Art of Reading Scripture*, edited by Ellen F. Davis and Richard B. Hays, 109–124. Grand Rapids: Eerdmans, 2003.

Jones, Henry Stuart, ed. *An Intermediate Greek-English Lexicon: Founded upon the Seventh Edition of Liddell and Scott's Greek-English Lexicon*. Oxford: Clarendon Press, 1959.

Jordán, Nassim Bravo. "Romanticism." In *Kierkegaard's Concepts: Tome V: Objectivity to Sacrifice*. Vol. 15 of *Kierkegaard Research: Sources, Reception and Resources*. edited by Steven M. Emmanuel, William McDonald, and Jon Stewart, 269–272. London; New York: Routledge, 2015.

K, Bob. "Ramen Jiro." *Ramen Tokyo* (blog). 20 January 2008. http://www.ramentokyo.com/2007/06/ramen-jiro.html.

Kähler, Martin. *The So-Called Historical Jesus and the Historic-Biblical Christ*. Translated by Carl E. Braaten. Philadelphia: Fortress, 1964.

Kaiser, Walter C., Jr. *The Christian and the Old Testament*. Eugene: Wipf & Stock, 2019.

Kaji, Nobuyuki. 沈黙の宗教 – 儒教 [*Religion of Silence: Confucianism*]. Tokyo: Chikuma-shobō, 1994.

Kajihara, Masaaki, and Hiroaki Yamashita, eds. 平家物語 上 [*The Tales of the Heike, Vol. 1*]. Tokyo: Iwanami-shoten, 1991.

Kant, Immanuel. *Critique of Pure Reason*. Translated and edited by Paul Guyer and Allen W. Wood. Cambridge: Cambridge University Press, 1998.

Kearney, Richard. "Kierkegaard's Concept of God-Man." In *Kierkegaardiana* 13, edited by Niels Jørgen Cappelørn, Helge Hultberg, and Poul Lubcke, 105–121. Copenhagen: Reitzel, 1984.

Keener, Craig S. *Acts: An Exegetical Commentary*: 4 vols. Ada: Baker Academic, 2014.

Kelly, Geffrey B. "The Influence of Kierkegaard on Bonhoeffer's Concept of Discipleship." *Irish Theological Quarterly* 41 (1974): 148–154.

Kempis, Thomas à. *The Imitation of Christ*. Translated by Leo Sherley-Price. Harmondsworth: Penguin Books, 1952.

Kierkegaard Association, ed. 新キェルケゴール研究 第12号 [*Kierkegaard Studies, Volume 12*]. Tokyo: Kierkegaard Association, 2014.

———. 新キェルケゴール研究 第13号 [*Kierkegaard Studies, Volume 13*]. Tokyo: Kierkegaard Association, 2015.

———. 新キェルケゴール研究 第14号 [*Kierkegaard Studies, Volume 14*]. Tokyo: Kierkegaard Association, 2016.

———. 新キェルケゴール研究 第16号 [*Kierkegaard Studies, Volume 16*]. Tokyo: Kierkegaard Association, 2018.

Kierkegaard, Søren. *Christian Discourses: The Crisis and a Crisis in the Life of an Actress*. Translated by Howard Vincent Hong and Edna Hatlestad Hong. Princeton: Princeton University Press, 1997.

———. *The Concept of Anxiety*. Translated by Reider Thomte in collaboration with Albert B. Anderson. Princeton: Princeton University Press, 1980.

———. *The Concept of Irony, with Continual Reference to Socrates; Together with Notes of Schelling's Berlin Lectures*. Reprint edition. Translated by Howard

Vincent Hong and Edna Hatlestad Hong. Princeton: Princeton University Press, 1989.

———. *Concluding Unscientific Postscript to Philosophical Fragments, Volume 1*. Translated by Howard Vincent Hong and Edna Hatlestad Hong. Princeton: Princeton University Press, 1992.

———. *Concluding Unscientific Postscript to the Philosophical Crumbs*. Translated by Alastair Hannay. Cambridge: Cambridge University Press, 2009.

———. *Diary of a Seducer*. Translated by Alastair Hannay. Rev. ed. London: Pushkin, 1999.

———. *Eighteen Upbuilding Discourses*. Translated by Howard Vincent Hong and Edna Hatlestad Hong. Princeton: Princeton University Press, 1990.

———. *Either/Or*. Translated by Howard V. Hong and Edna Hatlestad Hong. 2 vols. Princeton: Princeton University Press, 1987.

———. *The Essential Kierkegaard*. Edited by Howard Vincent Hong and Edna Hatlestad Hong. Princeton: Princeton University Press, 2000.

———. "The Expectation of Faith." In *Edifying Discourses: A Selection*, edited by Paul L. Holmer, 2–28. Translated by David F. and Lillian Marvin Swenson. New York: Harper & Brothers, 1958.

———. *Fear and Trembling* and *Repetition*. Translated by Howard Vincent Hong and Edna Hatlestad Hong. Princeton: Princeton University Press, 1983.

———. *For Self-Examination* and *Judge for Yourself!* Translated by Howard Vincent Hong and Edna Hatlestad Hong. Princeton: Princeton University Press, 1990.

———. *The Journals of Kierkegaard*. Translated by Alexander Dru. New York: Harper Torchbooks, 1959.

———. *A Kierkegaard Anthology*. Edited by Robert Bretall. New York: Modern Library, 1946.

———. *Kierkegaard's Concluding Unscientific Postscript*. Translated by David F. Swenson. Princeton: Princeton University Press, 1974.

———. *Kierkegaard's Journals and Notebooks, Volume 5: Journals NB6–NB10*. Edited and translated by Niels Jørgen Cappelørn, Alastair Hannay, Bruce H. Kirmmse, David D. Possen, Joel D. S. Rasmussen, and Vannesa Rumble. Princeton: Princeton University Press, 2012.

———. *The Moment and Late Writings*. Edited by Howard Vincent Hong and Edna Hatlestad Hong. Princeton: Princeton University Press, 2009.

———. *Philosophical Fragments, or a Fragment of Philosophy* and *Johannes Climacus, or De omnibus dubitandum est*. Translated by Howard Vincent Hong and Edna Hatlestad Hong. Princeton: Princeton University Press, 1985.

———. *The Point of View, Etc.* Translated by Walter Lowrie. London: Oxford University Press, 1939.

———. *The Point of View for My Work as an Author, The Single Individual, On My Work as an Author* and *Armed Neutrality*. Translated by Howard Vincent Hong and Edna Hatlestad Hong. Princeton: Princeton University Press, 1998.

———. *Practice in Christianity*. Translated by Howard Vincent Hong and Edna Hatlestad Hong. Princeton: Princeton University Press, 1991.

———. *Prefaces* and *Writing Sampler*. Edited and translated by Todd W. Nichol. Princeton: Princeton University Press, 1998.

———. *The Sickness unto Death: A Christian Psychological Exposition for Upbuilding and Awakening*. Translated by Howard Vincent Hong and Edna Hatlestad Hong. Princeton: Princeton University Press, 1980.

———. *Søren Kierkegaard's Journals and Papers*. Edited and translated by Howard Vincent Hong and Edna Hatlestad Hong, assisted by Gregor Malantschuk. 7 vols. Bloomington: Indiana University Press, 1967–1978.

———. *Stages on Life's Way: Studies by Various Persons*. Translated by Howard Vincent Hong and Edna Hatlestad Hong. Princeton: Princeton University Press, 1988.

———. *Purity of Heart Is to Will One Thing*. Radford: Wilder, 2008.

———. *Two Ages: The Age of Revolution and the Present Age: A Literary Review*. Translated by Howard Vincent Hong and Edna Hatlestad Hong. Princeton: Princeton University Press, 1978.

———. *Upbuilding Discourses in Various Spirits*. Translated by Howard Vincent Hong and Edna Hatlestad Hong. Princeton: Princeton University Press, 1993.

———. *Without Authority*. Translated by Howard Vincent Hong and Edna Hatlestad Hong. Princeton: Princeton University Press, 1997.

———. *Works of Love*. Translated by Howard Vincent Hong and Edna Hatlestad Hong. Princeton: Princeton University Press, 1962.

———. キリスト教の修練 [*Practice in Christianity*]. Translated by Yoshio Inoue. Tokyo: Shinkyō-shuppan-sha, 2004.

———. キルケゴール講話・遺稿集 1 [*Kierkegaard's Selected Works of Discourses and Journals and Papers*], vol. 1, ed. by Munetaka Iijima, 二つの建徳的講話 1843 年 [*Two Upbuilding Discourses* (1843)] and 三つの建徳的講話 1843年 [*Three Upbuilding Discourses* (1843)], trans. by Yasuo Fukushima; 四つの建徳的講話 1843年 [*Four Upbuilding Discourses* (1843)] and 牧師資格取得説教 [Trial Sermon held in Trinitatis Church (February 24, 1844) (*Pap*. IV C1/ *JP*, 4, 3916)], trans. by Masatoshi Yamada. Tokyo: Shinchi-shobo 1981.

———. キルケゴール著作集　第一巻 [A Selection from Kierkegaard's Works, Vol. 1], あれか、これか　第一部（上）[*Either/Or*, Part One], part 1. Trans. by Masao Asai. Tokyo: Hakusui-sha, 1963.

———. キルケゴール著作集　第二巻 [A Selection from Kierkegaard's Works, Vol. 2], あれか、これか　第一部（下）[*Either/Or*, Part One], part 2. Trans. by Masao Asai. Tokyo: Hakusui-sha, 1965.

———. キルケゴール著作集　第三巻 [A Selection from Kierkegaard's Works, Vol. 3], あれか、これか　第二部（上）[*Either/Or*, Part Two], part 1. Trans. by Masao Asai. Tokyo: Hakusui-sha, 1965.

———. キルケゴール著作集　第四巻 [A Selection from Kierkegaard's Works, Vol. 4], あれか、これか　第二部（下）[*Either/Or*, Part Two], part 2. Trans. by Masao Asai. Tokyo: Hakusui-sha 1965.

———. キルケゴール著作集　第八巻 [A Selection from Kierkegaard's Works, Vol. 8], 哲学的断片への結びとしての非学問的あとがき（中）[*Concluding Unscientific Postscript*, part 2]. Trans. by Yoshimu Sugiyama and Keiji Ogawa. Tokyo: Hakusui-sha, 1969.

———. キルケゴール著作集　第十七巻 [A Selection from Kierkegaard's Works, Vol. 17], キリスト教の修練 [*Practice in Christianity*]. Trans. by Yoshimu Sugiyama. Tokyo: Hakusui-sha, 1963.

———. キルケゴール著作集　第十八巻 [A Selection from Kierkegaard's Works, Vol. 18], わが著作活動の視点 [*The Point of View for my Work as as Author*], trans. by Ginsabrō Tabuchi; 野の百合、空の鳥 [*The Lilly in the Field and the Bird of the Air*], trans. by Yasushi Kuyama. Tokyo: Hakusui-sha, 1963.

———. 死に至る病 [*The Sickness unto Death*]. Translated by Keizaburō Masuda. Tokyo: Chikuma-bunko, 1996.

———. 死に至る病 [*The Sickness unto Death*]. Translated by Shinji Saitō. Tokyo: Iwanami-bunko, 1957.

———. 死に至る病 [*The Sickness unto Death*]. Translated by Yūsuke Suzuki. Tokyo: Kōdan-sha Gakujutsu-bunko, 2017.

———. 世界の名著40「キルケゴール」[World Masterpieces. Vol. 40, Kierkegaard] (containing 哲学的断片 [*Philosophical Fragments*], trans. by Yoshimu Sugiyama; 不安の概念 [*The Concept of Anxiety*], trans. by Gisaburō Tabuchi; 現代の批判 ["The Present Age" from *A Literary Review*] and 死にいたる病 [*The Sickness unto Death*], trans. by Keizaburō Masuda). Tokyo: Chūō Kōron-sha, 1966.

———. セーレン・キェルケゴールの日誌 第１巻 [*Journals*] [especially passages which are about Regine Olsen]. Translated by Jun Hashimoto. Tokyo: Mirai-sha, 1985.

———. 背後から傷つける思想 [Thoughts that Wound from Behind – for Upbuilding (from *Christian Discourses*)]. Translated by Jun Hashimoto. Tokyo: Shinkyo-shuppan-sha, 1976.

Kierkegaard, Søren, and John Updike. *The Seducer's Diary*. Translated by Howard Vincent Hong and Edna Hatlestad Hong. Reissue ed. Princeton: Princeton University Press, 2013.

Kikukawa, Miyoko. 矢内原忠雄の「日本的基督教」: 土着化論再考 ["'Japanese Christianity' of Tadao Yanaihara: Reconsidering Indigenization"]. 基督教研究 [*The Study of Christianity*] 73, no. 2 (2011): 91–104.

Kirkconnell, W. Glenn. *Kierkegaard on Ethics and Religion: From Either/Or to Philosophical Fragments*. London; New York: Continuum, 2008.

Kirkpatrick, Matthew D. "Kierkegaard and a Religionless Christianity: The Place of Søren Kierkegaard in the Thought of Dietrich Bonhoeffer." PhD diss., University of Oxford, 2008.

Kirmmse, Bruce H. *Kierkegaard in Golden Age Denmark*. Indiana Series in the Philosophy of Religion. Bloomington: Indiana University Press, 1990.

Kitamori, Kazō. 日本人と聖書 [*Japanese and the Bible*]. Tokyo: Kyōbunkan, 1995.

Koami Jinja. "神道の汎神論上価値観こそ、和と調和を生み現在の日本の繁栄に導いた" ["It Is Precisely the Values of Shinto's Pantheism That Gave Birth to Harmony and Balance, Leading to Japan's Present Prosperity"]. *Koami Jinja Blog*. Last modified March 19, 2022. https://blog.goo.ne.jp/koamijinja/e/2347d5bcaefcd2cce2965775b60be56f.

Kobayashi, Shinobu, and Kyōdō News Crew. 昭和天皇 最後の侍従日記 [*Shōwa Emperor's Last Chamberlain's Diary*]. Bunshun-bunko, 2019.

Koch, Carl Henrik. *Den Danske Idealisme 1800–1880* [*The Danish Idealism 1800–1880*]. København: Gyldendal, 2004.

Kojiki. Translated by Donald L. Philippi. Tokyo: University of Tokyo Press, 1968.

Kojima, Noriyuki, Kōjiro Naoki, Kazutami Nishimiya, Susumu Kuranaka, and Masamori Mōri, eds. and trans.日本書紀 1 (*Nihonshoki 1*) [The Chronicles of Japan 1]. Tokyo: Shōgakukan, 1994.

Kondō, Katsuhiko. キリスト教弁証学 [*Christian Apologetics*]. Tokyo: Kyōbunkan, 2016.

Kondō, Tomie. "Aware." In 日本を知る101章 (コロナ・ブックス⑦) [*101 Key Words for Understanding Japan* (Corona Books ⑦)], edited by Hiroshi Shimonaka, 238–240. Tokyo: Heibon-sha, 1995.

Kumazawa, Yoshinobu. キルケゴールとブルトマン [*Kierkegaard and Bultmann*], A Monthly Newsletter 16 in Kierkegaard's Works vol. 16. Tokyo: Hakusui-sha, 1964.

Kurano, Kenji, ed. 古事記 (*Kojiki*) [*Records of Ancient Matters*]. Tokyo: Iwanami-bunko, 1963; 2007.

Kurosu, Satomi, Noriko Tsuya, Kiyoshi Hamano, Aoi Okada, Osamu Saitō, Miyuki Takahashi, Hiroshi Kawaguchi, and Harald Fuess. 歴史人口学から見た結婚・離婚・再婚 [*Marriage, Divorce, Remarriage from the Perspective of*

Historical Demography]. Edited by Satomi Kurosu. Chiba: Reitaku Daigaku-shuppan-kai, 2012.

Langmead, Ross. *The Word Made Flesh: Towards an Incarnational Missiology*. American Society of Missiology Dissertation Series. Lanham: University Press of America, 2004.

Lappano, David. "Press/Journalism." In *Kierkegaard's Concepts: Tome V: Objectivity to Sacrifice*. Vol. 15 of *Kierkegaard Research: Sources, Reception and Resources*, edited by Steven M. Emmanuel, William McDonald, and Jon Stewart, 121–128. London; New York: Routledge, 2015.

Law, David R., "Cheap Grace and the Cost of Discipleship in Kierkegaard's *Self-Examination*" In *For Self-Examination and Judge for Yourself!* Vol. 21 of *International Kierkegaard Commentary*, edited by Robert L. Perkins, 111–142. Macon: Mercer University Press, 2002.

———. "A Cacophony of Voices: The Multiple Authors and Readers of Kierkegaard's *The Point of View for My Work as an Author*." In *The Point of View*. Vol. 22 of *International Kierkegaard Commentary*, edited by Robert L. Perkins, 12–47. Macon: Mercer University Press, 2010.

———. *Kierkegaard's Kenotic Christology*. Oxford: Oxford University Press, 2013.

———. "Redeeming the Penultimate: Discipleship and Church in the Thought of Søren Kierkegaard and Dietrich Bonhoeffer." *International Journal for the Study of the Christian Church* 11 (2011): 14–26.

Lee, Robert. "Paradigm Shifts from Ancient Jerusalem to Modern Tokyo: A Critical Expansion of Bosch." Accessed 8 February 2020. https://anabaptistwiki.org/mediawiki/images/b/b2/Vol._11supp_Lee%2C_Robert._Paradigm_Shifts_from_Ancient_Jerusalem_to_Modern_Tokyo-A_Critical_Expansion_of_Bosch.pdf.

Lee, Wonjung. 魚木忠一の「日本基督教」を再考する：挫折した土着化神学への試み ["Reconsidering 'Christianity in Japan' of Tadakazu Uwoki: An Attempt of Indigenous Theology Dwindled"]. キリスト教社会問題研究 [*The Study of Christianity and Social Problems*] 68 (2019): 91–115.

Levin, Judith N. *Japanese Mythology*. New York: Rosen Publishing, 2008.

Lie, John. "Ruth Benedict's Legacy of Shame: Orientalism and Occidentalism in the Study of Japan." *Asian Journal of Social Science* 29, no. 2 (2001): 249–261.

Lindsey, Hal. *Satan Is Alive and Well on Planet Earth*. Grand Rapids: Zondervan, 1972.

Lingenfelter, Sherwood G., and Marvin K. Mayers. *Ministering Cross-Culturally: An Incarnational Model for Personal Relationships*. 2nd ed. Grand Rapids: Baker Academic, 1986; 2003.

Lippitt, John. "Existential Laughter." *Cogito* 10, no. 1 (1996): 63–72.

———. *Humour and Irony in Kierkegaard's Thought*. London: Macmillan, 2000.

———. "A Philosophical Response: The Kierkegaardian Self and Person-Centered Therapy." In *Kierkegaard's Pastoral Dialogues*, edited by Helle Møller Jensen and George Pattison, loc. 2064–2418. Eugene: Wipf & Stock, 2012. Kindle.

Lippitt, John, and George Pattison, eds. *The Oxford Handbook of Kierkegaard*. Oxford: Oxford University Press, 2013.

Lisi, Leonardo F. "Faust: The Seduction of Doubt." In *Kierkegaard's Literary Figures and Motifs: Tome I: Agamemnon to Guadalquivir*. Vol. 16 of *Kierkegaard Research: Sources, Reception and Resources*, edited by Katalin Nun and Jon Stewart, 209–228. London; New York: Routledge, 2015

Lloyd-Jones, D. Martyn. *Preaching and Preachers*. Grand Rapids: Zondervan, 1971.

Lorensen, Marlene Ringgard. "Preaching as Repetition – in Times of Transition." *International Journal of Homiletics* 1, no. 1 (2016): 34–51.

Lorentzen, Jamie. *Kierkegaard's Metaphors* (International Kierkegaard Commentary). Macon: Mercer University Press, 2001.

Lowrie, Walter. *Kierkegaard*. London: Oxford University Press, 1938.

———. *A Short Life of Kierkegaard*. Princeton: Princeton University Press, 2013.

Lu, David J. *Japan: A Documentary History: v. 1: The Dawn of History to the Late Eighteenth Century (2nd Edition)*. London; New York: Routledge, 1996.

———. *Overcoming Barriers to Evangelization in Japan*. Eugene: Wipf & Stock, 2019.

———. 日本宣教を阻む5つの障壁 [*Overcoming Barriers to Evangelization in Japan*]. Tokyo: Inochino Kotoba-sha, 2020.

Lubańska, Stefania. "Pascalian Themes in the Philosophy of Søren Kierkegaard." *Studies in Logic, Grammar and Rhetoric* 20, no. 33 (2010): 89–98.

Lukács, Georg (György). *The Destruction of Reason*. Translated by Peter Palmer. Atlantic Highlands: Humanities Press, 1981.

———. 魂と形式 [*Soul and Form*]. Translated by Jirō Kawamura, Shūhei Enko, and Mitsuyoshi Sanjō. Tokyo: Hakusui-sha, 1969.

———. 理性の破壊 (上) [*Destruction of Reason vol. 1*]. Translated by Ryōzō Teruoka. Tokyo: Hakusui-sha, 1968.

Lyotard, Jean-François. *The Confession of Augustine*. Translated by Richard Beardsworth. Stanford: Stanford University Press, 2000.

———. *The Postmodern Condition: A Report on Knowledge*. Translated by Geoff Bennington and Brian Massumi. Minneapolis: University of Minnesota Press, 1984.

Lyrics Mode. "Death – Spiritual Healing Lyrics." Accessed 28 August 2020. https://www.lyricsmode.com/lyrics/d/death/spiritual_healing.html.

———. "Napalm Death – Practice What You Preach Lyrics." Accessed 28 August 2020. https://www.lyricsmode.com/lyrics/n/napalm_death/practice_what_you_preach.html.

———. "Testament – Practice What You Preach Lyrics." Accessed 28 August 2020. https://www.lyricsmode.com/lyrics/t/testament/practice_what_you_preach.html.

McElhinney, and David Will Heath. "75 Best Japanese Authors of All Time." https://japanobjects.com/features/japanese-authors (accessed 19 March 2025).

MacIntyre, Alasdair. *After Virtue: A Study in Moral Theory*. 2nd ed. Notre Dame: University of Notre Dame Press, 1984.

Mackey, Louis. *Kierkegaard: A Kind of Poet*. Philadelphia: University of Pennsylvania Press, 1971.

———. *Points of View: Readings of Kierkegaard*. Kierkegaard and Postmodernism. Tallahassee: University Press of Florida, 1986.

Makoto, Mizuta. 夏目漱石とセーレン・キェルケゴール – 「自己」への問いと発見 ["Natsume Sōseki and Søren Kierkegaard: Their Quest for 'Self'"]. 『比較思想研究』 [*Studies in Comparative Philosophy*] 27 (2000): 90–96.

Malantschuk, Gregor. *Kierkegaard's Concept of Existence*. Marquette Studies in Philosophy. Translated by Howard Vincent Hong and Edna Hatlestad Hong. Milwaukee: Marquette University Press, 2003.

———. *Kierkegaard's Thought*. Translated by Howard Vincent Hong and Edna Hatlestad Hong. Princeton: Princeton University Press, 1974.

Manis, R. Zachary. "'Eternity Will Nail Him to Himself': The Logic of Damnation in Kierkegaard's 'The Sickness unto Death.'" *Religious Studies* 52 (2016): 287–314.

The Manyōshū (*One Thousand Poems with the Texts in Romaji*). Translated by the Nippon Gakujutsu Shinkōkai. New York: Columbia University Press, 1965.

Marcuse, Herbert. *Reason and Revolution: Hegel and the Rise of Social Theory*. Boston: Beacon, 1960.

———. 理性と革命 [*Reason and Revolution*]. Translated by Keizaburō Masuda. Tokyo: Iwanami-shoten, 1961.

Marek, Jakub. "Anti-Climacus: Kierkegaard's Servant of the Word." In *Kierkegaard's Pseudonyms*. Vol. 17 of *Kierkegaard Research: Sources, Reception and Resources*, edited by Katalin Nun and Jon Stewart, 39–50. London; New York: Routledge, 2015.

Marino, Gordon. "Kierkegaard on the Couch." *Opinionator*, 28 October 2009. https://opinionator.blogs.nytimes.com/2009/10/28/kierkegaard-on-the-couch/?mcubz=1.

———. "Making the Darkness Visible: On the Distinction between Despair and Depression in Kierkegaard's *Journals*." In *Kierkegaard in the Present Age* (Marquette Studies in Philosophy), 99–111. Milwaukee: Marquette University Press, 2001.

Markwald, Rudolf K., and Marilynn Morris Markwald. *Katharina Von Bora: A Reformation Life*. Saint Louis: Concordia, 2002.

Marshall, Ronald F. *Kierkegaard for the Church: Essays and Sermons*. Eugene: Wipf & Stock, 2013.

Martens, Paul. "Kierkegaard and the Bible." In *The Oxford Handbook of Kierkegaard*, edited by John Lippitt and George Pattison, 150–165. Oxford: Oxford University Press, 2013.

Martín, José García "The Category of the Single Individual in Kierkegaard." *European Journal of Science and Theology* 13, no. 3 (June 2017): 99–108.

Masugata, Kinya. 日本に於けるキェルケゴール受容史 ["A History of Reception of Kierkegaard in Japan"]. In キェルケゴールと日本の仏教・哲学 [*Kierkegaard and Japanese Buddhism and Philosophy*], edited by Masaru Ōtani and Ōya Kenichi, 265–285. Tokyo: Tōhō-shuppan, 1992.

———. "A Short History of Kierkegaard's Reception in Japan." In *Kierkegaard and Japanese Thought*, edited by James Giles, 31–52. Basingstoke; New York: Palgrave Macmillan, 2008.

Matsuda, Kazunori. 日本の精神風土における福音の「文化内開花（インカルチュレーション）」事例研究—遠藤周作『海と毒薬』の場合— ["Inculturation of the Gospel as Seen in the Japanese Spirit and Climate: A Case Study of Shūsaku Endo's 'The Sea and Poison'"]. In 科学/人間 [*Journal of Science and Humanities*] 47, (March 2018): 119–143.

Matsuki, Shinichi, ed. キェルケゴールとキリスト教神学の展望 [*New Perspective of Studies on Kierkegaard and the Scope of Contemporary Christian Theology*]. Hyogo: Kwansei Gakuin University Press, 2006.

Matsunaga, Daigan, and Alicia Matsunaga. "The Concept of Upāya (方便) in Mahāyāna Buddhist Philosophy." *Japanese Journal of Religious Studies* 1, no. 1 (March 1974): 51–72.

McCarthy, Vincent A. *Kierkegaard as Psychologist*. Evanston: Northwestern University Press, 2015.

McDonald, William. "Kierkegaard and Romanticism." In *The Oxford Handbook of Kierkegaard*, edited by John Lippitt and George Pattison, 94–111. Oxford: Oxford University Press 2013.

———. "Music." In *Kierkegaard's Concepts: Tome IV: Individual to Novel*. Vol. 15 of *Kierkegaard Research: Sources, Reception and Resources*, edited by Steven M. Emmanuel, William McDonald, and Jon Stewart, 213–222. London; New York: Routledge, 2014.

McGrath, Alister. *Evangelicalism and the Future of Christianity*. Downers Grove: InterVarsity Press, 1995.

McKim, Donald K., ed. *The Westminster Handbook to Reformed Theology*. The Westminster Handbooks to Christian Theology. Louisville: Westminster John Knox, 2001.

McLuckie, John. "A Pastoral Response: Care and Conversation." In *Kierkegaard's Pastoral Dialogues*, edited by Helle Møller Jensen and George Pattison, loc. 2591–2602. Eugene: Wipf & Stock, 2012.

Meyer, Marvin, and Charles Hughes, eds. *Jesus Then and Now*. Salem: Trinity, 2001.

Miller, Mark C. "The Hipness unto Death: Søren Kierkegaard and David Letterman – Ironic Apologists to Generation X." *Mars Hill Review* 7, no. 7 (Winter/Spring 1997): 38–52.

Miller, Robert J. "What Do the Stories about Resurrection(s) Prove?" In *Will the Real Jesus Please Stand Up?*, edited by Paul Copan, 77–98. Grand Rapids: Baker Books, 1998.

Milton, John. "Areopagitica." In *Complete Poems and Major Prose*, edited by Merritt Y. Hughes, 716–749. Indianapolis; Cambridge: Hackett, 1957; 2003.

Minami, Connie. 「単独的普遍者」―サルトルのキルケゴール解釈をめぐって― ["'The Singular Universal': on Sartre's Interpretation of Kierkegaard"]. In 新キェルケゴール研究 第13号 [Kierkegaard Studies, Volume 13], edited by the Kierkegaard Association, 87–102. Tokyo: Kierkegaard Association, 2015.

Minear, Paul S., and Paul S. Morimoto. *Kierkegaard and the Bible: An Index*. Princeton: Princeton University Press, 1953.

Miura, Ayako. 塩狩峠 [*Shiokari Pass*]. Tokyo: Shinchō-bunko, 1973.

"Reconstruction of Japan." Modern Japan in Archives, accessed 23 March 2022. https://www.ndl.go.jp/modern/e/cha5/index.html.

Mooney, Edward F., ed. *Ethics, Love, and Faith in Kierkegaard: Philosophical Engagements*. Bloomington: Indiana University Press, 2008.

Montaigne, Michel de. *Essays*. Translated by J. M. Cohen. London: Penguin Books, 1993.

Morgan, Silas and Edward John Carnell. "A Skeptical Neo-Evangelical Reading." In *Kierkegaard's Influence on Theology: Tome II: Anglophone and Scandinavian Protestant Theology*. Vol. 10 of *Kierkegaard Research: Sources, Reception and Resources*. London; New York: Routledge, 2012.

Mortensen, Finn Hauberg, ed. *Kierkegaard Made in Japan*. Odense: Odense University Press, 1996.

Mounce, Bill. "Search the Greek Dictionary." Accessed 1 April 2022. https://www.billmounce.com/greek-dictionary/Kenoo.

Mulder, Jack, Jr. *Kierkegaard and the Catholic Tradition: Conflict and Dialogue*. Bloomington: Indiana University Press, 2010.

———. "Martyrdom/Persecution." In *Kierkegaard's Concepts: Tome IV: Individual to Novel*. Vol. 15 of *Kierkegaard Research: Sources, Reception and Resources*, edited by Steven M. Emmanuel, William McDonald, and Jon Stewart, 123–130. London; New York: Routledge, 2014.

Mullen, Douglas. *Kierkegaard's Philosophy*. New York: Mentor, 1981.

Mullins, Mark R. *Christianity Made in Japan: A Study of Indigenous Movements*. Nanzan Library of Asian Religion and Culture. Honolulu: University of Hawai'i Press, 1998.

Munch-Petersen, Laurits. *Forførerens Dagbog* [*Seducer's Diary*]. Drama. 2014.

Murphy, Francesca Aran, ed. *The Oxford Handbook of Christology*. Oxford: Oxford University Press, 2015.

Nakamasa, Masaki. 日本とドイツ – 二つの戦後思想 [*Japan and Germany: Two Post-war Thinkings*]. Tokyo: Kōbunsha-shinsho, 2005.

Nakamura, Satoshi. 日本キリスト教宣教史 [*The History of Mission in Japan*]. Tokyo: Inochino Kotoba-sha, 2009.

Nakano, Yoshio. "A Commentary" in Sōseki Natsume, 日本の文学14「夏目漱石（三）」 [A Treasury of Japanese Literature, vol. 14, Sōseki Natsume, no. 3] (『道草』[Michikusa], 『明暗』[Meian]), 537–551. Tokyo: Chūōkōron-sha 1966.

Namikawa, Takayoshi. ブッダたちの仏教 [*Buddhism of Buddhas*]. Tokyo: Chikuma-shinsho, 2017.

Nanda, Meera. *Postmodernism and Religious Fundamentalism: A Scientific Rebuttal to Hindu Science: An Essay, a Review and an Interview*. New Delhi: Navayana, 2005.

Natsume, Kinnosuke. 漱石全集　第八巻 [*Soseki Complete Works, Vol. 8*], 行人 [Koujin], Tokyo: Iwanami-shoten, 1994.

Natsume, Soseki. *Kokoro*. Translated by Edwin McClellan. Mineola: Dover, 1957; 2006.

———. *The Wayfarer*. Translated by Beongcheon Yu. Detroit: Wayne State University Press, 1967.

Natsume, Sōseki. 日本の文学13「夏目漱石（二）」 [*A Treasury of Japanese Literature, vol. 13, Natsume Sōseki, No.2*] (『三四郎』[Sanshirō], 『それから』[Sorekara], 『こころ』[Kokoro]). Tokyo: Chūō Kōron-sha, 1965.

Neto, José R. Maia. *The Christianization of Pyrrhonism: Scepticism and Faith in Pascal, Kierkegaard, and Shestov*. Archives internationales d'histoire des idées [*International Archives of the History of Ideas*]. Dordrecht; Boston; London: Kluwer Academic, 1995.

Nietzsche, Friedrich. *The Will to Power*. Translated by Walter Kaufmann and R. J. Hollingdale. New York: Vintage Books, 1968.

Nihon Kindai, Bungakukan, ed. 日本近代文学大事典 第四巻 事項 [*Dictionary of Modern Japanese Literature, Vol. 4: Literary Terms, Schools, or Organisations, and Literary Disputes*]. Tokyo: Kōdan-sha, 1977.

Nihongi: Chronicles of Japan from the Earliest Times to A.D. 697. Translated by W. G. Aston. Tokyo: Tuttle, 1972.

Nishida, Kitarō. *An Inquiry into the Good*. Translated by Masao Abe and Christopher Ives. New Haven: Yale University Press, 1990.

———. 善の研究 [*An Inquiry into the Good*]. Tokyo: Iwanami-bunko, 1960; 2012.

Nitobe, Inazō. "Bushido, the Soul of Japan." Accessed 28 March 2022. https://www.sacred-texts.com/shi/bsd/bsd09.htm. .

———. *Bushido, the Soul of Japan*. Philadelphia: Leeds & Biddle, 1900.

———. 武士道 [*Bushidō*]. Translated by Tadao Yanaihara. Tokyo: Iwanami-bunko, 1938; 1974.

Nitsch, Paul Friedrich A. *Neues Mythologisches Wörterbuch II* [*New Mythological Dictionary II*]. Revised by Friedrich Gotthilf Klopfer. Leipzig: Soran, 1821.

Nölke, Muhō. 日本人に「宗教」は要らない [*The Japanese Do Not Need "Religion"*]. Tokyo: Bestsellers, 2014.

Nowachek, Matthew Thomas. "Living within the Sacred Tension: Paradox and Its Significance for Christian Existence in the Thought of Søren Kierkegaard." PhD diss., Marquette University, 2016.

Nun, Katalin, and Jon Stewart, eds. *Kierkegaard's Literary Figures and Motifs: Tome I: Agamemnon to Guadalquivir*. Vol. 16 of *Kierkegaard Research: Sources, Reception and Resources*. London; New York: Routledge, 2015.

———. *Kierkegaard's Literary Figures and Motifs: Tome II: Gulliver to Zerlina*. Vol. 16 of *Kierkegaard Research: Sources, Reception and Resources*. London; New York: Routledge, 2015.

———. *Kierkegaard's Pseudonyms*. Vol. 17 of *Kierkegaard Research: Sources, Reception and Resources*. London; New York: Routledge, 2015.

Nutt, Derek. "Kierkegaard's Johannes Climacus on Faith and Reason." *Berkeley Journal of Religion and Theology* 4, no. 1 (2018): 46–73.

O'Collins, Gerald. *Christology: A Biblical, Historical, and Systematic Study of Jesus*. 2nd ed. Oxford; New York: Oxford University Press, 2009.

Odin, Steve. *The Social Self in Zen and American Pragmatism*. Albany: State University of New York Press, 1996.

Ohara, Shin. 内村鑑三の生涯 – 日本的キリスト教の創造 [*Biography of Kanzō Uchimura: Creation of Japanese Christianity*]. Tokyo: PHP-bunko, 1997.

Ōhashi, Hideo. はじめてのキリスト教 [*Christianity for the First Time*]. Tokyo: Ministry for Christ, 2016.

Okazaki, Yoshie. 漱石と則天去私 [*Sōseki and Sokuten Kyoshi*]. Tokyo: Hōbunkan-shuppan, 1968.

Olson, Roger E. "Was Kierkegaard an Evangelical? Part 1–3." *My Evangelical Arminian Theological Musings* (blog). August–September 2011. http://www.patheos.com/blogs/rogereolson/2011/08/was-kierkegaard-an-evangelical-part-1/; http://www.patheos.com/blogs/rogereolson/2011/08/was-kierkegaard-an-evangelical-part-2/; http://www.patheos.com/blogs/rogereolson/2011/09/kierkegaard-as-evangelical-part-3-final/ (accessed 29 Dec 2016).

Ōnuki, Takashi, Shirō Natori, Hisao Miyamoto, and Fumiaki Momose, eds. 岩波キリスト教辞典 [*Iwanami Christian Dictionary*]. Tokyo: Iwanami-shoten, 2002.

Ōtani, Hidehito. キルケゴール教会闘争の研究 [*A Study of Kierkegaard's Attack upon Christendom*]. Tokyo: Keisō-shobō, 2007.

———. キルケゴール青年時代の研究 正 [*A Study of Kierkegaard's Youth, Vol. 1*]. Tokyo: Keisō-shobō, 1966.

———. キルケゴール著作活動の研究 前篇 – 青年時代を中心に行われた文学研究の実態 [*A Study on Kierkegaard's Authorship, Part 1 – The Realities of Young Kierkegaard's Own Studies of Literature*]. Tokyo: Keisō-shobō, 1989.

———. キルケゴール著作活動の研究 後編 – 全著作構造の解明 [*A Study on Kierkegaard's Authorship, Part 2 – Investigation in the Structure of the Entirety of His Works*]. Tokyo: Keisō-shobō, 1991.

Ōtani, Hidehito, and Izumi Harunori. キルケゴール 死に至る病 [*Kierkegaard: The Sickness unto Death*]. Tokyo: Yūhikaku, 1980.

Ōtani, Masaru, and Ōya Kenichi. キェルケゴールと日本の仏教・哲学 [*Kierekgaard and the Japanese Buddhism and Philosophy*]. Tokyo: Tōhō-shuppan, 1992.

Ott, Craig, Stephen J. Strauss, and Timothy C. Tennent. *Encountering Theology of Mission: Biblical Foundations, Historical Developments, and Contemporary Issues*. Encountering Mission. Grand Rapids: Baker Academic, 2010.

Pannenberg, Wolfhart. *Jesus – God and Man*. Translated by Lewis L. Wilkins and Duane A. Priebe. London: SCM, 1968; 2002.

Park, Bradley. "Buddhism and Japanese Aesthetics. Department of Philosophy and Religious Studies, St. Mary's College of Maryland." https://communitycollegeoutreach.arizona.edu/materials/buddhism-and-japanese-aesthetics (accessed 3 April 2025).

Park, Chong Soon. 夏目漱石とキリスト教 ["Natsume Sōseki and Christianity"] 基督教学研究 [*Journal of Christian Studies*] 31 (2011): 177–187.

Parry, Richard Lloyd. "Akihito and the Sorrows of Japan." *London Review of Books*, vol. 42, no. 6. 19 March 2020. https://www.lrb.co.uk/the-paper/v42/n06/richard-lloyd-parry/akihito-and-the-sorrows-of-japan.

Pascal, Blaise. *Pensées*. Translated by W. F. Trotter. Seattle: Amazon Digital Services, 2012. Kindle.

Patrick, Denzil G. M. *Pascal and Kierkegaard: A Study in the Strategy of Evangelism*. Vol. II. London: Lutterworth, 1947.

Pattison, George. *Kierkegaard's Upbuilding Discourses: Philosophy, Literature, and Theology*. London; New York: Routledge, 2003.

Pedersen, Viggo Hjørnager, ed. *Dansk-Engelsk Ordbog, 3. udgave* [*Danish-English Dictionary*. 3rd ed.]. København: Gyldendalske Boghandel, 1990.

Penner, Myron Bradley. *The End of Apologetics: Christian Witness in a Postmodern Context*. Grand Rapids: Baker Academic, 2013.

Perkins, Robert L., ed. *Either/Or, I*. Vol. 3 of *International Kierkegaard Commentary*. Macon: Mercer University Press, 1995.

———. *Either/Or, II*. Vol. 4 of *International Kierkegaard Commentary*. Macon: Mercer University Press, 1995.

———. *Eighteen Upbuilding Discourses*. Vol. 5 of *International Kierkegaard Commentary*. Macon: Mercer University Press, 2003.

———. *For Self-Examination and Judge for Yourself!* Vol. 21 of *International Kierkegaard Commentary*. Macon: Mercer University Press, 2002.

———. *The Point of View*. Vol. 22 of *International Kierkegaard Commentary*. Macon: Mercer University Press, 2010.

———. *Practice in Christianity*. Vol. 20 of *International Kierkegaard Commentary*. Macon: Mercer University Press, 2004.

———. *The Sickness unto Death*. Vol. 19 of *International Kierkegaard Commentary*. Macon: Mercer University Press, 2001.

———. *Two Ages*. Vol. 14 of *International Kierkegaard Commentary*. Macon: Mercer University Press, 1984.

Petty, Josh. "Metamodernism: The Path Forward." 26 April 2018. https://medium.com/@joshpetty_31591/metamodernism-the-path-forward-9743d1748edf.

Plantinga, Alvin. *Warranted Christian Belief*. New York: Oxford University Press, 2000.

Podmore, Simon D. "Carl R. Rogers: To Be That Self Which One Truly Is." In *Kierkegaard's Influence on the Social Sciences*. Vol. 13 of *Kierkegaard Research: Sources, Reception and Resources*, edited by Jon Stewart, 238–258. Farnham; Burlington: Ashgate, 2011.

———. *Kierkegaard and the Self before God: Anatomy of the Abyss*. Bloomington: Indiana University Press, 2011.

Pohlmeyer, Markus. "Prometheus: Thief, Creator, and Icon of Pain." In *Kierkegaard's Literary Figures and Motifs: Tome II: Gulliver to Zerlina*. Vol. 16 of *Kierkegaard Research: Sources, Reception and Resources*, edited by Katalin Nun and Jon Stewart, 187–198. London; New York: Routledge, 2015.

Politikens Nudansk Ordbog, 19. udgave [*Politiken's New Danish Dictionary*. 19th ed.]. København: Politikens Forlagshus, 2005.

Poole, Roger. *Kierkegaard: The Indirect Communication*. Charlottesville: University of Virginia Press, 1993.

Pope, Mick. "Grappling for Christ: Incarnational Mission at the Margins of the Church." In *We Are Pilgrims: From, in and with the Margins of Our Diverse World*, edited by Darren Cronshaw and Rosemary Dewerse, 151–163. Dandenong: Urban Neighbours of Hope, 2015.

Popova, Maria "Why Haters Hate: Kierkegaard Explains the Psychology of Cyber-Bullying and Online Trolling in 1847." *Brain Pickings* (blog). 13 October 2014. https://internet.psych.wisc.edu/wp-content/uploads/532-Master/532-UnitPages/Unit-06/Popova_Kirkegaard_BrainPickings_2014.pdf.

Posch, Thomas. "Nature/Natural Science." *Kierkegaard's Concepts: Tome IV: Individual to Novel.* Vol. 15 of *Kierkegaard Research: Sources, Reception and Resources*, edited by Steven M. Emmanuel, William McDonald, and Jon Stewart, 227–230. London; New York: Routledge, 2014.

Possen, David D. "The Voice of Rigor." In *Practice in Christianity*. Vol. 20 of *International Kierkegaard Commentary*, edited by Robert L. Perkins, 161–185. Macon: Mercer University Press, 2004.

———. "The Works of Anti-Climacus." In *Practice in Christianity*. Vol. 20 of *International Kierkegaard Commentary*, edited by Robert L. Perkins, 187–209. Macon: Mercer University Press, 2004.

Pyper, Hugh S. *The Joy of Kierkegaard: Essays on Kierkegaard as a Biblical Reader.* London: Equinox, 2011.

Rae, Murray. "Kierkegaard and the Historians." *International Journal for Philosophy of Religion* 37 (April 1995): 87–102.

Rae, Murray A. "The Forgetfulness of Historical-Talkative Remembrance in Kierkegaard's *Practice in Christianity*." In *Practice in Christianity*. Vol. 20 of *International Kierkegaard Commentary*, edited by Robert L. Perkins, 69-94. Macon: Mercer University Press, 2004.

Reischauer, Edwin O., and Marius B. Jansen. *The Japanese Today: Change and Continuity*. Enlarged ed. Boston; Rutland, Vermont; Tokyo: Harvard University Press, 1995.

Ricœur, Paul. *Freud and Philosophy: An Essay on Interpretation*. New Haven: Yale University Press, 1970.

Robinson, G. D. "Paul Ricoeur and the Hermeneutics of Suspicion: A Brief Overview and Critique." *PREMISE*, vol. 2, no. 8. 27 September 1995. http://individual.utoronto.ca/bmclean/hermeneutics/ricoeur_suppl/Ricoeur_Herm_of_Suspicion.htm.

Rogers, Carl R. *On Becoming a Person: A Therapist View of Psychotherapy*. Boston: Houghton Mifflin, 1961.

Root, Jerry. "Why Must Evangelism and Discipleship Go Hand in Hand?" *Lausanne World Pulse Archives*. 2007. http://www.lausanneworldpulse.com/themedarticles-php/717/05-2007.

Rudolph, David J. *A Jew to the Jews: Jewish Contours of Pauline Flexibility in 1 Corinthians 9:19–23*. 2nd ed. Eugene: Wipf & Stock, 2016.

Salinger, Jerome David. *Raise High the Roof Beam, Carpenters*. https://mixi.jp/view_diary.pl?id=1959831813&owner_id=1737245 (accessed 25 March 2025).

Sanchez, Alejandro Cavallazzi. "Dialectic." In *Kierkegaard's Concepts: Tome II: Classicism to Enthusiasm*. Vol. 15 of *Kierkegaard Research: Sources, Reception and Resources*, edited by Steven M. Emmanuel, William McDonald, and Jon Stewart, 165–169. London; New York: Routledge, 2014.

Sanders, Van E. "A Theological Study of Point of Contact Theory." *Global Missiology* 4, no. 1 (July 2004): 1–52.

Sano, Tsunehiko, and Nicolas. 教法問答 [*Doctrinal Dialogues*]. Yamaguchi: Toyoshi Egi, 1890.

Sartre, Jean-Paul. "L' Universal singulier." [The Singular Universal] In *Kierkegaard Viviant: Colloque organise par l'Unesco a Paris du 21 au 23 avril 1964* [*Kierkegaard Alive: A Colloquium in Paris Organized by UNESCO 21-23 April 1964*], 20–63. Paris: Gallimard, 1966.

———. 実存主義はヒューマニズムである [*Existentialism Is Humanism*]. Translated by Takehiko Ibuki. Kyoto: Jimbun Shoin, 1955.

———. 存在と無 I [*Being and Nothingness, vol. 1*]. Translated by Shinzaburō Matsunami. Kyoto: Jimbun Shoin, 1956.

———. 存在と無 II [*Being and Nothingness, vol. 2*]. Translated by Shinzaburō Matsunami. Kyoto: Jimbun Shoin, 1958.

———. 存在と無 III [*Being and Nothingness, vol. 3*]. Translated by Shinzaburō Matsunami. Kyoto: Jimbun Shoin, 1960.

———. 普遍的単独者 ["The Singular Universal"]. In 生けるキルケゴール [*Kierkegaard Alive*], 16–50. Translated by Shinzaburō Matsunami. Kyoto: Jimbun Shoin, 1967.

———. 方法の問題 [*Question of Method*]. Translated by Hiroyuki Hirai. Kyoto: Jimbun Shoin, 1962.

Sasabuchi, Tomoichi. 浪漫主義文学 ["Romantic Literature"]. In 日本近代文学大事典 第四巻 事項 [*Dictionary of Modern Japanese Literature, vol. 4: Literary Terms, Schools, or Organizations, and Literary Disputes*], edited by Nihon Kindai Bungakukan, 533–536. Tokyo: Kōdan-sha, 1977.

Sasai, Shūrei. 必生 闘う仏教 [*Live without Fail, Fighting Buddhism*]. Tokyo: Shūei-shinsho, 2010.

Sawyer, Jacob H. *The Hidden Authorship of Søren Kierkegaard*. Eugene: Wipf & Stock, 2015.

Schaeffer, Francis A. *A Christian View of Philosophy and Culture*. Vol. 1 of *The Complete Works of Francis A. Schaeffer*. Wheaton: Crossway Books, 1982.

———. *A Christian View of the Bible as Truth*. Vol. 2 of *The Complete Works of Francis A. Schaeffer*. Wheaton: Crossway Books, 1982.

———. *A Christian View of the Church*. Vol. 4 of *The Complete Works of Francis A. Schaeffer*. Wheaton: Crossway Books, 1982.

———. *A Christian View of the West*. Vol. 5 of *The Complete Works of Francis A. Schaeffer*. Wheaton: Crossway Books, 1982.

———. *Escape from Reason*. London: InterVarsity Fellowship, 1968.
———. *The God Who Is There: Speaking Historic Christianity into the Twentieth Century*. London: Pickering & Inglis, 1982.
———. *How Should We Then Live?: The Rise and Decline of Western Thought and Culture*. Old Tappan: Fleming H. Revell, 1976.
Schmidt, Dennis J. Foreword to *Being and Time*, by Martin Heidegger. Translated by Joan Stambaugh. Albany: State University of New York Press, 2010.
Schnabel, Eckhard J. *Early Christian Mission: Jesus and the Twelve*. Downers Grove: InterVarsity Press, 2005.
Schreiner, Thomas R. *Galatians*. Zondervan Exegetical Commentary on the New Testament. Grand Rapids: Zondervan Academic, 2010.
Schulz, Heiko, Jon Stewart, and Karl Verstrynge, eds. *Kierkegaard Studies Yearbook 1999*. Berlin: de Gruyter, 1999.
———. *Kierkegaard Studies Yearbook 2000*. Berlin: de Gruyter, 2000.
———. *Kierkegaard Studies Yearbook 2017*. Berlin: de Gruyter, 2017.
Schweitzer, Albert. *The Quest of the Historical Jesus: A Critical Study of Its Progress from Reimarus to Wrede*. Translated by W. Montgomery. London: Black, 1911.
Scribe, Eugene. *First Love: A Comedy in One Act*. Adapted from the French by L. J. Hollenius. Chicago: The Dramatic Publishing Company, 1869. Accessed 24 July 2019. https://babel.hathitrust.org/cgi/pt?id=wu.89055731467&view=1up&seq=24.
Sekine, Seizo. *Philosophical Interpretations of the Old Testament*. Beihefte zur Zeitschrift für die Alttestamentliche Wissenschaft. Translated by J. Randall Short, and Judy Wakabayashi. Berlin: de Gruyter, 2014.
———. *Transcendency and Symbols in the Old Testament: A Genealogy of the Hermeneutical Experiences*. Beihefte zur Zeitschrift für die Alttestamentliche Wissenschaft 275. Translated by Judy Wakabayashi. Berlin: de Gruyter, 1998.
———. 旧約聖書と哲学 – 現代の問いのなかの一神教 [*The Old Testament and Philosophy: Monotheism in the Midst of Modern Questions*]. Tokyo: Iwanami-shoten, 2008.
———. 旧約における超越と象徴 – 解釈学的経験の系譜 [*Transcendency and Symbols in the Old Testament: A Genealogy of the Hermeneutical Experiences*]. Translated by Judy Wakabayashi. Tokyo: Tokyo Daigaku-shuppan-kai, 1994.
Silva, Moisés. *Philippians*. Baker Exegetical Commentary on the New Testament. 2nd ed. Edited by Robert Yarbrough and Robert Stein. Grand Rapids: Baker Academic, 1992; 2005.
Shimizu, Masayuki. 日本思想全史 [*A Complete History of Japanese Thought*]. Tokyo: Chikuma-shinsho, 2014.
Shimonaka, Hiroshi, ed. 日本を知る101章 (コロナ・ブックス⑦) [*101 Key Words for Understanding Japan* (Corona Books ⑦)]. Tokyo: Heibon-sha, 1995.

Shinran, *Tannishō; Shūjishō*. Translated by Mizumaro Ishida. Tokyo: Heibonsha, 1964.

Shinto Kokusai Gakkai. "神道とは" ["What Is Shintoism?"]. *Shinto Kokusai Gakkai*. Accessed March 19, 2022. http://www.shinto.org/wordjp/?page_id=2.

"Shiokari Pass: The Story of Separating Two Great Rivers – 4." *Hokkaido Magazine Kai*. Accesssed 24 March 2022. http://kai-hokkaido.com/en/feature_vol35_sidestory4/.

Sinnett, M. W. *Restoring the Conversation: Socratic Dialectic in the Authorship of Søren Kierkegaard*. St Andrews: Theology in Scotland for St. Mary's College, 2000.

Søltoft, Pia. "The Power of Eloquence: On the Relation between Ethics and Rhetoric in Preaching." In *Søren Kierkegaard and the Word(s): Essays on Hermeneutic and Communication*, edited by Poul Houe and Gordon D. Marino, 240–247. Copenhagen: Reitzel, 2003.

———. "Søren Kierkegaard on Mission in Christendom: Upbuilding Language and Its Rhetoric Understood as the Fundament of Mission." *Swedish Missiological Themes* 95, no. 4 (2007): 395–404.

Sophocles. *Sophocles I, Antigone, Oedipus the King, Oedipus at Colonus*. The Complete Greek Tragedies. Translated by Mark Griffith and David Grene. Chicago: University of Chicago Press, 2013.

"Søren Kierkegaard Forskningscenteret - Person." Accessed 26 February 2016. http://www.sk.ku.dk/medpers.asp?id=28.

Speidell, Todd, Greg Marcar, and Andrew Torrance, eds. *Søren Kierkegaard: Theologian of the Gospel*. Eugene: Wipf & Stock, 2021.

Sponheim, Paul R. *Existing before God: Søren Kierkegaard and the Human Venture*. Minneapolis: Fortress, 2017.

Spurgeon, Charles. *The Complete Works of C. H. Spurgeon, vol. 38*. Harrington: Delmarva, 2013.

Stalker, Nancy K. *Japan: History and Culture from Classical to Cool*. Oakland: University of California Press, 2018.

Stan, Leo. "Holy Spirit." In *Kierkegaard's Concepts: Tome III: Envy to Incognito*. Vol. 15 of *Kierkegaard Research: Sources, Reception and Resources*, edited by Steven M. Emmanuel, William McDonald, and Jon Stewart, 157–161. London; New York: Routledge, 2016.

Stewart, Jon. *Faust, Romantic Irony, and System: German Culture in the Thought of Søren Kierkegaard*. Copenhagen: Museum Tusculanum, 2019.

———, ed. *Kierkegaard and His Danish Contemporaries: Tome II: Theology*. Vol. 7 of *Kierkegaard Research: Sources, Reception and Resources*. London; New York: Routledge, 2009.

———, ed. *Kierkegaard and the Renaissance and Modern Traditions: Tome I: Philosophy*. Vol. 5 of *Kierkegaard Research: Sources, Reception and Resources*. Farnham: Ashgate, 2009.

———, ed. *Kierkegaard Secondary Literature: Tome V: Greek, Hebrew, Hungarian, Italian, Japanese, Norwegian, and Polish*. Vol. 18 of *Kierkegaard Research: Sources, Reception and Resources*. London; New York: Routledge, 2017.

———, ed. *Kierkegaard's Influence on Literature, Criticism and Art: Tome II: Denmark*. Vol. 12 of *Kierkegaard Research: Sources, Reception and Resources*. London; New York: Routledge, 2013.

———, ed. *Kierkegaard's Influence on the Social Sciences*. Vol. 13 of *Kierkegaard Research: Sources, Reception and Resources*. Farnham; Burlington: Ashgate, 2011.

———, ed. *Kierkegaard's Influence on Theology: Tome II: Anglophone and Scandinavian Protestant Theology*. Vol. 10 of *Kierkegaard Research: Sources, Reception and Resources*. London; New York: Routledge, 2012.

———, ed. *Kierkegaard's Internal Reception: Tome II: Southern, Central and Eastern Europe*. Vol. 8 of *Kierkegaard Research: Sources, Reception and Resources*. Farnham: Ashgate, 2009.

———. "Kierkegaard's Relation to the German Romantics and the Problem of Pseudonymity." In *Faust, Romantic Irony, and System: German Culture in the Thought of Søren Kierkegaard*, 307–338. Copenhagen: Museum Tusculanum, 2019.

———. *Kierkegaard's Relations to Hegel Reconsidered*. Cambridge; New York: Cambridge University Press, 2003.

———. "'Philosophy and Christianity Can Never Be United': The Role of Sibbern and Martensen in Kierkegaard's Reception of Schleiermacher." In *Kierkegaard Studies Yearbook 2017*, edited by Heiko Schulz, Jon Stewart, and Karl Verstrynge, 291–312. Berlin: de Gruyter, 2017.

Storm, Dan Anthony. *D. Anthony Storm's Commentary on Kierkegaard*. http://www.sorenkierkegaard.org/kierkegaard-commentary.html. (accessed 23 Jan 2012).

Stott, John R. W. *The Contemporary Christian: Applying God's Word to Today's World*. Downers Grove: InterVarsity Press, 1992.

Straus, Mark. "The Campaign to Eliminate Hell." *National Geographic*. 13 May 2016. http://news.nationalgeographic.com/culture/article/160513-theology-hell-history-christianity/.

Strawser, Michael. "The Indirectness of Kierkegaard's Signed Writings." *International Journal of Philosophical Studies* 3, no. 1 (1995): 73–90.

Sturluson, Snorri. *The Prose Edda*. Translated by Arthur Gilchrist Brodeur. New York: The American-Scandinavian Foundation, 1916.

Sutō, Takaya. キルケゴールと「キリスト教界」 [*Kierkegaard and "Christendom"*]. Tokyo: Sōbun-sha, 2014.

「日本の自殺死亡率」[Suicide rates in Japan]. *nippon.com*. http://www.nippon.com/ja/features/h00075/. (accessed 6 Feb 2015).

Suzuki, Daisetz. 日本的霊性 [*Japanese Spirituality*]. Tokyo: Iwanami-bunko, 1972.

———. *Japanese Spirituality*. Translated by Norman Waddell. Tokyo: Japan Society for the Promotion of Science, 1972.

Swenson, David F. Introduction to *Lectures on the Religious Thought of Søren Kierkegaard*, by Eduard Geismar. Minneapolis: Augsburg, 1937.

Symons, Stéphane, ed. *The Marriage of Aesthetics and Ethics*. Critical Studies in German Idealism. Leiden: Brill, 2015.

Szabados, Ádám. "Incarnational Mission: Søren Kierkegaard's Challenge to Evangelical Christianity." Acessed 6 February 2015. http://szabadosadam.hu/divinity/flashbooks/6-1_Incarnational.swf.

Tachibana, Takashi. 思索紀行 [*Thought Journey*]. Tokyo: Shoseki-jōhōsha, 2004.

———. シベリア鎮魂歌 – 香月泰男の世界 [*Siberia Requiem: The World of Yasuo Kazuki*]. Tokyo: Bungei Shunjū, 2004.

Tagawa, Kenzō. 新約聖書 訳と注 2下 使徒行伝 [*The New Testament, Translation and Commentary, volume 2(2): Acts*]. Tokyo: Sakuhin-sha, 2011.

Tajafuerce, Begonya Saez. "Kierkegaardian Seduction, or the Aesthethic Actio(nes) in Distans." *Diacritics* 30, no. 1 (Spring 2000): 78–88.

Takahashi, Tetsuya. 靖国問題 [*Yasukuni Issues*]. Tokyo: Chikuma-shinsho, 2005.

Tavor, Ori. "12 Religious Thought." In *Routledge Handbook of Early Chinese History*, edited by Paul R. Goldin, 261–279. London; New York: Routledge, 2018.

Taylor, Victor E., and Charles E. Winquist, eds. *The Routledge Encyclopedia of Postmodernism*. London: Routledge, 2001.

Teachman, Erin. "'Evangelicals' and Their Gatekeepers: A Case Study in Exploitation." *Medium*. 13 December 2016. https://medium.com/@newmethos/evangelicals-and-their-gatekeepers-98c4d9477951.

Teo, Alan Robert, and Albert C. Gaw. "Hikikomori: A Japanese Culture-Bound Syndrome of Social Withdrawal? A Proposal for DSM-V." *Journal of Nervous and Mental Disease* 198, no. 6 (2010): 444–449.

Thapar, Romila. *Time as a Metaphor of History: Early India: The Krishna Bharadwaj Memorial Lecture*. Oxford: Oxford University Press, 1996.

"日本国憲法 [The Constitution of Japan]" https://japan.kantei.go.jp/constitution_and_government_of_japan/constitution_e.html (accessed 13 May 2025).

死にいたる病「菊と刀」[*The Sickness unto Death "The Chrysanthemum and the Sword"*]; クリスチャン新聞福音版 [Christian Newspaper Gospel Version] Word of Life Press Ministries (March 2020), no. 522.

世界の宗教人口 ["The World's Religious Population"]. *Aikido World*, accessed 4 April 2025, https://aikido.mixh.jp/world-religious-statics-2/

Thomas, Andrew. "Money and Missionary Lifestyle in the Buddhist World." In *Complexity of Money and Mission in Asia*, SEANET9, edited by Paul. H. De Neui, 43–58. South Pasadena: William Carey Library, 2012.

Thompson, Curtis L. "Apologetics." In *Kierkegaard's Concepts: Tome I: Absolute to Church*. Vol. 15 of *Kierkegaard Research: Sources, Reception and Resources*, edited by Steven M. Emmanuel, William McDonald, and Jon Stewart, 71–75. London; New York: Routledge, 2016.

Thulstrup, M. M. "The Single Individual." In Bibliotheca Kierkegaardiana, vol. 16, Some of Kierkegaard's main categories. Copenhagen: Reitzels Forlag, 1988: 9–25.

Thulstrup, Marie Mikulová. "Søren Kierkegaard's Martybegreb." *Dansk teologisk Tidskrift* 27 (1964): 100–114.

Thulstrup, Niels. *Kierkegaard's Relation to Hegel*. Translated by George L. Stengren. Princeton: Princeton University Press, 1980; 2014.

Tietjen, Mark A. *Kierkegaard: A Christian Missionary to Christians*. Downers Grove: IVP Academic, 2016. Kindle.

———. *Kierkegaard, Communication, and Virtue: Authorship as Edification*. Philosophy of Religion series. Bloomington: Indiana University Press, 2013.

Tikkanen, Amy. "Shimabara Rebellion," *Britannica*, last modified [or revised] date not given, accessed 24 March 24, https://www.britannica.com/event/Shimabara-Rebellion.

Tillich, Paul. 生きる勇気 [*The Courage to Be*]. Translated by Hideo Ōki. Tokyo: Heibon-sha, 1995.

———. 近代プロテスタント思想史 (下) [*Perspectives on 19th and 20th Century Protestant Theology vol. 2*]. Translated by Toshio Satō. Tokyo: Hakusui-sha, 1997.

———. 組織神学〈第2巻〉 [*Systematic Theology II*]. Translated by Michio Taniguchi. Tokyo: Shinkyō-shuppan, 1969.

Tonon, Margherita. "Adorno's Response to Kierkegaard: The Ethical Validity of the Aesthetic?" In *The Marriage of Aesthetics and Ethics*. Critical Studies in German Idealism. Edited by Stéphane Symons, 185–199. Leiden: Brill, 2015.

Toren, Benno van den. "From Missionary Incarnate to Incarnational Guest: A Critical Reflection on Incarnation as a Model for Missionary Presence." *Transformation*: 32, no. 2 (April 2015): 81–96.

Torrance, Andrew B. *The Freedom to Become a Christian: A Kierkegaardian Account of Human Transformation in Relationship with God*. London: Bloomsbury T&T Clark, 2016.

Toya, Manabu. 神道入門 [*Introduction to Shintoism*]. Tokyo: Kawade-shobō-shinsha, 2016.

Turchin, Sean Anthony. "Offense." In *Kierkegaard's Concepts: Tome V: Objectivity to Sacrifice*. Vol. 15 of *Kierkegaard Research: Sources, Reception and Resources*, edited by Steven M. Emmanuel, William McDonald, and Jon Stewart, 7–13. London; New York: Routledge, 2015.

Turner, David L. *Matthew*. Baker Exegetical Commentary on the New Testament. Grand Rapids: Baker Academic, 2008.

Turner, Luke. "Metamodernist Manifesto." 2011. http://www.metamodernism.org/.

"U2 Lyrics." AZ Lyrics. Accessed 4 May 2020. https://www.azlyrics.com/u/u2band.html.

Uchimura, Kanzō. *Representative Men of Japan*. Tokyo: Keisei-sha, 1908.

———. "Two J's" in *The Japan Christian Intelligencer* 1/7 (Sept.) 1926 [reprinted in Uchimura] 1980–1984, vol. 30: 53–54.

Uda, Susumu, ed. 神の啓示と日本人の宗教意識 – 現代における宣教上の"接触点"を探る [*God's Revelation and the Japanese Religious Consciousness: Exploring the "Contact Point" in Modern Mission*]. Tokyo: Inochino Kotoba-sha, 1989.

Ueda, Shizuteru. 私とは何か [*What Is I?*]. Tokyo: Iwanami-shinsho, 2000.

Uoki, Tadakazu. 日本基督教の精神的伝統 [*Spiritual Tradition of Japan Christianity*]. Tokyo: Bunsei-sha, 1941.

Valčo, Michal. "The Value of Dietrich Bonhoeffer's Theological-Ethical Reading of Søren Kierkegaard." *European Journal of Science and Theology* 13, no. 1 (February 2017): 47–58.

Vidal, Dolors Perarnau, and Óscar Parcero Oubiña. "Spain: The Old and New Kierkegaard Reception in Spain." In *Kierkegaard's International Reception: Tome II: Southern, Central and Eastern Europe*. Vol. 8 of *Kierkegaard Research: Sources, Reception and Resources*, edited by Jon Stewart, 17–80. Farnham: Ashgate, 2009.

Wahl, Jean. *Études Kierkegaardiennes* [*Kierkegaardian Studies*]. Paris: Aubier, 1938.

Walsh, Sylvia. "Patterns for Living Poetically." In *Authorship and Authenticity: Kierkegaard and His Pseudonyms*. Vol. 1 of *Critical Assessments of Leading Philosophers*, edited by Daniel W. Conway and K. E. Gover, 278–291. London; New York: Routledge, 2002.

Watanabe, Kōki. 日本の宗教人口：2億と2-3割の怪の解 [Religious Demographics in Japan: A Mystery of Two Hundred Million and the Enigma of 20–30%]. 武蔵野大学仏教文化研究所紀要 [Journal of Institute of Buddhist Culture, Musashino University], (27), 2011-03: 25–37.

Watanabe, Naoki, ed. 宗教と現代がわかる本 2007 [*The Book You Can Understand Religion and Modern Age*]. Tokyo: Heibon-sha, 2007.

Watkin, Julia. *Historical Dictionary of Kierkegaard's Philosophy*. Lanham; Toronto; Oxford: Scarecrow, 2001.

———. "Judge William – A Christian?" In *Either/Or, II*. Vol. 4 of *International Kierkegaard Commentary*, edited by Robert L. Perkins, 113–124. Macon: Mercer University Press, 1995.

"Weblio" "英和辞典・和英辞典 [English-Japanese Dictionary, Japanese-English Dictionary]" s.v. "行住坐臥 [*Gyōjūzaga*]" https://ejje.weblio.jp/content/%E8%A1%8C%E4%BD%8F+%E5%9D%90%E8%87%A5 (accessed 29 Feb 2020).

Wells, Samuel. *Incarnational Mission: Being with the World*. Norwich: Canterbury, 2018.

Westphal, Merold. *Becoming a Self: A Reading of Kierkegaard's Concluding Unscientific Postscript*. West Lafayette: Purdue University Press, 1996.

———. *Kierkegaard's Concept of Faith*. Kierkegaard as a Christian Thinker. Grand Rapids:. Eerdmans, 2014.

日本浪曼派とはなにか ["*What is Japanese Romanticism?*"]. ユリイカ [*Eureka*], 7 (9). Tokyo: Seido-sha, October 1975.

Wright, Tom. *Paul for Everyone: Romans Part 1: Chapters 1–8*. Rev. ed. London: SPCK, 2006.

Yamagiwa, Tomoo. 破天 – インド仏教徒の頂点に立つ日本人 [*Unprecedented: A Japanese Who Stands on the Top of Indian Buddhists*]. Tokyo: Shūei-shinsho, 2008.

Yamaguchi, Yōichi. 「日本的キリスト教」の考察 ["Consideration of 'Japanese Christianity'"]. In 「日本的キリスト教」を超えて [*Beyond "Japanese Christianity"*], edited by Shinshū Summer Mission, 11–37. Tokyo: Inochi no kotoba-sha, 2016.

Yamamoto, Hirofumi. 殉教 – 日本人は何を信仰したか [*Martyrdom: What Did Japanese Believe?*]. Tokyo: Kōbunsha-shinsho, 2009.

Yiu, Angela. *Chaos and Order in the Works of Natsume Sōseki (Study of the East Asian Institute)*. Honolulu: University of Hawai'i Press, 1998.

Yoshimoto, Takaaki, Takeshi Umehara, and Shinichi Nakazawa. 日本人は思想したか [*Have the Japanese Ever Philosophised?*]. Tokyo: Shinchō-sha, 1995.

Young, Edward. *The Complaint: or, Night-Thoughts on Life, Death, and Immortality*. 9 vols. London: R. Dodsley, 1742–1744.

Yousef, Tawfiq. "Modernism, Postmodernism, and Metamodernism: A Critique." *International Journal of Language and Literature* 5, no. 1 (June 2017): 33–43.

Ziolkowski, Eric. *The Literary Kierkegaard*. Evanston: Northwestern University Press, 2011.

Langham Literature, with its publishing work, is a ministry of Langham Partnership.

Langham Partnership is a global fellowship working in pursuit of the vision God entrusted to its founder John Stott –

> *to facilitate the growth of the church in maturity and Christ-likeness through raising the standards of biblical preaching and teaching.*

Our vision is to see churches in the Majority World equipped for mission and growing to maturity in Christ through the ministry of pastors and leaders who believe, teach and live by the word of God.

Our mission is to strengthen the ministry of the word of God through:
- nurturing national movements for biblical preaching
- fostering the creation and distribution of evangelical literature
- enhancing evangelical theological education

especially in countries where churches are under-resourced.

Our ministry

Langham Preaching partners with national leaders to nurture indigenous biblical preaching movements for pastors and lay preachers all around the world. With the support of a team of trainers from many countries, a multi-level programme of seminars provides practical training, and is followed by a programme for training local facilitators. Local preachers' groups and national and regional networks ensure continuity and ongoing development, seeking to build vigorous movements committed to Bible exposition.

Langham Literature provides Majority World preachers, scholars and seminary libraries with evangelical books and electronic resources through publishing and distribution, grants and discounts. The programme also fosters the creation of indigenous evangelical books in many languages, through writer's grants, strengthening local evangelical publishing houses, and investment in major regional literature projects, such as one volume Bible commentaries like the *Africa Bible Commentary* and the *South Asia Bible Commentary*.

Langham Scholars provides financial support for evangelical doctoral students from the Majority World so that, when they return home, they may train pastors and other Christian leaders with sound, biblical and theological teaching. This programme equips those who equip others. Langham Scholars also works in partnership with Majority World seminaries in strengthening evangelical theological education. A growing number of Langham Scholars study in high quality doctoral programmes in the Majority World itself. As well as teaching the next generation of pastors, graduated Langham Scholars exercise significant influence through their writing and leadership.

To learn more about Langham Partnership and the work we do visit **langham.org**

www.ingramcontent.com/pod-product-compliance
Lightning Source LLC
Chambersburg PA
CBHW050300010526
44108CB00040B/1909